7 DEADLY SINS

7 DEADLY SINS

A VISUAL HISTORY

ED SIMON

CERNUNNOS

CONTENTS

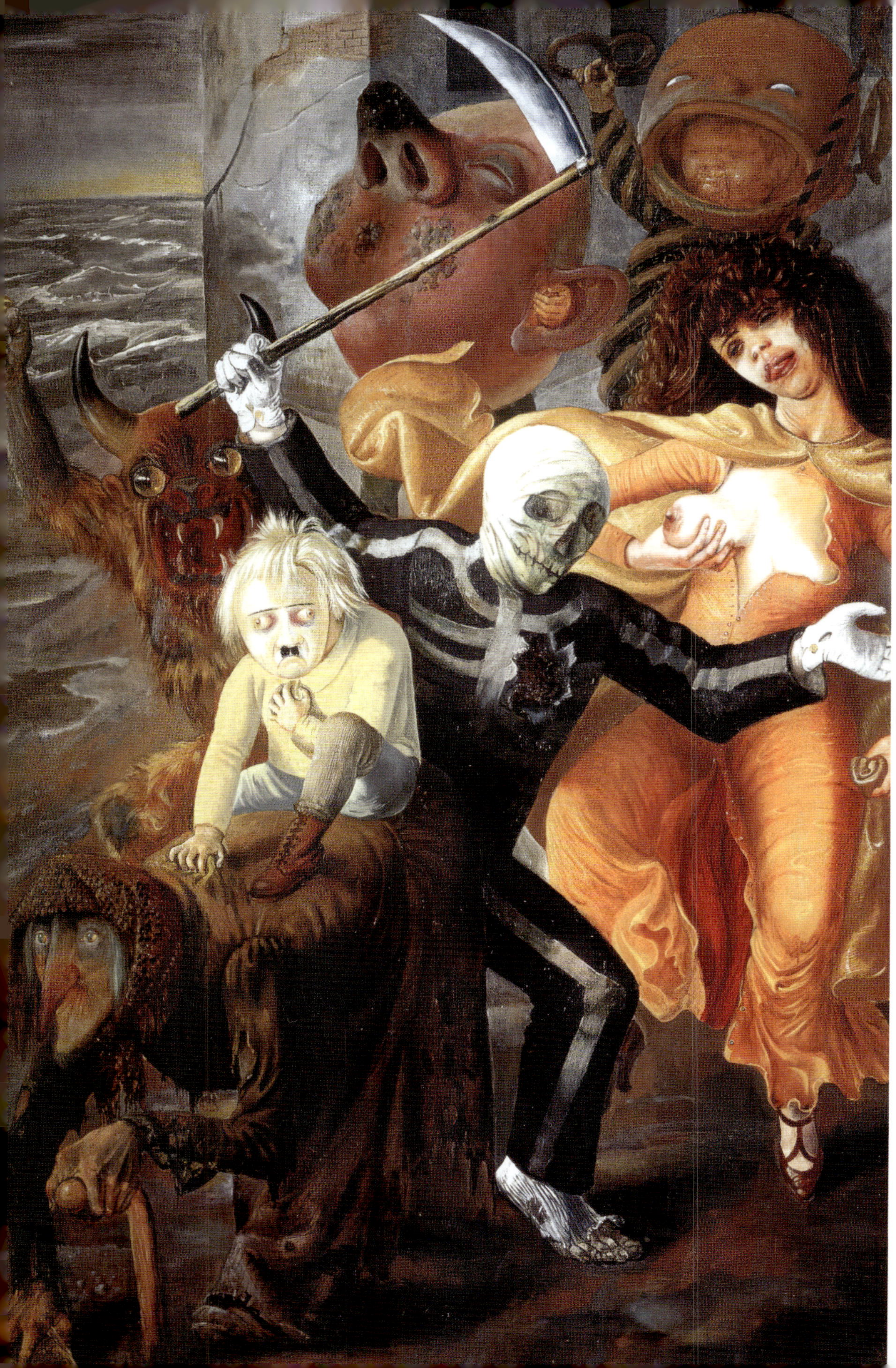

INTRODUCTION

ON VICE

"When I look back upon my life
It's always with a sense of shame
I've always been the one to blame
For everything I long to do."
—Pet Shop Boys, "It's a Sin" (1987)

Seen from behind, the woman in the red dress's face is only visible to us because of the mirror into which she is gazing, held aloft by a spindly black reptilian demon; the man is in repose, while his lover in her black dress and white habit sits beneath the canvas of a vermillion tent, the couple's conjugal recreations briefly in intermission while they are entertained by a pair of fools; a corpulent burgher in a scratchy green tunic stretched tight over his ample belly gnaws at a chicken bone while clutching a tankard of beer as he pushes his hungry son away from him; in parallel to the lazy dog curled and dozing at his feet, a man in heavy green velvet sleeps upright in his stiff wooden chair, with the dream of a stern, black-clad nun imploring him to abandon such acedia standing at his right; a wealthy man with pet hawk on wrist absent-mindedly stands while his servants unload his wares, as from a doorway a modest couple stares on in green-eyed covetousness; the rich merchant's compatriot, a judge, hears deliberations from an attorney while sitting on the wooden bench of an al fresco courtroom, a thatched-roof cottage beyond, while with his right hand he slyly accepts a bribe from opposing counsel; finally, two inebriated peasants, their faces twisted into a cruel rage, run toward each other with swords held aloft, their battle interrupted by a maiden who desperately tries to separate them. All of these scenes are arranged in a circle apportioned into seven equal sections, almost as if infernal place settings upon a table or diabolical hours on a clock. In the four corners of the composition are an equivalent number of smaller circles, each depicting one of the *last things*—Heaven and Hell, Judgment and Death—the remains of both vice and virtue. In Heaven, a multitude of the virtuous are admitted by St. Peter into the celestial kingdom beneath the benevolent gaze of Christ; in Hell, the sinful are tortured by an assemblage of bestial demons, women and men splayed out on racks and stabbed with knives underneath the ash-black sky of a burning pit; Christ floats in judgment above the multitude, accompanied by a host of triumphant angels, while in the final

OPPOSITE Otto Dix's 1933 *The Seven Deadly Sins*, original at the Staatliche Kunsthalle in Karlsruhe, Germany.

entry, a man on his deathbed anxiously awaits the chime of the bells, an angel and demon visible only to him weighing the measure of his soul.

More than five centuries ago, only eight years after Columbus's slipper touched the white sands of San Salvador and seventeen prior to Luther's hammer hitting the door of the Wittenberg Cathedral, either Hieronymus Bosch or a student of his purchased from a Brabant merchant a rectangle of Dutch poplar about five feet long and four feet wide and with oils as red as blood and as blue as Heaven, as green as the earth and as black as death, painted the aforementioned scenes in a composition entitled *The Seven Deadly Sins and the Four Last Things*. An entire moral universe recorded on wood from a tree felled in the Low Countries more than half a millennium ago, the vagaries of pride, lust, gluttony, sloth, envy, greed, and wrath rendered in exacting detail, and the costs of such transgressions indicated in the corners of the piece. Bosch, long celebrated for his cracked visions of corpuscular demons deep within the ravines of the earth, of surreal, nightmarish imagery called forth from a festering creative abscess, is relatively tame in this painting (despite the occasional devil here or there). Yet the image is no less arresting because of it, particularly as Bosch (or somebody in his stead) illustrated the sins as a circle (so evocative of the infamous wheel of fortune), harkening to the variability and inevitability of moral failing in all of our lives. At the center of Bosch's (or his student's) tableau is a small depiction of Christ, omniscient and omnipresent, a panopticon and all-seeing eye, sitting in condemnation of these minor foibles that so often can metastasize into grievous sin—for envy can turn into robbery, lust into rape, wrath into murder. Within the canon of the Roman Catholic Church, that is to say that the cardinal sins—those minor peccadillos and forgivable oversights, our vanities and appetites—can lead to mortal scenes. The Seven Deadly Vices may not themselves constitute the portal to Hell, but if unchecked they can be the key.

Seven days of creation, seven sacraments, seven wonders of the world and hills of Rome. So overdetermined is seven, that prime number associated by numerologists with divinity itself, that it feels expected that there would of course be a listing of Seven Deadly Sins. More surprising is that the list itself appears nowhere in Scripture, for in our secular age, where literacy of the Bible has become a rare virtue, there is perhaps an assumption that the Seven Deadly Sins are first encountered in the Hebrew Scriptures or the New Testament. Historically, though the Church Father Evagrius Ponticus drew upon classical precedents, any listing of fundamental sins which could lead to further perdition was first made by that fourth-century theologian who lived along the Bithynian coast of Asia Minor. Believing that the source of disunion could be physical, mental, or emotional, Ponticus attempted to tally all of those moods and dispositions that can lead to mortal sins and settled on eight, rather than seven (listing "sadness" as a sin). As translated into Latin by his younger contemporary John Cassian, the Eight Deadly Sins became a staple of spiritual contemplation among Catholics of the early Middle Ages. Pope Gregory I, the sixth-century pontiff who was the first to have the superlative "the Great" added after his name, redacted Ponticus's inventory from eight into seven, combining sadness into "Acedia," the rough modern corollary to sloth, while also more fully explicating the nature of envy. What exactly these individual sins might encompass and how they might be interpreted has changed over the course of many centuries, but since Gregory the Great the listing has remained uniform (even while a commitment to the Seven Deadly Sins themselves as a moral guide has declined over the past half millennium). Despite the relative disinterest which theologians have had in the subject since the Reformation, the Seven Deadly Sins have so long fascinated the general public in part because they describe average, regular, boring failures. To think too highly of oneself, to eat and drink too much, to find one's eye wandering toward unclothed flesh or to slack off at tasks, to desire something that doesn't belong to you or to stingily hold on too tightly to that which does, and finally to feel your blood pressure rise in anger, your palms go clammy with rage—well, it would take a saintly person to claim that they've never experienced these, or something near enough. Most of us (hopefully) aren't murderers or war criminals, but that we're a bit too proud or a bit too envious, sometimes lustful or gluttonous, lazy, greedy, or angry, is simply the lot of humanity. Because of their universality, and the seeming exhaustiveness of the listed transgressions that seem neither too few nor too many, the sins have often been a subject of great art and literature. Dante's epic *The Divine Comedy*, the first third of which deals with the poet's harrowing of Hell as guided by his Roman antecedent Virgil, provides a detailed cosmology of how the sinful are punished at the various circles of perdition. There is the second circle, where the lustful are forever buffeted about on eternal winds, the adulterous lovers Francesca da Rimini and Paolo Malatesta—condemned for an instance of rank carnality encouraged by a romance about Guinevere and Lancelot which they read together—tell Dante that "Love, which permits no loved one not to love, / took me so strongly with delight in him / that we are one in Hell, as we were above." In a circle below, the gluttonous wallow in their own fetid crapulence, the sweat and stank from their corpulent bodies, the flicks of spit-slicked food from the corners of their mouths, now a deep cesspool in which they eternally drown. The greedy, once with addresses on Florence's Ponte Vecchio, or maybe Park Avenue or Rodeo Drive, now rather reside in the fourth circle, where they are forced by demons to joust with one another with the treasures they once hoarded, a "nation of lost souls, / far more than were above: they strained their chests / against enormous weights, and with mad howls / rolled them at one another." There are nine circles in all, where not just the classical Seven Deadly Sins, but also heresy and treachery, among others, are punished with an exacting logic, all of which is enumerated by Dante in a complex topography of circles within circles, of vestibules and antechambers.

An obvious reciprocal logic animates "Inferno," whereby sins are punished in a manner in keeping with their appearance, a diabolical irony that sees the lustful whisked about in passionate vortices and the greedy weighed down by their own wealth. This has often been the obscene enjoyment of thinking about the Seven Deadly Sins, for nearly two millennia they have been represented in such a manner. David Fincher's grim, gothic, macabre 1995 noir film *Se7en*, in which a wizened old cop, played by Morgan Freeman, and his hotheaded new partner, portrayed by Brad Pitt, pursue a serial killer who gruesomely murders his victims by the logic of the Seven Deadly Sins, is probably the most popular contemporary example (it is certainly how most people remind themselves of just what exactly is on that original list). A morbidly obese man forced to gorge himself to death, a lay-about parasite strapped into a bed until he is transformed into a living cadaver covered in sores and pustules, a financier who bleeds out after being made to cut out a pound of his own flesh. "If we catch John Doe and he turns out to be the Devil—I mean, if he's Satan himself," says Freeman's character, Detective William Somerset, "that might live up to our expectations. But . . . he's not the Devil. He's just a man." Which has always been the pointof not just of the classification of the Seven Deadly Sins, but also of the moral sins which are their progeny—that they're committed not by devils, but men.

Some of the most arresting portrayals of the Seven Deadly Sins come in the form of the morality plays which were performed at open-air festivals and during feast days throughout medieval Europe. The Seven Deadly Sins were personified as characters visible to a soul strung between Heaven and Hell, paradise and perdition, goading a person on into the transgressions which ultimately lead to those wicked acts that earn somebody continual punishment. Part of what makes these characters so compelling, such as in the fourteenth-century anonymous English play *Everyman*, is that they can be interpreted as aspects of the human psyche, as elements of our multifaceted and polyglot, labyrinthine and intricate minds. Ambiguity as to where the sins come from implies that we condemn ourselves. "The tyde abydeth no man," warns Death in the play. This dramatic conceit of a beautiful Pride, obese Gluttony, and gold-bedecked Greed existing as not just broad archetypes, but as personages capable of convincing the fallible mind into sin, was still apparent in the earliest days of the secular theater, even after the Reformation. Richard Tarlton's lost 1585 play *The Seven Deadly Sins* is an obvious example, though less celebrated than Christopher Marlowe's 1593 play *Doctor Faustus*, wherein all of the sins arrive in their expected forms to discourse with the condemned scholar who has sold his soul to Satan. "If we say that we have no sin, / We deceive ourselves, and there's no truth in us," writes Marlowe.

Again, this is part of the theological significance of the Seven Deadly Sins, their moral power, ethical power, psychological power. The list of sins is pedestrian, prosaic, basic, and quotidian, a summation of the "banality of evil" long before Hannah Arendt coined that phrase in her study *Eichmann in Jerusalem*, describing the Nazi functionary who was personally responsible for the deaths of hundreds of thousands of Hungarian Jews. Part of what Arendt's controversial account suggested was that a man like Eichmann, far from being an incomprehensible monster, was all the more chillingly just an average person, like me or you. Yet sin shall pluck upon sin, the further somebody sinks into blood. As an ethical guide, it's this aspect that makes the Seven Deadly Sins compare in marked contrast to the abstractions and absolutism of other moral theories ranging from the Golden Rule to the eighteenth-century philosopher Immanuel Kant's categorical imperative. Most importantly, the Seven Deadly Sins—as a diagnostic tool, if not also as a set of instructions for how to actually live—is far preferable to the strictures of the Decalogue, a moral code which does actually appear in Scripture. The Ten Commandments as explicated in Exodus share a

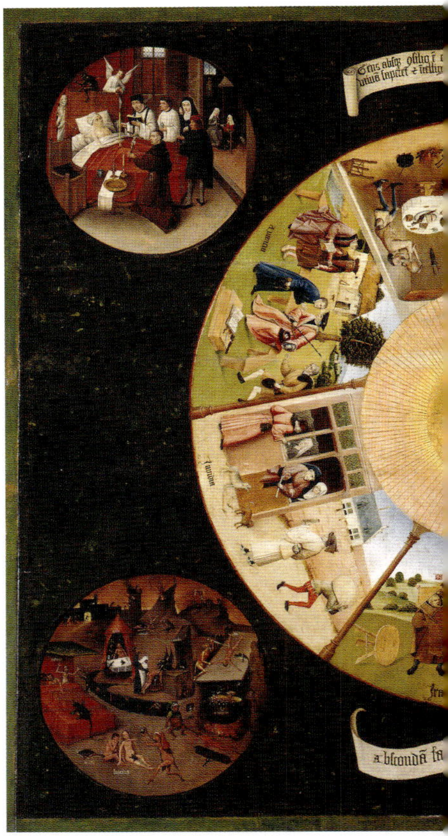

TOP *The Seven Deadly Sins and the Four Final Things* by either Hieronymus Bosch or his student, painted c. 1500 with the original in Madrid's Prado Museum.

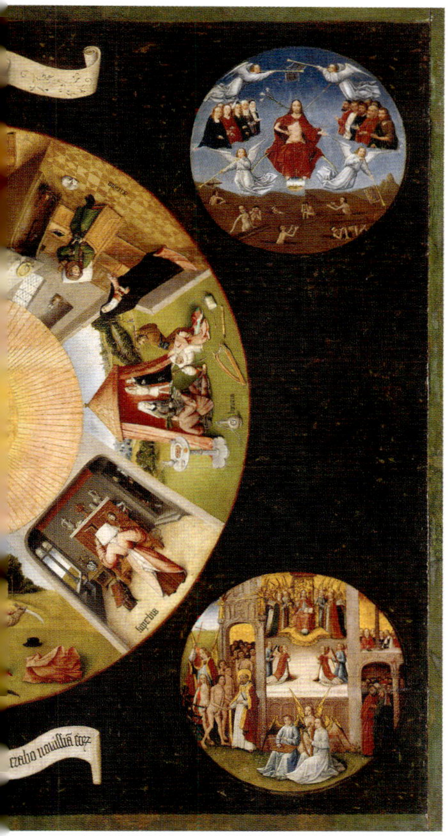

similar concern as does the listing of the Seven Deadly Sins, yet the former is ironically both more and less strict in what it proscribes. More strict because it's definitive in what thou *shouldst* and *shouldnst* do, but less in that the rules themselves become easier to follow than the broad and ambiguous guidelines of the Seven Deadly Sins. The Decalogue trades in certainty—*Thou shalt not murder, thou shalt not commit adultery, thou shalt not steal*—while the Seven Deadly Sins are more equivocal. *Avoid gluttony*, but how much can I eat? *Eschew sloth*, so how many hours should I rest? *Greed is a sin*, but how then should I best make my livelihood? By contrast, the Ten Commandments actually ask less of us; to not murder or steal should be comparatively easy. In that the laws of Exodus are so clear-cut, the punishments (whether civil or cosmic) are also more obvious, but those rules are also easier to follow. The result, counterintuitively, is that a culture which places more stock in the Decalogue than in the Seven Deadly Sins is a culture where the standards of what it means to be good are at a base minimum.

Such is our culture, obviously. The shift from seeing the locus of wisdom in the Seven Deadly Sins to rather the Ten Commandments has been a five-century process. Scholar John Bossy explains that the fifteenth and sixteenth centuries saw an alteration in Christianity's "moral arithmetic," where both Reformation Protestants and Counter-Reformation Catholics traded away the grand ethical edifice of the Seven Deadly Sins for the constraints of the Ten Commandments, in large part because the former didn't have scriptural precedent. In an epoch where faith in a traditional god is a more absurd leap than self-evident truth, who cares about the Decalogue's injunctions concerning idolatry and blasphemy? If the most that we can ask of treatment to our neighbors is that we don't murder them, then we've made the bare minimum of good behavior the basis for society. Imagine, then, a progressive restoration of the Seven Deadly Sins as not just a moral guide, but a moral guide based in the material conditions of the world. We're in need of such guidance at this particular juncture in history, for the Decalogue offers no prescriptions on the inequities which the Seven Deadly Sins always kept at the forefront. Fundamentally, from Ponticus onward, the sins were always defined as being attitudes which deprive the least of us from an equitable share of what human beings deserve. More than just being about morality, the Seven Deadly Sins are about justice. To talk about gluttony, where some enjoy Almas caviar and Romanée-Conti while 828 million people a day go to bed hungry, is to talk about justice. To discuss how two billion women, men, and children—a quarter of the globe's population—are victims of wrath living in active war zones from Syria to Haiti, is to have a discussion about justice. To understand that the greed of this planet's 2,153 billionaires led to an accumulation of wealth equal to that of the 4.6 billion people of the rest of the planet is to only begin to take the measure of injustice. Pride, lust, gluttony, sloth, envy, greed, and wrath are not archaic remnants of a distant past, medieval relics fit only for Dante—they are the apparatus by which we fully measure the fallenness of this world.

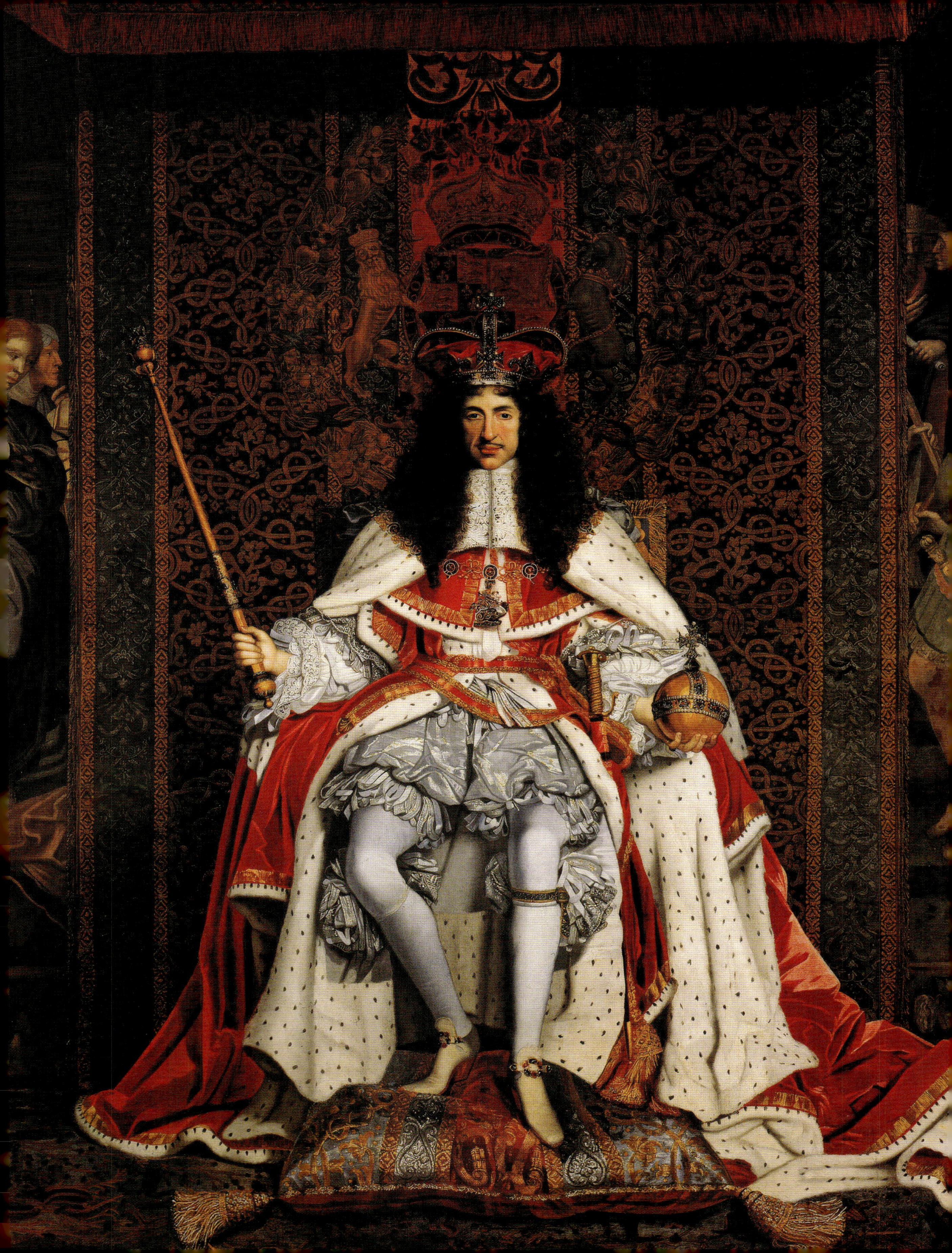

CHAPTER ONE

UNPAID-FOR SILK: PRIDE

"If God has bestowed on us any excellent gift, we imagine it to be our own achievement; and we swell and even burst with pride."
—John Calvin, *Golden Booklet of the True Christian Life* (1550)

"You're so vain, you probably think this song is about you."
—Carly Simon, "You're So Vain" (1972)

In the wisdom of the forty-seven translators of the King James Version of the Bible convened by order of the English monarchy in 1611, an ecumenical assemblage of both High Church clergy and lowly Puritans, the Hebrew phrase from Proverbs 16:18 would be rendered as "Pride goes before destruction, and a haughty spirit before a fall," though normally it's misremembered in popular parlance simply as "Pride comes before a fall." The choice of the indefinite article is an interesting one, for in the mythology of the Church it wasn't just *a* fall but *the* fall which resulted from Lucifer's overweening hubris, nature itself disordered because of the intensity of ego. That grammatical conflation of the indefinite and the definite is a crucial one, allowing for the eternal things of the mythological realm to intersect with the quotidian of our own lives; to explain how our human pride mirrors a mythic Pride. הַגָּאוֹן in the original scripture, the Hebrew translation for "pride" is a bit more than just self-esteem; it connotates a sense of regard that diminishes all other people and in the process courts destruction. In the fourth century, Evagrius Ponticus used the word "Υπερηφανία"—"hyperephania"—which, more than the milquetoast modern translation of "pride," is better translated as "grandiosity": not simply feeling good about yourself from time to time, but delusionally feeling as if you're more deserving than others simply by the reality of your being. John Cassian, a century after Ponticus, used the word "superbia" for pride, which was associated with that classical dramatic concept of hubris. As a narrative conceit, hubris referred to a fatal flaw embedded within the psyche, an inability to fully understand ourselves because of excessive self-love. In the examples from both literature and history which follow, from Lucifer to a contemporary central Asian strongman, Roman emperors to Hollywood stars, there's an intimation of the dangers such pride can make wrought.

PREVIOUS SPREAD John Michael Wright's portrait of Charles II, made between 1671 and 1676 and held today by the Royal Collection Trust, depicts the monarch in the full regalia of his position, holding aloft orb and scepter as the veritable representative of God on earth, an embodiment of the divine right of kings.

OPPOSITE The great nonconformist William Blake in this 1805 watercolor held by the Tate Britain depicts the archangel before his fall adorned and beautiful in Heaven with regal orb and scepter, just like Charles. "Thou wast perfect till Iniquity was Found in Thee," wrote the Prophet Ezekiel.

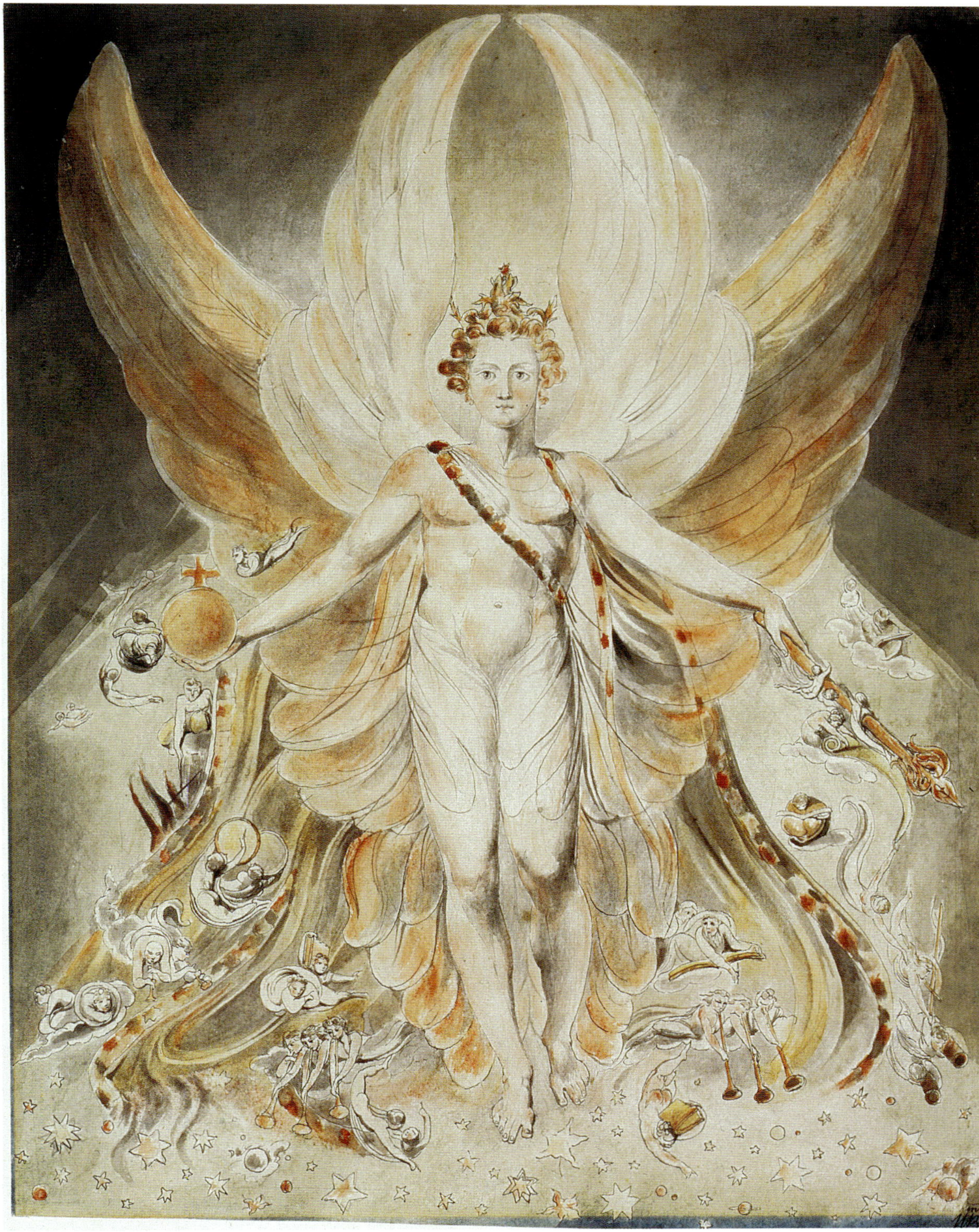

THEORY—MOTHER OF ALL VICES

Pride is the primogeniture of all sin, if you believe the Scholastic theologians. The origin, the genesis, the beginning, for it was that once-beautiful angel Lucifer who was driven by such sentiments, believing that he could launch a war against Heaven, eventually punished by being transformed into Satan. That misstep which initiated our fall is thus the ur-sin. All other transgressions are to follow from this primary sin, reflections of Lucifer's first disorder in this belief that you—the individual—are more deserving, more important, grander, and greater than those around you, and that as a consequence you are owed wealth, comfort, power, and perhaps most of all acknowledgment in larger sum than those lesser mortals who are lucky enough to occupy this same world with you, for a bit. Idolatry of the self is the modus operandi of pride, the valorization of your own consciousness and body beyond all proportion, the worship of your own identity as if it were a deity. Satan, the inventor of pride, was he who implored in Book IX of John Milton's seventeenth-century epic poem *Paradise Lost* to "loom on me! / Me who have touched and tasted yet both live / And life more perfect have attained than fate / Meant me, by vent'ring higher than my Lot!" Such sentiments, diffracted and dispersed, have imbued all of us with an occasional sense of inflated ego (some more than others, obviously). Ours is a society and culture that sees little problem with pride; it's both the dictum of self-actualized liberals and rugged individualist conservatives, perhaps the natural conclusion of an Enlightenment politics which has made the pursuit of happiness—rather than justice—the primary purpose of government. We are nothing so much like each other, for pride is when the admirable humanist axiom that elevates personal dignity metastasizes into self-adoration, when Protagoras's claim that "Man is the measure of all things" quite naturally mutates into "*This* man is the measure of all things."

If the humanist desire to understand the world as a window is the cause of much of the glories of the modern world—the advances in art and philosophy, science and technology—than its corrupted variation is to see the world as a mirror instead. Or, maybe more accurately, as a smartphone in which we are eternally scrolling, coveting that dopamine rush derived from the pure crystalline opioid which is continual attention. Many of the other sins are about consumption for the body, whether gluttony's filling of the belly or lust's emptying of the loins, but pride alone is about the rapacious appetites of the soul. There is something elemental, almost ethereal about pride, for where greed can be fed with riches or sloth with rest, pride is wholly more mysterious, self-regard intangible and inchoate, but as powerful as any other overweening hunger. To kill someone for a crust of bread if you're starving is understandable, almost forgivable, yet many more millions have perished due to the machinations of some mad tyrant, hell-bent on proving to somebody—the people, their teachers, God, their father—that they matter, that they're important. *More important.* Sins, however, are never just a matter of the soul, but far more importantly of the works which emanate from that source, so that whither the origins of pride (false or not), its destruction is measured in terms of the lives affected by the vainglory of an individual,

OPPOSITE The German painter Albrecht Dürer's self-portrait of 1500, held by the Alte Pinakothek of Munich, is a visual embodiment of Renaissance humanism. Turning his gaze inward, Dürer inaugurates the first year of the sixteenth century with this intense-eyed reflection of himself, an expression of the highest ideals of self-fashioning and individual creation which defined the period.

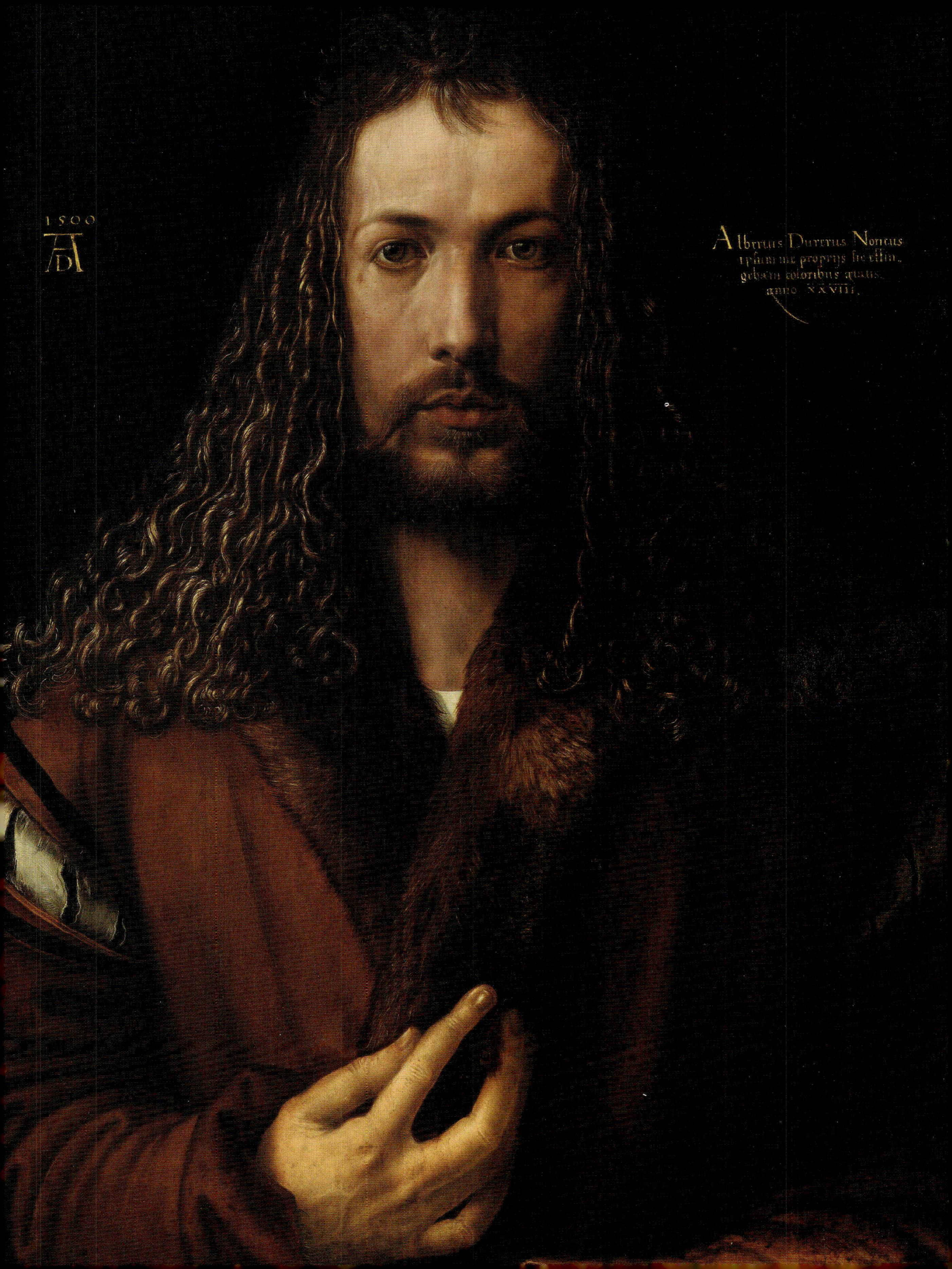
1500
AD
Albertus Durerus Noricus
ipsum me proprijs sic effin-
gebam coloribus aetatis
anno XXVIII.

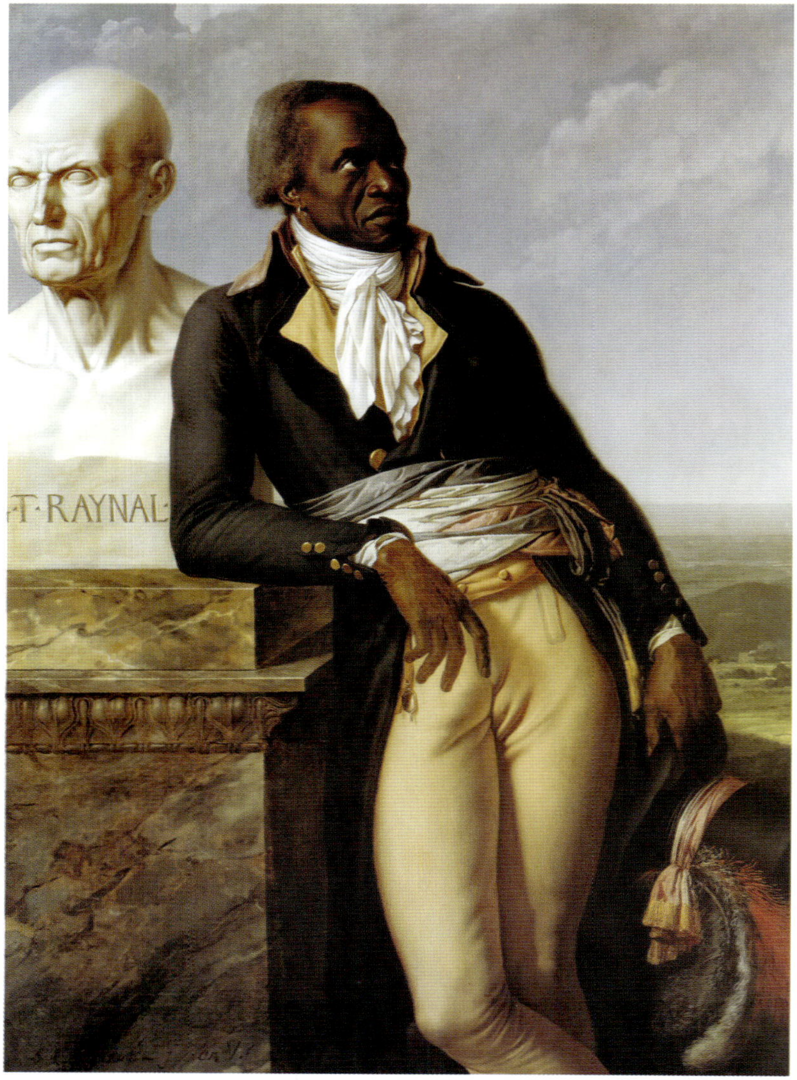

those dismissed or discarded as lesser, as unworthy of the attentions paid to the "main character" of the self-satisfied, conceited, narcissistic, hubristic man.

"It was pride that changed the angels into devils," as written by Thomas of Ireland in his fourteenth-century *Manipulus florum*, quoting Saint Augustine from a millennium before. Augustine meant this both literally and figuratively, but regardless of the mechanism whereby pride debases a man into a monster, the general thrust of such a transformation is largely agreed upon, at least by Christian theologians and their philosophical fellow-travelers. We are to understand pride, and all of its associated manifestations, as a uniquely pernicious sin, for it alone can justify to ourselves the utility of all of the other transgressions. Investigate pride's lineage, for from such perseveration on the self comes narcissism, vanity, arrogance, smugness, egotism, conceitedness. None of these are reducible to one another, but they're all arguably differing masks of elemental pride; from the haughty executive paying themselves an exorbitant bonus to the smug

ABOVE Famed neoclassical painter Anne-Louis Girode de Roucy-Trioson turns his gaze to the Haitian revolutionary and representative to the French National Convention Jean-Baptiste Belley in this 1797 portrait held by the Musée de Château de Versailles. Born in Senegal and enslaved in Santa Domingo, Belley's ascension to the political heights of the French Republic demonstrated the ideals of liberty, equality, and fraternity, and Girode's decision to depict him in the proud stance of classical portraiture is not a veneration of arrogance, but rather of dignity.

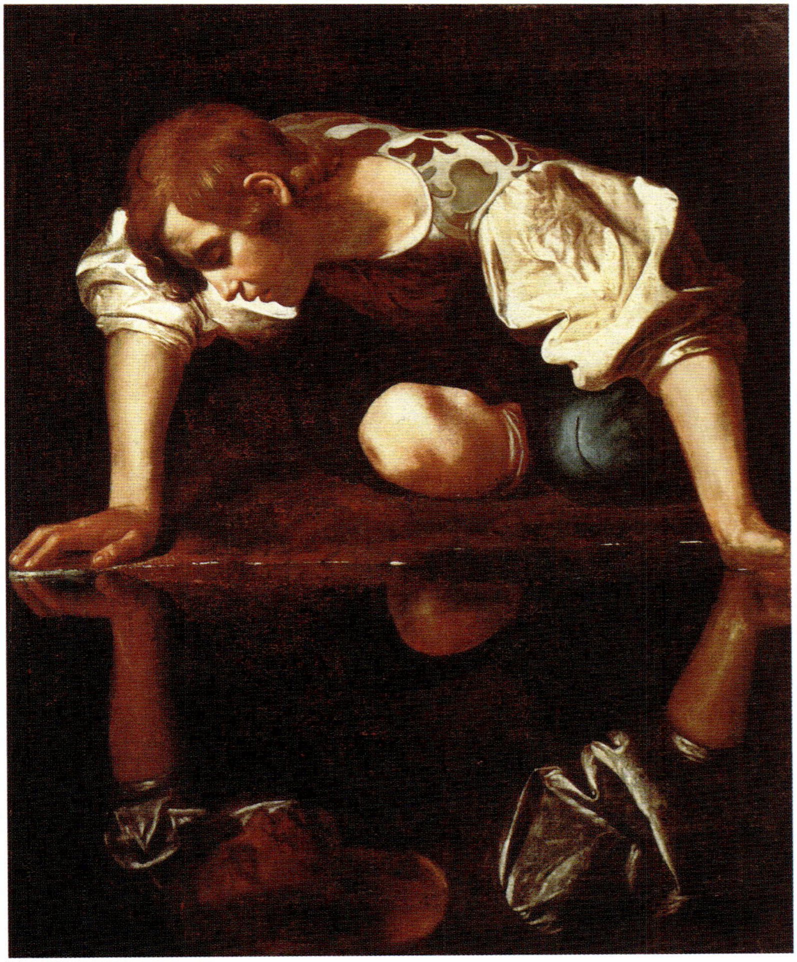

ABOVE Personally familiar with the emotion of pride, and of narcissism, the brilliant Italian painter Caravaggio interprets the legend of Narcissus in this work composed between 1597 and 1599, the original held at the Gallerie Nazionali d'Arte Antica, Rome.

activist tsk-tsking everyone else's conduct, in the conduct of the arrogant writer obsessively checking her reviews and the vain influencer altering the filter on his Instagram photos—these are the many legions of pride's children.

Pride need not always be condemned, for arguments could be made that in self-regard there is a kingdom of dignity and assertion, a realm of regality and respect. What can seem like pride is often simply poise, and all the better for it. There's a reason why "Pride" is so often the rallying cry for civil libertarians and those challenging injustice, why we can admiringly speak of Black Pride and LGBTQ+ Pride. What the term means in those contexts is different from the original term; rather than excessive self-regard, they are simple statements of basic self-regard in an unjust society that would render the marginalized voiceless and without agency. There is a potent subversion of the pride which is so often oppressive in those calls to equity, liberty, and justice, for it's not to say "I'm more important than you" to the proudful oppressor, but rather "I'm just as

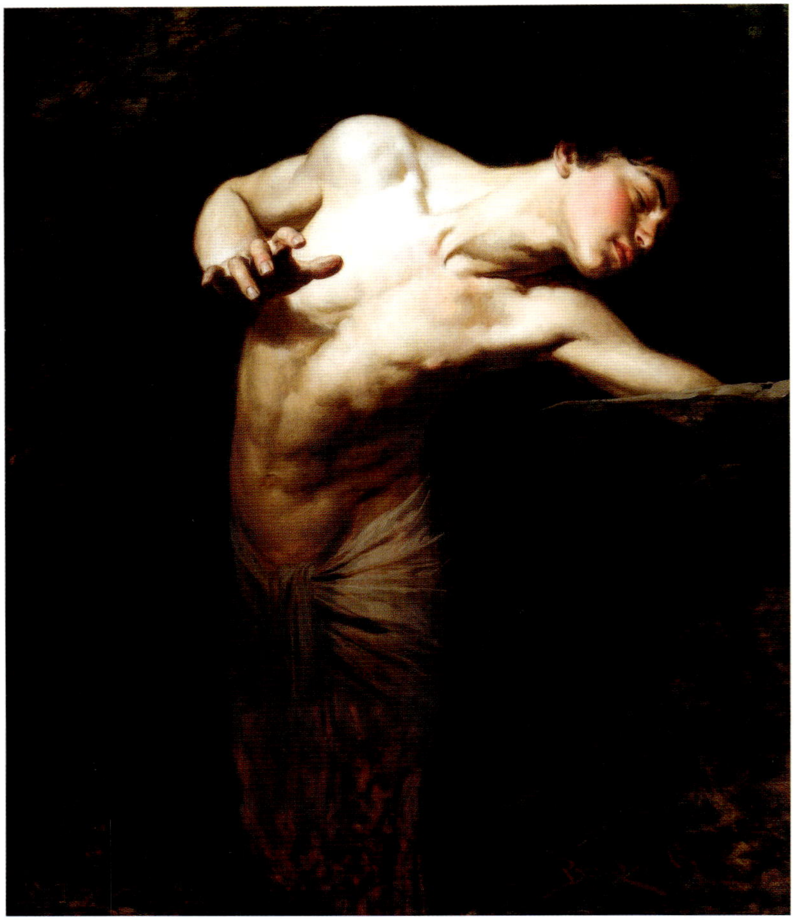

important as you," a rather different (and unassailable) proposition. Like the concept of respect, for whom some view everyone as worthy of such a quality but others think that it is their own singular purview, pride can come in varieties both noxious and emancipatory, the bars for a prison and the key for its release.

Doubtless we don't respect those who are craven, mealy, weak-willed, or worm-like; there is a reason why the opposite of pride can sometimes seem as bad, or worse, of a vice. A confident person can be many things, stalwart, loyal, and generous, while the prideful man can be thin-skinned, selfish, even cruel. Confidence is outward facing, while pride is a retreat into the self. Most psychologically potent of sins, the cerebral transgression if you will, pride is often the subject of great literature, the narrative of an individual brought low by flawed hubris when humility would have served them better. Self-regard is an internal tension, a rough knot in the wood of the soul. Ovid, that great Roman poet of the mercurial self, gives sense of the extremes of pride in his parable about Narcissus, a beautiful young hunter so enamored with his own reflection that he withers away while gazing with intense longing into a clear pool of water. Immune to the affections of other humans—and thus to any connection, any true union with a soul not his own—Narcissus thence for "outstretched / upon the overshadowed green, his eyes / fixed on their mirrored image never may know /

LEFT Clearly attracted to the master Caravaggio's love of formal beauty and striking chiaroscuro, the Hungarian painter Gyula Benczúr, in his *Narcissus*, rendered in 1881 with the original at the Hungarian National Gallery in Budapest, raises the question of whether its mythic subject perhaps had a good reason for being so self-infatuated.

their longings satisfied, and by their sight / he is himself undone." Lost in the eyes of another, we may discover infinite possibility, but our own reflections are a poor substitute, a shallow pool in which we're easily drowned.

Invented by Ovid, a point which deserves a little pride, the myth of Narcissus is an irresistible artistic subject as much as a cautionary tale: the beautiful young man in a sylvan grove, leaning over a clear spring and with intense fascination desiring to embrace and caress a mere reflection of himself. Visual imagery is oft the medium of pride, closely related to vanity, the idolatry of youthfulness, beauty, and vigor, for the font of Narcissus's failure was his physical perfection which ensnared him. Oscar Wilde, the Victorian dandy and aesthete who understood well the regenerative properties of beauty, the paradisical possibility of decadence, and the utopian potential of pleasure, also had the wisdom to warn about its potential demonic effects. *The Picture of Dorian Gray*, published in 1890, is Wilde's warning about vanity in its story about the titular, libertine muse who enters a Faustian covenant whereby his beauty shall not fade while his hidden portrait suffers the inevitable ravages of entropy instead. By the end of the novel, Dorian has ragefully destroyed his portrait in a pique of contrition, so that when his servants discover the slashed portrait, the figure within has been returned to youth while the hedonist suicide is as withered and infirm as should have been expected by his age.

Wilde understood that the "only thing in the world worse than being talked about . . . is not being talked about." More than anything beauty demands attention—pride demands attention—but what's echoed back endlessly is the solitary individual's own vanity, like a pair of mirrors in a tailor's shop reflecting each other in endless regress. Vanity is merely a permutation of pride. To glory in your own appearance, or in perception of your own beauty, sexuality, or sartorial style, is just pride translated. Arguably power is the stimulating impulse behind pride, to demand, to exploit, to commandeer, to subvert, to control being the primary purpose of the rebellion of Lucifer, who, though he was initially beautiful, spent more time admiring his own sovereign abilities than his reflection. Peg-legged Ahab stomping about the deck of the *Pequod* in Herman Melville's sublime 1851 *Moby-Dick; or, the Whale* is not a man enamored with his own visage, but he does hold limitless, rageful faith in his own sovereign abilities. Such pride is the hubris which the Greeks so eloquently warned about, the fatal flaw intrinsic to some whereby excessive belief in one's own abilities, strengths, and rights manifests tragically. For Ahab, his compulsion to harpoon and murder the titular white whale that was responsible for both the captain's infirmity and the death of his first mate is born from a wicked, almost Luciferian pride. "For could the sun do that, then could I do the other," Ahab says to his mate Starbuck, "Who's over me? Truth hath no confines," though the captain would finally sink with the *Pequod* and his crew, peg leg and all.

Naturally there is an etiology of this affliction, the disease of so-called narcissistic personality disorder, often associated with its partners in the Dark Triad of personality disorders that includes sociopathy and Machiavellianism. According to the *Diagnostic and Statistical Manual of Mental Disorders, Volume 5*, narcissistic personality disorder is characterized by a "grandiose sense of self-importance," marked by "fantasies of success, power, brilliance, beauty, or perfect love," as well as a sense of their own election or specialness, the need for excessive admiration,

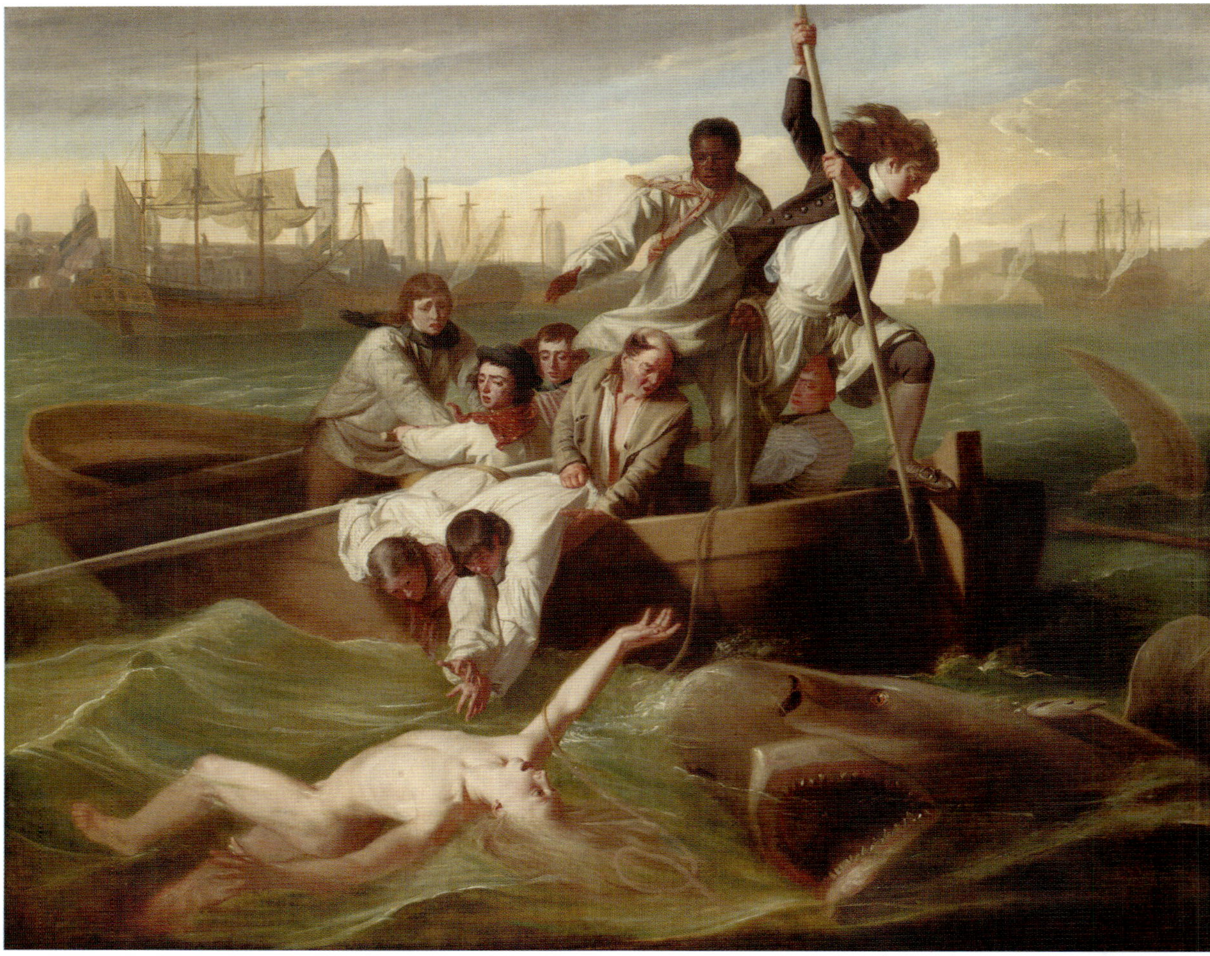

a grandiose sense of entitlement, an inclination toward both exploiting and envying others, and most disturbingly a lack of empathy. According to the *DSM-5*, somewhere between 1 percent and 15 percent of people in the United States could be diagnosed with the condition, meaning almost one out of six Americans may be helplessly narcissistic. Ultimately such pride is not just an obsessive self-regard, but also an instrumentalization of others, a lack of compunction about using your fellow humans as mere tools to further your own aims.

Bret Easton Ellis took such pride to its logical and terrifying conclusion in his 1991 satirical novel *American Psycho*, in which the narcissism of yuppie Wall Street investment bro Patrick Bateman manifests in the form of his becoming a sadistic serial killer. Such a conflation, between pride and murderousness, helps to illustrate the dangers of allowing the former to degenerate. Fundamentally, pride is anti-egalitarian, for it defines others as mere instruments of oneself. Some of this is unavoidable, an aspect of being human (as all the sins are), but when pride is elevated to such a degree that those separate from oneself become entirely insignificant, then the murder of other people for sadistic enjoyment might as well follow. *American Psycho*, an understandably controversial novel that seemingly

ABOVE The American artist John Singleton Copley's 1778 epic classic *Watson and the Shark*, original held at the National Gallery of Art in Washington, DC, depicts a moment of high drama in his imagining of an actual event that had occurred earlier that year when an English sailor boy was saved from a shark attack in the harbor at Havana. Though completed eighty-three years before Herman Melville would publish *Moby-Dick*, the image of the regal harpooner attacking the shark can't help but prefigure Ahab and his obsession with the whale.

OPPOSITE Contemporary Serbian painter Stojan Milanov's *A Busy Man*, original held by Saatchi Art, presents a briefcase-carrying businessman in a flurry of chaotic lines and jumbled colors, a figure who in his bifurcations radiates haughty sociopathy.

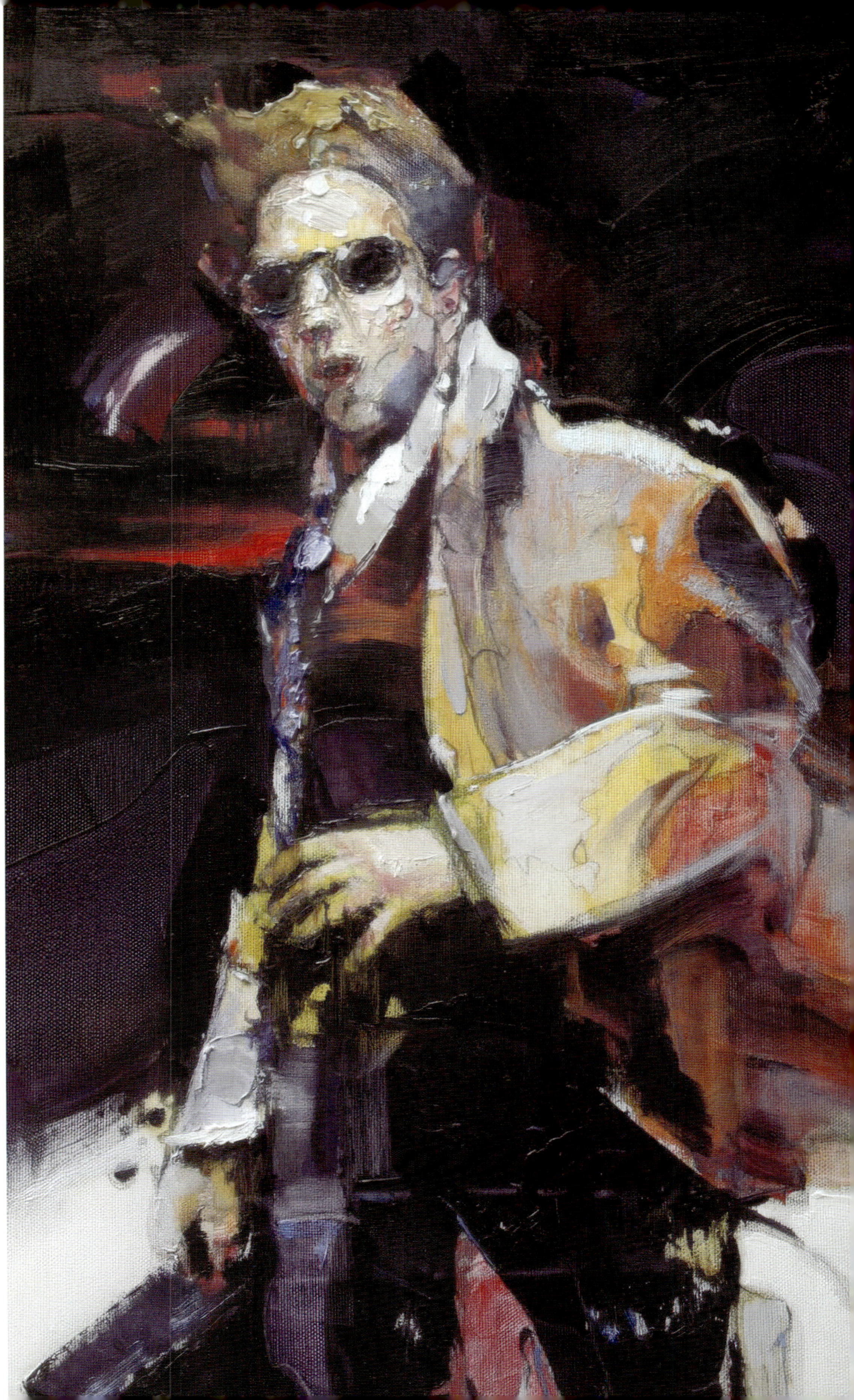

revels in horrific accounts of mutilation, cannibalism, and necrophilia, does convey a potent anthropology of pride, an understanding that at its center vanity is basically meaningless. Ellis writes that there is an "idea of a Patrick Bateman, some kind of abstraction, but there is no real me, only an entity, something illusory, and though I can hide my cold gaze and you can shake my hand and feel flesh gripping yours and maybe you can even sense our lifestyles are probably comparable: *I simply am not there*."

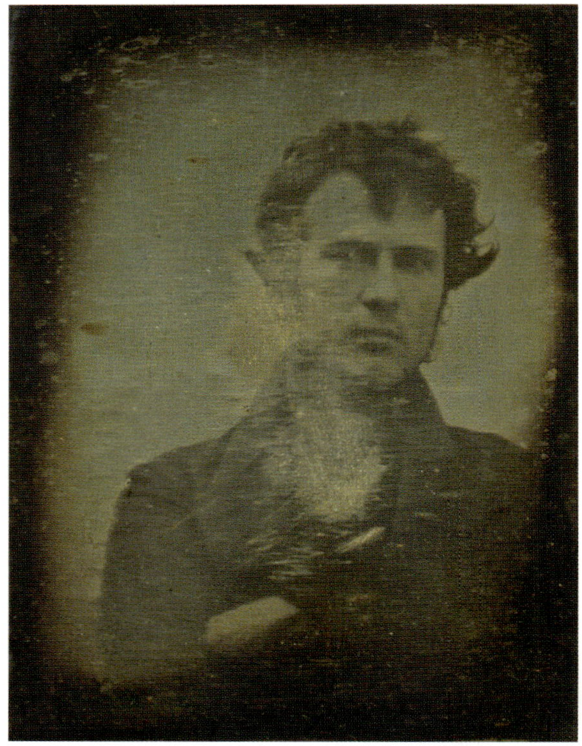

Pride is self-assertion, a desperate and anxious war of attrition against insecurity. This is the difference between pride and confidence, the former always suspecting that that which a person enthuses about is secretly lacking. Confidence has a certainty which pride is lacking. Sins are by their nature rapacious; but their feeding is rather like pouring alcohol upon a fire. The most modern of ailments, our age of selfie and social media post, of mugging for the camera, always checking to see how many "Likes" have been accrued. Endlessly scrolling on social media, staring at our avatars in the corner of Twitter or Facebook. Attempting conversation with others when the voice returning in the void is an echo. Looking toward the lens, we discard our fellow sisters and brothers; if the Scriptures are to be believed, in going into ourselves, we only spurn divinity. "Do not scornfully turn your face away from people," reads the Qur'an 31:18, "Do not walk around puffed-up with pride; God does not love arrogant and boastful people." Fundamentally pride is a sin not only against your fellow humans, or against God (whoever that might be), but also against yourself. To be bounded in a nutshell while counting yourself the king of infinite space is to collapse into a singularity of nothingness. Desiring the avoidance of pretension and at the risk of courting vulgarity, it's to vanish up into your own asshole. The journey from pride to solipsism is quick, and in the latter there is a disappearance into the self, where every window becomes a mirror, and there is no escape from the grim prison of your own skull. Communion with their fellow humans sacrificed for such a transitory thing, the promises of pride mere illusions and chimera, desert mirages. "'My name is Ozymandias, King of Kings; / Look on my Works, ye mighty and despair!'" quotes the narrator of Percy Shelley's 1818 sonnet, reading the obscured carvings on the base of the Pharaoh Ramses's once-monumental statue buried in the Sahara. "Nothing beside remains," writes Shelley. "Round the decay / Of that colossal Wreck / boundless and bare / The lone and level sands stretch far away."

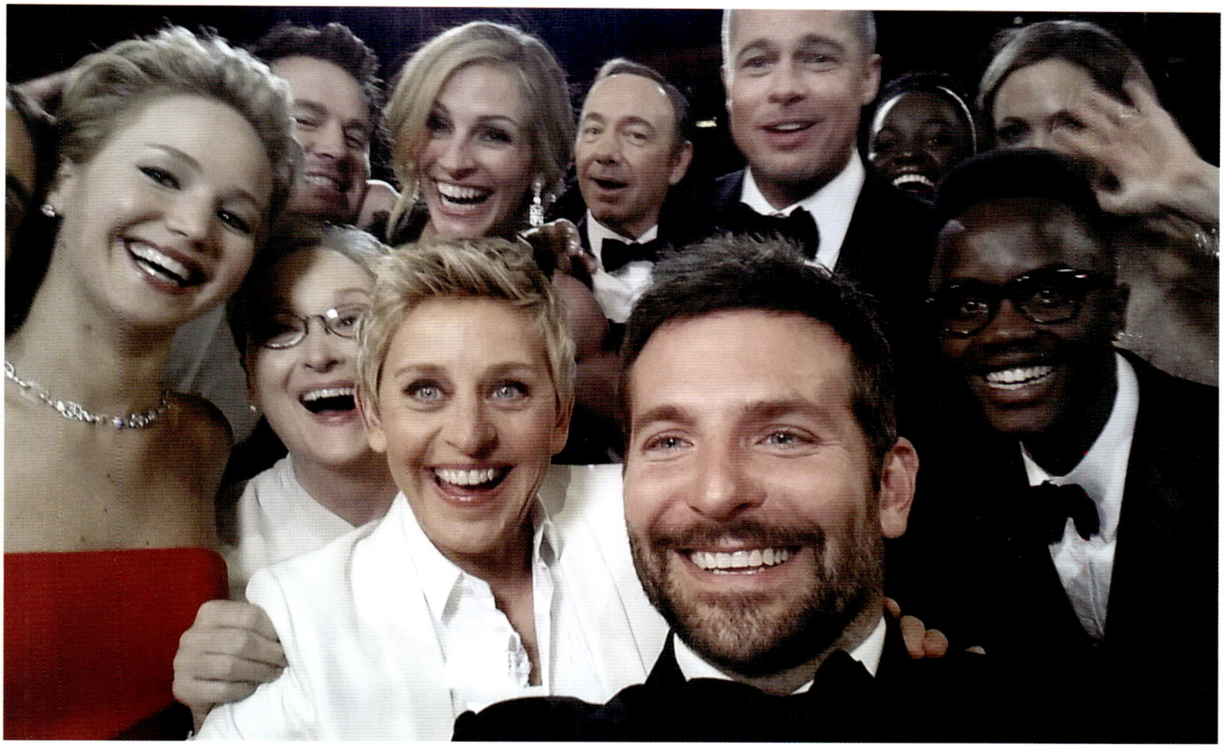

INTERLUDE—WILLIAM MCGONAGALL

OPPOSITE Thirteen years after the French had invented photographic techniques, the American daguerreotypist Robert Cornelius turned the lens toward himself, forever preserving his image in silver nitrate in this 1839 "selfie," the first of its type. In our current moment it's estimated that, using a smartphone, some ninety-three million selfies are taken every day.

ABOVE Hollywood celebrities, including Bradley Cooper, Ellen DeGeneres, Meryl Streep, Jennifer Lawrence, Brad Pitt, Kevin Spacey, and Julia Roberts, among others, turned the camera toward themselves in this selfie from the 2014 Academy Awards, which would be shared by 3.2 million people, among the most retweeted of such images.

It is unclear if Queen Victoria hid within Balmoral when Great Britain's worst poet, William McGonagall, walked sixty miles from Dundee so as to demand an audience in July of 1878, but I'd like to think so. Victoria in her mourning dress and diamond-studded tiara, in some drawing room with tartan wall-paper and oil portraits of the inbred Saxe-Coburg-Goethe family, peeking out at the corpuscular weaver insisting to the guards that he was the poet laureate. "You're not the queen's poet!" they responded. "Tennyson is the queen's poet!" Unable to enter, McGonagall walked back home. A year earlier, McGonagall had written asking that Victoria be his patron; he was rebuffed with utmost politeness. With an arrogance indistinguishable from delusion, McGonagall interpreted the rejection positively. Not all critics were as polite, because McGonagall has been remembered—accurately—as the worst poet to place one metrical foot in front of the other. "Beautiful railway bridge of the silv'ry Tay," McGonagall wrote in 1880, "Alas! I am very sorry to say / That ninety lives have been taken away / On the last sabbath day of 1879 / Which will be remember'd for a very long time." Obviously not Matthew Hopkins's "The Wreck of the Deutschland." If the affected elisions were the whole of it, maybe it would be forgivable. But the awfulness is all-consuming—his rhymes are yoked to subject matter incommensurate with their flippancy ("sorry to say . . . lives have been taken away"). Then there is his meter, which is less sprung rhythm than flung; unedited thoughts galloping away, with concluding sentiments dropped like a bowling ball. More than anything, there's McGonagall's pathological concreteness, for he is incapable of abstraction: "Beautiful new railway bridge of the silv'ry Tay, / With your strong brick piers and buttresses in so grand array, / And your thirteen central girders, which seem to my eye / Strong enough all windy storms to defy." For many poets, concreteness belies deeper abstraction—all of those red wheelbarrows and black boughs—but for McGonagall there are no metaphors. The railroad bridge is a railroad bridge, and he very much likes it.

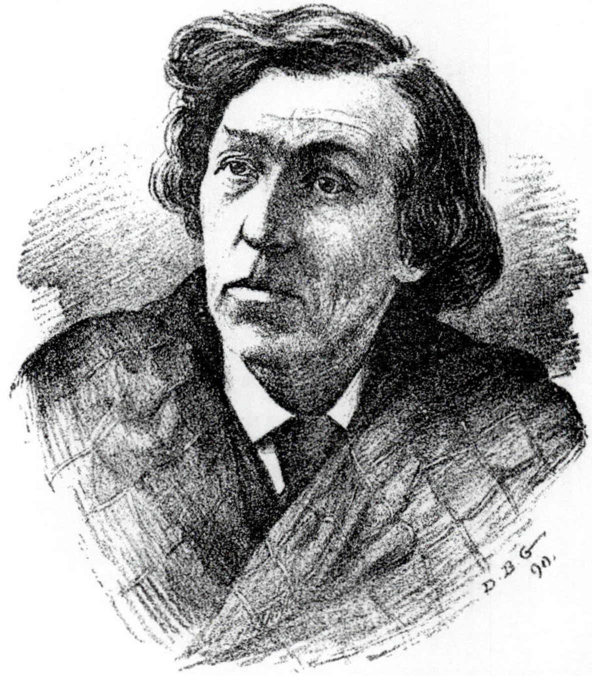

ABOVE *The Poet William McGonagall* as painted by William Bradley Lamond in 1891, with the original held by the Dundee Art Galleries and Museum Collection.

OPPOSITE, LEFT German painter Franz Xaver Winterhalter's *Prince Albert*, depicting his pompous subject in all of his regal imprimatur, composed in 1842 and held by the UK's Royal Collection Trust.

OPPOSITE, RIGHT Painted the same year as the portrait of her husband, Winterhalter's picture of Victoria, also held by the Royal Collection Trust, pairs well with its partner.

Whether or not McGonagall deserves the sobriquet of "worst" is subjective, but I can promise you that I've never read verse as bad, even in those undergraduate literary journals featuring black-and-white photographs of trees dappled in rain, or self-published anthologies of Christian verse. Poetry by children—even by stupid children—is better than his. A weaver by training, McGonagall was most likely born in Ireland, though he claimed to be from Edinburgh. Just as well to reject that land of druids and bards, for McGonagall had little magic and no poetry. Despite that, he claimed a supernatural touch, explaining that he was "seized with a strong desire to write poetry, so strong, in fact, that in imagination I thought I heard a voice crying in my ears—'Write! Write!'" In an 1890 *Weekly News* essay, McGonagall notes that he told his unseen muse, "I know nothing about poetry," and that incompetent force never rectified that. His first attempt was doggerel about Rev. George Gillifan: "He preaches in a plain, straightforward way, / The people flock to hear him night and day, / And hundreds from his church doors are often turned away, / Because he is the greatest preacher of the present day." I don't know whether or not the minister suffered some crisis of ability after reading that, though the preacher's estimation that "Shakespeare never wrote anything like this" is charitable, accurate, and hilarious.

Other citizens were far less generous. When McGonagall was received by the Dunfermline chapter of the International Organization of Good Templars (he was a member), the chair told "William, his poetry was very bad"; when reading temperance verse he was showered by pub-goers with mushy peas, and he was hired by a local circus to read while pelted with rotten eggs, fetid herring, and stale bread. Finally, the mistreatment was too much, and he wrote, "Welcome! thrice welcome! to the year 1893, / For it is the year I intend to leave Dundee, / Owing to the treatment I receive." Determined, unbowed, and unbroken, McGonagall wrote while oblivious to just how untalented he was, performing the title role in a production of *Macbeth* where he made up additional lines after refusing to die, and declaring as if he were William Blake (if Blake were an idiot) that "Dame Fortune has been very kind to me by endowing me with . . . genius." Something admirable in such single-minded dedication, his "strong desire to write poetry." No pride is quite as singular as that of the conceited madman.

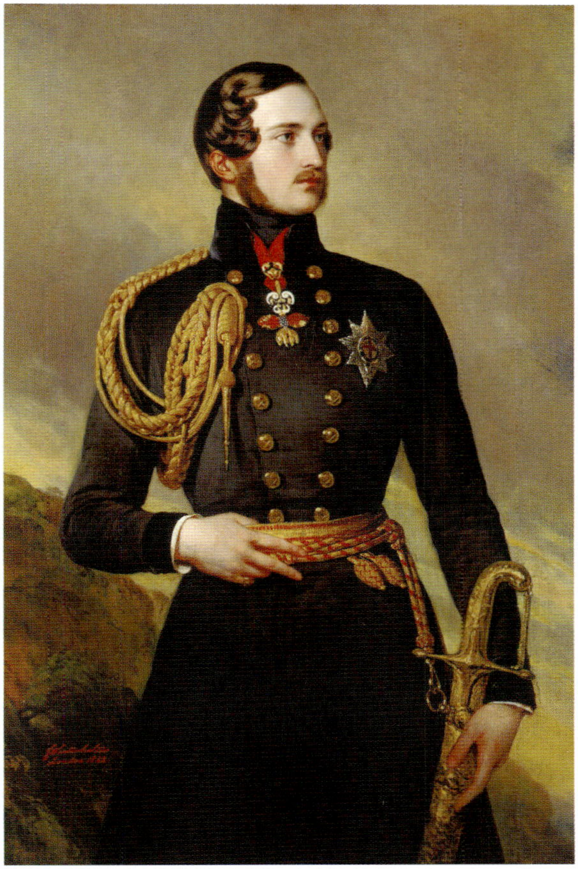

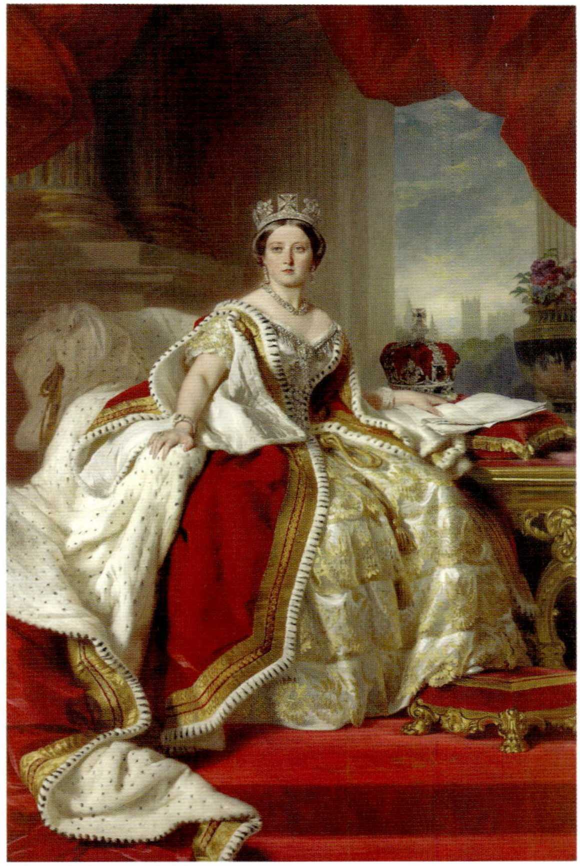

The writer "seemed inured to insult," notes Norman Watson in *Poet McGonagall: The Biography of William McGonagall*, "his deadpan response to ridicule being his greatest character trait . . . [for] he wasn't concerned by verbal insults, and didn't flinch before fusillades of missiles." To be a poet—or any type of writer, really—necessitates a bit of hubris. We'd do well to each have a Roman servant behind us, whispering "Remember that you too shall fall out of print," and to be reminded that McGonagall will remain available longer than most. He almost deconstructed the idea of poetry, performing the conceitedness, the arrogance, the narcissism that defines it, even (maybe especially) the best of writing. "He was so giftedly bad," writes Stephen Pile in *The Book of Heroic Failures*, "that he backed unwittingly into genius." Those that pelted him with pub food, the "ignorant rabble" who "lifts stones and snowballs, throws them at me" exhibited their own rancid pride, for at least McGonagall was delusional. The mob had the far crueler arrogance of glorying in the fact that they weren't him. The pride of all of his critics—hilariously bitchy though it often was—was still pride. McGonagall isn't just the patron saint of awful poets—he is the avatar of us all. His burnt-cheeked conceitedness, his endearing self-regard, are the embodiment of pride's absurdity. And his pride was so harmless by comparison. In his Balmoral journey, it's taken as a given that he's the foolish one and not Victoria, who styled herself the "Queen of India," which she never visited and knew nothing about.

Power is a fiction far more dangerous than mere poetry. Unlike a monarch who pretends to represent millions who live unwillingly under her reign, McGonagall actually did what he claimed to do, albeit poorly. Remembered as a poet—even if terrible—he still had a sense of vocation. For all of the abuse which he suffered, all of the derision and mocking, when McGonagall died and was buried in Edinburgh's Greyfriars Kirkyard, his tombstone described him as a "Poet and Tragedian," which is exactly what he was.

PRAXIS—DEADLIEST OF ALL SINS

Almost 250 feet tall, constructed for around twelve million dollars in a nation where the average income is $122 a month, the garish Monument of Neutrality looks like an unfolding white metal tripod as framed by the gleaming, tacky marble skyscrapers of Turkmenistan's geographically massive but barely populated staged capital city of Ashgabat. Looking out over Ashgabat's gridwork of manicured gardens and empty highways, was a thirty-four-foot-tall golden statue of Turkmenistan's former dictator Saparmurat Atayevich Niyazov, universally known by the cultish honorific Turkmenbashi, or "Head of All Turkmen." For the fifteen years of his reign, Turkmenbashi governed with an increasingly erratic personality, policy based on whim and paranoid delusion more than any ideology, though always with Niyazov as the fundamental arbiter of, well, everything. Turkmenbashi banned all colors for cars except white; in a pique of Caesarism he renamed the months of the year after his family members; and, fancying himself prophet, philosopher, and poet within the position of chief executive, he penned an unreadable epic entitled the *Ruhnama*, which, despite appearing as if a cross between the Persian *Shahnameh* and Stephen R. Covey's self-help bible *The 7 Habits of Highly Effective People*, was elevated to holy writ.

Within this otherwise pious Muslim nation, Turkmenbashi demanded that the *Ruhnama* be placed next to the Qur'an in mosques. Curricula throughout Turkmenistan emphasized only memorization and familiarity with the narratives and philosophy of the *Ruhnama*, insomuch as it evidenced such things, and to even receive a driver's license required a test on the finer points of Turkmenbashi thought. Not far from the Monument of Neutrality, there was a massive sculpture made to look like an open copy of the *Ruhnama*, with scheduled nightly light shows wherein it appeared as if the pages were turning. "I'm an envoy from Heaven on high!" reads Turkmenbashi, ostensibly the president of a modern nation who governed from 1990 until 2006. "Just laws, sacred spells do I bring / giving wings to the fold who would fly / and swimsuits to those who would swim." Strangely for a man whose pride was less arrogant than idolatrous, the golden statue atop the Ashgabat memorial isn't particularly flattering, with his arms outstretched and a billowing flag behind him, though perhaps that reflects its subject's self-delusions. The apotheosized dictator is rendered largely as he

OPPOSITE The French painter Auguste Toulmouche's 1889 *Vanity*, held in a private collection, satirizes the narcissism of the ostensibly moralistic Victorian era.

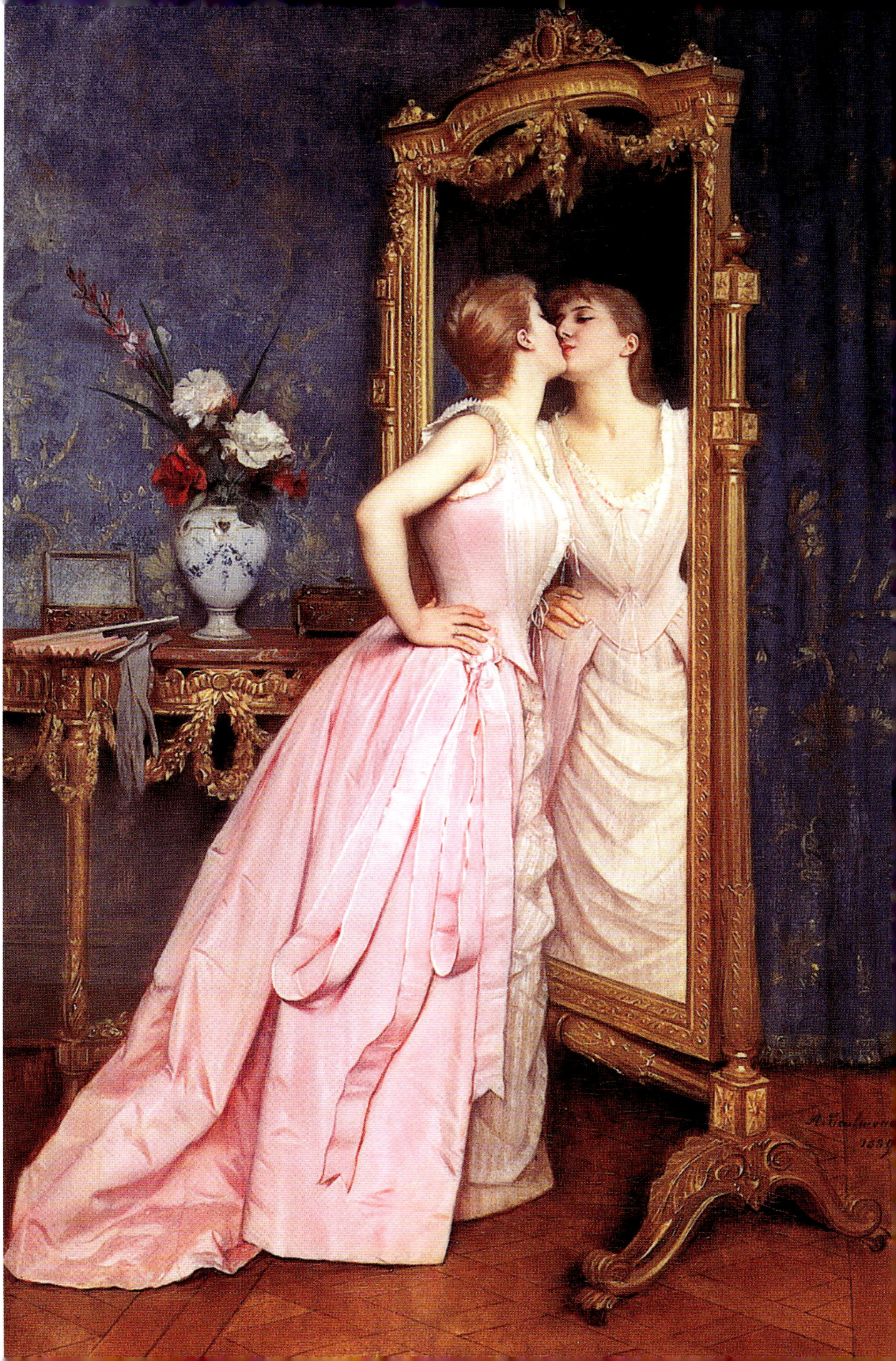

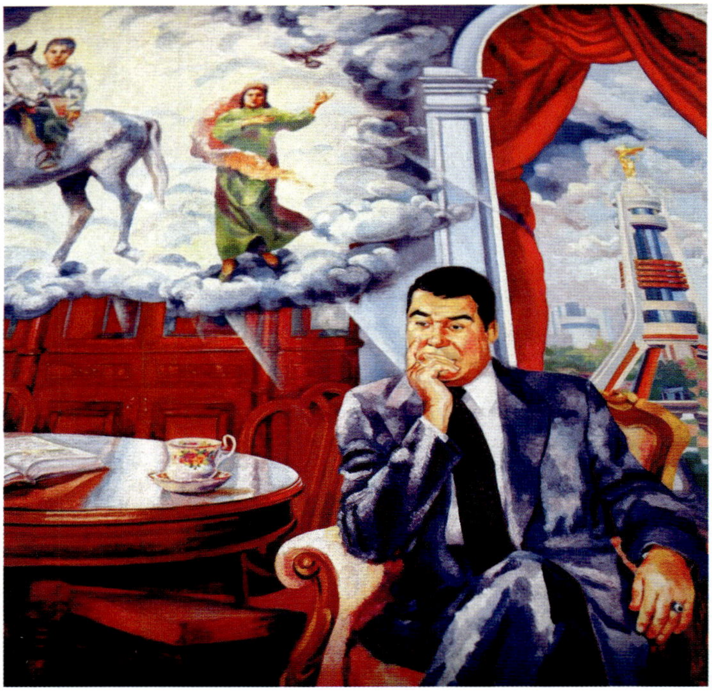

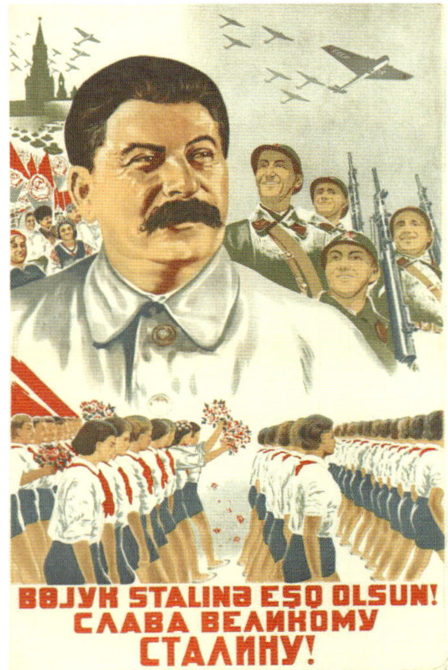

appeared, paunchy and in an ill-fitting suit, while the helmet of golden hair doesn't convey how Turkmenbashi's once-gray mane miraculously became shoe-leather black within an evening. Despite the relative representational modesty of what is, after all, a thirty-four-foot-tall golden statue, it should be noted that an internal clockwork mechanism in the base turned Turkmenbashi's face toward the rising sun every morning.

Nothing as dramatic as the imagined fate of the statue of Ramses in Shelley's "Ozymandias" happened to Turkmenbashi's monument—it was simply moved by his successor to Ashgabat's suburbs while he went on to consolidate his own growing personality cult—but it is an adequate demonstration of the absurdity of pride pushed to its extremes. Here in this dismal capital of a totalitarian state a man named Niyazov fancied himself lord of all of his people and a prophet for extra measure, so to honor that divination he erected a statue whereby he looked like a doughy nobody working in middle management within a midwestern office park somewhere. "All this will pass in a few years, when the people no longer depend on me," Niyazov said, for he claimed that his people have "always bowed to something; once it was fire, then Islam, then Marx." Perhaps, for it is crucial to remember that though the mechanism in the base of Turkmenbashi's statue may have been novel, the idea of such a memorial is very much not, for the history of civilization is less a litany of Great Men than it is a sad and often dangerous, pathetic but frequently tragic, litany of small but powerful men enraptured by their own overweening pride. Totalitarianism is perhaps simply monarchism amended by mass media, but the nature of authoritarianism has always been that of a cankered individualism writ large, where the sacred sovereignty of the person is conflated with an entire nation or people. "The tyrant is a child of

LEFT Propaganda poster of Turkmenbashi in a moment of introspection, apparently dreaming up scenes from his turgid *Ruhnama*.

RIGHT Representative Soviet propaganda poster depicting Joseph Stalin as the figurative father of the nation, surrounded by children from a variety of backgrounds, with a bust of Vladimir Lenin looking on approvingly.

OPPOSITE "I am the state," the Bourbon ruler of France Louis XIV supposedly said before the Parliament of Paris in 1655. Hyacinth Rigaud's 1700 *Portrait of Louis XVI in Coronation Robes* is displayed in the former royal palaces of the Louvre.

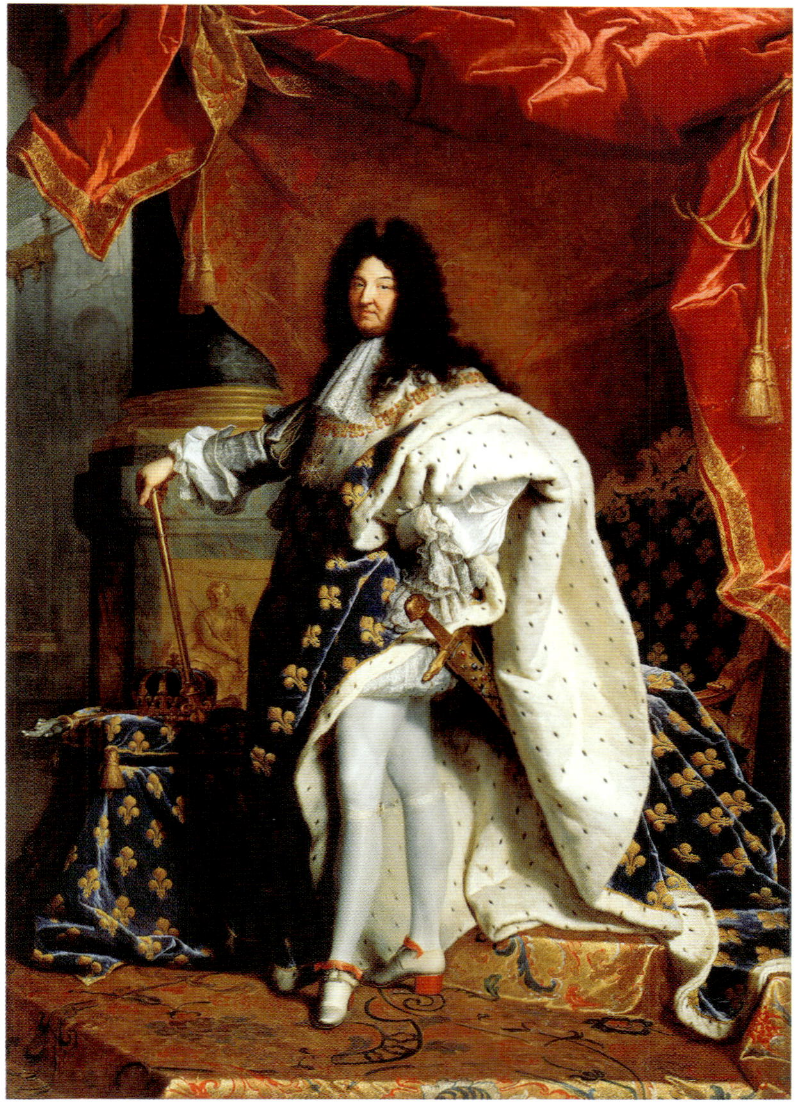

Pr de," writes Sophocles in *Oedipus Rex,* "Who drinks from his sickening cup / Recklessness and vanity, / Until from his high crest headlong / he plummets to the dust of hope." When given the power to reshape an entire world in their own visage, the vanity of the tyrant demands reform, rebellion, revolution that remakes an environment by their stipulations. And so, there is the forging of statues to greet the sun, renumbering of the calendar with their familiar names. Fundamentally pride is a selfish overflowing of the personality beyond the confines of the individual; it speaks in a language of domination and dehumanization, and left unfettered to burn like a fire in a dry wood, it ultimately can lead to the re gn of the dictator, the rule of the tyrant. For every wise Solomon there are ten degenerate Nebuchadnezzars; humble Cincinnatus is answered by decadent Caligula, stoic Marcus Aurelius by the madman Nero. Power need not imply pride per se, though that's certainly most often the script.

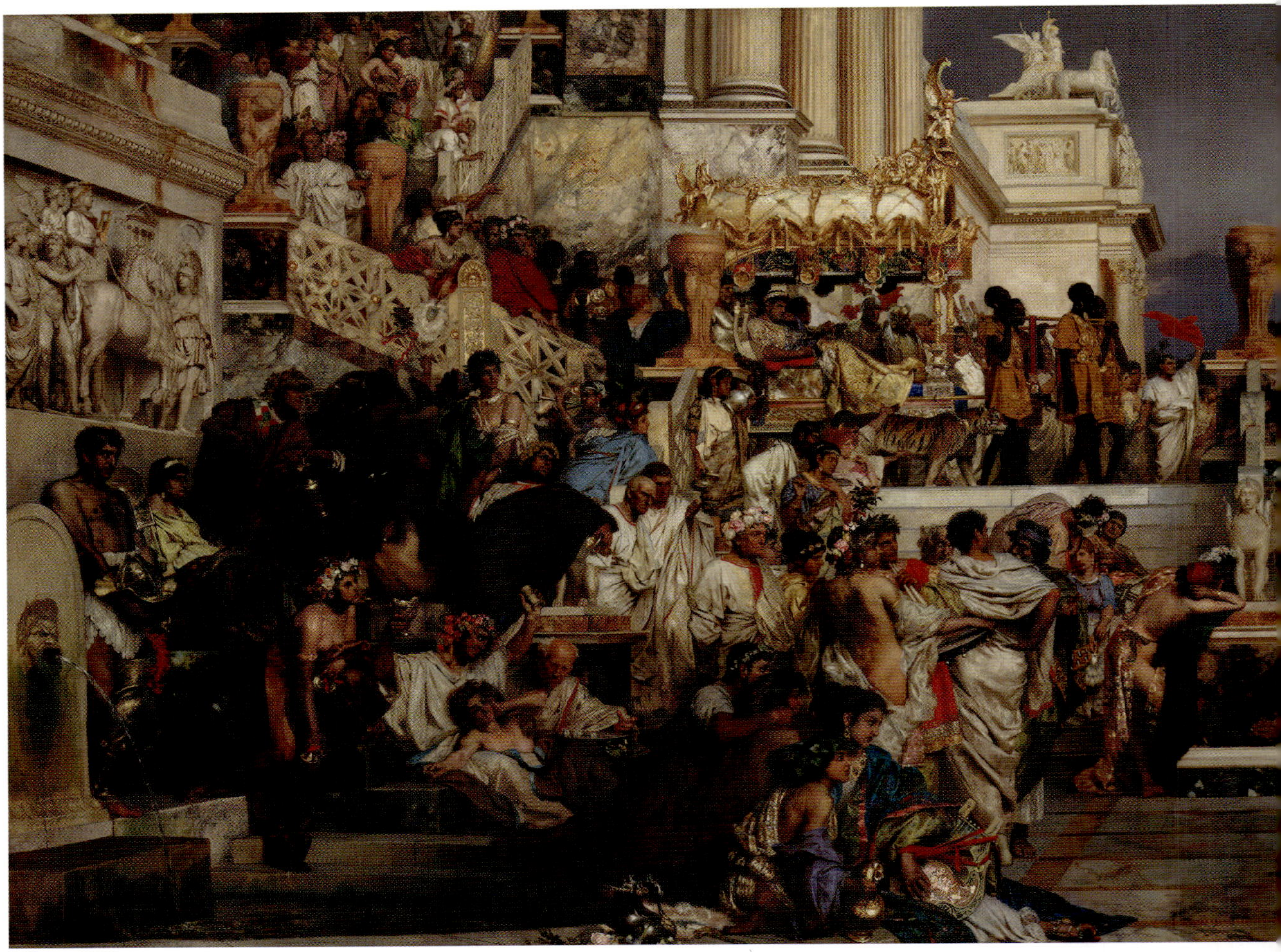

That final Roman Emperor listed is arguably the archetypal dictatorial personality, mad Nero who dressed in drag before the Senate, orchestrated the assassination of his own mother in a planned shipwreck upon the Bay of Naples, and most notoriously (and possibly archetypally) absent-mindedly plucked upon his lyre while the city burned, later blaming the conflagration on the early Christians who were then martyred in scores. Arguably the model for the Antichrist of Revelation, Nero was he who assembled Christians as burning pyres to light the entrance of guests to a garden party within his massive palace, a man whom Edward Gibbon in *The Decline and Fall of the Roman Empire* labeled "profligate and cruel." Part of the pride of Nero, as pushed to its utter extremes, was the firm faith in his own abilities—and rights—to reconstruct the world as he saw fit, to use others as players in his drama, pigments in his painting, clay in his sculpture. The distinction of impulse between the creative artist and the tyrant is unnervingly permeable, for both possess the hubris toward creation, even if the latter is frequently marked more by lack of talent. Nero with his lyre, Henry VIII claiming to have composed "Greensleeves," Adolf Hitler with his easel and oils, Joseph Stalin with his red pen moving deftly between poetry edits and drafting

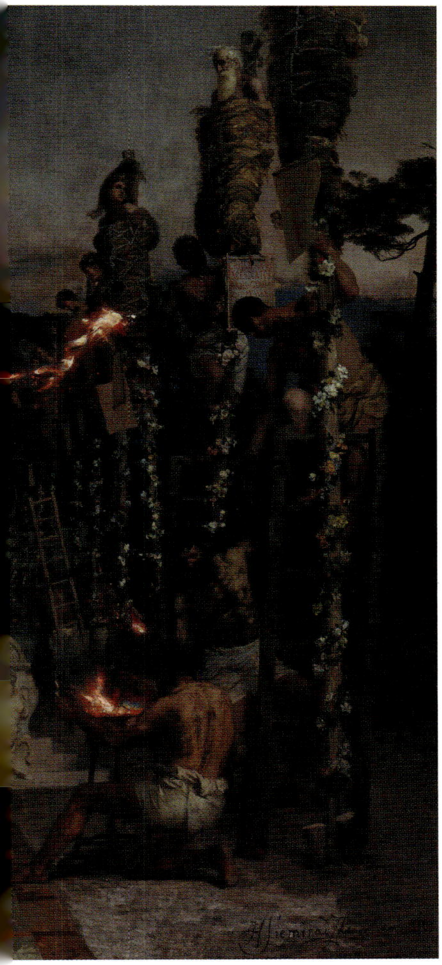

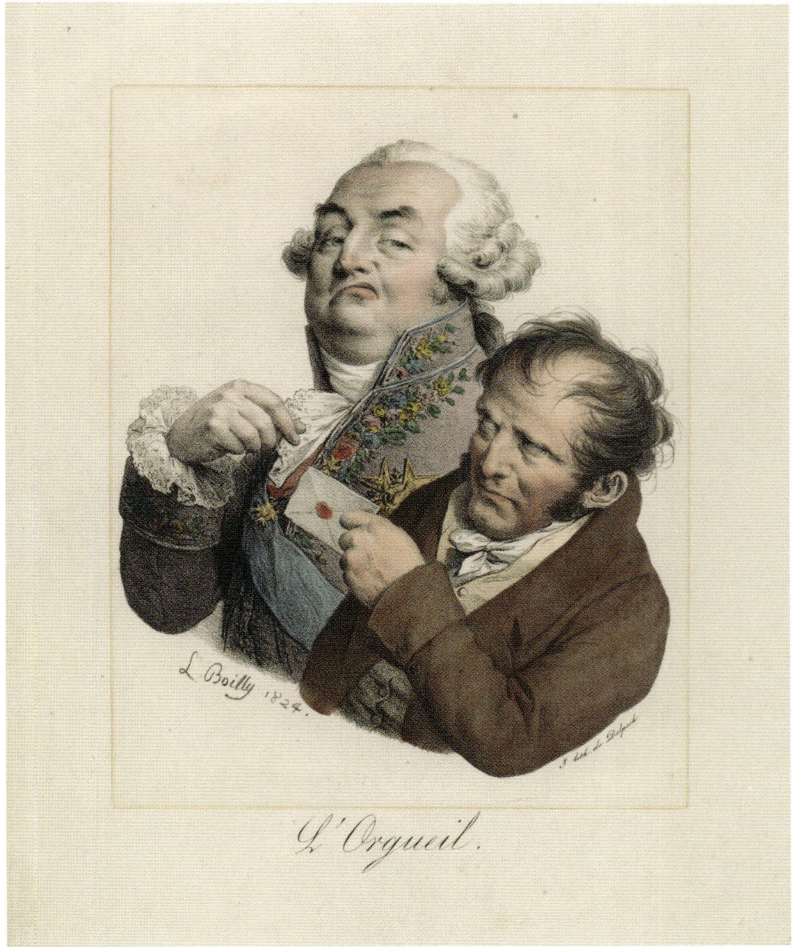

TOP LEFT Henryk Siemiradzki's 1876 historical tableaux *Nero's Torches*, original held at the National Museum in Krakow; a cautionary warning about the full tribulations of unchecked pride.

TOP RIGHT French artist Louis-Léopold Boilly's satirical cartoon *Pride*, from an 1824 series on the seven deadly sins.

lists of who was to be sent to the gulag. What artists and tyrants share is that sense of pride, that sense of entitlement which holds that they have the ability to re-create the world, and the wounded aggrievement when they don't receive the attention which they feel is theirs.

Of course rarely is the writing of dictators particularly *good*; few syllabi include Saddam Hussein's romance *Zabibah and the King* or Karadžić's *Under the Left Breast of the Century*, though the Ayatollah Ruhollah Khomeini's verse is surprisingly nimble. At the risk of being uncharitable, a dictator with artistic aspirations evokes the nut pushing their self-published pamphlets, convinced of their own genius and unwilling to countenance any revision by an editor. This, obviously, raises the issue of those who are proud, and are absolutely accurate in the estimation of their genius. Wolfgang Amadeus Mozart and Ludwig von Beethoven both infamously lacked humility; the former claimed that it would be an impiety not to admit that he was a superior talent, while the latter said that there might be thousands of princes, but "there is only one Beethoven." Here is the thing, however—both were absolutely correct. Mozart, who started composing when he was six, gave us the *Jupiter* Symphony, *The Magic Flute*, *Don Giovanni*, and the Requiem

Mass; Beethoven composed Symphony no. 5, "Pathetique" no. 8 in C Minor op. 13, and the *Moonlight* Sonata. Disdain Beethoven's arrogance as uncouth, but the composer of "Ode to Joy" isn't wrong that that piece alone is worth any number of forgotten princes within the Holy Roman Empire. Michelangelo and Pablo Picasso, James Joyce and Ernest Hemingway, Akira Kurosawa and Stanley Kubrick, Miles Davis and Bob Dylan—all megalomaniacal egos. But who can't forgive them for the Sistine Chapel ceiling and *Guernica*, *Ulysses* and *For Whom the Bell Tolls*, *Rashomon* and *Dr. Strangelove*, "So What?" and "Like a Rolling Stone"? The man shoving photocopied pamphlets into your hand at the bus stop probably doesn't have the next *Finnegans Wake* in his clammy fists—probably—but that doesn't alter the fact that even if the delusional and the truly brilliant share an arrogance, only the latter category obviously can justify it. If pride is a sin, however, it's arguably not exonerated merely because an artist is capable of greatness. The delusional can after all be forgiven their enthusiasms as the product of a diseased mind, but the genius who forgets that there is something mystical about their gifts is not unlike the rich man who inherited his wealth but attributes it to his own boot-strapping.

If tyrants are proud of their power and geniuses of their talent, then a third category of arrogance is in those who revel in their riches while attributing such luck to their own presumed talents, rather than, more realistically, luck (or a trust fund). The Gilded Age robber barons in the United States lived in opulent mansions on the Upper East Side and in summer palaces in Newport, Rhode Island; they cut their steak on gold plates with pewter knives, and drank from Baccarat crystal. Greed, as with all of the remaining seven deadly sins, can be related to pride, but while avoiding speaking too much of avarice rather than arrogance, it's worth noting the vanity which often presumes that one *deserves* that Newport mansion more than the worker in a steel mill, that one is *entitled* to the Upper East Side townhome in a way that the coal miner isn't. And thus they convince themselves that not only is their greed good, but their pride is justified as well, the logic of the eighteenth-century British political Bernard Mandeville, who in his 1714 work *The Fable of the Bees* argued that "Luxury / Employ'd a Million of the Poor, / And odious Pride a Million more; / Envy it self, and Vanity, / Were Ministers of Industry . . . The very Wheel that turn'd the Trade," an early version of the trickle-down reasoning that has since eroded society, community, and the sentiment of mutual charity between humans. Mandeville's reasoning remains how the powerful, rich, and pride justify their personal comforts, this foolish myth that the rich innately deserve their wealth because of their harder work, though it's beyond the scope of this book to crunch the numbers comparing hours put into inheritance when compared to hours deep within the earth carving anthracite from the walls.

Lest this be seen as too optimistic an appraisal of the inner seat of the soul for the working class, consider how often the gapping, internal emptiness of our current-day proud captains of industry announces itself, the tech titans of Silicon Valley who shoot octogenarian TV stars into space or contemplate cloning themselves, all to quiet the inner suck of the void where most people's hearts are. When considering pride, the identical wellspring of this sin can be apparent in far less dire circumstances than tyrants and robber barons; the hot-cheeked and flushed impulse that demands a husband snap at his wife for correcting him, that commands a woman to speak to the manager or a student to berate their teacher is but a smaller sliver of the same noxious impulse that erects

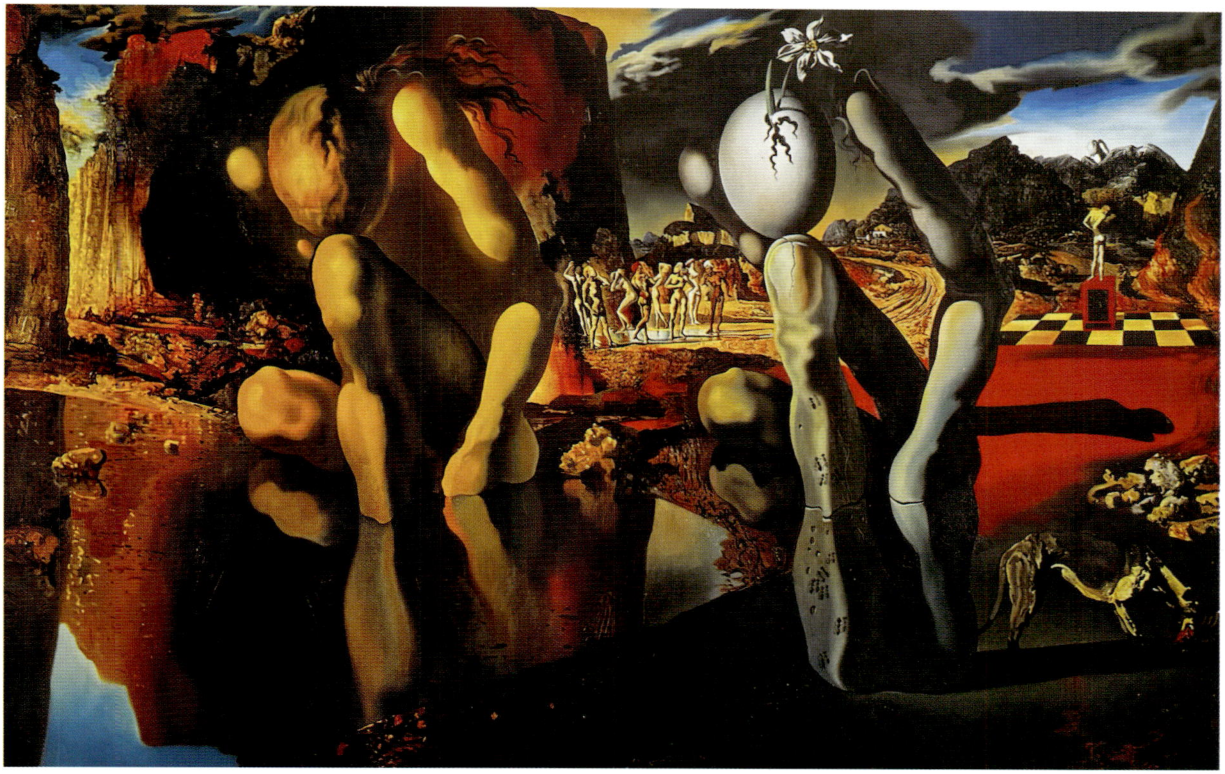

ABOVE Intended as an expression of his own disturbed mental state and composed through the principles of what he called his "paranoic-critical period," Spanish surrealist painter Salvador Dalí's 1937 *Metamorphosis of Narcissus* uses a number of optical illusions to convey the atomized and alienated, insular and interior dimension of the narcissist.

statues and portraits throughout gleaming marble capitals where everybody else is perceived as microscopic in egotistic leaders' estimation. More recently, the vampiric self-consumption of empty, nihilistic pride may have reached its consummation in the digital masters of the contemporary tech industry, for if dictators aimed to control our bodies and artists our minds, then the silicon Sibyl has commandeered our souls. Now we can all be the mad tyrant; now pride has finally been democratized, Lucifer's first sin spreading its tendrils outward through every retweet and Facebook "Like." Examine what pride has wrought, a generation of myopic young men who are self-declared incels enacting hideous violence out of their wounded ego, the entitlement of jackbooted culture warriors enraged that they no longer have complete control over every aspect of society, the narcissism of the wealthy who would prefer not to be bothered by income disparity, or disenfranchisement, or dispossession. We're told that to even speak of their being something like "privilege"—just another word for "pride," incidentally—is too divisive. Perhaps the solution to such narcissism, to such arrogance and hubris, lay in that ancient, innate, human sense of connection which comes to view others not as an audience, but as interlocutors, to submit ourselves to the dignity of our brothers and sisters. As scripture says, "The best way is the modest way. The modest way is the Golden guide!," as it is written in the great Turkmenbashi's *Ruhnama.*

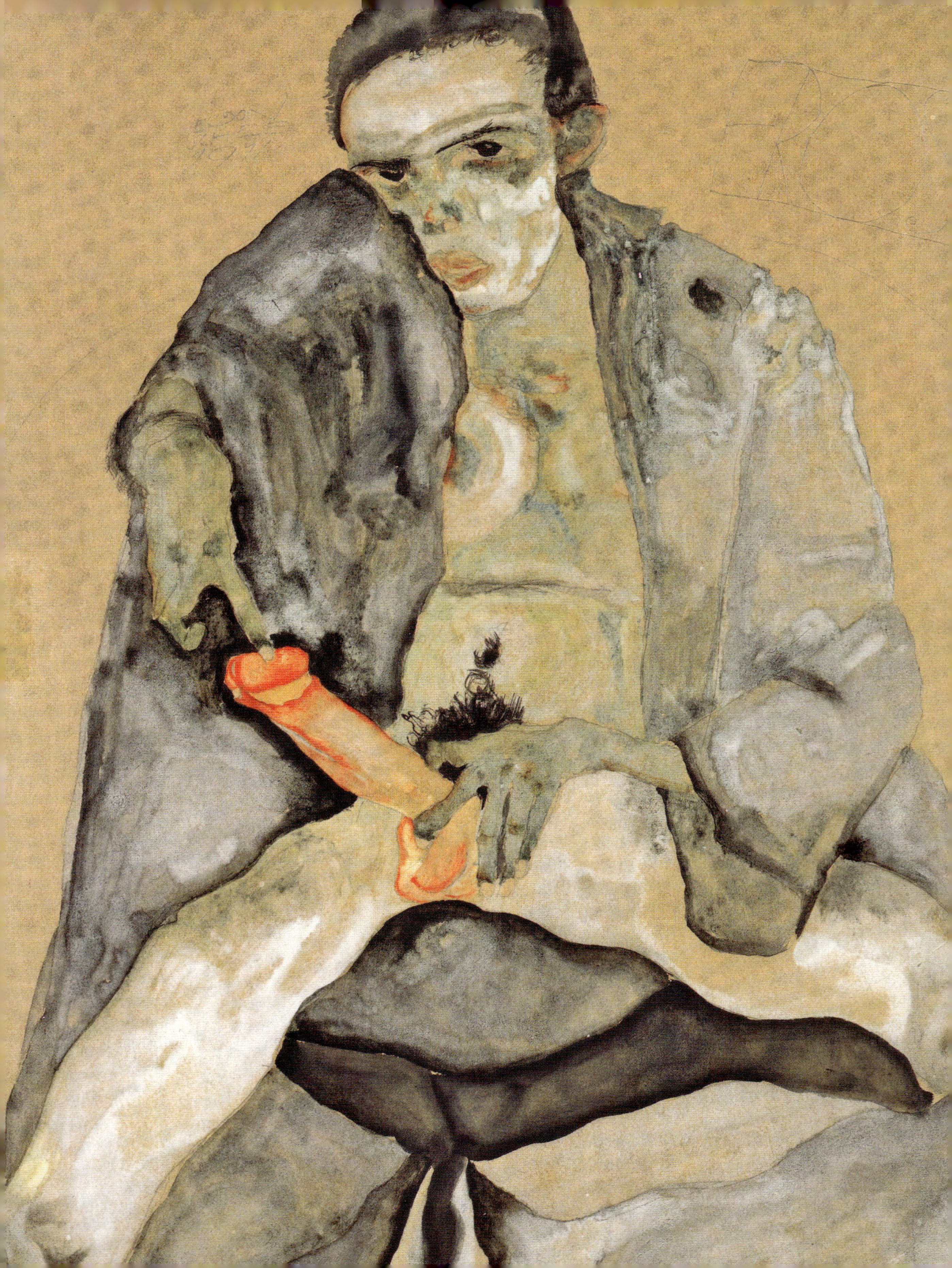

CHAPTER TWO

A SHARP WHIP AT HER OWN GIRDLE: LUST

"Blow upon my garden, / That its spices may flow out.
Let my beloved come to his garden / And eat its pleasant fruits."
—Song of Songs, 4:16

"There should be bells ringing, dams bursting, bombs going off."
—Linda Lovelace in *Deep Throat* (1972)

The reductionist stereotype which contrasts the libidinal Greeks and Romans of the classical past with stern and prudish Christians is a hatchet job, a gross simplification which ignores that the policing of sex organs has always been an imperative of the authoritarian psyche. After all, it was Caesar Augustus, the enlightened despot of Mediterranean pagan civilization, who exiled the brilliant poet Ovid to the barbarous woods of Romania, where he rusticated among illiterates for having written lines like "All right, boys, skewer me." A reading of the "Song of Songs" in the Hebrew Scriptures, which tradition holds is the erotic lyrics of King Solomon and the Ethiopian beauty the Queen of Sheba, should disavow anyone of the misapprehension that the Bible is a chaste manual. Surely much of the carnal nature of the Bible is explicated only to condemn sex, perversions from Lot and his daughters to David espying Bathsheba recounted as instances of human failure, but even in these instances sexuality is more complicated. Throughout Scripture, the attitude toward sex is often more progressive than all of those celibate monks writing exegesis centuries later might indicate. Nor is scripture unequivocally prohibitive of same-sex desire, as the "friendship" of David to Jonathan evidences, wherein the two become "one in spirit." Even the most denunciatory of passages, such as when God destroys Sodom and Gomorrah, doesn't have to do with homosexuality as is often stated, but rather with the crowd outside of Lot's house demanding to rape the strangers he is lodging. Contrary to centuries of homophobia, Genesis condemns not homosexuality but rather valorizes consent. Yet it's also true that many passages of the Hebrew Scriptures are stern in their outlining of sexual propriety. The authors of the New Testament, arguably, are even more reactionary, with Christ claiming that even to look upon a woman with lust is to commit adultery in your heart. When Pope Gregory I made his authoritative list of transgressions, it was lust who notably became the "Queen of Sins," almost usurping pride of its traditional place, and solidifying the Church as an institution that largely eschewed sexuality as a most heinous aspect of the human soul.

PREVIOUS SPREAD German artist Egon Schiele used wicked satire to investigate the sundry aspects of human nature, as in his 1911 painting *Eros,* now held in a private collection. Fascinated by the torrid and ugly aspects of sexuality, Schiele's painting is notable for something rarely seen in fine art—a turgid, tumescent, throbbing erection. If erotic, *Eros* nonetheless lacks beauty, an apt summation of lust at its most capacious and hungry.

OPPOSITE Schiele's 1914 *Seated Female Nude, Elbows Resting on Right Knee*, now held at the Albertina Museum in Vienna, is a paramount example of his approach toward depicting an unidealized sexuality.

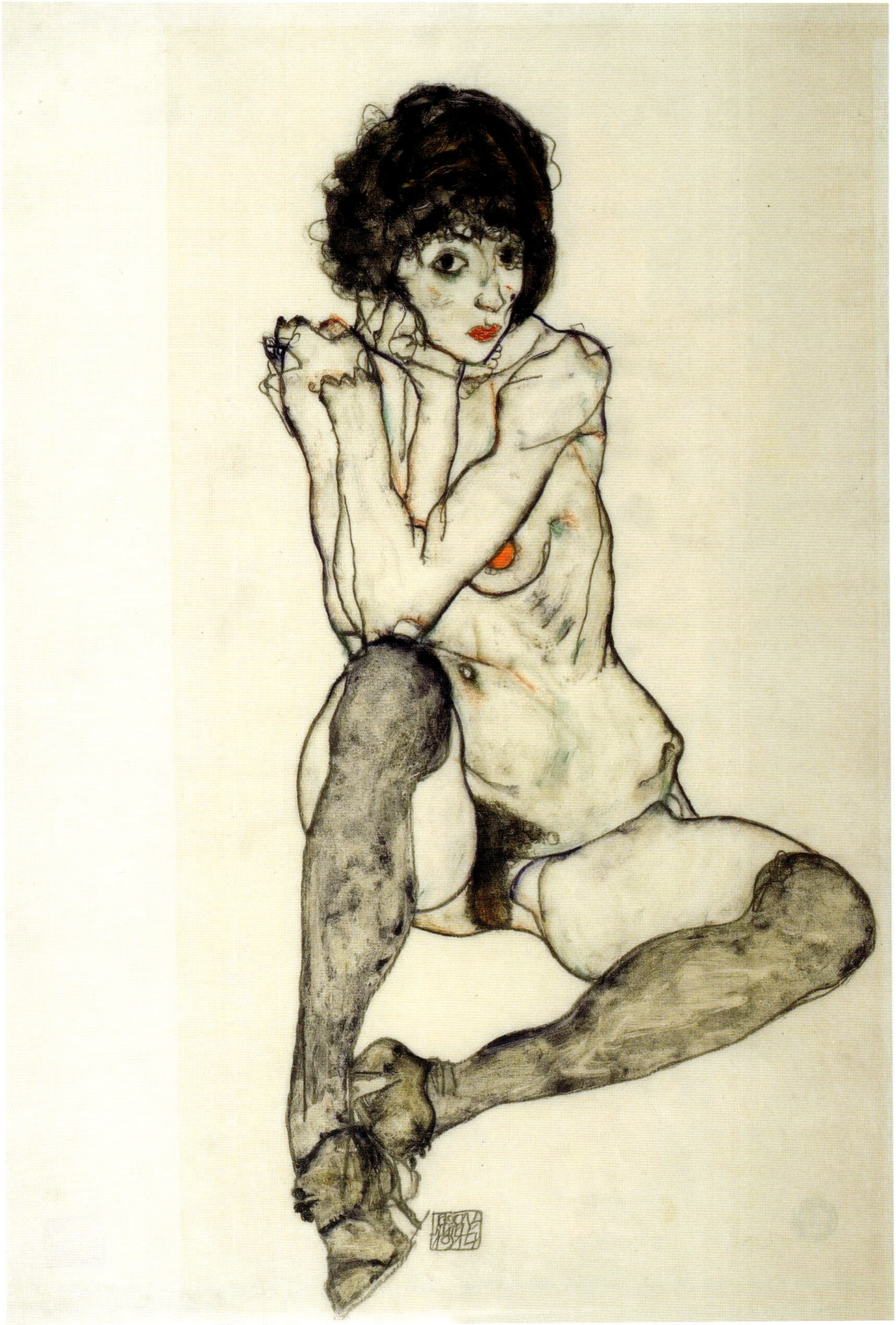

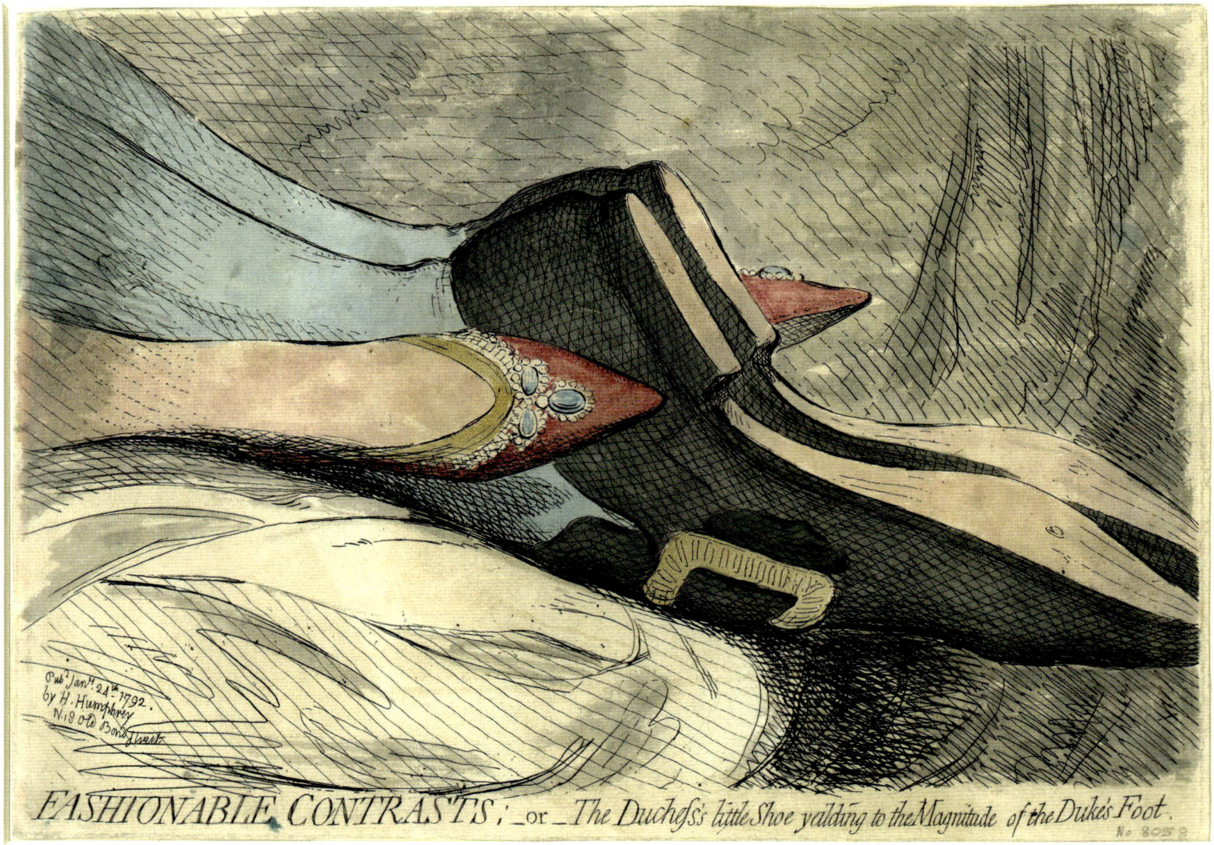

THEORY—THE BIGGEST ORGAN

The dictates of mythic propriety might prefer that the infernal Marquis de Sade's 1782 philosophical tract *Dialogue Between a Priest and a Dying Man* was written with ink composed of a mixture of the debauched libertine's thin, sickly brown shit and piss as smeared across the rough stone fourteenth-century walls of the Château de Vincennes, where he was then imprisoned for sodomy and debauchery under direct order of the king, but unfortunately for a good story he merely rendered his work on paper. Within that short tract, de Sade presents a disputation between a priest coming to offer last rites to a man who wishes that he had lived a dissolute life devoted only to his prick, mouth, and asshole. The dying man offers as a confession that "I only plucked an occasional flower when I might have gathered an ample fruit," his only regret that he hadn't fucked more and longer. Ultimately the priest is converted, and joins the dying man in a life of profligate indulgence. By the time that de Sade had written this earliest of his works that can accurately be dated, he had already been punished for various sexual crimes, from sado-masochistic romps to hosting orgies at his chalet with adolescents of both genders, and

ABOVE With more than a bit of wit and humor, British caricaturist James Gillray's 1792 cartoon *Fashionable Contrasts; or, the Duchess's Little Shoe Yielding to the Magnitude of the Duke's Foot* gives a granular view of some recreational activities during the Age of Reason. Original held by the British Museum.

of blasphemy and profanation of public morals when he hired a whore named Jeanne Testard to join him in masturbatory sacrilege involving a crucifix, a eucharistic chalice, and shouted onanistic denunciations of Christ. Lest Sade's punishment be dismissed as the mere prudishness of an antique time, the marquis's crimes were often far from consensual, as with his 1768 kidnapping and rape of Rose Keller. Saved from harsher punishments by virtue of his aristocratic station, de Sade somehow survived both the Bourbons and the Jacobins, while penning some of the most scurrilous and disturbing pornography ever committed to manuscript, such as *The 120 Days of Sodom, Justine, Philosophy in the Bedroom,* and *Juliette*.

Steadfast materialist and zealous atheist, de Sade pushed the philosophies of the Enlightenment to a nihilistic conclusion, interpreting the highest regard as being nothing as abstract as morality or ethics, but merely pleasure. *Dialogue Between a Priest and a Dying Man* enumerates the reasoning of de Sade, though whether or not his actions resulted from his philosophy or the latter was merely convenient justification for the former is the perennial biographical question. What de Sade offers is a type of libertine doxology, an affirmation of the doctrine that we're all "Created by Nature with very keen tastes, with very strong passions; placed in this world solely to yield to them and to satisfy them; and these consequences of my creation being no more than necessities arising from the first designs of Nature." The marquis rejects transcendence for the glandular; no communion but fucking and no eucharist but cum, no god but the prick and de Sade is its prophet. No doubt most Enlightenment proponents of liberty did not degenerate into libertinage, but de Sade's zealotry was rendered from an honest accounting of things driven to their natural conclusion. If all is but atoms, and the swerve of those particles, then the only ethic which matters to a man like de Sade is how those atoms in aggregate rub against each other. For the moralizer, lust is a sin, but for the libertine, lust is simply a problem that can be solved through friction.

Christianity, a casual observer might note, has had more than a bit of a perseveration on human sexuality, being a religion codified by stiffs with stiffies. The most transcendent of prosaic human experiences capable of generating an otherworldly ecstasy—for not even food or sleep can compete with the orgasm—sex in many ways offers a rejoinder to religious epiphany, a mysticism of the gonads beyond that of the spirit. Hence the rigorous scrupulosity about not just what acts are performed, but even thinking about such acts. Libertinage then could only really be a phenomenon in a society that's fully repressed; it is the ejaculatory eruption of all of that which the Church demands you not indulge in, experience, or even contemplate. In many ways de Sade becomes, dialectically that is, the most Christian of figures, for masturbating with a crucifix can only be shocking for those living within a Christian society. Christian prudery ebbs and flows, there is no essential anti-sexuality within the faith per se, as the example of every moralizing Puritan can be matched with a medieval pilgrim sporting a metal badge shaped like a cock or vulva, a Caravaggio painting of a hard-bodied Christ who is beautiful in more than just spirit. If anything, lust and chastity exist within tense symbiosis throughout the faith, for arguably the greatest benefit Christianity ever supplied to sexuality was sin.

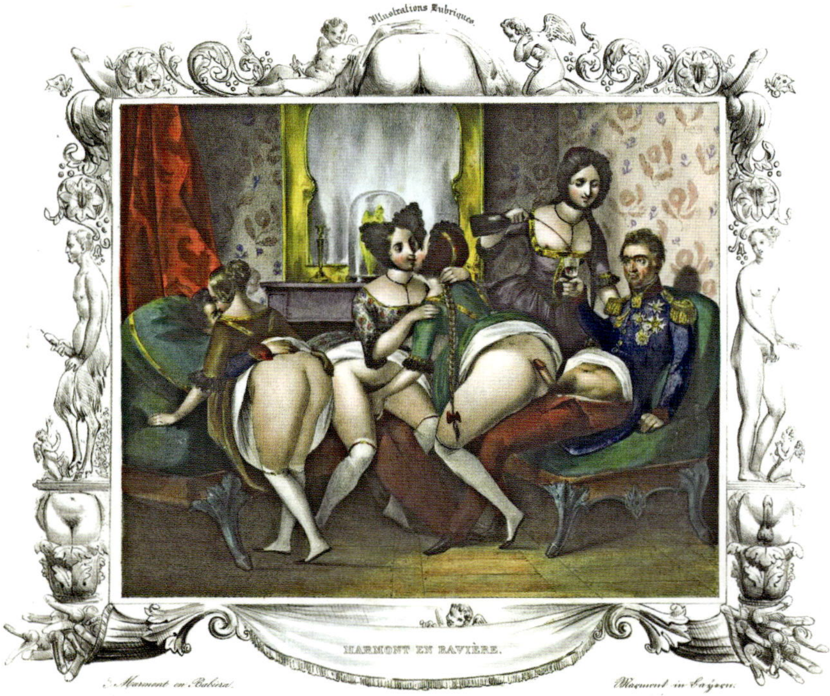

Transgression and temptation are, after all, estimably sexy. It would be historical revisionism to claim that Christian orthodoxy was sex-positive, for there is certainly no shortage of source quotes to demonstrate the stern and doctrinaire denunciations of what the body can do. Thomas Aquinas, who unlike Augustine was celibate his entire life, says in *Cardinal Virtues* that kink is a sin, denouncing the "use of an improper instrument or other strange ways of copulating." Perhaps an even more draconian conclusion is rendered in *Summa Theologica,* where Aquinas argues that a "man who is too ardent a lover of his wife acts counter to the good of marriage." Furthermore, lust is often a *mental* crime. Augustine argues in the *City of God* that the first couple was capable of purely rational intercourse in Eden before the Fall, Adam willing his member to turgidity through logical syllogism rather than the white hot heat of passion, for it is the latter and not the former which is actually dangerous. Punishment for such passion—a necessary and appropriate punishment—is the pain of childbirth; for lover of prostitutes that the pre-reformed Augustine was, lust was primarily the woman's fault. As an example of priorities, Thomas Aquinas thought masturbation more of a sin than rape.

Within the West there has always been a counter-tradition, an argument for the naturalness and healthiness of the beast with two backs. Some of this is less an intellectual system than it simply is what people do, how they live their lives. There has, after all, thankfully always been a disjunct between what religious authorities have preached and what believers have actually practiced. Historian James Brundage provided a helpful flowchart in his classic study *Law, Sex, and Christian Society in Medieval Europe*, which specified on which days married couples would be allowed to fuck. Brundage explains that for the Church,

TOP Along with the Belgian Felicien Rops, the French illustrator Martin van Maele was a master of erotic draftsmanship, such as in his 1908 *De Sceleribus et Criminibus* or *Fellatio in Mockery of a Crucifix.* The regalia and ritual of Catholicism naturally lent itself to images of bondage, which in Protestant countries was frequently sectarian propaganda, in Catholic countries such as Belgium and France was a fetish, but that was perhaps everywhere an expression of sublimated desire. .

OPPOSITE, LEFT A 1906 illustration of an ancient Greek youth masturbating to the thought of various figures in sexual congress, rendered by the French artist Edouard-Henri Avril for the anthology of classical erotic writings *On the Figure of Venus.*

OPPOSITE, RIGHT Contemporary Spanish artist Pictor Mulier unabashedly celebrates feminine self-pleasure, as in this 2018 painting of a shirtless woman masturbating while reading Pauline Reage's 1954 pornographic BDSM novel *The Story of O.* Original represented by Saatchi.

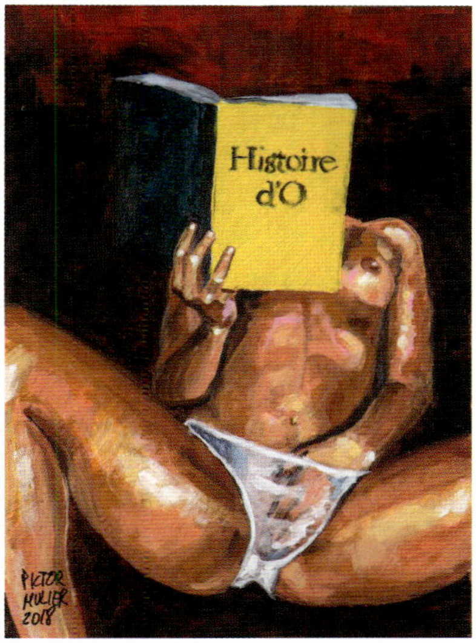

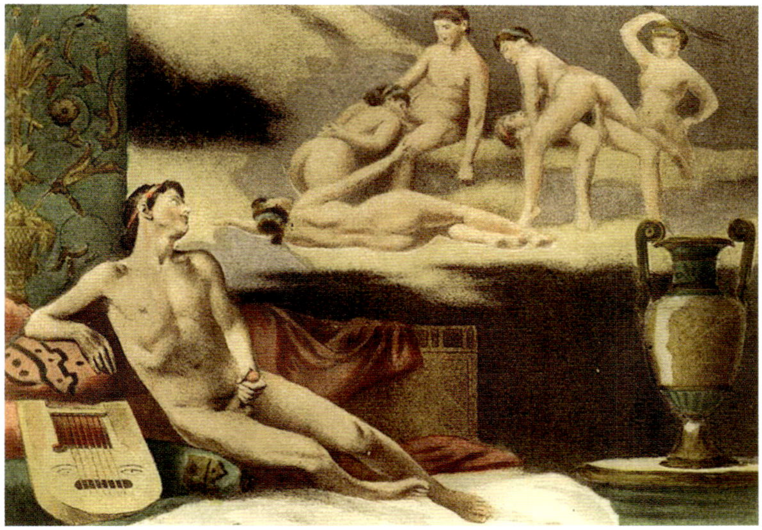

perilously few days of the calendar year would be considered appropriate for fornication, even among sacramentally married couples. If your wife is menstruating or pregnant, if it's Lent or a fast day, if it's Easter or Whitsun Week—no fucking. If it's the daytime—no fucking. If you've been married less than three days—no fucking. If it does happen to be the handful of days out of 365 when you're allowed to have sex with your spouse, you must be partially clothed, there must not be fondling or passionate kissing, and both parties must do their best not to enjoy it. Don't even think about oral sex, or, Christ save us, anal. Here is the thing, however—Brundage derived his diagram from an analysis of Penitentials, the guidebooks that priests used to decide on the proper acts of contrition for various sins which might be confessed to them. That means that people must have done all of these things that were considered lewd, and frequently. Not so different from today.

Beyond the true philosophy of lust which is generated not by brains but by genitals, and not in the seminar or church but between the sheets, there has been a long history of intellectual defenses of sexuality. Four centuries before the Common Era, the licentious post-Socratic philosophical movement known as the Cyrenaics promulgated an ethic which turned Epicureanism's command to avoid pain on its (smaller) head, rather arguing that the highest goal of life is to acquire pleasure. If the Epicureans might enjoy a simple bowl of stewed lentils and a pleasant conversation about goodness with friends, then the Cyrenaics found that a feast and an orgy were more conducive a symposium, arguably the first thinkers to intellectually advocate for hedonism. "The best thing is to possess pleasure," intoned the Cyrenaic founder known as Aristippus, for all the rest is commentary. Despite Christianity's reputation for being anti-sex, classical

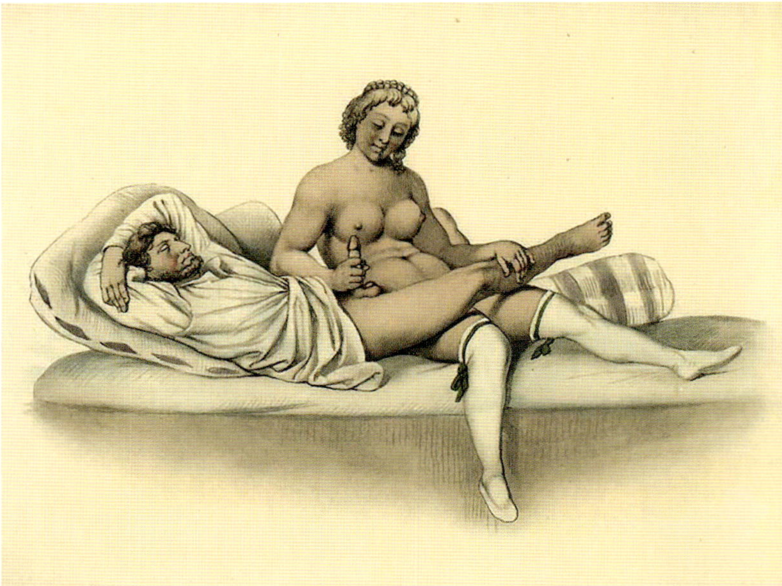

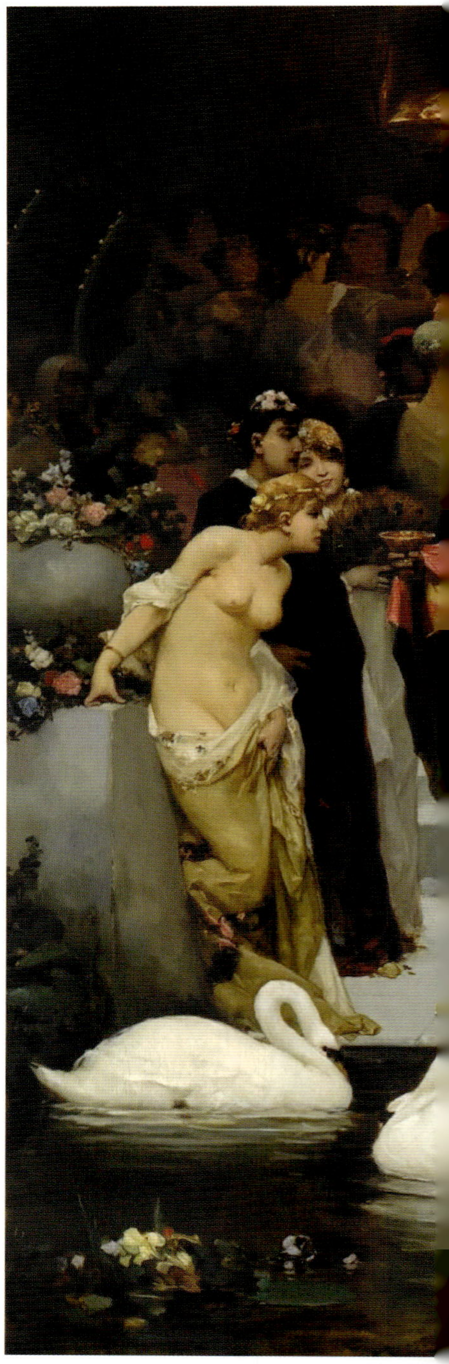

pagan critics of what was then simply a Jewish cult often ironically slandered the followers of Jesus with having committed behavior more in keeping with the Cyrenaics. Hearing of clandestine, nocturnal meetings of Christians to celebrate the Eucharist, many Romans assumed that this persecuted sect was engaging in orgiastic frenzies, with a third-century apologist named Minucius Felix recording in his dialogue *Octavius* that "Some people claim that the Christians actually worship the penis of their high priest, and adore the generative organ as if it was their own father"—kinky. Not that such slander was only directed to early Christians by pagans, for there was internecine libel as well, with groups such as the Cainites and Adamites supposedly practicing intricate forms of lustful sex magic. There's disagreement as to how accurate those claims are, but there was a potent suspicion that in sexual transgression therein lay transcendence.

Advocacy for debauchery was largely dormant in the Christian West until the Enlightenment brought forth the figure of the libertine, often in the mold of de Sade, the antinomian and amoral advocate for sexual pleasure as a means unto its own end. De Sade was merely the most notorious of this new type of man, the unrepentant rake and gladly debauched philosophe. Maybe predictably, libertinage was most well-expressed not in dry syllogism, but in itchy-palmed pornography, among the most enduring literary productions of this moment in the seventeenth and eighteenth centuries being smut. Strident, confident, and unashamed, this literature embodied the ancient Roman Catullus's warning that as concerns puritanical critics of such verse, "I will sodomize and face-fuck you" (figuratively, at least). In the tradition of Catullus were writers such as John Wilmot, the 2nd Earl of Rochester, among the most stunning of libertine poets, fusing cock and consciousness in his defense of lust. "In liquid raptures I dissolve all o'er," writes Wilmot in a 1680 poem, "Melt into sperm, and spend every pore." An embarrassment among the uptight English, the clear genius of Rochester has often been passed over in silence, while

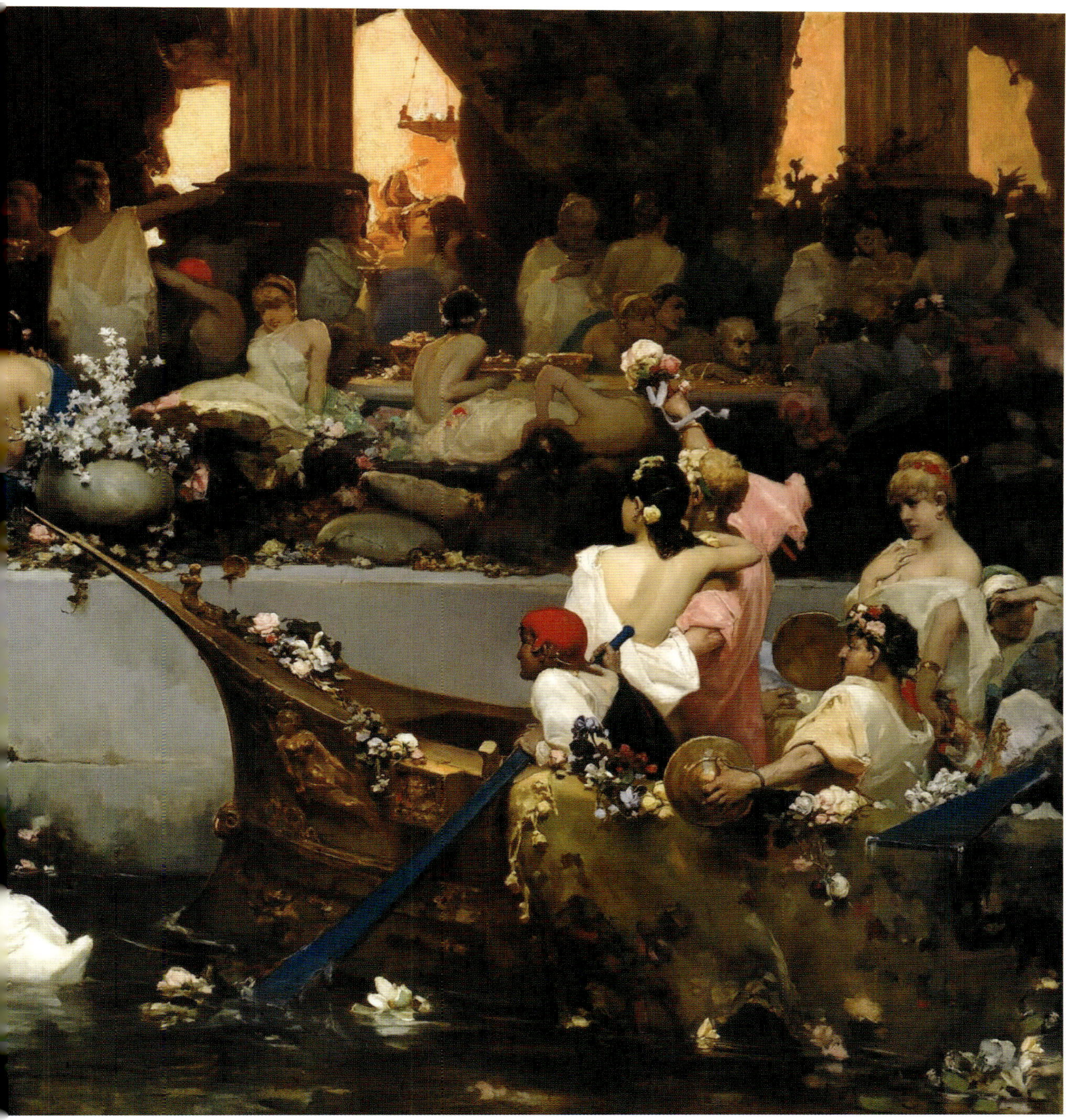

OPPOSITE An 1840 watercolor by the Austrian artist Peter Johann Nepomuk Geiger of a man enjoying a hand job.

ABOVE Polish artist Vasily Alexandra Kotarbinsky lets his imagination roam in this lush 1898 painting of a decadent Roman orgy, where dozens of beautiful young men and women congregate within magisterial architectural environs. For being an orgy, however, there seems to be a surprising dearth of actual sex occurring. Original in private collection.

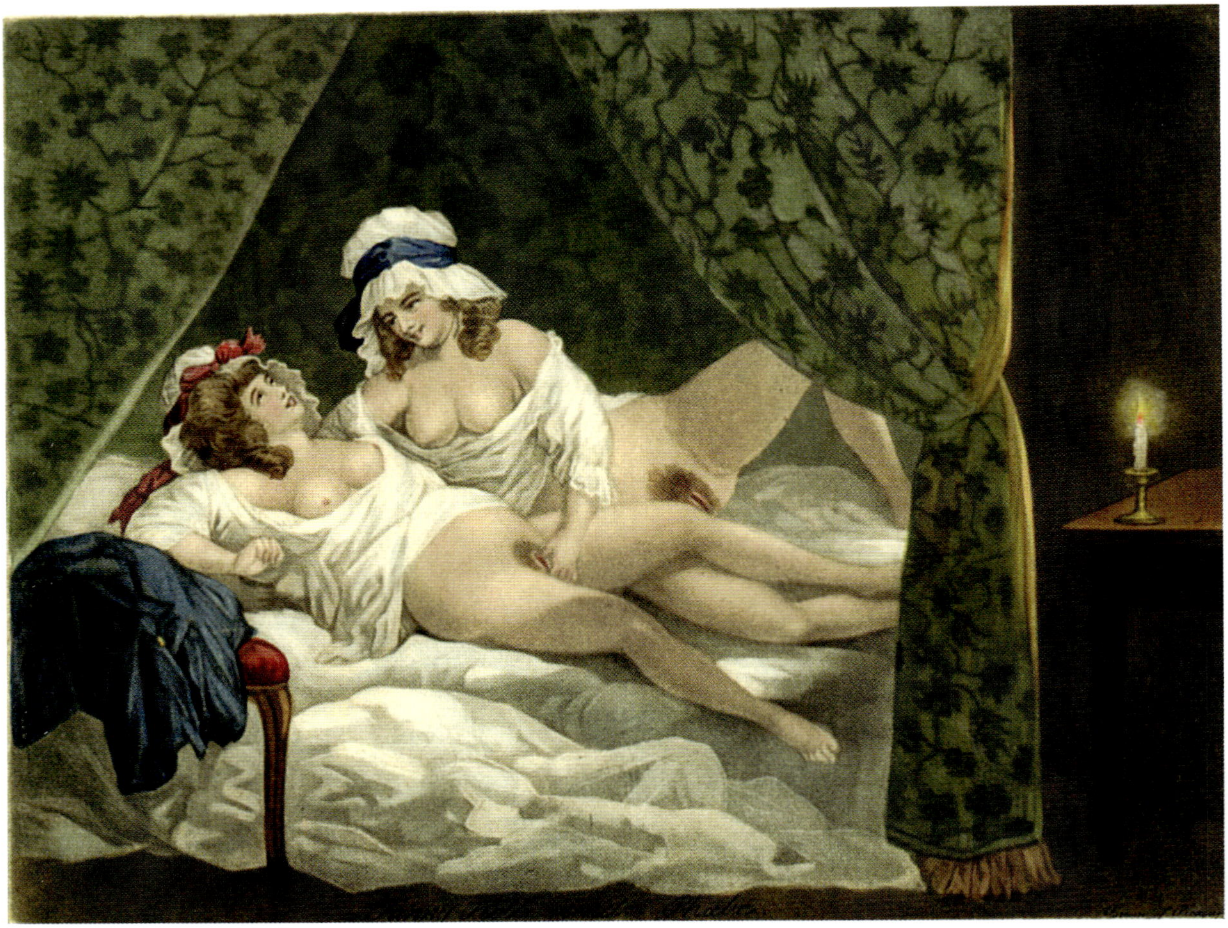

to the south amongst the Latinate French there has been more comfort with their canon of decadence, as with Pierre Choderlos de Laclos's 1782 epistolary novel *Dangerous Liaisons*, or the Enlightenment philosophe Denis Diderot's anonymous first novel *The Indiscreet Jewels* from 1748, in which the inventor of the encyclopedia provides an erotic portrait of Louis XV's mistress Madame de Pompadour. Not that the English have lacked in erotic scribblings—no place that invested in order and decorum ever could—with the 1722 Daniel Defoe novel *Moll Flanders* (by a Puritan!) surprisingly tolerant as concerns female sexual agency, while John Cleland's 1748 *Fanny Hill; or, Memoirs of a Woman of Pleasure* was unrepentant in its celebration of sexual vitality. Literature, which at its best is simply philosophy with self-awareness, can express more of the world than mere abstraction and argument does, the stanza far more appropriate than the syllogism, or as Cleland notes, most people's "foundation in virtue was no other than a total ignorance of vice." These were novels of engorgement and tumescence, of fellatio and cunnilingus, spanked bottoms and canned backsides, of pussy and pricks, regardless of all of the powdered wigs characters might be wearing.

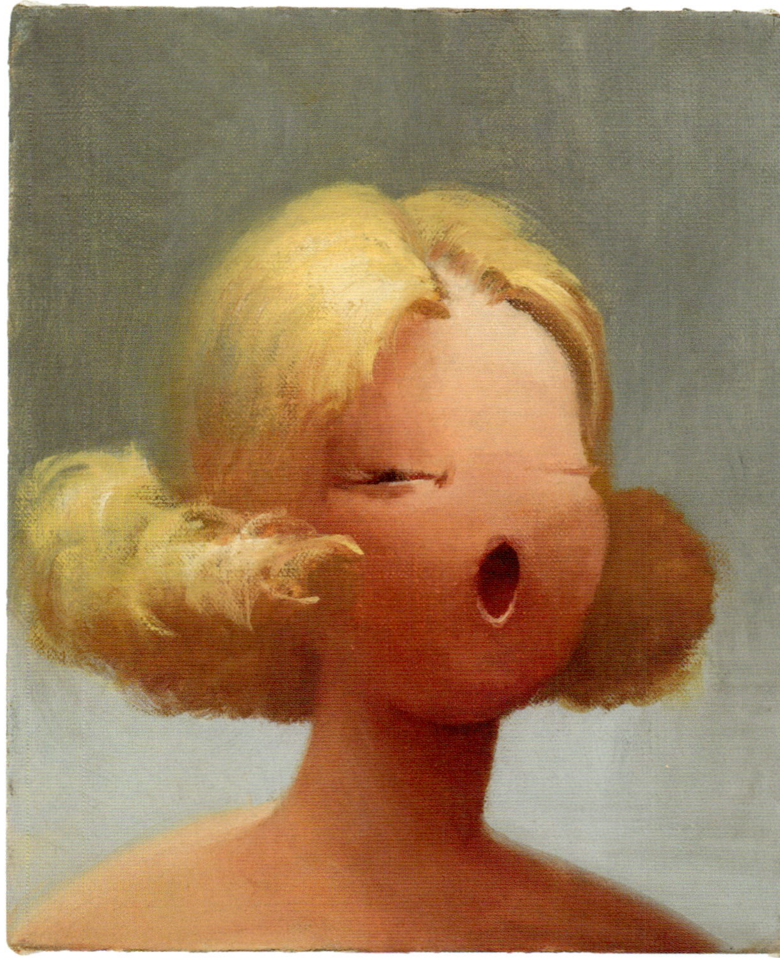

OPPOSITE Attributed to artist William Ward, this mezzotint from a 1787 edition of John Cleland's *Memoirs of a Woman of Pleasure* shows the characters of Fanny and Phoebe in Sapphic repose. "Truth!" wrote Cleland, "stark naked truth, is the word, and I will not so much as take the pains to bestow the strip of a gauze-wrapper on it."

TOP Contemporary American artist Lisa Yuskavage portrays the sexual revolution in all of its complexity, such as in this 1995 painting *Oh 2* in which a woman has been reduced to the most base essentials.

D. H. Lawrence in his 1928 *Lady Chatterley's Lover*—a novel that in no small part was instrumental in the twentieth century's movement toward sexual liberation—soberly observes that "however one might sentimentalize it, this sex business was one of the most ancient, sordid connections and subjections." In castigating the prudery and reserve of those Church Fathers who did intone against the conjugal act, we also obscure the ways that sexuality is frequently a method of dehumanization, frequently a violence and a trauma. Even among the most austere of theologians, it was rarely fucking alone that was the sin—it was the lust. The predilection toward control, possession, dominance; the viewing of another human being's body as merely a tool for one's own pleasure. De Sade, for example, is not a man who delights in the pleasure of others—clearly it's the exact opposite. More importantly, this was a man who saw no ethic in the consensual, yet that is the highest ethic of all sexuality, whether among spouses or strangers, as expressed conventionally or kinkily. At its best, sexuality is a means of breaking down boundaries between individuals, an expression of care and concern, of mutual pleasure and exploration, perhaps of love. A celebration of what bodies can do, of full connection in a consensual shared freedom. At its worst, lust can reduce another person into a mere body.

The Viennese psychoanalyst Wilhelm Reich wrote in his 1927 study *The Function of the Orgasm* that the "unity and congruity of culture and nature, work and love, morality and sexuality, longed for from time immemorial, will remain a dream as long as man continues to condemn the biological demand for natural (orgastic) sexual gratification." Well, maybe—and we'll note Reich's suspiciously convenient use of a male pronoun in the excerpt, arguments for sexual freedom often for a specifically *masculine* sexual freedom. For it's not what organ is put into what orifice wherein sin resides; it's not the number of people or their genders, the desire or its consummation. The true risks of lust are in the possibility of turning a human being into a mere object, a woman into a hole and a man into a dildo. As is the case with so many of the vices in the contemporary era, economics and technology outline the sins in stark relief. There is an ugliness to this commodification, where lust transmogrifies into greed, the worship of Venus really a supplication to Mammon. "I will bite into your clitoris and spit out two franc pieces," wrote novelist Henry Miller in his 1934 *Tropic of Cancer*, which more than anything liberatory reveals much of what's risked when sex is severed from spirit, when de Sade's materialism is taken seriously.

INTERLUDE—PIETRO ARETINO

In the first year of the sixteenth century, within the Palazzo Apostolico gathered the Cardinal Cesare Borgia and his sister Lucretia, along with their father Pope Alexander VI and fifty Roman prostitutes. According to the *Liber Notarum* of the Protonotary Apostolic Johann Burchard, who acted as Master of Ceremonies, the courtesans danced with those in attendance, performing elaborate strip-teases until all were naked. "After dinner the candelabra with the burning candles were taken from the tables and placed on the floor," writes Burchard, "and chestnuts were strewn around, which the naked courtesans picked up, creeping on hands and knees between the chandeliers, while the Pope, Cesare, and his sister Lucretia looked on." Finally, the guests convulsed into a lustful mass, as the Pope and his bastards awarded prizes "such as tunics of silk, shoes, barrettes, and other things" for those who could copulate the most prodigiously. In *A World Lit Only by Fire*, William Manchester claims that "Servants kept score of each man's orgasms, for the pope greatly admired virility and measured a man . . . by his ejaculative capacity," though no historian takes *that* detail seriously. Regardless, the whole thing is a lot. Not every pope is a saint.

Whether the "Banquet of Chestnuts" happened, it's indisputable that Alexander had a permissive definition of celibacy, as his children can attest to. If the age is remembered for Niccolò Machiavelli and Giordano Bruno, Raphael and Donatello, Claude Monteverdi and Galileo Galilei, then Guido Ruggiero reminds us in *Erotic Cultures of Renaissance Italy* it was also marked by "nightlife in the urban heart of Florence, the smell of flesh in the streets, the Medici buildings

OPPOSITE German painter Heinrich Lossow's aptly named 1880 work *The Sin* depicts two members of the clergy *in flagrante delicto* while attending Pope Alexander VI's infamous Banquet of Chestnuts.

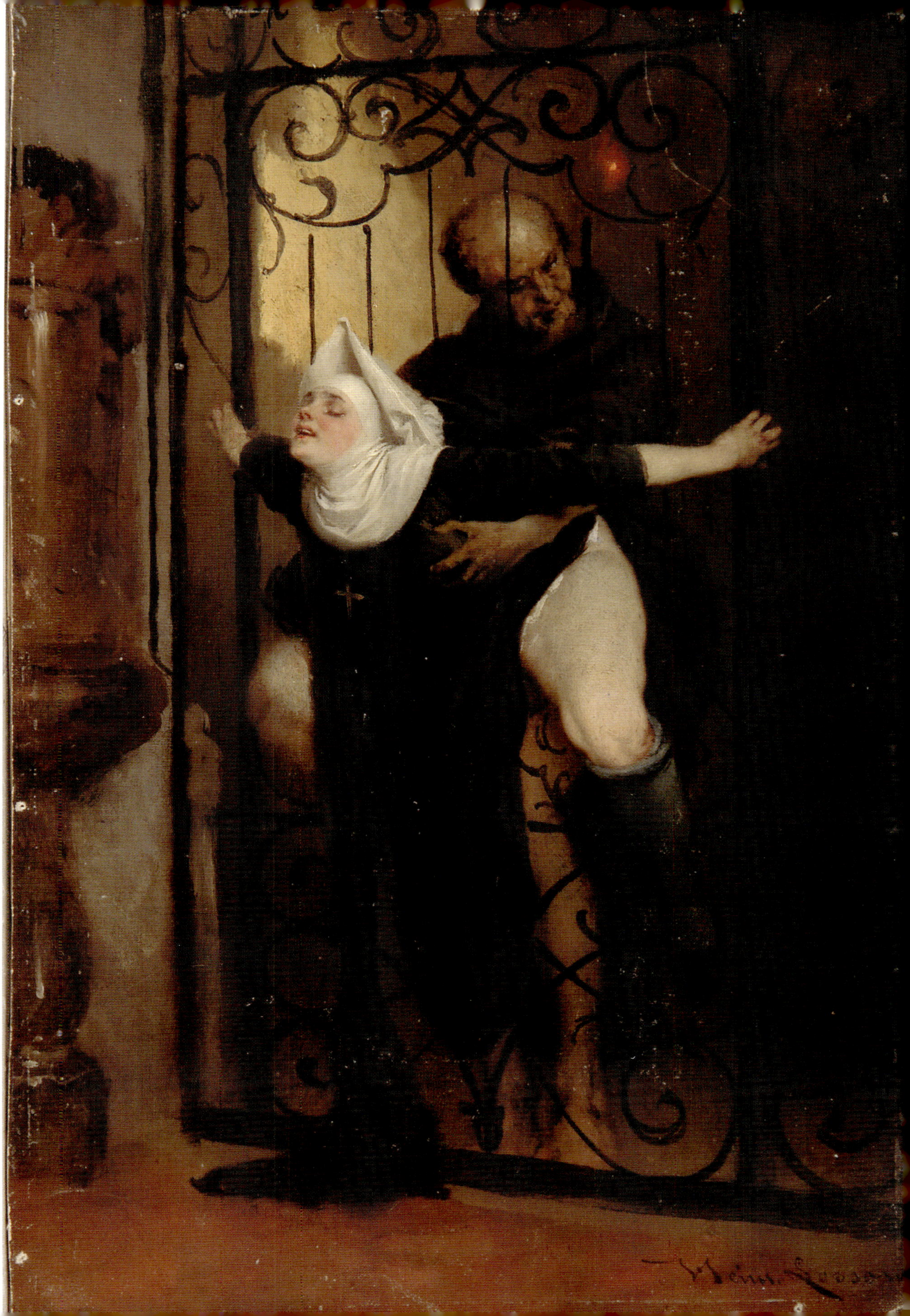

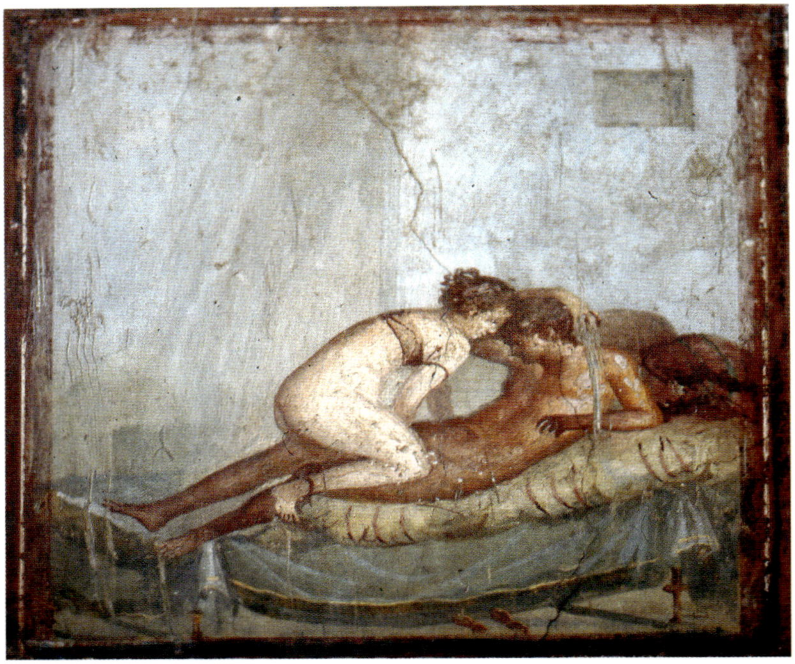

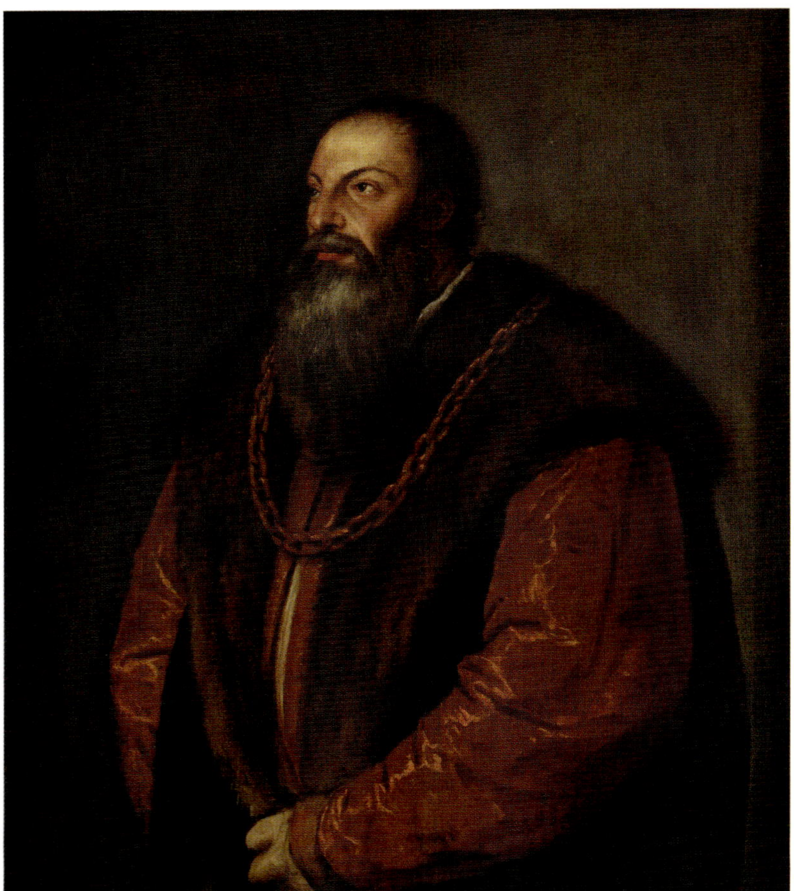

rented to prostitutes and bath houses." There was no humanism without the body. Part of what shocked Martin Luther on his Roman pilgrimage wasn't just the corruption, but the general permissiveness. From Alexander VI himself up through the dashing eighteenth-century Venetian adventurer Giacomo Casanova, northern Europeans have often projected their fantasies onto Italy. "The chief business of my life has always been to indulge my senses," Giacomo Casanova confessed. "I never knew anything of greater importance. I felt myself born for the fair sex, I have ever loved it dearly." During the cinquecento, no man sang as ecstatic a song as Pietro Aretino, poet laureate of filth.

Before Bob Guccione's *Penthouse* and Hugh Heffner's *Playboy*, there was Aretino's *Dubbi amorosi*; before the Marquis de Sade's *120 Days of Sodom* and the 2nd Earl of Rochester's *The Quintessence of Debauchery*, there was *La cortigiana*. Across poetry, prose, and plays, Aretino inverted the pretensions of humanism and the pieties of Neo-Platonism, finding the quivering body underneath metaphysical obtuseness. If Dante and Petrarch wrote of the heart, then Aretino wrote of the head and shaft, vulva and clitoris. "Speak plainly and say 'fuck,' 'prick,' 'cunt,' and 'ass' if you want anyone except the scholars at the University of Rome to understand you," Aretino argues in *The School of Whoredom*, an effective motto for his aesthetics. Born to a poor Tuscan cobbler, Aretino ascended by virtue of quick wit and cruel sarcasm. In 1516, Aretino announced himself as a poetic genius with a pamphlet mocking the funeral of Pope Leo X's beloved pet elephant Hanno (a gift from the king of Portugal). Despite his wicked humor (or maybe because of it), he ingratiated himself with the Medicis, and ironically became a common Vatican presence, kept close as the "Scourge of Princes," a jester with poison pen. When a Medici was pope, there Aretino found his home; when some usurper came in, the poet spent his days on the murky canals of Venice. Always Aretino wrote, dialogues and treatises, sonnets and romances, and letters threatening to blackmail the numerous men he had dalliances with, since he was proudly "a sodomite," noting that only once did he fall in "love with a female cook and temporarily switched from boys to girls."

Not exactly handsome, Aretino is a severe if wicked-looking man of arched eyebrow and keen eye, his bulky figure weighed down beneath brown fur and heavy red satin, a bronze necklace looking nothing so much like a chain. His beard, the sort already sported by those chaste, severe, and ascetic reformers beyond the Alps, appears less like it belongs to an Old Testament prophet and more to Pan. Titian painted Aretino several times, including as Pontius Pilate presenting Christ; captured in paint by Giorgio Vasari, Jacopo Tintoretto, and several lesser-known artists, his image was also caste on medals, a particular favorite being one that depicts him as composed entirely out of cock-and-balls. It was through imagery that he'd be remembered, due to the intervention of the architect and painter Giulio Romano and the engraver Marcantonio Raimondi. The first made a series of pornographic paintings known as *The Sixteen Pleasures* showing men and women, men and men, women and women, in multiple combinations, in a contortion of bodies. The second made engravings of that series for mass purchase, images to be kept under straw-filled mattresses and hidden within the binding of Jerome's Vulgate. And Aretino? He supplied poems to accompany, entitled *Sonetti Lussoriosi*—"The Lust Sonnets." So filthy

OPPOSITE, TOP King Francis I of Naples was scandalized in 1819 upon viewing pornographic works excavated from the ruins of Pompeii and Herculaneum and ordered them to be locked away, with the murals and sculptures still only occasionally allowed to be exhibited. Used as decoration in both brothels and residences, such imagery reflects the relatively laissez-faire sexuality of the ancient Mediterranean.

OPPOSITE, BOTTOM A girthy man, in all senses of that phrasing, Pietro Aretino is depicted here by his great friend the Renaissance master Titian in this 1537 composition held by the Frick Collection in New York.

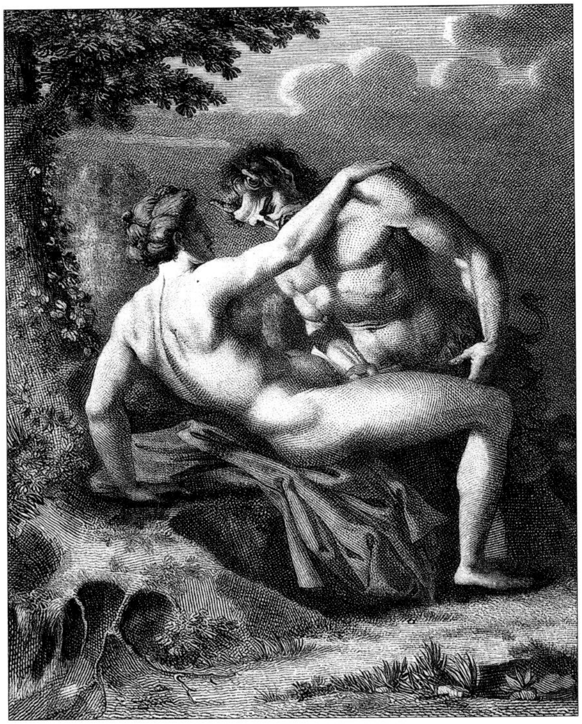

LE SATYRE ET LA NIMPHE.

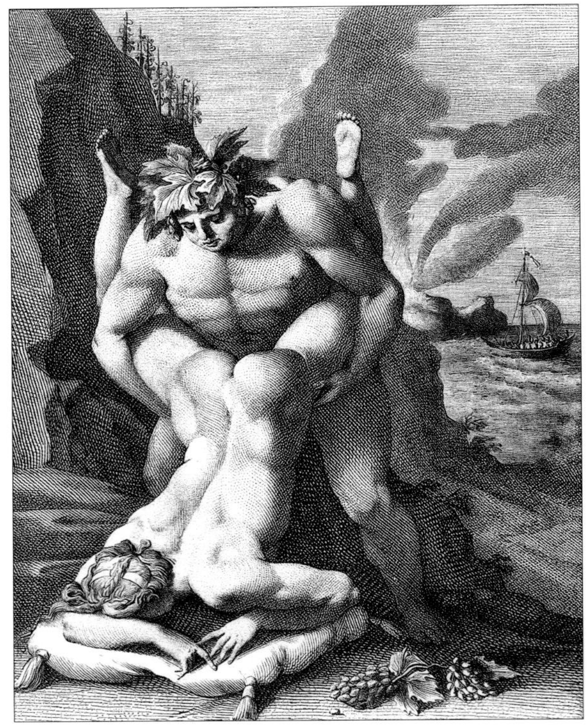

BACHUS ET ARIANE.

was Aretino's poetry, that when the English composer Michael Nyman scored the sonnets, the programs which contained their translations were withdrawn by the London theater premiering the piece. The year was 2008.

"Dear old man, stick a finger up my ass," writes Aretino in the first line of his third sonnet. There's also "I want him in the ass, you will forgive me," "Give me your tongue and support yourself with your feet on the wall," and "Because I try such a thick cock," and, well, it goes on like this. Aretino loses something in the rendering, but he was regarded as a master stylist, and when combined with Raimondi's admittedly filthy engravings, the effect was something never quite seen before. What they had produced was *pornography*. Ever since pheromones first defused eroticism has existed; art and literature had always celebrated it. But with the mass production of what was basically a dirty magazine, Aretino did something new. Not to disparage him; there is consummate smut and terrible literature, and as proficiency is to be respected, one should always prefer to be the talented pornographer over the hack poet. The definition is simply an issue of intent.

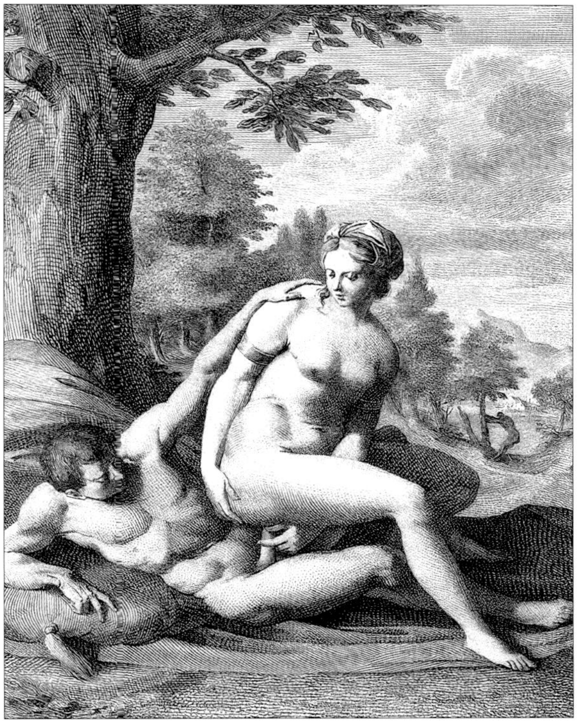

ANGELIQUE ET MEDOR.

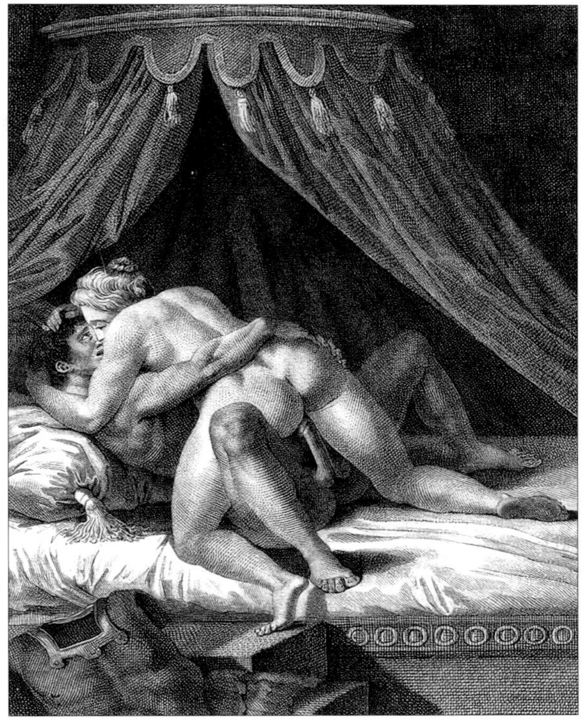

MARS ET VENUS

ABOVE Four graphic engravings by the Italian artist Marcantonio Raimondi from his 1524 pornographic masterpiece *I Modi* or *The Sixteen Pleasures*, original held by the British Museum.

Ironically, if Aretino saw a sanctity in anything, it was the sacredness of the bordello, which was why he was outraged when he heard about renovations at the Vatican. The chief artist overseeing this project was similar to Aretino; both were lovers of men, both were adept poets, both imbued their works with frank eroticism, albeit to different ends. Yet Aretino was enough of a traditionalist to be incensed about naked angels adorning the Vatican's ceilings, writing in a 1545 letter to the artist that "your art would be at home in some voluptuous brothel, certainly not in the highest chapel in the world." The artist's answer would be, in some ways, ambiguous—as the relationship between love and lust always must be. When Michelangelo painted St. Bartholomew on the Sistine Chapel's *The Last Judgment*, he rendered the martyr in the traditional image of Écorché; that is, the resurrected apostle is shown holding his own flayed skin. The sagging, drooping, leathery face dangling from the arm of Bartholomew is none other than that of Michelangelo. And the face of the living saint? That belongs to Aretino.

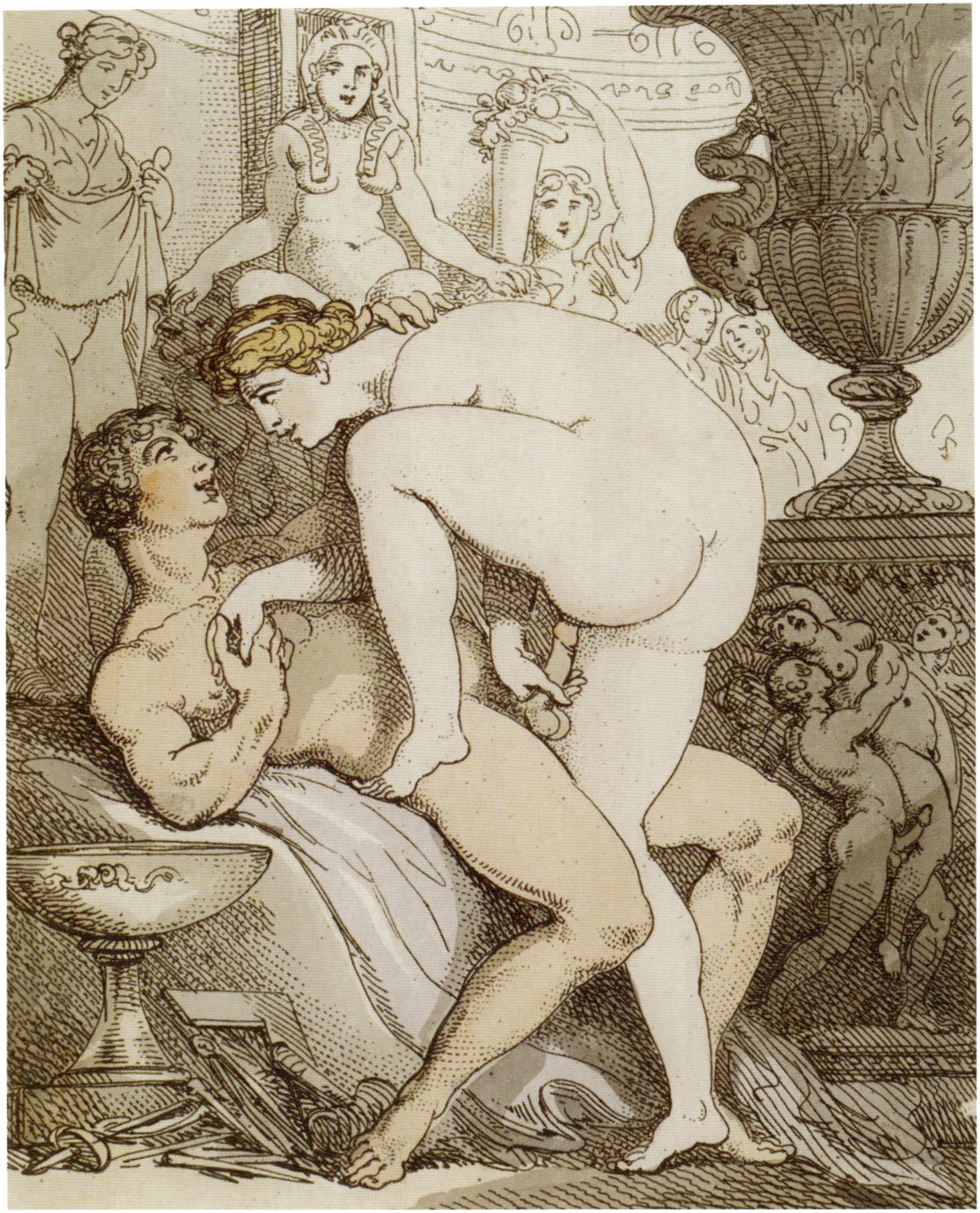

ABOVE English caricaturist Thomas Rowlandson turns his satirical eye toward the classical legend of Pygmalion, a sculptor who falls in love with his own creation. In this 1810 print made as part of an erotic series, Rowlandson envisions the sculpture coming to life and mounting Pygmalion.

OPPOSITE French painter Anicet-Charles-Gabriel Lemonnier's 1812 painting *In the Salon of Madame Geoffrin in 1755*. Original held at the Château de Malmaison.

PRAXIS—GRANT ME CHASTITY, BUT NOT YET

They would gather in Manchester, that gloomy northern English town of dark Satanic mills; behind darkened doors up the steep, cobble-stoned alleys of melancholic Edinburgh; and before either of those chapters would be found, in the small town of Anstruther, next to the clear waters of the Firth of Forth. There, gentlemen such as the antiquarian David Erskine (11th Earl of Buchan) would sup with Sir Hugh Cleghorn (colonial administrator of Ceylon) or would share a dram of whiskey with the celebrated composer Thomas Erskine (the 6th Earl of Kellie). Ben Franklin was an occasional guest. These were men of discernment and taste who might discuss David Hume's theories of induction over sirloins of beef roast or wild venison, could consider Adam Smith's arguments while enjoying port or sherry, ruminate on the pragmatism of Thomas Reid's common sense philosophy while eating treacle tart or nursery pudding. Gathering for more than a hundred years starting in 1732, this club with its most respected of members was an embodiment of the Scottish Enlightenment, of that movement's sober, judicious, convivial, good-spirited, and pragmatic commitment to reasoned discourse. At least until

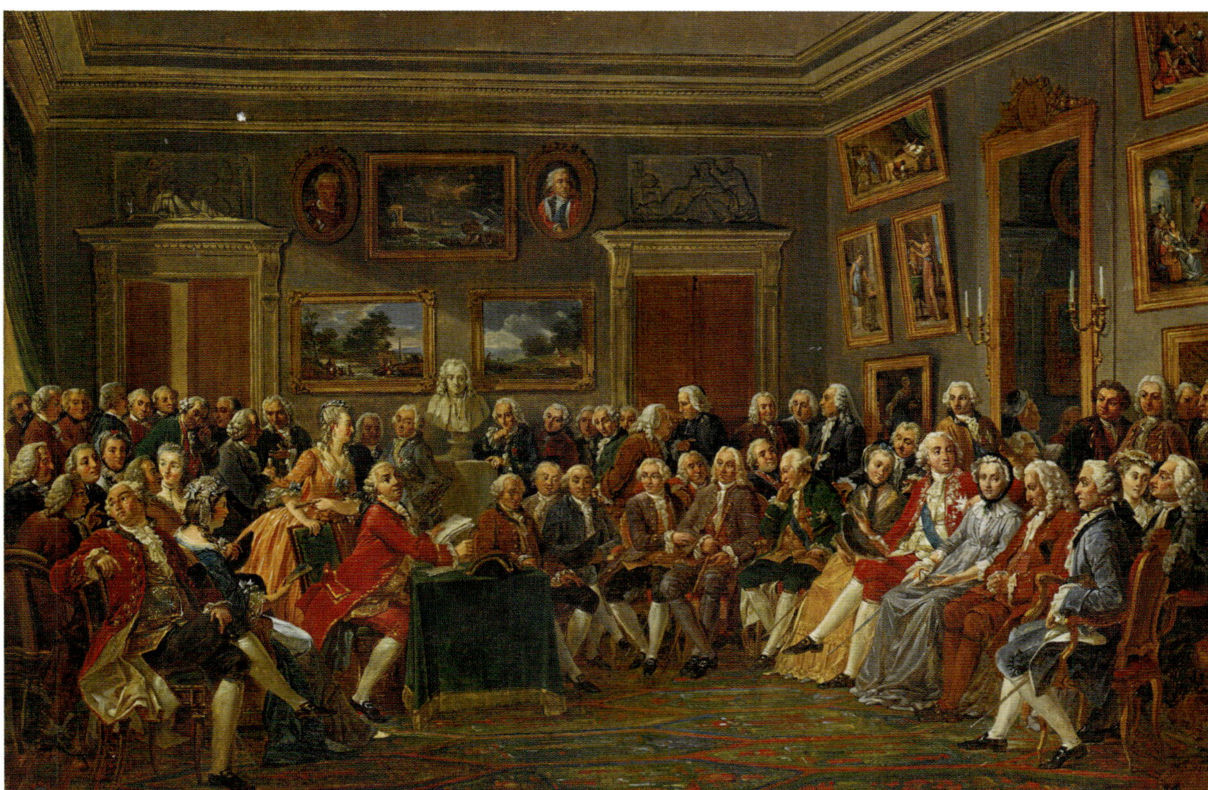

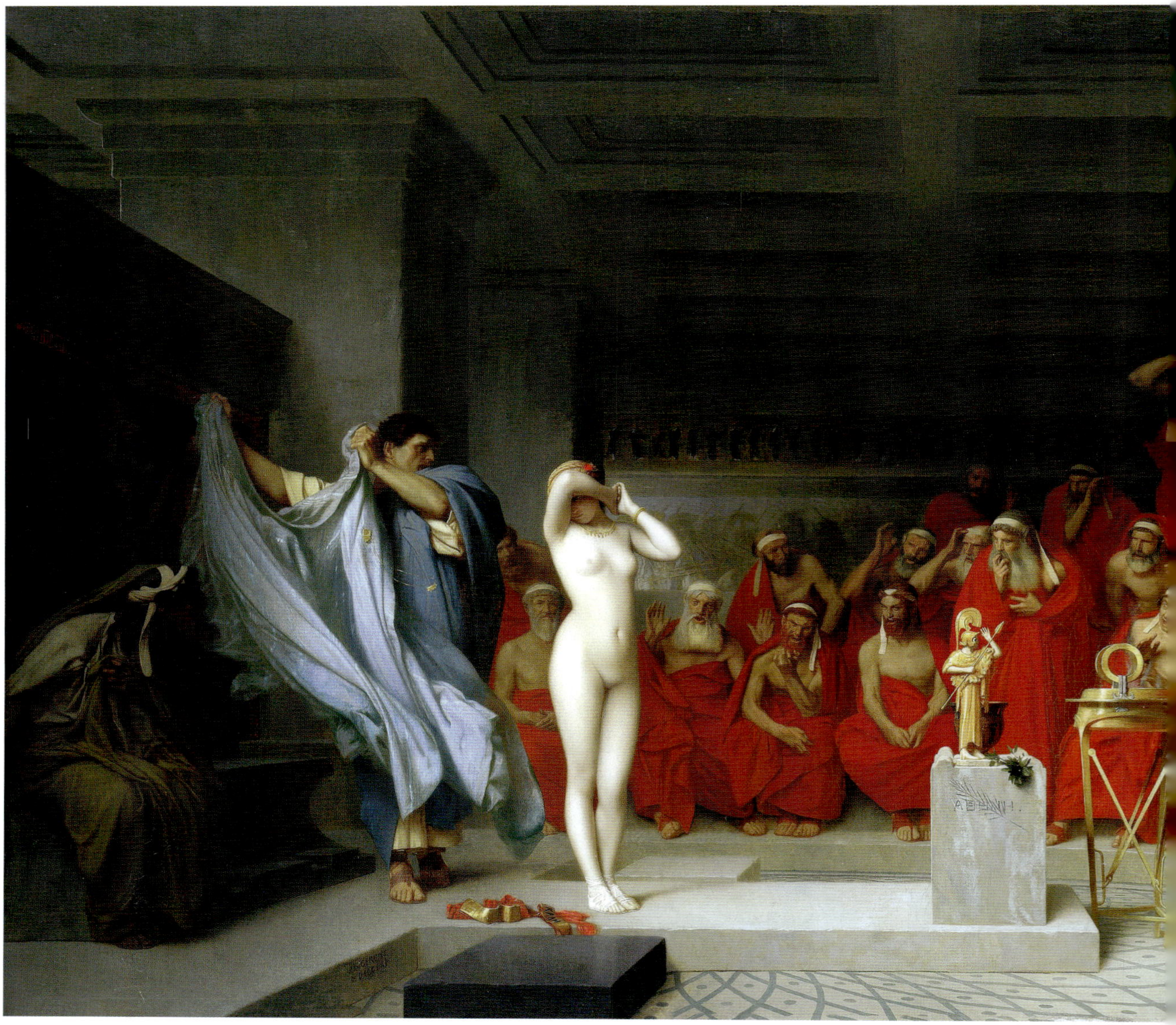

after dessert. For after the table was cleared and those minor appetites of stomach and mind were satiated, the esteemed members of the Most Ancient and Most Puissant Order of the Beggar's Benison and Merryland would retire to their actual purpose.

In a room decorated with oil paintings depicting powdered wig nobles and adorned with carpets from the Hindu Kush, two or three "posture girls," so-called "nymphets" of eighteen or nineteen, would enter and disrobe, while a first of the members would unveil his chubby, short cock, then another, then a third, and soon the entire assemblage of statesmen, aristocrats, and scholars were all of them pumping away to completion. Unusual as such collective self-gratification might seem, even more homoerotic was the initiation into the

Beggar's Benison, as a new member would be fluffed to excitement by a volunteer, and then according to the book of rules would be "ordered by the Sovereign to place his Genitals upon the Testing Platter . . . The Members and Knights two and two came round in a state of erection and touched the Novice Penis to Penis. Thereafter the special Glass, was filled with Port Wine." After all of the penitents in the Cult of Onan had drank their fill, there would be readings from the Song of Songs, or perhaps more contemporary fair, such as *Fanny Hill*. Lest all this seem scurrilous legend, let it be known that the relics of Beggar's Benison still exist, preserved in the archives of St. Andrews University. Squirreled away are the implements of lust used by these otherwise impeccable men—a glass shaped like a shaft and balls, from which port would be drunk; the pewter "testing platter" emblazoned with an engraving of a cock and on which that organ would often be examined, though the plate was most often used for collecting the copious quantities of club members' semen; and most infamously a wig made from the pubic hairs of King Charles II's mistress Nell Gwynne, the infamous "Protestant Whore." Theirs was a confraternity dedicated to a single axiom as expressed in their motto—"May prick nor purse ne'er fail you."

The cavorting of the Beggar's Benison embodies much of what we suspect about men in power. In their dim-lit room with the sound of furious rubbing and occasional ejaculatory moans, there is not a sense of romance or certainly of love, much less even eroticism or sensuality, but rather a type of predation, the vaguely pathetic collective fraternal hazing of wealthy and powerful figures feeling free to exploit working-class girls. Who were the "posture girls"? Sex workers, presumably, though there is little detail in the surviving records about their identities, their personalities, or even appearance, since their presence appears almost incidental. We're assured that they were eighteen or nineteen, and there is a thankfulness in that relative maturity, though how much they would have enjoyed the sight of this frigging elderly audience is debatable. Between the docked cocks and the collection of cum, one suspects that the presence of the nymphets is mere afterthought, except their purpose is to provide a locus for the Beggar's Benison's lust, the entire cracked sacrament a union of the voyeuristic and exhibitionistic. "In a world ordered by sexual imbalance," writes the critic Laura Mulvey in *Visual Pleasure and Narrative Cinema*, "pleasure in looking has been split between active / male and passive / female." The women within that darkened parlor existed only to be looked at, while the activity of sexual pleasure was the domain of the men. In patriarchal culture, lust is the privilege of men but the responsibility of women. A profound inequity, which is why among men lust is prized as a quality of virility, of "boys being boys," while mere enjoyment of sexual pleasure by women has historically been castigated as sluttiness. That's why the eighteenth-century Venetian adventurer Giacomo Casanova is celebrated as the stud who seduced hundreds of women, while his contemporary Czarina Catherine the Great of Russia, who merely enjoyed sex like any other person, has long been slandered as having been crushed to death by a horse she was fucking, since supposedly she could only climax from the turgidity of the creature's prodigious cock (an untrue story incidentally, which is the point).

The archetypal figure of the fictional Spanish lover Don Juan, celebrated by the French playwright Molière, the Austrian composer Wolfgang Amadeus Mozart, and the English poet Lord Byron, a deflowerer of virgins who lives by

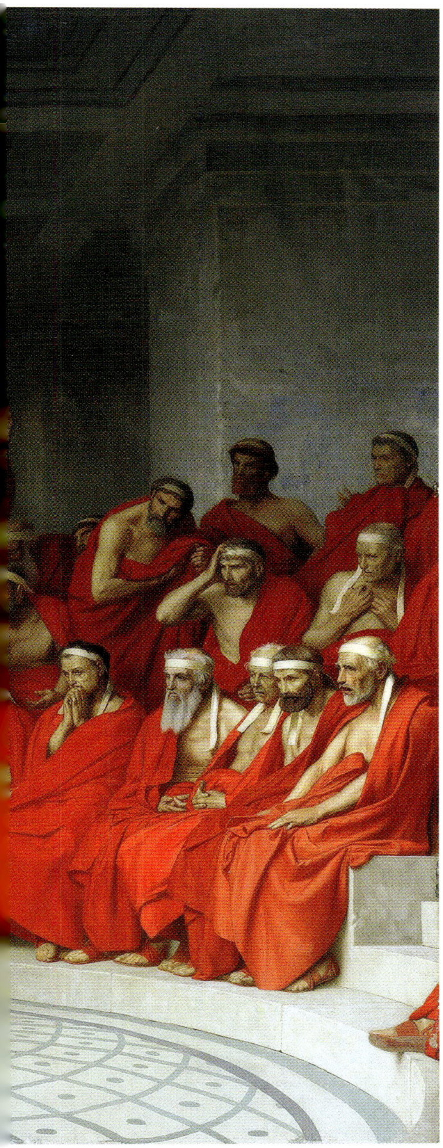

ABOVE French artist Jean-Léon Gérôme's 1861 painting *Phyrne Before the Areopagus* depicts the historical incident in which an ancient Athenian woman on trial for impiety was stripped by her defender in a successful gambit to sway the hearts of the jury by the fact of her beauty. Original at the Kunsthalle Hamburg.

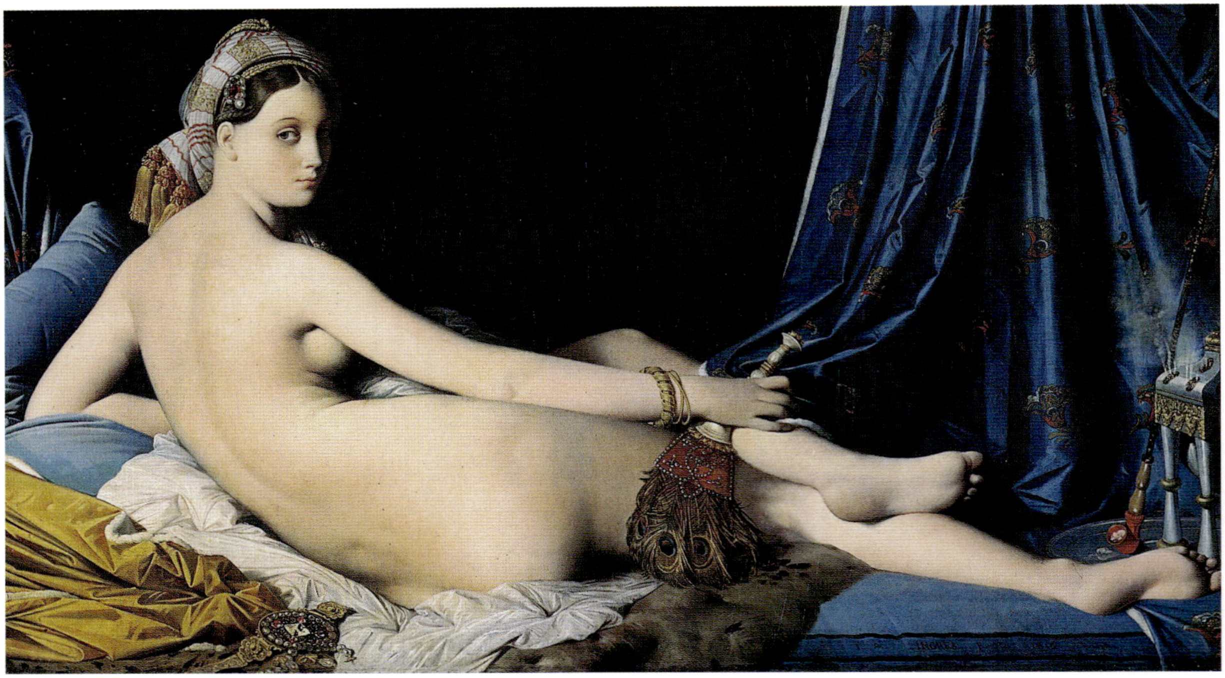

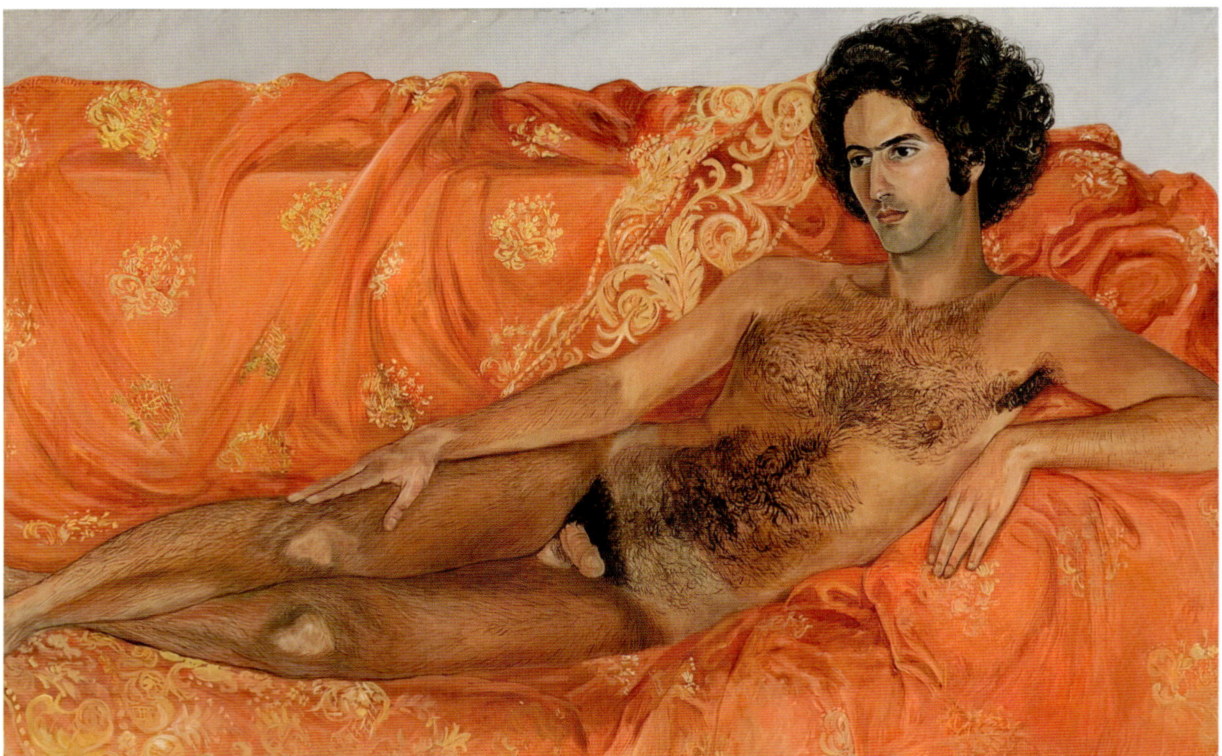

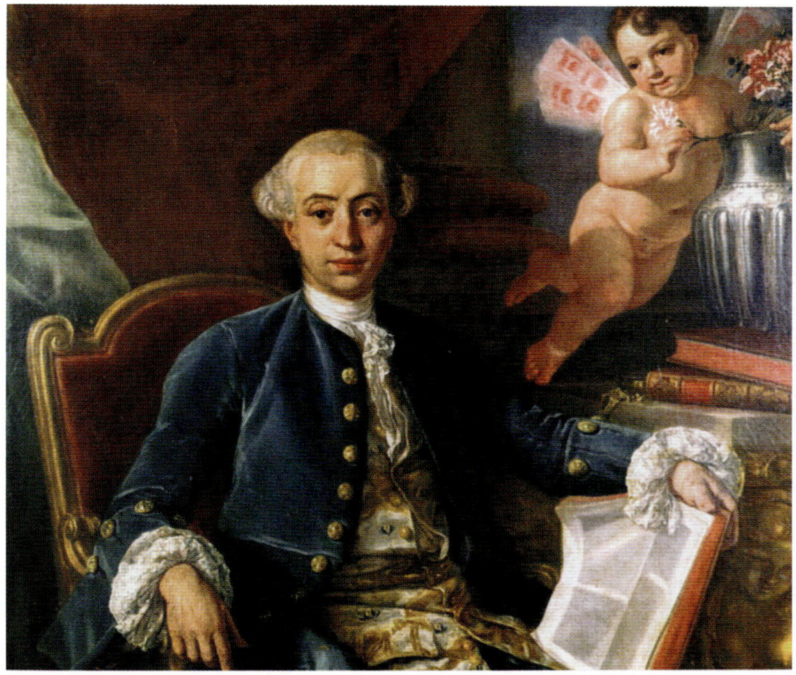

OPPOSITE, TOP French artist Jean-Auguste-Dominique Ingres's 1814 masterpiece *Grand Odalisque* was unveiled to outrage when first displayed, and in many ways the controversy over the reclining, nude courtesan hasn't diminished, even if the politics around it have. Original at the Louvre.

OPPOSITE, BOTTOM British artist Sylvia Sleigh brilliantly subverted the expectations of sexualized imagery in her reversal of the gaze, such as in her 1977 painting *Imperial Nude*.

TOP Italian painter Francisco Narici records the visage of his fellow countryman Giacomo Casanova in this 1760 portrait, the libertine watched over by Cupid, the son of Venus and the angel of love.

the maxim that of in "her first passion woman loves her lover: / In all the others, all she loves is love," should be contrasted with the first-century Roman empress Messalina. Both have earned a reputation for fucking thousands of women and men; in Don Juan's case that's fictional and for Messalina it very well could be slander, yet the former is a synonym for sensuality and the later for debased whoreishness. The more women a man fucks, the more there is to gain—in esteem, respect, envy. A woman is viewed in the exact opposite way, but of course the physical act itself isn't so different, sex simply being a matter of where you put certain things in particular places.

Casanova is again the standard case of masculine virality, fucking his away from Rome to St. Petersburg, London to Constantinople, claiming to have bedded 136 women. Even when comparing that number to KISS front man Gene Simmons's claim of having slept with 4,800 women, or the supposed 20,000 notches on the bedpost of NBA star Wilt Chamberlain, only Casanova is remembered as the consummate Lothario, the man whose name simply means "Lover of Women." He's rather blunt on the score himself, describing his attraction to women as a "feeling which . . . became my ruling passion" in his twelve-volume autobiographical picaresque *Story of My Life*, written over the course of nine years starting in 1789, admitting that "I have loved women even to madness." A nonfiction bildungsroman in which the author becomes a veritable symbol of Europe during the Age of Reason itself, his journeys taking him from Venice to Vienna, Prague to Paris. Casanova exhibits a lust for all experiences, describing conversations with Voltaire, Goethe, and Franklin inhis travails which included a

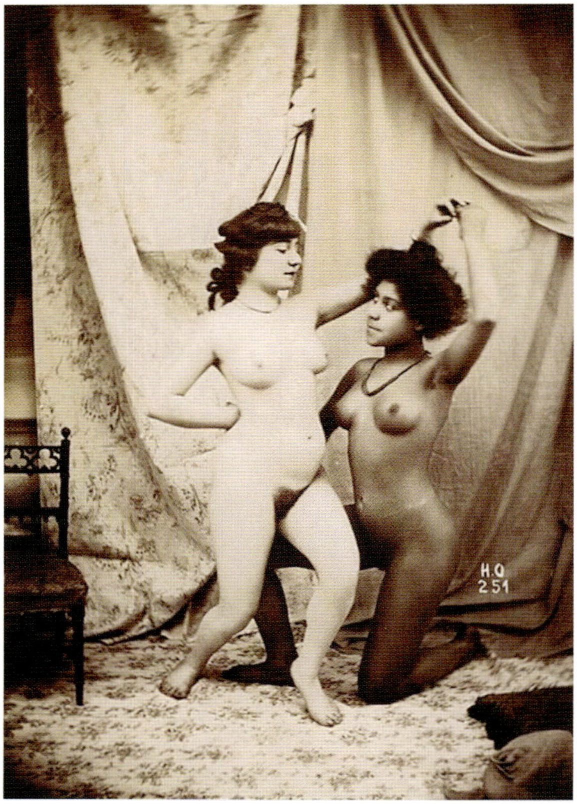

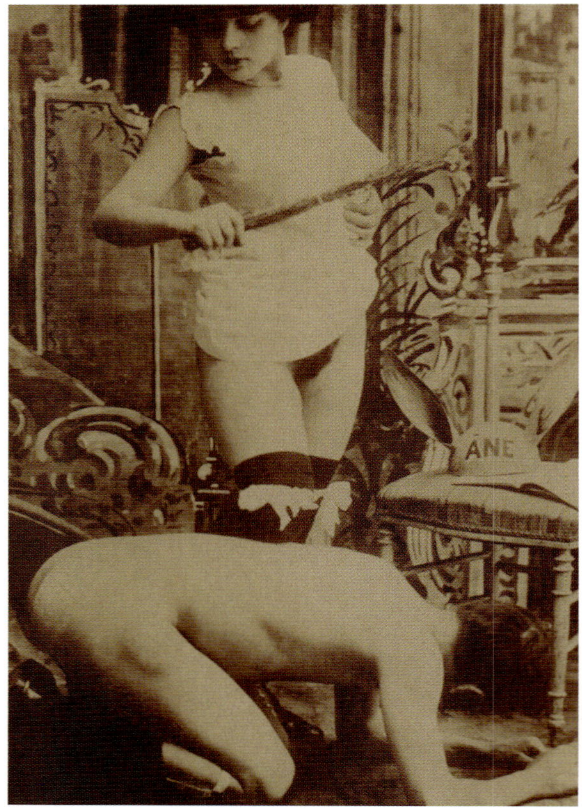

thrilling prison escape, as well as his stints working as a lawyer, an ecclesiastical secretary, a military theoretician, a natural philosopher and occultist, a professional gambler, a spy, and finally as the world's most fascinating librarian. A man as lucky as libidinous, tall but hook-nosed, dapper but smallpox-scarred, of whom his own friend Charles de Ligne remarked that he "would be a good-looking man if he were not ugly," but such was his charm. Through all of it, even while Casanova honestly accounts to his being "addicted to every kind of dissolute living," he still bluntly declares, "Worthy or not, my life is my subject, and my subject is my life."

Somebody has to have fucked long and hard for their name to remain synonymous with fucking for three and a half centuries, to be transformed into a quasi-mythic folk hero of sex. Even in our century, an era of free pornography and streaming live sex, of the inevitable coming epoch of artificial intelligence sexbots and fetish-on-demand simulated movies, the name Casanova endures. Ours is an era of continual, omnipresent neon fucking, but Casanova's prick still stands tall (just type his surname into any of the free porn sites if you don't believe that). Possibly only the name Lolita, from Vladimir Nabokov's novel of that title, can compare in its associations, but the differences between the connotations is instructive. Nabokov's narrator, the unctuous pedophile Humbert Humbert, may claim that Dolores Haze is the "light of my life, fire of my loins. My sin, my soul," but really she's a twelve-year-old girl incapable of consent.

TOP Pornography is the carriage pulled by the horse of technology. The desire to ever better simulate, facilitate, and propagate erotic imagery is an unheralded impetus for progress. Joseph Nicéphore Niépce took the first photograph—of a static view outside of his window—in 1826. The first pornographic images—far more interesting—only waited until 1839 to be developed. Depicting both heterosexual and same-sex desire, pornography of the period was liberating in the face of the conservative conventions of an otherwise restrictive century.

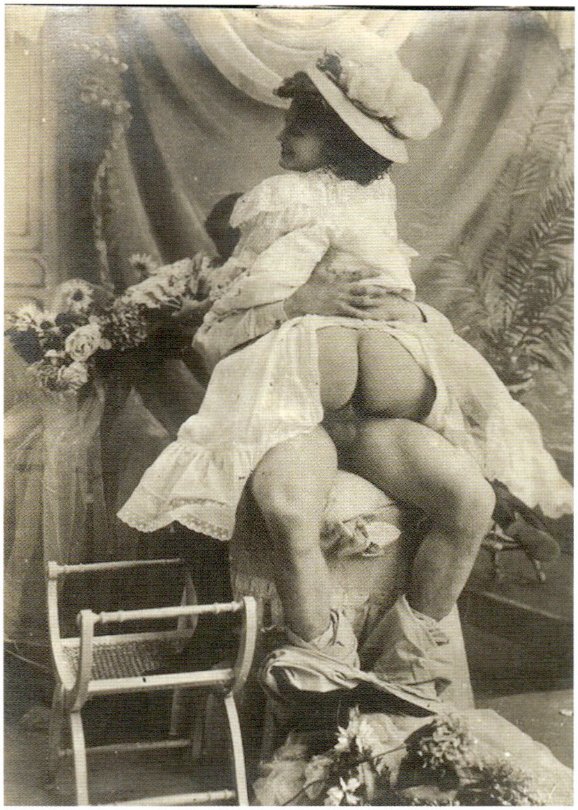

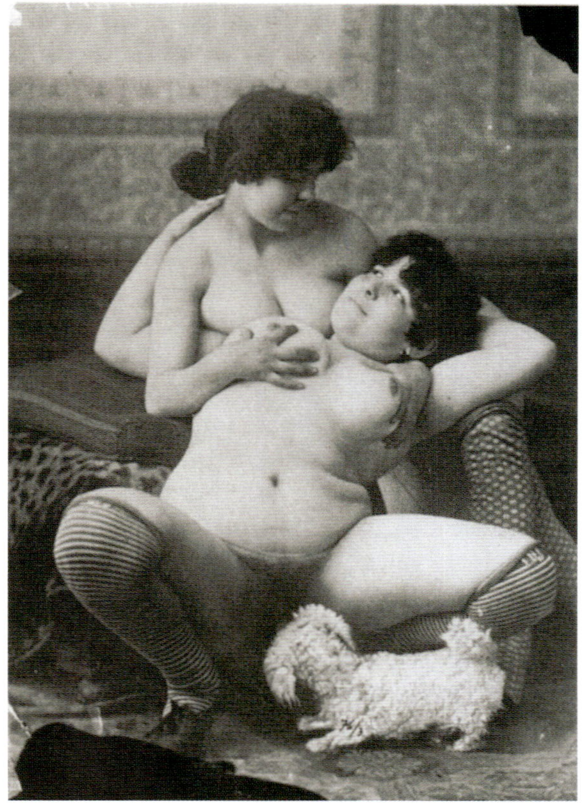

The culture portrays a Casanova as a daring sexual adventurer and a Lolita as a coquettish nymphomaniac, a seducing nymphet (an interpretation which requires a willful misreading of Nabokov's subtle novel), but it's more complicated than that. Beyond the fact that Casanova was real and that Lolita isn't, there is the fact that the former was as much a predator as a protagonist, and the latter was always meant to be read as the fantasy of a self-justifying pervert. If Casanova was an archetype of a particular Enlightenment model of lust, then Lolita (as Humbert calls Haze)—the passive, receptive, immature, inactive paragon of impure male sexual desire—became a modern archetype. Obviously—*obviously*—"Lolita" is a category of porn in the contemporary era, available to everyone, everywhere, all of the time. Erotica, whether relegated to a shoebox under the bed or the secret archives of the Vatican, was long something hidden, but now it's as available as the nearest Android phone. Though ours didn't invent any of these acts, we've become the epoch of gang bangs and bukkake, three-ways and cum shots, double penetration and ass-to-mouth; people reduced to categories, to body parts—Asian, MILF, Ebony, Lolita. That which is hidden in the confines coming to the light has its own intransigence. Once there may have been a sexual utopianism which imagined a free and pleasurable exploration of human erotic potential, but that has been commodified, privatized, and marketed. We were promised free love, but instead we just got a subscription to the exclusive section of YouPorn.com.

The prophets of the coming pornocracy, men like *Playboy* founder Hugh Hefner, *Penthouse* editor Bob Guccione, and *Hustler* CEO Larry Flynt, may have been many things—advocates for their versions of sexual freedom, free speech enthusiasts, and decriers of American puritanism—but they were primarily businessmen. *Playboy* is a magazine you'd be embarrassed to be caught reading by your grandparents; you'd be mortified if your parents found a copy of *Penthouse* under your mattress; and your cheeks would burn red if you found yourself flipping through *Hustler*, but ultimately they're all just products being sold, even if behind a counter and put in a brown paper bag. Hefner, he of the silk pajamas and bathrobe, the Playboy Mansion's infamous grotto and the invention of the centerfold, has sometimes been enshrined as the John the Baptist of sexual liberation, a man who along with the birth control pill was midwife to a less prudish culture, and who could wisely intone that "sex is the driving force on the planet. We should embrace it, not see it as the enemy," for who in their right mind would ever disagree with that? Yet he'd also be the man who confessed that the "notion that *Playboy* turns women into sex objects is ridiculous. Women are sex objects." There's that fap-fap-fap of the old men in the Beggar's Benson again, which sounds like freedom but is anything but. Ethical prerogatives demand that we also label Casanova for what he truly was: not just an advocate for sexual freedom, not even just a lover of over a hundred women, but also a man guilty of incest, pedophilia, and rape. Therein lay a fundamental element of lust, clear in that loaded phrase of Hefner's—"object." The dictum that people can be purchased, traded, discarded. This is the irony, that in our pornographic obsessions, we're just as puritanical as our forebearers. Tragically postlapsarian, for indeed there can be liberation in sex, there can be freedom, pleasure, love. But it all depends on how you greet your partner. Otherwise, a libertine is just a puritan with a more dynamic social life.

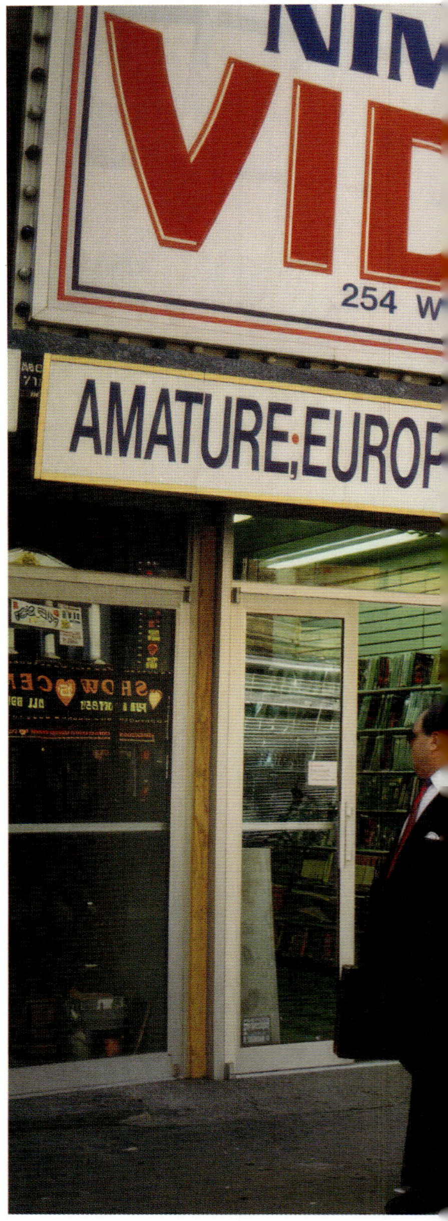

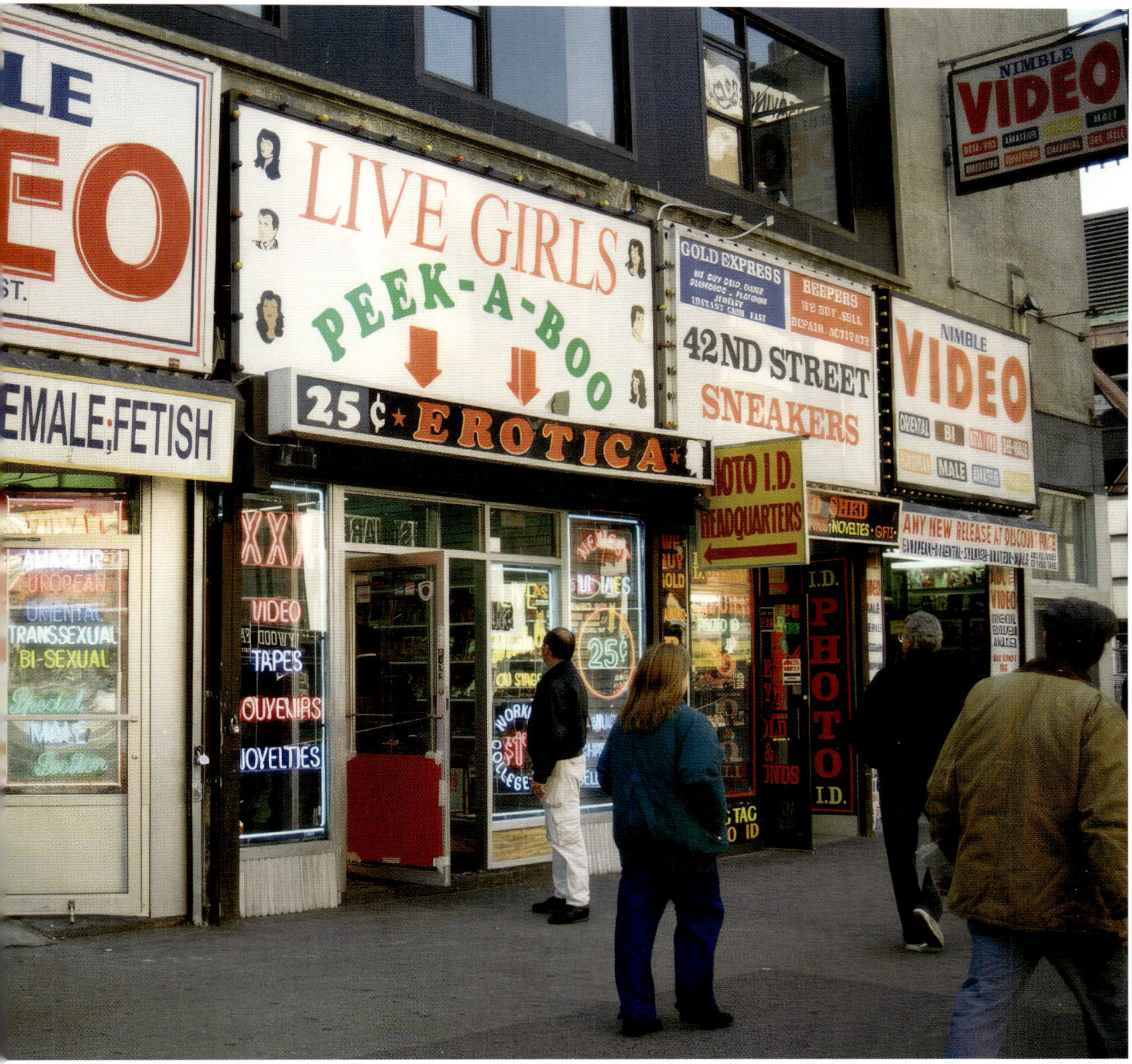

ABOVE Today in New York's Times Square, you're far more likely to encounter midwestern families going to Red Lobster or the Olive Garden for an overpriced dinner before seeing *The Lion King* than you are an aviator-shaded, trench-coated masturbator coming out of a live sex show, but a generation ago this was a national red light district.

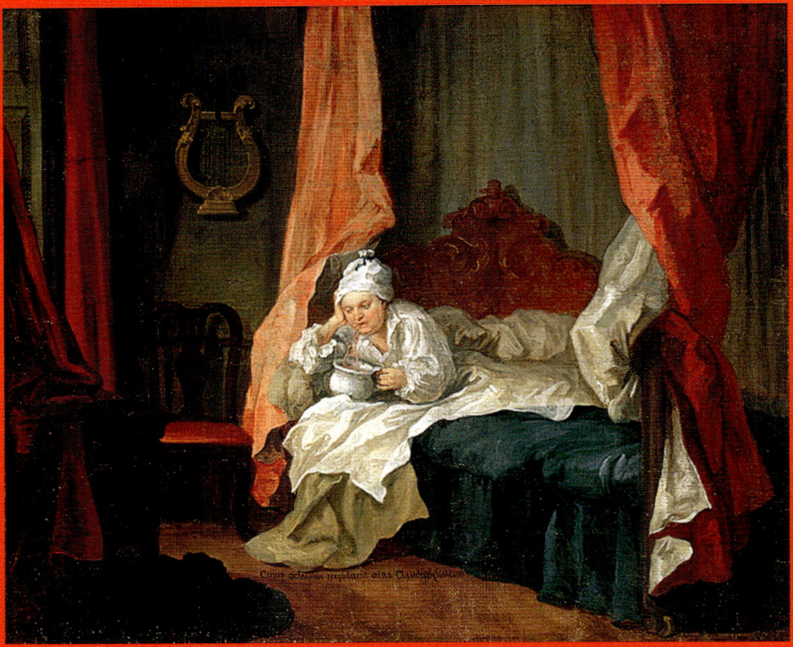

CHAPTER THREE

A FILLED STOMACH: GLUTTONY

"In Cockaygne food and drink are had without worry, trouble or toil.
The meat is choice and the drink is clear at every meal . . . There are fine, great rivers
of oil, milk, honey, and wine; water serves no purpose except as a sight and for washing."
—Anonymous, *The Land of Cockaygne* (c. 1350)

"An ounce of sauce covers a multitude of sins."
—Anthony Bourdain, *Kitchen Confidential: Adventures in the Culinary Underbelly* (2000)

The author of Proverbs 23:20–21, whom tradition claims was King David, warned the pious to "Be not among winebibbers; among riotous eaters of flesh: For the drunkard and the glutton shall come to poverty: and drowsiness shall clothe a man with rags." Such a denunciation of excessive living remains the operative wisdom. We sit in moral judgment of the over-eater, of the addict, of the glutton. Gregory the Great distinguished the activities and attitudes which constituted gluttony, so that the simple eater of a simple meal could rest assured that he had not accidentally fallen into a transgression. According to the sixth-century pope, gluttony involved eating before proscribed meals, seeking out the most expensive ingredients, overly preparing your food, eating more than you need, or enjoying it too much. From that austere rubric, the ranks of gluttony divide into two classes—gourmets and gourmands. The first are those who are overly enamored with the *quality* of cuisine; the foodie who searches out delectable dishes and rare delicacies, the patron of the Zagat guide and the pilgrim of Michelin-starred restaurants. The latter, by contrast, are obsessed with the *quantity* of food, with devouring heaping platters of fried chicken wings and plates of pizza, the joyless and engorged addict of eating. Much opprobrium was reserved for the glutton, who may seem to ultimately be victim of a sin which only harms himself. Gregory denounces physical enjoyment; his is a staid and austere hatred of materiality. Yet it would be disingenuous to assume that gluttony only ever harmed the glutton, for in late antiquity and the Middle Ages, when the caloric intake of the average peasant was often at famine levels, to eat more than your fair share was to literally take food from the starving. To love food more than people is to elevate the transitory above the human, for as the Greek poet Callimachus mourned three centuries before Christ, "All that I have given to my stomach has disappeared."

PREVIOUS SPREAD The greatest painterly satirist of an excessive century, English artist William Hogarth gave wicked shape to the foibles and failings of both rich and poor. This 1750 painting shows the aristocrat Francis Matthew Schutz, third cousin to the Prince of Wales, in his bed after a night of debauchery, hungover and vomiting into a pewter chamber pot within the lush environs of his private bedchamber. Original held by the Tate Britain.

OPPOSITE Bohemian artist George Emanuel Opiz's 1804 work *The Glutton* presents a gentleman of both enormous appetites and carriage, with five courses already before him as one meaty palm grabs an appetizer from a servant. At the foot of the table, a pampered lap dog guarding some bones from a lean and hungry greyhound has the exact same facial expression as his master, a handy encapsulation of both the mentality and immorality of gluttony.

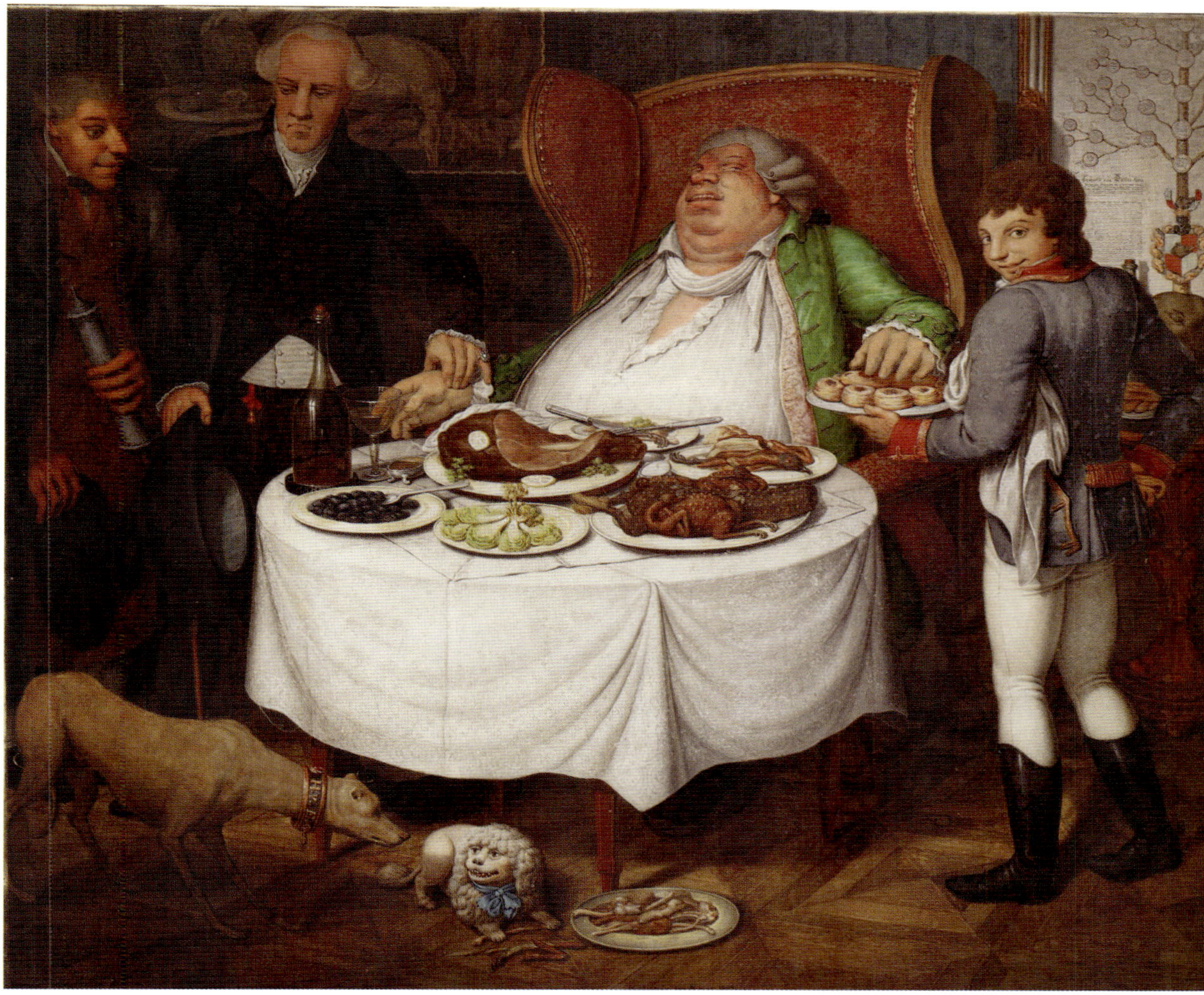

THE SCIENCE OF THE COOKSHOP—THEORY

Here is what you need—two pounds of dried, white beans; two large, sliced yellow onions and a few tablespoons of tomato paste; sprigs of parsley and a generous heaping of minced garlic; a half-teaspoon of thyme and two bay leaves; four pounds of lamb, at least a pound of fatty salt pork, two pounds of cured Toulouse sausage, and five pounds of fatty goose, with cracklings included; three cups of beef bouillon, two of cups of breadcrumbs from a baguette, and two from a bottle of *Sauvignon de Touraine*. Some butter, but goose fat is better. And salt to taste. This traditional French cassoulet only needs to bake at around 400 degrees for twenty minutes. All this was prepared before the public television audience of WGBH Boston in 1962 for the second season of Julia Child's iconic cooking show *The French Chef*, and she announces in her trademark operatic voice, "Baked beans! But these are not Boston baked beans, these are beans with a French accent! This is *cassoulet*!," she says, drawing out the last word with a singular, affected, Gallic precision. American audiences had never watched anyone like Child before, she a former member of the U.S. government's Office of Strategic Services in World War II who would graduate from the prestigious Parisian culinary academy Le Cordon Bleu. "Cassoulet, that best of bean feasts, is everyday fare for a peasant but ambrosia for a gastronome," said Child, and it's an encapsulation of her entire culinary philosophy. Not rarity of ingredient, but quality; not formality of presentation, but the experience's sensuality; and always a dedication. This was a gluttony not necessarily of the stomach, but of the mouth; not of satiation, but of the senses. Nobody watching WGBH in the early '60s in that cold Puritan city of hardtack and clam chowder had seen anything like Child. From Brockton to Braintree, Saugus to Swampscott, she revolutionized the kitchens of Massachusetts, and then the United States.

For lunch, postwar Americans dined on greasy SPAM and sickly sweet white-bread sandwiches and for supper grainy meatloaf and oily chicken pot pie; where the most adventurous dining was the seemingly endless variety of foods preserved in quivering, gelatinous aspic. If Anglo-American culture envisioned food as a means for survival, Child rather introduced the nation to a far more romantic approach. Americans watching the six-foot-two-inch Child in her television kitchen extol the virtues of coq au vin and beef bourguignon imagined grander possibilities. In Child's *Mastering the Art of French Cooking*, the chef argued that you "learn about great food by finding the best there is, whether simple or luxurious. Then you savor it, analyze it, and discuss it with your companions, and you compare it with other experiences." Breakfast was an epiphany, lunch a theophany, dinner a sacrament. The point wasn't to make the most expensive dish, the most complicated meal, the most impressive dinner, but rather it was simply to *enjoy* yourself. To taste the richness of salted butter and the creaminess of brie, the sweetness of fresh strawberries and the gaminess of rabbit. Unless you were from recent immigrant stock, this was a deeply foreign conception to most Americans, who saw three square meals a day as a means of caloric intake. Where even if the amount of hot dogs, hamburgers, and apple pie ingested could be copious in portion—and a nation that survived the Second World War with minimal rationing was already learning the virtues of second and third portions—Child offered something else. To not just eat—not just to enjoy, but to love—eggs and butter, cream and sugar, cheese, and cheese, and cheese.

All of it an irredeemable sin, of course; at least if we're to take the most adamant theological scolds seriously. The same distaste for the physical which justified sexual prudery also disdained the overenjoyment of food, and just as those who lusted with their gonads were branded sluts, those who fed the mouth were condemned as hogs, fatsos, lardasses. In the United States especially, where most are not thin, there are few things more universally hated than the fat. Gluttony, however, has little to do with mere corpulence; in fact such an association emerges relatively late, in only the last few centuries. By contrast, it was the inordinate enjoyment of eating, in addition to over-indulgence, that tarred somebody as a glutton. A sin of the epicure more than anything. Indeed, if pride was cosmically the first sin in Lucifer's rebellion, then gluttony was the first of the human sins, our fall solidified with the bite of a crisp apple (or pomegranate, or pear—the Bible isn't exact in this regard). For the Church Fathers of

OPPOSITE More subtle and loving than William Hogarth, contemporary American painter Noah Verrier nonetheless displays a satirical sensibility in his popular renderings of junk food, composed as if they were classical European still-life paintings. His 2022 painting of a meal from the fast-food chain Taco Bell, depicting a crunchy taco shell wrapped in a soft tortilla known as a "Gordito," a plastic thimble of neon-orange nacho cheese, a bag of nachos, and an extra-large plastic cup of a glowing green soda, all garnished with a flower in a mason jar, is an affectionate portrayal of American gastronomy at its most decadent.

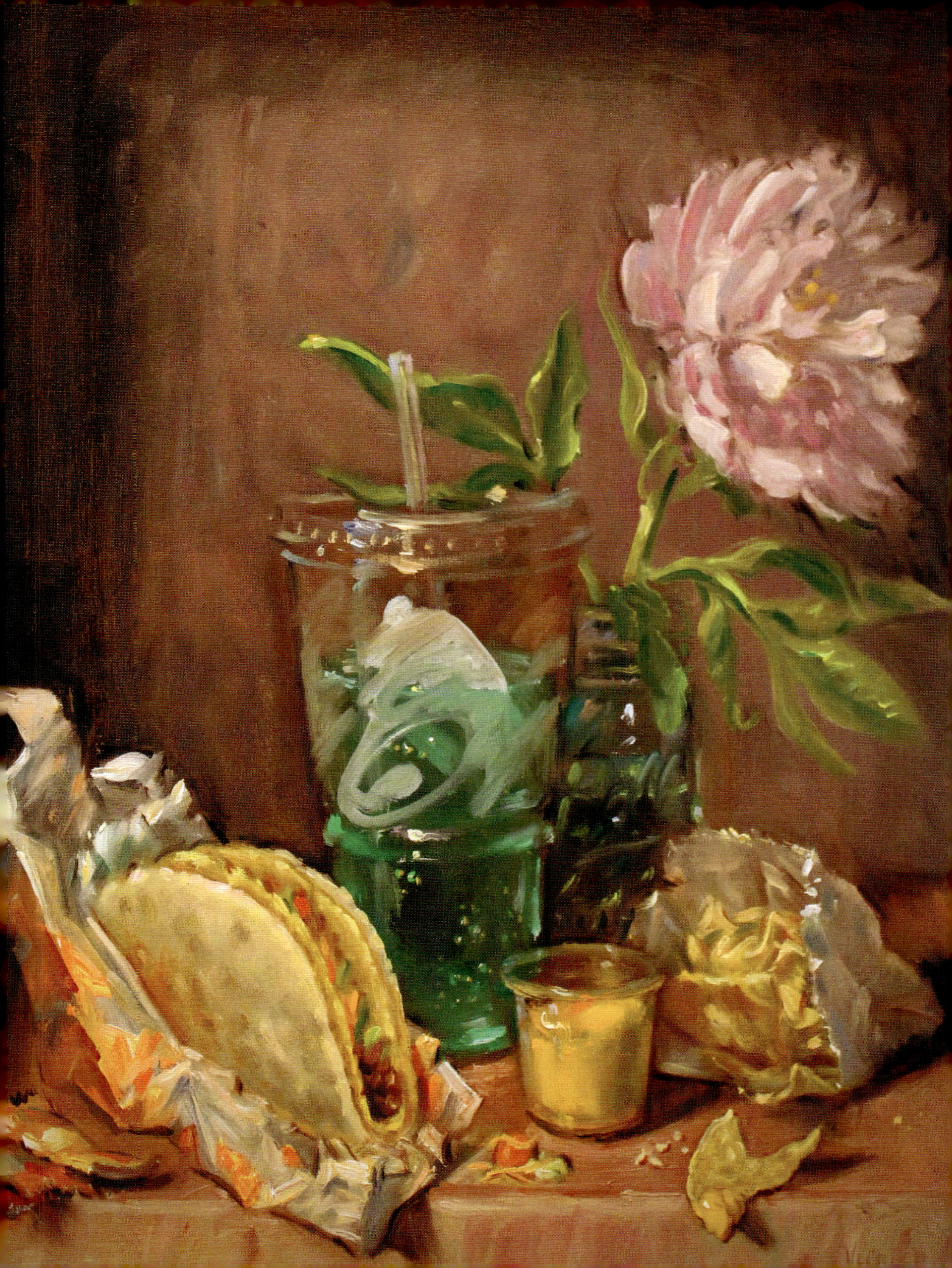

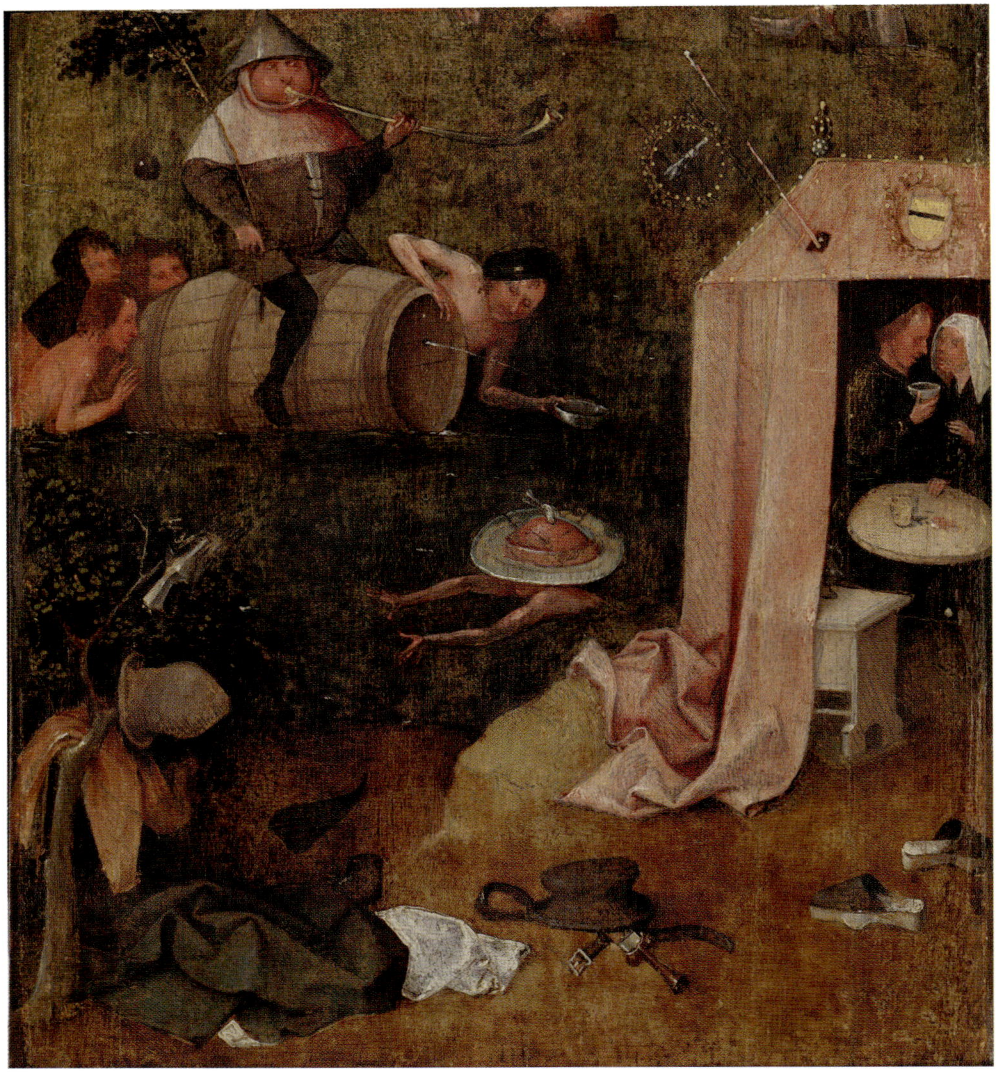

late antiquity and the Scholastic theologians of the Middle Ages, it wasn't necessarily the orgiastic scarfing of food alone that constituted gluttony (though that would be included); rather, it was the *misuse* of food. To eat without gratitude, to indulge without thought, to luxuriate without limit: all of that would qualify as misuse, regardless of how many courses you ate. Eating your feelings was just as bad as going back for seconds and thirds (not that they're always unconnected). Serious stuff, for as the fourth-century Byzantine theologian John Chrysostom would opine, "By the belly's incontinence was Adam expelled from Paradise." Such condemnation has a long afterlife, born from the idealist metaphysics of Christianity which disdained the material world as at best a trap and at worst irredeemably fallen. This was the sentiment of the Roman philosopher Seneca, asking in his *Epistles*, "What is more shameful than a costly meal which eats away the income even of a knight?" to which we could respond, "Being a philosopher who helps prestige-launder the crimes of Nero."

ABOVE Hieronymus Bosch, the greatest artist of a (sometimes inscrutable) morality from the late Middle Ages, makes the connection between lust and gluttony clear in the painting *Allegory of Intemperance*. Not just sins of the flesh, but fleshy sins: the drunken burgher mounting a cask of beer as if it were a woman is guilty of a related sin to that of the libertine, a feeding of base sense rather than the cultivation of higher faith. Painted sometime between 1496 and 1500, with the original at the Yale University Art Gallery in New Haven, Connecticut.

Because those sins of the stomach are estimably comprehensible, for *eating feels good*. Let he who has not enjoyed the hot salty crunch of a French fry, the velvet smoothness of vanilla ice cream, the snap of a grilled hot dog or the juiciness of a rare hamburger be he who castes the first dinner roll. In response to the Church Fathers, our greatest theorists of gluttony have naturally been chefs. They write not in dialectic and syllogism, but rather recipe; not within the symposium, but the kitchen. Marcus Gavius Apicius, the compiler of the first-century *On the Subject of Cooking*, endures as the patron of gourmands, a figure denounced by both Pliny and Seneca for his inordinate love of food, but who in turn answered the Stoics' paeons to frugality with goose-liver pâté and glistening red mullet, piglets fed on honeyed wine and astringent, fermented, savory garum as salty as the Aegean. As the stock glutton of ancient Roman moralizing, those official censures denounced Apicius, who lived for the sensory delights of Libyan shrimp and dried figs. Seneca, doubtlessly thinking of the transitoriness of the body and the supposed peace which comes from accepting our morality, said that as concerns the amount of denari Apicius paid for food, "such sums are called disgraceful if spent on the appetites." As a spiritual response, Apicius could have responded with something in *On the Subject of Cooking*, and that would be to put "lamb or kid into a pan. Finely chop an onion and coriander, pound pepper, lovage, cumin, garum, oil, and wine. Cook, turn into a shallow pan, thicken with wheat starch. If you take lamb you should add the contents of the mortar while the meat is still raw, if kid, add it while it is cooking." Against the theorizing of Seneca, Apicius's experience to me seems unassailable. *On the Subject of Cooking*—with chapters that have titles like "The Butcher," "Pulses and Legumes," and "The Quadruped, Four-Legged Animals," and that even included a recipe for roast flamingo tongue tart and dolphin meatballs—featured Apicius's name as the author, but such attribution is most likely apocryphal. Still, Apicius endures as the author of the first cookbook, which in manuscript and then in print would sit next to bubbling cauldrons of oily mutton and plucked pigeons in kitchens from Gaul to Britannia.

The Middle Ages saw a proliferation of guides, especially as regional cultures differentiated themselves in the imperial dusk. If cookery was first explicated by an Italian, then it was elaborated on by the French. During the Middle Ages, that nation contributed tomes like Guillaume Tirel's *Le Viander* from 1300, which advocated haute cuisine based in the balance of spices, while a century later Maistre Chiquart, the chef to the Duke of Savoy, assembled his 1420 *Du fait du Cuisine*. Stereotypically late to explicating a philosophy of gastronomy was that island of boiled meat and gravy, that corner of God's earth, England. An anonymous chef edited *The Method of Cooking*, a guide to the preparation of sumptuous savory and sweet banquets for the scions of the Plantagenet regime, in 1390. This book, contrary to the slur which holds the English largely allergic to flavor, is a testament to the medieval affection for cardamom and cinnamon, nutmeg and pepper. *The Method of Cooking* is not just an *English* cookbook, but a *European* one, including recipes for French vinaigrettes and Italian pastas, in addition to offal pies and boiled meat. More impressively, the editor compiled not just a practical guide, but systematized a full philosophy of cuisine. Taking into consideration the presentation of the food, and the balance of colors and flavors within a dish, *The Method of Cooking* is written in the poetry of "sage, parsley,

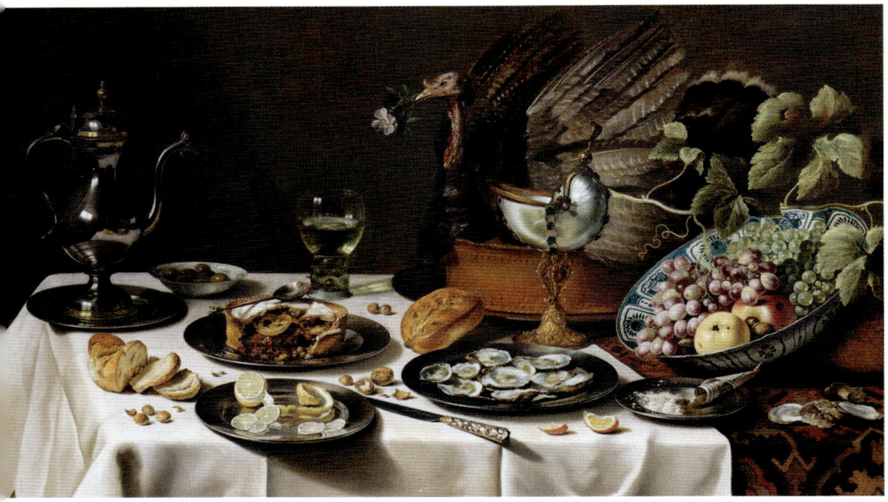

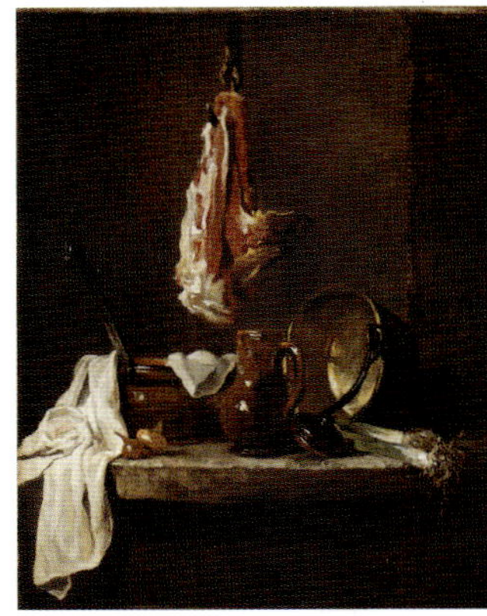

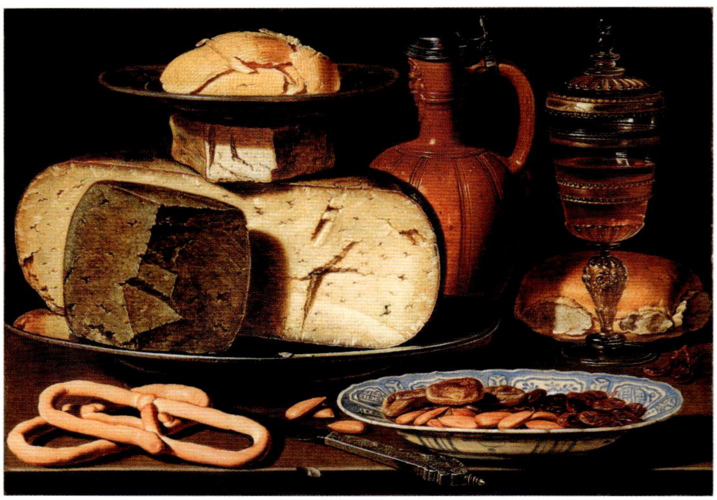

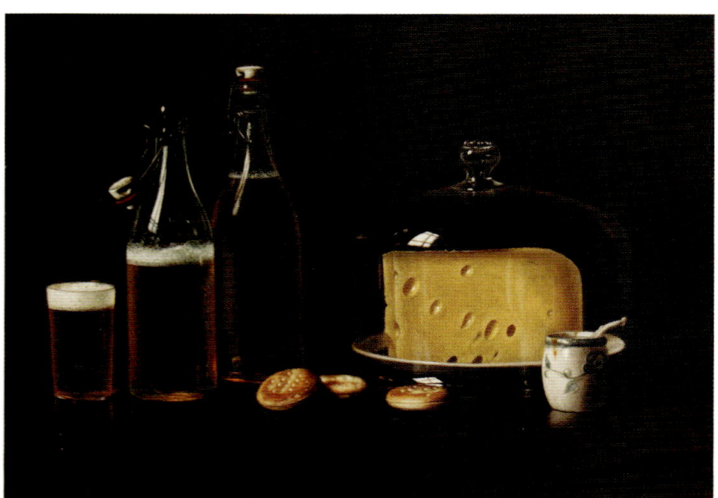

THIS PAGE Among the most distinctive and unusual of artistic subjects is that of the still-life, immaculately rendered and posed inanimate objects, quite frequently of food either before or after a meal, but always lacking the presence of any actual people. Popular in the seventeenth-century Low Countries, still-lifes supplied a way for masters to display their technical brilliance. From top to bottom, left to right: *Still Life with a Turkey Pie*, completed by the Dutch painter Pieter Claesz in 1627, with the original at Amsterdam's Rijksmuseum; French painter Jean-Baptiste-Simeon Chardin's 1739 *Still Life with a Rib of Beef* at the Allen Memorial Art Museum in Oberlin, Ohio; *Still Life with Cheeses, Almonds, and Pretzels*, painted by the Flemish artist Clara Peeters in 1615, with the original at the Mauritshuis Museum of the Hague; and American painter Albert Francis King's 1900 *Late Night Snack* at the Carnegie Museum of Art in Pittsburgh.

OPPOSITE A most unusual recipe appears in the English chef Geoffry Fule's fourteenth-century cookbook, which begins "Taketh one unicorn" and then counsels on how to marinate the mythic beast in cloves and garlic, all of it cooked over a spitfire. Fule being chef to Phillipa of Hainault, the Queen of England, his compendium has more accessible recipes as well (at least relatively speaking), including roast hedgehogs and blackbirds. Original at the British Library.

hyssop and savory, quinces and pears, garlic and grapes." Chefs like Tirel and the compiler of *The Method of Cooking* innately understood something about cuisine despite the monkish schoolmen's condemnation of gluttony—eating food can be pleasurable, and there's nothing wrong with that.

Naturally it took a humanist and—even more naturally—an Italian to express an intellectual commitment to dinnertime. Bartolomeo Platina's 1475 *On Honest Indulgence and Good Health* was the Renaissance's great cookbook, and the first to benefit from the printing press. Drawing largely from the recipes of his contemporary the great papal chef Martino de Rossi—"the prince of cooks"—the author argued that food "leads to happiness, just as medicine restores health to the sick." Much of Platina's table of contents is unusual to us today. Every familiar recipe, such as vermicelli, is matched with something incongruous, such as chicken in rosewater. But the impact was what was important, for drawing from Galenic medicine and a commitment to moderation, Platina gave Renaissance gastronomes permission to ingest without guilt. Ironic that the first great modern cookbooks, rolling off the presses of Bologna and Venice, should seem strangely *un-Italian*, but Platina and de Rossi were chefs, not prophets, and *Honest Indulgence and Good Health* would be published seventeen years before their fellow countryman Christopher Columbus would disembark in the Western Hemisphere and begin that process of importing the most Italian of fruits, the tomato. Not just that lurid red vegetable rumored to overly excite the passions, but a whole litany of New World produce. Tomatoes and potatoes, cranberries and blueberries, artichokes and avocados, gourds and corn, beans and peppers. Chocolate! Imagine what de Rossi could have done were he capable of making red sauce? Or tiramisu?

As it was, de Rossi was supplanted a century later as the Lombard-born Bartolomeo Scappi, personal chef to both Pope Pius IV and Pope Pius V, compiled his 1570 *Work of the Art of Cooking*. Perusing those recipes, the home chef can learn how to make Scappi's capon tortellini, chestnut zeppole, lasagna, tagliatelle, and ravioli, in a litany of sauces, including iconic red, as well as encountering the cook's spirited defense of parmesan. Looking at the red-tiled dome of Bruneschelli rising over Florence or the intricate marble inlay of Michelangelo's St. Peter's Basilica, Scappi would discover a potent metaphor, saying that the chef must be as a "wise Architect who, following his careful design, lays out a firm foundation and on it presents to the world useful and marvelous buildings." Platina and Scappi were the first of an incongruous new type, the celebrity chef.

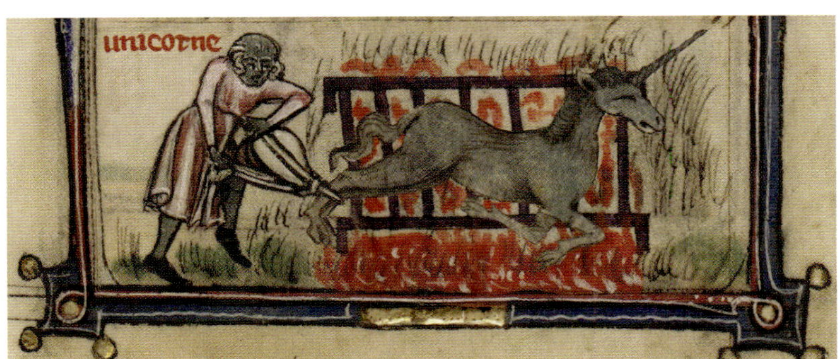

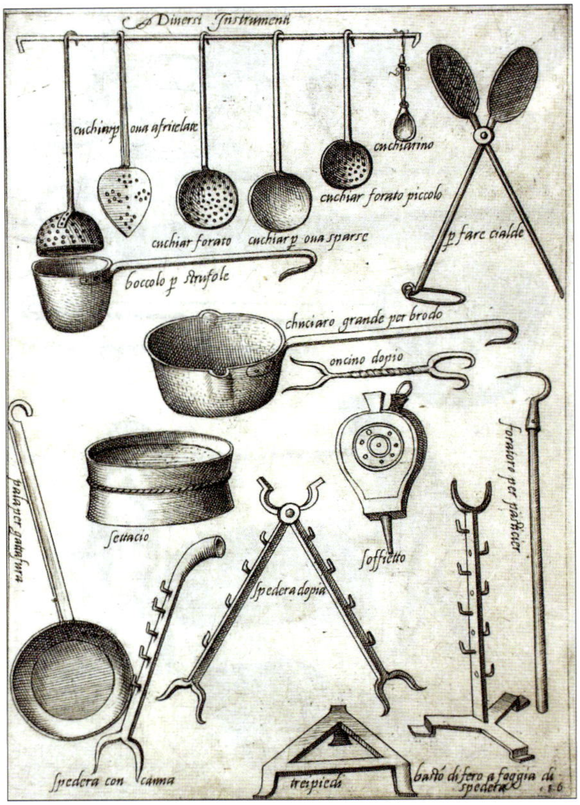

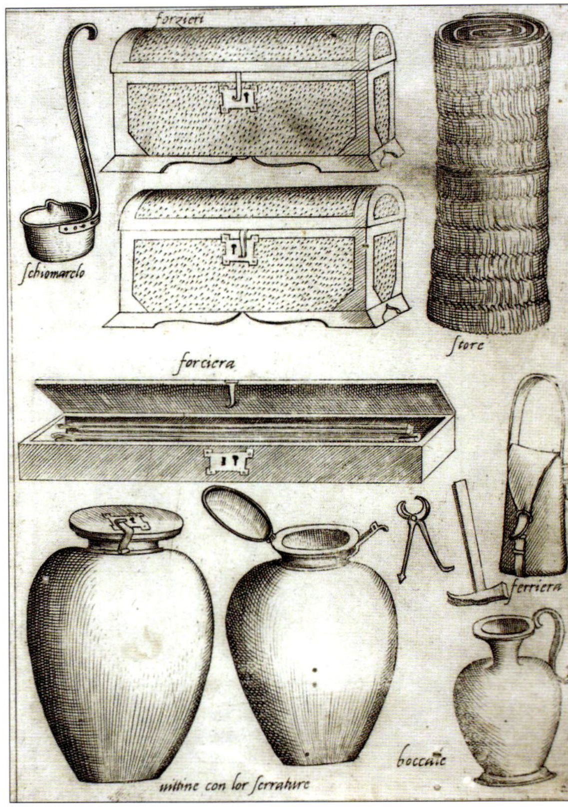

ABOVE The master chef's tools from Bartolomeo Scappi's *Work of the Art of Cooking*.

From their example there would be others over the centuries, masters of consommé and molders of antipasto, rebels of tapas and revolutionaries of dessert. *Architects of food*. Antonin Careme, the great nineteenth-century French pâtissier who prepared bechamel for Talleyrand, allemande for King George IV, and espagnole for Tsar Alexander I; Alexis Soyer, who supped both Queen Victorian at his Reform Club and the starving Irish in the network of soup kitchens established since the former refused to feed the latter; the great Auguste Escoffier, who canonized the five "Mouther Sauces" of France. Then there are their twentieth-century descendants: Julia Child, of course, Jamie Oliver and Lidia Bastianich, Gordon Ramsey and Anthony Bourdain. Even day-glo-tipped and goateed Guy Fieri, biting into a bacon-covered, guacamole-besmirched, mayonnaise-inundated multipound burger, has his role in taking us all on a pilgrimage to Flavortown.

A meal is, by its nature, transitory. An art that is circumscribed by time, that is ingested and then expelled. Beautiful in part because of that, for a chef's medium is impermanent, and always will be. The closest that we have to recording such fleeting sensations—the bite of salt on a crispy potato chip or the chill creaminess of vichyssoise, the earthy granularity of a chili cheese dog or the ocean-benediction of a silty raw oyster—is in words. Not even the lurid, dripping orifices of food porn photography can quite match the solidity of poetry and prose in this regard. Wallace Stevens counting out iambs in Hartford, alliterating about "kitchen cups in concupiscent curds," for the "only emperor is the emperor of ice-cream," or, as he composed in

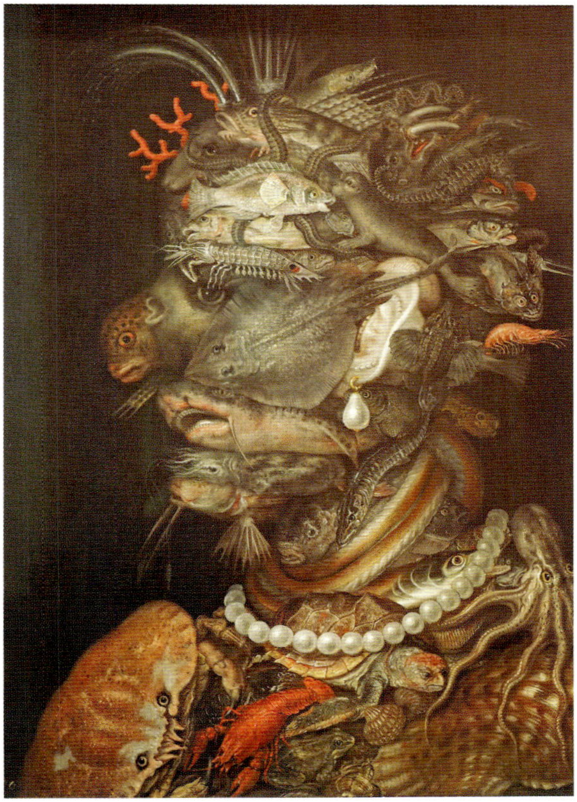

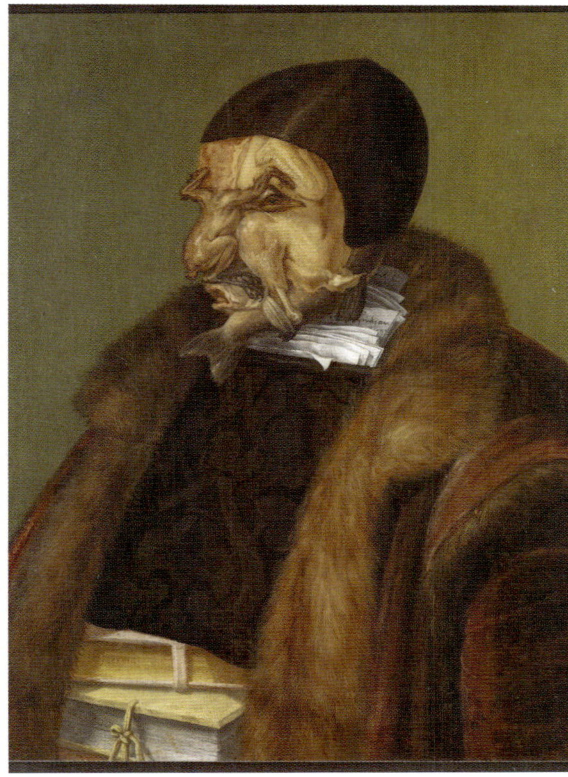

ABOVE True to the cliché which has that you are what you eat, Giuseppe Arcimboldo gives us a damp and fishy gentleman on the left in his 1566 composition *Water*, held by the Kunsthistorisches Museum in Vienna, and on the right an unpleasant barrister assembled from plucked fowl in his painting *The Jurist* from that same year, held at the National Museum of Sweden in Stockholm.

between delivering babies, William Carlos Williams's late-night apology letter for eating those chilled ice-box plums, because "they were delicious / so sweet / and so cold." Sterling modernists, they affixed those sensory details with an iconoclastic parsimony, but who doesn't taste the teeth-chattering sweetness of ice cream through the assonance of Stevens's final line, and who can't imagine the perforated purple flesh of the cold, sweet plum in the monosyllabic conclusion to Williams's poem which puckers your lips as surely as the tang of that fruit itself? Then there is the layered complexity of description in the great prose scenes of gastronomy, the menu of meals and feasts across literature like a trail of fish bones and cheese rinds. Leopold Bloom from James Joyce's *Ulysses* is one of the great relishers of food; given over to not just salty gorgonzola sandwiches, but the "inner organs of beasts and fowls . . . thick giblet soup, nutty gizzards . . . stuffed roast heart, liver-slices fried with crustcrumbs, fried hencods' roes," and most of all "grilled mutton kidneys which gave to his palette a fine tang of faintly scented urine," for in such offal there is vitality, there is the flavor of earth. Then there was the warm and inviting bounty of the sea enjoyed by Ishmael and his honest cannibal confidant Queequeg at the Try Pots Tavern of Nantucket in Herman Melville's *Moby-Dick*, a creamy chowder composed of "small juicy clams, scarcely bigger than hazel nuts, mixed with pounded ship biscuit, and salted pork cut up into little flakes; the whole enriched with butter, and plentifully seasoned with pepper and salt." For all that will come within *Moby-Dick*, perhaps it was all worth it for that small crock of fortifying chowder.

By the Renaissance, gluttony took on the implications of not just loving food too much, but eaten too much of it as well, a slide from gastronomy to corpulence. The first titular character in Francois Rabelais's fifteenth-century romance *Gargantua and Pantagruel*, true to his descriptive name, is a sweating, farting, mouth-breathing orifice-monster of a human being, while the drunken fat coward Falstaff across a variety of William Shakespeare's plays is less monstrous, though his fleshy physiognomy marks him as a figure of fun, a fatso to be mocked. "There live not three good men unhanged in England," says Falstaff with his typical drunken bravado, a buffoon who claims with thumb pressed into his fleshy chest, "and one of them is fat and grows old." Sitting at the Boar's Head Inn, Falstaff is a hail-fellow-well-met sort with a tankard of sack and a gammon at hand, and though we love him because we see in the errant knight a bit of ourselves in all of our protuberances, it's certainly his obesity that in part designates him as a figure of scorn.

The same impulse led to the exhibitions of circus fat ladies in freak and geek shows to the contemporary cable television abomination of *My 600-lb Life*, for if it's true that being fat is a sin, then it's one for which people cruelly jeer and mock those supposed transgressors of the moral order. There is an irony to such cruelty, for 43.4 percent of Americans are considered obese, and an astounding 70 percent over the age of twenty are. Yet 25 percent of Americans are also food insecure—and, as counterintuitive as it might seem, these two categories are a Venn diagram with a substantial overlapping midsection. The reality is that for the millions of people condemned by poverty to live in food deserts, the only affordable options are Big Macs and Double Quarter Pounders, Whoppers and KFC, the sin being that of the wider society. This is not gluttony but something else. Perhaps the true gluttons, then, are those who can afford the nutritionists and Peloton subscription, the GOOP fantasists and the exercise freaks with the money and time to sculpt themselves while condemning the rest of society to McDonald's and Wendy's. Unfortunate, since McNuggets can't compare to a fresh apple from the branch: the crisp tartness, the sweet juice, the forbidden extravagance of the whole thing.

INTERLUDE—THE CONSTITUTIONAL CONVENTION

Fifty-four bottles of Madeira, sixty of claret, twenty-two of porter, twelve bottles of beer, eight of cider, seven large punch bowls (spiked with rum). The "55 gentlemens" gathered in September of 1787 within the dim confines of Philadelphia's redbrick City Tavern, candlelight flickering on the white walls with green molding, also included on their bill various "dinner, fruit, relishes, and olives." The assembled could have dined on pepper pot (a West Indian beef stew), trout from the Schuylkill or crab from the Chesapeake, mallard duck and chicken braised in Madeira, Atlantic oysters fried in cornmeal, braised rabbit, and escallops of veal. For dessert, it's possible they enjoyed rich French pastries. There were nine musicians and seven servants who shared twenty-one bottles of wine, as well as a budget for cigars. On average, each guest had around a bottle—or a gallon—of alcohol. Adjusted for inflation, the tab was $17,253. As the night wore on, fingers were greased with oil from fish bones and mouths were smeared with gravy, hands wiped on ruffled collars and wigs askew, and the guests got progressively drunker. Voices raised, food spilled, bottles dropped. It must have been—in its wanton gluttonousness—grotesque. And one hell of a collective hangover. Two days later and those men gathered again, just a few streets over at Independence Hall, where they signed the Constitution of the United States.

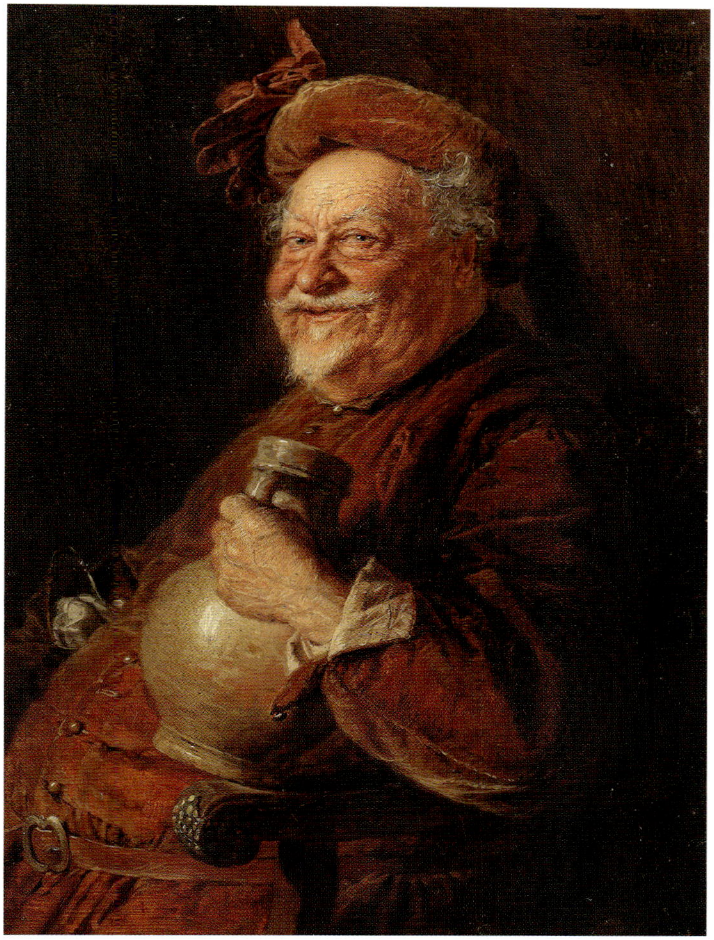

ABOVE German painter Edouard von Grützner turned to one of his favorite subjects in this 1906 depiction of the patron saint of all those who enjoy dinnertime just a bit too much: *Falstaff*. Original held in private collection.

When a sweet cracknell went into the gaping maw of Virginia delegate George Mason, its confection was procured by brutal methods, such as those practiced by the English slaver Thomas Thistlewood, who noted in a diary entry from 1754 that on his Jamaican sugar plantation he punished one enslaved man named Derby by having him whipped, "pickled him well . . . shit in his mouth, immediately put a gag whilst his mouth was full & made him wear it 4 or 5 hours." The sweet spiced rum that was quaffed by James Madison was produced in a horrific manner on Antigua, Barbados, Cuba; as when Thistlewood had tortured two enslaved men, one named Quacoo and the other ironically christened Punch, by having their feet flogged "then washed and rubbed in salt pickle, lime juice & bird pepper." And the cigars, clenched between the ivory teeth of George Washington (his own dentures extracted from the mouths of humans he owned at Mt. Vernon) came from Cuban plantations every bit as brutal as Jamaica's, marked by murder, rape, and torture, as when Thistlewood punished Coobah by putting "a chain about her neck . . . flogged her well & brand marked her in the forehead." What's too often occluded in our public knowledge is just how much of the slave trade was driven by *appetite*. Saccharine pleasure, cotton's softness, the intoxications of nicotine. Since a few people thirsted for rum, other people had their backs broken; because other humans had a sweet tooth, some humans were tortured. A globalized economy, where a lawyer in Philadelphia could eat rice from South Carolina, and then put sugar from Saint Dominique in tea from Ceylon, but the exploitation happened elsewhere. Same as it ever was.

Luxury and justice are not easily paired. An irony that the Haitian revolutionary

Louverture was inspired by Thomas Jefferson, seeing a radical kernel that wasn't necessarily realized, and then using that rhetoric against the colonialism that exchanged flesh for rum, blood for sugar. When those powerful men gathered in Philadelphia, it was in reaction to the comparative social, cultural, economic, and racial freedom that existed in several former colonies under the admittedly haphazard Articles of Confederation. The Revolutionaries themselves thus strangled the Revolution, forging what several decades later the abolitionist William Lloyd Garrison would call "a covenant with death," a document which counted Black people as three-fifths of a human. Edward Said writes in *Orientalism* that "every single empire in its official discourse has said that it is not like all the others, that its circumstances are special, that it has a mission to enlighten, civilize, bring order and democracy," and yet every single empire has also brought "misery and death." Jefferson's fabled "Empire of Liberty" is no different. Save perhaps in one peculiar particular, for eleven years before the Constitutional Convention many of the same men ratified a different document which promised that the goal of any sacred political order was "life, liberty, and the pursuit of happiness." The American Revolution's radicalism has always rested on the definition of each one of those terms—and maybe more importantly who is doing the defining.

How appropriate that America's real birthday, in 1787—which all but erased 1776—should be inaugurated with a decadent feast, as gluttony is our reigning ideology. Gluttony is just consumption, and our economics are defined by mastication, digestion, defecation: of resources, of humans, even of the earth. When Jefferson penned the declaration, he was shamelessly cribbing from John Locke's *Second Treatise on Government* where our inalienable rights include

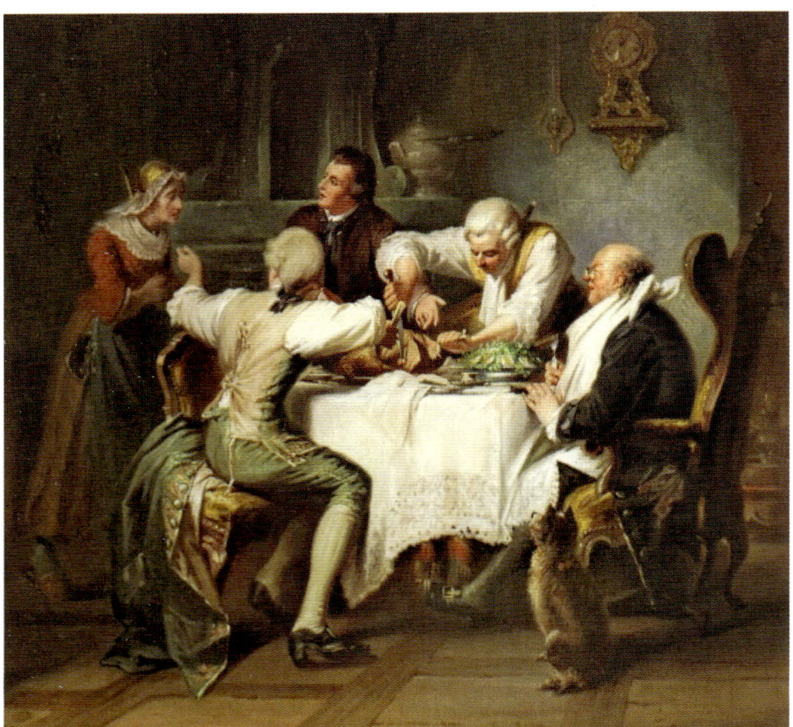

LEFT Nineteenth-century German painter Jakob Emanuel Gaisser's *Rococo Society at a Gluttony*.

"life, liberty, and property." Such a precipitous alteration, for though the vast majority of Americans have always said Jefferson's words while thinking Locke's, the actual language promises something otherworldly. Whether that "happiness" is just another iteration of material power—or something entirely different—is what everything depends on. We were promised utopia, but what we got was a government of the gluttonnous, for the gluttonnous, and by the gluttonnous, as it's forever been in our otherwise hungry nation.

THE HEART OF A KING—PRAXIS

Human flesh, if accounts are to be believed, tastes a bit like sweetened pork. American adventurer William Seabrook, in his 1931 account *Jungle Ways*, slightly amended the normal appraisal of this rarest of delicacies, describing from experience how human tastes like "good, fully developed veal." First maintaining that he'd sampled the dish while in West Africa, he later admitted that he'd procured his goods from a disreputable Parisian morgue and cooked the steaks himself. According to rumors, to be served as a dish of long pig was the ultimate fate of the bookish and athletic Michael Rockefeller—son of a future Vice President of the United States, grandson to the powerful financier, great-grandson of the magnate John D. Rockefeller, and thus scion to the massive wealth of Standard Oil—roasted and eaten by members of the Asmat tribe in South Papua in November of 1961. Graduate of Phillips Exeter and of Harvard, Rockefeller had little interest in business or politics, preferring to explore the torrid regions, making multiple expeditions to the southern Indian Ocean to collect art for the Peabody Museum and the Metropolitan Museum of Art. Largely accepted by the Asmat, Rockefeller went missing after his pontoon capsized. Despite accounts that the heir to the Rockefeller fortune had gone native and was ruling over a fiefdom deep within the island highlands like Colonel Kurtz, a documentary film crew several years later would meet a number of tribesmen who confirmed that they'd killed and eaten the explorer because they wished to avenge the death of a tribesmen murdered by the colonial Dutch. All that remained of Rockefeller was a bleached skull.

Raised on pâté and caviar, Beef Wellington and Beef Bourguignon, champagne and gin, the millionaire would in turn find himself served as long pig, the other white meat. European colonists maintained that the euphemism "long pig"—a rough translation of the Marquesan word "puaa oa"—was enthusiastically uttered by the Korowai and other tribes in the misty confines of Papua New Guinean highlands, a remote place whose inhabitants were treated as fearsome anthropophagi, described in lurid, cartoonishly racist language as naked savages with bones through their noses stewing missionaries in pots over open hearths. It's possible to analyze the presence of such a practice, whether in Papua New Guinea, the Andaman Islands, or the Amazon highlands, without condoning it; more importantly, it's crucial to place it within its context, to understand the differences between ritual cannibalism and the

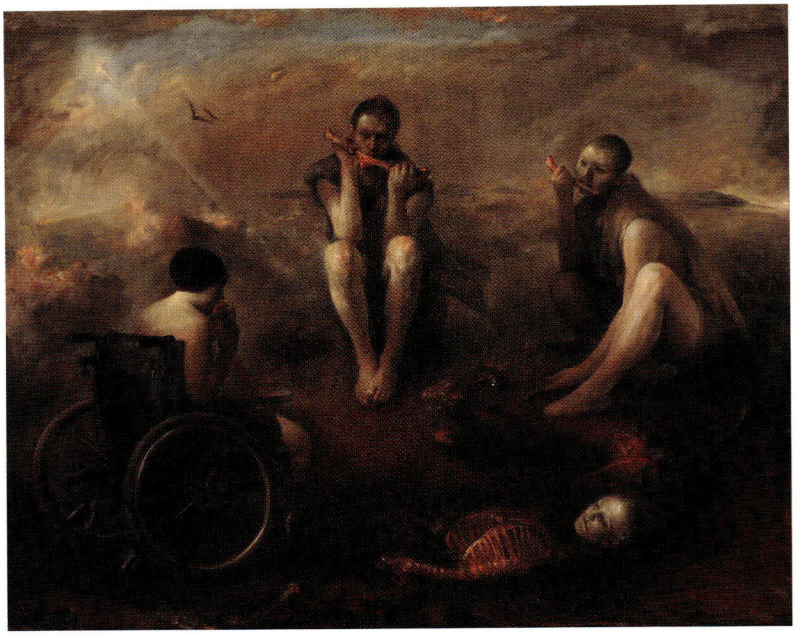

ABOVE Contemporary Norwegian artist Odd Nerdrum's politically and morally ambiguous 2005 kitsch painting *The Cannibals* presents a trio gorging themselves on the mutilated body of one of their companions.

slur of rapacious primitivism born from the fevered imaginations of colonists looking for justification in acquiring the land and resources of indigenous peoples, to literally cannibalize the earth. By contrast, in the sixteenth century, the French essayist Michel de Montaigne in a consideration of the Tupinamba people of South America, noted that despite reports of their ritual cannibalism of those who are already dead, he maintained that "there is nothing barbarous and savage in this nation, by anything that I can gather, excepting, that every one gives the title of barbarism to everything that is not in use in his own country."

Freud maintained that the only universal taboos are incest and patricide; but these are carefully delineated taboos, for what constitutes a transgression is contextual. Cannibalism has exceptions within every culture, whether eating your fellow humans is necessitated for survival or ritual. No anthropologist today doubts that the Korowai ate human flesh—maybe even a Rockefeller—but cannibalism is in evidence across all cultures, even in the West, such as with cruel circumstance during the ill-fated Donner Party or with the survivors of the 1972 Andean crash of Uruguayan Air Force Flight 571, but there are also encouraged incidences, as with the strange phenomenon of "medical cannibalism," when people would collect the detritus left from public executions or pay a premium for the ground remains of mummified Egyptians in the erroneous belief that such practices could cure infirmities. Cannibalism is metaphor more than anything else, the instrumentalization of other people in the most base and despicable of ways transcending your neighbors in a Crock Pot. "Prying so narrowly into the cannibals' faults," wrote Montaigne, " we are so blinded in ours," claiming that his own civilization was marked by "lying, treachery, dissimulation, avarice, envy, [and] detraction" far more than that of the Tupinamba. Indeed, while Rockefeller himself was innocent and didn't deserve his fate, an honest accounting must admit that his family, cannibalizing the very innards of the earth and promulgating the environmental collapse we now all face, did immeasurably more harm than a few dozen members of the Korowai in distant New Guinea. *Eat the rich.*

Obviously most of the eating in history has been done by the rich, from whose rank comes a legion of auspicious gourmands. Few positions come with more material plenty than being supreme hegemon of Rome, and even with Nero, Caligula, and Claudius, the less-famous but no-less-decadent third-century Emperor Marcus Aurelius Antoninus, better known by his name Elagabalus, is among those with a particularly inauspicious reputation. Edward Gibbon in *The Decline and Fall of the Roman Empire* castigated Elagabalus as having "abandoned himself to the grossest pleasures with ungoverned fury," which apparently included a discerning palette for delicacies like camel hump, Baltic sea-wolf, and dormice-and-honey-pie. Governing for only four tumultuous years before his assassination, even more ill-reputed were the entertainments at his lavish twelve-hour and twenty-two-course banquets, such as when several guests, including Roman senators, were smothered to death under a pile of violet and rose petals released from a trap ceiling. An empire of gross economic disparity, the urban peasantry might be able to afford boiled lentils and some watered wine, while the historian Suetonius records how the Emperor Vitellius—some two centuries before Elagabalus—was famed for inventing the "Shield of Minerva," which was made of the "livers of char-fish, the brains of pheasants and peacocks, with the tongues of flamingoes, and the entrails of lampreys, which had been brought in ships of war as far from the Carpathian Sea, and the Spanish straits."

King Henry VIII endures as a signifier of crapulent tastes; a man who, though reputed as among the most handsome in his own realm while still a prince, would die after thirty-eight years on the throne as a four-hundred-pound behemoth with a festering sore on his leg. Swathed in velvet and ermine, the Tudor king was continually drenched in his own spittle and sweat, the gamey waft of musk and fecal incontinence a miasma about his flesh-folded form. Depicted

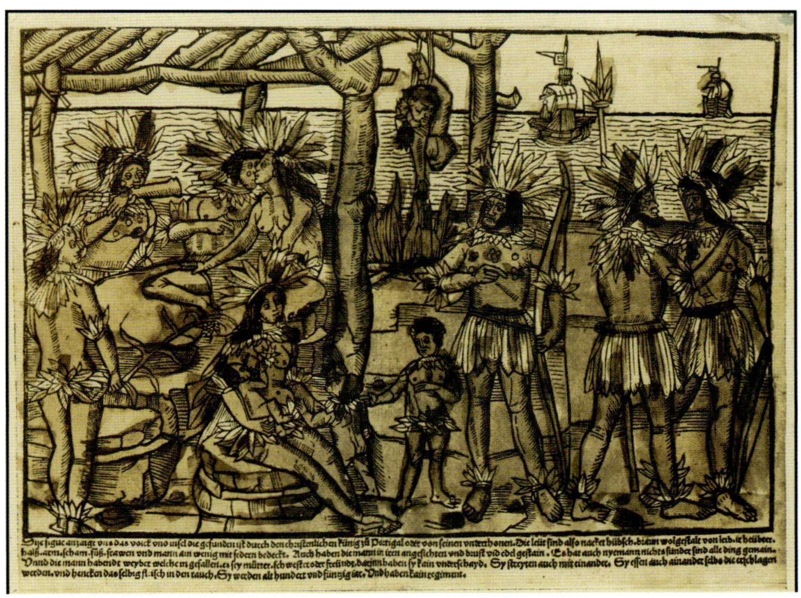

RIGHT Imagined scene of New World cannibalism in this colored woodcut engraving by German artist Johann Froschauer in 1505.

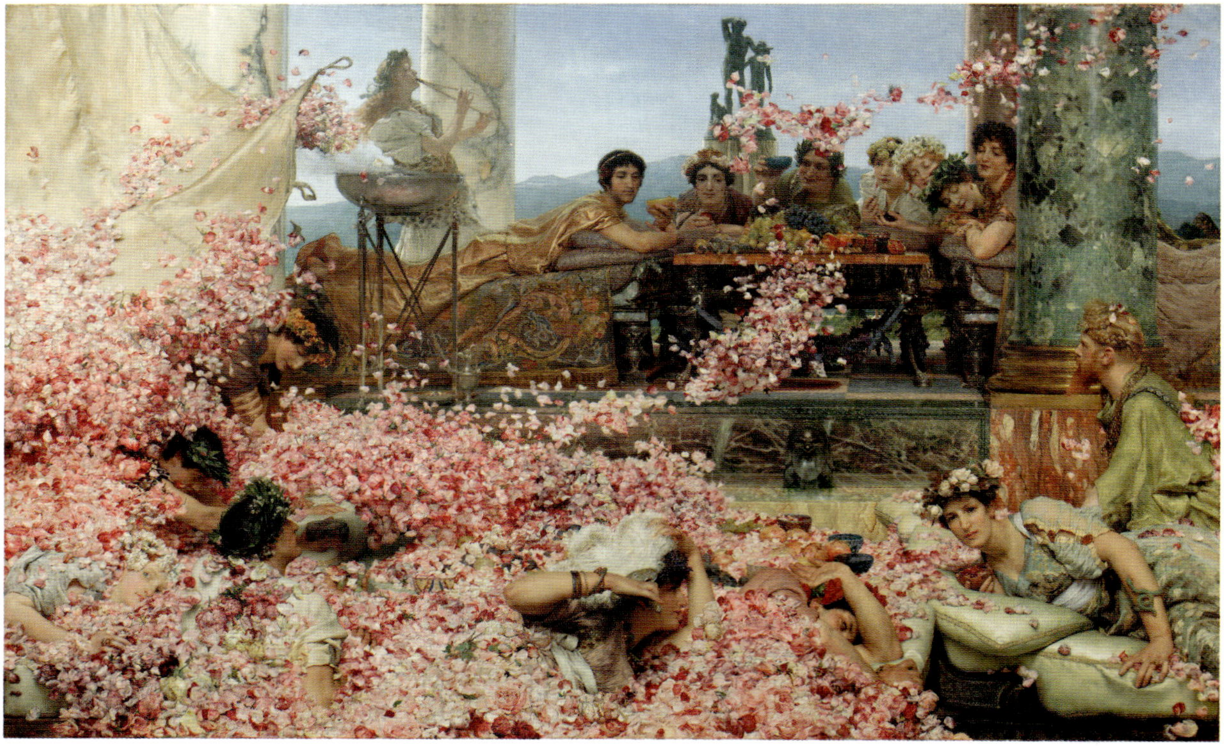

as a monumental knob of meat by the great Dutch painter Hans Holbein the Younger—though still featuring the shapely calves as clothed in silk tights which were Henry's life-long pride—the king was as geographical as he was anatomical. A typical feast as hosted by Henry at Hampton Court Palace, with as many as fourteen courses fed to well over a hundred courtiers, could include lamb, sheep, oxen, venison, veal, pig, and always roasted boar, so that within a typical year the kitchen would prepare on average a veritable zoological garden of 14,453 animals. Fowl was on Henry's menu, including the ever-popular roasted pheasant, swan, and peacock , as well as gamey black pudding and a variety of offal pies from the lung, intestines, stomach, kidneys, livers, and brains of those 14,453 slaughtered beasts. With some regularity, boiled North Sea whale meat was a popular entrée. In addition to such pursuits carnivorous, Henry was partial to a dessert of thick gobs of marzipan or spiced twelfth night fruitcake, all washed down over a twelve-month period with the equivalent of 75,000 gallons of mulled wine and an astounding 600,000 gallons of flat, warm English ale.

As if to stake our own claim to gluttonous superiority, the Gilded Age American railroad magnate James "Diamond Jim" Brady ruled over his own economic fiefdom from the dimly-lit booths of Rector's Restaurant on Broadway, whose owner described the industrialist as the "twenty-five best customers I ever had." Diamond Jim being an industrialist and gambler, philanthropist, and unlikely lover of the beautiful actress Lillian Russell, his typical day included a breakfast of hominy, cornbread, muffins, flapjacks, several steaks, fried potatoes, and a gallon of orange juice; a lunch of three dozen raw oysters, deviled crabs, multiple boiled lobsters, a joint of

TOP A supposedly fun thing we'll never do again at the conclusion of an evening's bacchanal in Dutch painter Lawrence Alma-Tadema's 1888 *The Roses of Heliogabulus*, original held in the private collection of Mexican telecommunications billionaire Juan Antonio Pérez Simón, though previous owners include billionaire right-wing lobbyist Fred Koch, and even the *Candid Camera* host Allen Funt, all of which proves that irony echoes through the centuries.

beef, and a large salad (healthy), followed by several pies and a few gallons of lemon-lime soda; while dinner at the restaurant included another order of oysters bigger than the last, six crabs, several bowls of terrapin soup, around six more lobsters, two roast ducks, sirloin steak, and a platter of French patisserie. Before bed, Diamond Jim would finish the evening with no less than two pounds of candy. When he died at the surprisingly ripe age of 60 in 1917—from complications including Bright's disease, coronary heart disease, diabetes, hypertension, gallstones, kidney stones, and an inflamed prostate—doctors discovered that Diamond Jim's stomach was six times larger than that of the average man's.

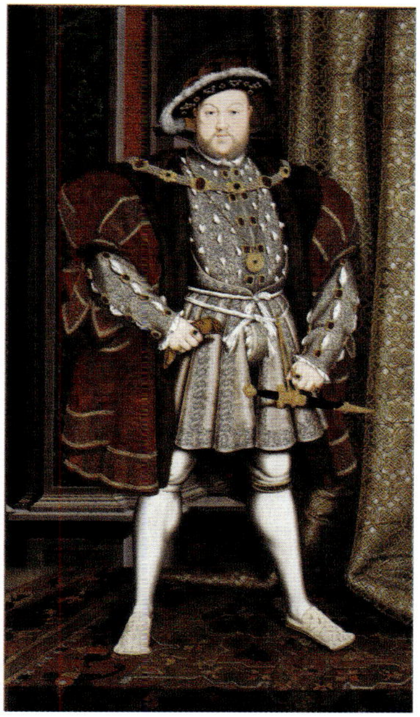

ABOVE *Portrait of Henry VIII* by Hans Holbein the younger, painted in 1536, but the original was destroyed in a fire by 1698. This copy is in the Walker Art Gallery of Liverpool.

If Diamond Jim's transgressions were those of quantity, they were not necessarily sins of quality. After all, there's nothing particularly exotic about eating scrambled eggs and hominy; it was the engorgement that was remarkable. Yet many of the most auspicious gluttons gravitate toward exotic tastes, toward food which is prohibited. Sometimes this is done within the network of religious and cultural codes. Unless one is Jewish or Muslim, there's no sin in enjoying bacon or pork chops, but when the seventeenth-century Kabbalistic pseudo-messiah Shabbatai Zevi entered a synagogue on Shabbat while eating treyf, it was a consciously blasphemous act, heresy as mediated through gastronomy. A similar impious menu was suggested by the Protestant theologian Heinrich Zwingli, who in 1522 advocated for eating smoked sausage on a Lenten Friday, with said meal being enjoyed in Zurich's cathedral following the minister's sermon, a shocking act remembered as the Affair of the Sausages. Both Zevi and Zwingli understood how much of belief is tied up in what we eat, how food codes from kashrut to Lenten prohibitions are connected to faith, and how the flouting of those codes is itself a form of religious disputation.

Synagogue, church, and mosque are hardly the only institutions to regulate food, as any Liquor Control Board or Health Department can attest to. There are dishes that are illegal for reasons of health or morality, but which endure in pop-up kitchens and secret restaurants, in banquets of the wealthy and at shady corner trattorias and cafes. Ikizukuri, the practice of preparing live sashimi for consumption, makes the boiling of lobsters seem positively humane. A Korean dish called San-nakji features still-alive octopi (among the most intelligent animals in the world), chopped into still-writhing tentacles and doused in sesame oil. The possibly mythic Dojo Tofu from Japan, meanwhile, features a loaf of tofu in a pot of water filled with baby eels, which is brought slowly to a boil as the fish try to escape into the loaf, which is then sliced like a cake from hell. Another cuisine which relies on living creatures, albeit ones with a less complex central nervous system, is the notorious Casu Martzu cheese of Sardinia, wherein a wheel of parmesan is allowed to ferment into an astringent, acerbic, shredded wet mass by the injection of fly's eggs into the whey, the popping and jumping of living maggots within one's mouth considered central to the enjoyment of the delicacy.

Of all of the prohibited dishes in Western culture, few are as iconic as the French delicacy of eating an ortolan whole. The ortolan, whose population dropped to dangerously low levels because of the practice, is a gorgeous, ethereal, and dainty bird of slight brown and orange plumage, well-regarded for its sweet early morning song. During their winter migrations to Africa, ortolans are captured in nets at the rate of around fifty thousand a year and later force-fed millet until they double in size, their livers and kidneys failing before they die. Then, preparation of the meal involves drowning the birds in Armagnac brandy, in which they are marinated. After that, the ortolan is roasted for eight minutes and plucked clean; it is consumed whole, and as the flesh and organs are worked from their skeleton, the bones are spit out, the whole disgraceful act done underneath a linen napkin. French president François Mitterrand enjoyed a meal of ortolan shortly before his death, though this was in 1995, four years before the government in both Paris and Brussels made the hunting and preparation of the bird illegal. For those who've eaten the bird, the ortolan is lauded as a creature whose taste is as beautiful as its song, the sacrifice of the creature worth the transitory pleasure. Rachel Galvin describes in a lyric from *Poetry* magazine how "Mediterranean salt emerges as flight bursts / in your mouth . . . Fifteen minutes of savoring a supple, burning ball of fat until you exhaust / its roast juices. When you finally swallow, you will regret / the end of a sensual experience." An obvious decadence to that, a kind of self-hatred as the gastronome hides beneath napkin, but not the only meal which shares in self-abnegation.

The Fool's Gold Loaf is a meal as American as the ortolan is French. Perfected at the Colorado Mine Company Restaurant in Denver, the Fool's Gold Loaf consists of an entire loaf of white bread cored out and then filled with a jar of smooth peanut butter, a jar of blueberry preserves, and a pound of drained bacon cooked in oil, the whole dinner an astounding eight thousand calories. Just as Mitterrand enjoyed the ortolan shortly before his demise, so did Elvis Presley dine upon the Fool's Gold Loaf a year before his death, flying his private jet to Denver and ordering twenty-two of the sandwiches, which were eaten by him and his crew on the airport tarmac, supplemented by cases of champagne. In 1977, only a few months later, the king's heart would give out as he sat upon his toilet at Graceland, such debauchery of food and pills finally taking their toll upon the organ that had once beat as Elvis brilliantly performed "Hound Dog" and "Jail House Rock." A strong organ, a beautiful organ, but a human one. More than a century before, the English paleontologist William Buckland—the man who'd

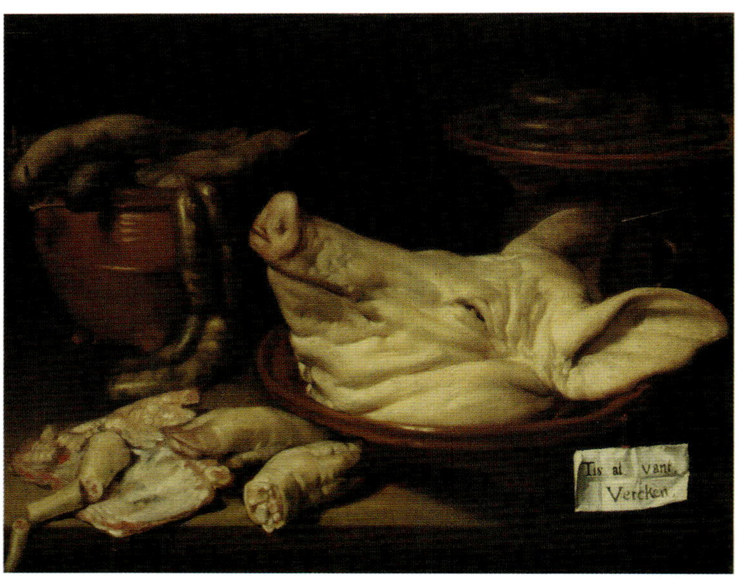

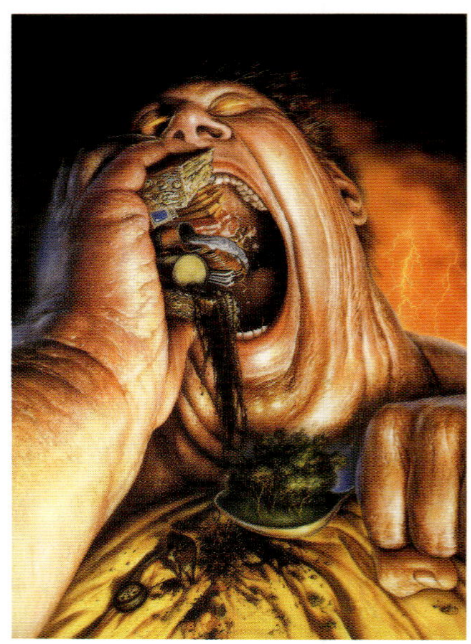

LEFT Protestant Good Friday dinner from 1650 *Still Life with Pig's Head, Pig's Knuckles, and Sausage* by anonymous artist, original at Rijksmuseum.

RIGHT Contemporary American illustrator Mark Frederickson's filling *Gluttony*.

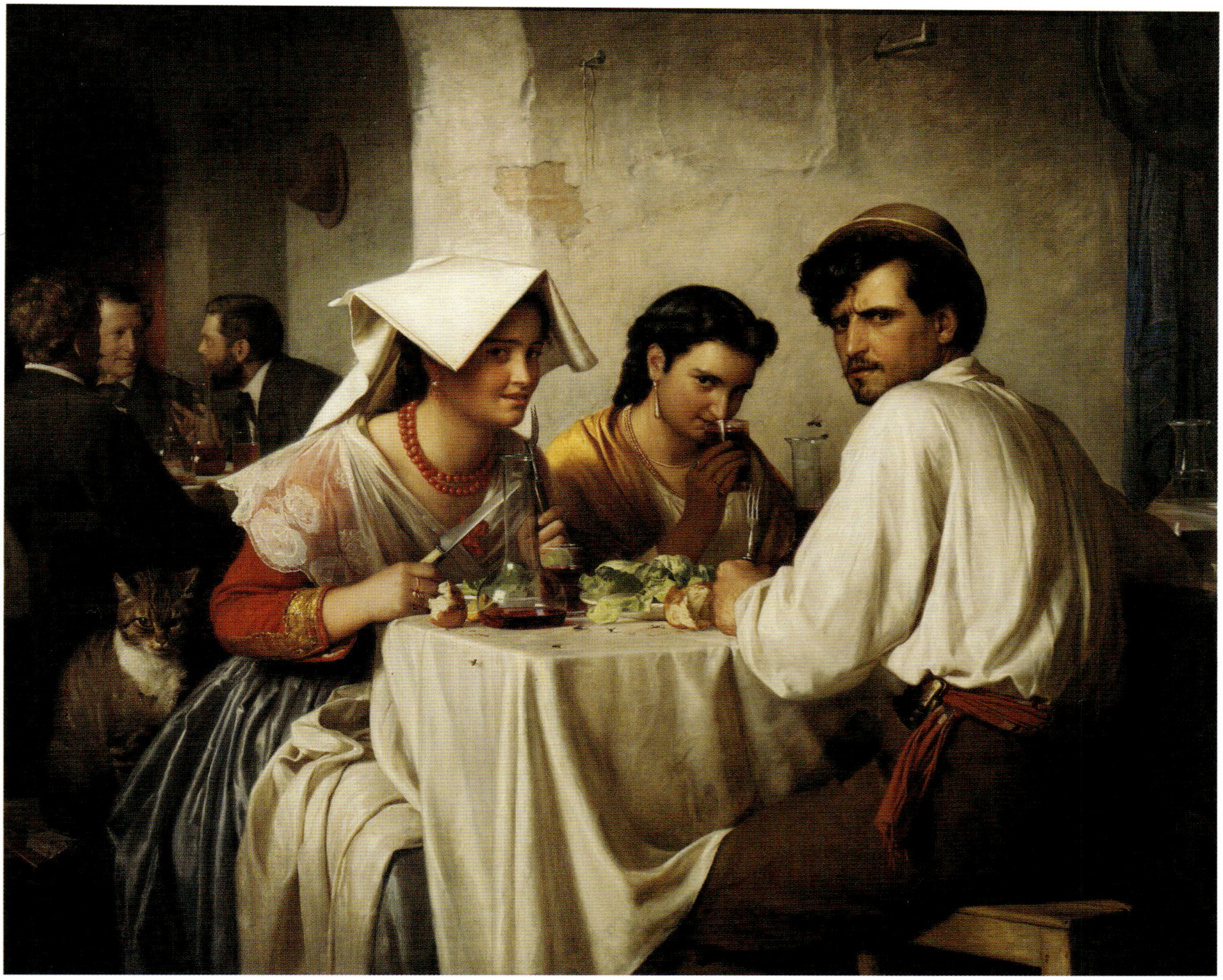

ABOVE Danish painter Carl Bloch's 1863 *In a Roman Osteria*, original held at the National Gallery of Denmark in Copenhagen. Perhaps the ortolan has already been consumed, but the bride here wears a napkin much as Mitterrand would have.

discovered and named the ancient gentle herbivore Megalosaurus—had considered a different king's heart. In between his work on dinosaurs and sparing with Darwin over evolution, Buckland advocated for zoophagy, the practice of exotic gastronomy, as he enjoyed dishes from rhinoceros steak to bluebottle fly pie. When presented with the mummified heart of Louis XIV, the scholar couldn't help but serve himself up a bit, commenting, "I have eaten many strange things, but I have never eaten the heart of a king before."

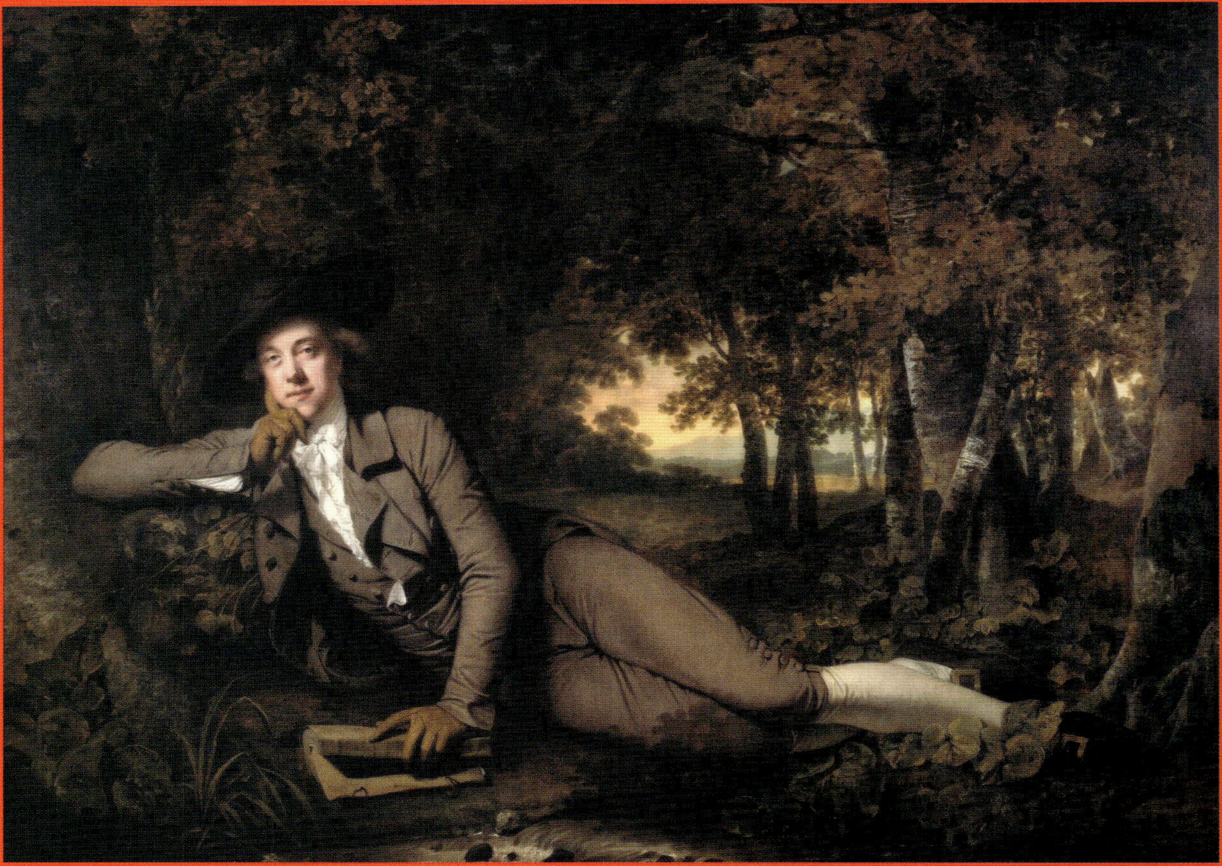

CHAPTER FOUR

THAT ALLURING WITCH: SLOTH

"Sleepiness and laziness in a man are the beginning of his misfortune."
—Genesis Rabbah 17 (450 C.E.)

"I would prefer not to."
—Herman Melville, *Bartleby, the Scrivener: A Story of Wall Street* (1853)

A most counterintuitive of vices. for while all the others assume some action, laziness is marked by inaction. Of the deadly sins, "sloth" altered the most, arguably demonstrating an ambivalence about laziness. Evagrius Ponticus's listing of eight deadly vices included two separate sins similar to sloth which would be combined by Gregory. Instead of sloth, Ponticus counted both "sadness" and "dejection." As concerns the first in Ponticus's *Philokalia*, the author meant "sadness" less in the conventional sense then as the negative feeling about another person's good fortune, a vice much closer to envy than sloth. Dejection, which in Greek is *acedia*, was a disposition closer to depression. When Gregory merged these two, he preserved the word "acedia," and for the entirety of the Middle Ages that's largely what was meant. Today, categorizing depression as a sin is anathema, an offense against people who suffer from a medical condition. However, Ponticus and Gregory knew nothing about dopamine and serotonin; for them acedia wasn't an issue of neurotransmitters, but a hubristic sin against hope itself. In addition to acedia's association with melancholy, dejection, and sadness, there was an implication of boredom, disinterest, incuriosity. An affliction which often bedeviled monks, as the fourth-century desert father John Cassian bemoaned how the suffering "look about anxiously this way and that, and sigh that none of the brethren come to see them, and often goes in and out of their cell, and frequently gazes up at the sun, as if it was too slow in setting, and so a kind of unreasonable confusion of mind takes possession of them like some foul darkness." Acedia, as with all of the sins, shouldn't be interpreted as something over which the afflicted has complete agency; such infirmities were understood as part of the natural (and universal) failings of the human soul. By contrast, today sloth is very much interpreted as willful laziness, a sin against economics. With that new status quo, then, sloth becomes something else as well: a means of resistance.

PREVIOUS SPREAD Brooke Boothby could afford to be a man of leisure. Son of Sir Brooke Boothby Ashbourne Hall, Derbyshire, the younger Boothby was a lay-about, a dilettante, a loafer. Conversant with the Swiss philosopher Jean-Jacques Rousseau and a fellow traveler in English literary circles, Boothby was a living embodiment of the fact that the aristocracy has the means to enjoy their unemployment, preferring rather to dream and imagine than to labor (should everyone be so lucky). English painter Joseph Wright conveys some of the proto-Romantic sentiment of young Boothby in this composition from 1781, held by the Tate Britain.

LOOKING FOR A GOOD MAN—THEORY

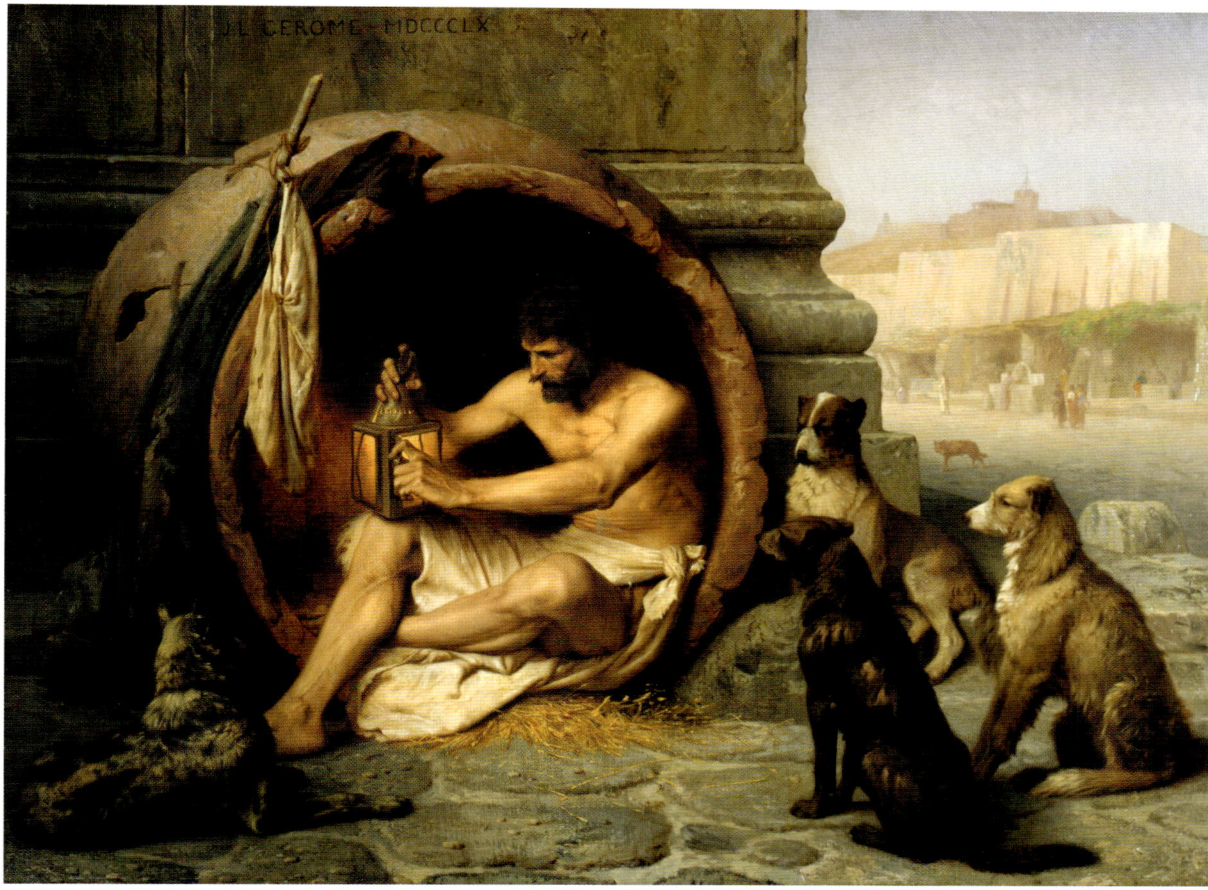

ABOVE French history painter Jean-Léon Gérôme romantically imagines Diogenes in his natural abode, preparing the lantern by whose light he snarked he'd be able to find at least one honest man in the daylight of Athens, as he's watched over by several of his canine compatriots. Painted in 1860, the original is at the Walters Art Museum in Baltimore, Maryland.

Not far from Plato's Academy, there was a very different thinker who resided in the Agora. Amidst giant, rough, earthenware pots filled with wine and oil, olives and dried figs, there was another jar which contained a most unusual product: Diogenes of Sinope. Curled up inside like a fetus, Diogenes spent his day sleeping, screaming obscenities at people, and publicly masturbating. "I wish it were as easy to banish hunger by rubbing my belly," he is reported to have said. Appropriate to remember Diogenes by his nickname, and that which was applied to those in his stead—"dogs," or in Greek, "Cynics." Author of thirty-five philosophical dialogues and thirteen letters across some half-a-million words, Plato is favorably compared to Diogenes, who wrote less than half of that, of which virtually none has survived, his encomiums to transgression and liberty only recorded by later historians. Where Plato was industrious, ambitious, and dedicated, Diogenes was a lay-about, a vagrant, a hobo, and for that reason he's the far superior intellect. Alfred North Whitehead may have claimed that all of philosophy could be

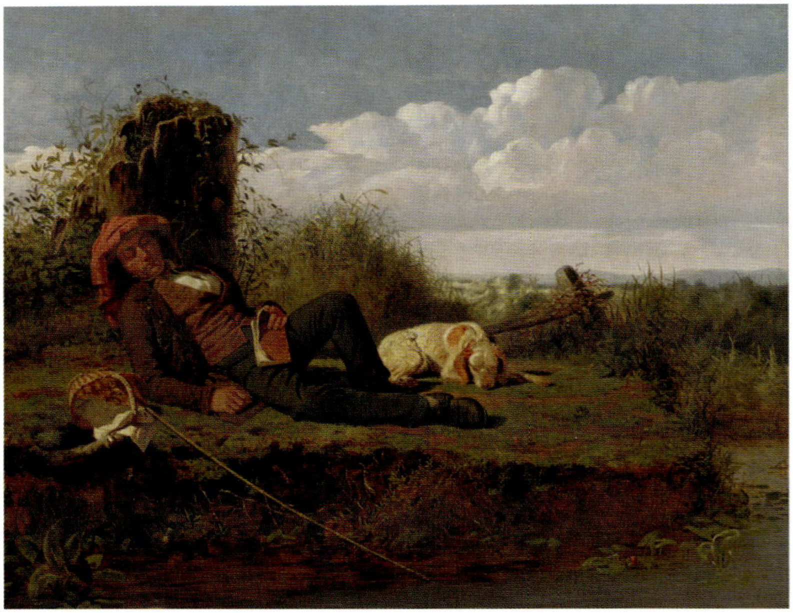

considered mere footnotes to Plato, but Diogenes offered far than mere citation—he gave us unbridled, unadulterated, unapologetic experience. Plato loved Truth, but Diogenes was committed to freedom, and that made all of the difference. What Diogenes counselled was to tune in, turn on, and drop out.

Superficially similar to Socrates, the Cynic shares none of Plato's teacher's unctuous moralizing. Socrates flattered himself as having probed inconsistencies in thought, but Diogenes truly demonstrated the self-serving hypocrisies of those Athenian values of excellence, honor, and nobility. For more than two millennia Socrates has been configured as emblematic of skepticism, free thought, and curiosity, while Diogenes is thought of—when he's thought of at all—as a kind of lazy hippie, a weirdo, a punk, a dropout, but it was the former who attached himself to the tyrannical rulers of the state, and the noble Cynic who lived his values unto the end. In beautiful contrast, when Alexander the Great (student of Aristotle) visited Diogenes, odor of grilled lamb and oregano permeating the Agora, it was after having conquered the entirety of the honey-scented Peloponnese, the pomegranate orchards of Persia, salt-aired Egypt, and the distant environs of the Hindu Kush, realm of the wise gymnosophists. Alexander the Great asked the resting philosopher if there was anything which he could do for him. "Yes," said filthy Diogenes laying inside of his jar, "you can get the fuck out of my light." Centuries later, Plutarch would write that the emperor had said afterward, "If I were not Alexander, I should wish to be Diogenes."

Laziness, indolence, sloth—what is more castigated than these virtues disguised as vices? For the Church Fathers, idleness was threatening because it allowed us time to get into trouble, to conspire and ruminate, plan and contrive. Work, we're told, fortifies the spirit—it "makes you free," as a certain notorious Teutonic slogan had it, so that diligence and sloth are more completely contrasted than any of the other vices and their attendant virtues. The most

TOP Unlikely that the model for the sleeping man in the American painter William Tylee Ranney's 1850 composition *The Lazy Fisherman* knew that he was in the stead of the great Diogenes, but perhaps his canine companion did.

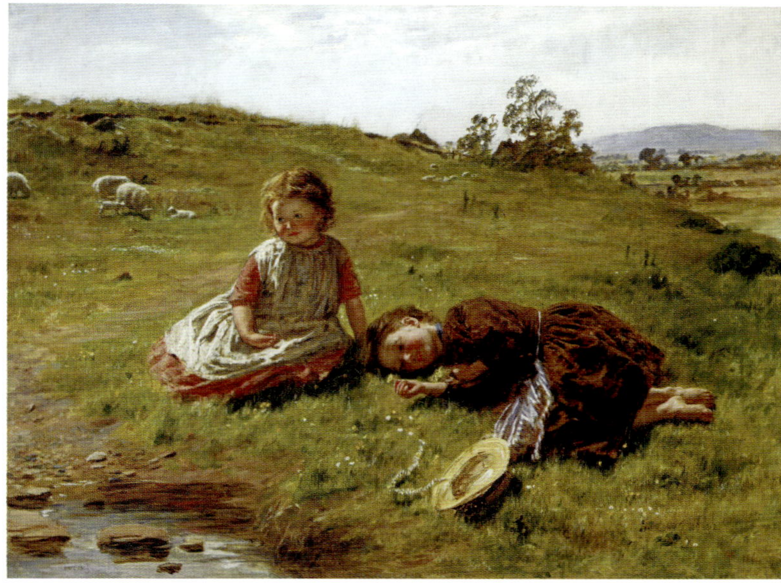

distasteful of sins, especially in a society and economic system which so totally relies on the labor of the mass of humans, even while the work ethic of those who most fully benefit from that said labor which is not their own remains frustratingly unquestioned. Moralizers thrill to the redemption narrative of the junkie who got clean or the whore who is now on the straight and narrow, but stories about people who finally get to work after daydreaming too much seldom receive the same admiration. We viscerally react with anger toward the lazy, the deadbeat, the slacker. So much of the valorization of work for its own sake masks the systemic exploitation of that same labor; the lash of poverty and the carrot of wage chains millions to the cubicle and the nine-to-five workday. "Hell is a collection of individuals who spend their time working on a task they don't like and are not especially good at," writes the anthropologist David Graeber in his landmark essay "Bullshit Jobs." How the manager, the administrator, the owner keeps everyone else tethered to the desk and checkout line, the factory and the delivery car, isn't just in the very real, material threat of unemployment, but also by denigrating those who valorize the acts of dreaming and creating, loafing and leaning, resting and playing, to "lean and loafe at my ease," as Walt Whitman enthuses in *Leaves of Grass*.

In almost all modern contexts "cynicism" is taken to mean this pose of worldly dissatisfaction, a misanthropic perspective that understands reform is an illusion and progress a chimera. Yet the officinal Cynics didn't just choose not to offer a positive philosophy; they outright denounced such things as mere emptiness, rather embracing an all-consuming lifestyle based on a rejection of societal virtues in favor of radical poverty, radical behavior, and most of all radical speech, known as *parrhesia*. The result was a form of critique so potent that it was as lived dialectic, deconstruction made flesh. We're told in several different sources that a group of respectable men were throwing bones

TOP What the prig calls slothfulness, a child simply calls play. At its core, recognizing slothfulness is, if anything, a recognition of the right to simply be. Scottish painter William McTaggart's 1864 composition *Spring*, original at the Scottish National Gallery in Edinburgh, exemplifying Whitman's belief that "I exist as I am, that is enough."

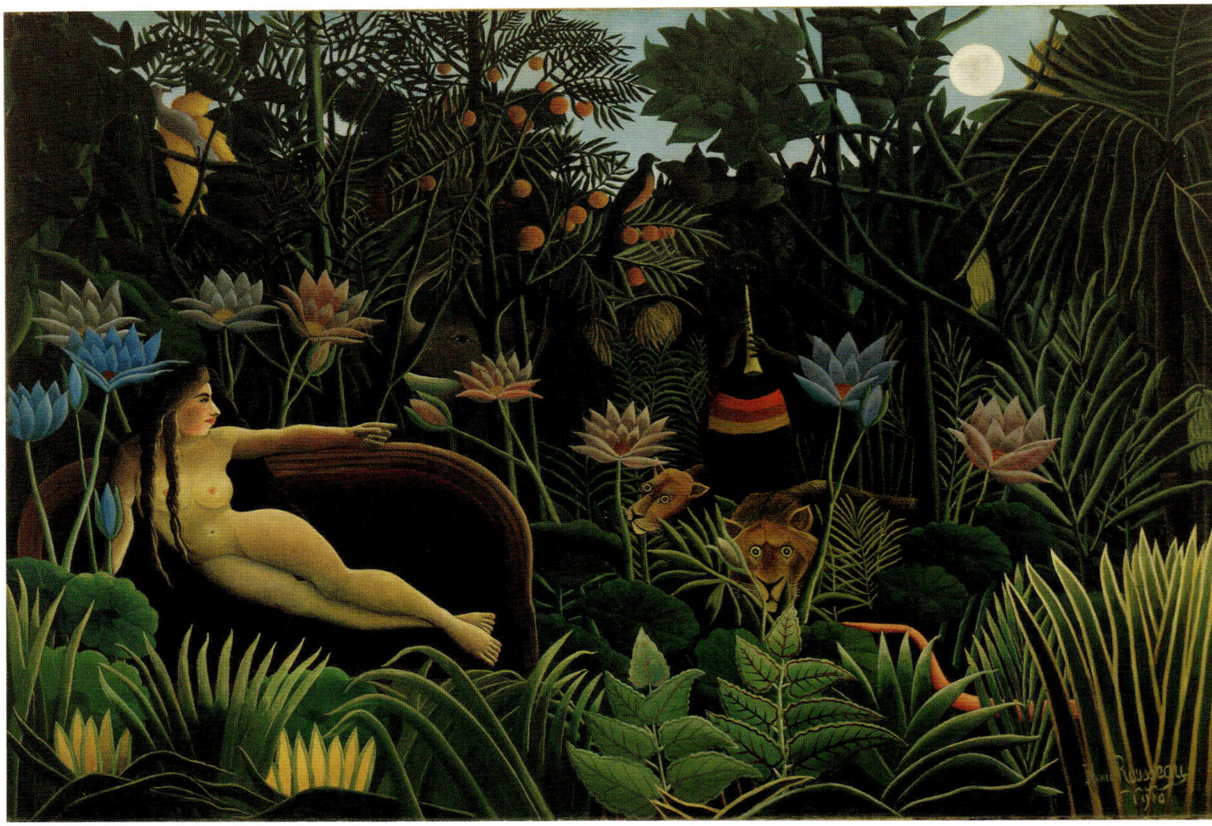

at Diogenes, so the philosopher took a piss in their direction, declaring that if they would treat him as a dog than as a dog he shall be, hence the origin of "Cynicism," which rejects the emptiness of the philosopher for the freeing wisdom of the dog content to sun himself lazily. Such blunt speech, such *parrhesia*, was a way of using honesty to puncture civilized hypocrisies, not out of a misguided romantic notion of returning to nature, but as a form of radical analysis. If Socrates could smugly declare himself to be a gadfly, then Diogenes was a fat, black horsefly drawn to the shit which respectable Athenians thought that they had disposed of.

In Diogenes's behavior there is far more of the punk rock provocateur G.G. Alin—masturbating and self-mutilating on stage while he smears feces on himself—then there is of Plato; more of Pussy Riot in his gambits than there is of Aristotle. Ancient Cynicism was vehemently opposed to the hierarchies of the world, a perspective embellished by an impoverished weirdo who threw away his drinking ladle when he was shamed by seeing an orphan who had the ingenuity of drawing water with only his cupped hand. An error to see Diogenes as the first troll, for what he was after was all the stranger and more mysterious than simply trying to piss people off. Rebellion for its own sake is simply a branding opportunity, for capitalism is able to endlessly appropriate

ABOVE The French Neo-Primitivist and Impressionist Henri Rousseau's celebrated 1910 painting *The Dream*, originally at New York's Museum of Modern Art, was both produced from a bohemian milieu that imagined alternative ways of organizing our time and labor, and exemplified those very same values.

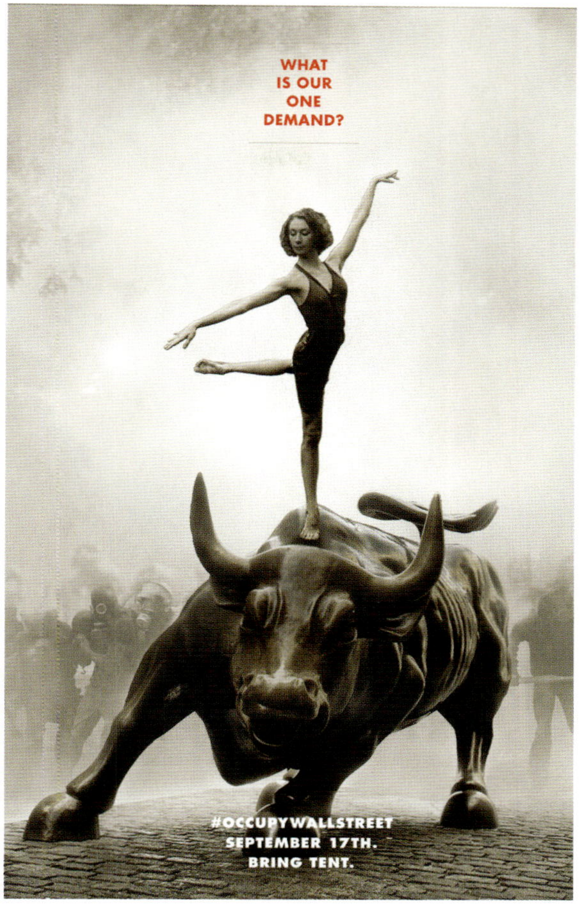

any challenges to it, so that you can buy a rare copy of *Rock 'n Roll Terrorist* by G.G. Alin on Amazon for the low price of $902.81.

Cynicism was always dangerous; persecuted by Emperor Nero, attacked by the Christian apologist Justin Martyr, and tamed into milquetoast lifestyle adage by the Emperor Julian the Apostate. But there is a greater gulf between what's possible today and Diogenes's mission than possibly at any other time in Western history, the ultimate victory of lower-case cynicism. Four centuries before the Common Era and Diogenes gained a reputation for uncommon wisdom; today if you scream obscenities at Jeff Bezos and jerk off in Whole Foods, it'll only get you a psych eval as a best-case scenario. Meanwhile, the very word used to designate such an anarchic movement as Cynicism is now redefined to mean the most abject of conservatisms, the smug neutered perspective of the worldlier-than-thou commentator who rejects out of hand the possibility of a better world. Contemporary cynicism is "enlightened false consciousness," writes the German philosopher Peter Sloterdijk in *Critique of Cynical Reason*. How did we get to this point, from directly challenging Alexander the Great in the Agora to being catty on Twitter, all the while suspecting that since things will never get better, that we've got no responsibility to even try?

Sloterdijk argues that it's literature's fault (as usual), since writers like the second-century Roman satirist Lucian transformed the reclining Cynic into being a mere character type in dialogues like *The Runaways* and the *Passing of Peregrinus*. "Every city is filled with such upstarts," bemoans Lucian in *The Runaways*, condemning the itinerant Cynics whom he saw as fit only for the gutter, those who "enlist in the army of the dog." By contrast, Lucian advocated for a more genteel cynicism, a cultured, lettered, privileged, and distanced position. Drawing inspiration from the satirist Menippus, a student of Diogenes for whom all of his works are lost, Lucian turned cynicism from critical method into "a function of literature," as Sloterdijk writes, with the ramification being that its original manifestation would be forever foreign to contemporary experience. Rather than being in the Agora, cynics would now be found in the books of "Desiderius Erasmus, Thomas More, François Rabelais, Jonathan Swift, Henry Fielding, and Denis Diderot," as Ansgar Allen enumerates, all of whom for their many writerly virtues of wit still lack the pungent stink of Diogenes's radicalism. As such, "cynicism" in the popular meaning of the world would naturally exert an influence on political thought, the neutered Diogenes limping through the pages of Niccolò Machiavelli, Thomas Hobbes, and Bernard Mandeville. Regardless of whether it is on the left or right, such cynicism is by definition conservative, but the real Cynic is an idealist.

Still, there is something unsatisfying in desiring Diogenes's subversions but only being able to afford Twitter snark. Mammon is a dark god, and the manner

ABOVE Prefiguring the current zeitgeist by a decade, the #OccupyWallStreet movement was an example of an anarchic social, economic, and cultural mass protest that advocated redefinitions of both work and the political left. Countercultural political movements have long been tarred with the accusation of "slothfulness," and such accusations were the same against thousands who spent several months in Lower Manhattan's Zucotti Park in 2010. Yet slothfulness is always a convenient slander against those who question for whom exactly it is that we're supposed to be laboring. Will Brown's iconic poster that appeared in *Adbusters* Magazine several months before #Occupy began plays with imagery of leisure and activism, the ballerina's choice to do something viewed by the wider culture as unpractical or non-instrumental its own form of resistance against the riot police in the background.

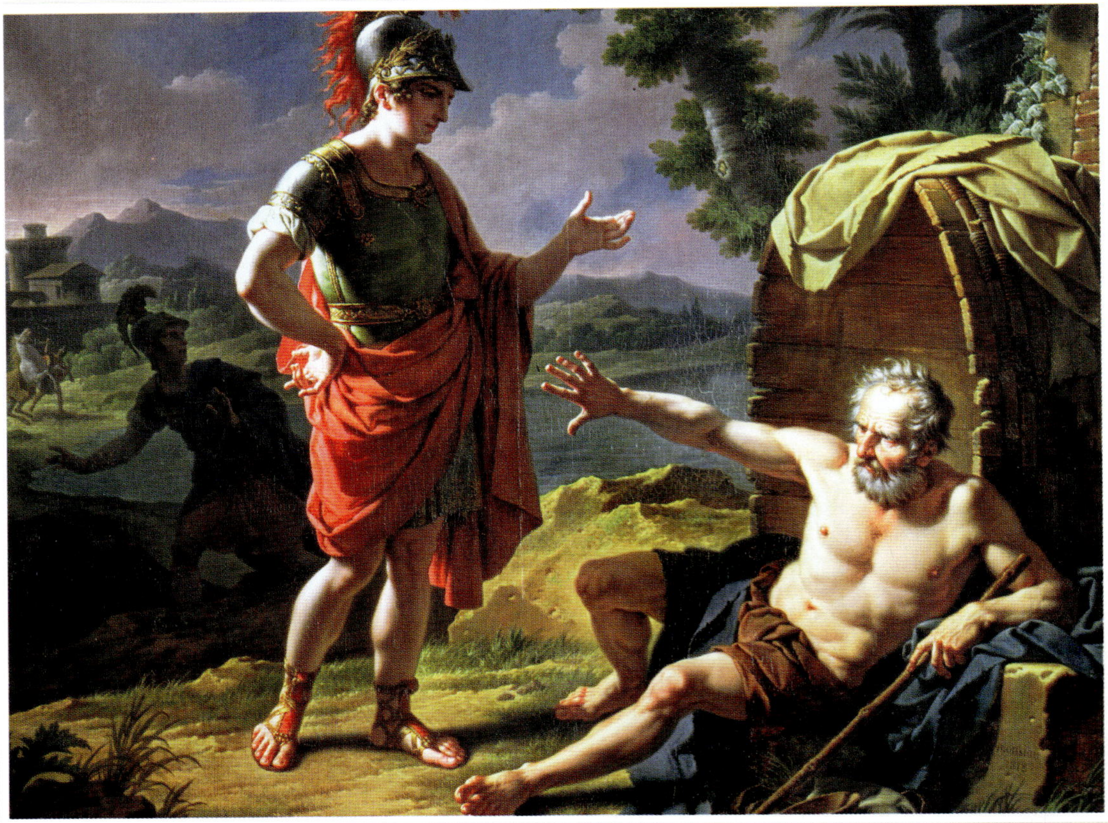

in which he's combatted must always be resolutely through the transcendent, in the realm of meaning: thus, something the materialist left blanches at as sacred deviance is sublimated back into the market. "From Cynic humiliation to Christian humility," writes Michel Foucault in *The Courage of Truth*, there is "an entire history of the humble, of disgrace, shame and scandal through shame, which is very important historically." Perhaps what's needed more than the Cynic is a heretic, the absolute blasphemy of rejecting the empty work of this society in favor of that inviolate pleasure of simple existence. When Alexander the Great had finished marching his martial elephants over the Hindu Kush, he despaired at having no more worlds to conquer, dying only a few short years later in a drunken binge through occupied Persepolis, the maw of his ambition all that was unconquerable. Diogenes, by contrast, was content to sleep in his jar and tell the emperor to get out of the light. Despite doing everything, Alexander failed to conquer the world; but regardless of having done nothing, Diogenes was able to acquire the sun.

ABOVE Diogenes tells Alexander the Great precisely where he should go in the French artist Nicolas-André Monsiau's 1818 painting *Alexander and Diogenes*, original held by the Musée des Beaux-Arts de Rouen.

INTERLUDE—THE GOLIARDIC POETS

By burning charcoal and mixing the ash with resin and water, or by fermenting the oak galls where a wasp has laid her egg and combining it with iron sulphate so as to extract dark-colored tannins, medieval craftsmen produced deep black ink. Manufacturing parchment was also laborious. After long strips of cow or sheep skin had their hair scraped away, they were soaked in lime and then stretched on a wooden frame where a parchminer ran a lunellum across the flesh to thin it out. The resultant pages were buffed with a pumice stone and then chalked. To make one large Bible necessitated the slaughter of around three hundred sheep. If all of medieval writing is simply stains on animals' corpses, then the monks who created that corpus were sustained on the meat of literature and scripture, their bowls filled with lamb and beef stews mixed with carrots and turnips as they scribbled on the skins of those creatures sacrificed for this cause. Copyists worked six hours a day, all of that skritching of nibs across vellum and pen-knives scratching mistakes away the only dun in the otherwise silent scriptorium. Talented scribes were commanded to work even longer, given special dispensations by their abbots from the canonical liturgy of hours to rather copy the prophets and the Gospels, Plato and Aristotle, Augustine and Aquinas. Evagrius Ponticus. That Church Father had a word for something which the monks often succumbed to—*acedia*. His student John of Cassian called acedia the "Noonday Demon," describing his own affliction as marked by much anxiety and sighing, a disease of "some foul darkness." Torpor, listlessness, exhaustion. According to Evagrius, acedia was a sin, but by the time of Gregory, it had been replaced by sloth. A telling change, as work began to be understood as a means unto itself, so that rest, recreation, and leisure were slurred as a sin. Today we'd understand acedia as the walking blues; the rote, joyless, and mechanical completion of that which needs to be done. For the scribes preserving Western civilization, illuminated by scant candlelight long after Vespers, the work was marked by calloused hands, sprained wrists, and strained eyes. Ironic, then, that one of the great works of indolence came from such a place.

In 1803 a Bavarian librarian discovered in the Benedictine monastery of Benediktbeurn a manuscript of 226 lyric poems written in a combination of Latin, Middle High German, and a dialect of French Provençal. Most of the poems are from as early as the eleventh century and a few as late as the thirteenth; the largely anonymous lyrics are paeons to indulgent living. Oft described as the greatest example of Goliardic poetry (of the name of the movement itself having an uncertain etymology), that genre was written by clergy who mocked Catholic theology, producing complex liturgies devoted to drinking, gambling, and so on. Goliards were the avant-garde of their day, staging satirical protests in Saxony and Provence, Occitan and Bavaria. A thirteenth-century complaint from the rector of the University of Paris said that Goliardic "Priests and clerks . . . dance in the choir dressed as women . . . they sing wanton songs. They eat black pudding at the altar itself, while the celebrant is saying Mass. They place dice on the altar." Poets like Hugh Primas, Walter of Chatillon, Petrus Blesensis, and especially the anonymous writer known only as the Archpoet contributed to this anthology extolling the virtues of drunkenness, fornication, gambling and most of all idleness, all of which was regulated by the pagan figure of Fortuna. "The time of joy is here now—come every girl! / Now share in the revels—come every lad!" Published to great acclaim after their uncovering, the *Songs of Benediktbeurn* are better known by their Latin title: *Carmina Burana*. That's the title whose lyrics the twentieth-century German composer Carl Orff set to music, and his eerie and demonic-sounding cantata conveys the blasphemous content of those satirical poems. "I am the Abbot of Cockaigne," says one narrator, and "and my pleasure is in the order of gamblers and whoever seeks me early in the tavern will leave naked after vespers."

There are the Middle Ages of Lent—quiet, dutiful, sacred; and then there is the medieval period of Carnival—bawdy, earthy, irreverent. Goliardic poets inhabited both of those worlds, and their legacy touches on traditions like the Shrovetide crowning of a Lord of Misrule and the imagined utopia of Cockaigne. Pronounced like the drug, though possibly derived from the name of a French cake, Cockaigne is neither the neutered paradise of Christian heaven nor the staid bureaucracy of Thomas More. Rather it's a lusty, decadent, fleshy place, a utopia of the common man, a heaven of the exhausted laborer. A mainstay of folklore, Cockaigne was supposed to be a realm where roasted capons would fly right into hungry mouths and cooked pigs roamed the countryside, where ale trickled down the streams and most of all where the tired could sleep on the banks. "To you, consummate drinkers, / Through little be your drought, / Good speed be to your tankards, / And send the wine about," a *Carmina Burana* poet slurrily enthused. Within that collection is included the so-called Drinkers Mass, which so convincingly imagined a coterie committed to lethargy that latter scholars believed such a group must be real. That passage honors "all those who dedicate themselves to the game: the dice enjoy their nakedness and honor the son of Bacchus," as gambling promises to clothe the peasantry in the garments of royals. Not just for the scribe toiling in the scriptorium, but for the serf surviving through subsistence farming on the land of a feudal lord, or the wife of that tiller raising and burying their children, Cockaigne offered a very human heaven—a place to finally rest. With the coming of Protestantism there would be even less rest as all of those feast days disappeared; with the coming of positivism the purpose of humanity was reoriented toward the instrumental. Lent may have been abolished, but carnival was too, replaced with the assembly line, the factory farm, the office cubicle.

Technological capitalism promised us liberation, but what it delivered was a gig economy and smartphone apps, a culture where answering emails at midnight and working multiple jobs was normalized, even compulsory. According to Evagrius, the sin was working so hard that one fell into despair, but our culture has long shifted the sin to not toiling hard enough. What Cockaigne symbolized was the idyl of *not working*; a realm for the non-instrumental, the refusal of practicality and pragmatism. In its place was the garden of leisure, the pleasure of mere existence, whose blessings are only unequally distributed in sleep (when it comes). Our Gordilacs are partisans of repose, joined by the Ranters and Romantics, the Beats and the hippies, and a thousand other bohemians who dreamt of leaning and loafing and inviting one's soul. Castigating sloth is to condemn a sacrosanct human right, the holy and blessed prerogative *to simply be*.

OPPOSITE With tasks that seemed neverending, the Goliardic poets imagined the joys of frivolity, of indolence, of wantonness, of laziness in the thirteenth-century *Codex Buranus*. "We are the ones whom everyone scolds," complains the poet, "and thus we are destitute."

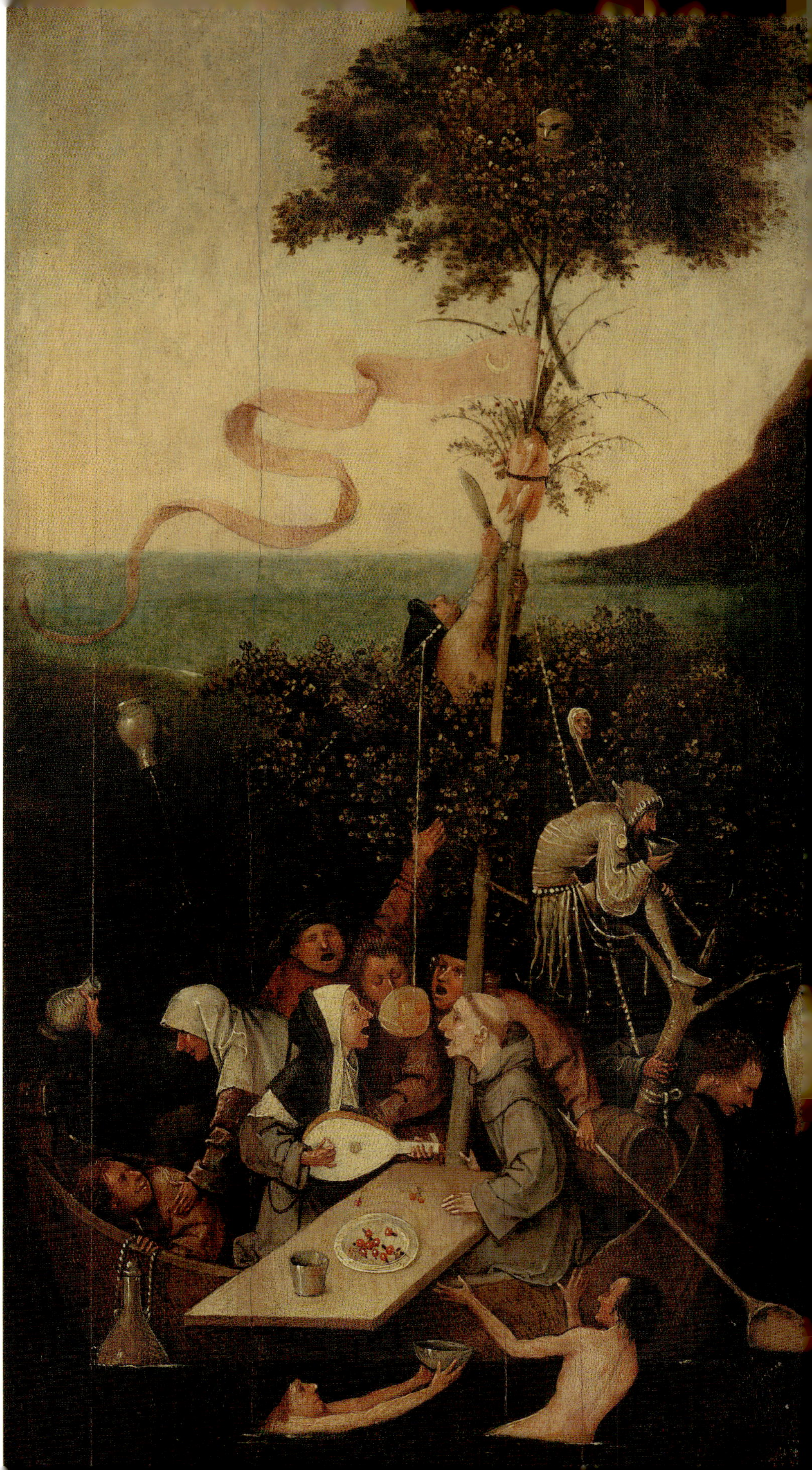

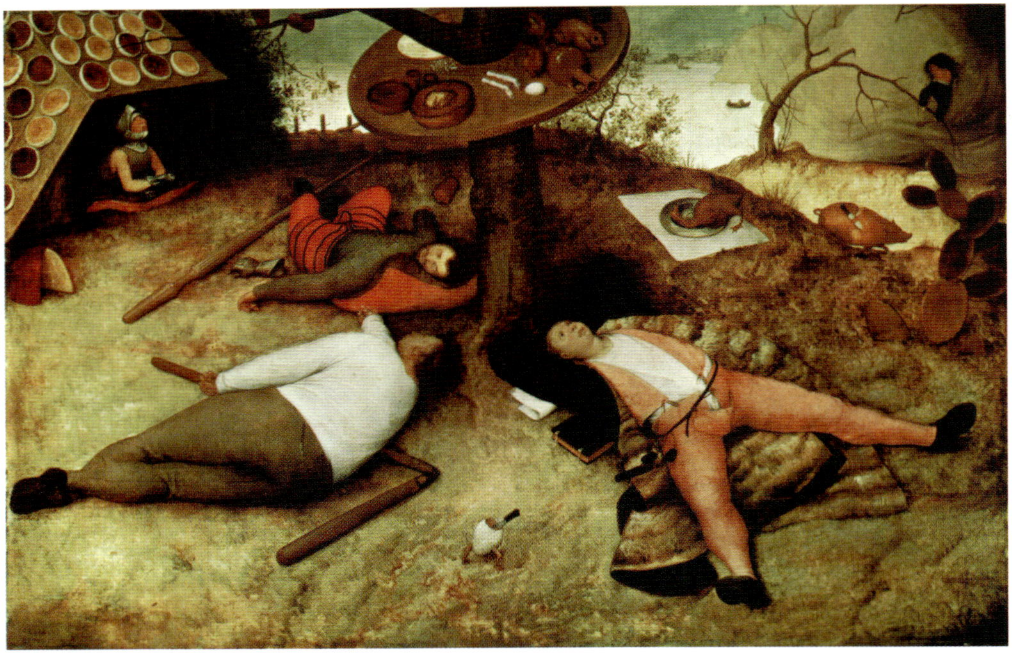

TURNING THE WORLD UPSIDE DOWN—PRAXIS

Following the Church of England emerging from the schism of Henry VIII and then on to the religious settlements of his children—the austere Protestantism of Edward VI, the Inquisition-friendly Catholicism of Mary I, and the *via media* Protestantism of Elizabeth I—the Lord of Misrule was endangered. The Lord of Misrule is one of those archetypes of the Middle Ages, a fragment of halcyon Merry Old England. During the Christmastide season, a layperson would be chosen as a jester-ruler over the festive commonfolk celebrating the solstice, a motley fool who mocked piety, subverted hierarchies, and challenged faith and state. Similar to the court fool, the Lord of Misrule is a dancing, farting, squawking, drinking, blaspheming, lounging, lazy challenge to the status quo, begrudgingly sanctioned by the medieval Church, but with scholars long arguing about just how radical the position actually was; whether he promised something that was revolutionary, or was mere pressure gauge. By the Elizabethan Age, the polemicist Philip Stubbes would rail in his 1585 *Anatomy of Abuses* against this "heathen company" with their "pipers piping, their drummers thundering, their stumps dancing, their bells jingling, their handkerchiefs swinging about their heads like madmen, their hobby horses and other monsters skirmishing." What Stubbs objected to was the *carnivalesque*.

The Russian theorist Mikhail Bakhtin invented this critical term, with its evocation of roasted chestnuts and stewed lamb, belled hats and checkered pants, warm ale and spiced wine, of unbuckling pantaloons and sleeping

TOP Maybe the most celebrated representation of Cockaigne, the Flemish painter Pieter Brueghel the Elder's 1567 *The Land of Cockaigne*, held in the Bavarian State Art Collection, enshrines three indolent peasants in slothful repose, in an imagined utopia where all work has been abolished and every luxury is as near as thought itself.

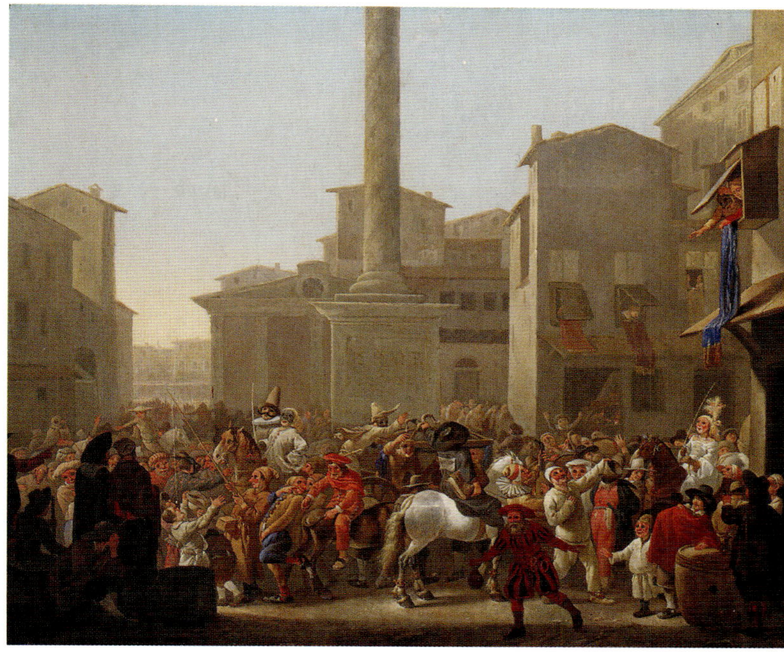

TOP Protestants like the Dutch painter Johannes Lingelbach were drawn to the traditions of carnival that endured among the more relaxed denizens of the Latin south. Training and living in Italy for most of his career, Lingelbach had ample opportunity to consider the lackadaisical attitudes of the romance nations, such as in this 1650 composition *Carnival in Rome* held by the Museum of Art History in Vienna.

underneath the nearest oak tree, a term that's both noun and adjective, that can describe how in the sixteenth century a man like the nobleman Richard Evelyn's retainer Owen Flood could be invested with "full power and authority [from] his lordship to break up all locks, bolts, bars, doors and latches, and to fling up all doors out of hinges." No concept derived from Bakhtin has been quite as evocative and contested as "carnivalesque" from his 1940 study of the seminal French Renaissance writer in his titular dissertation *Rabelais and His World*, a consideration of grotesque medieval subversions at the dawn of modernity. What Bakhtin defined as the "principle of laughter and the carnival spirit . . . [which] destroys this limited seriousness and all pretense of an extratemporal meaning and unconditional value of necessity. It frees human conscious, thought, and imagination for new potentialities." For Bakhtin, living under the at best drab uniformity of Soviet bureaucracy and at worst the totalitarian nightmares of Stalinism, the carnivalesque was a way of describing the ribald, lusty, and earthy rituals coming to an end in Rabelais's century as well as identifying a mode of critique to the positivist obsession with work. His was a methodology of collective joy and mocking humor, of promiscuous pleasures and wanton excess intended to turn the world upside down. Part of the brilliance of *Rabelais and his World* was that Bakhtin was purposefully agnostic on whether or not the carnivalesque was revolutionary or not; when somebody like Evelyn allowed his servant to knock the door off its hinges, did that gesture toward genuine utopian possibility, or was it simply a way of letting the lumpenproletariat blow off some steam? The other possibility, as Bakhtin considers, is that the carnivalesque allows for both. There is no definite answer to the question of whether the carnivalesque is heavenly revolt or mere bread-and-circuses, because sometimes it's one and sometimes it's the other, though when it's which can often be hard to discern.

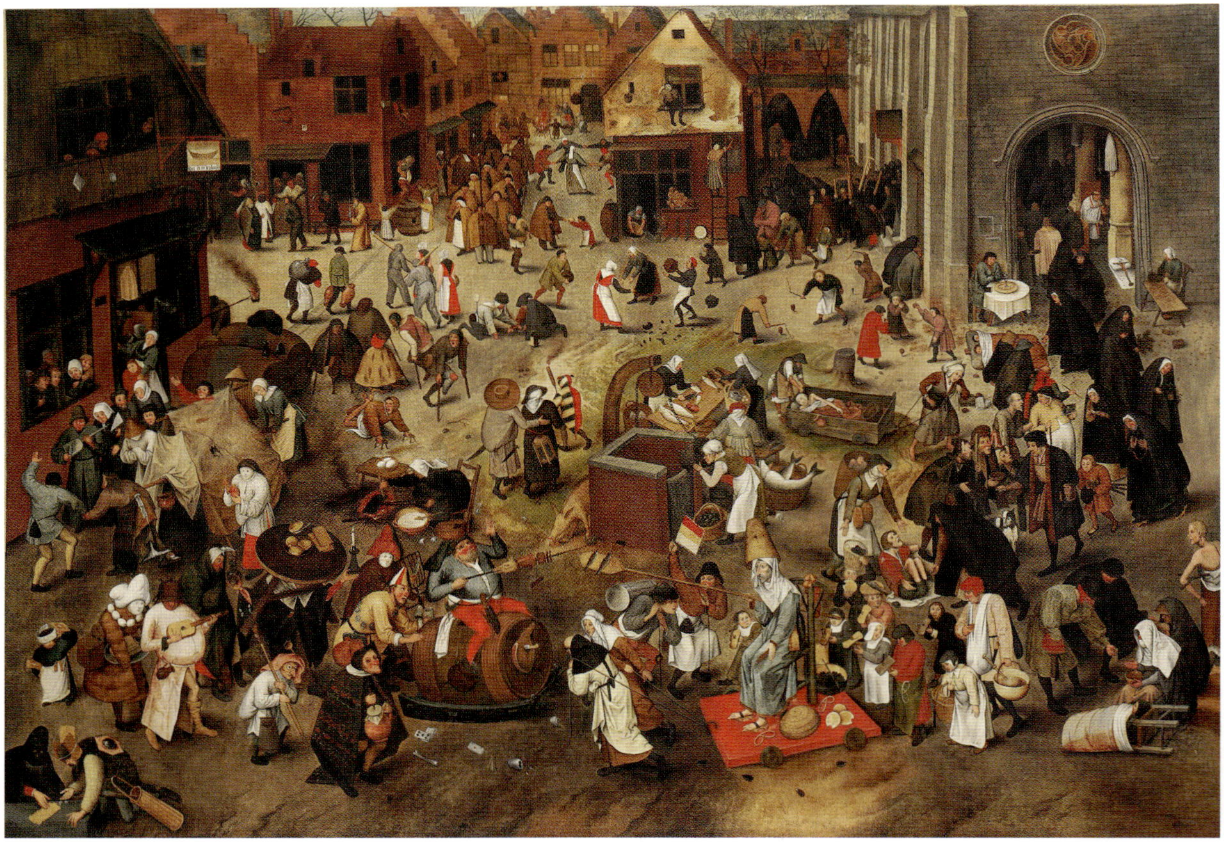

TOP Pieter Brueghel the Elder's 1599 *The Fight Between Carnival and Lent*, original held at the Museum of Art History in Vienna, imagines the former as a jolly man in red pantaloons riding a keg as a horse and the latter as a haggard, gaunt, corpuscular man in monastic robes. Allegorically representing the rhythms of the liturgical calendar, Brueghel's vision is an apt summation of modernity, whereby the convivial joyfulness of indolent Carnival would lose.

Strangely, however, the carnivalesque doesn't seem to enter much into our discourse today. Protestant religious authorities and increasingly the Catholic Magisterium overseeing the Counter-Reformation decreed that the crowning of a Lord of Misrule was more trouble than it was worth, and so throughout Europe, but especially in the north, such practices became rare. Protestantism ushered in another totalizing worldview allergic to the slovenly delights of the carnivalesque, and that was capitalism. As countryfolk crowded into cities and industrial capitalism developed, the carnivalesque wasn't just a threat to organized religion, but the factory system as well. However, if it were ever true that the Calvinist work ethic made capitalism possible, the former has long outlived its usefulness in that regard, for the satiation of appetites, the unleashing of libidinal energy, the unhampered celebration of the grotesque is what modern commercial capitalism thrives upon. Today, festivities have many redeeming qualities to the businessmen who operate them, the landlord who leases the property for them, the advertiser who promotes them.

Silicon Valley has always been the City on a Hill for a particular type of commodified dissent that tames the carnivalesque in the service of neoliberalism, the clarion call to "Think Different" inaugurating our epoch of surveillance capitalism, algorithmic omnipotence, and billionaire "rebels" in the form of Thiel, Bezos, and Zuckerberg. While it's true that the earliest days of the digital revolution grew out of countercultural commitments, a kind of Esalen Institute meets

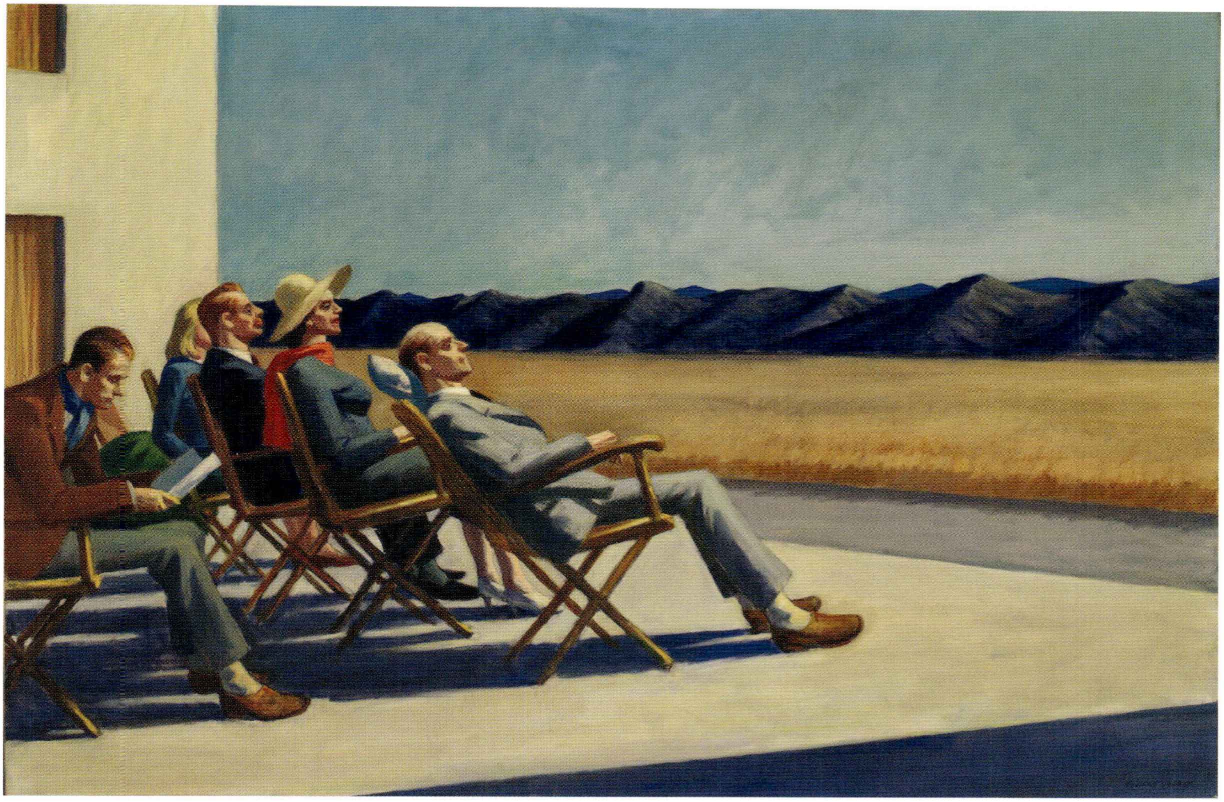

TOP The drunken carnivalesque was replaced with sober leisure, the anarchic festival with the stolid vacation. Capitalism trumpeted non-working time both as a commodity to be sold and as a way for workers to recharge so that they could do more work. Edward Hopper, America's great painter of loneliness, explores this slightly dehumanizing contemporary condition in his 1960 composition *People in the Sun*, with its middle-class figures reclining while visiting a stark desert landscape. Original at the Smithsonian Museum of American Art in Washington, DC.

The Whole Earth Catalogue creed, any of the utopian hacker ethos of a shared internet commons has long given way to a new Gilded Age. Northern California naturally imbued the industry with a particular style that's long been superficially carnivalesque in its appearance; nowhere is that evidenced more than in the one-time sacramental ritual of Nevada's Burning Man. With its crunchy bohemian performance art displays, the declared intent of upending hierarchies and expanding consciousness, the sacraments of MDMA, ayahuasca, and ibogaine, and even with its own court-sophist in the form of the Neo-Sufi Hakim Bey intoning about "Temporary Autonomous Zones," Burning Man commodifies the carnivalesque, with 2021 tickets starting at the low price of $425. The hippie vibes aside, its libertarian politics has long attracted participants like Larry Page and Sergey Brin of Google and Eric Schmidt of Alphabet, with another annual resident of Black Rock, Nevada, named Elon Musk declaring that "Burning Man is Silicon Valley." Lest there be any doubt about how rebellious Burning Man is, when Grover Norquist attended in 2014 he gushed how it was an example of "radical self-reliance." Now the king knows that it's better to pretend to be the Lord of Misrule himself, the better to keep the peasants in line.

When medieval peasants crowned an Abbot of Unreason, that daring act of blasphemy paradoxically depended on an acknowledgment of the sacred, heresy and the divine mutually reinforcing and always dependent on one another. Just as the Roman Catholic Church represented the overreaching ideology of

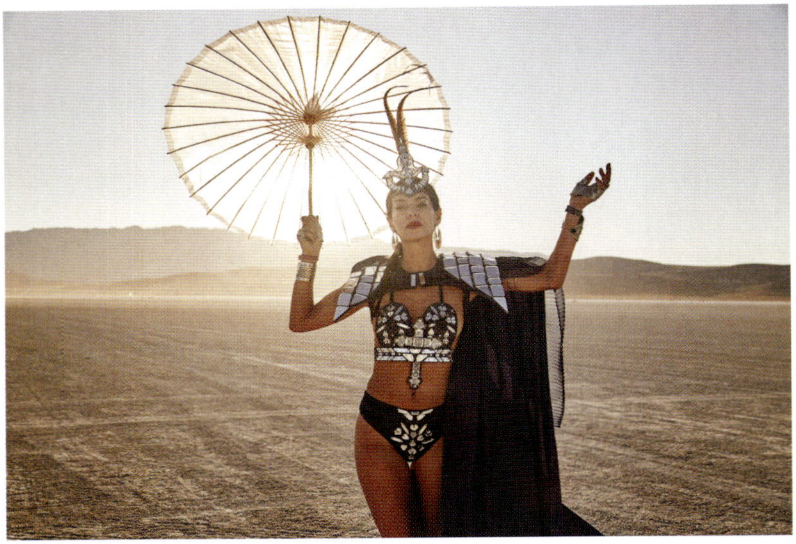

Western Christendom in the era when the Lord of Misrule poked at the pieties of both pope and prince, now our hegemonic faith is deregulated, privatized, free-market absolutist capitalism. If secularism means anything at all, it's not the demise of religion, but rather its replacement with capitalism. Yet all of those modern forms of the carnivalesque, whether in the form of Silicon Valley tech-utopianism or its darker twin of shit-posting pop-fascism, only offer the illusion of subversion while actually acting as High Mass for the new faith of our world. That so many of the New Atheists of a half generation ago have gravitated toward a toxic politics—call it the Dark Enlightenment, neo-reaction, or the alt-right—isn't surprising, for in their own bourgeois way that inchoate movement never challenged the gods who actually deserved the iconoclast's hammer.

Just as the medieval carnivalesque challenged the faith of its centuries, so too must we develop a mode of cultural resistance commensurate with the gods that reign during our own era. It is imperative to remember that the only methods of resistance are religious because the only things worth resisting are also religious. As soon as with clear eye we can identify late capitalism for what it is—a malignant, cannibalistic, rapacious, occult faith—the better we can craft our own spiritual revolts against it; the better we can develop impiety against this sect which deserves it, heresy leveled at this denomination that's earned it, blasphemy directed toward this church that warrants it. "Under capitalism, money occupies the ontological throne from which God has been evicted," writes Eugene McCarraher in *The Enchantments of Mammon: How Capitalism Became the Religion of Modernity*, and with that principle firmly in mind, a new carnivalesque to answer its imitation revanchist version comes into focus. What really deserve our scorn are different gods, such as the Market, the Invisible Hand, the Golden Calf of Wall Street. What made the Abbot of Unreason powerful was that there was an awareness that the system they were up against was sacred, even if it wasn't good. A similar consciousness is needed today, for what oppresses us is sacred, even if not good. To mock the rituals of state and Church during the Middle Ages acknowledged the charged

TOP *Think different* at Burning Man, that is, if you can afford it. Photograph of festivalgoer taken by Karim Tabar in 2019 for *Harper's Bazaar*.

OPPOSITE A very different form of carnivalesque subversion from those values offered at Burning Man, the #Occupy movement harkened back to the genuine resistance offered by medieval and early modern forms of economic critique, an awareness that the line which separates the festival from the protest can simply be one of intent. For some, such freedom is called sloth; for others it's democracy. Photograph from New York, 2010.

power and holy aura of those things; to be able to mount an effective campaign against capitalism requires a similar acknowledgment. That's always the problem with much anti-capitalist discourse—vulgar materialism prevents the well-meaning from understanding that what we're facing is a transcendent faith, and that the only way of resisting it is by recourse to a different and better religion. The Lord of Misrule no longer needs to target kings and priests; better to mock bosses and landlords. Perhaps this seems like a desire that's not enough as well as too much, but in a culture where the exorbitantly wealthy billionaire class with its privatized power occupies a position that no medieval ruler could have imagined, the faux-carnivalesque toothlessness of a podcaster or stand-up comedian is abundantly apparent. What then would a new carnivalesque even look like, if it's not to be found at Burning Man or on Twitter, in a comedy club or on the Dark Web?

In the past generation, so-called "culture jamming" was one method, though of limited utility. Today, the inspiring movement for unionization and the anarcho-medievalist r/Antiwork movement, along with the Great Resignation, is another. Despite the pandemic, the authoritarianism, the war, there is room for hope at this moment. But what the carnivalesque finally offers isn't seriousness, but joy. Joy is a revolutionary act. If our enemies are having fun, we must have more fun; if they're laughing, than we laugh louder; we drown their music out with our own ferocious drumming, we obscure their jackboot marches with ecstatic dances, we answer them with the derision, mocking, and snark that they so abundantly deserve. Our puritanism serves nobody but our enemies. Capitalism offers us the industrial ready-made, but the carnivalesque we build with our own hands. While we wait for the millennium to come, best to remember that the path of puritanical seriousness is the path of defeat. Better to put upon thine head the jester's hat and the mottled pants of the Lord of Misrule and try and turn the world upside down again.

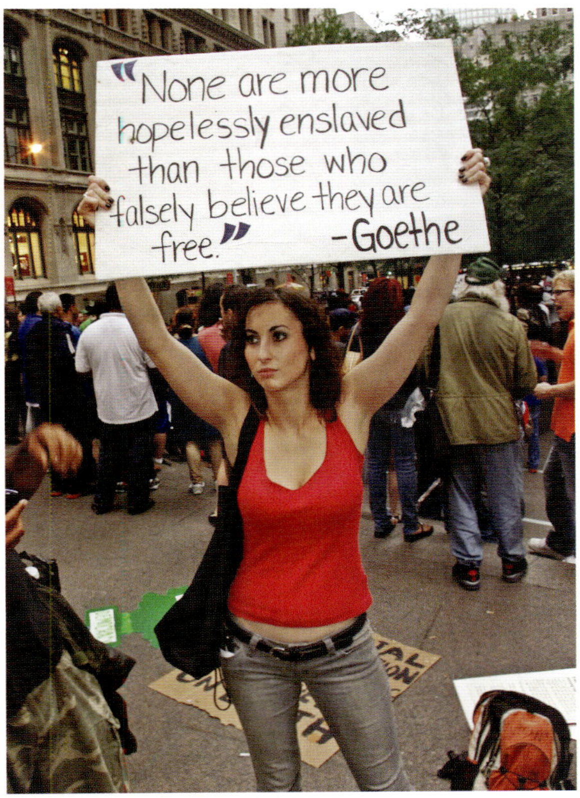

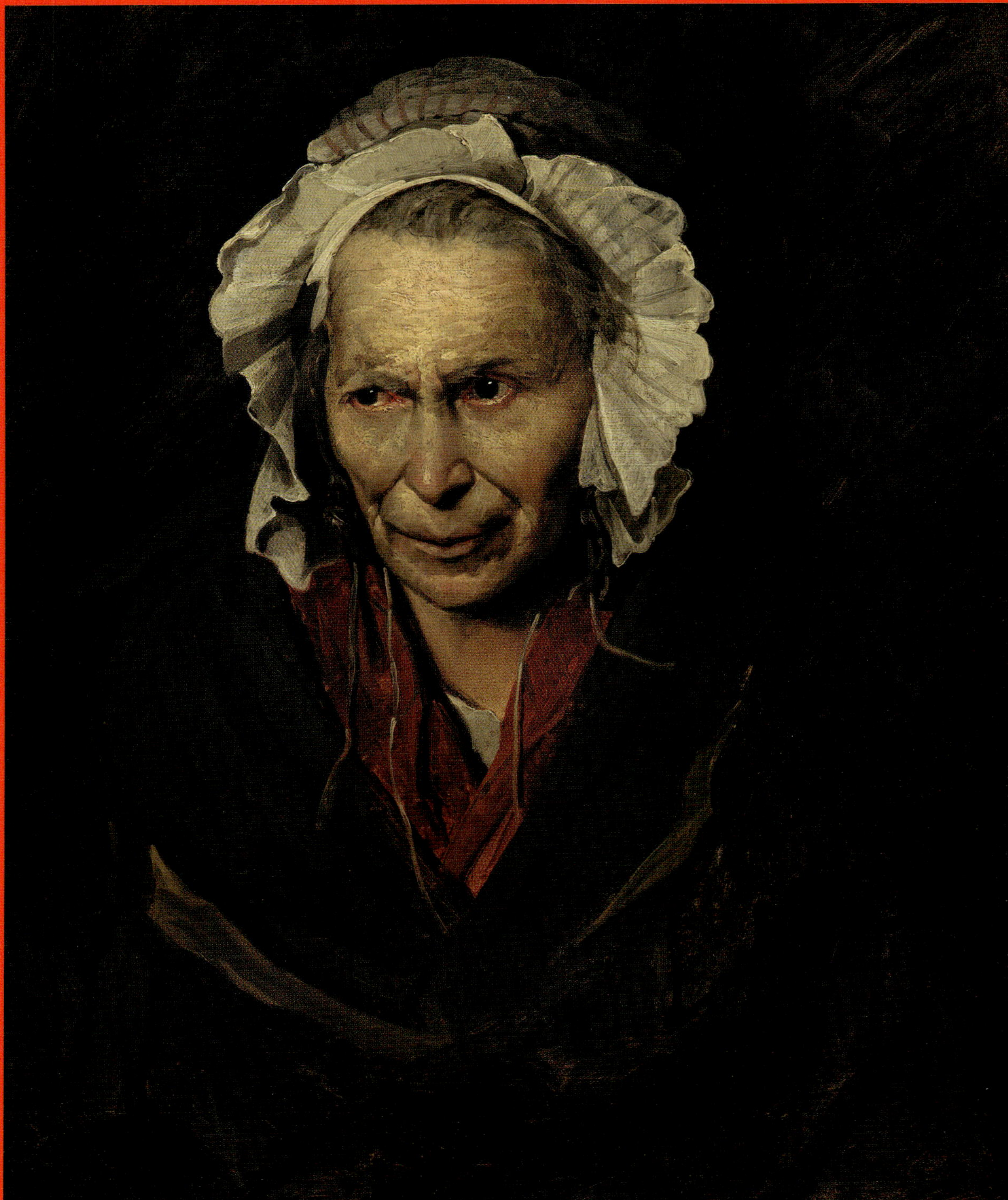

CHAPTER FIVE

ALONE NEVER CEASETH: ENVY

"It is in the character of very few men to honor without envy a friend who has prospered."
—Aeschylus, *Agamemnon* (c. 500 BCE)

"I feel it comin', it's flushing my face, / I feel it comin', jealously baby."
—Iggy Pop, "Jealousy" (1993)

The green-eyed monster of envy, as is memorably described by William Shakespeare in *Othello*, is by far the least enjoyable of the vices. If there are benefits to gluttony and lust, envy affords no such physical pleasure; if we exult in pride and even wrath, jealousy imparts no flush of satisfaction. The most dismal of the seven deadly sins, envy can seem punishment enough for its own transgressions. However, what makes the sins dangerous isn't necessarily how they initially act upon the sinner himself, but rather where they lead him. Envy, as a catalyst to criminal behavior, is no different from the other vices. Jealousy and envy arguably have as high a body count as those more alluring of vices, for those who covet that which belongs to another, who wish to possess that which is not theirs, can be capable of the most heinous of acts, the most despicable of decisions. The third-century Carthaginian bishop St. Cyprian argued in his *Tenth Treatise* that "envy is the root of all evils, the fountain of disasters, the nursery of crimes, the material of transgressions," for not even pride concerns itself so much with dominating others, whereas jealousy always desires to take and take and take. Jealousy has an illuminating etymology, deriving from the same Latin root as the word "zeal," underscoring the vice's hot-tempered state of emotional excitement, the way in which the heart-palpitating, face-flushing indignity of envy is closely related to its sister vice of wrath. This is a dangerous passion, for though the sin of coveting is the final transgression listed in the Decalogue, the Greek-speaking Jewish author of the apocryphal *Wisdom of Solomon*, composed a century before the Common Era, noted astutely that "through the devil's envy death entered the world, and those who belong to his party experience it."

PREVIOUS SPREAD French Romantic painter Théodore Géricault's c.1820 composition *Portrait of a Demented Woman* or *The Monomaniac of Jealousy*, original held at the Museum of Fine Arts of Lyon, captures the intensity of envy, the rapacious hunger of that vice.

OPPOSITE English Romantic painter James Ward's 1838 composition *Ignorance, Envy, and Jealousy* draws upon a rich tradition of medieval iconography and allegory. A beautiful, pure, white-robed woman represents Truth, in keeping with the Neo-Platonic tradition of interpreting cosmic Wisdom in feminine terms (normally using the term "Sophia" for that quality), with the bewinged figured of Ignorance and his twin children, Envy and Jealousy. Because of the historical misinterpretation of the subjects being Miranda and Caliban from Shakespeare's *The Tempest*, the painting remains in the collection of the Royal Shakespeare Company.

THEORY—THE INFLUENCE OF ANXIETY

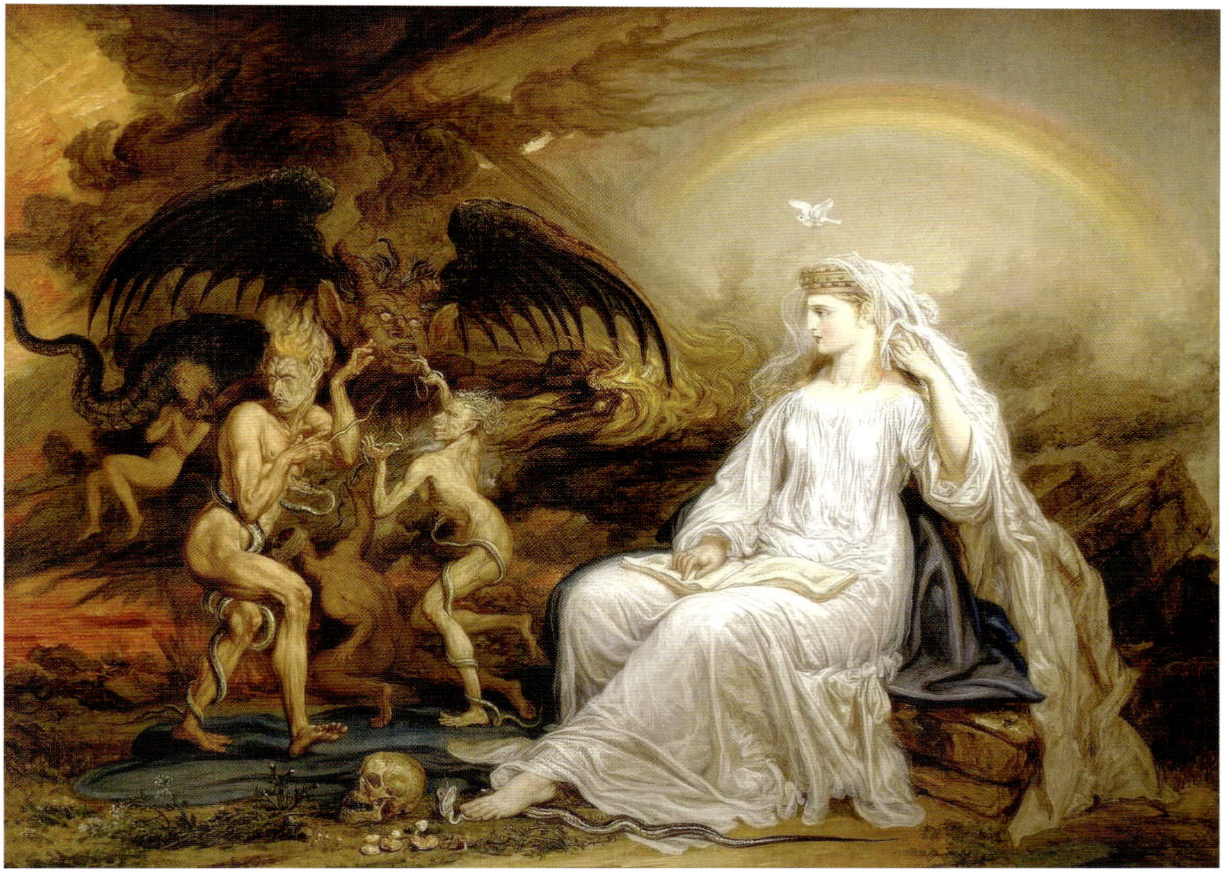

Amid the gentle green Midlothian hills and a little under eight miles from the steep, winding cobblestoned streets and alleyways of medieval Edinburgh is an odd but beautiful little church named Rosslyn Chapel. Commissioned by William Sinclair, the 1st Earl of Caithness, the 2nd Earl Sinclair, and the Last Earl of Orkney, the chapel was to be a place of worship and repose for the aristocratic Scots-Norman family who'd made their fortune during the religious campaigns fought in the Levant. Built of limestone that glows during the eerie orange-tinged dusk of a late-night northern summer, Rosslyn Chapel bears a unique mythology, this forlorn building with its slender outer buttresses silhouetted in the Scottish evening. There have long been rumors that the site was associated with esoteric beliefs rather than orthodox Christianity. The earl's relationship to the mysterious order of the Knights Templar has exacerbated such legends, with a popular iteration claiming that Rosslyn Chapel remains a site of meeting for secret societies from the Rosicrucians to the Freemasons, while more audacious conspiracy theorists conjecture that the shallow crypt of the church hides the Ark of the Covenant or the Holy Grail. Certainly, Rosslyn Chapel is beautiful, celebrated for a multitude of unique and technically ingenious carvings within its interior. Botanical carvings line the tops of the main sanctuary, including an abstracted plant, conical, nubbly, cellular, and pockmarked; it could be an acorn or a strawberry, while the more fantastical of interpretations maintain that it's new corn, espied in America by Sinclair in a forgotten voyage undertaken before Columbus. Beneath such features are a multitude of *woodwoses*, the green men of medieval fancy, bestial wild beings with vines and branches growing from their hair, their noses, their uncanny smiles, reminding the earl from whence humanity comes and to where it shall return, a pose of humility rendered in unspeakably beautiful skill.

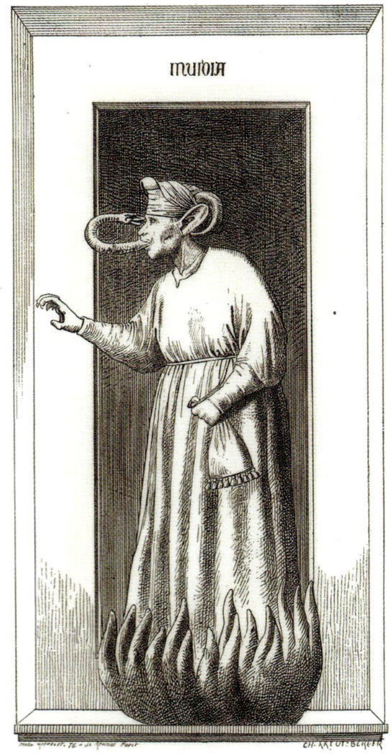

L'ENVIE

Fresque de Giotto à l'*Arena* de Padoue, quatorzième siècle. — L'Envie « est à la fois haineuse et avare, car, si elle a des ongles crochus pour déchirer, elle tient aussi une bourse serrée dans l'une de ses mains ». (De Grimouard de Saint-Laurent, *Guide de l'Art chrétien*, III, p. 446.) Un serpent lui sort de la bouche et se dresse contre ses yeux. — « La Démocratie, c'est l'Envie. » (Prudhon.)

TOP The Italian Renaissance master Giotto de Bondone's 1306 panel for the Scrovegni Chapel in Padua depicts Envy as an old crone, her feet already in the flames of hell, her face being supped on by a snake which bursts from her own mouth, the circular, self-devouring nature of the jealous mind represented with startling accuracy.

OPPOSITE American allegorist Paul Cadmus, drawn to fusing modernist sensibility with a magical realist idiom, turns that treatment to his series on vice, as in this 1947 composition *The Seven Deadly Sins: Envy*.

And then—most infamously—there is one of the thirteen interior supporting columns, this one known as the "Apprentice's Pillar." The Apprentice's Pillar is architecturally *sui genius*, a singularity of artistry that was never surpassed. Designed by the master mason, this central column was meant to evoke the Yggdrasil Tree of Nordic legend, that *tempus mundi* of all creation from which reality itself is generated. To a modern viewer, the twisted column with its swirled ribs slinking from the sculptures of hungry dragons at the base to the entwined tree branches at the top appears as if the double-helix of the DNA molecule, though regardless of perspective the symbolic import of the structure remains that of *creation*. An irony then, because it was envy over the skill of the artist that has led to this feature's infamy, while it should more rightly be celebrated for its beauty. According to the narrative when construction began on the chapel in 1446, the master mason traveled to the continent to learn from more proficient artisans. Leaving behind his young, untutored protégé to oversee the most basic carving in the chapel, the mason was gone for several months, carefully laboring and learning in hopes of understanding the way to make stone appear as if liquid, of coaxing solidity into the shape of water. More of a craftsman than an inspired artist, the mason nonetheless worked hard, and through diligence and determination he forged himself into a sculptor whom Sinclair was willing to trust in overseeing the construction of Rosslyn . . . hence his horror upon returning to the chapel, where he found that his foolish young mentee had already carved the column perfectly. Standing before such magnificence, a testament to humanity's capacity for beauty, the master mason should have felt awe—he should have trembled before the column's sublimity. Instead, his cheeks burned, his pulse raced, his eyes welled. And so, the mason took his mallet and pulverized the brains of his apprentice into a sticky, sickly, metallic spray against the sandstone. With some irony, carved on the architrave was a selection from 1 Esdras reading "Wine is strong, a king is stronger, women are stronger still, but truth conquers all." Ay, but what, then, of envy?

All of the mortal sins trade, at some level, in rapaciousness: greed most obviously, but also pride in its coveting of acclaim, wrath in its desire for vengeance, both gluttony and lust in their hunger for respective indulgences of

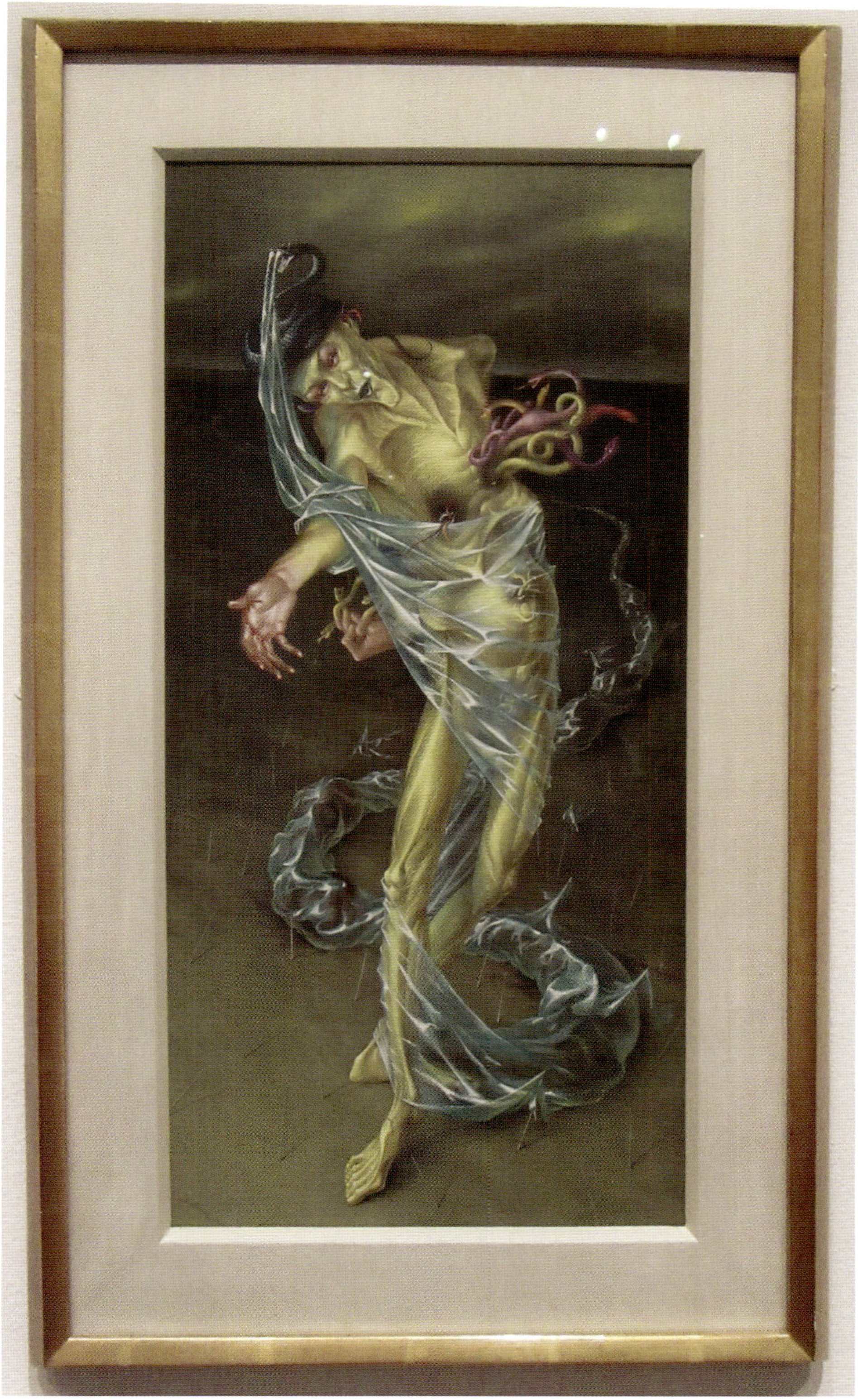

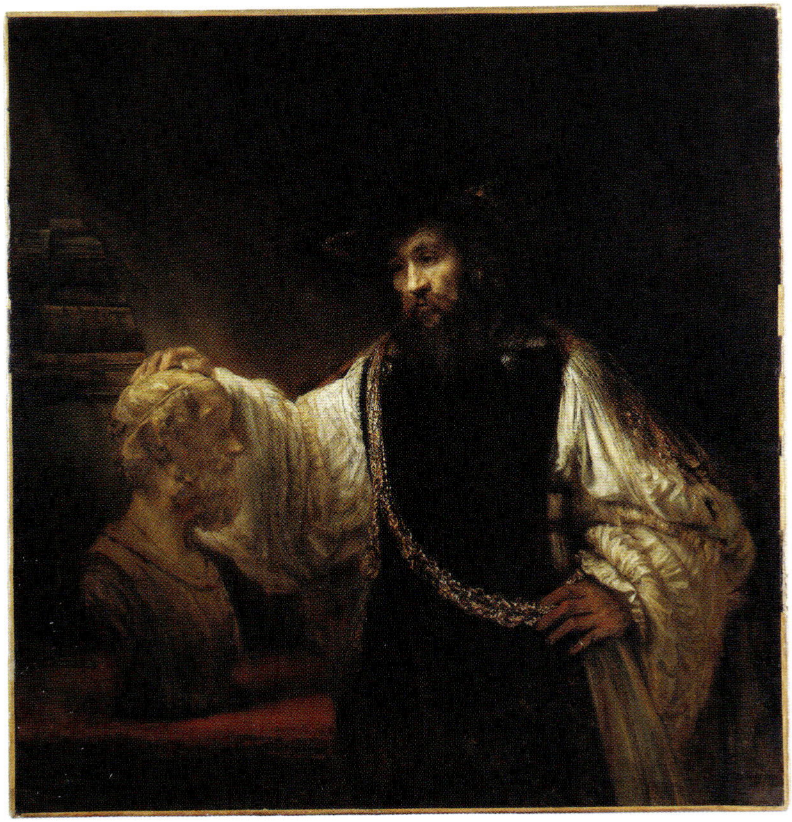

the flesh. Envy is no different, for what it craves is that which rightly belongs to somebody else, whether it be house or wife, career or wealth, talent or respect. Unlike those other sins, however, envy is difficult to mollify. Robert Burton noted as much in his massive seventeenth-century compendium of psychological observations *The Anatomy of Melancholy*, arguing that "every other sin hath some pleasure annexed to it, or will admit of an excuse; envy alone wants both. Other sins last but for awhile; the gut may be satisfied, anger remits, hatred hath an end, envy never ceaseth." That's not to say that the truly gluttonous is ever full or the carnally lustful is ever satiated, but other than misfortune visited upon the object of envy, such a sin is rarely materially compensated. This is, of course, even more true when those objects of jealousy are of an abstract nature. One can always eventually (theoretically) purchase a bigger house or marry a more beautiful woman, achieve greater professional success or earn more money, but talent, brilliance, and skill are attributes of a more ethereal nature. Per Burton's observation, even more crucial a difference between envy and its partner vices is that it's the only one of seven which is not remotely pleasurable. Attend the bacchanals of the glutton or the orgies of the lustful, the shopping sprees of the greedy or even the battlefields of the wrathful, and you will discover some species of enjoyment. But when it comes to envy, nobody enjoys feeling lesser, desiring that which you feel rightly belongs to you. Nearest the opposite of envy is possibly that emotion for which the Germans have a phrase,

ABOVE Doctor of all who know, tutor to Alexander the Great, the most important philosopher in the Hellenistic World, and yet Aristotle must contemplate a bust of the master Homer, for while the former deigns to circumscribe the rules of rhetoric through analysis, the latter merely possessed that sublime quality of mimesis. Rembrandt van Rijn in his 1653 *Aristotle Contemplating a Bust of Homer*, original held by the Metropolitan Museum of Art.

that infamous tingle of *Schadenfreude*, whereby the mediocrity who resides in the glass-lined corner office is fired or your neighbor is left by his sexy wife. In these instances, the jealous soul is briefly placated, but even then the paranoid suspicion remains, the anxious whisper still rings out, fears unalloyed and entitlement unassuaged—"*Why*," the envious person asks, "*did such an undeserving person have those things in the first place, rather than me?*"

For all of its deficiencies, envy does justify its philosophical import through sheer narrative drama. Only wrath is more capable of pushing people to the extremes of behavior encouraged by envy and jealousy, the first being an emotion that results in throttled neighbors and murdered spouses. If the nature of the Seven Deadly Sins is that they encourage us into unpardonable crimes, then envy has been responsible for a much bigger share of hell-bound souls than mere gluttony. Immanuel Kant, in his indomitably straightforward Prussian way, defines envy in *The Metaphysics of Morals* as the "propensity to view the well-being of others with distress" (also notably the exact opposite of Schadenfreude). Jealousy is an attendant emotion to envy, though the two are not synonymous. If envy is the desire of possessing that which is naturally somebody else's, then jealousy is the fear that that which is yours will be taken by another person. Both are marked by panic and a sensation of powerlessness; they are defined (like all of the sins) by the close-held belief that one individual is somehow more important than others. Envy is fundamentally antiegalitarian, just as jealousy is threaded with possessiveness. As the seventeenth-century raconteur and memoirist François de La Rochefoucauld remarked in his collection of *Maxims*, "In jealousy there is more self-love than love"; earlier he had described envy as "more implacable than hatred." The envious woman, the jealous man, does not take the object of their desire on its own terms; theirs is the inclination to dominate. An envious person can't enjoy the beauty of nature without wishing to put a fence about it; they can't appreciate the beauty of art without desiring to surpass it; they can't learn in the presence of genius without hoping to best it.

However, in a different realm from the material covetousness which makes somebody desire his neighbor's BMW or a coworker's corner office, a spirit of competition between people—artists, writers, musicians—need not necessarily be the same as envy, though it can often curdle into it, even if such friction isn't always unproductive. Accolades and awards can be ultimately empty; yet wishing to write a more perfect sonnet than Petrarch, compose a more beautiful sonata than Beethoven, or break the home run record of Babe Ruth can result in an excellence that the rest of us would have otherwise been denied (for then we would not have Shakespeare, Chopin, or Hank Aaron). Envy was the catalyst in the American critic Harold Bloom's theory of creative inspiration, an idiosyncratic but not unconvincing account of how the desire to prove one's worth in opposition to those whose brilliance and success you covet is the mechanism by which all groundbreaking art and literature is produced. In *The Anxiety of Influence: A Theory of Poetry*, Bloom describes "creative envy." He argues, "Poetic history . . . is held to be indistinguishable from poetic influence, since strong poets make that history by misreading one another, so as to clear imaginative space for themselves." That is to say that the young boy studying verse at the base of the master's statue feels an Oedipal envy of their influence, and that the only way to surpass those earlier achievements is to willfully misinterpret those achievements. Regardless of the specifics of Bloom's theory, this anxiety is marked by envy, by a desire not to stand on the shoulders of giants, but to cut them down to size. John Milton could only dream of *Paradise Lost* because of Edmund Spenser's *The Faerie Queene*, Spenser's achievement only made possible because of Dante's *The Divine Comedy*, the Florentines having had to first study Virgil's *The Aeneid*, with that Roman being a student (as is everybody) of Homer.

Gustave Flaubert, the inventor of the modern novel, modern literature, modern perspective, and modern consciousness, makes envy the great subject of his 1856 *Madame Bovary*, the eponymous heroine escaping from her tedious marriage by devouring romance novels that inculcate her into the caste of the envious. "At the bottom of her heart," the author writes of Bovary, "she was waiting for something to happen. Like shipwrecked sailors, she turned despairing eyes upon the solitude of her life, seeking afar off some white sail in the mists of the horizon." The humanity of Flaubert is such that he acknowledges how much of envy is kin to imagination, how the former is less a vice than it is a means of propelling oneself—even momentarily—out of the drabness of an unfulfilling life. An even deeper imagination, bordering on madness, animates that earlier novel, Miguel de Cervantes's sixteenth-century *Don Quixote*, where the titular aspiring knight is so jealous of the chivalries and romances of a departed medieval past that he constructs a mirage of them in his head. "Where envy reigns, virtue can't exist," writes Cervantes; yet he endows the desire to propel oneself out of prosaic circumstances, a manifestation of envy itself, with quasi-heroic, if tragic, implications. In a manner different from "envy," "jealousy" can't help but bear certain sexual associations, that particular vice associated with the possessive insanity of those who (rightly or wrongly) suspect their beloved of secretly "belonging" to someone else. The intensity of sexual jealousy naturally lends itself to tragedy, most frequently visited against women (the same case in life as in literature). For example, there is the matricidal Pozdnyshev in Leo Tolstoy's 1889 novella *The Kreutzer Sonata*, a despicable misogynist whose entitlement leads to his wife's murder, a man whose creed holds that if there is "no vanity in this life of ours, there is no sufficient reason for living." Then there is Angel Clare's pathological jealousy of his wife's rapist in Thomas Hardy's 1891 *Tess of d'Urbervilles*. Angel, in his damning coldness, claims that Tess was "more sinned against than sinning," admitting more about himself, his obsessions with purity and virginity, and his inability to direct anger in the direction where it deserves to go than he realizes. Even more monstrous, obviously, is Vladimir Nabokov's immaculately rendered Humbert Humbert, of the 1955 novel *Lolita*. An urbane, sophisticated, and sociopathic pedophile, Humbert murders another child rapist who has kidnapped the prepubescent Dolores Haze from under the former's gaze, telling the latter man that "because of all you did / because of all I did not / you have to die."

No work of literature in the Western canon quite so savagely expresses the wanton damage, intense cruelty, and myopic horror of sexual jealousy as William Shakespeare's *Othello*, a most potent work about the violence which men so frequently enact on their partners. "Damn her, lewd minx! O, damn her!" curses the titular Moorish general of the play, ensconced in the Venetian camp upon a Cyprus abandoned by the Turks, fuming over imagined infidelities of his beautiful, young, and loyal wife Desdemona that have been whispered to him by his

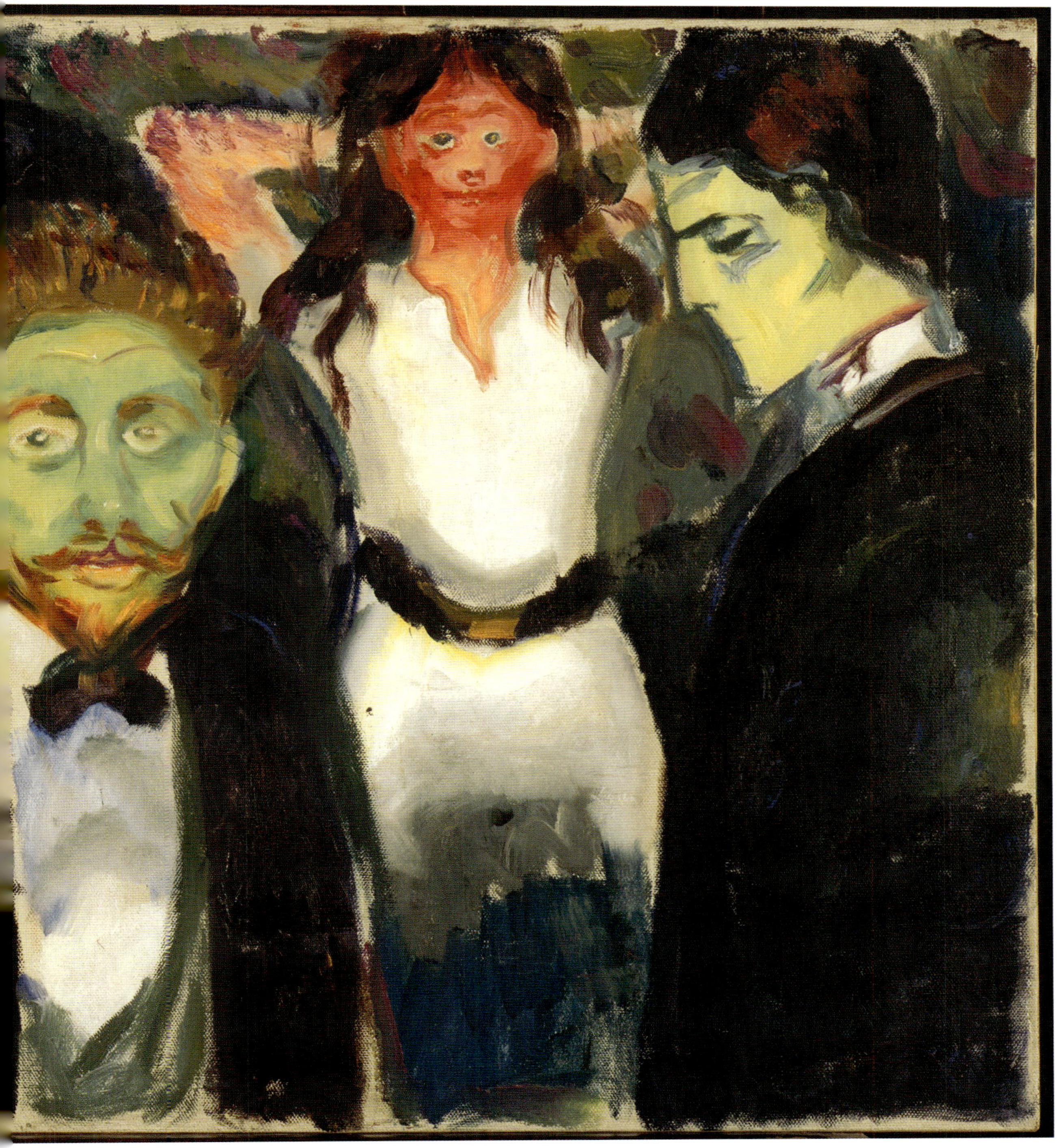

ABOVE An artist who knew of what he painted, the Norwegian Symbolist Edvard Munch's 1907 *Jealousy* (of which there are several iterations, this one featured at his single-artist museum in Oslo) exemplifies the masculine anxieties of his subject.

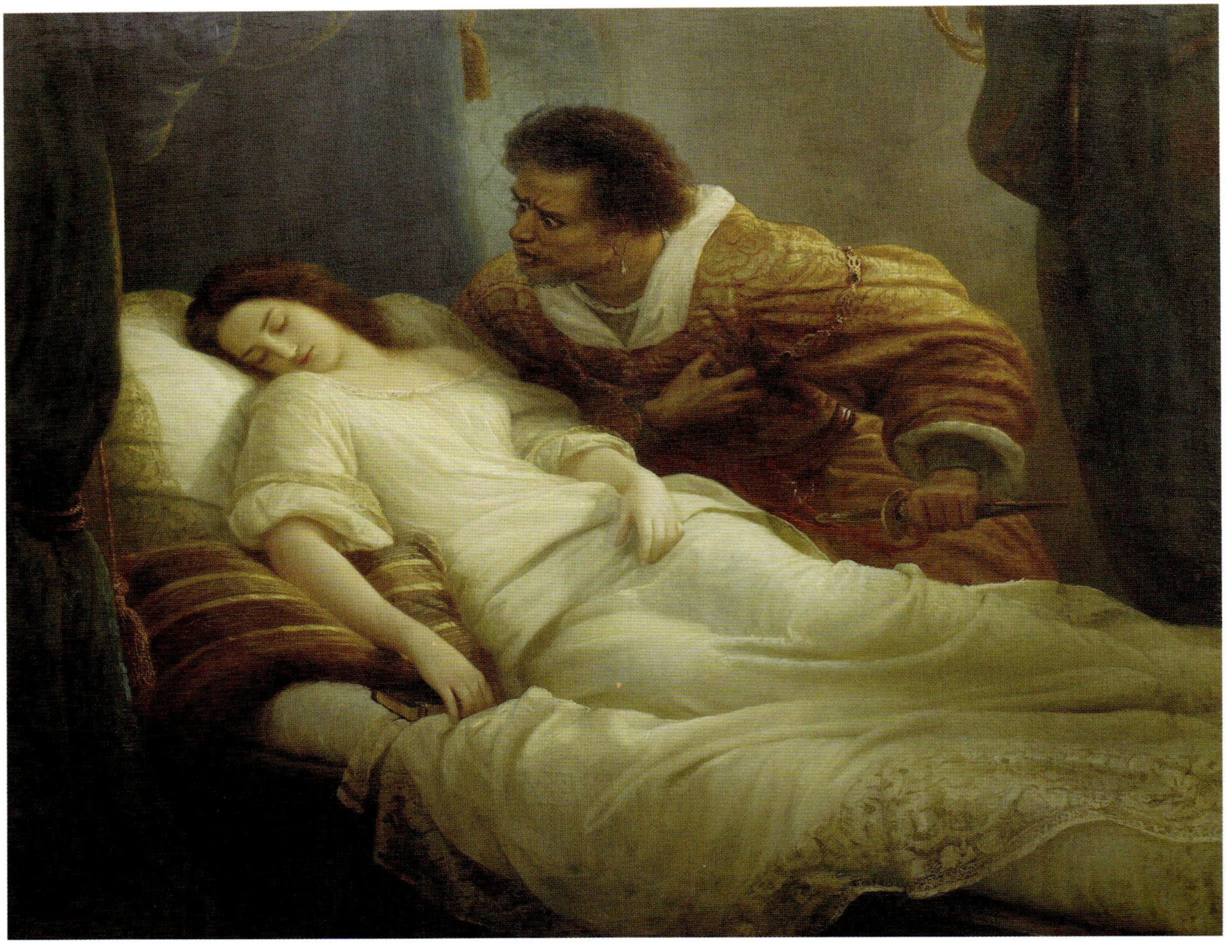

sociopathic counselor Iago. "Come, go with me apart; I will withdraw, / To furnish me with some swift means of death / For the fair devil." Shakespeare potently depicts how what is supposed to be love can transform into rage, how the possessiveness of the former is a catalyst for the latter. Iago, perhaps driven by envy at Moor's elevation over him, or maybe the sort of man who enacts wickedness for its own jaundiced purposes, is the immediate cause of Desdemona's smothering, but the demons capable of such a crime weren't placed within Othello by his counselor; that was always their home. By any estimation, Othello had everything: despite being a stranger to Venice, he had ascended the ranks of the city's military and enjoyed the faithful love of his beautiful wife. Yet all that was required was a moment of willfully placed doubt to drive him into insane paroxysms of jealousy, Desdemona murdered over suggestion and a misplaced handkerchief. A powerful man thus makes himself small, haunted by the imagined fingerprints of other lovers upon the skin of his wife. "I must weep," says Othello, pillow placed over the sleeping Desdemona's face. "But they are cruel tears. This sorrow's heavenly; / It strikes where it doth love."

A paradox in heavenly sorrow, but Othello does accidentally glance onto a potent aspect of jealousy: the vice's frequently divine associations. Zeus was

ABOVE Othello before his sleeping wife in her last moments of innocent life before her murder. As Dr. Johnson described it, "this dreadful scene; it is not to be endured." The German Romanticist Christian Köhler renders this scene about what envy wrought with great pathos in his 1859 painting *Othello*, original in private collection.

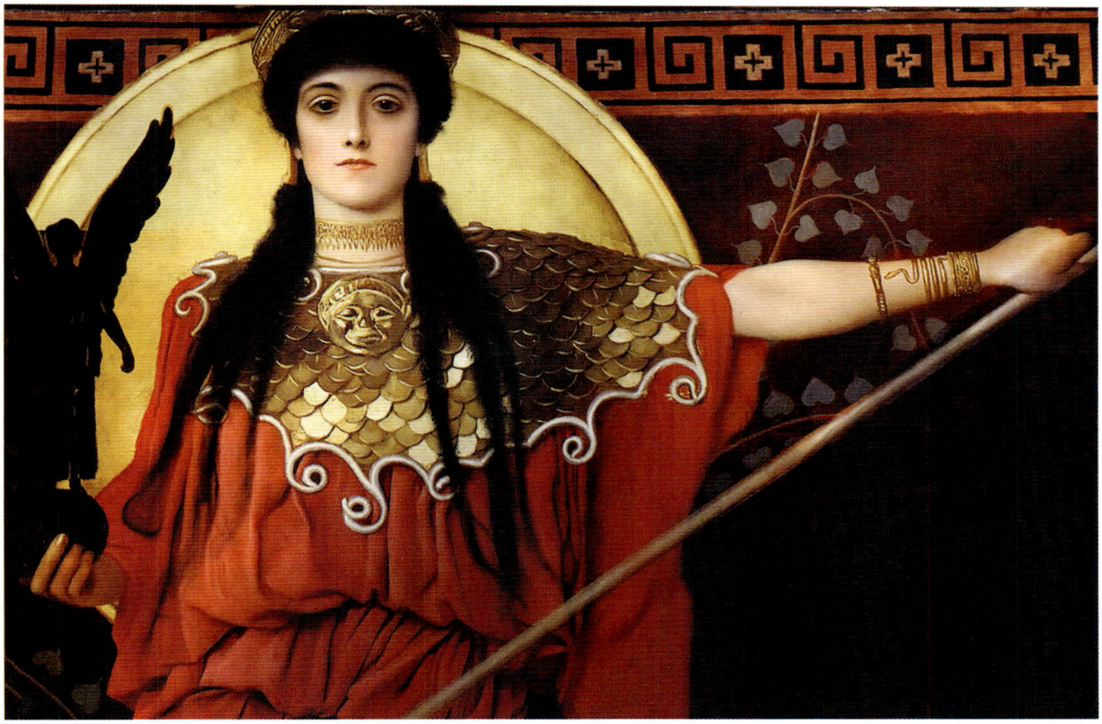

ABOVE Austrian Art Nouvelle master Gustav Klimt's depiction of the goddess Athena from his 1891 mural *Ancient Greece and Ancient Egypt*, original at the Kunst History Museum in Vienna. Despite being the goddess of wisdom, Athena is wracked by jealousy, an apt summation of the attitudes of some of the most brilliant artists, writers, and musicians, which is conveyed in her simultaneously haughty and hungry gaze.

notoriously a jealous deity, despite being the ruler of Olympus; his daughter Athena inherited that same trait. Yet of all of the mythological gods imbued with that defect, none was as guilty as the being worshiped by Jews, Christians, and Muslims. God, in the Hebrew Scriptures, makes clear that He is a jealous being. Along with wrath, envy is the only one of the seven vices attributed to the Lord, for we never hear of His hunger or His horniness, but He emphatically thunders in Exodus 20:5 (among other passages) that "I, the Lord your God, am a jealous God." This is the reason for envy's being considered a sin, for in desiring that which does not belong to you, the guilty courts idolatry. To take upon yourself the prerogative of envy is to ascribe to your own being something which is reserved for God and God alone. Monotheism by its very nature is a position riven by jealousy; that was the intent of the aforementioned passage in Scripture, for when Exodus was written the various panoplies of deities were still believed to have existed. God is clearly stating that devotion should be afforded only to Him and not Zeus, or Osiris, or Marduk, or Baal. But even after belief in Zeus, Osiris, Marduk, and Baal had waned, God's jealous disposition remained. That's because as the singular ground of being, as the Alpha and the Omega, a human's perseveration on things separate from the Godhead, their envy of things separate from the Lord, is still to court blasphemy. Which brings the issue of jealousy back to creative envy. If the painter is jealous of the competitor with better command of brushstroke and color, the writer jealous of the adversary more adept at dialogue and exposition, the musician jealous of the colleague more harmonious and spritely, then the suggestion is that such envy is actually being directed at the solitary and lonely God who makes all such things possible.

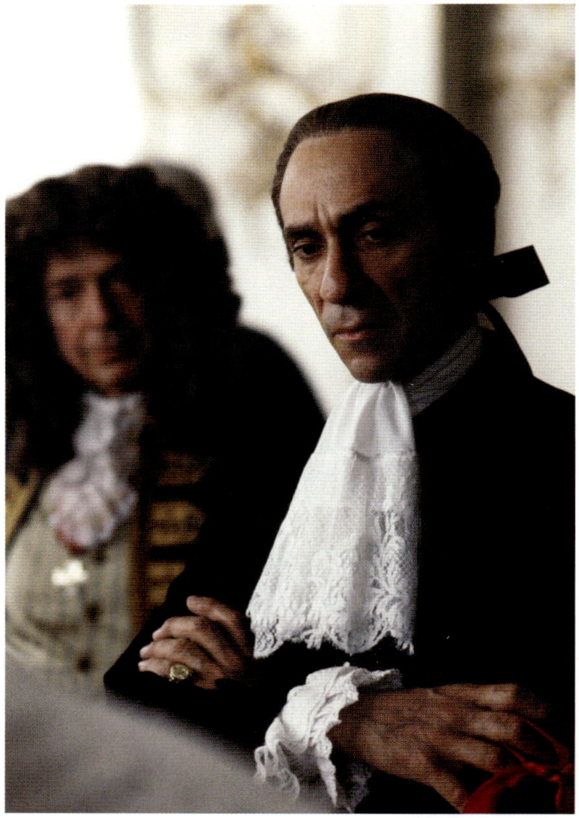

This was the idée fixe of the greatest exploration of creative envy made in the past century, Peter Schaffer's 1979 play *Amadeus* and the director Milos Forman's film adaptation of five years later. Presenting a heavily fictionalized account of the relationship between the eighteenth-century Austrian court composer Antonio Salieri and the prodigious Wolfgang Amadeus Mozart, both Schaffer and Forman illuminate the flesh-flushing, heart-racing, damp-faced reality that envy and hatred are frequently attendants. Salieri, as portrayed with oily, unctuous efficacy by an F. Murray Abraham in powdered wig and britches, is an Italian orphan who ascends to the heights of Vienna's artistic circles, becoming the most important composer in the world's most musical city. Dogged, diligent, and dutiful, he practices and molds himself into a passably talented composer, attributing his gifts to God and comporting himself with a seriousness which his role necessitates. Yet Mozart, a laughing, squawking, farting baboon who dedicates his time to drinking and womanizing, is capable of writing music not just immeasurably better than that of Salieri, but preternaturally better than that of anyone else who has ever placed a finger on a harpsichord key, held a quill above paper affixed with musical bars. What makes the pain of Salieri's jealousy even more acute is that while he's not talented enough to compose such music, he's intelligent enough to appreciate it.

"On the page it looked nothing," he recounts to his confessor decades after he has driven Mozart to madness and then poisoned him. "The beginning simple, almost comic. Just a pulse. Bassoons and basset horns, like a rusty squeezebox. And then suddenly, high above it, an oboe. A single note, hanging there, unwavering. Until a clarinet took over and sweetened it into a phrase of such delight . . . This was a music I'd never heard." For Salieri, this was like "hearing the voice of God," but he could never reconcile such gifts with the unserious man who produced that music. "All I wanted was to sing to God," protests Salieri. "He gave me that longing . . . If He didn't want me to praise Him with music, why implant the desire? Like a lust in my body! And then deny me the talent?" What Salieri's envy evidenced was a deficiency of faith, for when the composer's life was successful, he offered genuflections before the crucifix, but when Mozart arrives in Vienna, the Italian immolates that same cross—"From now on, we are enemies—You and I." Whether or not Salieri could understand why Mozart was to be endowed with gifts which the former could never access was not for him to understand—it was the purview of God to make such decisions. So Salieri's revenge on Mozart is

TOP The face of envy as Antonio Salieri hears Mozart play for the first time in Forman's *Amadeus*.

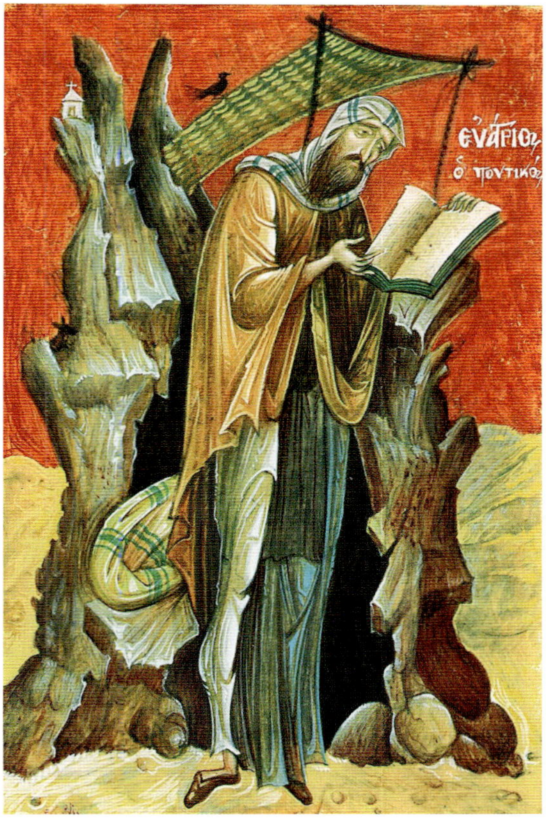

ultimately a revenge on the Lord, commissioning his better to compose a requiem Mass with the intention of killing the prodigy and then passing off the symphony as his own when the inevitable national funeral is held. Mozart's shrill, nasal, honking laugh is rather the last to echo out, however, for he has already spent any money which he's made, and there will be no elaborate funeral, history's greatest composer rather consigned to a pauper's grave and Salieri to the madhouse. That same shrill, nasal, honking laugh, a disgusted Salieri discovers, is the chuckle of God.

INTERLUDE—EVAGRIUS PONTICUS

When Evagrius Ponticus sat in his sunbaked anchorite's cell, picking pebbles out of his dried chickpeas and swallowing Egyptian grit with his warm water, do you think he spared a few envious thoughts for the residents of Alexandria strolling in the cool of the evening, retiring after pomegranates to enjoy the wind blowing off the Nile? Evagrius wasn't a saint, after all. Only a Church Father. He could just as easily kindle jealousy with memories of his past, the years teaching in Constantinople, where he lusted after lapis lazuli-bedecked married women who were perfumed with aloeswood and ambergris; or, when after absconding to Jerusalem at the behest of an angel, he still backslid into old ways, haughtily wandering narrow alleys in Byzantine silk and Lombard embroidery. No line is more truthful—or funny—than St. Augustine's plea in his *Confessions*, when he implored, "God, give me chastity and continence—but not yet." Evagrius was finally stricken with illness around 385 (a year before Augustine would convert to Christianity), and according to his fifth-century Irish biographer Palladius, St. Melania demanded of him, "Promise by the Lord that you mean to aim at the monastic life . . . I will pray that you be given a lease on life."

TOP Detail from fifteenth-century Byzantine illustration of Evagrius.

Conversion—or reconversion—followed, as he lived among the severe and ascetic cenobites and then spent his final fourteen years in a solitary cell,

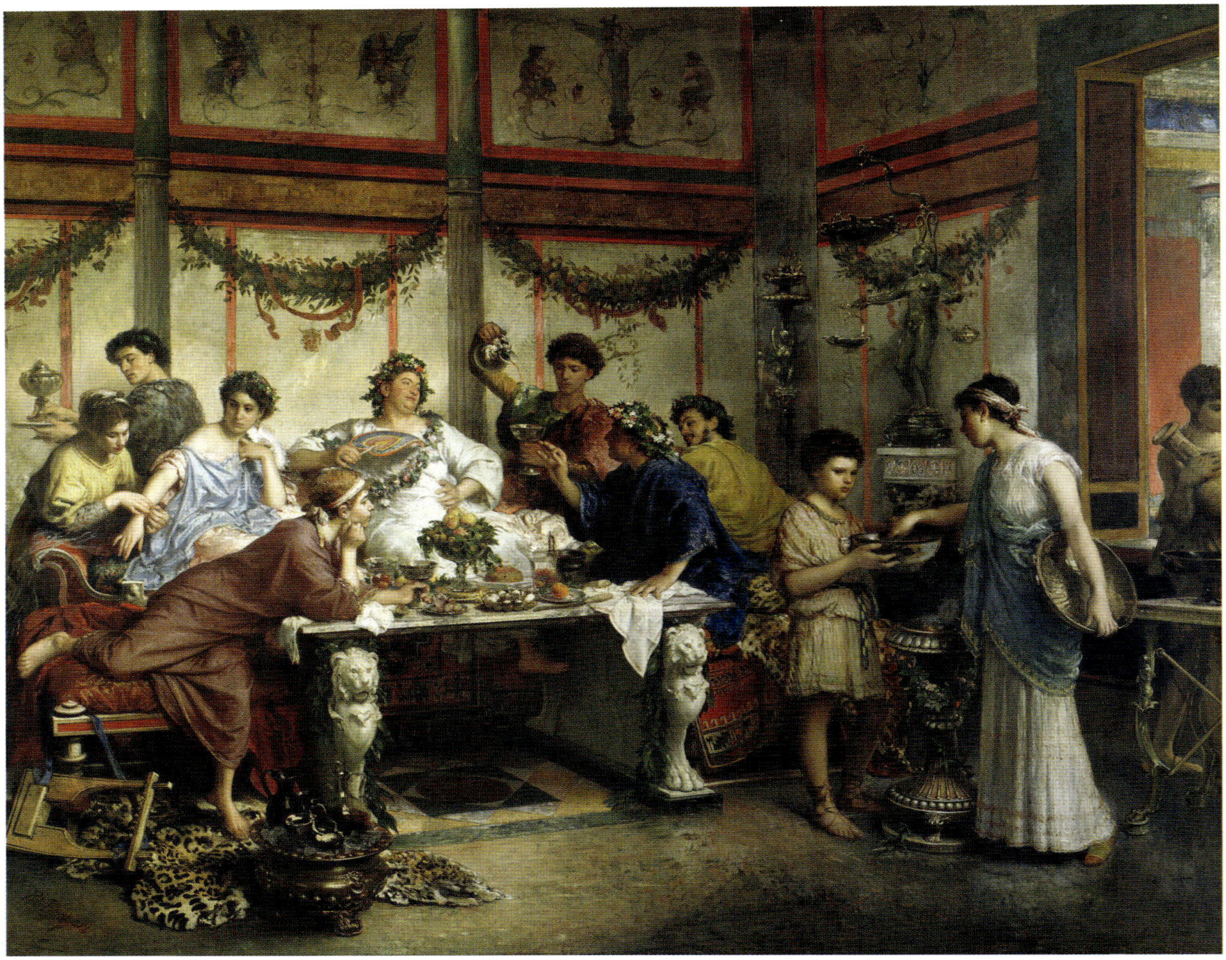

meditating, praying, atoning. "First of all pray to be purified from your passions," Evagrius advises in *The Praktikos*. "Secondly, pray to be delivered from ignorance. Thirdly, pray to be free from all temptation and abandonment." But, as Evagrius himself admitted, change is difficult. Impossible that in the desert sun he didn't spare a thought for the cool fountains of Byzantium or the shaded date trees of Jerusalem. Such euphoric recall, or the envious consideration of those free to eat, drink, and be merry, must have chafed Evagrius's soul. Having "embraced this life of solitude and . . . seeked out the blessings of stillness," as he writes in *The Philokalia*, Evagrius had opportunity to think about sin, taxonomize it, categorize it. What resulted—bolstered by his own ample experience—was a system of organization. In Evagrius's *The Eight Evil Spirits*, damnation is purchased with gluttony, fornication, avarice, sadness, wrath, acedia, boastfulness, and pride. By the late sixth century, Pope Gregory the Great amended this list by combining sadness and acedia into sloth and replacing boastfulness with a sin which Evagrius had overlooked—envy.

Had Evagrius not been dead for three centuries then perhaps he'd feel resentful, but as it was, Gregory's form became the enduring touchstone. Part of what

TOP "Eat, drink, and be merry," Solomon intones in the Book of Ecclesiastes, but it's an axiom more fit for the Hellenic world than the Hebraic. Roberto Bompiani's 1875 *A Roman Feast*, original held by the John Paul Getty Museum in Los Angeles, imagines decadent spreads and lascivious serving women at the celebration of Saturnalia. The austere pontificating of an Evagrius was in opposition to the classical world's celebration of the senses, yet it's hard to believe that the cenobite didn't have moments when he wished that he could join in.

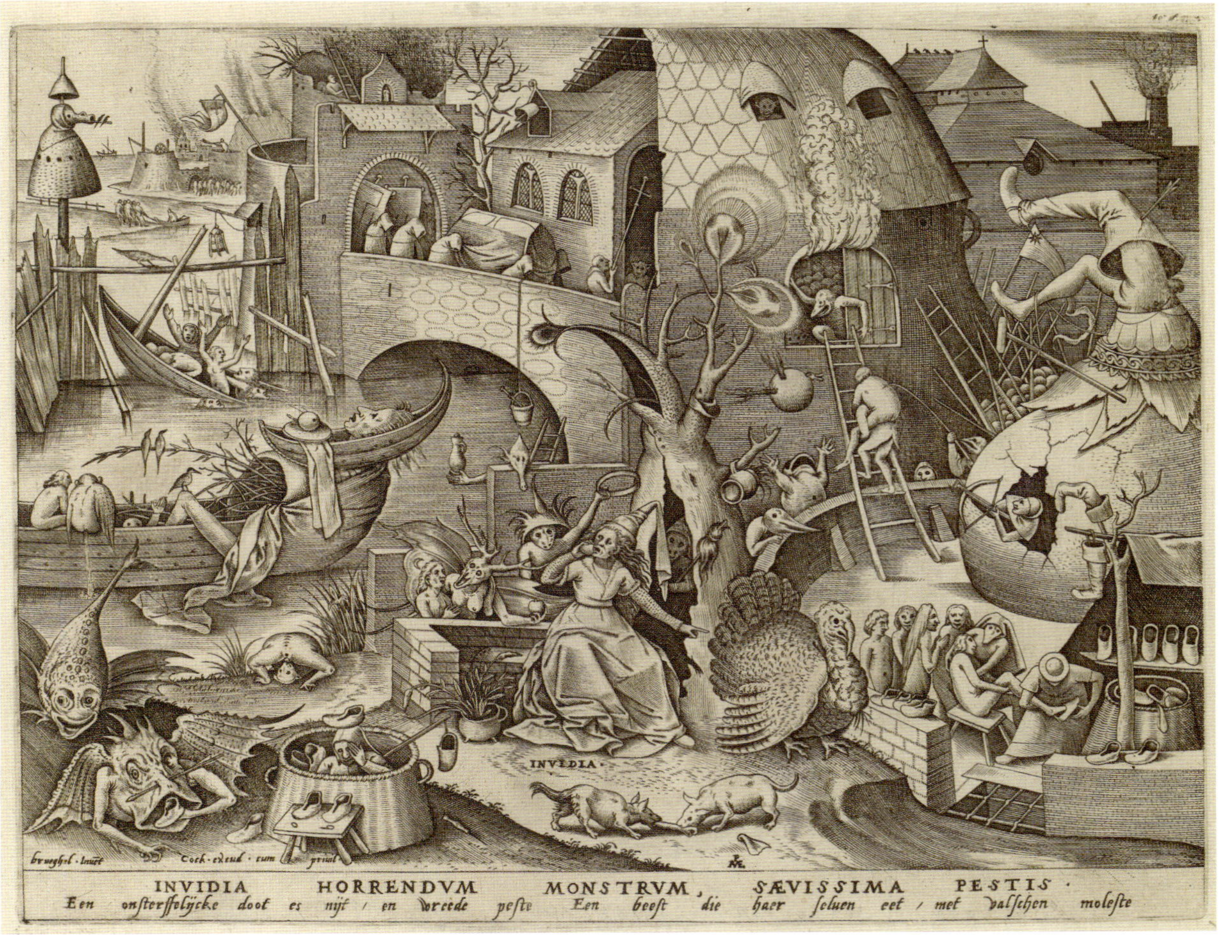

TOP The Flemish artist Pieter van der Heyden's 1558 allegorical engraving of *Envy* after Pieter Brueghel the Elder, original held by the Allen Memorial Art Museum in Oberlin, Ohio. Envy herself is in the center, devouring her own heart, while a variety of figures illustrate the theme (note the two dogs fighting over a bone).

makes the Seven Deadly Sins evocative is that, unlike the Decalogue or the 613 mitzvoth of Leviticus, they're neither proscriptions nor prohibitions, but rather elemental aspects of human psychology. God's commandments tell us to do this or to not do that, but the Seven Deadly Sins are more flexible and damning, because what they offer isn't strictly delineated but rather situated on a spectrum.

Such sins are universal, for every variety of wickedness constitutes something that, in moderation, is required. We all must eat, but shouldn't be gluttonous; we all must rest, but slothfulness has to be avoided; sexual feeling is natural, but lustfulness is something different. None of the sins describe anything particularly heinous; they're the provenance not just of serial killers, but of everyone. It is instructive to know that a better translation of "sin" is "thought"; human instinct and desire is neutral, but it's indulgence that is damning. The idolatry of natural thoughts often leads to excuses, such that greed causes an executive to defraud an investor, anger can lead to murderous road rage, and pride can push anyone down the path of heresy. This way, venial sins—every little white lie, early escape from the office, and filched hotel shampoo bottle—can metastasize into mortal sins: adultery, corruption, theft. Gregory's list isn't arbitrary; in a

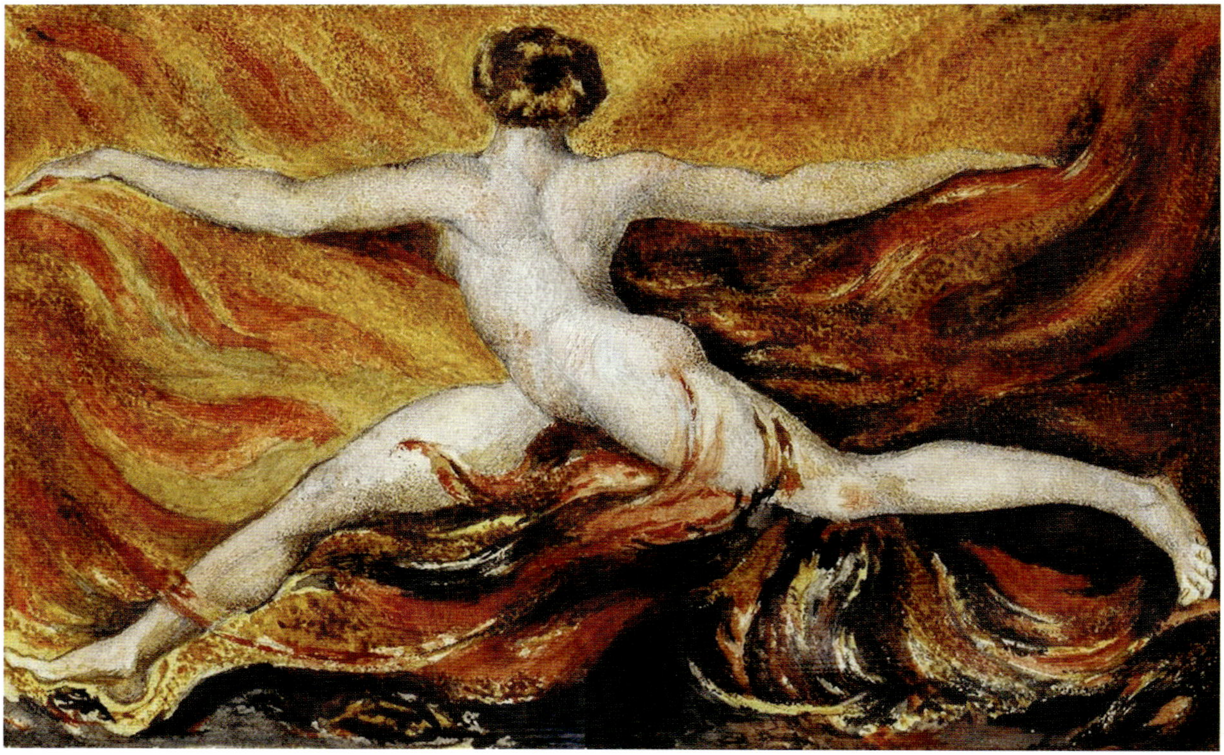

world of limited resources, gluttony takes food out of the mouths of the hungry, sloth necessitates that others have to pick up your slack, and greed exploits the impoverished. That the Seven Deadly Sins often grow out of that which people find enjoyable—most of us relish eating, delight in sleeping, enjoy fucking—is the point. Even wrath has its own piquant pleasures, as anyone who has ever read the comments section with flushed face and heightened blood pressure can attest. It's the perversion of the natural that leads to perdition. But envy? It's not even enjoyable.

Except it is. Walk down Fifth Avenue past the windows of Barneys or Bergdorf Goodman and tell me that envy doesn't have its joys; get lost clicking through Zillow entries for eight-bedroom homes with recessed lighting and built-in wine bars, kitchens with black granite tabletops and decks with views of the Napa Valley, and tell me that you don't enjoy envy; walk through Zabar's or Balducci's salivating at the cheese you can't afford, the obscenely expensive olives, the cuts of veal that you know are wicked to eat, and say that envy isn't fun. Our entire economy is built on envy, the doctrine of what sociologist Thorstein Veblen famously termed "conspicuous consumption," with the scriptures of our prophets written on Madison Avenue. Not only that, but envy often has the added pleasure of judgment, the ecstasy of shit-talking. *Why did that writer get a New York book contract? She's terrible. How could he get a tenure track job? He's a moron.*

Taxonomizing sin is itself defined by envy, the transgressions of imagination, the tribulations of fantasy, the barely sublimated projections of desires deferred. This is obvious in the more prurient of tomes: thirteenth-century Bernardo Gui's

TOP Envy is desire is passion is erotic, as the English visionary and prophet William Blake understood perfectly well and demonstrated in his 1794 watercolor *Flames of Furious Desire* from *The First Book of Urizen*.

The Inquisitor's Guide or Heinrich Kramer and Jacob Sprenger's fifteenth-century *Malleus Maleficarum—The Hammer of the Witches*—with its description of orgiastic Black Masses. Even our orthodox theologians indulge in the sin of judgment, which is often just envy turned inside out, with Thomas Aquinas noting with salacious glee in his thirteenth-century *Summa Theologica* that the "saints may enjoy their beatitude . . . more abundantly [as] they are permitted to see the punishment of the damned in hell." Such is the cracked, malignant brokenness of us all, that original sin which Augustine was just defining as Evagrius descended into infirmity.

THE CONSUMPTION OF CONSPICUOUSNESS

The outline of the small hand is clear, carved into the uneven limestone of Judea, three short fingers and a thumb mirrored on the other side with that same digit where a pinkie should normally be. This Israelite grave was prepared some seven centuries before the beginning of the Common Era. Whomever was once entombed within the cave in what is today the Palestinian West Bank has long since vanished due to the inevitability of entropy, but the distinctive markings upon their memorial survive, the carving of this open palm intended as apotropaic magic, the use of a symbol or amulet to keep someone safe. The figure would come to be known as the *hamsa*, derived from the Semitic root for the word "five" after the number of digits upon a hand, and roughly a cognate between Hebrew and Arabic. On a Carthaginian tomb the sign of the goddess Tinnit is rendered as the open hand of benediction, while in Egypt a three-fingered symbol representing Osiris, Isis, and their falcon-headed son Horus was similarly used to protect whoever inscribed it upon a wall or wore it as jewelry. By the Middle Ages, the hamsa was etched onto the vellum pages of Kabbalistic texts like the mystical Zohar, Sephardic Jews drawn to the three middle fingers' visual congruence with the Hebrew letter shin, the first phoneme in the word "Shaddai," one of the many synonyms for "God." The hand was often re-created not just on parchment or lambskin, but molded in silver or tin, adorned with lapis lazuli or rubies, affixed to the front of doors and over fireplaces, next to marital beds and always near an infant's crib.

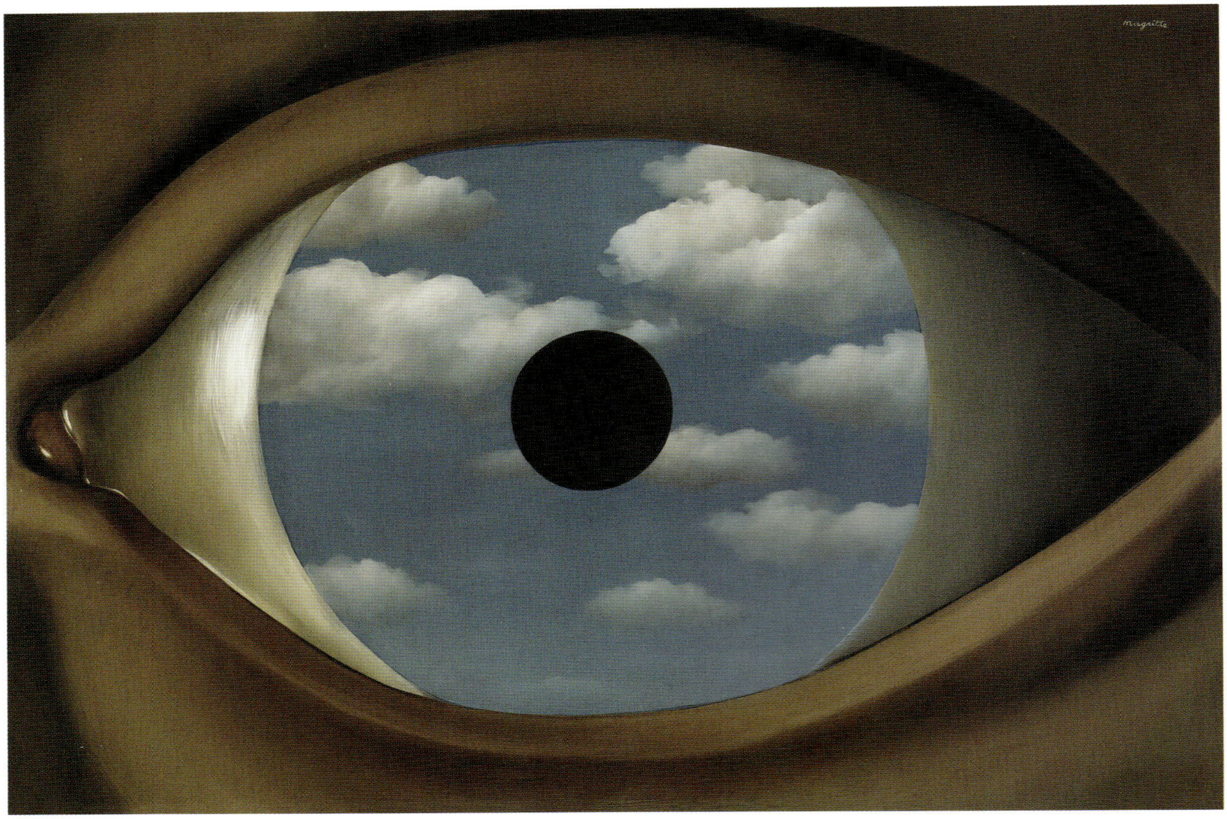

Today the hamsa can be found in high-end jewelry shops in New York and Tel Aviv or rendered as a cheap trinket for sale in stalls from Damascus to Jerusalem, on the Orthodox Jewish marriage contracts known as ketubah and as an emblem of the Islamic nation of Algeria. The hamsa of the Jews, the Hand of Fatima for Muslims, the Hand of Mary for Middle Eastern Christians, is as unifying a symbol as is the patrimony of Abraham. Whether as once an appendage of Tinnit, or Osiris, or the Lord, the hamsa has always been something more mysterious and ineffable, a hand grasping from the subterranean realms of our deep history, from the darkened corners of the mind, trying to hold all of us upright when threatened by those who wish to do us harm, who wish to take from us that which is ours. The magical function of the hamsa should be made clear by one of the most common features of the symbol, for often in the middle of the palm of this symmetrical hand, frequently affixed with a jewel or painted, sometimes merely a depression that was set by a stylus into the soft metal as it cooled from the workshop, is a single, unblinking eye. This eye promises protection against what the Jews call *ayin ha'ra*, the Romans call *malocchio*, and in its many permutations from the Maghreb to Mexico, Sudan to Sicily, is often known as the "evil eye."

An incantation, a hex, a curse. The risk is when you are in possession of anything which the green eyes of your fellow humans may light upon, which your friends or family, colleagues or neighbors, may envy. A bit of good fortune in romance or career. Betrothal to a beautiful woman, delivery of a perfect baby. Something that makes those around you tingle with jealousy. And then, often

TOP Belgian Surrealist René Magritte's 1928 *The False Mirror*, a title as unnerving as its imagery of clouds superimposed atop a large, unblinking, vacant abyss of an eye, original held by the Museum of Modern Art in New York City.

OPPOSITE The Dutch illustrator M. C. Escher's 1946 self-portrait of his eye is, from one perspective, an arresting memento mori, reminding both the artist and the audience that we all shall die; but it's also an invocation of the deadly covetousness which can dwell within the gaze.

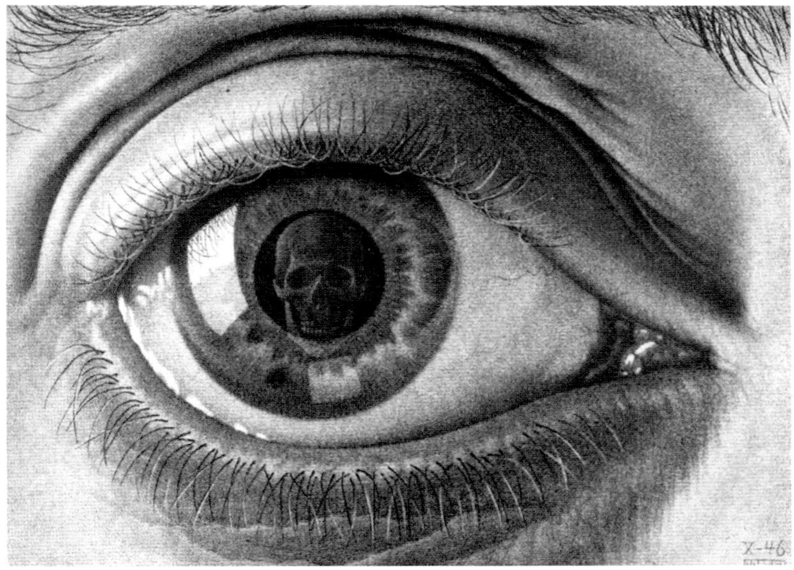

subconscious to even the one who wishes to do you harm, some tragedy will befall the fortunate woman or man; the rapacious evil eye will deprive them of their greatest joys. When success comes, the evil eye always wanders. A feature of the collective folk wisdom of Mediterranean cultures on both sides of the sea, as well as the Latin American inheritors of the Iberian branch of that aforementioned tradition, the evil eye is misattributed to mere superstition by the partisans of disenchantment, but the rest of us know to be wary of the compliment that's uttered a bit too enthusiastically.

And so the hamsa is but one means of warding off the pernicious dangers of such envy. In southern Italy there is the wearing of the *corno*, the goat's-horn-shaped amulet that also sometimes takes the form of a curled red pepper, worn on gold chains from Benevento to Bensonhurst. Italians can also protect themselves with an adept wielding of the infamous Neapolitan hand signal of a raised pinkie and index finger which is also used as an obscenity to signal the desire that someone be cuckolded. Among the Turkic peoples from Istanbul to Urumqi, strings of flattened, glass disks known as Nazar, decorated with a colorful turquoise teardrop-shaped eye at their center, are displayed to dispel any malignant feelings of envy that should radiate toward you, while in the Caribbean, palm trees are adorned with strings of blue Milk of Magnesia bottles whose clanging frightens off the feelings of jealousy which can be directed toward someone. So widespread is the belief in the evil eye throughout the non-Anglo world that it's close to a universal superstition, as varied as the methods of protection might be. Yet to even call it a superstition is fallacious, for even without the intercession of the supernatural, envy can function as a societal cancer, a means by which thankfulness is ignored and covetousness indulged, to the detriment of everybody. "You shall not covet your neighbor's house," reads Exodus 20:17, the final commandment of the Decalogue as given to Moses at Sinai. "You shall not covet your neighbor's wife, or his male and female servant, his ox or donkey, or anything that belongs to your neighbor." The prohibition on envy was as solemn as it was serious, yet since the pyrotechnic, neon dawn of postmodernity a half-century ago, covetousness has been encouraged and has transformed into the very currency of our existence.

Greed is now merely an ancillary to envy. Modern economics is not driven so much by material *want* but by material *desire*, two slightly different things. Wealth is less crucial than its aura; gold is less important than its glow. Image, and the inculcation of desire, of envy, of jealousy in others, is what the entire edifice of consumer capitalism is built upon; now we positively demand the evil eye's attention upon us. The Joneses are nothing unless they have jealous neighbors pining to keep up with them. During the mid-nineteenth century, an economist enthused that capitalism has generated impressive emotional stores of want, having "created more massive and more colossal productive forces than have all preceding generations," name-checking the marvels of "steam-navigation, railways, electric telegraphs . . . canalization of rivers," while asking "what earlier century had even a presentiment [of] such productive forces?" This economist was a paragon of bourgeois tastes, an avid reader of the sentimental novels of Honoré de Balzac, a fan of maudlin Romantic music, and a perennial smoker of cheap cigars. Today he'd no doubt enjoy a pumpkin spice latte at the Mall of America. His name was Karl Marx, and the selection quoted is from *The Communist Manifesto*. Marx's critique is pertinent because he acknowledges what's seductive about capitalism, how it is built on desire, on envy. Any radical analysis which ignores *what's so great about owning stuff* isn't really a radical analysis at all; any claim that *television isn't actually amazing*, or *junk food never tastes good, or pop music is anemic* is just bohemian posturing. Marx's denunciations of capitalism—written with the support of his wealthy friend Friedrich Engels—were trenchant because he didn't confuse ethics with aesthetics.

"Modern bourgeois society," Marx writes, "is like the sorcerer, who is no longer able to control the powers of the nether world whom he has called up by his spells." Dispute the prescription if we must, but Marx was perceptive in his diagnosis: for all of the material plenty which industry supplied to some, capitalism *depends* on exploitation, it is *defined* by inequity, it *requires* alienation. "If our religion is capitalism, then our theology is consumerism and our god is the Invisible Hand; the greatest of commandments then becomes to covet your neighbor's house, his wife, his male and female servants, his ox and his donkey. Our prayers are "Have It Your Way," "Think Different," and "Just Do It"; our avatars are Ronald McDonald, Mr. Peanut, and the Kool-Aid Man; our relics are the Golden Arches, the Mercedes trinity, and the Pepsi Tao. Our liturgy, that's advertising. It's produced some great and beautiful art. Television commercials and print advertisements, marketing campaigns and logo designs, all constitute the United States' artistic patrimony; our great literature is the jingle, the copy, the billboard, the TV spot, because all of it speaks to the elemental nature of desiring something.

OPPOSITE English pop artist Richard Hamilton's iconic 1956 collage *Just what is it that makes today's homes so different, so appealing?*, original held by the Kunsthalle in Tubingen, Germany, features among other images the bodybuilder Irvin "Zabo" Koszewski and an unidentified burlesque performer from a pornographic magazine situated in cutouts of midcentury modern furniture and mass consumer products, in a parody of consumptive postwar suburban aesthetics. Understanding how advertising operates, Hamilton satires the manner in which consumerism encourages want, which is to say envy.

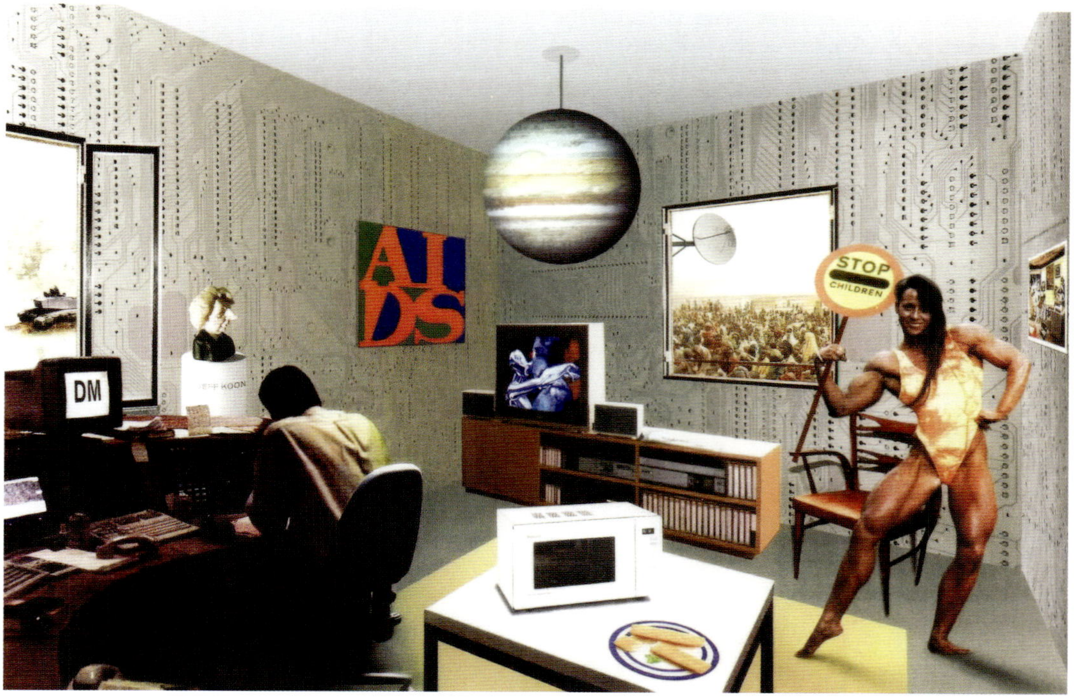

James Walter Thompson, who filched the Rock of Gibraltar for the Prudential Insurance Company in 1890; Doyle Dane Bernbach and their lemonish Volkswagen; Ogilvy and Mather with contracts for Schweppes, Guinness, Rolls-Royce, Sears, Dove, and so on. The little narratives constructed by these (mostly) men, tiny portraits and miniature novels, weren't created just to sell people things, but to also package fantasy. Wherever people are hungry they'll purchase food, wherever they're thirsty they'll buy drink, but commercials sell you an entire worldview. Every culture has myths, ordering stories of reality. In Athens, to live the good life depended on reason; in Jerusalem it was to commit yourself to faith; and on Madison Avenue it's to live for consumption. We don't have Hesiod's *Theogony* or the Torah; our scripture is a thirty-second spot. Our myth tells you that you are incomplete, disordered, and unhappy, but that the solution involves the accumulation of things—beautiful things, tasty things, sexy things, amazing things—and that through such commodities you become perfectible, as surely as an ancient Greek making offerings at Delphi ensured his favor among the Olympians, as much as a medieval penitent paying an indulgence ensures release from Purgatory. Does any of it work? Well, in the immediate sense, paying the indulgence makes you feel better too. But today the churches are defunct and our faith is dying as our shopping malls are boarding up, our prayers as unanswered as the next shipping delay. Still, as the Sibylline Oracle at the Mall of America says,

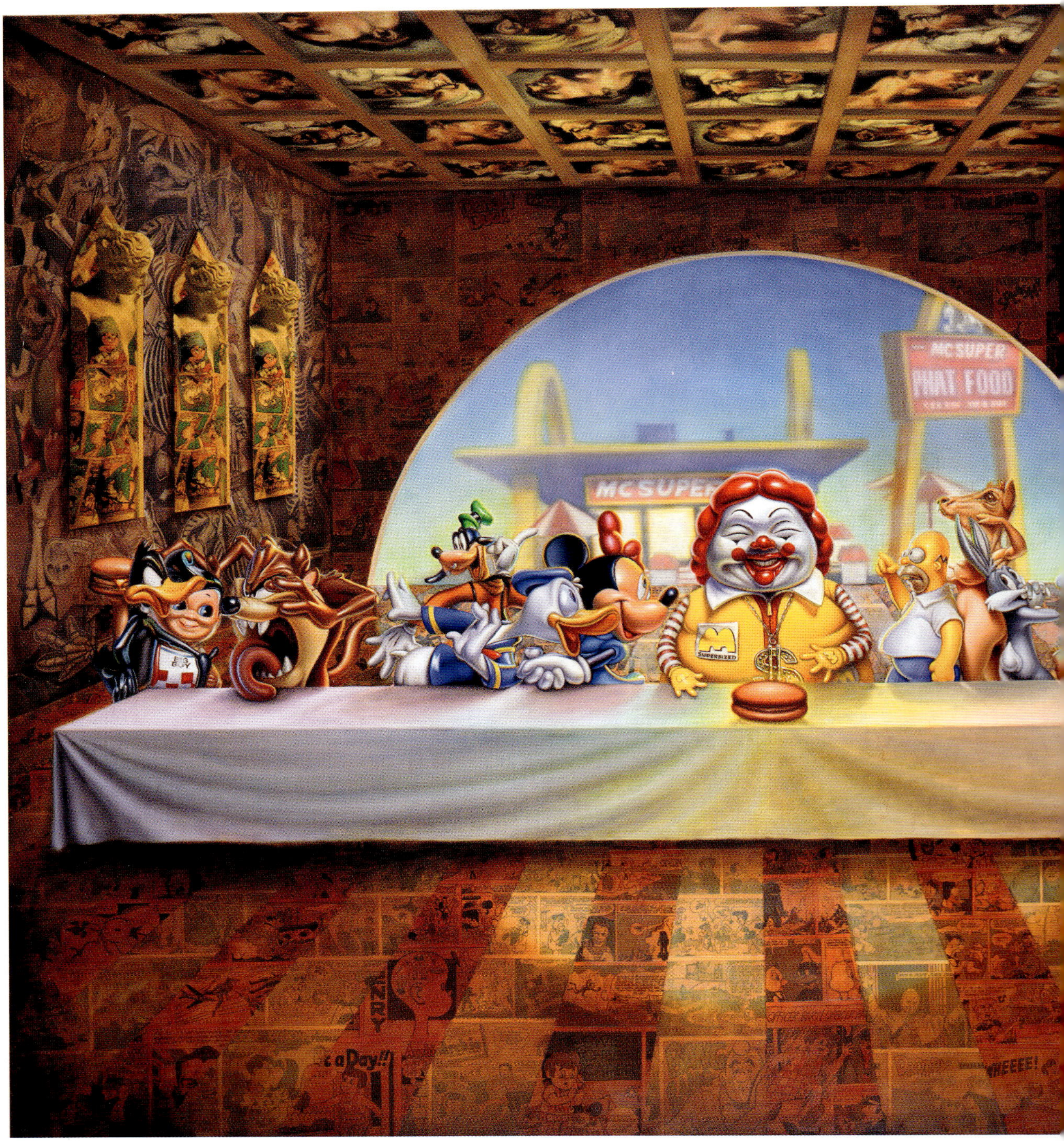

ABOVE Contemporary American painter Ron English's "popaganda" paintings satirize the wanton excess of American consumer culture, where the throne of God is vacated and replaced with the empty signifier of the advertisement, as in his 2010 parody *Super Supper*, with a corpulent Ronald McDonald sitting in the chair intended for Jesus Christ.

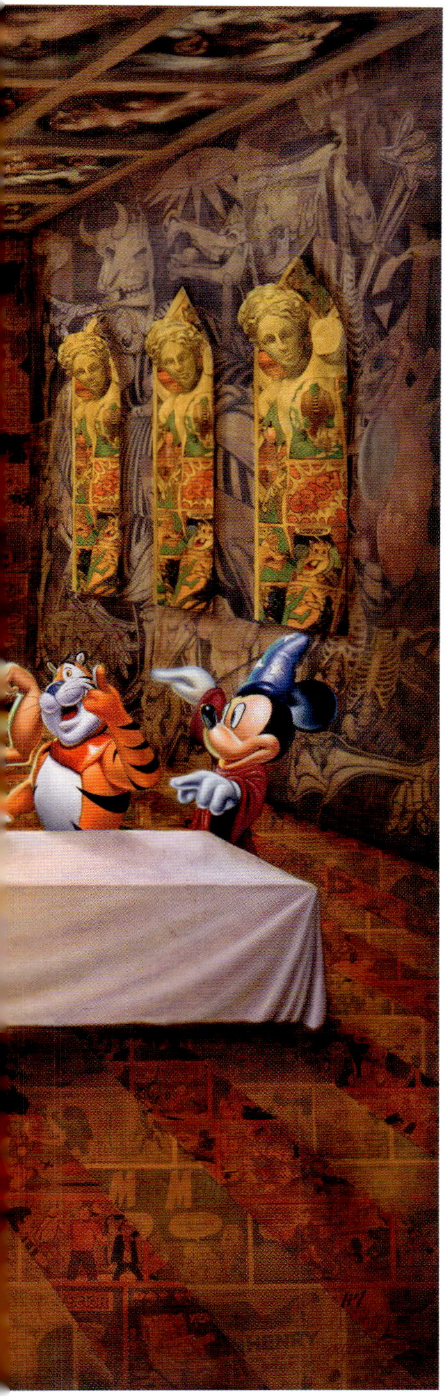

THE HEARTBEAT OF AMERICA IS OPEN HAPPINESS, WHEN A DIAMOND IS FOREVER IN THE HAPPIEST PLACE ON EARTH.

BECAUSE YOU'RE IN GOOD HANDS, SO DON'T LEAVE HOME WITHOUT IT.

WE BRING GOOD THINGS TO LIFE, AND GO THE EXTRA MILE. THE POWER OF DREAMS IS THE RELENTLESS PURSUIT OF PERFECTION, GOOD TO THE LAST DROP.

EAT FRESH, EXPECT MORE, AND PAY LESS–ANYTIME, ANYWHERE. BECAUSE YOU'RE WORTH IT.

CAN YOU HEAR ME NOW?

Critique this cento, but whatever way you arrange it, some version of this lyric will endure longer than anything by T. S. Eliot or Ezra Pound. If you can feel sublime only in a cathedral you deserve pity, because the numinous can be smuggled into these commercial prayers, however empty their promises. Virgil, Donatello, and Shostakovich all exploited emotions, and they were servants of nefarious masters as well; yet it would be a fool who thought that *The Aeneid*, *David*, and Symphony No. 5 in D minor, Op. 47 don't intimate the shores of eternity, the breath of transcendence. Materialism in its most raw and literal form has little to do with it. "It isn't the whiskey they choose," wrote David Ogilvy in *Ogilvy on Advertising*, "it's the image."

Ad men completely reshaped the mental topography during the initial post-war years, transforming envy into the operative sentiment of modernity. Theirs was the silver age of mental coercion (ours is the golden), when Soviet writers like Mikhail Sholokhov and Nikolai Ostrovsky were used to produce official literature which extoled collectivization and the command economy, where in the latter's novel *How the Steel Was Tempered* a character could shout "all my life, all my strength were given to the finest cause in all the world—the fight for the Liberation of Mankind!" Capitalist propaganda is far more subtle; rather, we have "those Golden Grahams / Graham cracker tasting cereal / That taste is such a treat!" Madison Avenue, where F. Scott Fitzgerald, Salman Rushdie, and Don DeLillo all worked as copywriters, has always housed an outsized concentration of literary ambition. Rushdie may have penned *The Satanic Verses*, but he also wrote "Naughty! But Nice" for Fresh Cream Cakes while working at Ogilvy and Mather; Fitzgerald wrote *The Great Gatsby* with its description of "such beautiful shirts," that rain of blue, and green, and yellow that Daisy sends down onto Jay, but while first living in Iowa, the author saw his line "We Keep You Clean in Muscatine" emblazoned on laundry trucks throughout the city.

There's no simple correspondence here, no one-to-one symbiosis, but the experience of DeLillo at Ogilvy and Mather must have informed his writing. In DeLillo's *White Noise*, erstwhile professor of Hitler studies and small liberal arts faculty member Jack Gladney exists, like all of us, in the medium of commercials. Thomas DiPietro records the author as saying in *Conversations with DeLillo* that America's central commandment is "consume or die," and that's on display in the novel. Commodity fetishism is the contrition through which the capitalist soul is formed, where one "found new aspects of myself, located a person I'd forgotten existed. Brightness settled around me . . . I was bigger than these sums. These sums poured off my skin like so much rain. These sums in fact came back to me in the form of existential credit." In *White Noise*, Jack mumbles the prayers of our faith—"Mastercard, Visa, American Express." *White Noise* expresses a truth of advertising—all of this purchasing isn't about stuff; it's about identity. Before the omnipresence of consumer culture, if you needed to plow—you bought a plow. If you needed to shovel—you bought a shovel. But as the sacrament of Jack's purchasing demonstrates, the simulacra of reality that is late capitalism asks you to buy (and sell) your soul. *White Noise* is an example of the advertising turn in literature, where a character's personality is signaled through the products that he buys. Victorian novels let you understand characters through phrenology, the slope of a brow signaling criminality or the distance between eyes demonstrating intelligence, but in postmodernism it's the brand of ice cream somebody eats or the type of car they drive.

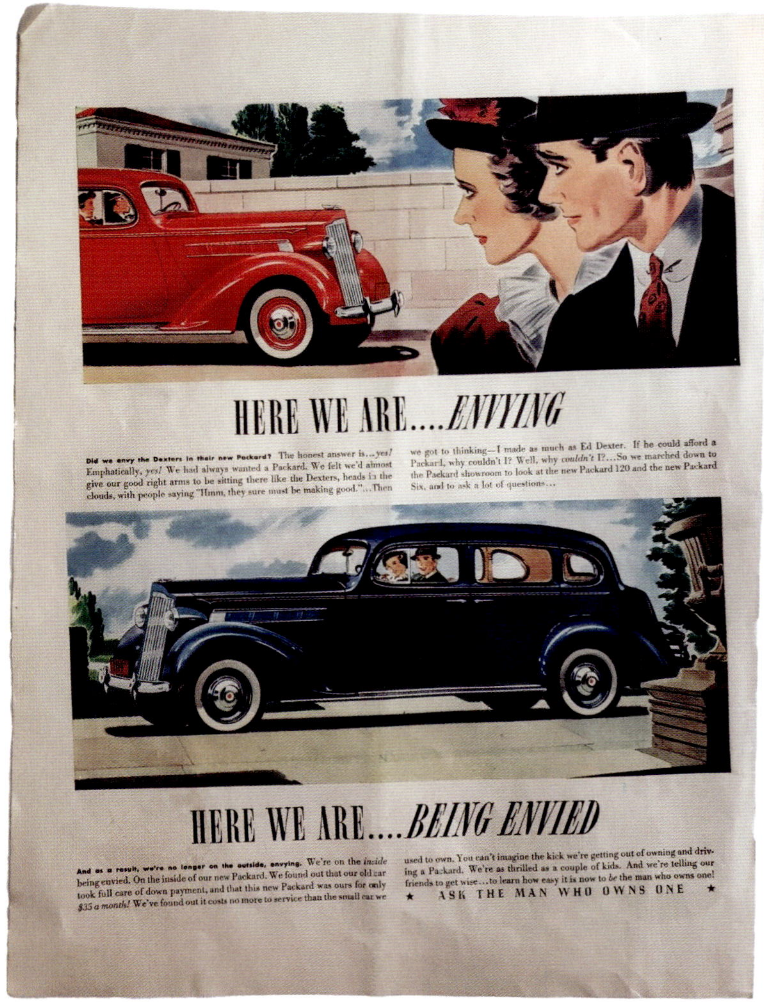

If you didn't already know that Patrick Bateman is a sociopathic serial killer in Bret Easton Ellis's *American Psycho*, or that he imagines himself to be, then you at least understand that he's a conceited prick with his "six-button wool and silk suit by Ermenegildo Zegna . . . cotton shirt with French cuffs by Ike Behar . . . Ralph Lauren silk tie and leather wing tips by Fratelli Rosetti," along with all those Eddie Money cassettes. By comparison, a very different personality is conveyed in the brands named by Jeffrey Eugenides in *The Marriage Plot*, where "Sometimes Madeline made him tea. Instead of going for an herbal infusion from Celestial Seasonings, with a quotation from Lao Tzu on the package, Madeline was a Fortnum & Mason's drinker, her favorite blend Earl Grey." The vaguely New Age-y affectations of Celestial Seasonings with its sleepy bear on the box, rejected in favor of the stolid, slightly stodgy, sort-of-fussy Fortnum & Mason's with the Royal Seal on its packaging, signals that Madeline is (rather than some hippie) a serious person, an Anglophile even (or, at least, that's what she's trying to convey; she owns both brands, clearly). Not even poetry

TOP Bluntly literal 1937 Packard car magazine advertisement.

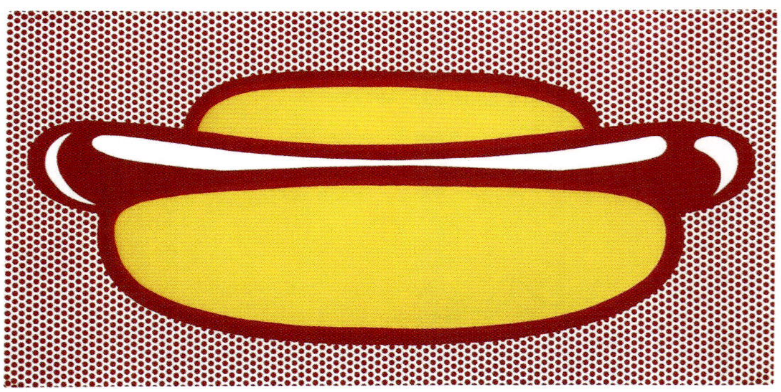

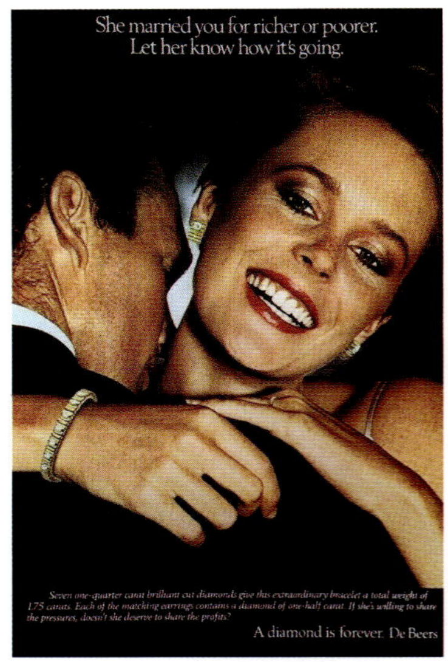

is so otherworldly to ignore capitalism's siren; Frederick Seidel has been writing about his luxury Italian motorcycles for decades, of Ducatis "all around, all red, all beautiful, / Ducatis as far as the eye can see, / Each small and perfect as a ladybug," these words published in 2019 in *The London Review of Books*. Bateman with his business cards and Madeline with her tea; Seidel on a motorcycle and Sissman's song of Pucci; all of these brand names tell us something, a poetics of envy.

It becomes impossible to imagine anything different, what Mark Fisher describes in *Capitalist Realism* as the process by which the market "subsumes and consumes all of previous history." Marxists use the term "late capitalism" as an optimistic shorthand, when the internal contradictions usher in the millennium of socialism. However, as with anything consumed without respite, you eventually run out, and history is no exception. How will we define ourselves when the final bill comes due, when the eternal credit card is maxed out, especially since we're incapable of imagining anything other than capitalism? "What

TOP LEFT American pop artist Roy Lichtenstein's iconic 1964 *Hot Dog*, original held by the Museum of Modern and Contemporary Art of Trento and Rovereto, Italy, is the postmodern still-life par excellence. Lichtenstein understands that contemporary consumer advertising does not sell things, but rather images of things. Reducing all specificity to a clean abstraction, Lichtenstein's painting is not of a hot dog, but of the *idea* of a hot dog.

TOP RIGHT The most effective advertising, of course, speaks for itself, or, as Veblen writes, to be respected the modern person assumes that it is "necessary to come up to a certain, somewhat indefinite, conventional standard of wealth."

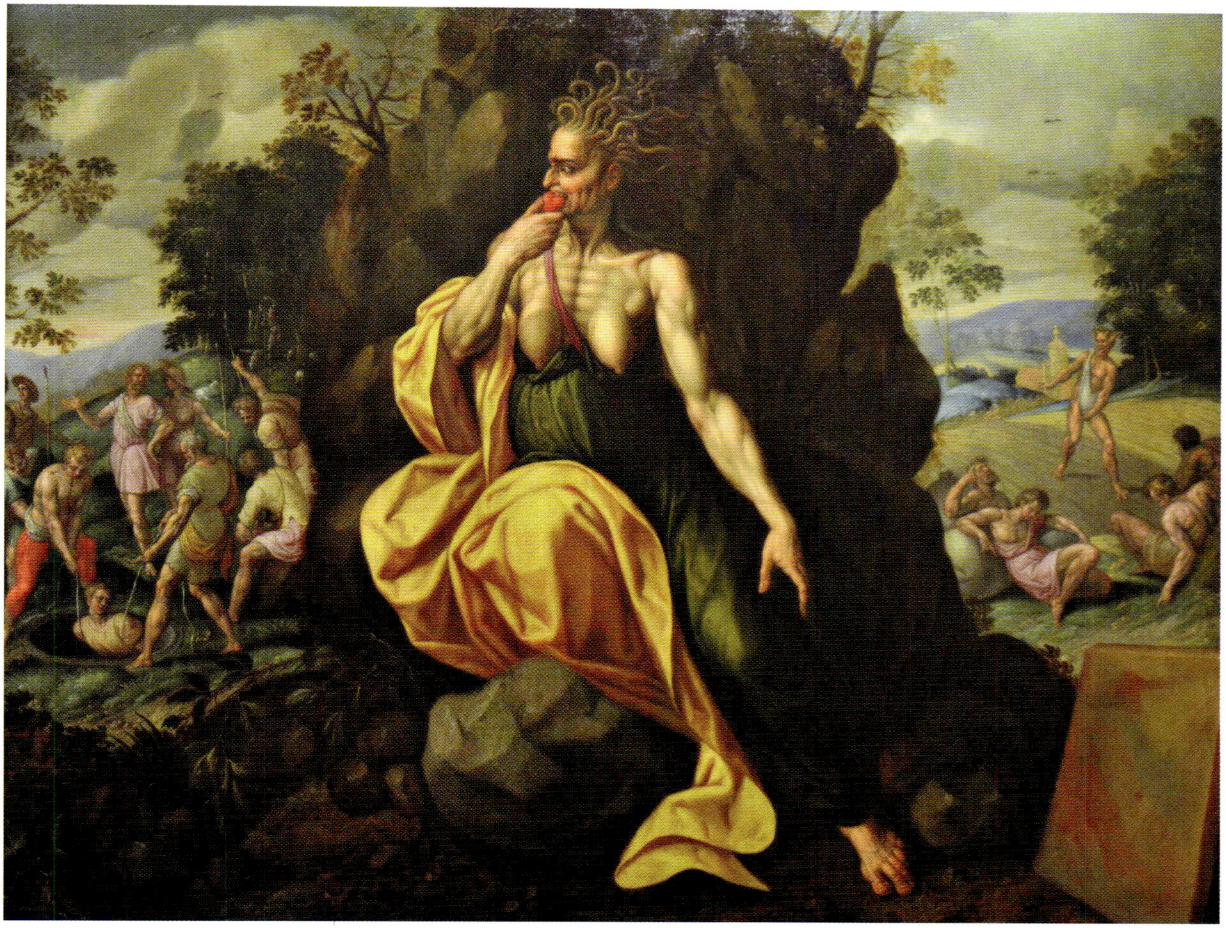

ABOVE A more traditional take on envy in the Flemish painter Jacob de Backer's c.1570 piece *Envy, One of the Seven Deadly Sins*, original held by the Museo di Capodimonte in Naples.

haunts me is not exactly the absence of literal space so much as a deep craving for metaphorical space," writes Naomi Klein in *No Logo: Resisting the Brand Bullies*; "release, escape, some kind of open-ended freedom." As Klein describes it, advertising and design mark everything in our reality, and we're so constricted we can't even imagine what wild open space would look like. For all that consumerism has promised us—comfort, security, identity—it was always the assurance that we could keep on purchasing our freedom which was the biggest illusion. Now the shipments are on backorder and the shelves are empty, but for the time being you can still have whatever it is you want delivered right to your front door, never mind that the driver can never stop working. What happens after collapse when we can no longer define ourselves through products? No clue—the burden of defining some better world falls to those left behind after the rest of us have already left. In the meantime, have a Coke.

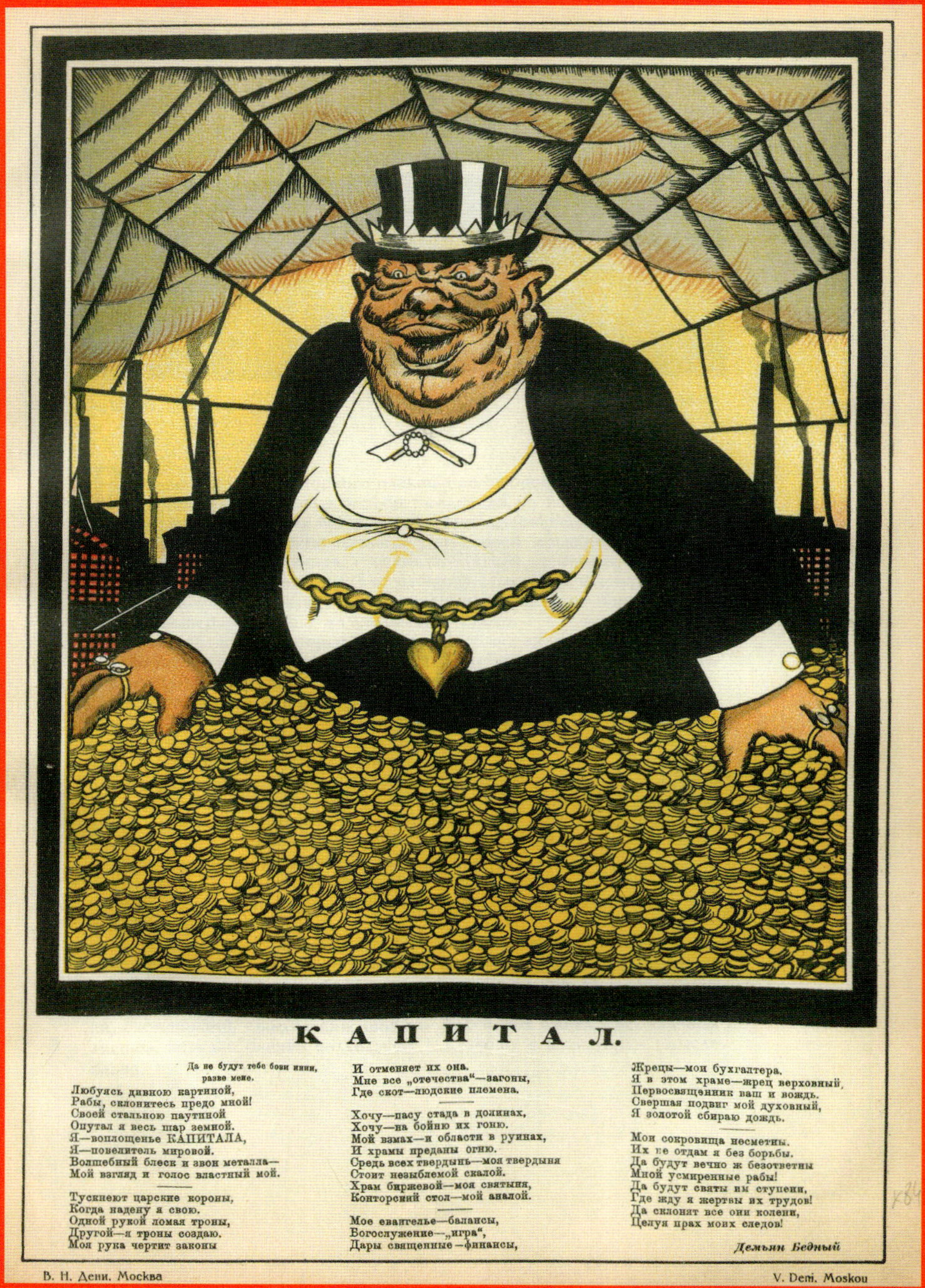
КАПИТАЛ.
Да не будут тебе бози инии, разве мене.
Любуясь дивною картиной,
Рабы, склонитесь предо мной!
Своей стальною паутиной
Опутал я весь шар земной.
Я—воплощенье КАПИТАЛА,
Я—повелитель мировой.
Волшебный блеск и звон металла—
Мой взгляд и голос властный мой.
Тускнеют царские короны,
Когда надену я свою.
Одной рукой ломая троны,
Другой—я троны создаю.
Моя рука чертит законы
И отменяет их она.
Мне все „отечества"—загоны,
Где скот—людские племена.
Хочу—пасу стада в долинах,
Хочу—на бойню их гоню.
Мой взмах—и области в руинах,
И храмы преданы огню.
Средь всех твердынь—моя твердыня
Стоит незыблемой скалой.
Храм биржевой—моя святыня,
Конторский стол—мой аналой.
Мое евангелье—балансы,
Богослуженье—„игра",
Дары священные—финансы,
Жрецы—мои бухгалтера.
Я в этом храме—жрец верховный,
Первосвященник ваш и вождь.
Свершая подвиг мой духовный,
Я золотой сбираю дождь.
Мои сокровища несметны.
Их не отдам я без борьбы.
Да будут вечно ж безответны
Мной усмиренные рабы!
Да будут святы им ступени,
Где жду я жертвы их трудов!
Да склонят все они колени,
Целуя прах моих следов!
Демьян Бедный
В. Н. Дени. Москва
V. Deni. Moskou

CHAPTER SIX

A KIND OF FEAR: GREED

"And again I say unto you, It is easier for a camel to go through the eye of a needle, than for a rich man to enter into the kingdom of God."
—Matthew 19:24

"Money, now this has to be some *good* shit."
—Martin Amis, *Money, a Suicide Note* (1984)

Greed is, in many ways, the most instrumental of sins. The most totemistic, the most archetypal, the most essential. Pride may be the font of all transgressions, but greed is at the center of our mythology in a different way, from the ancient despot hoarding gold and rubies, diamonds and pearls, to the corrupt miser sullenly counting pounds. Avarice can be easier to understand than mere pride—until it can't. Aristotle writes in his *Politics* that the origin of greed is in the disposition of those whose "desires are unlimited [so] they also desire that the means of gratifying them should be without limit." A fascinating implication here, for it subsumes virtually all of the other sins not into pride, but back into greed. What is sloth but greed for time, wrath as greed for vengeance, gluttony as greed for flesh, and lust as greed for just a different type of flesh? Even pride is nothing but greed for regard. If all of the sins are such because they imagine the individual as being more important than others, if their rapaciousness necessitates an expansion beyond their own little garden into other realms and dominions and then kingdoms, then greed must be the ur-transgression. Basil of Caesarea notes in the fourth century that far from being somehow innately deserving of the bounties which are a treasury for the earth, the rich "seize common goods before others have the opportunity, then claim them as their own by right of preemption," while a century later, John Cassian castigated those who "choose to love and care for images stamped on gold instead of God." Of course, among the most condemnatory of greed was Christ, who spoke virtually not at all about the current-day culture war issues which roil politics, but continually denounced avarice. This was the figure whose most public act in the week before his crucifixion was casting out the money changers in front of Jerusalem's Temple with whip in hand, turning over their tables and sending shekels and denarii tumbling into the dust of the courtyard.

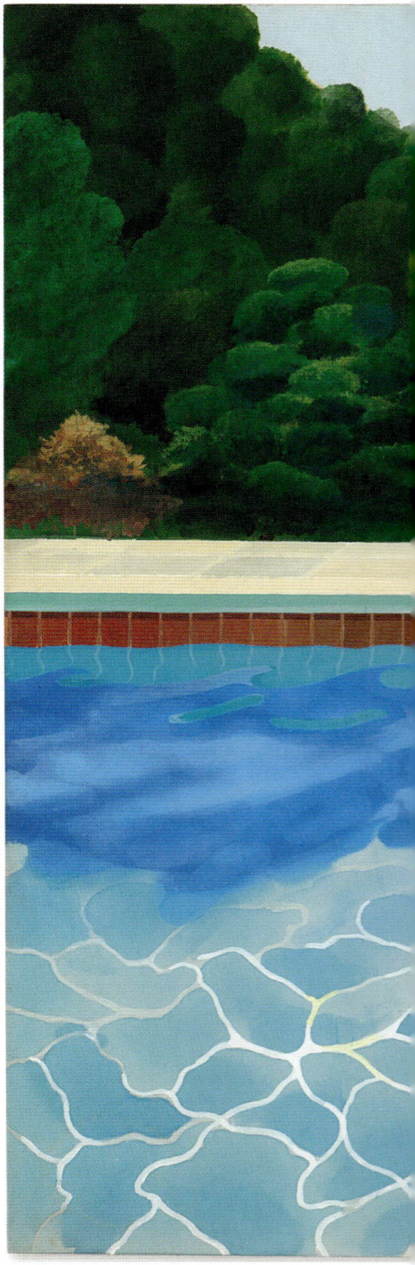

PREVIOUS SPREAD Bolshevik propaganda wasn't subtle, though it could be effective. Russian satirist Viktor Deni's much-reproduced 1919 image *Capital*, made only two years after the start of the Revolution and in the midst of a brutal civil war, draws from a century of radical Western iconography in making the business class the object of derision. Deni's visual idiom is instantly recognizable, found in Western pop culture from the cartoon Scrooge McDuck to the Monopoly board game's Mr. Moneybags.

RIGHT English pop artist David Hockney's 1972 composition *Portrait of an Artist (Pool with Two Figures)* presents a fascinating confluence of both content and context, for his evocation of the emptiness of a particular type of luxury existence enjoyed by the uber-wealthy is only matched by the fact that the painting itself sold at auction in 2018 for $90.3 million. Currently in private collection.

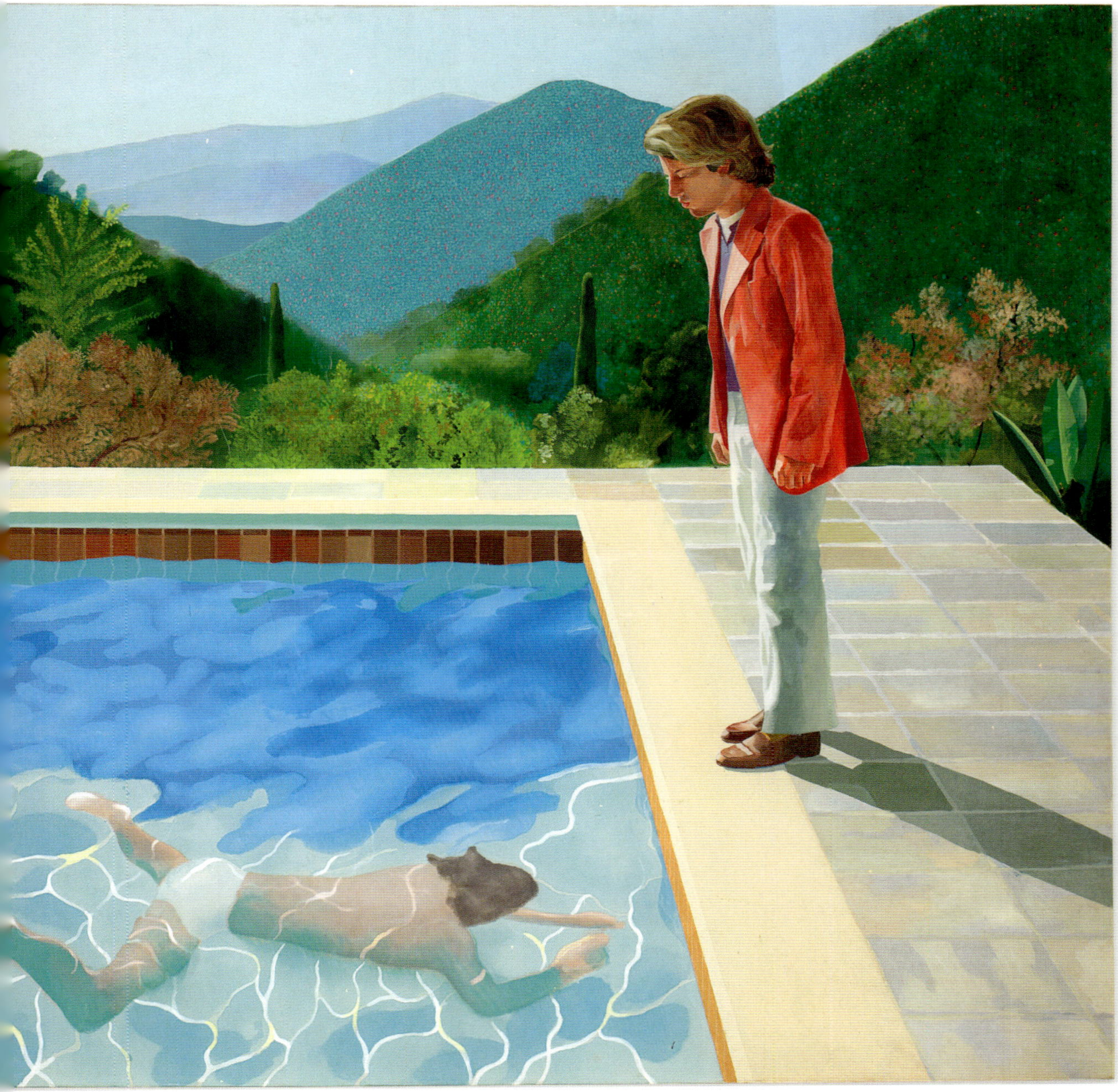

THE ROOT OF ALL EVIL

On a pristine, characteristically blue-skyed and sunny southwestern day, the City University of New York media theorist Douglas Rushkoff found himself spirited from the airport (could have been Palm Springs, Tucson, Sante Fe, etc.) by a private driver in a luxury car chartered by his hosts, soon traveling parallel to the main road on a private highway, the black-tinted windows of the solitary vehicle reflecting back the baking daylight of the desert. Long an advocate for a techno-optimism which affirmed the liberatory potential of Silicon Valley's innovations, Rushkoff had grown disenchanted with how digital robber barons had betrayed the earliest days of the computer revolution. Promised human connection, and we received noxious social media; assured of limitless knowledge, and we got racist memes and deepfakes, revenge porn and propaganda. Once we had the *Whole Earth Catalog*; now surveillance capitalism was our lot. When the Generation X firebrand first advocated for the limitless potential of digital technology in the 1990s, the world was on average a quarter of a degree cooler; in the time since, the ocean levels have risen almost four inches, and some 28 trillion tons of ice have melted, not to mention that around 60 percent of animal populations have been wiped out. If Rushkoff had once seen paradise, now he feared perdition, writing in *Survival of the Riches: Escape Fantasies of the Tech Billionaires* that theirs was a "future that had less to do with making the world a better place than it did with transcending the human condition altogether." While the world burned, Rushkoff realized, society fiddled on laptops and smartphones, the real traded for the virtual, and all of it powered with billions of tons of burnt fossil fuel.

Despite Rushkoff's growing concern over the direction in which the industry was going, and with increasing fears about everything from the dangers of virtual reality to artificial intelligence, many of the richest and most powerful in the technology world still deeply respected the opinions of this former cyberpunk advocate for open-source software and the internet. So it isn't entirely surprising that not long ago, during the second decade of this century, Rushkoff was offered a hefty sum—half of his annual salary—to address a gathering of tech bros and hedge-fund managers about the state of the future. "These people once showered the world with madly optimistic business plans for how technology might benefit human society," Rushkoff writes. Now, "they've reduced technological progress to a video game." Even as Rushkoff's own sympathies moved from the libertarian to the Marxist, he came to speak to these men, for as he explains with an admirable honesty, a gig is a gig; money is money. After being shepherded past the bleak and blasted highway, maybe framed by agave and yucca, or saguaro and autumn sage, they arrived at the front of the resort—a compound, almost—where Rushkoff was driven onto the property in a golf cart by two Patagonia-clad security men. When he finally arrived in the air-conditioned nexus of the facility, perhaps passing by minimalist gray walls and elegant water features, exquisite original art and sculpted bonsai trees, he expected a large auditorium, in which he'd deliver a lecture, the sort of stage we're all familiar with from TED Talks or Apple product demonstrations. Instead, he was ushered

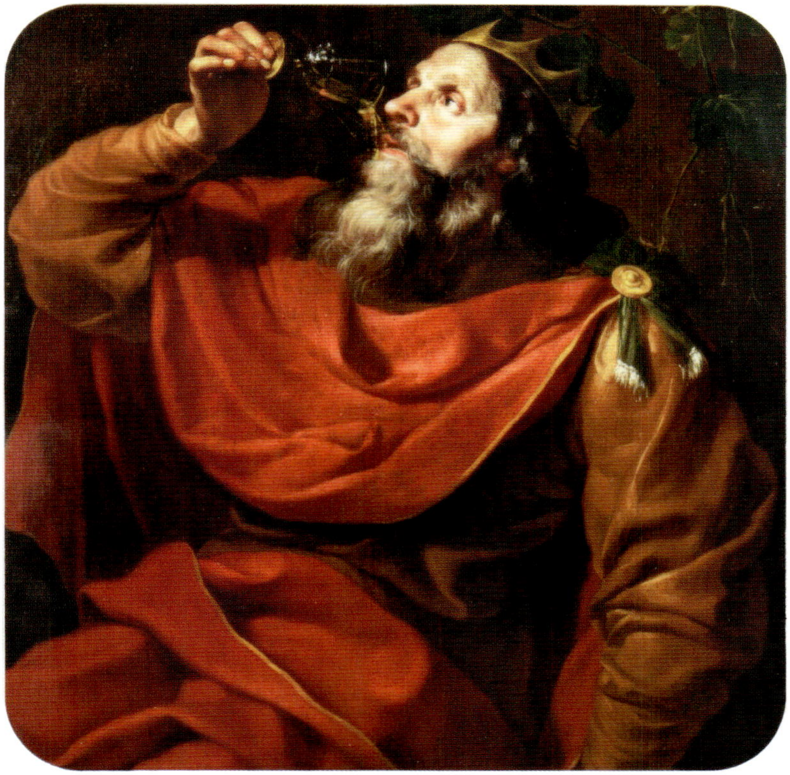

TOP French Baroque painter Nicolas Tournier's 1620 composition turns to a mythological figure (though is possibly based on an actual personage from the eighth century before the Common Era) synonymous with greed, the Phrygian ruler King Midas, who acquired the magical ability to transform anything which he touched into gold, to generate pure wealth as if it were only imaginary numbers on a screen. A dubious gift, this skill, as Tournier's painting shows the monarch valiantly trying to quaff a glass of now inedible wine that has been transformed into liquid gold. Appropriately enough, in a private collection.

into a sterile green room, in which five billionaires, titans of both private finance and technology, sat waiting for Rushkoff.

Jeff Bezos, Bill Gates, Richard Branson, Elon Musk, Peter Thiel—it was all of them, none of them. It doesn't matter who was in there; they're all interchangeable. Lords of Technology, Monarchs of Industry, pages of avarice. Whomever the mysterious billionaires were that invited Rushkoff, just know that they may have been clothed in Stuart Hughes or Alexander Amosu Vanquish II Bespoke, Gucci, Armani, Prada. Or at least they had these things back in the closets of one of their dozens of homes in Manhattan or Miami Beach, Marin County or Martha's Vineyard, along with garages full of Bugatti, Rolls-Royce, Astin Martin, Ferrari. Rushkoff doesn't mention the food, but expect it to have been exquisite; there's no perseveration on refreshment, but for a conference like this, Evian would have been appropriate, even if a bit pedestrian.

The conversation started normally enough; the gathered wanted the theorist's opinions on quantum cryptography and CRISPR gene editing, generative pre-training transformers and nuclear fusion. Then it veered into Silicon Valley woo, digressions about Martian colonization and the possibility of downloading your consciousness onto a hard drive. Finally, the billionaires nervously arrived at what they actually wanted to talk about with Rushkoff, something that they called "The Event." Rushkoff writes that their "extreme wealth and privilege served only to make them obsessed with insulating themselves from the very real and present danger of climate change, rising sea levels, mass migrations, global pandemics, nativist panic, and resource depletion," and so they wanted

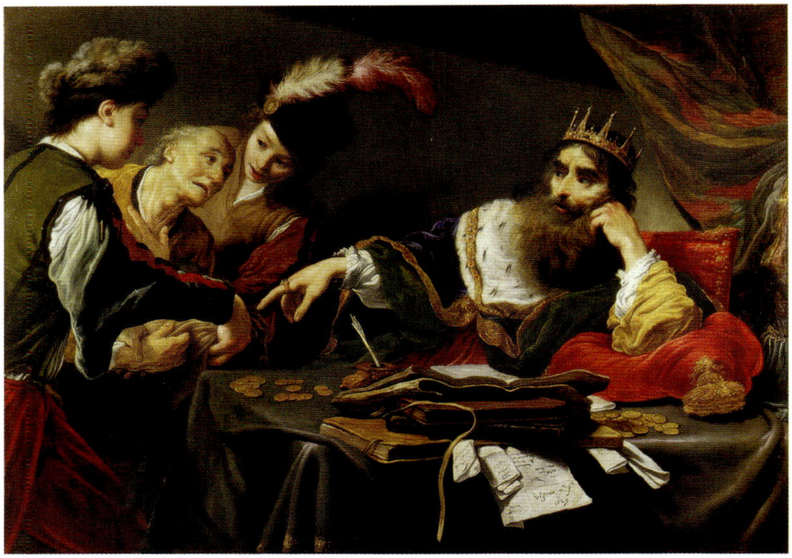

to know how their money could insulate them from the coming apocalypse. The billionaires, and their friends, had bought land in the highlands of New Zealand and amid the redwoods, in the rural Catskills and in remote Scandinavia, with the intent of constructing impenetrable, hidden compounds outfitted with theaters, swimming pools, wine cellars—all of the trappings of their taste and wealth, but insulated from the hungry world dying outside.

There was a problem, however. As they explained to Rushkoff: How should they tame the security forces whom they'd hired to protect them? These rich men were smart enough to know that when the famine comes you can't eat money—*even their blockchain cryptocurrency wouldn't work anymore*—but stupid enough to believe that having once had money still makes them exemplary. So, they brainstormed various schemes to make sure that the private protection firms and former Navy Seals whom they planned to use as muscle in their bunkers wouldn't turn on them once the lights went out. Some of the assembled were of the opinion that food rations should be apportioned from behind a locked room whose entrance combination only the resident billionaire would know, the better to dissuade some guard from bludgeoning the brain where those integral numbers resided. Others thought that they'd do better outfitting their servants with electric collars, even ones which contained explosives, just to prevent any erstwhile post-apocalyptic Spartacus from skirting his duties. Death robots—if the technology could be developed before the collapse—were also considered. A stunned and silent Rushkoff gathered his thoughts and "made pro-social arguments for partnership and solidarity as the best approaches to our collective long-term challenges," positing that loyalty is earned neither through threat of starvation nor electrocution, but rather by investments "in people and relationships." One of the billionaires maybe fiddled with his Patek Phillipe Grandmaster, another perhaps twisted a platinum wedding ring from his third wife. Finally, a tech executive rolled his eyes, then a hedge fund manager laughed. "At least they were getting their money's worth in entertainment," writes Rushkoff. Joviality can be fleeting. Regardless of their influence and their riches, those imaginary numbers on digital ledgers which

TOP Another Phrygian ruler renowned for his wealth and greed, albeit a monarch more firmly substantiated in the historical record, here King Croesus of Lydia reviews a peasant coming to offer scant tribute to a ruler who already has everything. French painter Claude Vignon's 1629 *Croesus Receiving Tribute from a Lydian Peasant* captures the flippancy and boredom of the king and the desperation of the hungry peasant. Original at the Musée des Beaux-Arts in Tours, France.

OPPOSITE As ridiculous and effectively useless as Midas's gold (which at least shines) is, the power of a hundred dollar bill is entirely symbolic; but symbolic power can still destroy the world if we consent to it. American painter Dominik Rutz's 2022 *Style break #1 money* overlays numerous bills over each other, the money then drifting down toward an X and what unmistakably looks like blood.

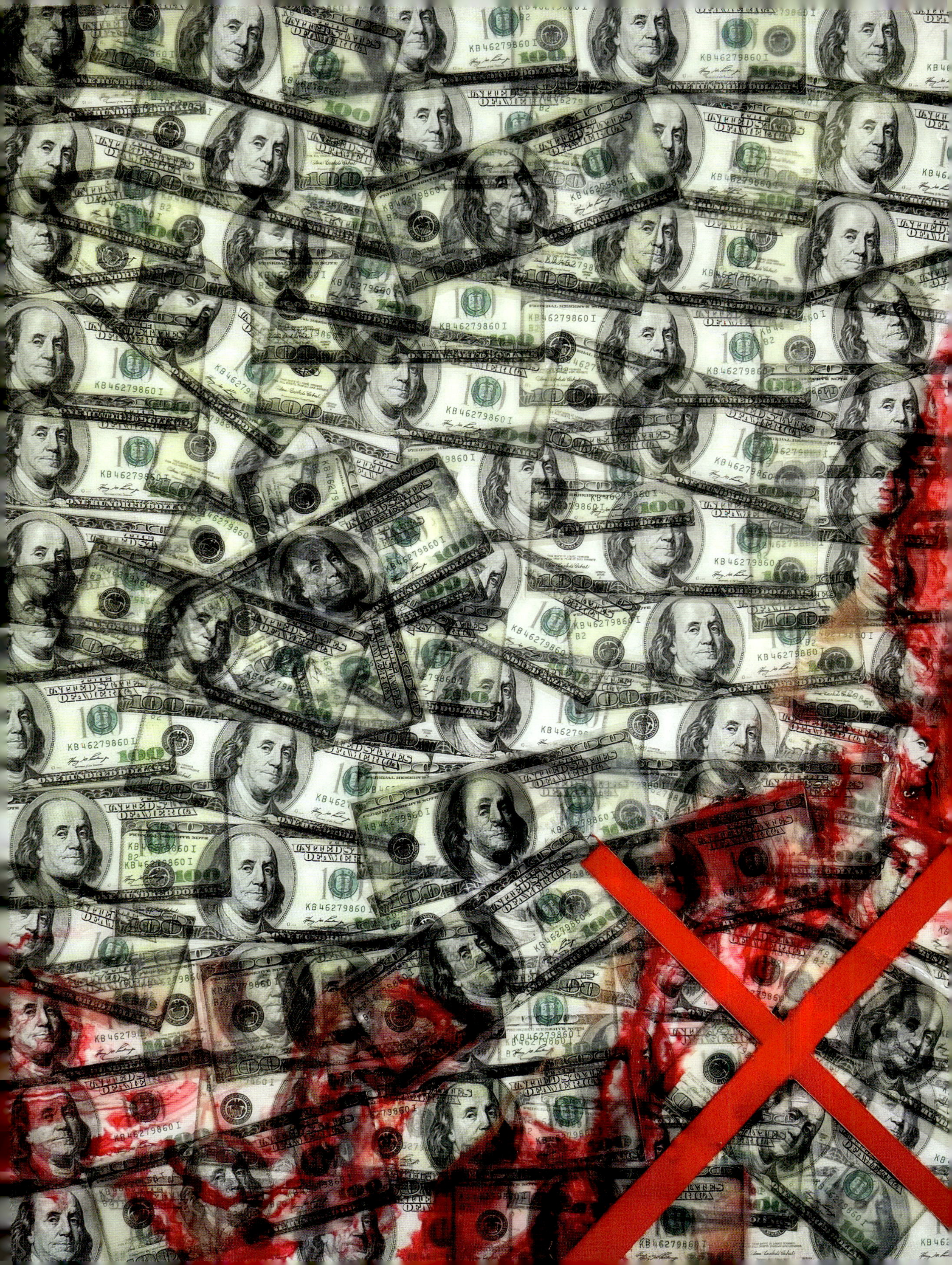

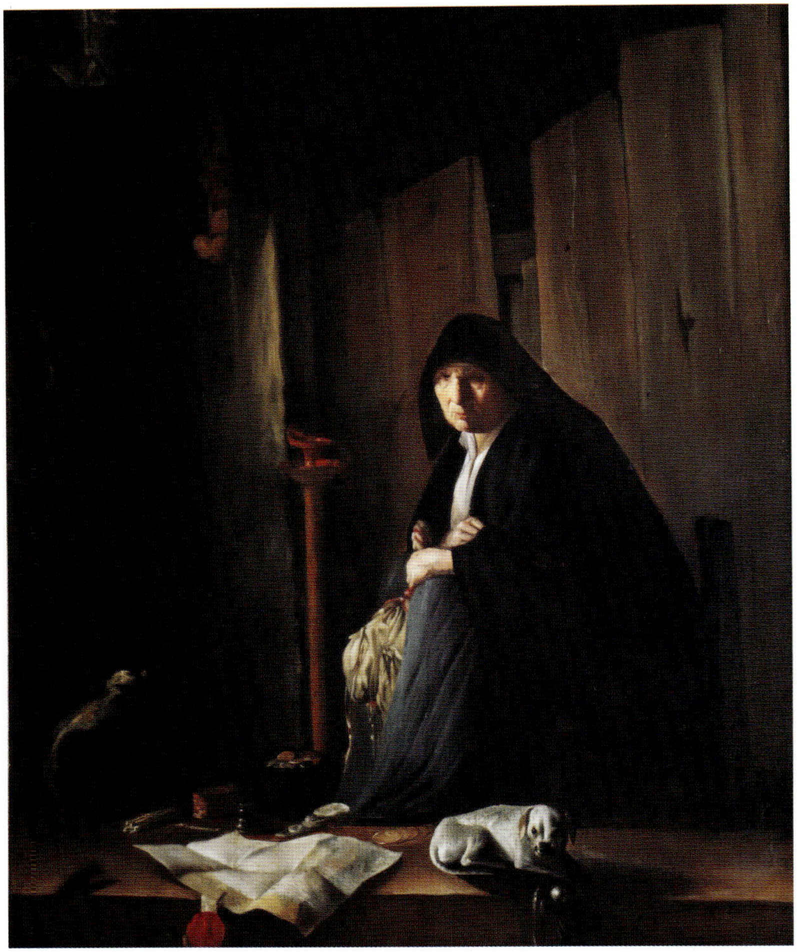

nonetheless increase exponentially without regulation, their privatized power accountable to nobody (which is all that wealth really is), these men were haughty, condescending, foolish, greedy, and deathly afraid. And they should be. There will be no escape hatch from the world which they created.

Because all of us are implicated in the network of associations that requires the arbitrary construction which we call money—whether we're capitalist or socialist, communist or anarchist, we all need cash—there is something about greed that innately makes sense, at least a little bit. Money is needed to pay electric and water bills, to make rent and buy groceries, which is to say, it signifies security. It would be a mistake, however, to think that the safety desired by Rushkoff's billionaires is just an issue of degree and not of kind. Genuine greed becomes jaundiced, cannibalistic. Regardless of what the Libertarian Party or the U.S. Chamber of Commerce might say, the accumulation of more and more is not dictated by inviolate rational principles as parsimonious as Euclid; rather, the origin of avarice is in a darker place, a more secret place, and it requires a rhetoric of theology rather than the inanities of economics.

Disregarding all but the most lefthand of paths, the preponderance of religious traditions have little good to say about greed (secular philosophies, from Bernard

TOP An anonymous seventeenth-century Dutch painting, though possibly attributable to Paulus Bor, entitled *Avarice*, allegorically depicting the sin as a crone only kept company by a guard dog, wealthy but without luxury, rich but without connection. Original at the Cummer Museum in Jacksonville, Florida.

OPPOSITE The Italian painter Jacopo Ligozzi also personified greed as a woman in the 1590 *Allegory of Avarice*, original at the Metropolitan Museum of Art in New York. As with the potential Bor composition, Ligozzi's Avarice sits shrouded in darkness, a bowl of jewelry at her feet; yet in this vision, winged death whispers in her ear. It's ambiguous as to whether death is the result of greed, or merely the universal inevitability for which wealth offers no rescue . . .

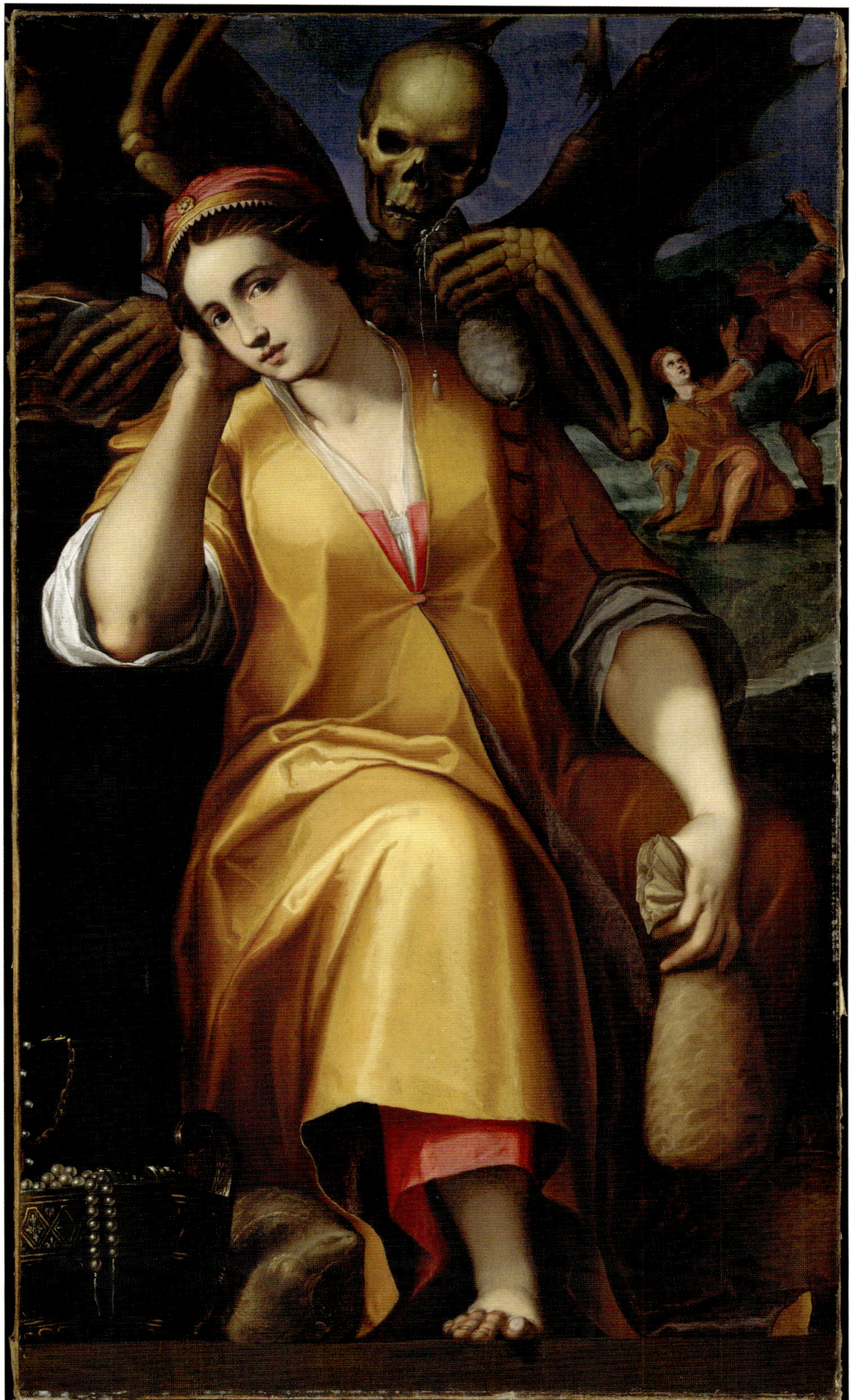

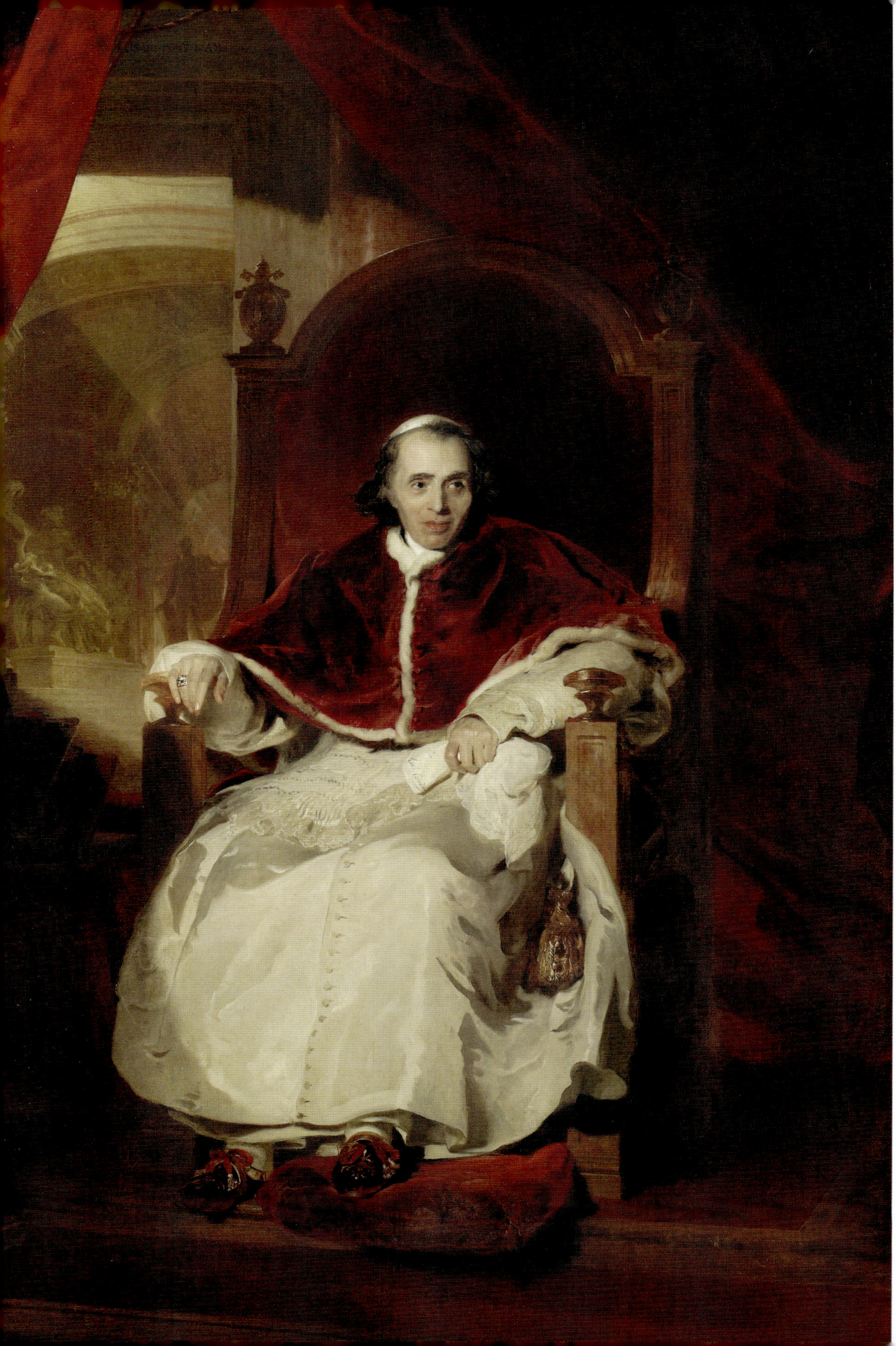

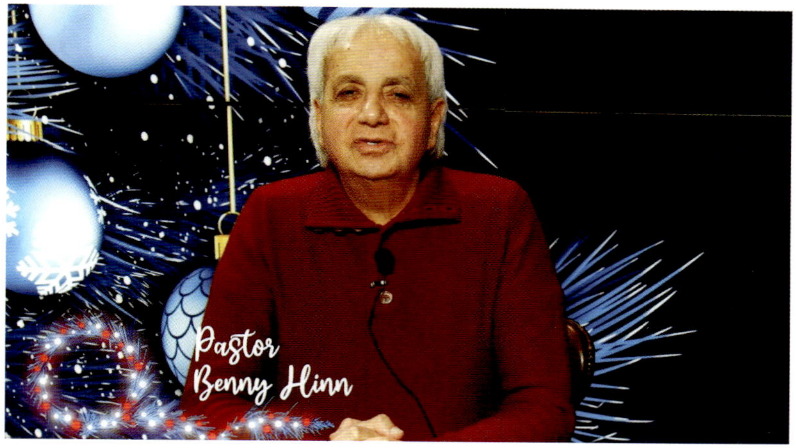

Mandeville to the entire University of Chicago Economics Department, can be rather different). The Decalogue, at least by condemning greed's close relation of envy, warns about avarice and thus marks all of the Abrahamic traditions that stem from Sinai. Yet this was hardly a novelty, as twenty-four centuries before, Christ had preached that it was easier for a camel to get through the eye of a needle than for the rich to enter God's Kingdom; the Egyptian vizier Ptahhotep warned his Pharaoh that he should "Beware an act of avarice; it is a bad and incurable disease." Ptahhotep's is among the earliest of a recurring theme when it comes to pathologizing greed, for while the pragmatic aspects of how covetousness can both upend social order and instigate conflict are obvious, many of the sages who condemn avarice do so by emphasizing how it can canker the soul. "The healthy man drinks and his thirst is gone: the other is delighted for a moment and then grows giddy, the water turns to gall, and he vomits and has colic," notes the first-century Roman Stoic Epictetus. "Such is the condition of the man who is haunted by desire in wealth." There is a distinction here to be made between rational self-interest, which can also upend social order and instigate conflict, and the insatiability of genuine greed, which only seeks to plug the hole in a sinking boat with more and more water. Solomon, among the richest of men in the history of the world, understood this well, writing in Ecclesiastes 5:10 that "He that loveth silver shall not be satisfied with silver; nor he that loveth abundance with increase." The failure is not in gold itself, but rather in the heart which covets it.

While most faiths condemn greed, few did so in as otherworldly a way as the anti-materialistic early Christians. It's hard to imagine today, after two millennia of pontiffs ruling in bejeweled robes and, more recently, evangelical mega-pastors bragging about their private jets and bespoke pastel suits, but the political theology of the early Church is arguably the most radically egalitarian of philosophies ever uttered. Christ's Sermon on the Mount, delivered in the Gospel of Matthew, is an obvious example of Christianity's urging of us to turn away from the gilded things of this world. "Blessed are the poor in spirit," intones Christ, "for theirs is the kingdom of Heaven," where the lowly shall be raised and the high struck down. Cynics may note the phrasing here, perhaps finding some wiggle room whereby one can be poor in spirit and rich in bank account (certainly that's been a way to slip through that eye of the needle), but there are other portions of

OPPOSITE A portrait of the eighteenth-century Pope Pius VII, ruler of the wealthy Papal States, as painted by Thomas Lawrence and held by the Royal Collection

TOP The American televangelist Reverend Benny Hinn, an advocate for the so-called "prosperity gospel," which teaches that any donations to the church will financially return ten-fold.

the New Testament where Christ's opinions toward the wealthy are delineated, Jesus making His feelings clear not just on the mount, but in utero as when Mother Mary prophetically thunders in the Magnificat that "He hath put down the mighty from their seats, and exalted them of low degree."

Christ's adopted brother James, author of the eponymous epistle and leader of the Jerusalem Church, and whose worshipers were known as Ebionites, writes in the earliest written portion of the New Testament, "Go to now, ye rich men, weep and howl for your miseries that shall come upon you. Your riches are corrupted, and your garments are motheaten. Your gold and silver is cankered; and the rust of them shall be a witness against you, and shall eat your flesh as it were fire." Not only does James castigate the capitalist—he raises up the worker. "Behold, the hire of the laborers who have reaped down your fields, which is of you kept back by fraud," a class analysis commensurate with a Bakunin or Marx. None of this was theory for those in the apostolic age, who believed that they were living during the end of history. Explicitly describing the social arrangements of the earliest Christians as "communistic," the contemporary New Testament translator David Bentley Hart explains that the gospel, "alarmingly enough, condemns personal wealth not merely as a moral danger, but as an intrinsic evil," adding that "Christ condemned not only an unhealthy preoccupation with riches, but rather the getting and keepings of riches as such." For those who try to ascribe modern politics to the first generation of Christians, pretending that they're either conservatives or liberals, the only ideology which can even roughly fit is a sort of low-church anarchism; collectives of women and men neutered of wealth, family, identity, sharing all in common and abiding by the belief that private property is a sin. As to the greedy, the miserly, the wealthy, James looks through the green-hued mists and sees bunkers with luxury theaters and wine cellars, swimming pools and garages filled with sports cars, all guarded by hungry security forces, noting to the Anthropocene's billionaires that "Ye have heaped treasure together for the last days."

Taking their cue from religion—often the horse that pulls the cart of so-called secular philosophy—a wide gauntlet of thinkers similarly chastised greed. Following Aristotle, the bulk of these arguments against avarice were focused on that personality defect's tendency to abrogate disunion and strife. Jean-Jacques Rousseau, that great fantasist of man's nobility in some presumed state of nature, contrasted the simplicity and egalitarianism of that condition with the stratified social reality which is visible to even those unwilling to look. In his 1755 tract *On the Origin of Inequality,* Rousseau describes the final iteration of the wealthy man's soul, explaining that "after a long course of prosperity, after having swallowed up treasures and ruined multitudes, the hero ends up by cutting every throat till he finds himself, at last, sole master of the world," and then

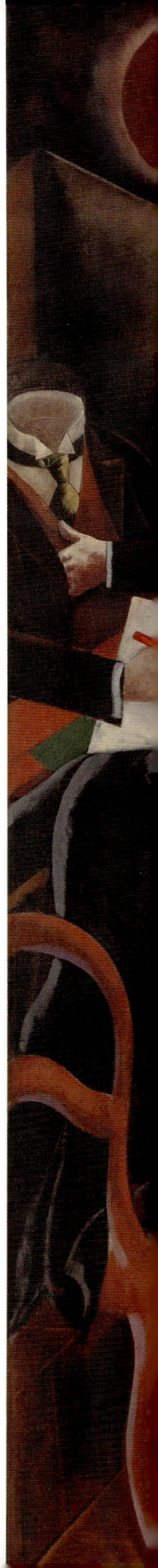

OPPOSITE Weimar-era satirist George Grosz takes a jaundiced view of the intersections of German militarism and capitalism in his 1926 *Eclipse of the Sun,* original held at the Heckscher Museum of Art in Huntington, New York.

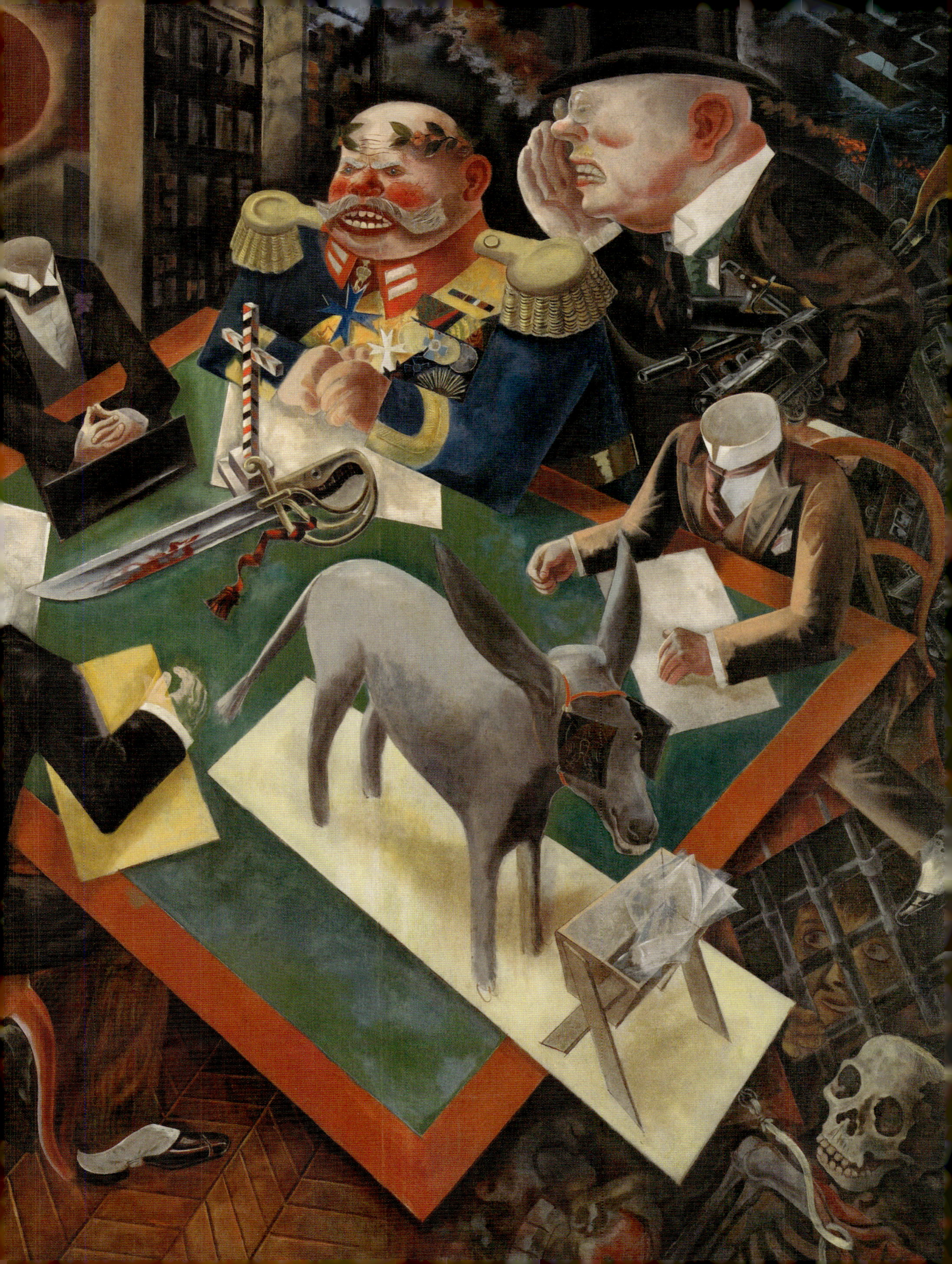

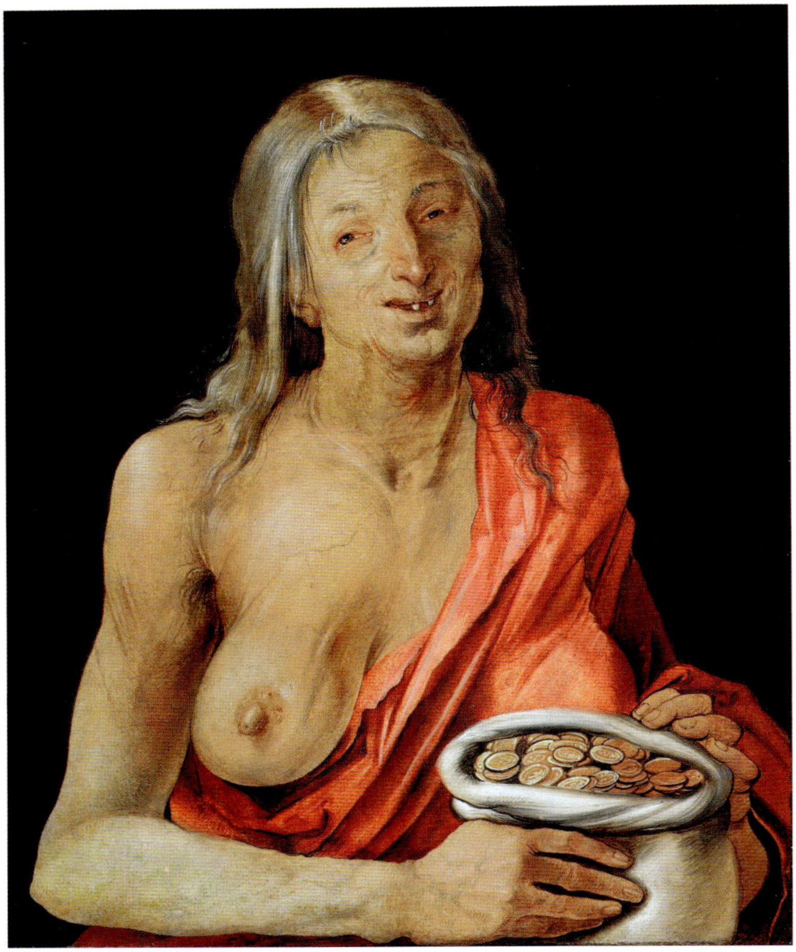

whether with, like Alexander, no other worlds to conquer, the rich man might not press cold blade to his own warm flesh. A century later, that Russian count Leo Tolstoy, who had as of late affected the persona of a peasant, was capable of seeing greed from both sides of the class divide, developing a Christian anarchism that as with the original variety eschewed the lures of materialism, concluding in his 1886 tract *What Then Must We Do?* that "Money, in itself, is evil." His contemporary Karl Marx was more damning than even the mystic Tolstoy, understanding greed not merely as a facet of some individual psyches, but as a permeating structure throughout the organization of society. Despite being an avowed materialist, Marx's vision was not so different from that of the Orthodox contemplative when it came to seeing the spiritual canker which avarice encouraged in everything, the way that it figuratively curdles milk and rots food. According to Marx in the first volume of his *Capital*, "avarice and the desire to get rich are the ruling passions" of the capitalist class, a toxic condition which ultimately inculcates a "Faustian bargain" within the soul of the miser and the manager, the boss and the owner.

Of course, the poets—a hungry vocation, though rarely a greedy one—have put their thoughts about avarice onto the pages of eternity's guest book. Dante,

ABOVE Despite her sack of golden marks, the allegorical figure in Albrecht Dürer's 1507 painting *Avarice* is threadbare and withered, a toothless hag naked and cackling, without shame but seemingly enmeshed in a strange, joyless fever dream. The point is abundantly clear—all of that money does nothing to actually make this woman happy. Original at Kunst History Museum in Vienna.

OPPOSITE Mexican painter and adamant Marxist Diego Rivera presents another satirical image of the corpulent and spoiled wealthy wallowing in their own luxury in his 1928 mural *The Capitalist Dinner*, original mural at the Secretariate of Education Building in Mexico City.

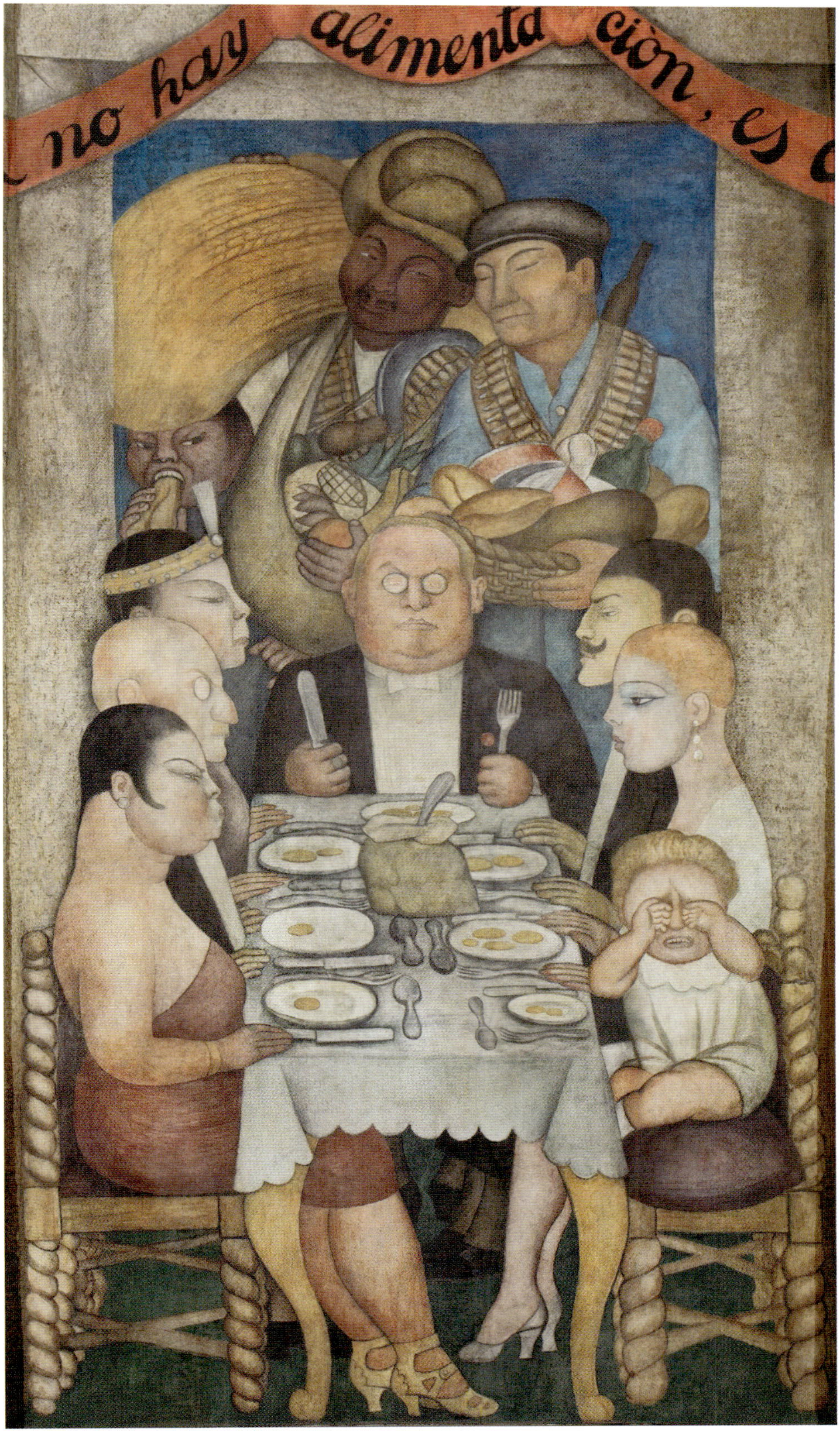
no hay alimenta ción, es

inheritor of a Christian civilization which was still vigorous enough to condemn greed (if not always to be consistent about it), places those guilty of avarice in the fourth circle of his nine circles of Hell. The Italian poet divides the greedy between two classes: the frugal misers who cling to so much wealth that could do good for others; and their opposites, the lavish spenders who enjoy all of the sensual pleasures which money can purchase. Both are within the tribe of the greedy, and both fundamentally waste wealth either by holding on to it or using it, abusing their fortune by rejecting the charitable option of finding those who could benefit from it and giving it away. Now, in perdition, they forever joust one another, weighed down by their own riches which now hang on them as if anchors. "I saw a nation of lost souls," Dante recounts of his vision, "they strained their chests / against enormous weights, and with mad howls / rolled them at one another. Then in haste / they rolled them back, one party shouting out: / 'Why do you hoard?' and the other: 'Why do you waste?,'" the ticker tape of the stock counter now mattering little over the dun cacophony of the inferno. Whatever metaphysical associations greed may have once had, its material damages are still obvious, and contemporary poets are sometimes no less lurid than Dante and just as concerned with the cost of so much wealth. The Harlem Renaissance poet Claude McKay's 1922 lyric compares the wealthy to birds of prey, making the primal, animalistic, bestial nature of avarice clear, writing that their "shadow dims the sunshine of our day . . . They swoop down for the spoil in certain might, / And fasten in our bleeding flesh their claws . . . And tugging and tearing without let or pause, / They flap their hideous wings in grim delight, / And stuff our gory hearts into their maws." Positively Dantean in his imagery, McKay is describing hawks and falcons, vultures and kites, but he's writing about strike-breakers and landlords, developers and managers.

Secular philosophy—even though historically, it's been as critical of greed as has religion—also has had less difficulty for the large part in squaring the circle of righteousness and wealth when it wants to, so that the pious can be hypocritical, but the clever are often merely wicked. There are, of course, the dictates of religion and culture, the pious platitudes uttered by priests and poets about the degradations of greed, but as has often been observed, few of us are willing (or, more fairly, able) to always turn away cash. Still, the ranks of those who publicly denounce greed include quite a few who in their souls are more than fine with pursuing their own selfish aims (sometimes while denouncing greed itself—check the price on this book). Arguably, this is a class of honest philosophers, figures like the seventeenth-century Bernard Mandeville, who in his 1714 *The Fable of the Bees* called greed "that noble sin," hypothesizing that "private vice can be publicly beneficial." This was a hinge moment in intellectual history for attempting to justify avarice, though the Protestant Reformation of two centuries before had done much to placate the minds of the greedy about the virtues of financial accumulation (though spending it on anything other than further investments was another matter), and Italian bankers since the Renaissance, then followed by the rest of Europe, had had little trouble practicing usury. Mandeville suggests that all of this might be good. According to him, there was no shame in greed; such private selfishness could be tethered to the collective progress of the economy, of the society. Arguably the first libertarian, Mandeville was far more unsparing in his encomiums to avarice than was, several decades later, Adam Smith, the English

OPPOSITE An anonymous fifteenth-century Flemish painting by a follower of Marinus van Reymerswaele. It's unclear whether the figures in *The Two Misers* are bankers or tax collectors, but regardless, the sense of greed is palpable, particularly in the knowing sneer of the figure on the right. Renaissance bankers overcame their squeamishness about charging usury (or interest), the foundation of all speculative investment. Original held by the British Royal Trust.

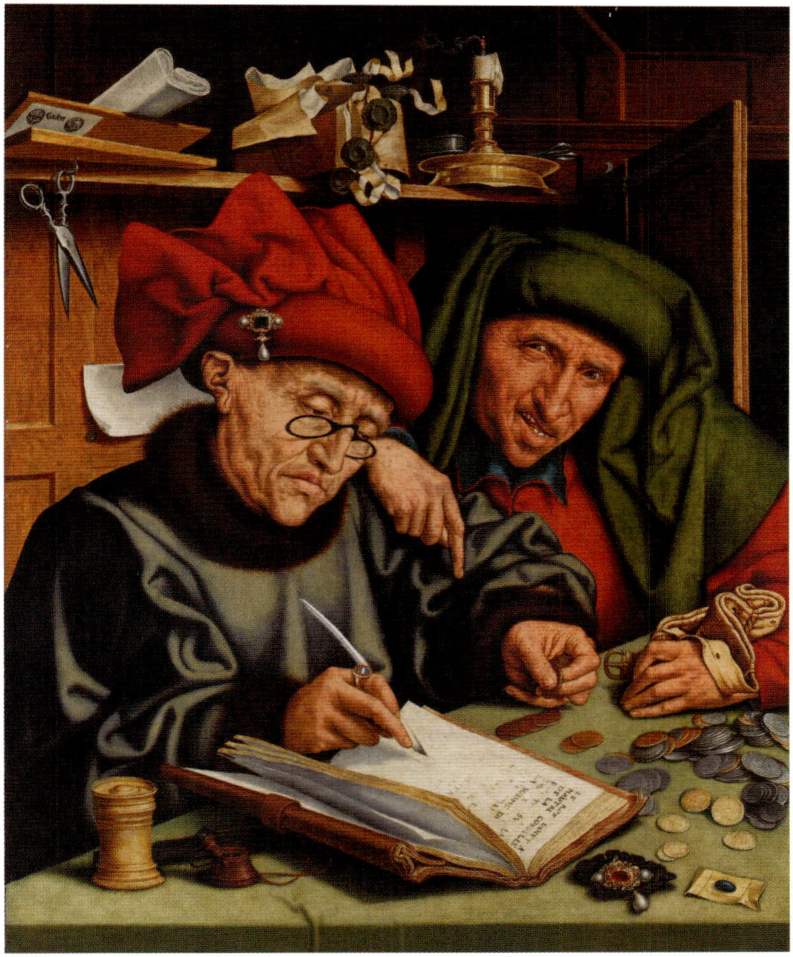

economist who has often been blamed for capitalist excess. Smith in fact offered a far more circumspect celebration of the free market than his reputation would suggest, one which maintained that the natural tendency to avarice must be kept in check with strong regulation. Modern libertarianism, condemning the tyranny of the government but celebrating the privatized equivalent from the wealthy, had no such scruples, despite the fact that Smith lauded the wisdom of a mythic "Invisible Hand" that would right the ship of the economy through the rational interaction of self-interested men.

Twentieth-century economists like Friedrich Hayek, Ludwig von Mises, and Milton Friedman were responsible for, depending on your perspective, either expelling hypocrisy from the greedy heart of an intelligentsia that had long prided poverty and condemned wealth, or who had with gleeful abandon welcomed the money changers back into the Temple. First trained in the context of Austrian economics departments, many of these luminaries would settle along Lake Michigan in the University of Chicago Economics Department, developing an ethos which held that taxation was theft, regulation was strangulation, and greed was good. Von Mises's 1951 paper "Profit and Loss" emphatically declares

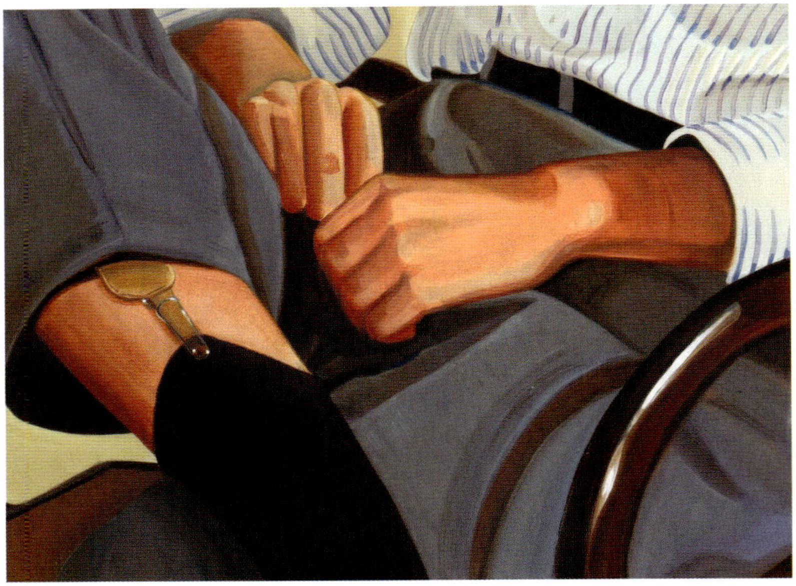

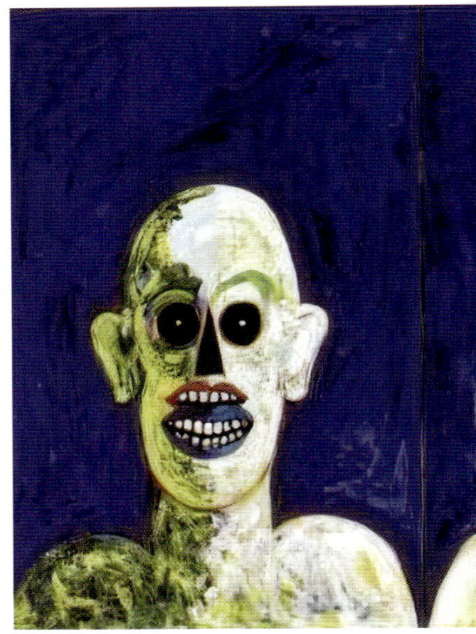

that "There is no reason why capitalists and entrepreneurs should be ashamed of earning profits," proudly displaying his own black soul by stating that nobody "has the right to talk as if he were Francis d'Assisi" (of course St. Francis presumably has that right, but that's of no accounting). Most mainstream economists were unconvinced by the libertarian claims to the goodness of eliminating regulation and allowing greed to propagate unfettered; beyond even the moral qualms about such thinking, figures like John Maynard Keynes had long maintained that such avarice was simply irrational, that it was in no way the ideal way for a society to function properly, even if it was the ideal way for a small number of people to become spectacularly rich.

Yet by the 1980s, the supply-side partisans were no longer just in Hyde Park, but now advising in London and Washington, the court philosophers of the Reagan and Thatcher regimes who began privatizing government services, slashing taxes for the wealthy, and removing even the barest of regulations holding them toward a common good. Underneath a mantle of "Liberty," while ignoring that nothing is free if you're poor, the libertarian credo became the faith of our soulless world. This was the variety of grotesquerie that allowed Murray Rothbard, the father of anarcho-libertarianism who was often even anathema to his ideological companions, to opine in his 1982 *The Ethics of Liberty* that he found the right of the individual to be greedy so sacrosanct, and the responsibility of the state to enforce even a minimum of goodness so objectionable, that he could only conclude that a parent "should not have a legal obligation to feed, clothe, or education his children," that the law could not "compel the parent to feed a child or to keep it alive." Those who, like Rothbard, are so enmeshed within sin that they can no longer even see it, acquire an almost admirable honesty, the sort of bluntness that allowed the stock trader Ivan Boesky to remark in a 1986 graduation speech at the University of California, Berkeley, where two decades before students had dreamt of a utopia but had long since traded in their

TOP LEFT American painter Leonard Baby's 2022 composition *Keeping It Up* is part of a new trend of depicting so-called quiet luxury, markers of wealth and class that are more inauspicious than during the cocaine eighties and the dot-com nineties, but which nonetheless celebrate money (not least among those who can afford to buy such luxury items). "I think about materialism and capitalism all the time," Baby told *Artsy*. "It's my closest friend and worst enemy."

TOP RIGHT Contemporary Greek-American painter Lucas Samaras's aptly named *The Collectors,* featured in the apartment of the character Gordon Gekko, as played by Michael Douglas, in the 1987 film *Wall Street*, Oliver Stone's classic exploration of eighties excess. Partially based on Boesky, Gekko famously claims, "Greed is good."

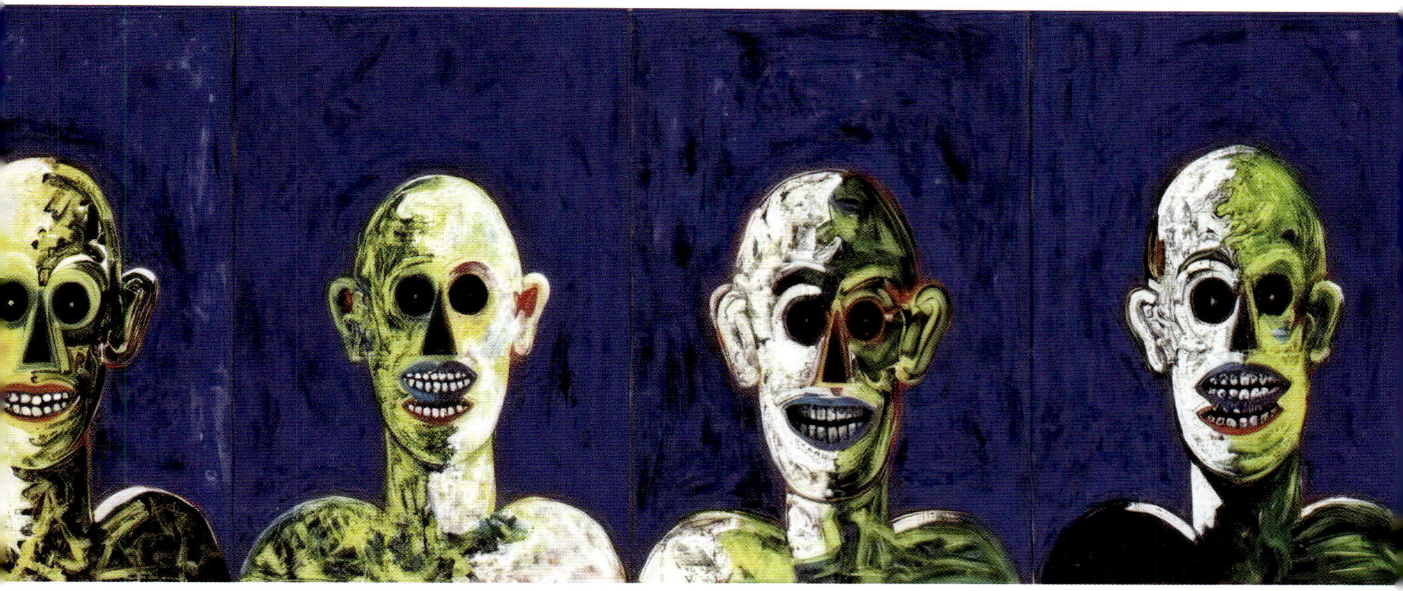

hippie values for their yuppie benefits, that "Greed is all right, by the way. I want you to know that . . . You can be greedy and still feel good about yourself." All the guilt had been drained from the feeling, but that doesn't mean the cold metal of Rousseau's blade isn't still at all of our throats.

Because the most salacious lie of the sectarians of selfishness wasn't that greed doesn't feel good—it does, sometimes. It wasn't that greed isn't a powerful engine for accumulating profit—of course it is. And it's not that greed isn't an aspect of human nature—clearly that's the case. It's that greed is *rational.* It's all those millions of words written by libertarian philosophers and free market economists claiming that the unrepentant, unredeemed, unapologetic rapacious accumulation of more and more and more in any way makes sense. Perhaps it does for the individual, for a bit, but sooner or later the Invisible Hand takes that blade to all of our throats, and five hedge fund managers find themselves in a conference room wondering how they'll prevent their own servants from killing them in the night. Were greed as rational as the Devil says it is, then the sleep of the wealthy would be blissfully uninterrupted—any choice that requires one to keep one eye open for fear of being smothered lacks in sense. The libertarian defending such beliefs would say that rational self-interest requires caution, that there is nothing unethical or irrational about locking the door, and perhaps that's true. But the all-knowing and all-seeing Invisible Hand is a deity that doesn't have human interests at heart, for that was the arm which dug the coal and drilled the oil, the hunger that demanded petroleum for money, and were it not for that appendage, we wouldn't currently be facing an apocalypse of its making.

Our current situation is not just irrational, or foolish, or even just stupid, but it's absurd in an almost cosmic sense, a divine sense. All of our tradition and culture, our philosophy and theology, has denounced the machinations of greed, but a carefully calibrated mechanism of duplicity and bad faith convinced

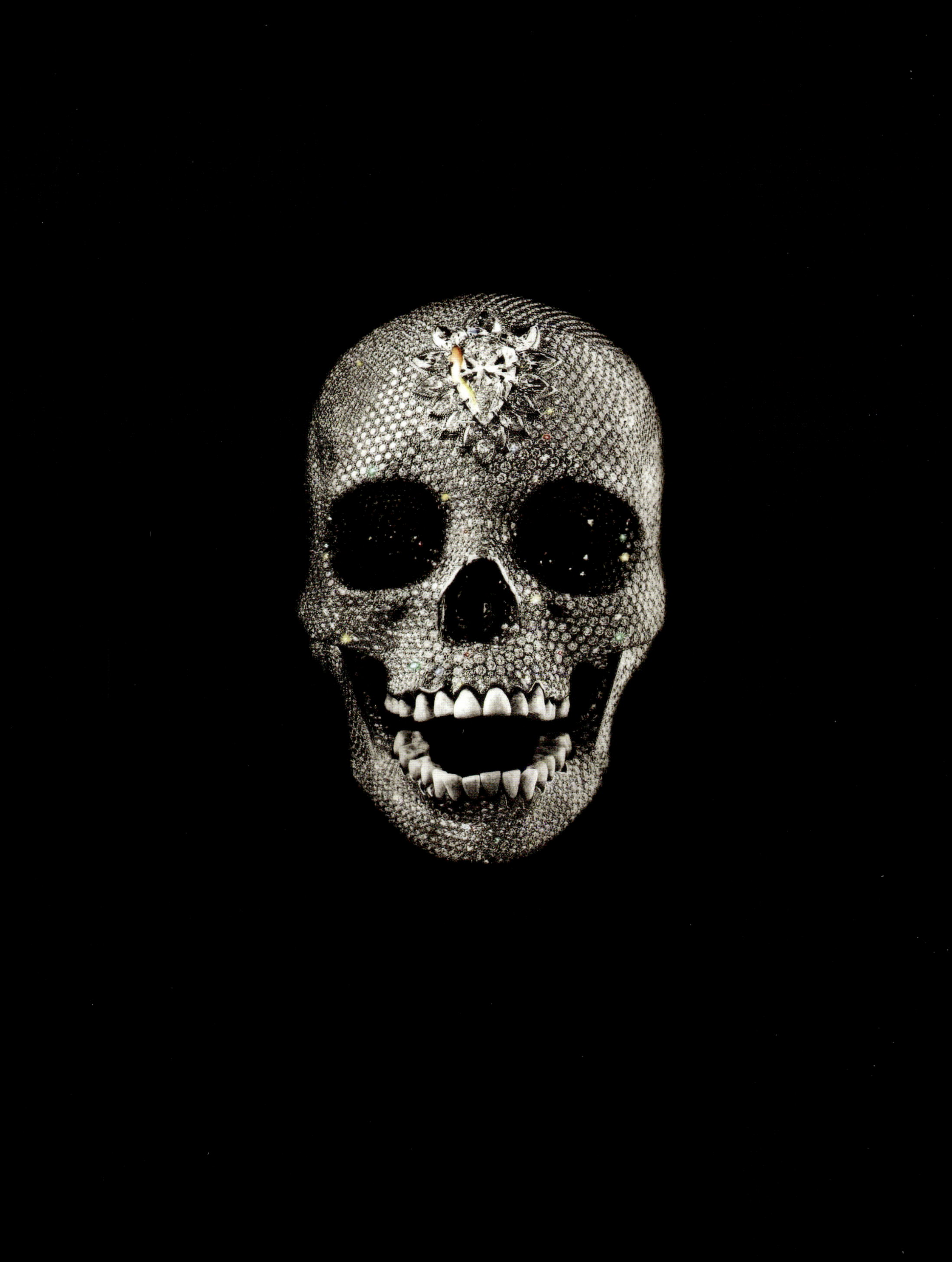

industrialists and politicians alike that that which we all know to be a nihilistic evil was secretly very logical—a parsimonious, elegant, and sophisticated way to order a society. The price we pay for that nonsense is complete economic collapse. And yet those mavens of industry who have written this conclusion for the human species dig on, they drill on, they make money onward, and they know that the end is coming for all (but maybe not them, they believe). The psychologist Erich Fromm described such a mentality aptly in his 1941 study *Escape from Freedom,* writing that "Greed is a bottomless pit which exhausts the person in an endless effort to satisfy the need without ever reaching satisfaction." More pragmatic than that is the ancient Cree prophecy which states that "When the last tree is cut down, the last fish eaten and the last stream poisoned, you will realize that you cannot eat money." With any justice, may this be the last fleeting thought of some billionaire in some bunker.

INTERLUDE—AYN RAND

Next to Ayn Rand's open casket at her 1982 funeral there was a six-foot-tall floral arrangement in the shape of a dollar sign, sent by her sometime lover, and always acolyte, future Federal Reserve chairman Alan Greenspan. Beyond the obvious reasons, it was appropriate for Rand, because where the intent was elegance, the result was tackiness; meant to advertise wealth, it actually exhibited cheapness; understood as clever, it was actually prosaic. No "writer" has so valorized avarice; no "philosopher" has so enshrined greed. Rand's ideology strips away even a gesture toward morality in its supply-side, free-market fantasies of individualism. "I refuse to apologize for my ability—I refuse to apologize for my success—I refuse to apologize for my money," one of Rand's numerous mouthpieces declares in her 1,168-page *Atlas Shrugged*—though she'd have done well to ask for forgiveness for all of those things. Her hatred of any sort of government assistance, it should be noted, didn't stop Rand from enlisting in Social Security and Medicare a few years before she died.

Born to an upwardly mobile couple in St. Petersburg, Rand's family lost everything to the Bolsheviks. A permanent hatred for altruistic economic policies—whether from communists or New Deal Democrats—or that tribe of now-extinct liberal Republicans, for that matter—marked her tenure in the United States. Desiring to be seen as a serious intellectual, the chain-smoking Russian was at heart a natural entertainer, and she took to the ethos of her adopted country. California was where she met her husband, Frank O'Connor; drawing on Rand's experience in the Russian theater, both were extras in the Cecil B. DeMille film *The King of Kings,* with Rand successfully negotiating being cast as an aristocrat rather than a peasant. A screenwriter in Hollywood and playwright on Broadway, she found the success she coveted with *The Fountainhead*, a novel about a modernist architect who refuses to alter his totalizing creative vision and must battle with

OPPOSITE In part because it was so critically hated, cool Britannia *enfant terrible* Damian Hirst's 2007 sculpture featuring an eighteenth-century skull covered in 8,601 perfect diamonds and entitled *For the Love of God* is the greatest work of art produced in this century. Manufactured for twelve million pounds, this grinning skull from Adam Smith's time period carries a sacrilegious air, cackling out to us like a Yorick from the origins of capitalism.

insipid bureaucrats and the lumpenproletariat not worthy of living in his universe. Howard Roark barks that "I do not recognize anyone's right to one minute of my life. Nor to any part of my energy. Nor to any achievement of mine. No matter who makes the claim, how large their number or how great their need." Boastful is the man who changed his own diapers in infancy.

Rand's innumerable flat and wooden characters, such as her idealized businessman John Galt in *Atlas Shrugged,* with his turgid sixty-page speech about the goodness of greed, announced her philosophy of rapacious avarice and feigned rationality known as Objectivism. A system that reads like Friedrich Nietzsche crossed with Adam Smith and covered in a sprinkling of Herbert Spencer, though as if none of them had never said a single interesting thing, Objectivism brandishes the word "reason" as a totem while advocating for naked self-interest as the only coherent way to organize a society. Too much credit would be given if we blamed Rand alone for economic privatization, the increasing gulf between rich and poor, and ecological degradation, but she certainly supplied the sticky veneer of pseudo-intellectual justification for the greed.

She may be anathema in the elite academy, but though Rand snobbishly hated the mob, the public has loved her (and besides, her own tastes veered toward Mickey Spillane and *Charlie's Angels*). A Library of Congress poll revealed *Atlas Shrugged* to be Americans' second-most favorite book following the Bible, and a Modern Library survey placed that book at number one—and *The Fountainhead* at number two. An astounding six-and-a-half million copies of *The Fountainhead* have been sold; half a million more of *Atlas Shrugged* have been purchased. Were Rand read only by the one college freshman you avoided, that would be one thing, but she's enjoyed by some of the worst and most powerful people. Silicon Valley weirdos like Elon Musk, Peter Thiel, and Mark Zuckerberg have all voiced their admiration; Ivana Trump reports that other than the book of Hitler's speeches her husband used to keep by their bedside, *The Fountainhead* is one of the few novels

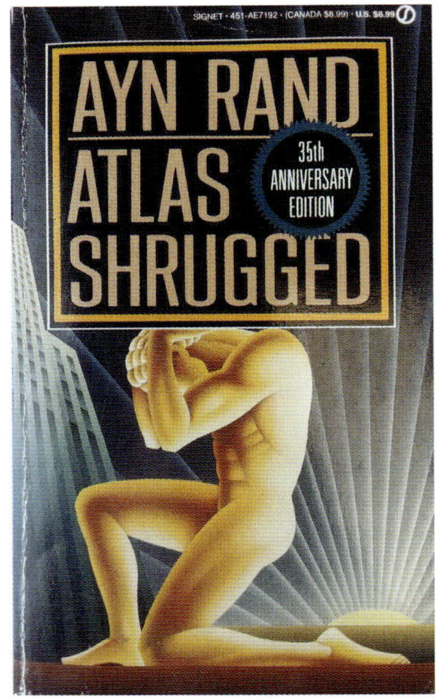

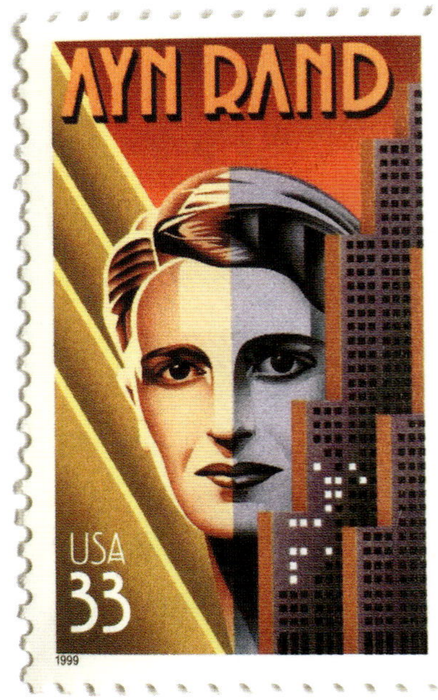

TOP Despite her supposed valorization of liberty and freedom, Rand's own aesthetics—drawing from a diversity of sources, notably art deco design—also evoked the visual idiom of totalitarianism, as seen in this muscular figure on the cover of her 1957 novel *Atlas Shrugged*.

BOTTOM A striking art deco–influenced image of Rand rendered in 1999, almost two decades after her death and reflecting her popularity, which endures despite her lack of critical accolades. Having sold over thirty-seven million copies, and regularly topping surveys of the most widely read books, Rand has earned a spot in a sort of "shadow canon" separate from academic approval. With some irony, then, that's perhaps why this particular portrait was painted for a postal stamp, an artifact of the United States Postal Service, among the most popular and massive of government bureaucracies. Courtesy of the National Postal Museum, Washington, DC.

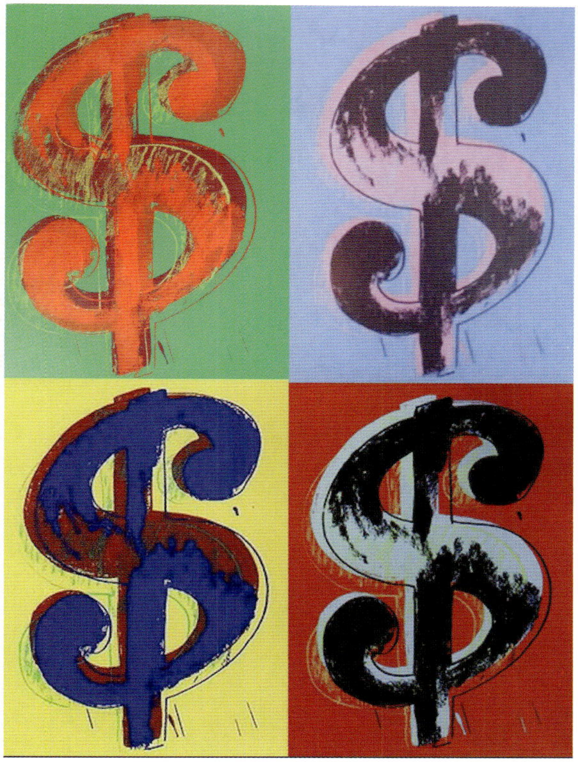

he's ever gotten through. Since the Reagan revolution (a president for whom she had little affection), Rand's vision has been cultishly promulgated by those failed academics who skulk the halls of conservative Beltway thinktanks like the Cato Institute and the Heritage Foundation, ghouls who publish position papers about cutting funding for school lunch programs and deregulating food safety.

"Let anyone who believes that a high standard of living is the achievement of labor unions and government controls ask himself the following question," Rand wrote in *Capitalism: The Unknown Ideal:* "If one had a 'time machine' and transported the united labor chieftains of America, plus three million government bureaucrats, back to the tenth century—would they be able to provide the medieval serf with electric lights, refrigerators, automobiles, and television sets?" To which I respond, would Mark Zuckerberg? Jeff Bezos? Give me a coterie of carpenters, mechanics, contractors, electricians, and plumbers and I imagine that I'd do a lot better. That's the thing with the capitalism that's our dominant faith: not just that it's immoral—though it is—but that's its so singularly stupid. Idolatrizing the greedy has been a disaster, for a year before Rand died, and in a private communication, Exxon executives revealed that anthropogenic climate change was real, and rather than mitigate global warming while it was still possible, they formulated a disinformation campaign, lest regulation cut into their profit margin. "I would give the greatest sunset in the world for one sight of New York's skyline . . . What other religion do we need?" Roark gushes, something we can meditate on as we watch the warm water rapidly swallow Manhattan and everything else in its path.

PINCHING A PENNY

Five minutes after midnight, as the drizzly and damp Saint Patrick's Day of 1990 came to a close, far from the green-clad revelers ponying up for last call of Guinness or Jameson from Sommerville to Southie, two men dressed in the uniforms of the Boston's finest parked on Palace Road in Fenway-Kenmore, Olmstead's Back Bay Fens with its honey locust and callery pear trees across the street, the Red Sox's eponymous ball park less than a mile away. A few minutes after they arrived, the faux police officers were given access at the side entrance of the elegant Isabella Stewart Gardner Museum, ostensibly responding to a security alert. Once inside, the pair of counterfeit

ABOVE Four studies made as part of Andy Warhol's 1982 dollar sign screen-print portfolio, made the year that Rand died.

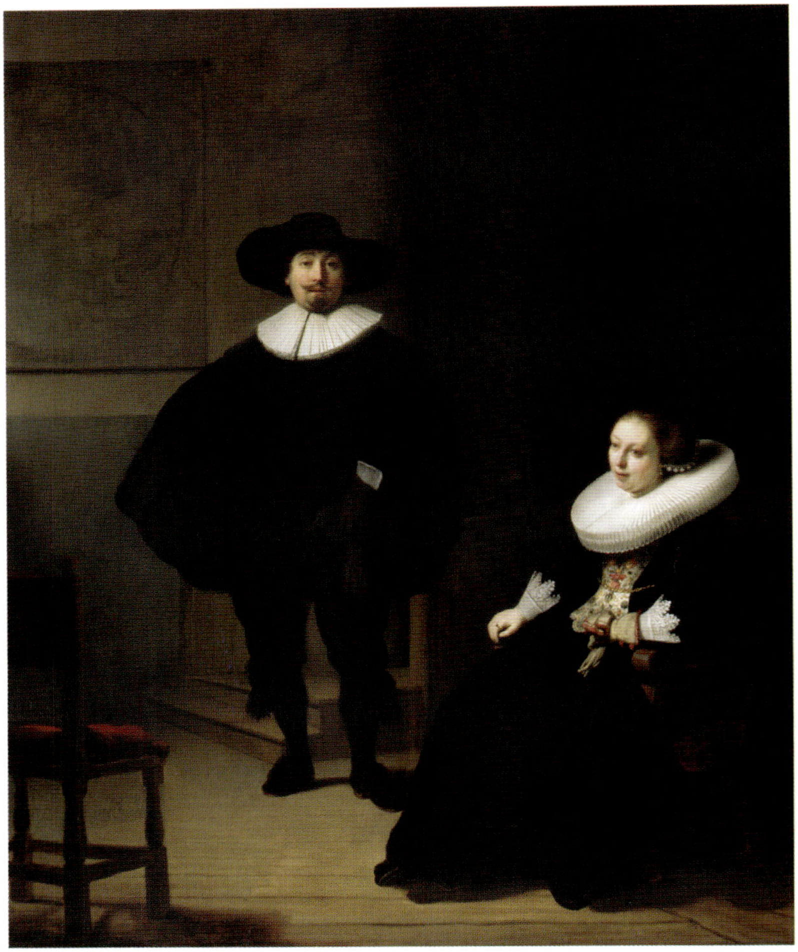

cops restrained the two evergreen security guards on shift that night, duct-taping both of them to chairs, and over the course of the next eighty-one minutes they conducted the most spectacular art heist in history. Moving from room to room in the Gilded Age mansion, the thieves used razor blades to cut paintings from their canvas stretchers, rolling them up into tubes and quickly moving on. Thirteen pieces would be stolen that night, including Johannes Vermeer's *The Concert* (out of a provenance of only thirty-four substantiated compositions), Rembrandt's *Storm on the Sea of Galilee* (the Dutch Master's only seascape), and a set of five sketches made by Edgar Degas, along with some relatively worthless tchotchkes, including a finial shaped like an eagle which had once been affixed to a Napoleonic standard. Having completed that portion of their heist, they removed videotapes of any security camera footage that might implicate them and then politely checked in to inquire about the comfort of the restrained guards. Securing several of the most sterling Dutch Renaissance works into their battered hatchback, the two men drove off into the Boston night with six hundred million dollars' worth of art in their trunk. Neither they nor the thirteen works have ever been located.

ABOVE Among the first trade empires to grow rich through financial speculation and investment, the Dutch Republic of the seventeenth century saw the emergence of a spectacularly wealthy elite right at the emergence of modern capitalism, as captured perfectly in Rembrandt's 1633 composition *A Lady and Gentleman in Black*. Owned by Boston's Isabella Stewart Gardner Museum, though its current whereabouts are unknown.

OPPOSITE Both patron and muse, Isabella Stewart Gardner herself was the subject of Swedish painter Anders Zorn's 1894 portrait of the socialite in Venice. Elegant, refined, sophisticated—all adjectives that are the children of wealth, which is the handmaiden of greed.

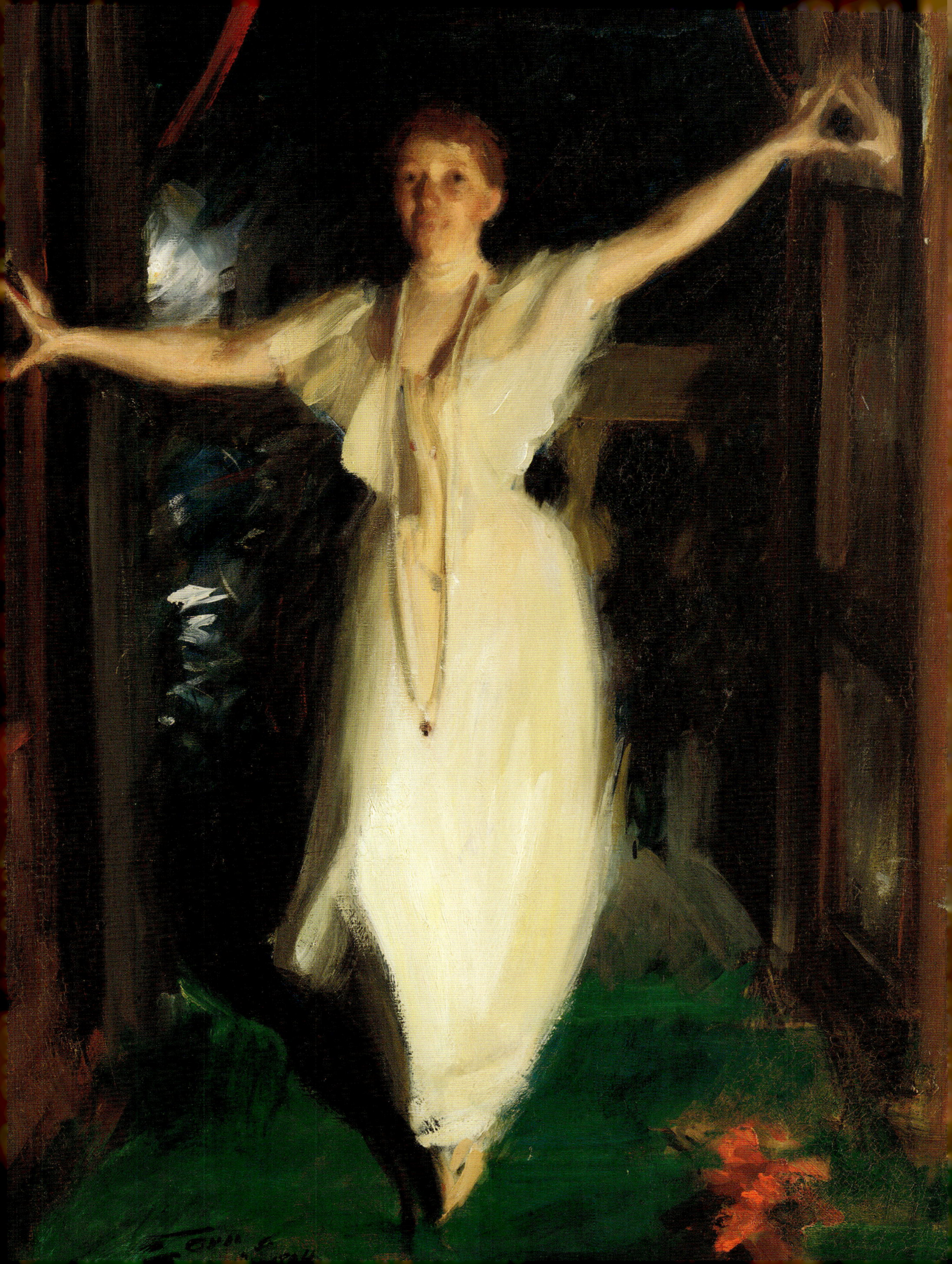

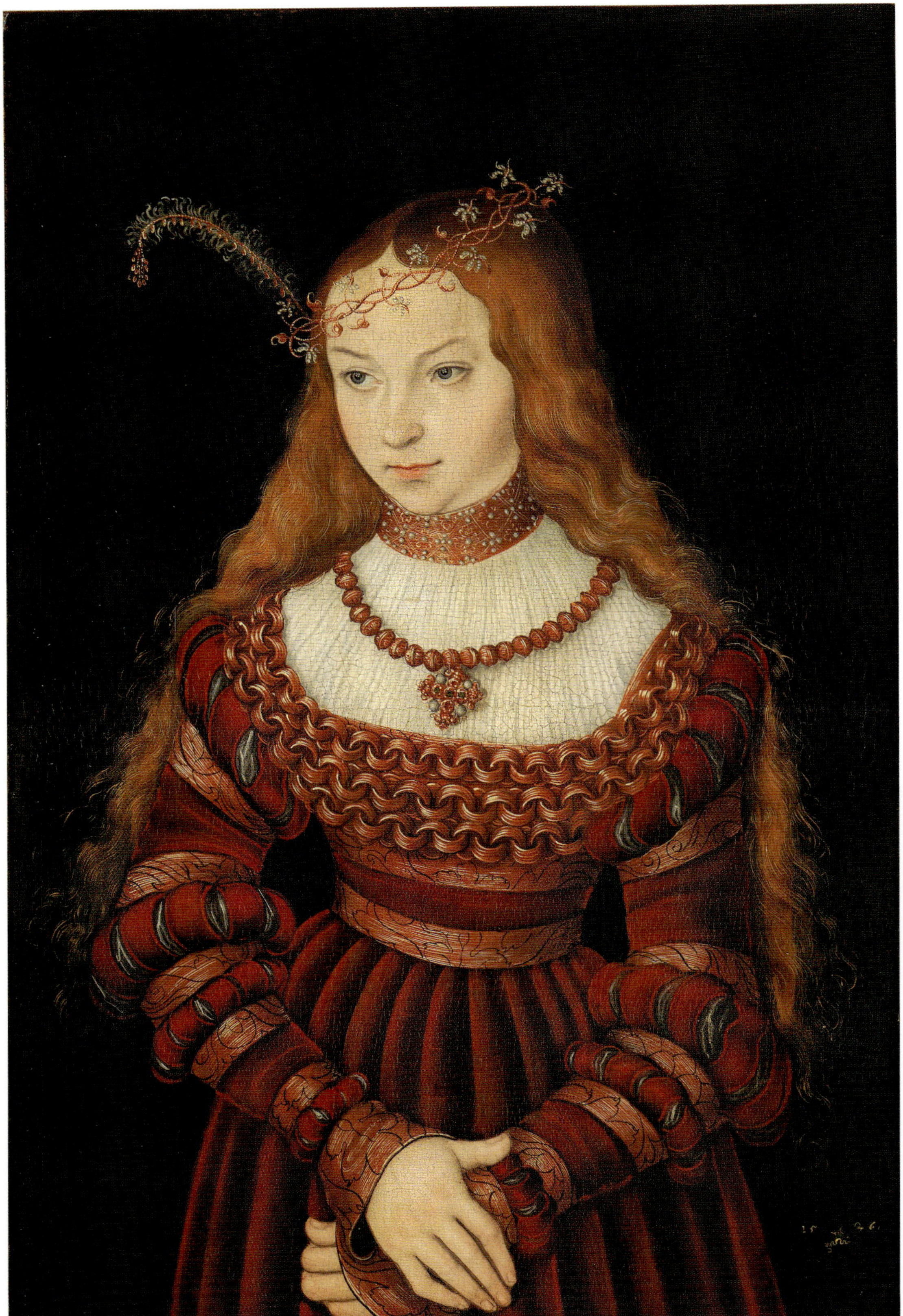

Consistent with the staid but simultaneously elegant environs of Fenway with its eponymous public park and the nearby Museum of Fine Arts, the Isabella Stewart Gardner Museum is an Italianate *palazzo* within the core of the Puritan City on a Hill. The visionary socialite and philanthropist who affixed her name to the museum—which was Gardner's house, constructed after her husband's death, and then carefully curated with a variety of old masters collected while on European holiday—is among one of the most striking galleries in the Western Hemisphere, a testament to the Brahmin's very un-Puritanical love of art. To label Gardner's desire to be in the presence of such treasures—to feel the cool ceramic of a Chinese gu or to marvel at the brushstrokes of a Titian—as "greed" would be a categorical mistake, not least of all because she made allowances to gift her collection to the people, to bequeath a public treasure unto generations yet unborn. But the eye for beauty, the wish to be in the presence of exquisite objects, is not unknown among those who are greedy. It is an aspect of the type from Midas to Henry Clay Frick, Croesus to J. Paul Getty. Gardner stipulated the exact contours of each of the respective galleries that opened in her former estate after her death, organizing less with a concern toward movements or chronology than with contrast and congruence in mind, the aesthetic argument being more crucial to Gardner than a mere scholarly one. The bombastic canvases of Titian and the color-poems of John Singer Sargent, the quietism of Rembrandt and Manet's capture of the eternal moment. Raphael, Botticelli, Degas, Whistler. Few collections amassed by a private individual boast both the scope and significance of the Isabella Stewart Gardner Museum. As with the Frick Collection in New York or the Barnes in Philadelphia, Gardner's museum is a testament to the curatorship of the woman who founded it, but even by the standards of those other collections, she was able to exert a profound control over the details of these galleries—where exactly canvases would be placed or vases and tapestries displayed—which posthumously still holds a gravitational pull.

Some irony ensues: because Gardner had contractually limited the ability of future curators to alter her collection in any manner, including prohibiting

OPPOSITE Bedecked in a luxurious finery of fabric and a luscious sheen of jewelry, Sibylle of Cleves was rendered upon her marriage to Electoral Prince John Frederick by Lucas Cranach the Elder in 1526, a gorgeous evocation of the tremendous wealth amassed by Renaissance princes. Exhibited at the castle in Baden-Baden, this portrait was stolen by Stéphane Breitwieser in 1995, part of the overall billion dollars' worth of art which he filched over several years.

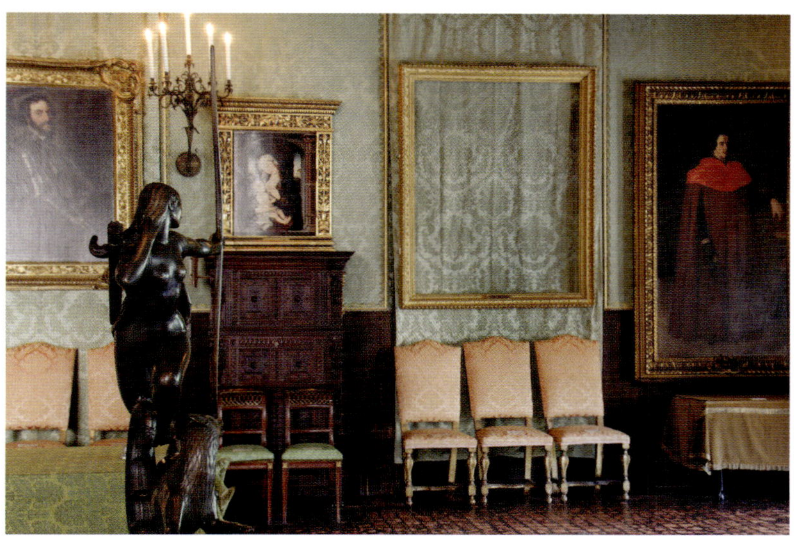

RIGHT Gaze into the framed nothingness that is the single greatest act of performance art accomplished in the twentieth century.

the purchasing or selling of works, when the art thieves absconded with their bounty, leaving behind their empty wooden frames, the trustees of the museum were forced to leave these stark lacunae as a reminder of the heist. Now only the immaculate red or green patterned wall paper is visible through the squares of mahogany, a nothingness displayed where once there hung a Rembrandt or a Vermeer. For the curators and trustees, the members and the visitors, Bostonians and art lovers throughout the world, the Isabella Stewart Gardner Museum heist is not just a beguiling mystery, but a vandalism, a travesty.

Of the various theories proffered as to who the guilty parties are in the Gardner heist—including Whitey Bulger's Winter Hill Gang, the Irish Republican Army, or the Mafia branch known as the Merlino Family—there have been a variety of potential justifications for the theft, from funding arms shipments to acquiring a bargaining chip for the release of inmates then serving RICO charges. Aesthetics, however, is rarely considered as a reason for why *The Concert* or *The Storm of Galilee* no longer graces the museum's walls. Yet whether or not Vermeer is now in the backroom of a North Boston restaurant or in a Miami drug kingpin's estate, the result was supremely aesthetic. Those empty frames now cradle a nothingness, an abyss. An arresting display of the nihilism at the core of greed, so that the theft itself elevates avarice into the realm of pure art, of infinite beauty. What those two criminals accomplished in 1990—whether members of the Merlino crew or some Dorchester toughs, whether to sell on the black market or to fund gun runners—was a sublime act, the greatest work of performance art ever rendered. The purest incident of greed that can be imagined. "Aesthetics are higher than ethics," claimed Oscar Wilde in his 1891 essay "The Critic as Artist."

Three decades of amateur sleuths and true crime enthusiasts have been attracted to the tale of the Gardner heist because it fulfills all the expectations of the genre—mysteriousness, high drama, and the allure of a puzzle—without the prurience, a guilt-free crime to enjoy with no body count (even while over the decades the FBI has linked, potentially, some mob whacks with the theft). This of course is a relative interpretation; art thievery may have connotations of the urbane sophisticate in the form of *The Thomas Crowne Affair*, but in reality it is more often the colonial pillaging of Asian and African nations or the Nazis' infamous rape of Europa, Hermann Goering running his fingers through a bowl of pilfered diamonds on his desk while staring at old masters stolen from Jewish families. Perhaps it's hyperbole to think of the Gardner heist as relatively innocent, for the victims are in the form of a humanity deprived of its cultural inheritance, some mafioso enjoying *The Concert* in his Block Island beach house or a gang member displaying *Christ on the Sea of Galilee* above his bed in Charlestown. The rest of us, by comparison, have to make due with the melancholic simulacra of reproduction.

Greed by its very nature desires exclusivity; it stands in opposition to both egalitarianism and free access. In modern capital, diamonds and gold matter less than the privatized power which money represents. Finance was first the domain of the ledger and now of the algorithm, but regardless what's important isn't material holdings so much as the arbitrary constructs of money, invisible numbers fluctuating on a mainframe somewhere. What the Gardner heist did, in a strange way, was reenchant material; it gave gold back its luster. Of course, the raw materials of

OPPOSITE Leonardo da Vinci's 1489 *Lady with an Ermine*, one of only four paintings of a contemporary woman by the master, depicts Cecillia Gallerani, the favored mistress of Ludovico Sforza, Duke of Milan. Northern Italy became spectacularly wealthy as a result of banking, the fruits of such greed obvious in the finery worn by Gallerani. Original held at the Czartoryski Museum in Krakow, though following the German invasion in 1939 the Nazis stole the Da Vinci and exhibited it at Berlin's Kaiser Friedrich Museum, before ultimately transferring it to party functionary Hans Frank's Bavarian country estate, where it was recovered by a special contingent of the United States Army known as the "Monuments Men," art historians convened for the express purpose of recovering works plundered by the Nazis.

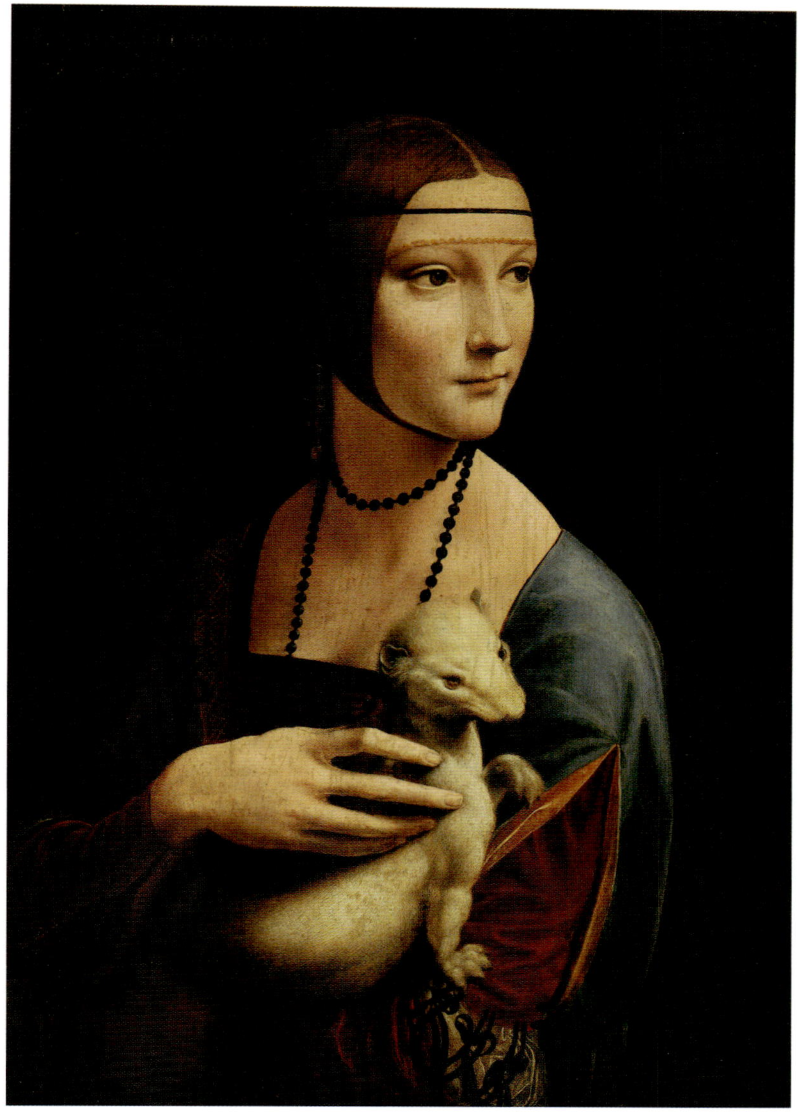

a Vermeer or a Rembrandt are worth little, maybe a few hundred dollars at most for canvas and what's now four-century-old decayed paint. The price of the painting is a construct as well, but that it's *beautiful* and *singular* recalls not the binary code on a banking computer that tells Michael Bloomberg how rich he is, but rather Spanish galloons secured with tons of Aztec and Incan gold, Qin Shi Huang with his jade-covered terra-cotta soldiers, or the British Crown Jewels gleaming in pilfered diamonds and rubies from the sundry lands of the earth. What the Boston heist underscores is how much of what appeals about wealth was originally a primal materiality, the shine of precious metal or the luxury of some rare decadent good. As charming as the stories which maintain that Warren Buffett enjoys a frugal Grand Slam breakfast every day at his local Omaha Denny's might be, what titillates about the otherwise boring investor is not that he lives cheaply, but that he could very much not if he chose to.

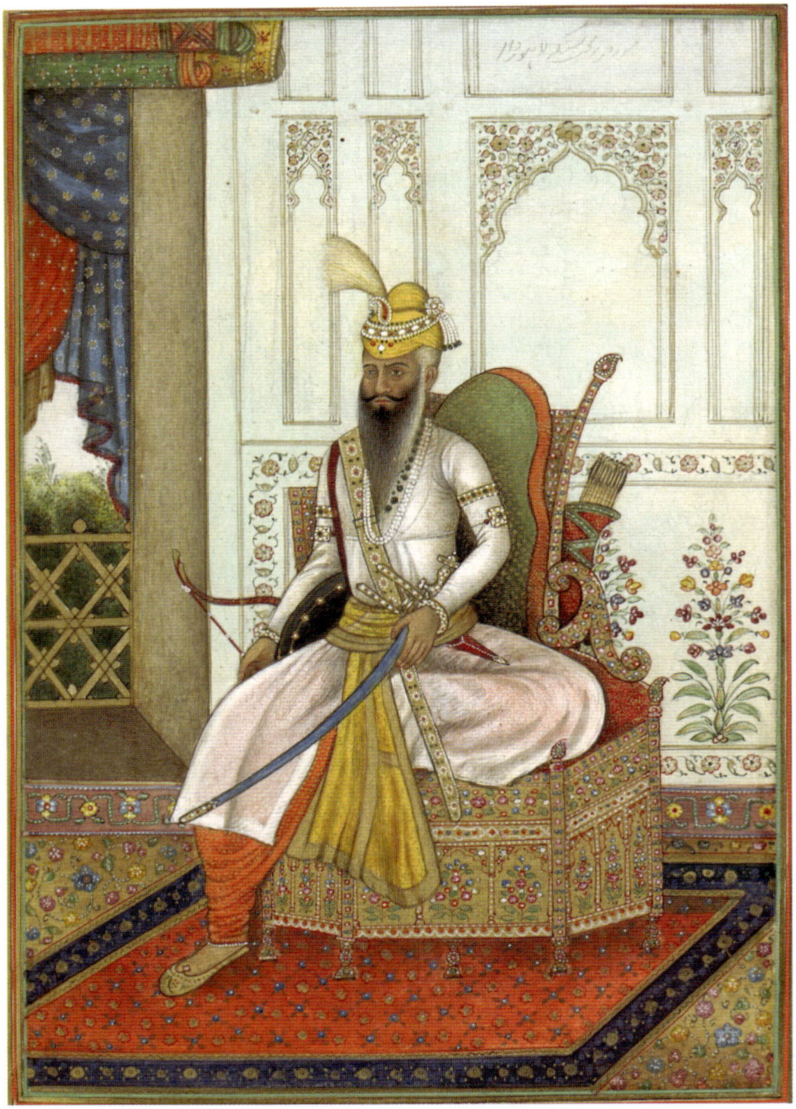

ABOVE A portrait of the nineteenth-century founder of the Sikh Empire Ranjit Singh as imagined by contemporary painter Manu Kauer Saluja in 2009 and exhibited at the Royal Ontario Museum in Toronto. Around his right bicep is a setting of the Koh-i-Noor diamond, a stunning 105.6 carat jewel that's among the largest cuttings in the world. Following the ruler's death, the diamond would be placed in a temple, only to be stolen by the British upon the conclusion of the Second Anglo-Sikh War in 1849. Given to Queen Victoria, it still remains part of the British Crown Jewels.

The abstractions of money as a concept aside, a massive amount of imaginary numbers are capable of purchasing some fairly not imaginary things. A million-and-a-half dollars will get you an evanescent Aston Martin Valour sports car, a triumph of British engineering as parsimonious, seamless, and most of all, as *quick* as a Bach concerto. A Stuart Hughes bespoke Diamond Edition suit goes for a cool $892,500, with only three ever sold. Almas Caviar, fished from the Persian sea with an umami taste as delicate as its black membrane, a flavor as primal as the ocean itself, goes for $34,000 per kilogram. The price of a single car or suit is already the same amount as a rich man's annual salary, a single swallow of caviar as much as a working-class woman's or man's. Inevitably we are drawn to the exploits of the wealthy, their ability to spend money in such a manner, greed manifesting as an almost athletic act of prowess. The Manor in Beverly Hills, next to Hugh Hefner's Playboy Mansion but far larger, was once owned by television producer Aaron Spelling, but is now home to some lucky billionaire content to leave obvious traces of their name off the lease. Twenty-one times the size of the average American home, the Manor features two butterfly staircases, a barbershop, and a 7,500-square-foot master bedroom. Bill Gates, paradoxically through either cluelessness or a surfeit of self-awareness, resides in a Seattle-area estate named Xanadu 2.0, a techno-friendly update of the fictional Charles Foster Kane's mansion in Oscar Welles's *Citizen Kane*. Within Xanadu 2.0, Gates can avail himself of seven bedrooms, twenty-four bathrooms, and a library which includes an original Leonardo da Vinci manuscript, as inaccessible to anyone reading this as the pilfered paintings of Boston are. Then for sheer American crapulence, there is the tone-deaf Versailles Mansion, this one built not outside Paris but in Florida, a monstrosity of ugly rococo excess that includes a thirty-car garage, six pools, and two elevators, one of which is built of gold, all for a hundred million dollars. The Bourbons, it should be noted, never had an infinity pool.

Austere Utilitarianism condemns the prioritizing of a night out to dinner over contributing to famine relief, the purchase of a movie ticket or weekend in the mountains when one could fund vaccinations in the third world. Imagine, then, the tremendous good that could come not just by deciding to eschew movie tickets

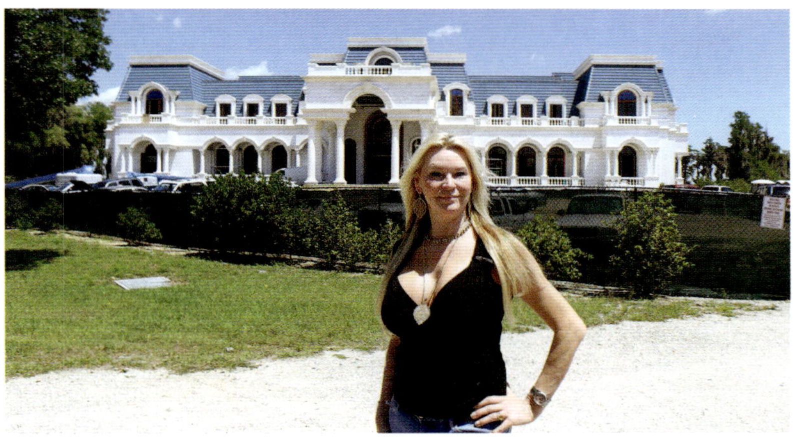

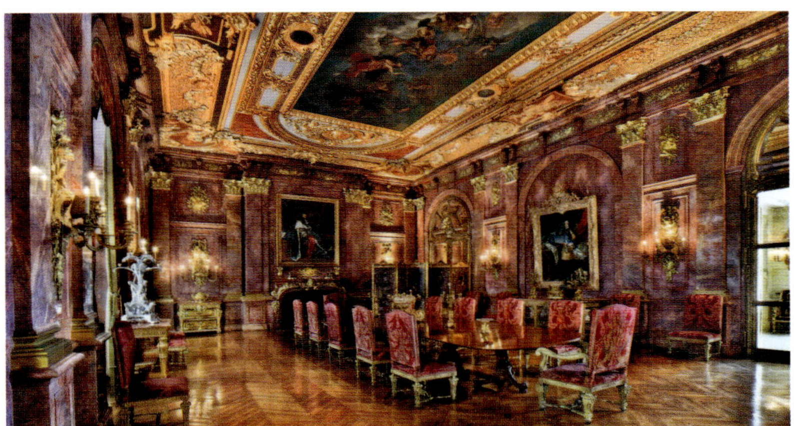

TOP Jackie Siegel, wife of Westgate Resorts founder David Siegel, in front of their as of now still uncompleted 90,000-square-foot estate Versailles, which will be the largest single-family residence in the United States and is appraised at a hundred million dollars, though its obvious excessive garishness should dissuade anyone from thinking that there is a connection between price and beauty. Picture courtesy of the *Orlando Sentinel*.

BOTTOM Gold leaf ceiling at the Breakers, the summer home of the Vanderbilts at Newport, Rhode Island, constructed in 1893.

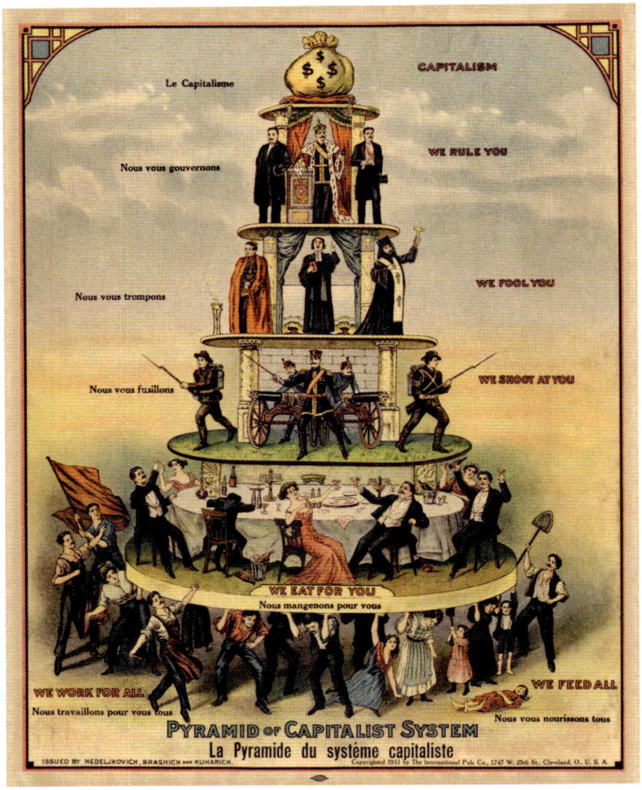

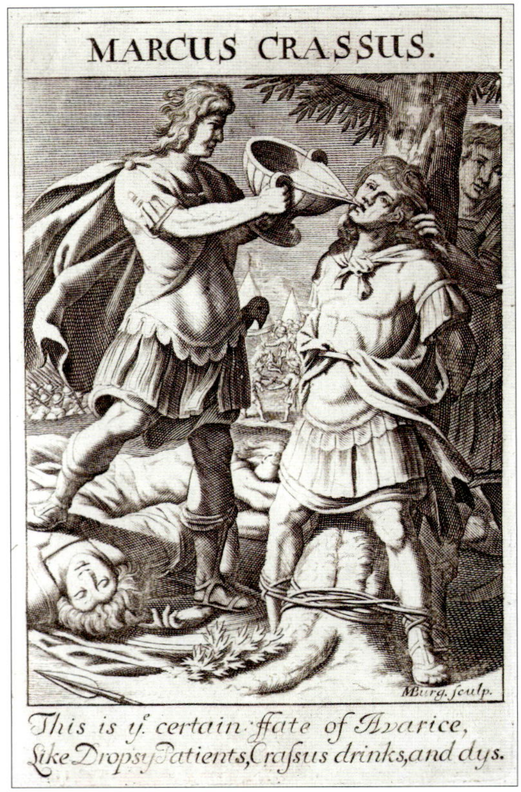

or a vacation, but instead to not buy that Aston Martin Valour, the Stuart Hughes bespoke Diamond Edition suit, the kilogram of Almas Caviar spread thick on a water cracker? Let us not fall into that trap that mistakes philanthropy—that mere exercise in prestige laundering and tax evasion—with genuine social justice, much less solidarity. Were resources infinite, every person could be the king of their own personal Biltmore. But in the world of limited (and always declining) material goods, the luxuries of the rich are theft from the rest of us.

Touring the grand Gilded Age mansion of Newport, Rhode Island, the Breakers and the Elms, Marble House and Rough Point, upon their stunning, rocky, windswept cliffs overlooking the Atlantic, is as if viewing a history of atrocity; for think of all those in the tenements and ghettos who could have been fed, educated, and healed with the money that went into a platinum-coated ceiling or an intricately chiseled Italian marble staircase. The mansions of Bel-Air and the townhomes of the Upper East Side, the condominiums of Kalorama and the ranches of Jackson Hole, all are monuments to the wastefulness of the greedy, the manner in which even the barest amelioration of suffering can be ignored in favor of the decadence of the rich. This is a tale as old as Ramses, but there have been variations throughout history. More recently, following decades of deregulation, the inequities between the wealthiest and everybody else have yawned into an insurmountable gulf. Let them eat cake, indeed.

Accounts of the ancient general and real estate speculator Marcus Licinius Crassus describe how as the owner of the city's private fire company, he allowed

TOP LEFT By the time that the Cleveland-based *Industrial Work,* an organ of the radical IWW, published its 1911 cartoon *Pyramid of the Capitalist System*, the basic contours of the diagram had already been familiar from French and Russian antecedents. Attributed to Nedeljkovich, Brasich, and Kuharich, the cartoon describes the socioeconomic system as being supported by a multitude of the proletariat, pressed down by the bourgeoisie, the army, the clergy, and the aristocratic and capitalist classes.

TOP RIGHT Rewarded for his loyalty to the Roman Triumvirate by being given the governorship of the Syrian provinces, Cassius would mount an ill-advised invasion of Parthia, captured by his adversaries and executed by being force-fed liquid gold in an ironic comment on his avarice. Other accounts record that his dismembered head would be used as a stage prop in a production of Euripides's *The Bacchae*.

whole blocks of Rome to burn so that he could buy lots up cheaply—not so different from the shock doctrine developers of today, scooping into paradisical locations following a natural disaster to build luxury resorts upon the ashes of the poor. Getty refused to pay a three-million-dollar ransom for his kidnapped grandson, a paltry sum for the billionaire, even after he was mailed the boy's dismembered ear. Perhaps this is shockingly heartless, but it's of the same kind as the sociopathy which allowed the executives at EXXON to be fully aware of anthropogenic climate change while spending billions in public disinformation to continue extracting and burning fossil fuels. If so many of the sins are defined by hunger, then greed's is the most gnawing, for it requires the elevation of mere possessions above God, even more shockingly by raising them above our fellow humans. "The public be damned!" shouted William H. Vanderbilt: "I only care about my property." Even more than hunger, even more than control, greed is an obsession with possession. The amount of money required to live a life of comfort is amazingly low compared to that which the mavens of finance and industry have accumulated. A million dollars would make one rich in most of the United States; ten million dollars would basically make it possible to, within reason, do anything which any person would ever realistically want to do in terms of leisure and enjoyment. Such wealth wouldn't make it possible to purchase a super yacht or a private island, but this is precisely the point. A thousand millionaires makes a single billionaire, or a hundred fortunate enough to have ten million. Oracle founder Larry Ellison has 134 billion dollars, Jeff Bezos 162 billion dollars, and Elon Musk an astounding 235 billion dollars. The average annual pay for an Amazon worker—those who packaged the book you're reading and then delivered it to you—is $28,446, or a few thousand less than a single spoonful of jet-black Almas caviar. By comparison, Bezos earns in one hour around $8,961,187. The Amazon worker would need to work continuously, 24 hours a day for 68 years, just to make what their boss earns in a single hour.

Beyond even the parameters of asking if all of the work that an Ellison, Bezos, or Musk does deserves such otherworldly compensation—simple arithmetic makes it hard to be convinced that the CEO of Amazon works 315 times harder in sixty minutes than a theoretical automaton laboring continually for 68 years—there is the even more prosaic question of just what all that wealth is capable of doing. Yes, there is Peter Singer's point about how such money could be used to address suffering, but in an even more straightforward sense, what does such wealth do for Ellison, Bezos, and Musk? Somebody can have a twenty-two-bedroom mansion, but they're still only capable of sleeping in a single bed in a night. That's to say that beyond even the wildest imaginations of a hedonist, the pleasure which such money imparts is marked by the simple fact that every human is a limited, finite, mortal being. They too shall die, and 235 billion dollars makes no difference in that inviolate fact, even with fantasies of somehow being able to download your consciousness to the Cloud. Which is where greed differentiates itself from the hungers of gluttony or lust, because in addition to such rapaciousness, there is also the quality of needing to hoard wealth. There is a joyless and perfunctory nature to this, the compulsion to squirrel away not just money but things of value, the miserly fear of always being at risk of theft, the frugal skinflint's need not to enjoy things, but to prevent others from enjoying them (even from one's twenty-two-room mansion).

Ulrich Boser in *The Gardner Heist: The True Story of the World's Largest Unsolved Art Theft* imagines a gallery "filled with all of the world's stolen artworks . . . the most impressive collection ever created." As it is, such a collection does effectively exist, at the Geneva Freeport warehouse, a temperature-controlled bunker which operates under the opaque rules of Swiss banking and where stupendously wealthy art collectors (including Nazi fugitives and ISIS) store their valuables, with journalist William Gompertz describing it as the "greatest art collection that nobody gets to see." Babylonian and Roman antiquities, Renaissance masters, Modernist classics, works by Da Vinci, Picasso, Renoir, Van Gogh. Most gallingly, most obscenely, the majority of these works haven't even been appreciated by those who ostensibly own them, the tremendous price paid for works of art since the 1980s making them a valuable commodity in investment and speculation (money laundering as well), so that a painting can pass between any number of hands (figuratively) all while remaining in the same cryonic chamber in Switzerland.

Perhaps *Christ on the Sea of Galilee* is under a bed in some Sommerville rowhouse, or *The Concert* now hangs in a Braintree bathroom, but is this any more horrific a cultural crime than the hiding of treasures by faceless tyrants in the Geneva Freeport, these works as impossible for the public to access as anything stolen from the Isabella Stewart Gardner Museum? If such things must be reduced to the language of finance, the theological vocabulary of our fallen modernity, then it's worth considering that while the thirteen paintings stolen from Boston may have been worth some six hundred million dollars, the thousands of works hidden in the Geneva Freeport are valued at an astounding hundred billion dollars. Regardless of whether paintings hang in a mobster's suburban home or a billionaire's bunker, these are works which you'll never be able to see. The greedy have long denied the people bread; now they preserve our roses in hermetically sealed chambers as well. A crime—a theft—a heist—of audacious proportions.

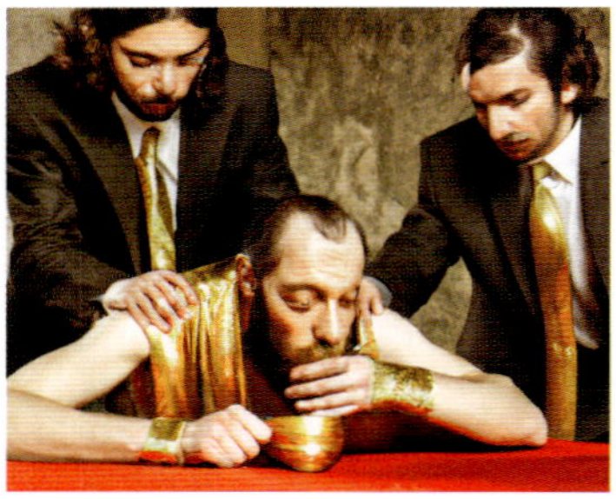

ABOVE Currently the lords of Silicon Valley are most titillated by artificial intelligence and the profit-making incentive in managers able to eliminate the pesky particulars of humans and their creativity. This image was generated by an AI program; it depicts Marcus Licinius Crassus as a modern businessman being forced to drink molten gold by some of his associates.

OPPOSITE Da Vinci's otherworldly *Salvator Mundi*, depicting Christ as monarch of the cosmos holding a celestial sphere in his left hand while raising the other in a sign of benediction. Painted in 1499, the composition spent decades unseen in a warehouse at the Geneva Freeport, before briefly being displayed in a landmark exhibition at he National Gallery of Art in London. Auctioned at Christie's for 450.3 million dollars in 2017, the single largest amount any work of art has ever been sold for, the Da Vinci was purchased by Saudi prince Badr bin Abdullah Al Saud on behalf of the crown prince and de facto absolute ruler of Saudi Arabia Mohammad bin Salman, who promptly hid the painting once again in a private collection, supposedly displaying it on his yacht. You will most likely never be able to stare into *Salvator Mundi*'s unblinking eyes with your own.

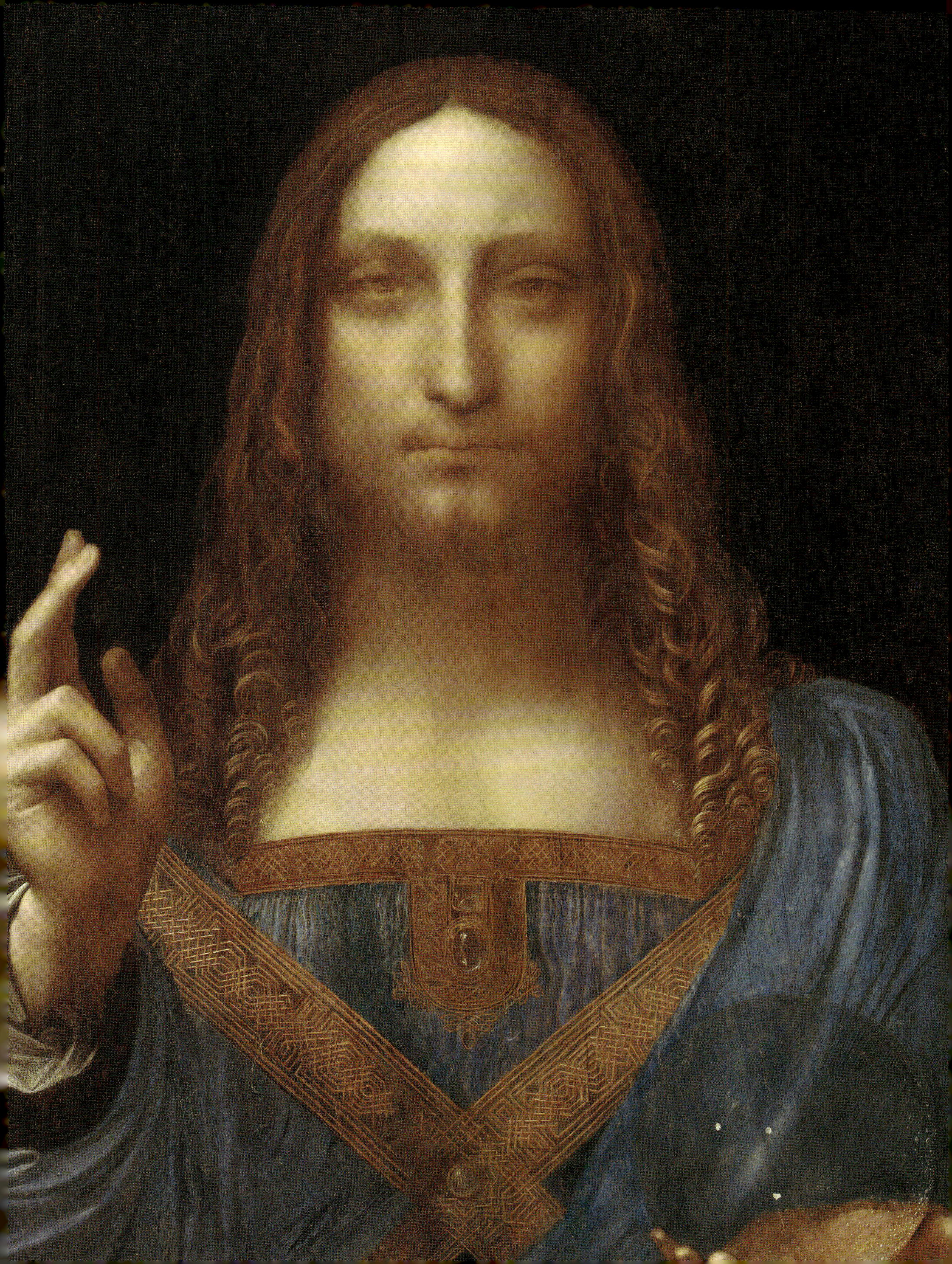

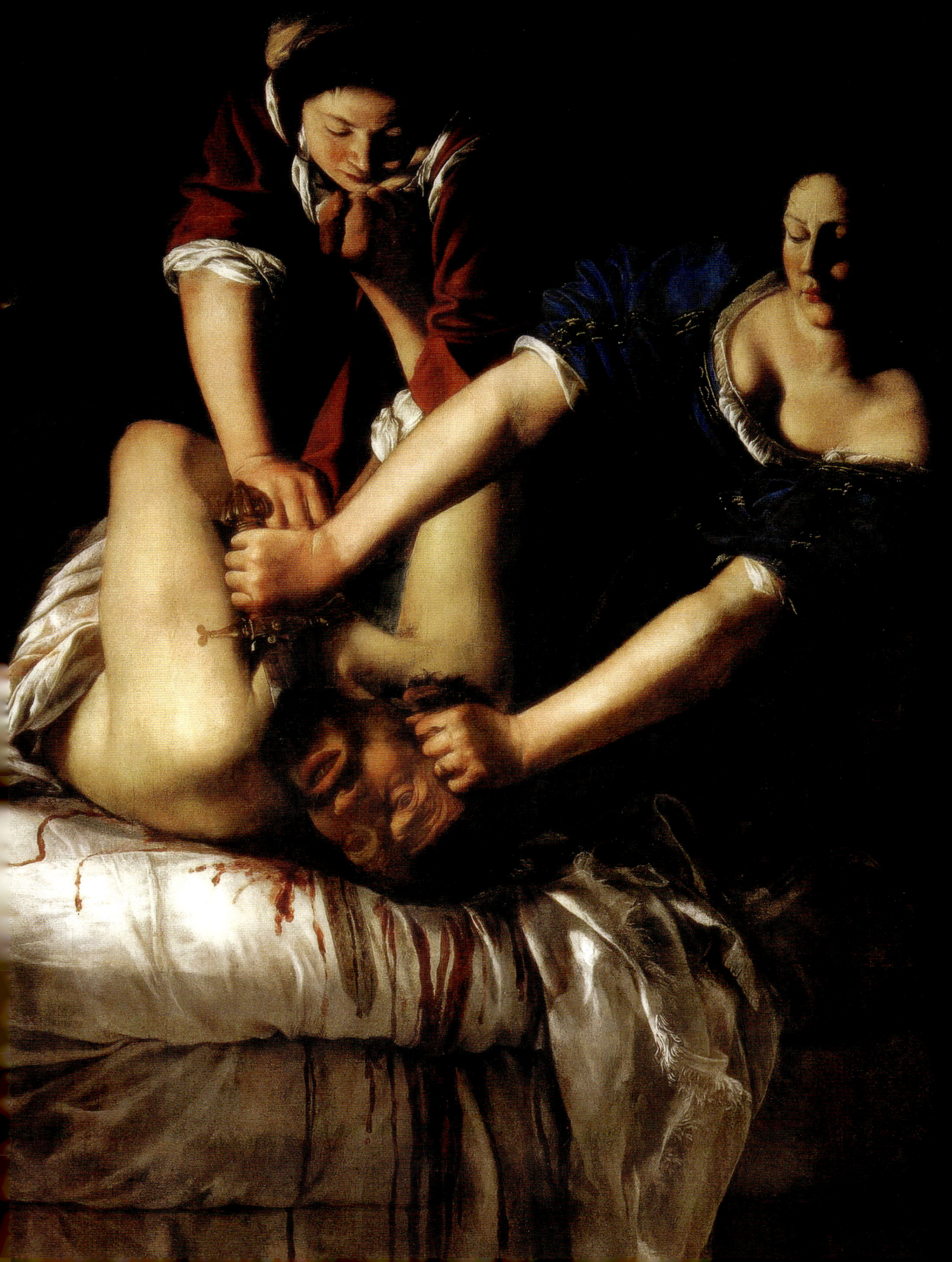

CHAPTER SEVEN

SINEWS OF THE SOUL: WRATH

"Now will I shortly pour out my fury upon thee, and accomplish mine anger upon thee: and I will judge thee according to thy ways, and will recompense thee for all thine abominations."
—Ezekiel 7:8

"And I hope that you die / And your death will come soon / I'll follow your casket / By the pale afternoon / And I'll watch while you're lowered / Down to your deathbed / And I'll stand over your grave / Till I'm sure that you're dead."
—Bob Dylan, "Masters of War" (1963)

Anger, rage, fury, even annoyance and irritation—wrath. Of all of the seven deadly sins, wrath is the most marked by uncontrollable irrationality, by the white-hotness of the poor decision, by the loss of propriety and good sense. And of the seven deadly sins, wrath is most obviously responsible for violence, where rage directly inculcates heinous actions in a manner that sloth or gluttony obviously doesn't. If the Church Fathers and Scholastics warned about this litany of sins precisely because they could lead the sinner to hell, then wrath has frequently marked the shortest distance to that burning place. "Be not hasty in thy spirit to be angry," says Solomon in Ecclesiastes 7:9, "for anger resteth in the bosom of fools." This aphorism is phrased in an unusual manner, for note the adjectives "hasty" and the verb "resteth." The prohibition is not on *anger*; it's on being quick to wrath without thinking; it's on being in a state of perennial rage. Wrath itself, it should be noted, is included alongside envy as the only two of the seven deadly sins which are ascribed to God. That's to say that the writers of Scripture—a collection not without its own troubling recounting of wrath—saw a sacred mission in anger. John 3:36 records that the "wrath of God abideth" on the unjust person, but the issue always remains: to whom shall Lord's retribution be entrusted? The history of religion is in large part a history of the evil done by religion, by those who claim the mantle of God's vengeance. Yet the history of religion's resistance to evil is, in large part, also a history of those who claim the mantle of God's vengeance. Among the most understandable of the sins, especially in our own volcanic epoch, wrath exhibits the duality of these transgressions, the great extent to which what's a vice and what's a virtue can depend on reasoning and context.

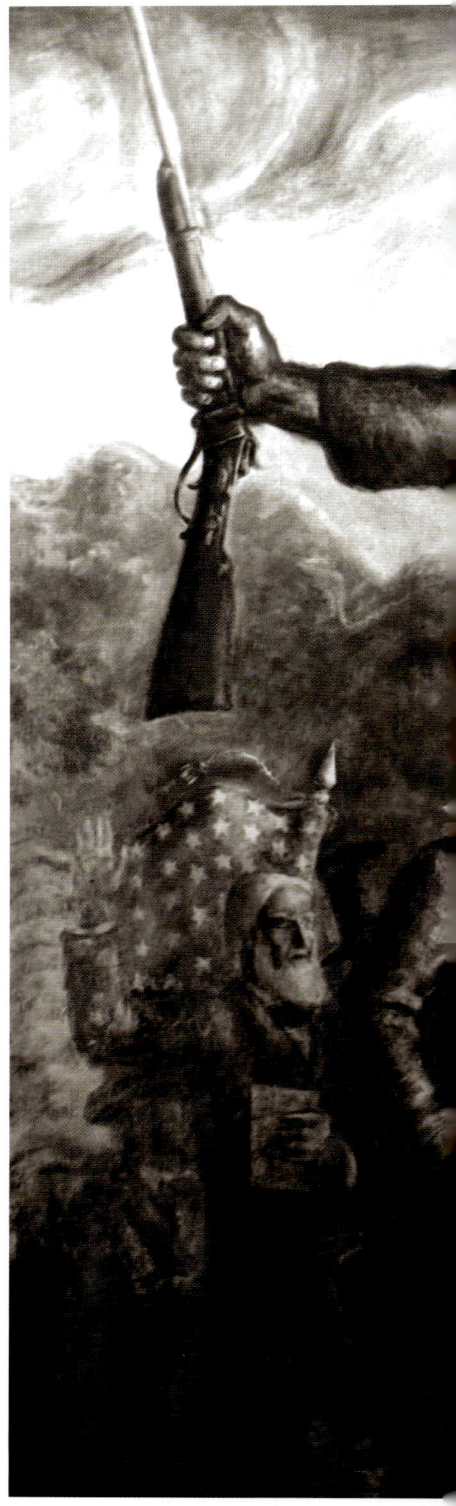

PREVIOUS SPREAD Few compositions have so deftly portrayed feminine vengeance and wrath like Baroque painter Artemisia Gentileschi's iconic and infamous 1612 *Judith Slaying Holofernes*, startling in its gruesome verisimilitude. Seeing in the tale a means of expressing her own righteous wrath, at the age of only twenty Gentileschi had modeled Judith after herself, and the Holofernes whose neck is in the process of being severed from his head bears the face of Agostino Tassi, who had raped the painter only a year before the composition's realization. Original held by the Museo di Capodimonte in Naples.

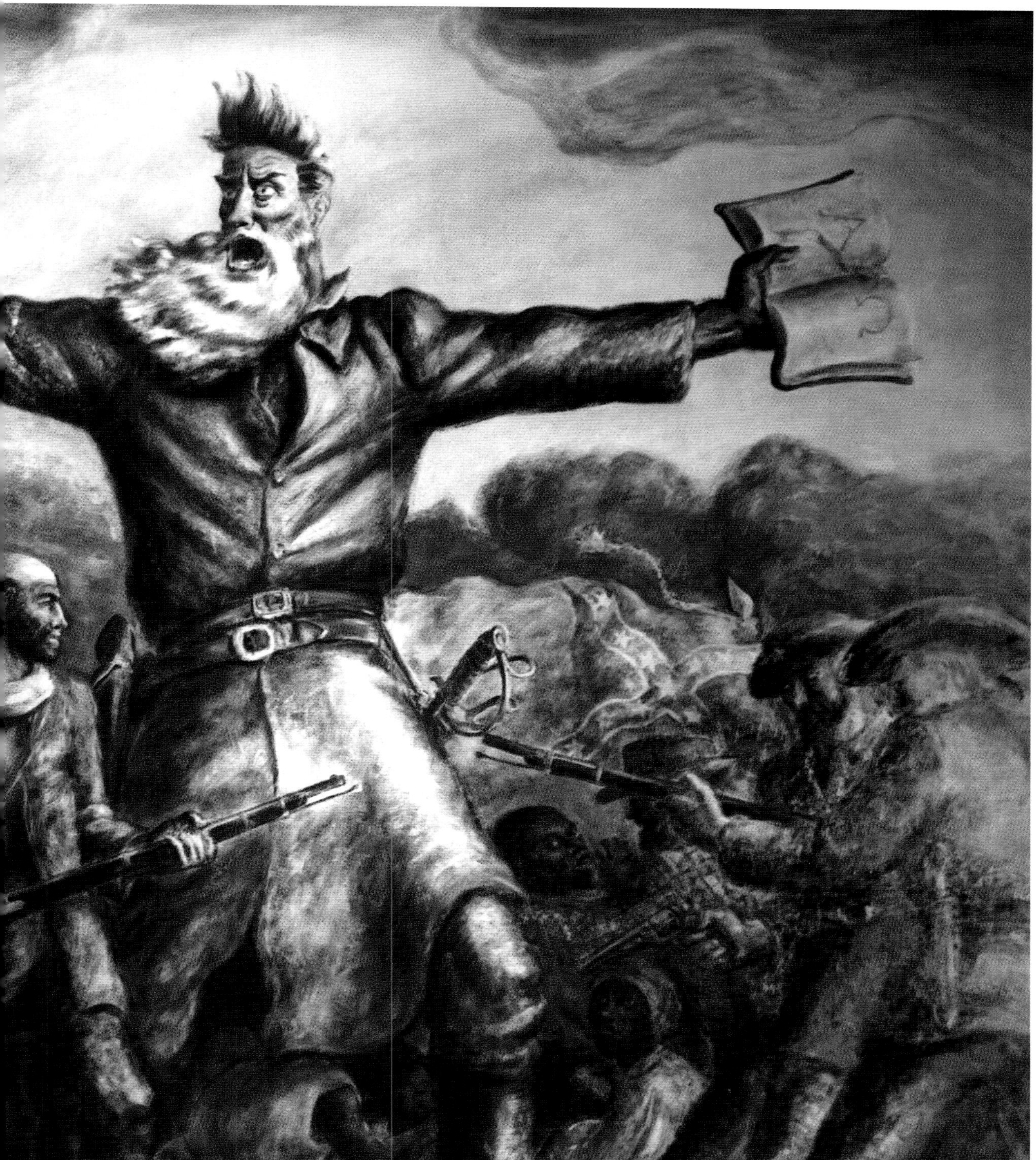

THE ARMY OF THE NORTH

By the silver light of the moon on a clear spring night in 1856, John Brown (lately of Osawatomie, Kansas, but originally from Torrington, Connecticut) and three of his sons used broadswords to kill five men whose deeds rightly and justly marked them for death. The men killed at Pottawatomie—"massacred," said the press—were cruel slave-catchers, those who'd settled in the Kansas territory in hopes of bringing the state into the United States as a dominion where bondage would rule. They had harassed and murdered those who'd prayed that Kansas would remain a place of free soil; the pro-slavery contingent had destroyed abolitionist printing presses, harassed and even murdered those opposed to the enslavement of Black Americans, and had even recently laid siege to the anti-slavery stronghold of Lawrence. Brown, a fervent evangelical Christian who believed in the equality of the races, held no communion with slavers, and affirmed the liberty of humanity over the tyranny of the plantation. At an 1837 memorial service in the austere First Congregational Church held for the abolitionist publisher Elijah Lovejoy, who had been lynched by a rabid, pro-slavery mob, Brown arose and with his right hand aloft declared that "Here before God, in the presence of these witnesses, I consecrate my life to the destruction of slavery"—and so he did. With a face as cragged and lined as the deep hollows and peaks of his beloved Allegheny Mountains, in which he'd spent his youth, Brown carried about him the aura of the warrior-prophet, especially when that face was adorned with a scripturally long beard that gave to him the appearance of an Old Testament patriarch. William Sherman, Allen Wilkinson, and James P. Doyle, along with the latter's two sons, William and Drury, who were in their twenties, would be killed at Pottawattamie. The justification for these men's deaths are obvious to anyone who has seen those terrible daguerreotypes, of the enslaved whose backs have been split into jagged wounds, of women whose mouths have been clamped shut with cruel metal implements, of families separated on the auction block. Brown was a Christian, and Christ did say "Blessed are the peacemakers." Brown was a Christian, and Christ did say "I came not to send peace, but a sword." So Brown did so on his behalf.

"Therefore I am full of the fury of the LORD; I am weary with holding in," reads Jeremiah 6:11, the prophet declaring that "I will pour it out upon the children abroad, and upon the assembly of young men together: for even the husband with the wife shall be taken, the aged with him that is full of days." From the genocide of Amalekites in the Book of Deuteronomy to the Psalmists' invocation of desiring to dash the heads of Babylonian infants upon the rocks, Jeremiah's sweltering anger is only a small example of the rage which percolates through Scripture, but it's a familiar human emotion that's expressed, and all the more disquieting in that it's a divine emotion as well. Jeremiah's description of fury is shockingly recognizable to contemporary readers, for whom the language of "holding in" such feelings is still how people often speak of anger. We think of hot emotions as needing to be constrained, contained, managed, and ameliorated, like a scalding fluid that threatens to boil over. Wrath is marked by *intensity* of emotion, even more so than the other deadly sins, for it's erratic, chaotic,

PREVIOUS SPREAD Painter John Steuart Curry's 1942 mural *Tragic Prelude* adorns the eastern wall of the Kansas State Capitol's rotunda in Topeka. With symbolic import, Curry imagines a massive John Brown clutching a rifle and a Bible (the later opened to Revelation, an Alpha and Omega visible) between clashing Union and Confederate troops.

OPPOSITE The identification of anger with masculinity performs the dual injustice of denying the validity of that emotion in women while denying the validity of all other emotions in men, yet the connection of wrath with testosterone endures. German symbolist painter Franz Stuck's 1905 composition *The Struggle for Women* reduces the expectation of masculine bestial rage to its broadest particular. Original at the Hermitage in St. Petersburg.

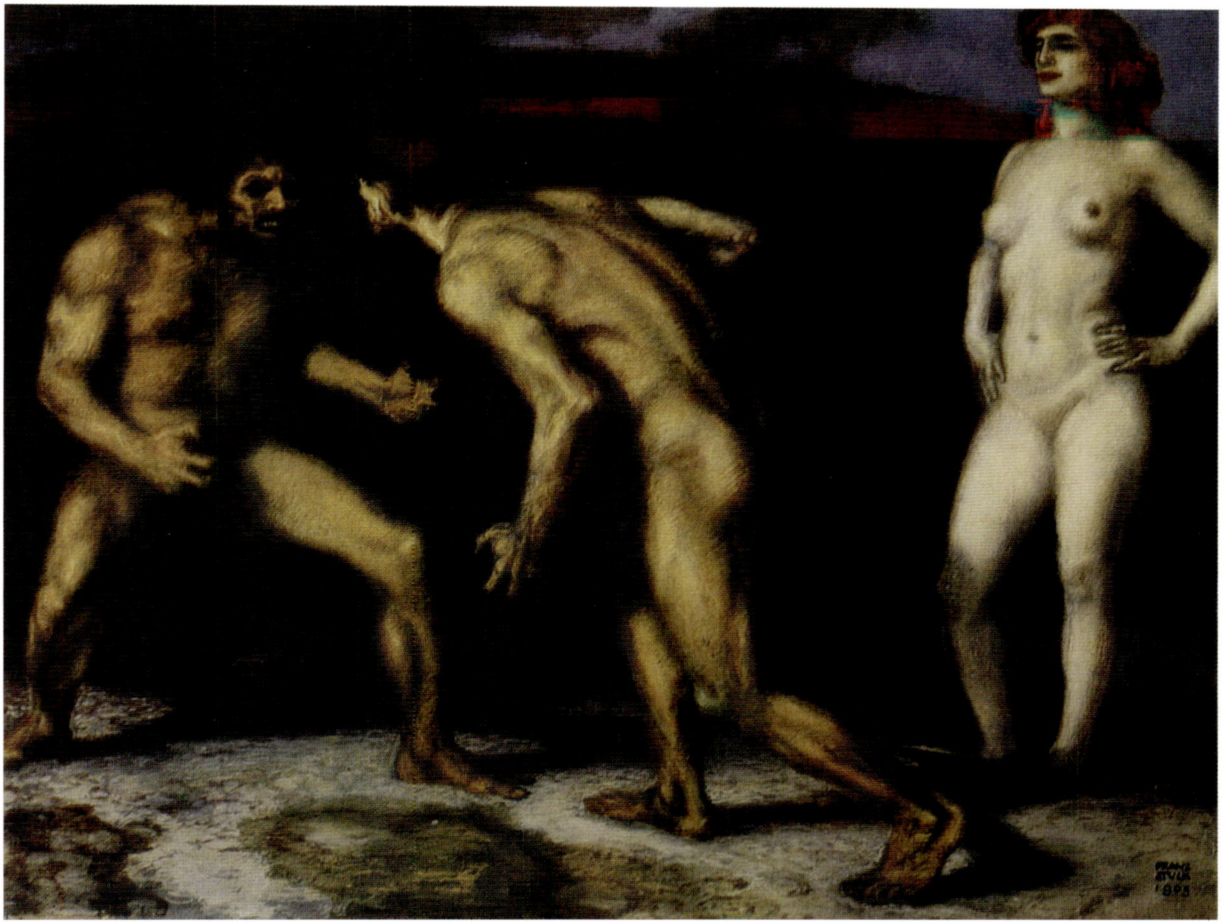

irrational. An emotion of high blood pressure and red-flushed cheek, of quivering extremities and shouted insults. To lose one's cool is to let baser instincts commandeer your body, to give into the animalistic and the bestial, to be motivated by instinct rather than conscience. Part of a constellation of emotions, wrath is joined by Jeremiah's fury, but also rage and anger, even annoyance. All of these feelings differ more in degree than kind, for the operative tenor of them is the loss of control, the subsuming of the self into darker chthonic forces. The anger which causes somebody to scream invective and obscenity at a car that's cut them off in traffic may differ in temperature from the hatefulness that sees a paramilitary moving from house to house hacking his neighbors to death with a machete, but both come from the same psychic wound, the same desire to inflict pain upon somebody else, the same loss of agency. Maybe even more than that, anger is often the recourse of those who perceive themselves to be slighted or embarrassed, impotent or powerless (regardless of the reality). Oftentimes the result is bloodshed, for violence is the daughter of wrath.

Anger is both an evergreen emotion and seemingly the operative register for our own era. Today, all manner of emotions are running at a deficit; contentedness and peacefulness, obviously; goodwill and brotherhood, clearly; happiness

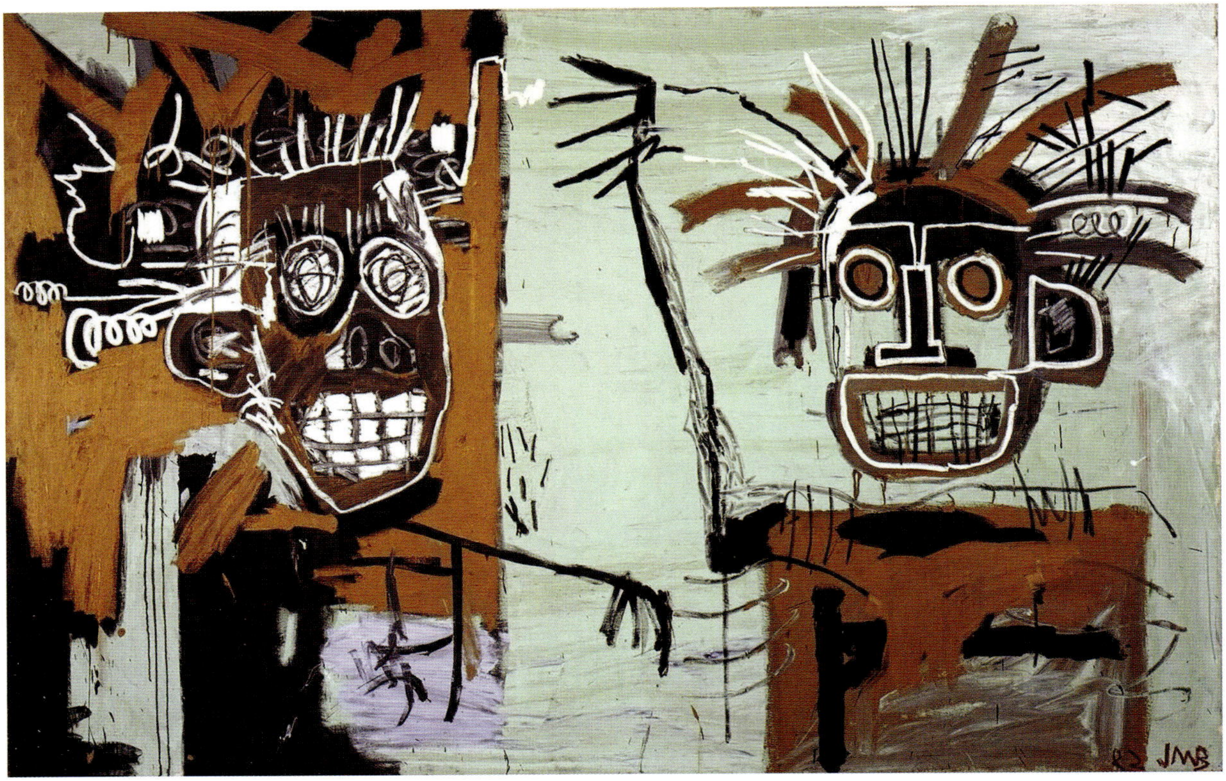

and hopefulness, undoubtedly. But rage, rage is the dominant disposition of our moment, where even sadness, melancholia, and depression are converted into white-hot fury, especially since those things are often but anger turned inward. People experience rage while being stuck in traffic or being placed on hold; in line at the Starbucks or in the Department of Motor Vehicles; both at work and at home, and also within the digital morass of online life, where capitalization and creative punctuation indicate the sputtering anger of this century. Everything is faster, more interconnected, and more confusing, while possibilities ever diminish, the result an inchoate wrath that simmers only to erupt more than occasionally in the form of mass shootings or the stochastic terrorism which marks American society (though the rest of the world is increasingly losing its immunity as well). According to a Gallup poll of 2021, almost a quarter of respondents throughout the world reported feeling irrational anger at least once a day. Two years before that, an NPR-IBM Watson Health poll had discovered that 84 percent of Americans felt that society had become increasingly enraged. These are the aftereffects of talk radio and sports television, professional wrestling and reality TV, where a rage-tweeting sociopath can commandeer the highest political position in the nation and subsequently raise the temperature for partisans across all sides of the political divide.

Rage can be Janus-faced—there is the righteous hatred of injustice and the wicked hatred of the marginalized, the liberatory fury of the marginalized and the authoritarian fury of the status quo, the necessary wrath of the disposed and

ABOVE A Black American of Haitian descent, the artist Jean-Michel Basquiat understood both the utility and perils of rage—who is allowed to exhibit it, how it must be repressed, and how it sometimes can't be. His 1986 self-portrait, held by the National Museum of Contemporary Art in Barcelona, reduces his own figure to a base archetype. For Basquiat, rage was both imprisoning and liberating.

BOTTOM Remembered by many as a gauzy white lamb, Christ acts in anger at least five times in the New Testament, once so arbitrarily as to miraculously wither a fig tree because it didn't bear fruit. His most spectacular eruption of rage—possibly that which led directly to his crucifixion—was the casting out of the money lenders in the courtyard of the Temple, the messiah knocking over tables and scourging the speculators with a whip. God's wrath would answer humanity's greed, for as Matthew 21:12 notes, Christ declared that "My house shall be called the house of prayer; but ye have made it a den of thieves." A favorite subject of El Greco, his 1600 composition *Christ Driving the Money Changers from the Temple*, held by the National Gallery in London.

the capricious wrath of the powerful. It is a mercurial and difficult-to-tame emotion, the tiger of the psyche. Wrath is at the core of every liberation movement but also at the center of every genocide. James, the brother of Jesus, warns in his epistle that "For the wrath of man worketh not the righteousness of God." Indeed, for as often as we're warned of the Lord's wrath (while also being reassured that the celestial Father is slow to anger), we're also counseled by Scripture to control our own passions, because the justice which fury pursues is not humanity's responsibility. That doesn't mean that organized religion has eschewed wrath, as a cursory reading of history surely demonstrates. An unusual thing, then, wrath; for no other sin is necessarily justified or coupled into the Church in the same manner. If some waggish antinomian were to try and transform all of the vices into virtues, nearly two millennia of theological precedent have already performed exactly that sleight of hand with wrath, repurposed it into a cleansing means of moral instruction and punishment (you're just not supposed to enjoy it too much).

Despite moments of rage within Christ's ministry—withered fig tree, money changers at the Temple—a fairly literal reading of the New Testament should affirm that those Christians who embrace a variety of pacificism have chosen a political theology most congruent with Scripture itself. Yet the utopian, millennial yearning for a pacific existence is frequently bludgeoned by the universal reality of rage. "And the life of man solitary, poor, nasty, brutish, and short," noted seventeenth-century political philosopher Thomas Hobbes in his *Leviathan*. The general consensus of so-called realists has oft been a variation on that

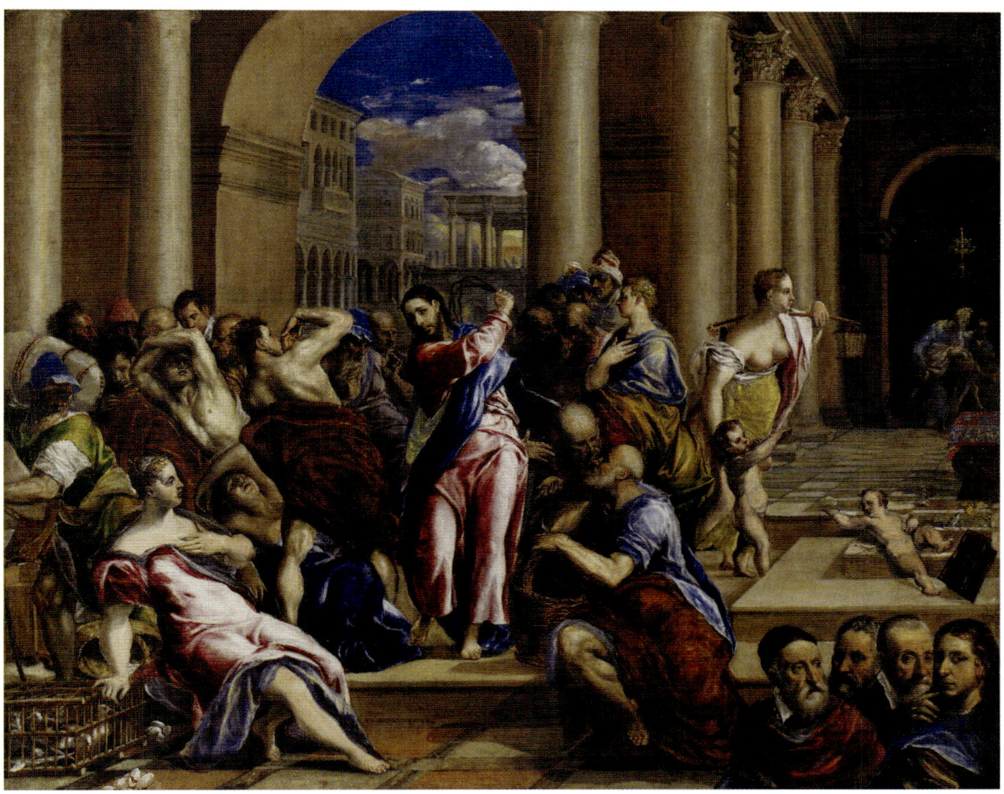

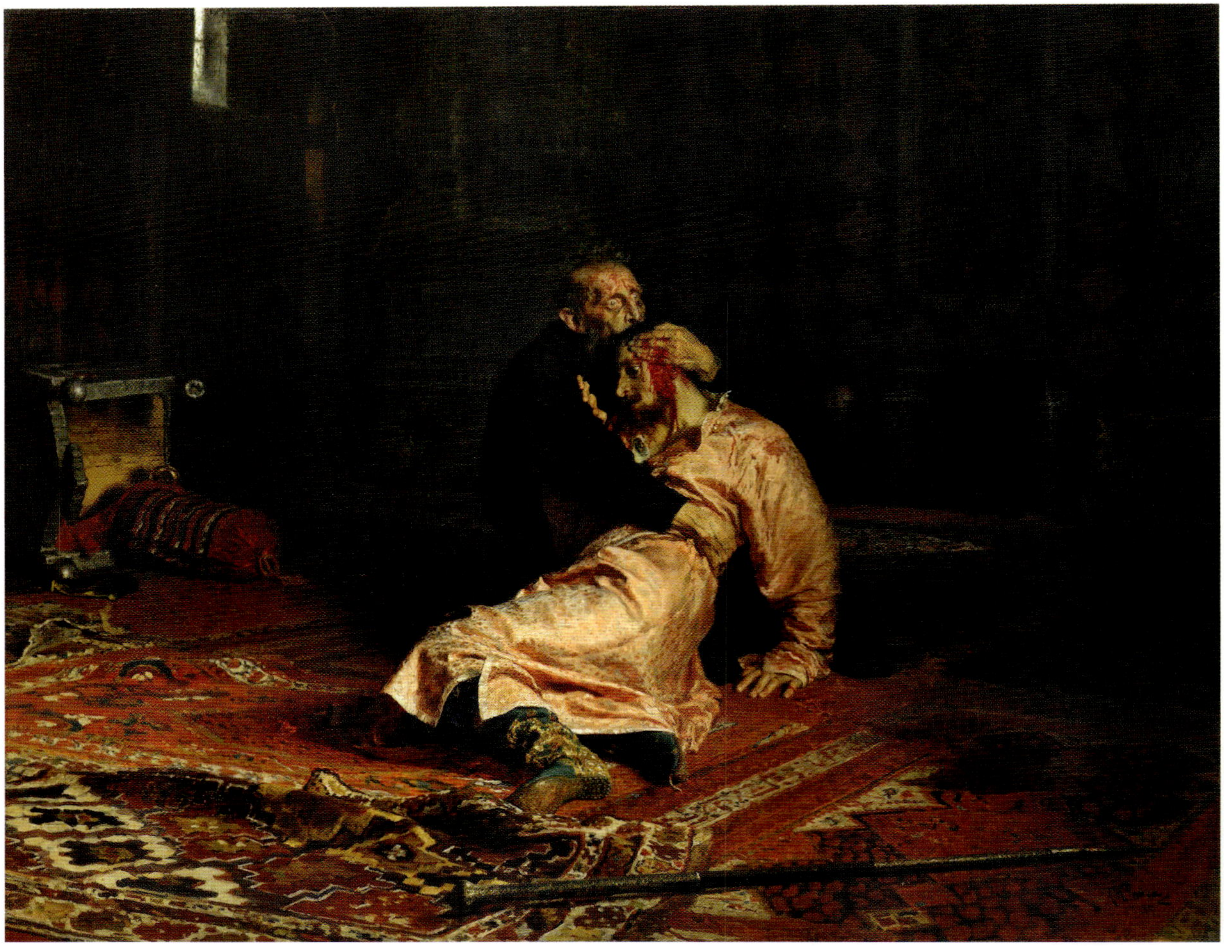

conclusion. Behind Charles Darwin's natural selection, Friedrich Nietzsche's will to power, Sigmund Freud's Id, is always that frothing, foaming, rageful countenance. Wrath, according to such thinkers, would seem to be the natural state of humans, a function of adrenaline and testosterone. More than two millennia before Hobbes, Aristotle largely concurred, arguing in the *Nicomachean Ethics* that "anyone can become angry, that is easy . . . but to be angry with the right person, to the right degree, at the right time, for the right purpose, and in the right way . . . this is not easy." Acknowledging the omnipresence of rage is different from then tabulating the manner in which it might be tamed, even if we only must tame those things which we recognize as dangerous. For the Stoics of the Hellenistic Age, anger was another irrational human emotion—like envy or fear—that could be carefully controlled with psychological training. The second-century philosopher Epictetus framed the issue of anger as being one where the rageful person was controlled by impulses, writing that "Any person capable of angering you becomes your master; he can anger you only when you permit yourself to be disturbed by him." Seneca, the Roman philosopher of that same century and the tutor to the cruel Emperor Nero, wrote an entire

ABOVE The effective opposite of Marcus Aurelius in terms of wise leadership, Tsar Ivan the Terrible had a title that could only do so much to fully encompass the depravities of his rage, one notable instance recorded by Russian painter Ilya Repin in his 1883 composition *Ivan the Terrible and His Son Ivan on 16 November 1581*. Having been struck by the tsar, who erupted in anger at his son's questions, the twenty-seven-year-old would die in his remorseful father's arms, Ivan supposedly yelling, "May I be damned! I've killed my son! I've killed my son!" Original at the Tretyakov Gallery in Moscow.

OPPOSITE Pieter Brueghel the Elder's 1563 *Dull Gret*, original held by Museum Mayer van den Bergh in Antwerp.

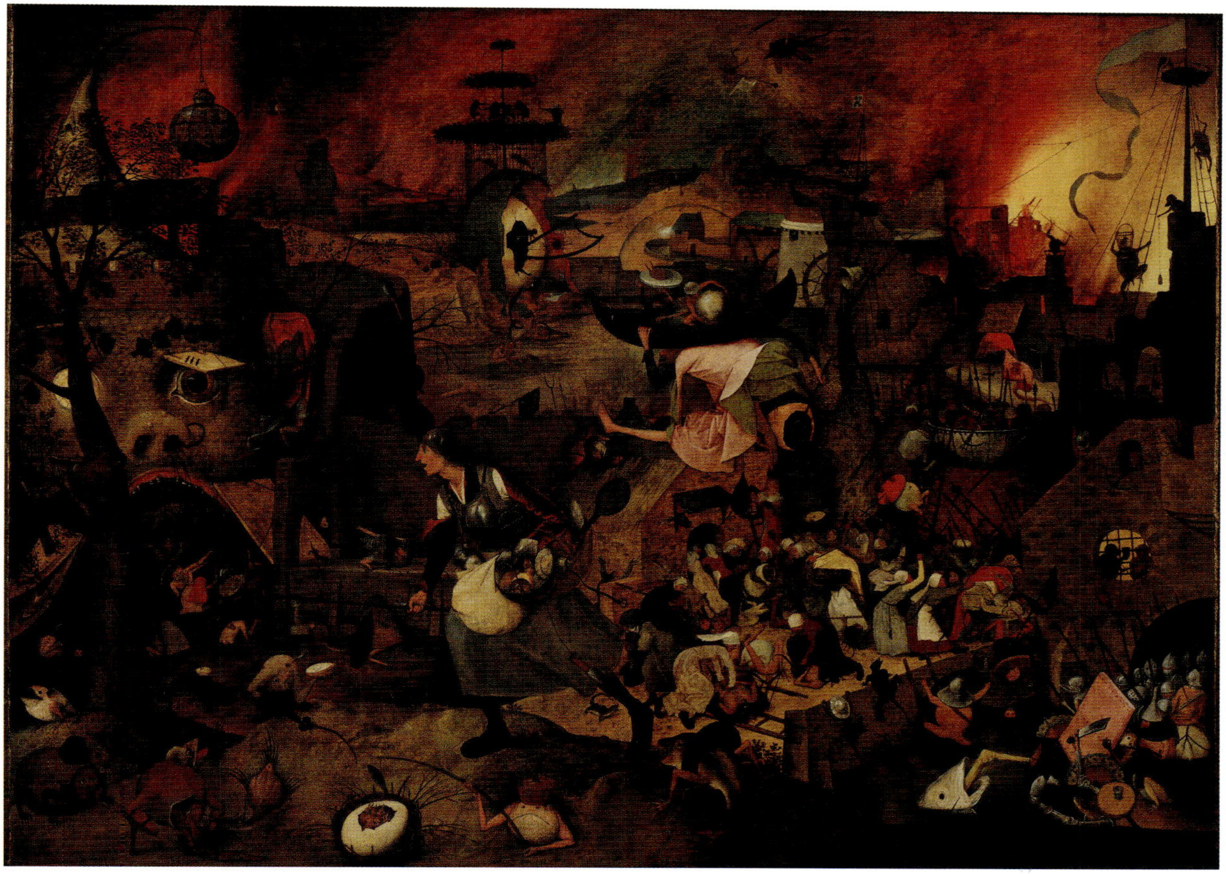

treatise on wrath, arguing in *On Anger* that "my anger is more likely to do me more harm than your wrong," while Marcus Aurelius, himself a Roman emperor, would claim in his *Meditations* from that same time period that "anger and the sorrow it produces are far more harmful than the things which make us angry." Notably, Marcus Aurelius began writing the *Meditations* in the midst of his successful Marcomannic campaigns, wherein he conquered vast swaths of central Europe and vanquished the Vandals, among other Germanic tribes, presumably in a spirit of calm equanimity.

Among the Scholastic theologians of the Middle Ages there developed just such a schema, a theory of just war, which necessitated how one was to militarily engage an adversary in a just and humane manner. Christ's pacifism may have been rejected, but indiscriminate anger was still a sin, and so when war was counseled it had to be under certain circumstances. "Those who have waged war in obedience to the divine command, or in conformity with His laws, have represented in their person the public justice of the wisdom of government, and in this capacity have put to death wicked men; such persons have by no means violated the commandment 'Thou shalt not kill,'" writes St. Augustine in his fourth-century *City of God*. This may seem mere sophistry, yet just war theory existed in part to expunge wrath from the waging of war. According to thinkers like Augustine, war could be justified under certain conditions, and certain values had to be upheld during the waging of a military campaign. The entire litany of such a philosophy of rights in battle, from the Geneva Conventions to the Law of the Hague, are in the tradition of just war theory; they conceive of liberal, universalist, and rational dictates on how war should be fought, if it is indeed to be fought at all. The fair treatment of captured combatants, the prohibition on certain weapons and punishments, the protection of civilian populations, are all in the legacy of just war theory, and the violation of those stipulations is rightly derided as barbarism. Far from paradise, for sure, but in a fallen world, just war theory is an attempt to ameliorate the dark passions that simmer in rage.

Yet a function of wrath can also be liberation; it can be to harrow those same dark, Dionysian places from whence such emotions, and such oppressions, emerge. For example, in the imagination of the Flemish painter Pieter Brueghel the Elder, when the dread virago Dull Gret invaded hell, she put on an armor of kitchenwares—a breastplate made from a baking pan, a helmet made from a colander, and a skillet alongside her sword. Across a red-burnt Flemish countryside, Dull Gret gathered a legion of her fellow women—wives, domestics, cooks, midwives, servants—and marched them as a conquering army toward a bloated whale-like demon's hellmouth that acted as a portal between our world and the realms beneath. Above Dull Gret's army, the sky blazed an eye-watering red, as if the sun itself had broken like rotten yolk over the very earth; set on the horizon are collapsing brick towers; upon the fields which they maneuver, an already engorged hell has expelled some of its inhabitants to defend the kingdom against the conquering women. One appears as a rotting wooden barrel, a flat face pressed against its head; another as a sort of anthropomorphic fish, with bent legs scuttling across the Flemish countryside; silhouetted on the decks of burning ships that crowd the distant horizons are hominid amphibians

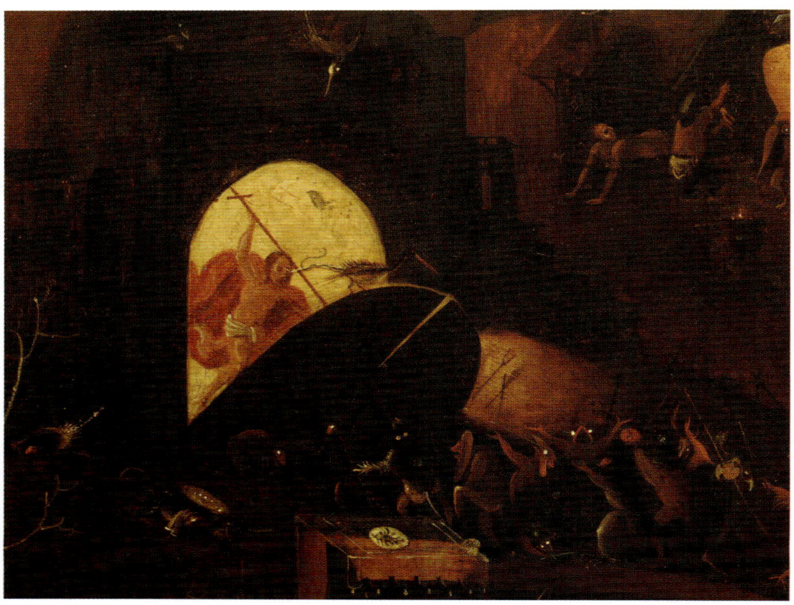

LEFT Detail from *Christ Breaking Down the Gates of Hell*, a painting by a follower of Hieronymus Bosch, painted sometime around the middle of the sixteenth century, with the original held at the Kunsthistoriches Museum in Vienna. "For Christ also hath suffered for sins, the just for the unjust, that he might bring us to God, being put to death in flesh, but quickened in spirit," reads the first epistle of Peter. During Holy Saturday, strung between his crucifixion and resurrection, doctrine holds that Christ "harrowed" Hell, invading Lucifer's domain and freeing the righteous Jews imprisoned there before the incarnation.

hanging from hulls. But the Boschian array is insignificant to Dull Gret. These bestial visages and deformed bodies aren't terrifying to the warrior, who with the countenance of a grim fanatic marches onward toward hell, not oblivious, but confident. Confident that even upon the very entrance to hell, it is Satan and his legions within who must shake at her approach, for as the Flemish proverb has it, "She could plunder in front of hell and return unscathed."

Such is the subject of Brueghel's *Dull Gret*, his disturbing, nightmarish, hallucinogenic 1563 painting of the Flemish legend that imagined a warrior so disgusted with the ways in which the most pernicious and evil of inequities were continually enacted upon her fellow women that she decided to take the battle directly to the source and so invaded hell. However, as the patriot Thomas Paine reminds us, "Tyranny, like hell, is not easily conquered." Brueghel's painting has had as convoluted a history of ownership as it has of proper interpretation; variously held by the Museum Mayer van den Bergh in Antwerp, Vienna's Kunsthistorisches Museum, and in the Prague galleries of the sixteenth-century occult-obsessed Holy Roman Emperor Rudolf II. Dull Gret's inspiring intransigence has flitted about the consciousness of those who imagine abolishing the very confines of perdition. As Christ had once harrowed the halls of hell, so too would this peasant woman of the Low Countries command an army into the capital of Diss, pillaging and marauding along the way. Demons would pass fearsome account of her uncompromising acts, so that by the time Dull Gret would brandish her skillet before the throne of Satan, the fallen angel would quake at her approach. In dramatist Caryl Churchill's feminist classic *Top Girls*, a character based on Dull Gret explains her justifications for battle in simple, earthy Dutch colloquium: "I've had enough. I was mad, I hate the bastards. I come out my front door that morning and shout till my neighbors come out and I said, 'Come on, we're going where the evil come from and pay the bastards out.'"

There's an ambiguity to Brueghel's painting, as to whether or not we should read the battle scene of Dull Gret as a misogynistic joke about the intemperance of pushy women, or as a mystical proto-feminist allegory in which oppression, injustice, and inequity can be defeated as if by an army that fears not even hell. Whether or not our heroine is destined to be the object of respect or mockery, whether she is fearsome or ridiculous, the theme of harrowing is one that goes back to Orpheus, Odysseus, and Aeneas in Hades, to Christ in hell. Not everyone who journeys to the underworld and returns unscathed does so as a conqueror, and in that Dull Gret shares far more with Christ than she does with those classical antecedents. Maybe the very idea is nonsensical, if we're talking about a Flemish peasant woman and not the Son of God, and yet how much more inspiring for it? The idea that all which is required to abolish those evil systems which oppress us is the requisite bravery, the commanding confidence, and a colander on your head?

Because whether or not this was his intent, what Brueghel depicted in *Dull Gret* is a type of utopian yearning, rendered in red and black oils. Maybe the legend of the fearsome Amazon who marauds into Pandemonium is meant to be mocking; maybe she's supposed to be a figure of levity. Or perhaps it's a paean to subversion, an ode to resistance, an epic of what it means to carve out a space for emancipation even within the sulphureous smoke of the hellmouth. Imagine that—is it hubris to think that a mere human can abolish Satan's kingdom? Or is it the very essence of what it means to hope? Because whether or not there

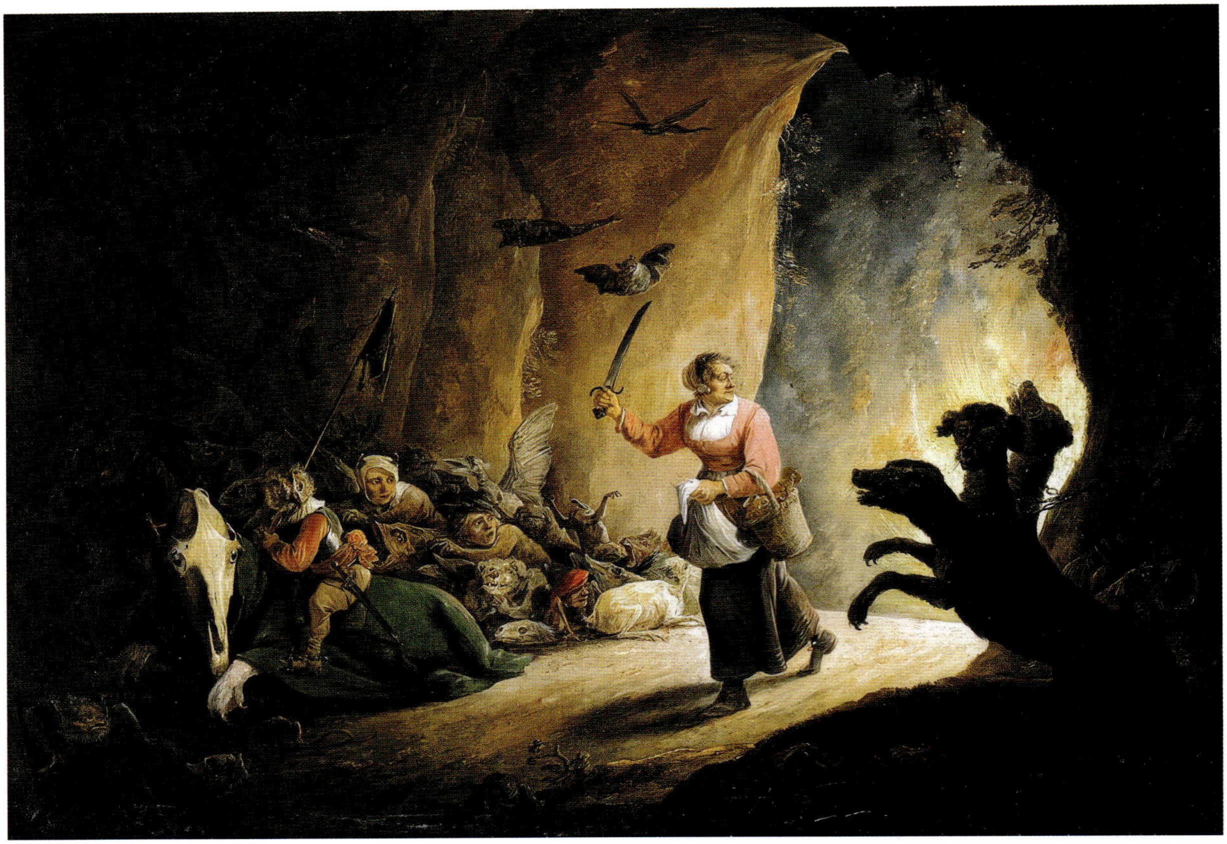

was a Dull Gret, whether or not there is actually a hell, and whether or not after her death the Flemish spinster would find herself returned to those confines as a prisoner punished for her intransigence, the message of Brueghel's painting announces itself as clearly as those trumpets that punctuate Revelation. *Dull Gret*'s message concerns not whether it's possible to conquer hell, but the necessity of living our lives so that we imagine it could be, for in that sublime possibility we can see the demons trembling, if only a little bit. The grapes of wrath crushed for the finest vintage.

ABOVE From Dull Gret to the English-language traditions of Mad Meg, early modern people were fascinated by tales of domestic women conquering Hell. In David Teniers the Younger's 1645 invocation of the legend, held in private collection.

INTERLUDE—DANIEL BERRIGAN

Napalm is composed of kerosene or diesel and a gelling agent to thicken the consistency. Frequently the latter consists of aluminum naphthenate or aluminum salts derived from fatty acids, often synthesized out of coconut oils. Whether discharged from a flame-thrower or dropped from an F-100D, napalm sticks and burns. The material would become synonymous with the American involvement in Vietnam between the French defeat at Dien Bien Phu in 1955 and then the fall of Saigon two decades later. The amount of napalm dropped on Vietnam dwarfs its earlier uses in Japan (and to a lesser extent Germany) and during the Korean War. The forerunner to the U.S. Air Force released 14,000 tons of napalm in World War II; the amount used in Vietnam was 373,000 tons. Sven Lindquist reports in *A History of Bombing* that the "explosive power of these bombs corresponded to about 640 Hiroshimas," with South Vietnam littered with "ten million bomb craters covering a total area of 100,000 hectares." U.S. involvement in Indochina—when also considering the resultant deaths triggered by destabilization—probably led to more than three million deaths. Such are the cold and merciless calculations of the Pentagon, raining fire over a poor nation in another hemisphere. "The war is simply an obscenity, a depraved act by weak and miserable men," wrote Noam Chomsky in his 1969 book *American Power and the New Mandarins*. "It is not pleasant to say such words, but candor permits no less."

In 1968, a high school physics teacher named Dean Pappas manufactured a small amount of napalm and, with eight others, including the brothers Philip and Daniel Berrigan, both of whom were ordained priests, broke into the Catonsville, Maryland, Local Board No. 33, retrieved six hundred draft cards, and then immolated them in the parking lot. On those cards were the numbers of men who would not die in Vietnam. All nine of the trespassers were faithful Catholics, and they aimed their righteous sabotage not just at the military, but also at the "Roman Catholic Church," guilty of "silence and cowardice in the face of our country's crimes." The Berrigan Brothers were not new to this; six months before, they'd destroyed draft cards in Baltimore by dousing them in pig's blood. Nor would their activities stop; similar protests against the military-industrial complex took place in Harrisburg, Washington, DC, Milwaukee, and King of Prussia, Pennsylvania. "Our apologies, good friends, for the fracture of good order, the burning of paper instead of children, the angering of the orderlies in the front parlor of the charnel house," wrote Daniel, who was a Jesuit, in a meditation which was entered as trial evidence. "We could not, so help us God, do otherwise."

Perhaps Zeus is lusty, but not the God of Abraham; maybe Dionysius is gluttonous, but not the Lord of Israel. Because justice is the prerogative of the Lord, so wrath is the only indulgence which He allows. "The time is past when good men can remain silent, when obedience can segregate men from public risk, when the poor can die without defense," Daniel wrote. The Berrigans were persecuted by the FBI, prosecuted by the court system, and they spent years in prison—though having killed no one (quite the opposite, actually). How could wrath directed at those responsible for our age's apocalyptic injustices ever be interpreted as a sin? Philip, who was a member of the Josephite order, was also a veteran who had served in the Bulge. He had seen what war does, he'd seen shrapnel embedded in corpses and bodies crushed under debris. Daniel and he were pacifists as a result. But a pacifist can express wrath—maybe especially. And what differentiates wrath from rage is the clear-minded rationality of the former, the understanding not that God's on your side but that you're on his. Justice is the theory, wrath is the practice; love of humanity necessitates anger at the powerful, at wickedness. Both brothers were accomplished poets as well, particularly Daniel, and in one lyric he aptly expressed that ethical understanding: "God is fire, is love."

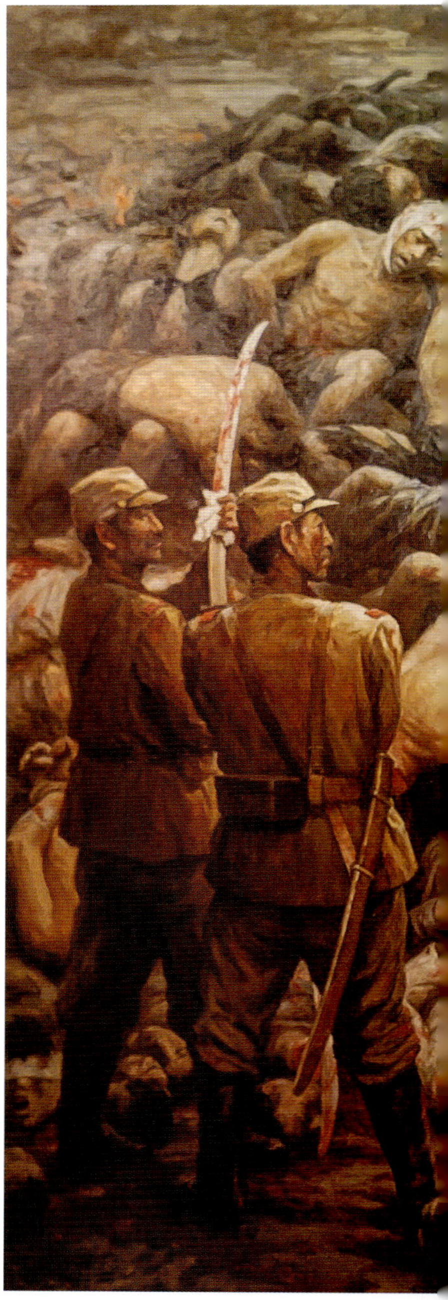

A WASTELAND CALLED PEACE

While it is not the most wicked injustice of war, it is still a barbarity that so much of our attention is on the murderers and not the murdered. To focus only on the monsters is to reduce the innocent dead to corpses. Piles of rubble, of shoes and books and toys, of twisted bodies. We imperil our own conscience if we forget such evidence of life. This is why we must not repeat the names of the two Japanese Imperial Army officers who, according to the *Tokyo Nichi Nichi Shimbun*, engaged in a contest to see who could first kill a hundred Chinese civilians during the invasion of Nanjing. According to the paper, one man had killed 106 innocent humans and the other 105, with "both . . . lieutenants going into extra innings." This book will not record the names of those two officers because we do not know the names of the 211 women, children, and men whom they murdered. You will not find the names of these lieutenants in this book because we don't know the names of the 150 additional people they killed the following day. Such atrocities "did not penetrate the world consciousness," writes historian Iris Chang in *The Rape of Nanking: The Forgotten Holocaust of World War II*, "because the victims themselves had remained silent," and so we will not say the perpetrators' names, for they had their own opportunity to speak at their trials.

During the six weeks of invasion that started in December 1937, more than two hundred thousand Chinese civilians were murdered, with at least twenty thousand incidences of rape (both of these numbers are likely lower than the real ones). Robert O. Wilson, an American physician in Nanjing, recorded in his diary that the "slaughter of civilians is appalling. I could go on for pages telling of cases of rape and brutality almost beyond belief," and he does, and if you need to read those, you can. The doctor would testify at the International Military Tribunal for the Far East after the war's end; in 1948 that same commission executed the two officers involved in that horrific contest. Whether or not it's good and righteous and just to execute those who commit such crimes is a matter of debate. As to if it's true or not that an eye for an eye makes the whole world blind, it's difficult to form an opinion. The idea of taking any human life is cause for

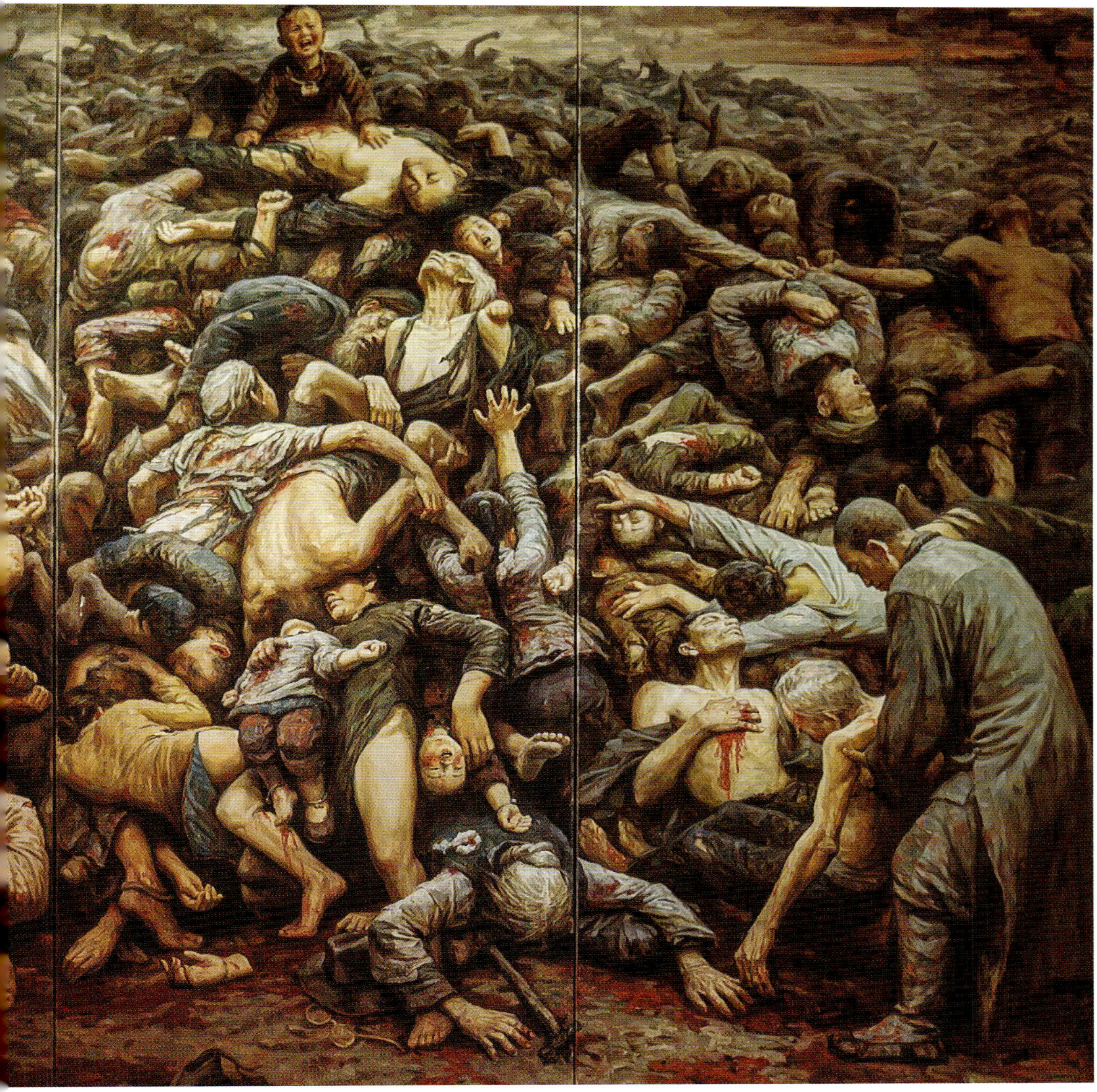

ABOVE Chinese painter Li Zijian's 1992 mural *Nanjing Massacre* gives a sense of the barbarity and horror of the Japanese invasion, a pile of dismembered bodies and body parts only a fraction of the hundreds of thousands who were tortured and killed within the city. To the side, Zijian depicts two Imperial officers laughing at the evil which they've committed, the unthinking dehumanization at the center of wrath manifested in this pyre of corpses. Original held in private collection.

unease, but it's undoubtedly an ethical travesty to mourn for those two officers on the gallows, nor should the thought of them in Hell bother you, though whatever that says about us is something that we probably should have more concern about. Atrocities are so often committed by perfectly normal people—those two may have grown up in loving families; they may have delighted in their wives and children. Those soldiers were not demons, but humans, and that is all the more terrifying.

"Almost all people have this potential for evil, which would be unleashed only under certain dangerous social circumstances," Chang writes. It is also important to remember that if everybody is capable of committing atrocities, only a small percentage of humans actually do, lest we obscure evil in the gauzy miasma of moral universalism. Yet the question of what drives men to such wickedness is forever unanswerable. Why are some Adolf Eichmann or Josef Mengele and by contrast others are Mahatma Gandhi or Óscar Romero? Chang's research involved discovering the involvement of German businessman John Rabe, who established the Nanking Safety Zone, where through diplomatic immunity he was able to protect civilians and saved two hundred thousand people. Rabe was also a dedicated member of the Nazi Party. The only thing more mysterious than human beings is grace, whatever its origin might be. Separate from historical scholarship, intelligence reports, and national security briefings, war literature exists to help us comprehend the arbitrary nature of grace and damnation. If war literature is written to impart meaning, then all war literature is failure. Nothing is so incomprehensible as war; not logistics, or strategy, battles for land, glory, riches, or liberation, all of which can be perfectly logical, but the *actual act of war*, of waking up knowing that your life could be taken or that you must take a life. We're told this is our animal nature, but the organized barbarity at Andersonville, or Dachau, or Nanjing has no corollary in the natural world. War literature exists not to impart meaning, but rather the appearance of it, so to gesture at something beyond this veil of darkness; something unutterable, and ineffable, and silent, and strange. War literature, at its best, exists not as scripture but as liturgy, not to explain but to remember. Chang writes that "to forget a Holocaust is to kill twice," and such writing ensures that we don't become complicit.

Literature replaces the aridity of numbers with the texture of humanity, while somehow grappling with the full scope of atrocity. When Joseph Stalin was Commissar of Munitions during the enforced famine known as the Holodomor, which killed almost four million Ukrainians in the mid-'30s, he told a group of his colleagues that "If only one man dies of hunger, that is a tragedy. If millions die, that's only statistics." What is grotesque is that this ruthless theorist of the human abyss was correct. When death tolls mount from the hundreds, to the thousands, to the millions, the brain is only capable of processing so much. For who is forgotten is Myshko Cherkasy, whose mother, when he died and was to be buried, discovered that his grave was already occupied by another child; Michael Kovrak who starved to death in front of his young brother; Olya Sturko forced to give birth upon the wheat fields at a collective farm, who died from eating a small amount of food after weeks of starving. The task of war literature is to transform shadows into pictures, to put flesh upon the bones of mere statistics. To square individual tragedy with the horror of mass atrocity, to mathematically transform the number one into an infinity. Ethically, the writer and their reader

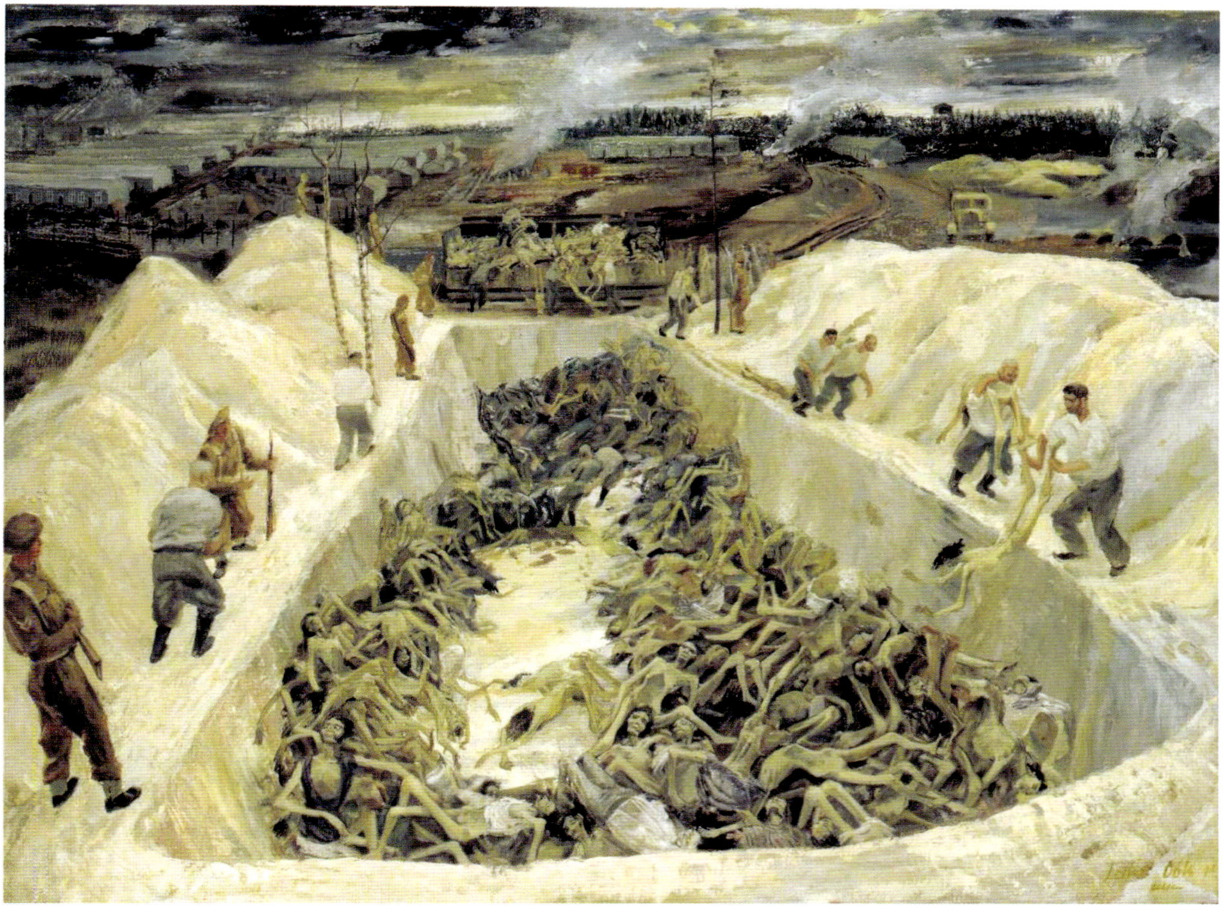

ABOVE Embedded with the British Army during the Second World War, painter Leslie Cole was tasked with recording the atrocities committed by the Nazis that were revealed as the Allies liberated Europe. His 1945 painting *One of the Death Pits, Belsen* depicts a massive tangle of bodies in one of the most notorious of Nazi death camps.

must *attempt* to comprehend that each singular murder is but one of four million. With one, or two, or three deaths in mind, we must try and imagine all of the deaths. Holding to particularity, we must mourn for the multiplicity. That this is by definition impossible does not alleviate our responsibility; if anything, our own actions become all the more imperative. What is asked of us is something theological, to grasp toward the enormity of all that which we are incapable of understanding.

Every human is a universe; each individual in victory and defeat, love and hatred, desire and revulsion, is more complicated than all great literature, more beautiful than every painting, more true than all of the axioms of philosophy. The human soul is inviolate and, in its own flawed way, a species of perfection; which is why murder is a sin and to take millions of lives is a crime against humanity. "The violence of war is random," writes journalist Chris Hedges in *War Is a Force That Gives Us Meaning*. "It does not make sense. And many of those who struggle with loss also struggle with the knowledge that the loss was futile and unnecessary." War literature which does something as sacrilegious as to *make sense* scarcely deserves to be called literature. Reduced to its basest formulation, war is the practice of resolving disagreements, or acquiring land, or erasing

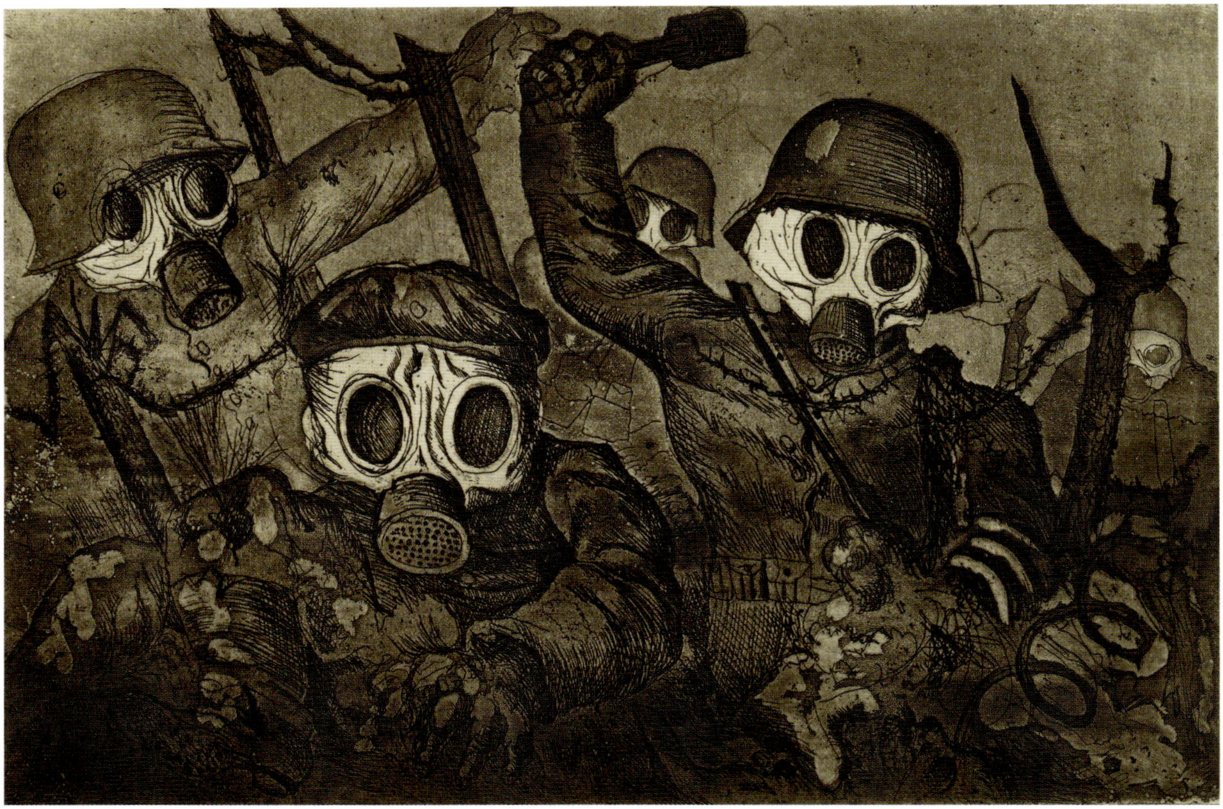

humans whom you hate by organizing men with weapons who then kill people until everyone is tired of all the killing, or everyone's dead. That is irrational, stupid, inexplicable, there is no making sense of that, and so any honest war literature refuses to concern itself with such theodicies.

There is a risk in reducing gun and wound to axiom and postulate, bullet to arid argument. You can't summarize a null point of meaning with anything as quotidian as a syllogism. That shining and polished-black-jack-booted Prussian general Carl von Clausewitz claimed in *On War* that "war is a continuation of politics by other means." Perhaps, though, often the opposite is just as true. Let's not impugn von Clausewitz's instilling of bravery, loyalty, and respect within his troops, his inspection of ammunition and armories, his evaluation of the Cannae model of troop formation in imitation of Hannibal's victory during the Second Punic War; but give us rather that grizzled frontiersman General William Tecumseh Sherman's opinion as he marched all the way to Savannah that "war is hell." Those three words seem at least truthful. War isn't just hell, of course. War is also strategy, war is distraction, war is horror, war is entertainment, war is propaganda, war is spontaneous, war is planned, war is boring, war is exciting, war is oppressive, war is liberatory, war is wasteful, war is necessary, but most of all war is meaningless. At least the actual pulling of the trigger is. Being able to kill a man, the uncertainty of whether you'll return, the knowledge you may never see your family again, the reality that somebody else might never see theirs again because of you—none of that can quite be circumscribed by logic or

TOP Detail from the German painter Otto Dix's 1924 *Stormtroopers Advancing Under a Gas Attack*, original at the British Museum. With their gas masks and their weaponry, the soldiers in Dix's fevered nightmare of a painting appear more robot than man, the central equation of all war being that of how the human can be subsumed into the merely mechanical, the transformation of people into matter, with wrath the catalyst.

OPPOSITE Uniforms and weapons are incidental to the central purpose of war, for war is always defined by the illogical act of murdering another human being on behalf of a ruler, or a state, or a religion, or an ideology. French artist Jean Fouquet's illuminated manuscript of 1460, depicting the ninth-century Battle of Fontenoy-en-Puisaye, may bear little aesthetic similarity to Dix's symbolist cartoon, but both literally imagine the exact same thing—a field of murdered bodies and their murderers, somewhere in France. Original held by the Metropolitan Museum of Art in New York.

poetry. All war literature must be failed literature because it gestures to where words themselves fail.

All honest war literature is fundamentally anti-war. That's not the same as saying that all war literature must be *pacifistic*. Consider Kurt Vonnegut's auto-fiction / science fiction account of the Allied firebombing of Dresden in *Slaughterhouse-Five*, Norman Mailer's indulgent but trenchant *The Naked and the Dead*, Joseph Heller's hilarious and terrifying *Catch-22*, Dalton Trumbo's disturbing account of being caged within one's own destroyed body in *Johnny Got His Gun*, the German writer Erich Maria Remarque's exquisite account of World War I trench fighting in *All Quiet on the Western Front*, each and every one exemplars, each and every one anti-war, each and every one pacifistic, and tellingly each and every one by a veteran. Remarque explained that his book was to be "neither an accusation nor a confession, and least of all an adventure, for death is not an adventure to those who stand face to face with it." But great war literature need not be pacifistic, only anti-war, which is to say that it comprehends barbarity. Two of the most poignant, brutal, and under-heralded mid-century war novels are Martin Booth's horrific *Hiroshima Joe* and John Horne Burns's *The Gallery*. Both books concern the ostensible "Good War" against the Axis powers, with Booth focusing on the war against Japan and Burns writing about the occupation of Naples by the Americans. And both, while not arguing against the reasons for the war, focus on brutality enacted against "enemy" civilians, how innocence is never a quality of those who fight, regardless of their side's righteousness.

The titular character of *Hiroshima Joe* is Captain John Sandingham, a British POW captured by the Japanese in Hong Kong and witness to the unspeakable horror of the atom bomb. Sandingham observes the incineration of whole city blocks, women and men turned to ash, shadows burnt into sidewalks, and children with skin hanging from their bodies; he sees "what no man should be made to see; he died fearing what we all must fear," a world where there is no distinction between soldier and civilian, where peace itself is conquered. *The Gallery* also disavows Manichean platitudes in fictionalized vignettes based on the American occupation of the author's beloved Naples, where the ostensible good guys were involved in extortion, racketeering, rape, murder. Burns's novel is a warning at the dawn of the true American century, that "unless we made some attempt to realize that everyone in the world isn't American, and that not everything American is good, we'll all perish together." An irony is that some of the greatest anti-war literature comes from the Second World War, arguably the most morally unassailable battle in human history. A generation after the Great War, and the "combatants were unillusioned from the start," writes editor Sebastian Faulks in the introduction to *The Vintage Book of War Fiction*. "They knew how gruesome war would be, they knew that they had been dropped into it by inept politicians, but in place of innocent patriotism of their fathers they had a proper moral cause to fight for." If war is necessary, there's still nothing glorious about it. Between

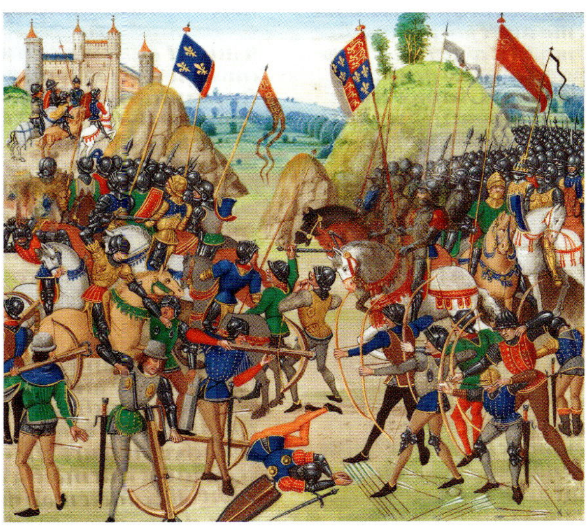

country or what's right, at the very least there's something to be said for fighting on behalf of the latter.

In a war of defense or liberation there can be many things—loyalty and courage, honor and fraternity. Glory, however, is invented by poets. War is blood congealing on the dead grass at Flanders Field and brains sprayed across Omaha Beach, it's a gangrenous foot being sawed off at Manassas and bits of flesh dotting Hill 488. "I sing of arms," as Virgil begins *The Aeneid*, a topic of utmost seriousness since a man first struck another man, our story of creation based not in Eden but in when Cain slew Abel. Triumph of kings and victory of the nation, glory of soldiers and the shame of the vanquished. Virgil's epic is great poetry, but it's also propaganda, albeit with its own anti-war moments studded like land mines within. The most antique of war literature, even when written to valorize, still has within it the seeds of truth. *The Iliad* of Homer, whether or not he had experienced war himself, is the great martial epic of valor, and yet within its opening lines there is the honesty which compels him to describe war as "Black and murderous . . . Incalculable pain, pitched countless souls . . . bodies to rot as feasts / For dogs and birds." Achilles and Jason, Aeneas and Pallas, may fight with shields and spears, swords and helmets, while today soldiers wear Flak Jackets and brandish M4s, but the same absurd goal is at play—kill the other guy before you get killed. Despite the social Darwinian fallacy that understands people as living in a barely contained state of nature, just three days' worth of good meals away from total anarchy, to kill a man, especially a stranger, and particularly one who's done nothing to you, is a supremely unnatural thing.

When humanists extol the canon's universalism, they reduce and flatten our differences with the past, and the reality is that we neither love, pray, live, or work like our ancestors in Rome, or Greece, or Babylon, but the score of being made to kill a man—and the resulting wounds—remains similar. Suffering isn't

BOTTOM Evocative of his earlier and far more famous *Guernica*, Pablo Picasso's 1951 *Massacre in Korea* castigates the barbarity of American troops involved in the slaughter of some 30,000 civilians in Sinchon. The victims on the left in their grief and their nudity, their innocence and their fear, are undeniably human, while the soldiers on the right appear more machine then men. Original held by the Museo Picasso in Malaga, Spain.

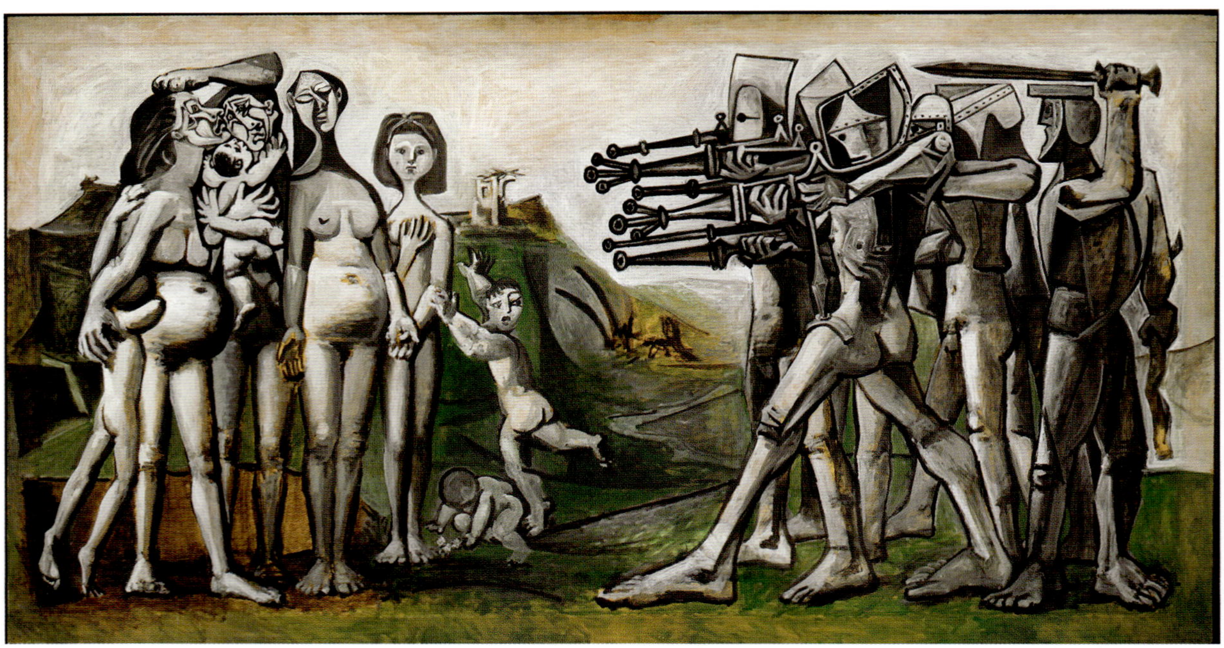

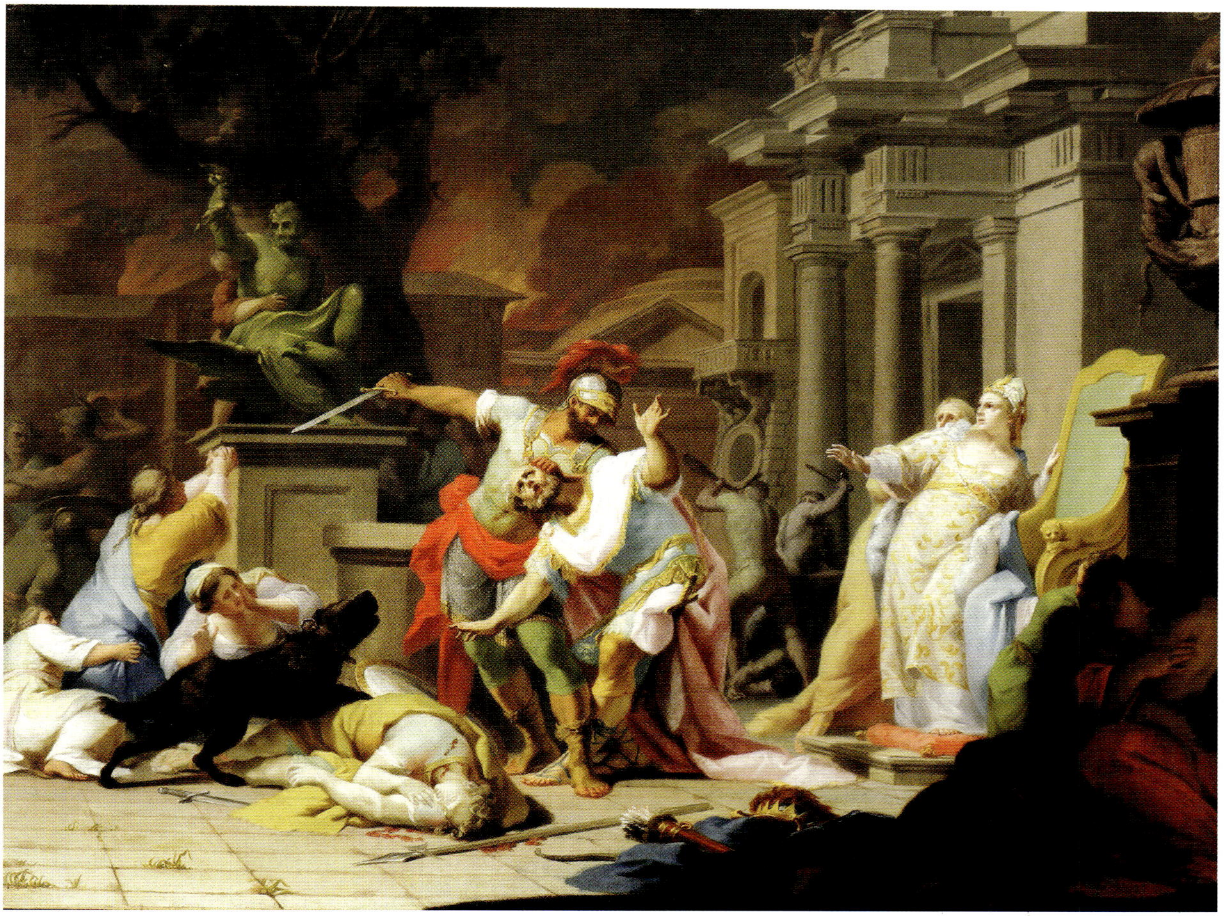

ABOVE "Rage—Goddess, sing the rage of . . . Achilles, / murderous, doomed . . . hurling down to the House of Death so many sturdy souls." Here, as the Greeks sack Troy, Achilles's son Neoptolemus prepares to murder Priam, as imagined by French historical painter Jules Lefebvre in this 1861 painting. The inconsolable women in the background, the corpse under Neoptolemus's foot, the flames beyond the pillars, the look on Priam's face—all of it underscores war's barbarity. And yet just like with Homer's beautiful lines, Lefebvre's elegant neoclassical brushstrokes obscure war's reality, turning it into allegory or stage-set. Original at the Beaux-Arts de Paris.

about meaning; to the contrary, it can often be about nothing. And yet suffering must still be endured, and so literature acts not to explain the inexplicable but rather to soothe, to say, *You are not alone, this has happened before, this will happen again, and not everybody survives, but some people do.*

"'Forward, the Light Brigade! / Charge for the guns!' he said: / Into the valley of Death / Rode the six hundred," wrote Alfred Lord Tennyson in 1854, mere days after the routing of the 4th and 13th Light Dragoons, 17th Lancers, and 8th and 11th Hussars during the Crimean War. Few poets seem stuffier than Tennyson, so patriotic, formal, traditional, and conservative, his verse ponderously Victorian while across the Atlantic Walt Whitman was breaking meter and Emily Dickinson was reinventing metaphor. All of those exclamation points, that equestrian rhythm, that sickly celebration of valor. Yet even Tennyson drew a distinction between the incompetent men who sent boys to their deaths and the boys themselves, who "Storm'd at with shot and shell, / Boldly they rode and well, / Into the jaws of Death, / Into the mouth of Hell." This, it could be observed, is still mythological language, Tennyson describing the campaign in the language of harrowing. He chose the wrong genre, for war literature isn't myth—it's horror. What's lacking in Tennyson is the physical experience of war; he describes "Cannon to

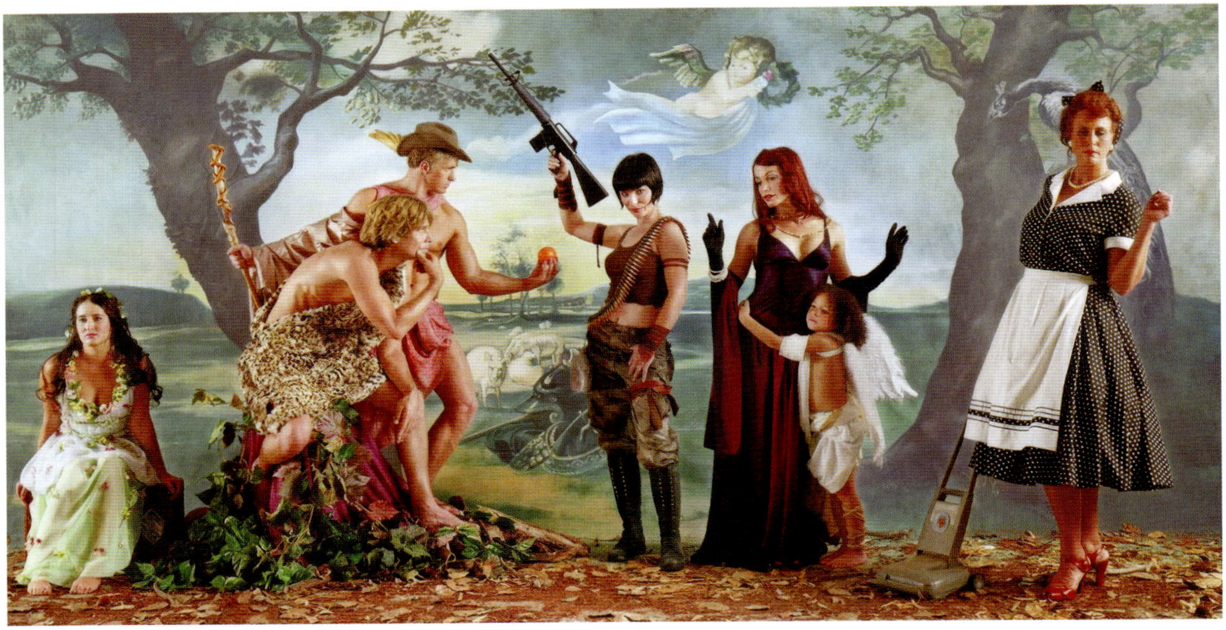

right of them, / Cannon to left of them, / Cannon behind them . . . While horse and hero fell, / They that had fought so well." This is basically a boy's fantasy of war. Tennyson might as well be describing soccer. The poet laureate wasn't a veteran, and it shows; it's what allows him to ask, "When can their glory fade? / O the wild charge they made! / All the world wonder'd. / Honor the charge they made! / Honor the Light Brigade!" Now, all that's remembered is a poem more pablum than Parnassus, each of those dead soldiers now forgotten other than for some cenotaphs and memorials in England. What's missing is blood—gouged eyes—protruding bones—first-degree burns—festering bullet wounds—severed hands and crushed bodies. What's missing is the sense that death isn't metaphor or simile or allegory, but that death is just death, a violent one all the more so.

Compare Tennyson's verse to Whitman's "The Wound-Dresser" from his collection of Civil War lyrics *Drum-Taps*. Of Quaker pacifist stock, though a vociferous supporter of the Union, Whitman left Brooklyn for Washington, DC, after hearing of his brother's wounding at Antietam, deciding to stay in the capital, where he worked as a nurse in war hospitals. The good, gray poet would tenderly minister to the beautiful boys of American death, wrapping their burns and cuts, setting their broken legs, distributing sweets and occasionally reading his verse to men who undoubtedly had no idea that he was the greatest of American poets. "Bearing the bandages, water and sponge, / Straight and swift to my wounded I go, / Where they lie on the ground after the battle brought in, / Where their priceless blood reddens the grass, the ground." Whitman is an abolitionist who comprehends that the Confederacy is defeated at Gettysburg and Antietam and nowhere else, but he is not delusional about the cost. Tennyson's Dragoons, Lancets, and Hussars are heroes, whereas Whitman asks in a parenthetical, "(was one side so brave? the other was equally brave)." The British poem lacks blood, it lacks corpses, it lacks bodies, replacing them with abstractions. In "The

TOP American performance artist Eleanor Antin's 2007 piece *The Judgement of Paris (After Rubens)* gives a postmodern gloss to both the old master and the section of Homer in which the eponymous Trojan gives an inscribed golden apple to Aphrodite instead of to two other goddesses, Hera or Athena. An instigating event in the Trojan War, the supposed goddess of love is here rendered by Antin holding that most American of weapons, the semiautomatic rifle, while outfitted in camo fatigues and tank top, a bandolier over her breasts. Love and wrath conjoined in *The Iliad* and the United States.

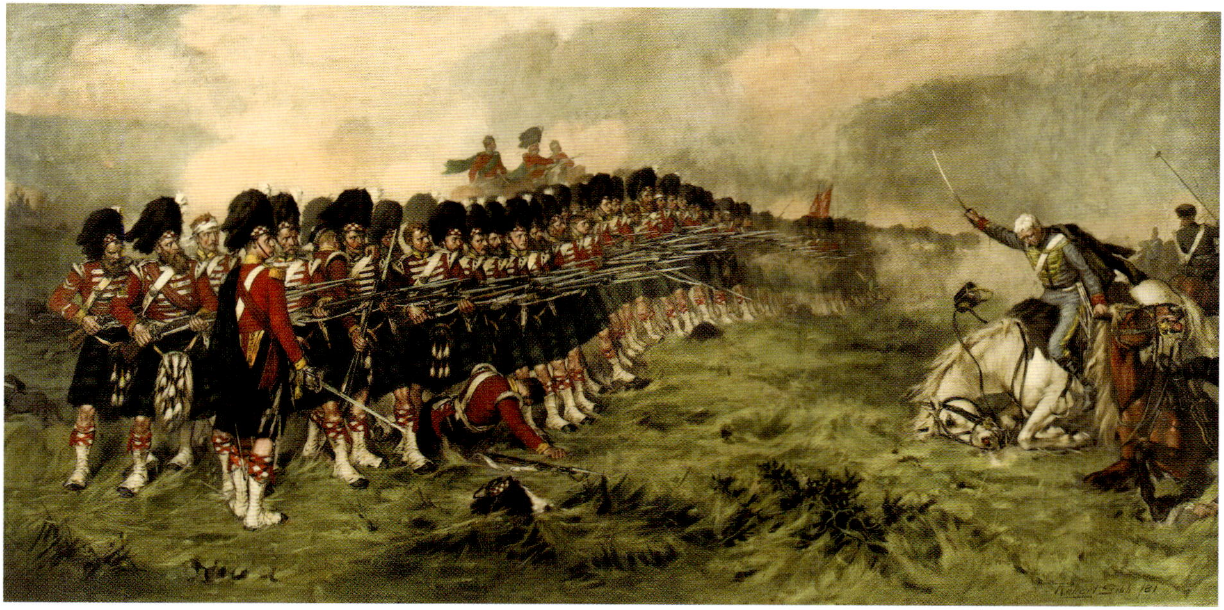

Wound-Dresser," Whitman describes "stump of the arm, the amputated hand . . . the clotted lint . . . the matter and blood." Whether or not a war is just, or justified, or righteous, or right, Whitman understands that it results in men like the soldier whose "eyes are closed, his face is pale, he dares not look on the bloody stump, / And has not yet look'd on it." The difference between the poems is that Tennyson described war in terms of glory, and Whitman knows that it's about "clotted rags and blood, emptied, and fill'd again." One poem works because it tells the truth and the other one doesn't work because it lies. As Remarque writes in the following century, "A hospital alone shows what war is."

Besides, meter, rhythm, and rhyme can be useful, for what war lyrics are more successful than that of Wilfred Owen's and Siegfried Sassoon's accounts of trench warfare written in the midst of the Great War itself? Owen was a working-class Shropshire lad tutored on Keats, Shelley, and Yeats; Sassoon was from a wealthy Baghdadi Jewish family and was educated at Cambridge. The two read and admired each other, and served at the same time along the crooked, burning gash of the Western Front. As inheritors of a classical English education, both men wrote in a cadence that owes more to the measured traditionalism of Tennyson than to the barbaric yawp of Whitman, and yet when war's madness can be barely constrained by formalism, its horrors are all the more pronounced. "Soldiers are citizens of death's grey land," wrote Sassoon in *The Counter-Attack and Other Poems*, "Drawing no dividend from time's to-morrows." Almost oracular, but the eloquence of Sassoon's rhetoric belies the horror it describes. In Owen's most famous poem, "Dulce et Decorum Est," written from the trenches themselves, he describes watching the burning, disintegrating, acrid death that results when a soldier is hit with mustard gas, for "someone still was yelling out and stumbling, / And flound'ring like a man in fire or lime . . . / Dim, through the misty panes and thick green light, / As under a green sea, I saw him drowning."

TOP Robert Gibb's 1881 *The Thin Red* Line takes part in the same mythologization as did Tennyson, the painter depicting the fabled 93rc Sutherland Highlands Regiment of Scottish soldiers (along with their Turkish allies) who held off a Russian contingent five times their size during the Crimean War's Battle of Balaclava in 1854. Original held by the National War Museum in Edinburgh.

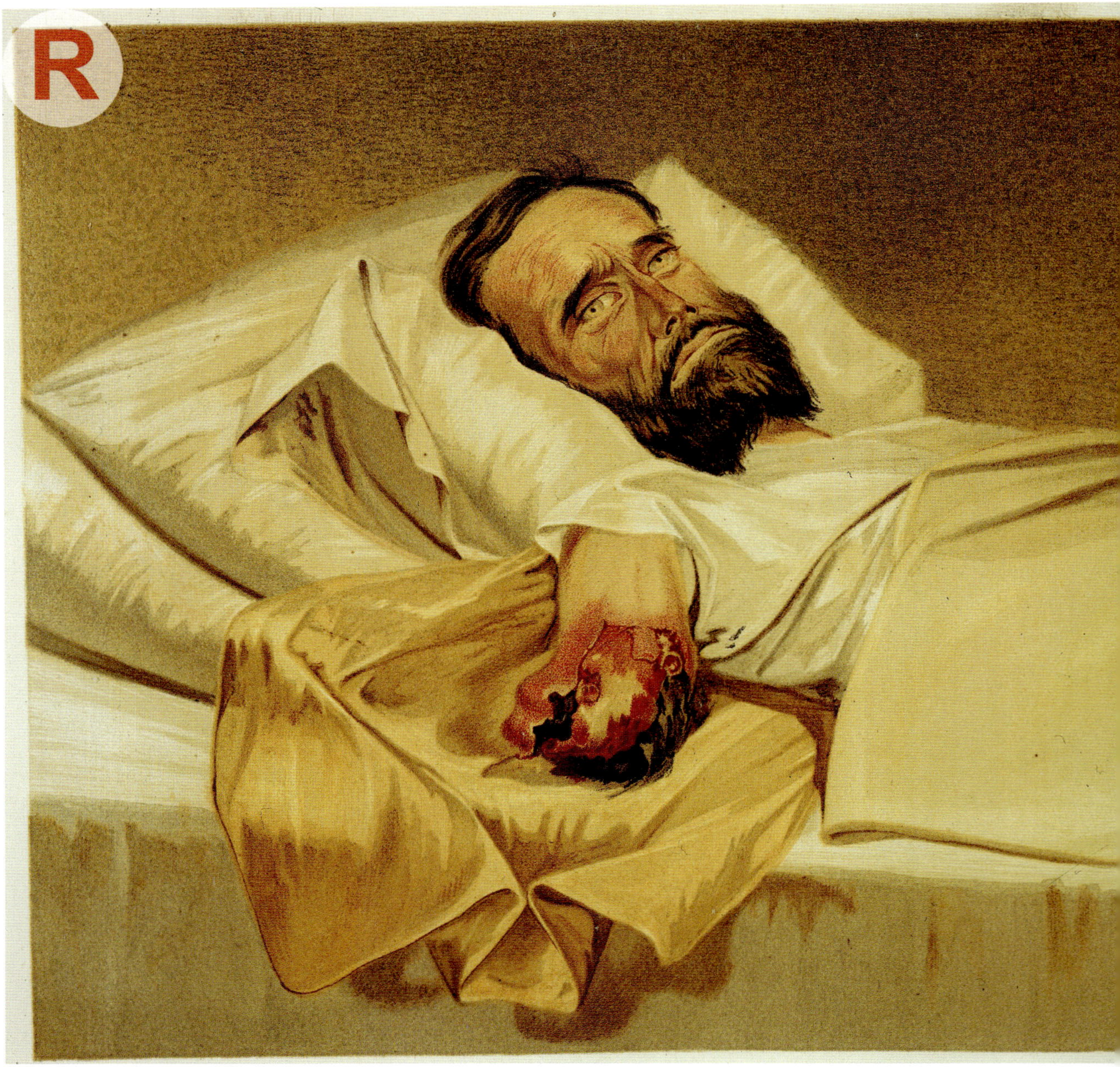

ABOVE Son of glory, soldier of bravery, scion of wrath. Not a painting rendered for aesthetic purposes, but an illustration for pedagogical ones, this painting meant to depict the affects of battlefield gangrene. The man in the picture isn't imagined: his name is Milton Wallen of the 1st Kentucky Cavalry, a Confederate regiment. The soldier was treated in a Richmond medical hospital administered by the Union Army. Painted by Edward Stauch, the image was reproduced in the *Medical & Surgical History of the War of the Rebellion*, first published in 1870 by the Surgeon General of the United States Army.

OPPOSITE After the rage—peace; after the fear—peace; or at least peace is what they call such silent devastation. British painter C. R. W. Nevinson makes clear his feelings about the supposed Great War through the irony of his harrowing 1918 painting's title—*Paths of Glory*. Original held by the Imperial War Museum in London.

The Great War surprised the great powers, doddering men who'd amassed massive armies and let their technology outstrip their empathy. The war was fought between the first cousins who ruled Britain, Germany, and Russia, offering up as sacrifice millions of young men cooked in mustard and shot at by Gatling gun on the barbed wire of broken Europe. The impact of Sassoon and especially Owen's verse is that they exist between the grandiosity of Victorian youth trained on myths of the Light Brigade when compared to the reality of Verdun, Somme, and Gallipoli. When Owen describes the dying man's "every jolt, the blood . . . gargling from the froth-corrupted lungs, / Obscene as cancer, bitter as the cud / Of vile, incurable soles on innocent tongues," he writes in an idiom that at the literal level of sounds is *beautiful*. Go ahead, read that bit out loud to yourself, listen to the cadence, the relationship of syllables to each other, the meter, the unforced rhyming, and admit that Owen has used beautiful language to describe an atrocity. And in that ironic gap, valor is erased by degradation. Owen expresses more about battle than propagandists ever could. He would die in 1918 while crossing the Sambre-Oise Canal. His mother received the telegram on Armistice Day, when bells were ringing in celebration throughout Shrewsbury. "The old lie: *Dulce et Decorum Est / Pro Patria mori*." Who knows what poems have been interrupted by a bullet, what novels disrupted by mortar attack?

Some of the surviving lyrics are assembled in Lorrie Goldensohn's remarkable *American War Poetry*, the first collection of its kind, including verse from colonial wars through Afghanistan, with sections dedicated to overlooked conflicts including the Spanish American War, the Indian Wars, and even the Spanish Civil War. Goldensohn writes that poetry is a way of conveying "battlefield advance and retreat, the daring and courage of leaders and men, as well as the despoliation of territory, the experience of prison camp and the making of refugees, the annihilation and wounding of human flesh, the grieving aftermath." Every emotion is expressed in such verse, from cruel jingoism to fear,

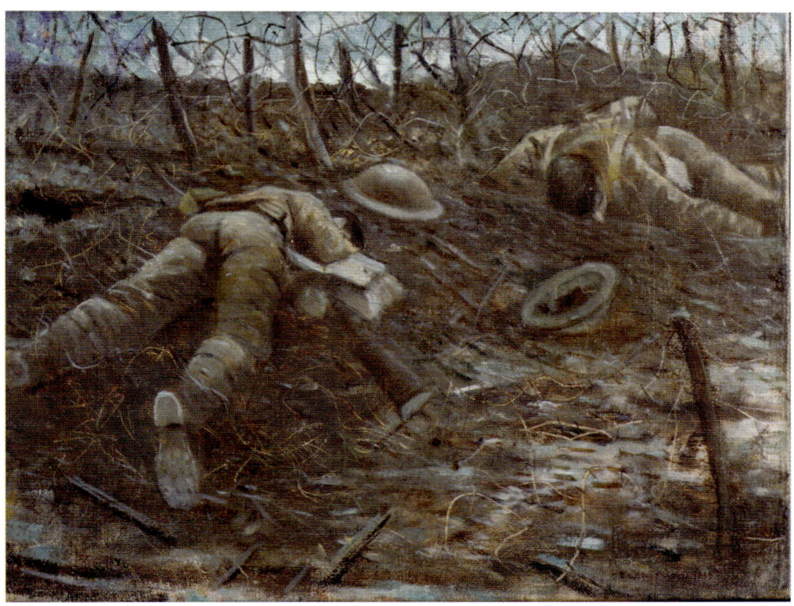

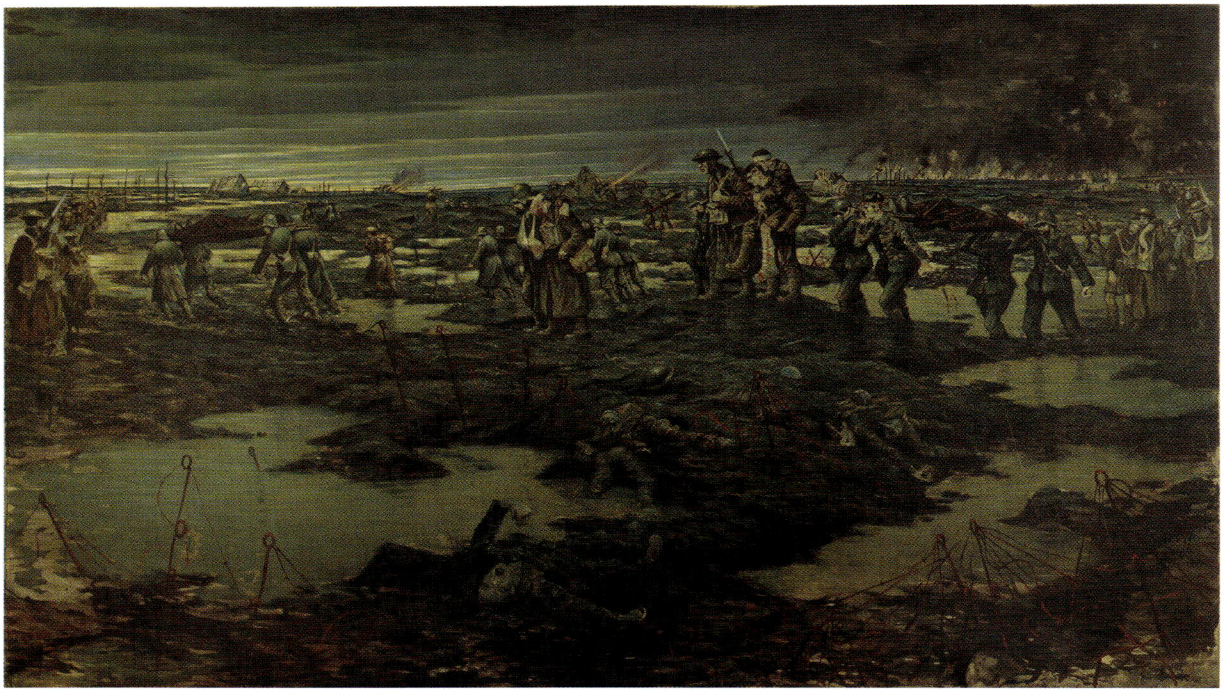

from patriotic loyalty to absurdity. James Dickey, American poet laureate and veteran of the Second World War, gives a meditation in incendiary and gasoline, writing of how "All families lie together, though some are burned alive." Yusef Komunyakaa presents the haunting experience of searching for the names of dead friends on the Vietnam Veterans Memorial, where "My black face fades, / hiding inside the black granite." For sheer methodical, scientific accuracy, however, Iraq War veteran Brian Turner's masterpiece *Here, Bullet* provides both autopsy report and psychological evaluation. "If a body is what you want, / then here is bone and gristle and flesh." That is what war poetry must be about: "where the world ends, every time."

If war requires any genre, it's not drama, or novel, or poetry, but journalism, Studs Terkel's interviews in *The Good War*, Philip Gourevitch's harrowing *We Regret to Inform You That Tomorrow We Will Be Killed with Our Families* about Rwanda, Aleksandar Hemon's evocation of a Sarajevo youth before the wars in *The Book of My Lives*. Anthony Swofford expresses dark truths in *Jarhead*, his account of the Marine Corps during the Persian Gulf invasion, writing that "as a young man raised on the films of the Vietnam War, I want ammunition and alcohol and dope, I want to screw some whores and kill some Iraqi motherfuckers." Waiting for the invasion to begin, the bored Marines sit in the Kuwaiti desert and watch movies about an earlier confrontation. Francis Ford Coppola's *Apocalypse Now*, Oliver Stone's *Platoon*, Stanley Kubrick's *Full Metal Jacket*. Swofford is blunt—all of those movies might ostensibly be anti-war, but the grunts' attempts to psych themselves up listening to Wagner's *Ride of the Valkyries* as U.S. helicopters drop napalm don't engender pacifism so much as an adrenaline boost. Which is the corollary to all war literature being anti-war, and that's that war

TOP Nevinson's 1918 *Harvest of Battle* is not a depiction of rage, but of its aftermath, the survivors of an assault picking out the corpses of dead comrades in the mulch of Flanders's trenches. "A typical scene after an offensive at dawn," notes Nevinson, having himself served in an ambulance unit during the war. Original at the Imperial War Museum.

OPPOSITE, LEFT Colombian painter Fernando Botero's 2005 series about the atrocities committed by U.S. troops at the Abu Ghraib detention center near Baghdad during the Iraq War presented not just the barbarity of war, but the dehumanization of wrath, the way in which it can reduce fellow human beings into nothingness.

OPPOSITE, RIGHT This among the most infamous of images from Abu Ghraib, prisoner Abdou Hussain Saad Faleh was hooded and forced to stand on a block, his arms outstretched, for hours at a time. From 2005.

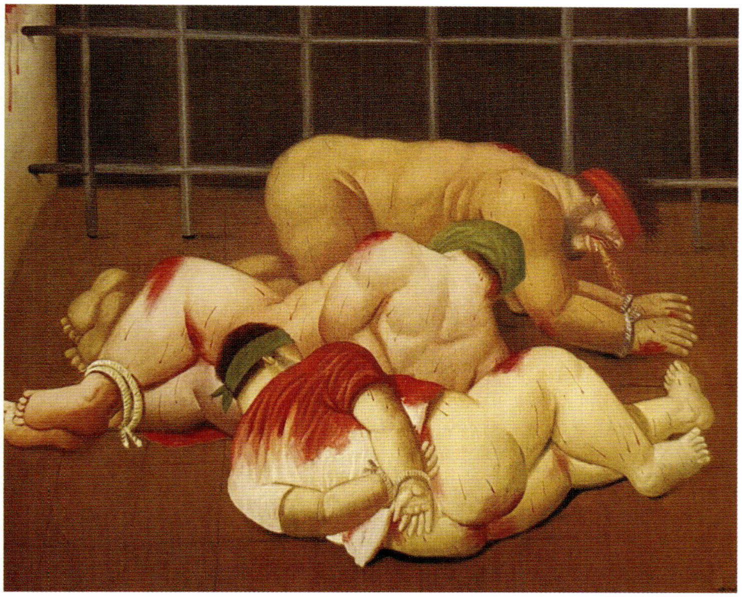

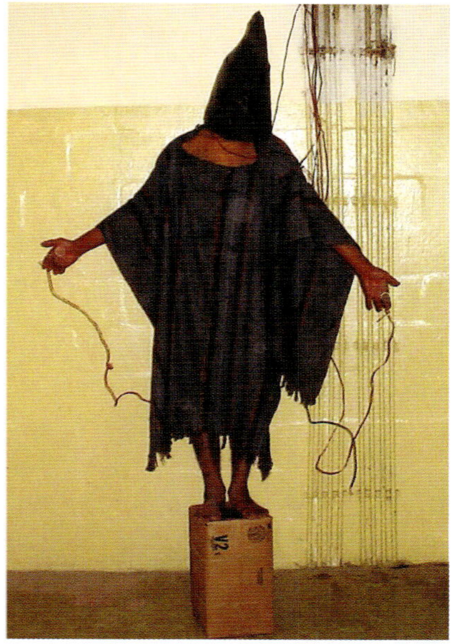

literature can't help but be prurient, exploitative, exhibitionistic, pornographic. The moment editing and revision happen, then you've made literature, a polite way of saying something with an agenda, and anything with an agenda is incapable of examining the unvarnished totality of something, especially a black hole like war. A true literature of war has never been written. It might not even be possible.

There's been some elision between violence and war in this argument. There is a sloppiness in that, because all war might be murder, but not all murder is war. Cain killed Abel, by himself. No general directed him. Violence might be natural (though so is cholera), but war is strange. "If wars were fought only by the men on the ground, the men facing one another in real battle, most wars would end quickly and sensibly," notes Swofford. "Men are smart and men are animals, in that they don't want to die so simply for so little." Often war is presented as a bestial return to a state of nature, but it's the exact opposite. With few exceptions, animals don't engage in war, though they kill each other all the time. War is not the daughter of nature, but rather the son of civilization. War is fought by men, but it's demanded by chiefs and priests, caesars and kings, czars and dictators, generals and presidents. Only six short lines constitute W. H. Auden's "Epitaph from a Tyrant," published in 1940, a year after the invasion of Poland, appearing in the collection *Another Time*:

PERFECTION, OF A KIND, WAS WHAT HE
WAS AFTER,
AND THE POETRY HE INVENTED WAS
EASY TO UNDERSTAND;
HE KNEW HUMAN FOLLY LIKE THE BACK
OF HIS HAND,
AND WAS GREATLY INTERESTED IN
ARMIES AND FLEETS;
WHEN HE LAUGHED, RESPECTABLE
SENATORS BURST WITH LAUGHTER,
AND WHEN HE CRIED THE LITTLE
CHILDREN DIED IN THE STREETS.

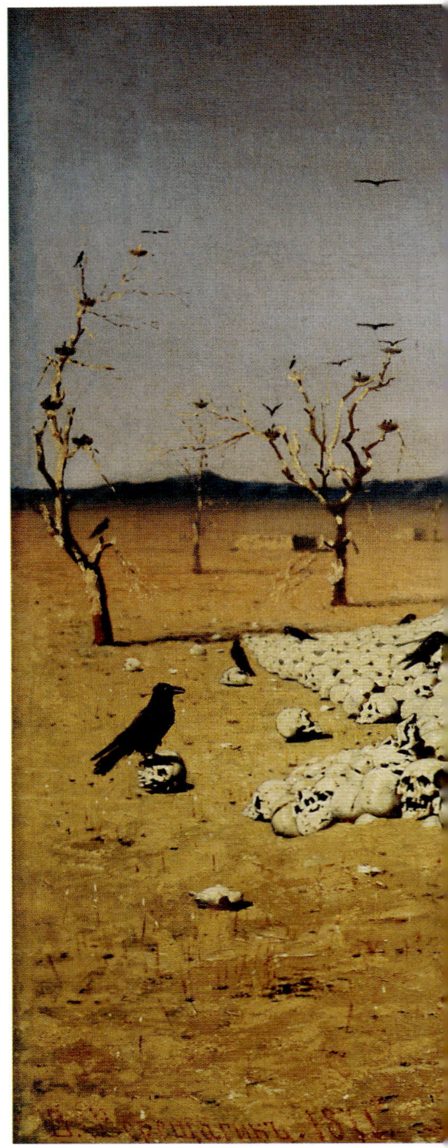

No human has ever been so physically powerful as to exert the authority which even the smallest war demands, so that the history of war is the history of tyrants somehow compelling men to violence. The Hitlers and Stalins, the Napoleons and Khans. Pharoah Thutmose III. The earliest written record of war, when the Egyptians crushed the Canaanites 1,457 years before the Common Era. Recorded on a stele are the details of this supposed "campaign of victory which his majesty made to extend the frontiers of Egypt, in valor, in victory, in power, and in justification." We are given laborious, self-satisfied, and grandiose detailing about Thutmose's forces, so that "everything which his majesty did to this town and to that wretched enemy and his wretched army is set down by the individual day and by the individual expedition and by the individual troop commanders." More than eight thousand Canaanites were killed and half that many enslaved in the first recorded war. When shall be the last, and under what circumstances? Shall swords be beaten into ploughshares or melted into radioactive dust? By a coincidence, Thutmose's army laid siege to the Canaanite garrison at Megiddo, which for separate reasons is today far more widely known by its Greek name—Armageddon.

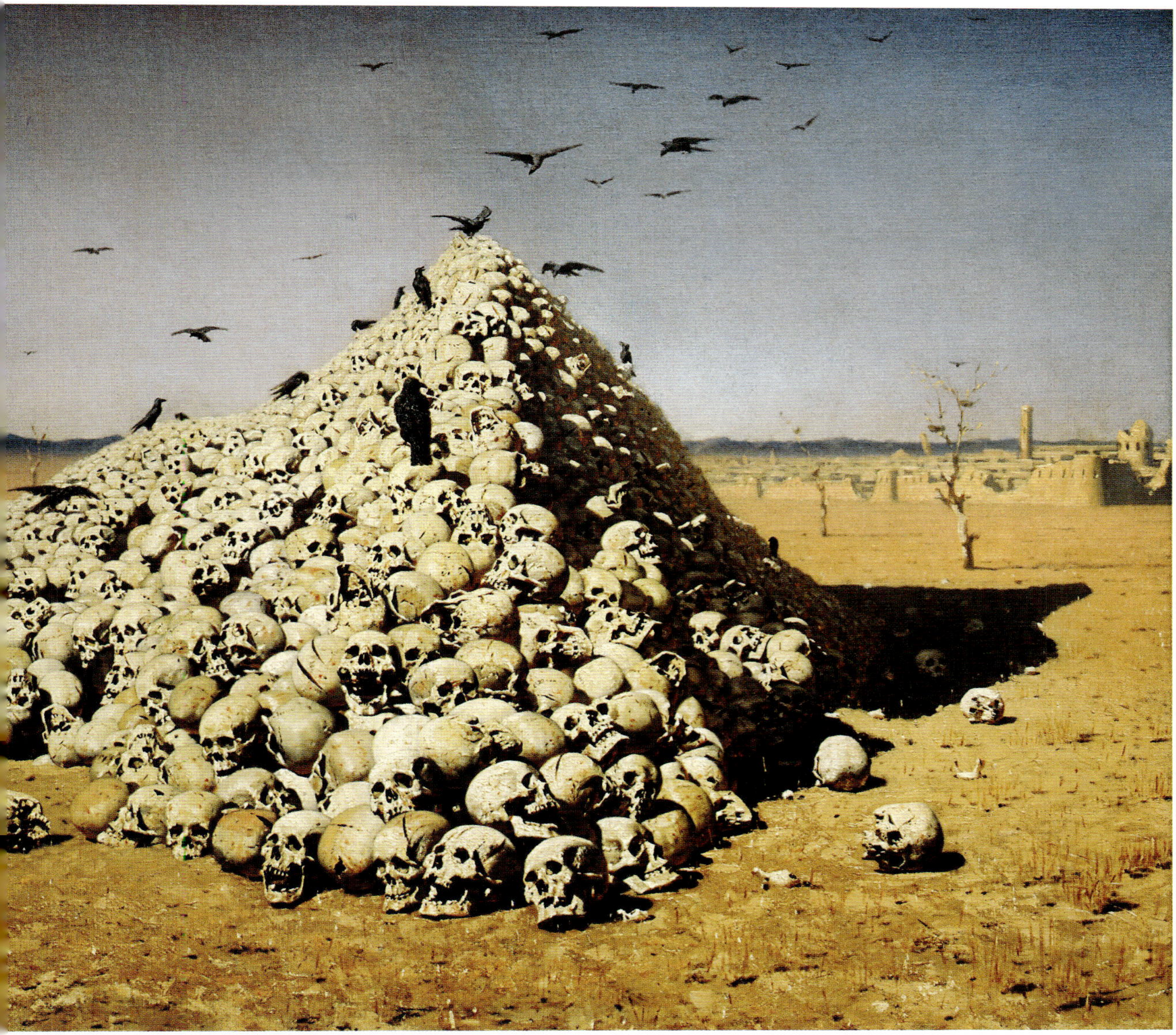

ABOVE Russian painter Vasily Vereshchagin's 1871 composition *The Apotheosis of War,* based on his own wartime service with the Russian Imperial Army in Central Asia, is, paradoxically, unnervingly realistic and strangely surreal, the pile of skulls as if something from a cryptic dream, although the painting recorded an actual event. After wrath, only quiet. Original at the Tretyakov Gallery in Moscow.

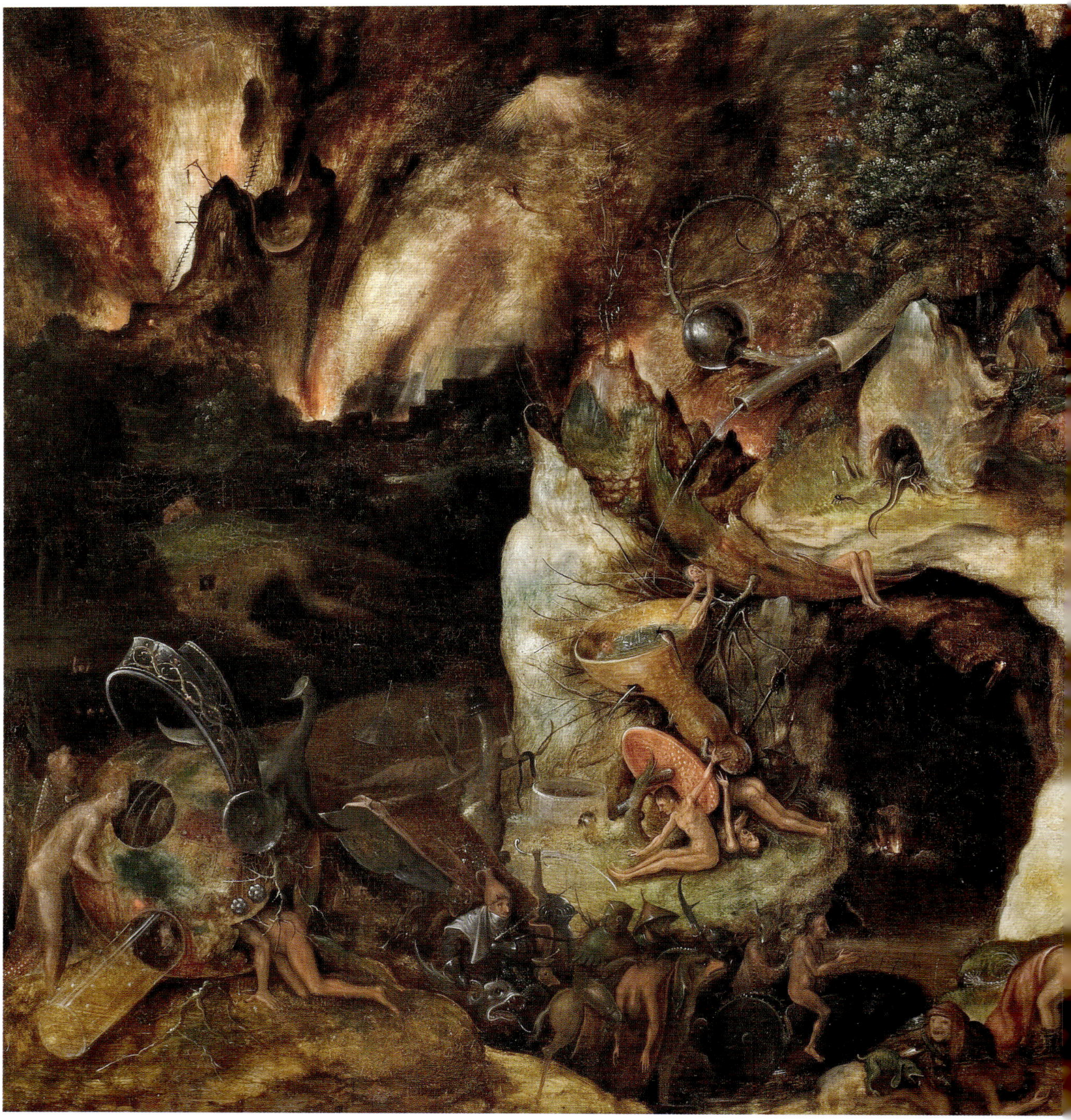

ABOVE A follower of Hieronymus Bosch depicts hell in this 1565 *Infernal Landscape*. The original is held at the Prado Museum.

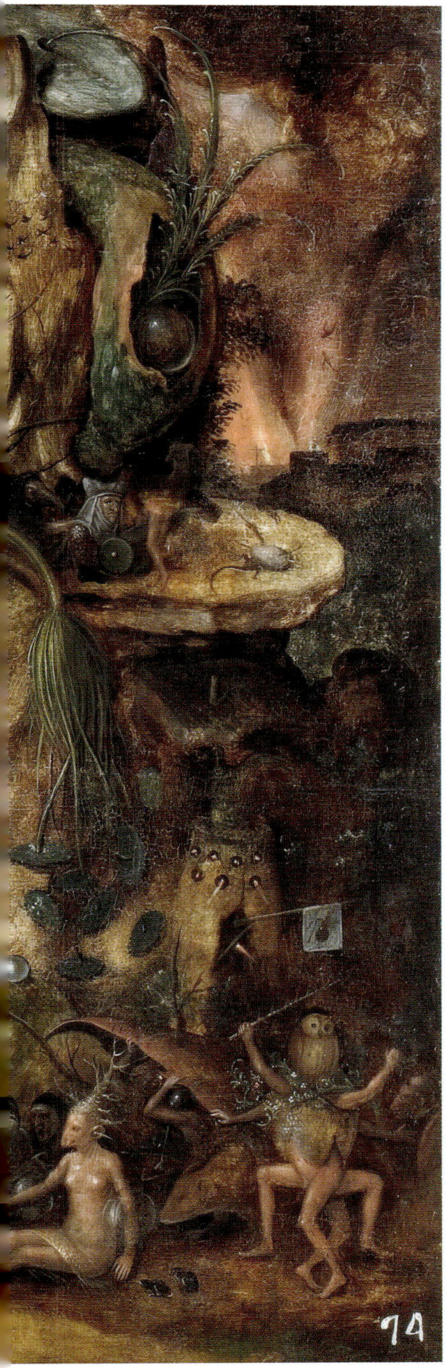

CONCLUSION

THE SEVEN CONTEMPORARY DEADLY VICES

Far from being archaic remnants of a medieval past, of moralizing censure and pious rectitude, both the Seven Deadly Vices and the Seven Capital Virtues constitute a system which accepts humanity in its variety and complexity, and more importantly, which accepts the human *individual* in their own variety and complexity, all of us in our capacities for both hatred and cruelty, empathy and kindness. Such an ethical calculus trades not in abstraction, but in the very real particulars of lived experience; we have within us all a chorus of sinners and saints, and the task of living a life worth living, especially when we are living our lives in responsibility and benefit for others. Fundamentally, both the vices and the virtues describe a limited world, one where we have no choice but to live in a community of others and where evil and goodness are both defined in part by the effects that our actions have on that community. A cursory reading of this volume should demonstrate that the listing of vices and virtues can be estimably ambiguous, that sometimes what appears as one can actually be the other. Despite that, we need not retreat into a noxious relativism, for regardless of the context, vice is entirely about a projection of the self outward, of imposing one's own agency without concern for permission to do so. Vice is always an idolatry of the self. In that spirit, then, a suggestion for the Seven Deadly Sins of our current moment.

I. ENTITLEMENT

PARTNER TO NARCISSISM, EGOCENTRICITY, SELF-DELUSION, AND PRIDE. ENTITLEMENT IS THE PRESUMPTION THAT YOU ARE MORE IMPORTANT THAN OTHERS, THAT YOU ARE OWED MORE THAN YOUR FAIR SHARE, THAT OWNERSHIP OF RESOURCES, ATTENTION, AND OPPORTUNITY IS YOUR GIVEN. THE VICE OF THOSE WHO UNDERSTAND THEIR PRIVILEGE AS A BIRTH RIGHT, OF HEDGE-FUND MANAGERS AND INFLUENCERS, OF TRUST-FUND CHILDREN AND LEGACY ADMITTEES.

II. WASTE

THIS VICE IS THE CREED OF THOSE WHO SEE NATURE AND ITS BOUNTY AS DISPOSABLE, WHO BELIEVE THAT DOMINION IS THE SACRED WRIT OF HUMANITY, AND IN PARTICULAR OF THEMSELVES. THIS IS THE SIN OF OIL EXECUTIVES AND CAR MANUFACTURERS, OF THOSE WHO ADVOCATE FOR DEREGULATION AND WHO ESCHEW RENEWABILITY.

III. MYOPIA

A SIN THAT DEFINES ANY WHO REFUSE TO SEE BEYOND THEIR OWN CIRCUMSTANCES, WHO HAVE NO CONCERN FOR THOSE WHO AREN'T LIKE THEM. THIS IS THE TRANSGRESSION OF THOSE WHOSE OWN DELIGHT IN AND CONCERN WITH THE SELF BLIND THEM TO THE HUMANITY OF THE STRANGERS IN THEIR MIDST.

IV. **IGNORANCE**

SEPARATE FROM MERE STUPIDITY, IGNORANCE IS RATHER A RELISHING IN INCURIOSITY, IN BEING PROUD OF ALL OF THAT WHICH YOU DON'T KNOW OR UNDERSTAND, A LACK OF CONCERN WITH THAT WORLD THAT IS LARGER THAN YOUR LIMITED EXPERIENCE. IT IS A REJECTION OF THE WORLD.

V. **BIGOTRY**

RATHER THAN INDIFFERENCE, BIGOTRY IS A FOCUSED OBSESSION WITH THOSE DIFFERENT FROM ONESELF. RATHER THAN EXPERIENCE THE WORLD IN A SPIRIT OF GRATITUDE AND GRACE, THE BIGOT MERELY PROJECTS THEIR OWN INNER SELF OUTWARD. FROM BIGOTRY COMES THE HIDEOUS CHIMERAS OF AUTHORITARIANISM, TOTALITARIANISM, FASCISM, AND GENOCIDE.

VI. **CRUELTY**

THE DELIGHT IN PAIN AND SUFFERING, SADISTIC ENJOYMENT TAKEN AT THE EXPENSE OF ANOTHER HUMAN BEING, OR AN ANIMAL, OR THE NATURAL WORLD. AN ANTI-GOSPEL, NIHILISTIC EMBRACE OF THAT WHICH IS SATANIC.

VII. **GREED**

NOW, AS THEN, GREED REMAINS THE FONT OF OTHER VICES.

Today, in our inequities and our sufferings, our injustices and our illiberalism, let us pray that we can identify the beams in our own eyes, and may such vice be exorcized from the soul collective.

BIOGRAPHY

Ed Simon is the editor of *Belt Magazine* and a staff writer for the literary site The Millions, as well as the author of several books. He has a PhD in English and is an expert on the literature and religion of the Renaissance and Reformation. His work has appeared in the *Atlantic*, the *Paris Review Daily*, the *Washington Post*, and the *New York Times*, among dozens of others. He is most recently the author of *Elysium: A Visual History of Angelology*.

ACKNOWLEDGMENTS

Thanks are due to the various institutions and libraries consulted in the writing of this volume, including, but not limited to, the Carnegie Library of Pittsburgh and the Hunt Memorial Library at Carnegie Mellon University. A labor such as this is made possible through the generations of scholars in fields as diverse as history, theology, philosophy, and literary study who are cited throughout the book. All of the scholars who I've consulted have shaped my own thinking on questions of ethics and morality; they were instrumental in the writing of this title. Special thanks must be given to editorial assistants Regan Mies and Ruby Pucillo, whose attention and discernment have immeasurably improved the work, as well as visionary editor Rodolph Lachat, with whom I'm proud to have now worked on three books for Abrams and Cernunnos. Finally, the bulk of my thanks must go to my family—my sons, Finn and Milo, and my wife, Meg.

7 DEADLY SINS

Library of Congress Control Number: 2024937748

ISBN: 978-1-4197-7410-2
eISBN: 979-8-88707-302-6

Cernunnos logo design: Mark Ryden
Book design: Benjamin Brard

Printed and bound in China
10 9 8 7 6 5 4 3 2 1

ABRAMS The Art of Books
195 Broadway, New York, NY 10007
abramsbooks.com

7 HEAVENLY VIRTUES

7 HEAVENLY VIRTUES

A VISUAL HISTORY

ED SIMON

CERNUNNOS

CONTENTS

INTRODUCTION

ON VIRTUE

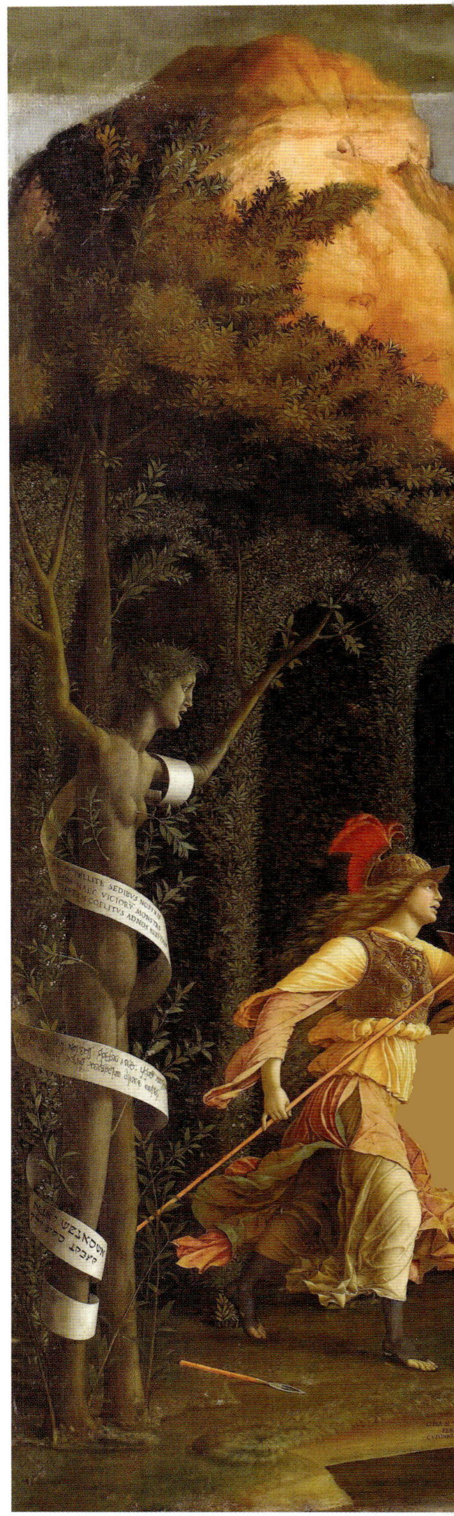

"Sail on silver girl

Sail on by

Your time has come to shine

All your dreams are on their way

See how they shine."

—Simon & Garfunkel, "Bridge Over Troubled Water"

(1970)

The population of the earth on September 26, 1983, was around 4.685 billion women, men, and children, and most of them would have been killed in under forty-five minutes during an all-out nuclear exchange between the Soviet Union and the United States if it hadn't been for a quick, and arguably irrational, decision made by a lieutenant colonel in the Soviet Air Defense services named Stanislav Petrov. In his official military identification photograph taken that same year, Petrov is an unremarkable man with a bouffant of swept-back black hair and a slight widow's peak, thin with high cheekbones, big ears, and unmistakable Slavic eyes. His green coat is decorated in several minor medals awarded by the USSR, but his most significant action never received official commemoration from his nation. That autumn evening in question, Petrov was stationed in the secret city of Serpukhov-15, around twenty miles south of Moscow, where he monitored computers deep within the subterranean command center of the Soviet nuclear missile early warning system. Coincidentally, a little under eight thousand miles away, a series of low storm clouds rolled in over the cold plains of North Dakota while a Soviet spy satellite which was part of the Oko warning system happened to be in orbit above. Rather than the rumble of a plains thunderstorm, the satellite detected one, and then four more, LGM-30 Minuteman intercontinental ballistic missiles being launched by the United States. In less than a minute, that information was relayed to Petrov, who sat a hemisphere away in front of his black computer screen with its blinking

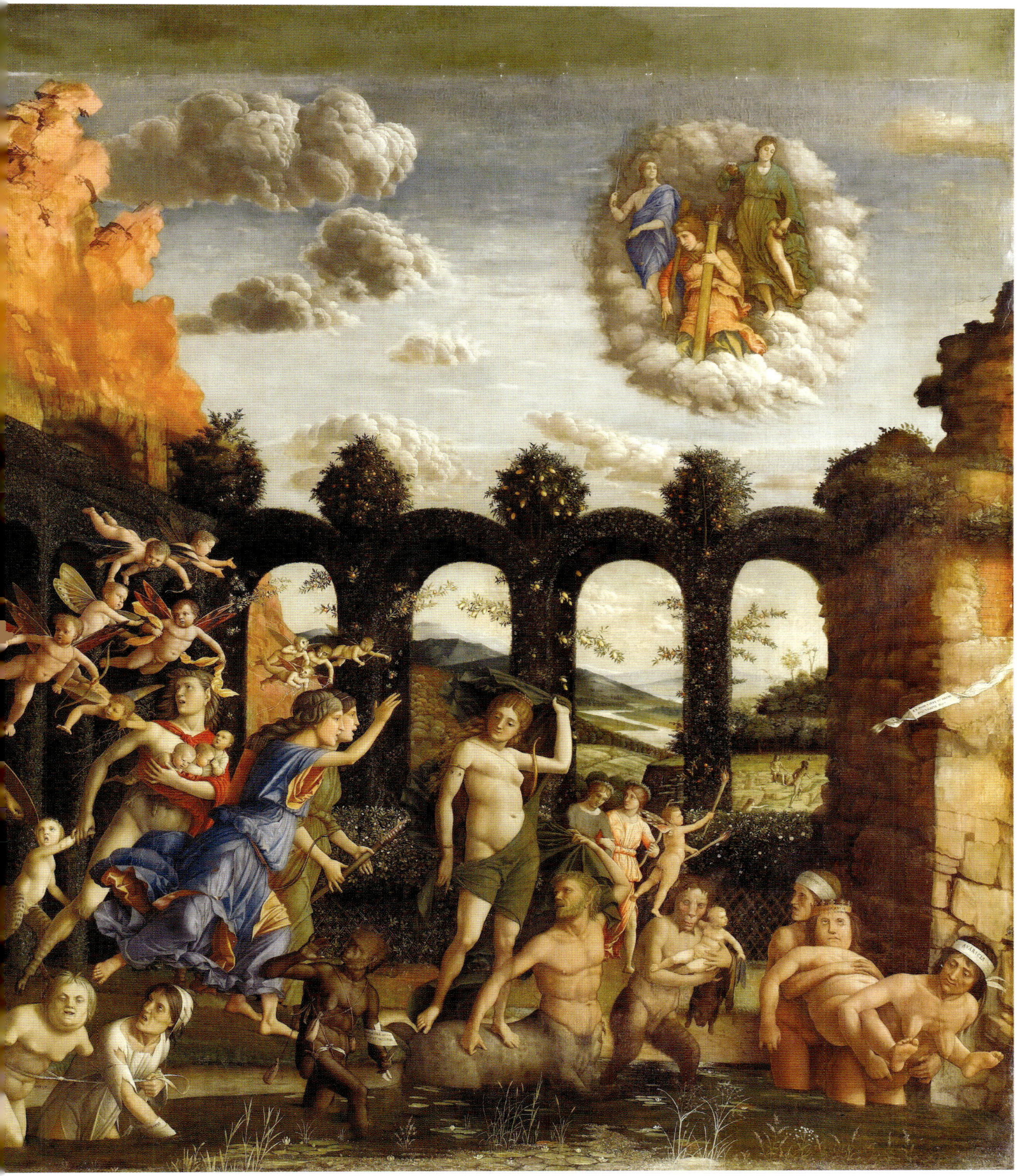

ABOVE Italian Renaissance painter Andrea Mantegna's 1502 *The Triumph of the Virtues*, original at the Louvre.

green Cyrillic letters. His responsibility—his military oath—was to immediately contact the next in the chain-of-command, so that in less than fifteen minutes the Kremlin would have the information needed to justify a retaliatory strike against the United States, and yet the lieutenant colonel performed the most radical act of goodness which has perhaps ever happened—he did nothing.

"My late wife for ten years knew nothing about it," Petrov told a documentary film reporter in 2012. "'So what did you do?' she asked me. 'Nothing. I did nothing.'" In later interviews, first with higher-ranking officers in the Soviet military and then Western journalists after the end of the Cold War, Petrov maintained that even though he acted in direct violation of his training, his gut feeling that night was eminently commonsensical, he having reasoned that the United States wouldn't begin a nuclear exchange with only five missiles, and thus (correctly) assuming that the alert was merely computer error. Had somebody else been on shift that September evening, or had Petrov reacted by the dictates of Soviet military bureaucracy, then undoubtedly Moscow would have responded with a nuclear attack on the West, which the U.S. erroneously would have believed was an act of retaliation. Had this come to pass, about half an hour after Petrov had received that alert, New York, Washington, DC, Los Angeles, Chicago, and San Francisco would be incinerated, followed by London, Paris, and Toronto. Regardless of the American military brass instantaneously killed at the Pentagon, those missile silos in North Dakota, now dappled in the cool rain from those clouds perilously misinterpreted as missiles less than an hour before, would still open up their vast chasms upon the earth, nuclear-tipped projectiles sent back toward the Soviet Union, so that less than sixty minutes after Petrov received his alert, Leningrad, Gorky, Saratov, Kazan, Tbilsi, and Moscow would be erased as well. Joseph Stalin was responsible for almost nine million deaths, Adolph Hitler for thirteen million between World War II and the Holocaust, while this nameless, faceless bureaucrat with minimal power and seemingly no ego was responsible for saving four billion lives. Stalin, Hitler, Mussolini, Franco, Pinochet, Pol Pot, Idi Amin, and Saddam Hussein were responsible for untold horror, bloodshed, and evil in their lives, motivated by overweening pride, but an unremarkable man named Petrov was able to save more lives than the rest of those monsters were ever able to take.

"Imaginary evil is romantic and varied," wrote the French Jewish philosopher Simone Weil in her 1943 *Gravity and Grace*. "Real evil is gloomy, monotonous, barren, boring." Weil foreshadows Hannah Arendt's two-decades-later argument in *Eichman in Jerusalem* about the "banality of evil," an observation about how we imagine evil as perpetrated by evocative creatures like Hannibal Lecter, Dracula, and Lucifer, but the reality is far more prosaic—boring men doing hideous things, atrocities committed by dim-witted and uninteresting people who might as well be insurance salesmen and yet are capable of the most twisted actions. Weil writes that by contrast, "Imaginary good is boring; real good is always new, marvelous, intoxicating." There seems to be a paradox here, for Petrov himself seems precisely that sort of boring figure, a minor military functionary in pressed uniform sitting in front of a computer screen, a man so dry he couldn't even be bothered to tell his wife about the time that he saved the world. Yet this is a good that makes Weil's point, because this figure—just as much of a seeming insurance salesman as Arendt's banal evildoer—is new, marvelous, and intoxicating. That such an average, regular person was capable of not just evil, but of good, is as beguiling and beautiful as any fact which can be conceived of. Imagine yourself in Petrov's situation in 1983. What gave him the fortitude not to immediately contact those above him so as to initiate a military response? Was it principle, fear? Were the alert accurate, Petrov and everybody else at Serpukhov-15 would be dead shortly enough, for had the United States launched ICBMs toward the Soviet Union it was already too late for Moscow to do anything other than to respond in revenge. Did Petrov know that and decide that even if he was to die—even if he was to be the victim of a monstrous evil in the form of a preemptive strike—he would unilaterally make the decision not to inform his superiors so that at least half the world's children would survive World War III? Or perhaps his self-effacing modesty at having simply done his job is the closest to the truth: Petrov really was knowledgeable enough about the nuances of false alerts to be able to recognize a blinking alarm as merely signaling some storm clouds on the other side of the planet. Maybe it's all of these, or perhaps it's none. I suspect Petrov himself, lying in bed at night and reflecting on that fateful choice, must have wondered which it was. Or maybe not—maybe radical good simply accepts what it is.

Weil's point about goodness is best paired with Arendt's observation about evil, for the former is just as important, and in some manner just as surprising. So much of our attention is spent parsing the intricacies of the sociopath's brain, the evil man's soul, but it's not often enough that we similarly acknowledge just how strange and counterintuitive radical goodness can be. The bystander who jumps onto subway tracks to save the life of a stranger whose name they don't even know, the volunteer who painfully donates bone marrow or a kidney for somebody whom they will never meet, the good Samaritan who risks—and perhaps loses—their life in the act of defending somebody from an assailant, or by running into a burning house, or by pushing a person out of the way of a wayward car and gets hit in the process. A mysterious force, every bit as ineffable as radical evil, the word "virtue" hardly seems fully appropriate for a phenomenon as revolutionary as pure goodness. "Virtue" has connotations of the maudlin, mid-century youth behavior-control propaganda "Goofus and Gallant" from *Highlights* magazine, or of the schmaltzy Claymation series *Davey & Goliath* produced by the Lutheran Church. The word, for better or worse, doesn't evoke radical goodness so much as it does being prim, prudish, puritanical, where the virtuous are a category that includes teetotalers, those who go to bed and get up early, clean and polite young people who eschew cuss words, and those who pass on dessert. There is nothing fun or sexy about virtue. This, I would argue, is a problem more with the word (or at least with the associations it has accrued over the generations) than it is with the quality itself. For if it's true that the listing of virtues compiled by the Church had something to do with social control, with behavior modification that keeps people docile and pliable, it's also true that *goodness* itself is an evergreen subversive quality, where to wish good and do good and be good are a means of challenging the inequity and cruelty that is too often the rule of this world.

Because goodness is so often understood, contra Weil's argument, as boring, there is much less focus on the Seven Capital Virtues in our popular culture than there is on the Seven Deadly Sins (check which half of this book is longer, after all). There is, for example, no converse of David Fincher's film *Se7en*, where do-gooders go around rewarding people for their humility or kindness, where a noble activist receives an anonymous financial contribution or a humble volunteer is given an award. Indeed, even the Church itself seemed content to be a bit more inconsistent with listing virtue than vice. The collection explored here are the Seven Capital Virtues, which are different from the Seven Heavenly Virtues, themselves composed of Four Cardinal Virtues and Three Theological Virtues, though it should be said that confusingly, there are attributes shared and similar across all of these variable enumerations. The Three Theological Virtues are the oldest of any such listing—predating the Seven Deadly Sins by four centuries—and the only ones which are explicitly mentioned in Scripture. Dealing with virtues connected to belief, Paul in his epistle to the Corinthians writes, "And now faith, hope, and love abide, these three; and the greatest of these is love," a moving sentiment from an apostle not often associated with them. The Four Cardinal Virtues took as their purview not belief, but action, first listed by Ambrose in the fourth century and then reaffirmed by his student Augustine; they are temperance, justice, prudence, and fortitude. Joined together, the cumulative seven of the theological and cardinal virtues were a schema that defined right belief and behavior, though they differ from the Capital Virtues, even while some remain the same (temperance, for example). Those Seven Capital Virtues, the ones which will be explored in the present volume, were formulated in direct reaction to their far more famous cousins of the Seven Deadly Sins.

Prudentius, an Iberian Latin poet of the fifth century living through the collapse of empire, was the first author to imagine the human mind as a battlefield between seven virtues and vices, in his psychologically astute *Psychomachia*. Long before modernists abandoned the simplistic Enlightenment myth of a unitary mind, of the *Cogito* in full and rational control of its faculties, Prudentius described how "War rages, horrid war / Even in our bones; our double nature sounds / With armed discord." The title of his poem directly translating to "soul war," Prudentius understood that to be human is to be strung between Heaven and Hell, to be capable of the most touching tenderness and cold cruelty, the most radiant goodness and the most wicked evil, sometimes within the single individual. Contradiction and paradox are our lot far more than boring consistency, with *Psychomachia* enacting that disunion. "Body of a man I bring thee," sings Prudentius's celestial choirs, "Noble even in its ruin." Prudentius didn't rely on the earlier list of the Cardinal Virtues in composing his own; rather, his character list (for they are humanized as personalities) is composed of Faith, Chastity, Patience, Humility, Sobriety, Good Works, and Concordia (the last roughly equivalent to agreeableness). Here the enumeration is much closer to the final draft, which would be the Seven Capital Virtues, though there are some important differences (surprisingly, Good Works doesn't appear in the ultimate version, nor Concordia). Rather, the list as you will see it in this book—humility, chastity, temperance, diligence, kindness, charity, and patience (which I've rendered as "peacefulness")—was finalized, appropriately enough, by the same thinker responsible for the definitive iteration of the Seven Deadly Sins: the sixth-century pontiff Pope Gregory the Great. For more than a millennium, with inevitable shifts in the meaning or implications of each individual virtue and vice, this has been the authoritative listing of both. As understood by Gregory, the virtues and vices in their numerologically significant groupings of seven were a way of understanding in totality the divided consciousness of humanity, whereby each virtue has an equal and opposite vice, binary oppositions riven through the soul of man.

OPPOSITE Stained-glass window in Christ Church Cathedral, Dublin, depicting the Seven Capital Virtues.

Regardless, the Seven Capital Virtues have never occupied the same space in the artistic consciousness of the West as have the Seven Deadly Sins, for our greater loss. Despite the superficial ways in which the Seven Deadly Sins—Lust! Greed! Wrath!—are fascinating, there is a deeper strangeness to virtue, as Weil would have understood well, that radiates in its own powerful beauty. At their most basic, the Seven Capital Virtues ask of us how we shall lead a good life. Not an enjoyable life, not a productive or even a happy one, but a *good* life. They ask us how we shall interact with our families, our neighbors, with strangers. As with the ancient Greeks, such "virtue" is a question not of platitudes and pieties, but of excellence, of what it means to engage with the world in a spirit of magnanimity, fairness, charity, and empathy. "For some identify happiness with virtue," writes Aristotle in the *Nicomachean Ethics*, "some with practical wisdom, others with a kind of philosophic wisdom . . . while others include also external prosperity," and while the philosopher allows that these can all theoretically be related to the good, they are not entirely reducible to it either.

Goodness is neither wisdom nor wealth; ironically, like evil, in its purest form good is not instrumental, utilitarian, or even pragmatic. To be sure, good and evil can be used to further some aim, and perhaps virtue and vice are the shadows cast from Heaven and Hell of those more pure attributes, but in their elemental state, good and evil are singularities; they are foreign and alien. With some irony, it can be noted that there was an equivalent justification given by Stanislav Petrov and Adolf Eichmann for what they had done—they were both just doing their job, following orders. But they weren't; theirs were both acts beyond normal rationality, albeit one was done for pure good and the other for pure evil. To be in the presence of pure good—a moment of pure benevolence, a disinterested sacrifice, a charity, an instance of complete tenderness or kindness—is not unlike being within the presence of pure evil. That's not to say that good and evil are the same—not at all. By definition they are complete opposites. It's to say that good—like evil—is something that when we've really experienced it, as either the recipient or dispenser of its fortunes, we may understand just how distant and different the divine is from our prosaic lives, but how it nonetheless also thrums through the particulars of everyday existence as well. Today, in the sweltering summer of collapse, when there seems to be such a deficit of goodness, the virtues themselves radically remind us that the unlikeliest of things—connection, kindness, love—remain not just possible, but common.

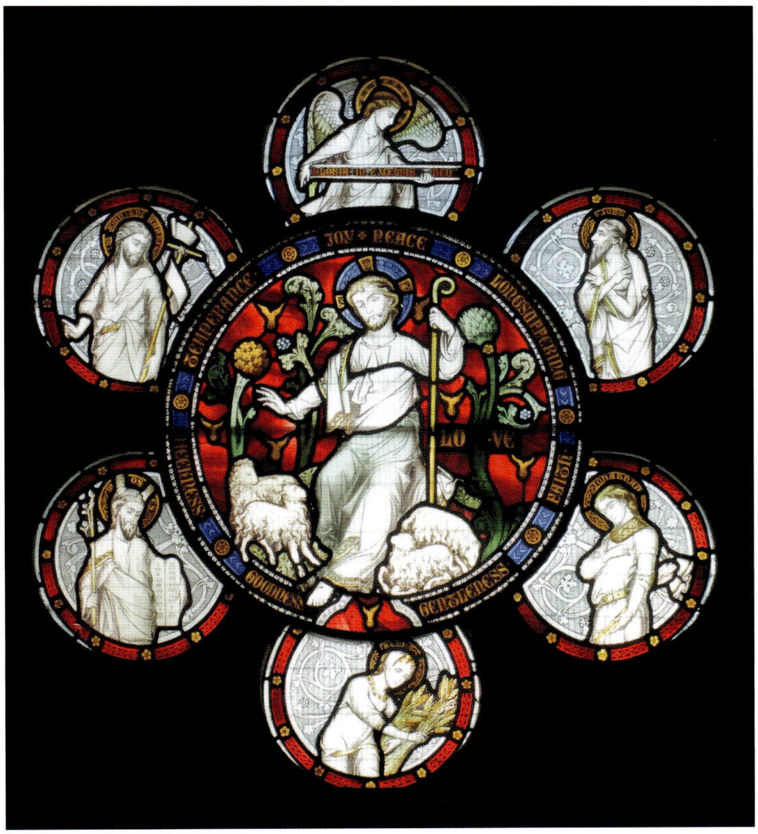

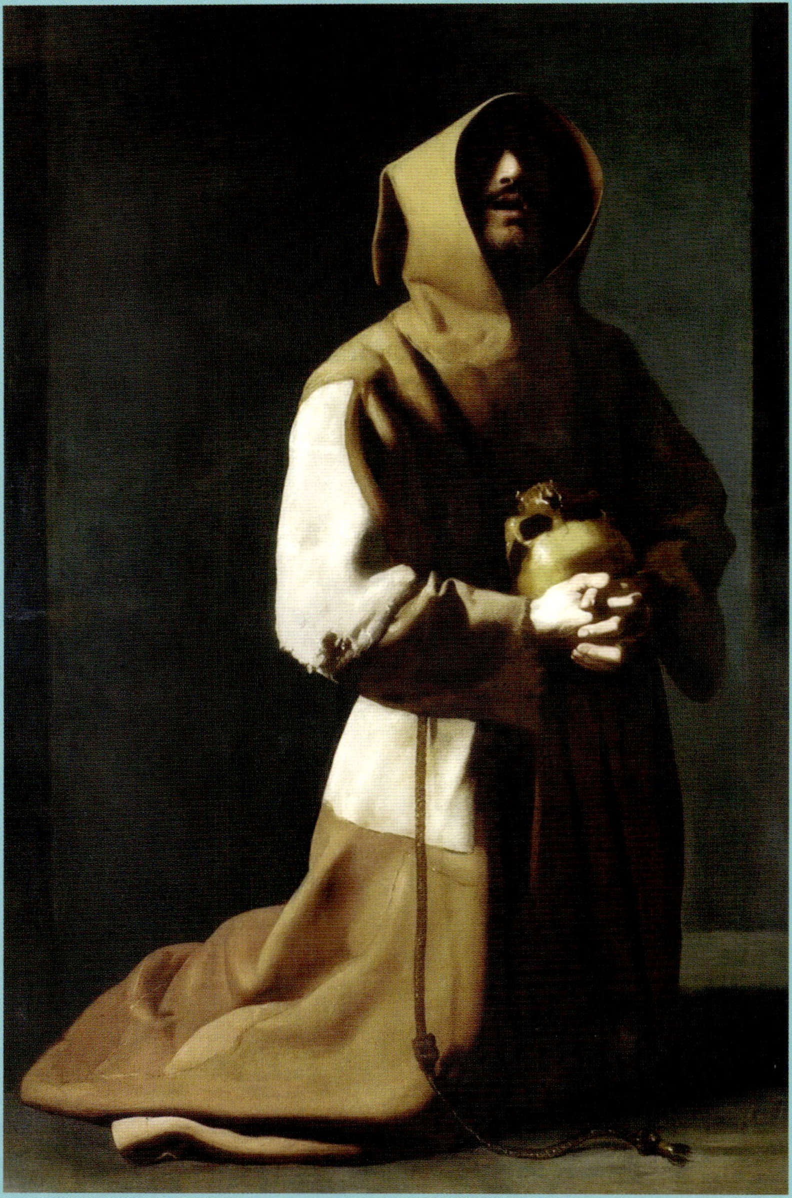

CHAPTER ONE

MAKING MEN ANGELS: HUMILITY

"Every one that exalteth himself shall be abased;

and he that humbleth himself shall be exalted."

—Luke 18:14

"'Umble we are, 'umble we have been, 'umble we shall ever be."

—Charles Dickens, *David Copperfield* (1849)

The Church Fathers—an assortment of oddballs, weirdos, and eccentrics—were responsible for enshrining not just the theology of Christianity in its first few centuries, but also its tenor, mood, soul, and aesthetic. These were men like Saint Benedict who cloistered themselves away in monasteries, or caves, or, as for some of the heartiest of spirits, high atop columns where they would make their homes for years, waste trickling down the side like wax from a melting candle. Naturally, and maybe with a bit of ironic self-regard, they would establish humility as the chief of virtues. Even while there is ample precedent in the Hebrew Scriptures for valorizing humility, such self-abnegation was a particularly Christian enthusiasm, drawn from the Beatitudes themselves wherein Christ could exhort his followers that "Blessed are the meek." Within the ancient Mediterranean, even as philosophical movements like the Stoics and Epicureans advocated for a radical simplicity, Christ's elevation of humility had a revolutionary caste. Ironically, it took a few centuries for humility to be officially listed as a numbered virtue. Paul—more responsible for Christianity than even Christ, and no stranger to celebrating humility—famously listed the theological virtues as "faith, hope, and love" in his first epistle to the Corinthians. Both Ambrose and Augustine some three centuries later celebrate temperance and justice, prudence and fortitude, but humility hadn't quite coalesced into the final list yet. The fourth-century Christian poet Prudentius, toiling away in what today would be northern Spain, provided an early example of humility as paired with its infernal adversary pride in his allegorical poem *Psychomachia*. Roughly translating to "soul war," *Psychomachia* is a psychologically astute work, a poem which understands the competing appetites within the human mind, and the bifurcated complexities of dueling antipathies of the self. What Prudentius would think of as the battle between good and evil but which modernity has recategorized as the slippage of Id and Superego. According to Prudentius, humility is a "princess in her own right, yet reliant on the aid of others," a quality which is the canvas for great things rather than the paint, for the rigorous soul has learned to "lay aside arrogance . . . to beware the pit at your feet, whoever threatens lofty things." From a twentieth-century French philosopher and resistance fighter to a medieval pope who rejected earthly glory, humility can generate figures of goodness as fascinating as their opposites.

PREVIOUS SPREAD Spanish Baroque master Francisco de Zurbarán's *St. Francis in Meditation*, painted between 1635 and 1639 with the original held at the National Gallery in London, is an exemplar of Counter-Reformation aesthetics and mysticism. Turning to the beloved thirteenth-century Saint Francis of Assisi, a minor aristocrat who spurned his inheritance in favor of a life of simple piety, Zurbarán's intense chiaroscuro conveys the interior humility of the monk, the darkness surrounding him a visual testament to the ways in which modesty serves to make our very souls as if a cloister in the fallen world, for, as Francis preached, "Where there is patience and humility, there is neither anger nor vexation."

OPPOSITE Arguably all faith-traditions teach about the utility of self-effacement, yet Christ's Beatitudes as recounted in the Gospel of Matthew stress humility in a manner which seems impossible for the regular person to attain (though that's part of the point). This anonymous c. 1480 composition from a Netherlandish painter known only as Master of the Housebook depicts Christ washing the feet of His apostles on Maundy Thursday. Original held by the Staatliche Museum in Berlin.

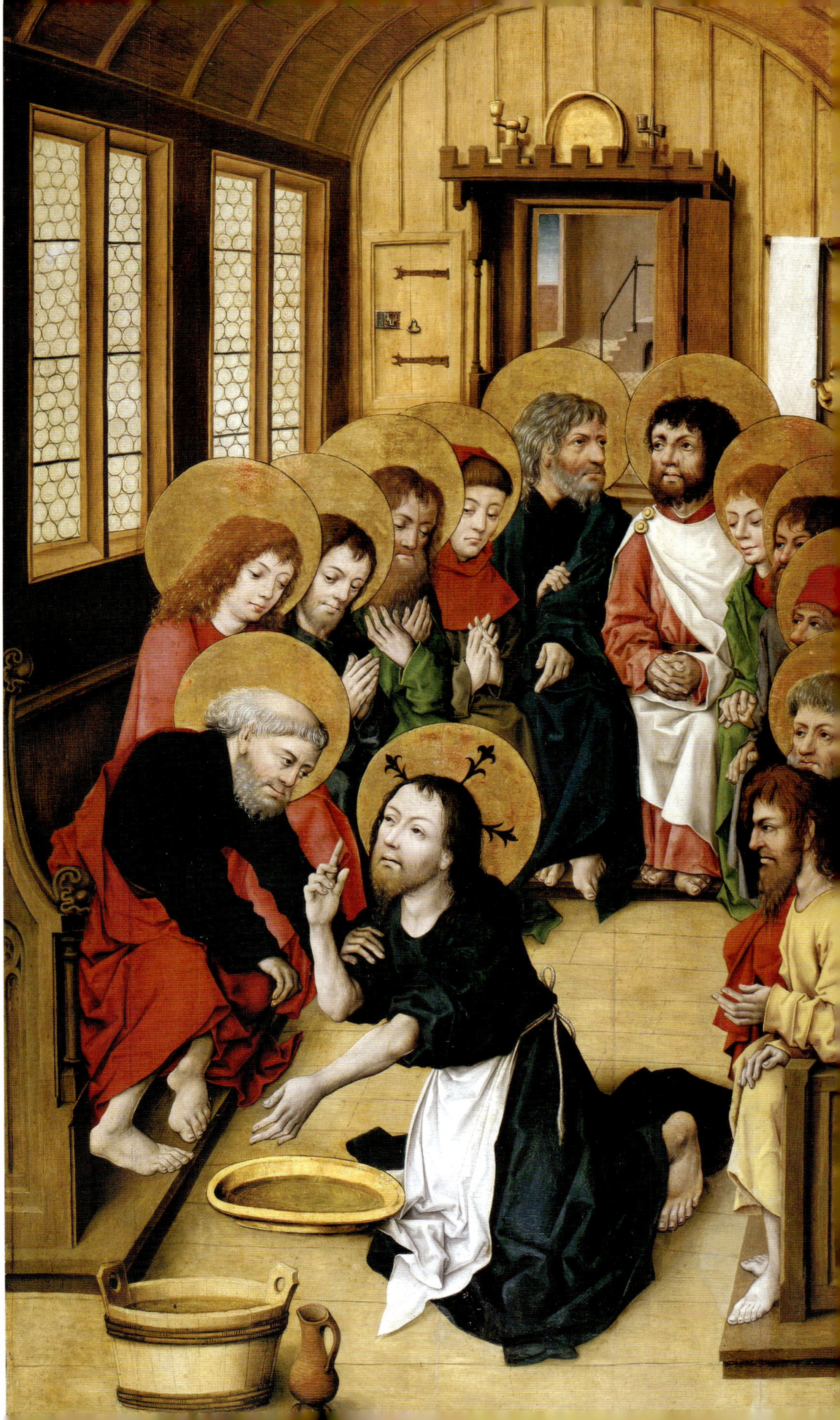

THEORY—THE BASE OF EVERY VIRTUE

Two years before the German surrender, the mystical anarchist Simone Weil would die at the Grosvenor Hall sanitorium in Ashford, Kent, where she was undergoing treatment for tuberculosis, having refused to eat more than she imagined her fellow countryman got for daily rations in occupied France, so that she ultimately starved to death of her own volition. Otherworldly, eerie, saintly, Weil is an uncategorizable philosopher at the nexus of Judaism and Catholicism, anarchism and faith, Marxism and mysticism. Beyond any categories however, Weil ultimately put her own theories about abasement and abjection, humility and humiliation into the final choice she ever made. Part of a grand intellectual tradition from Socrates to Seneca, the philosopher indebted to the mind but felled by the body, for all of us exist within the parameters of the dialectic, the rigorous stipulations of the paradox. She was the pacifist who marched with the Duruti Column as part of the International Brigades during the Spanish Civil War; the aspiring anchorite who before her death was undergoing military training in England for the French Resistance. These were experiences witnessed with keen eye by the sleight, bookish woman in her thick spectacles, a humanist for whom no type of person should be foreign. "In the intellectual order," Weil wrote in her theological study *Gravity and Grace*, "the virtue of humility is nothing more nor less than the power of attention."

Known by her classmates at the École normale supérieure as variously the "Red virgin" or "The Martian," she was the top student in exams for "General Philosophy and Logic" (the second highest scores went to Simone de Beauvoir), but despite her clear brilliance, Weil radiated a sense of utmost humility, true to her own definition of that virtue. This was, after all, the woman who in a 1942 essay claimed that humility was a "far more precious treasure than all academic progress . . . it is perhaps even more useful to contemplate our stupidity than our sin." *Attention* was the core of Weil's metaphysics and epistemology, her aesthetics and ethics. Born Jewish, Weil's late life saw her increasingly drawn to a mystically inflected Catholicism, and though she studied with a Dominican friar it's believed that she most likely never converted. Nonetheless, and with a fascination for the perennialism of all faiths, Weil would write of attention in her book *Waiting for God* that the "beauty of this world is Christ's tender smile coming to us through matter." According to Weil, every single mundane moment, prosaic place, profane experience was thrumming with the numinous, transcendent, and sacred. What being aware of this required was a limitation of the ego; the muffling of the internal monologue so that one could hear, the turning away from the reflection so one could truly see. In abandoning the self, she believed, a person could simply acquire God. When Weil died, she was a year older than Christ at Golgotha.

What virtue appears less satisfying than humility? Even by the standards of good behavior, which are already rarely counted as good fun, humility is the dreary purview of sackcloth and ashes, for if one can brag about charity or chastity, then by its very definition humility can't countenance pride in itself. The diligent can admire their own work well done and the kind can appreciate

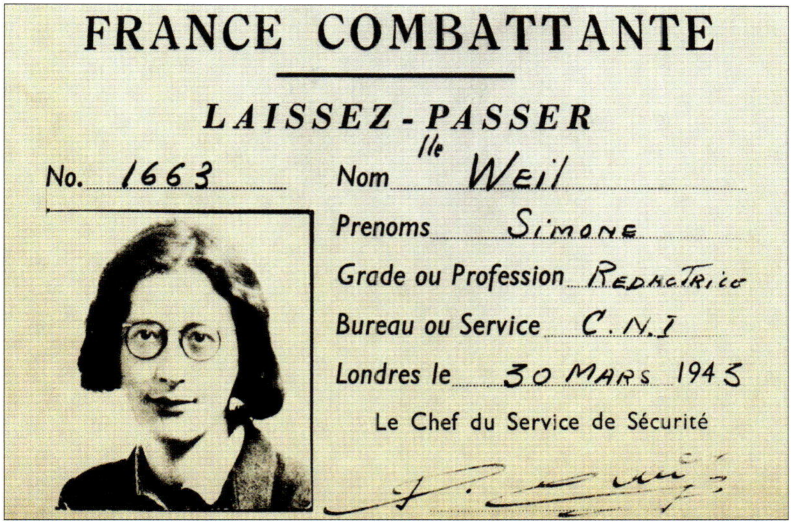

FRANCE COMBATTANTE

LAISSEZ-PASSER

No. 1663 Nom Mlle Weil

Prenoms Simone

Grade ou Profession Redactrice

Bureau ou Service C.N.I

Londres le 30 Mars 1943

Le Chef du Service de Sécurité

universal admiration, but the humble person is better pathologized as having a self-esteem problem. Especially in the modern context which privileges individual self-promotion most of all, those with humility appear borderline mentally ill. Yet if pride is the font of all sins, then its opposing virtue must be the font of all which is good, unsexy though it may be. Political equality is the daughter of humility, democracy the ethos of the humble. The mystics speak of a process called *kenosis*, the emptying out of the self so that God may come in (an understanding which Weil knew well), but even in less abstract terms, humility allows the individual to meet if not the Lord, then their fellow humans. In quieting their own ego, there is room for the brother and sister, the neighbor and fellow citizen, the stranger and the dispossessed to fully come into the *attention* of the blessedly humble person. With humility, we can have the necessary awareness that sees others on their own terms, which makes connection and communion possible. Humility is the prerequisite for a true empathy, for the former requires a keen awareness of the awesome sublimity of standing before another human in all of their strangeness, beauty, and worth. The individual of true humility has turned themselves into a great eye and ear of experience, for as the fifteenth-century German priest Thomas à Kempis wrote in *The Imitation of Christ*, the "humble man enjoys peace in the midst of many vexations, because his trust is in God, not in the world. Hence, you must not think that you have made any progress until you look upon yourself as inferior to all others."

As with all of the virtues and vices—indeed as with any intellectual concept at all—humility exists in a matrix of relation to other attributes, not of synonyms per se, but a web of connotations. Humility is not necessarily sibling, but perhaps close cousin, to qualities as various as shame and guilt, though more than those rather derogatory terms it's most congruent with simplicity. To claim that humility is reducible to shame, guilt, and so on is erroneous. They're not at all the same thing, yet their significance and function isn't entirely diametrically opposed either. What all of these various concepts share is the necessity of minimizing the ego, of standing athwart the human inclination toward pride and accepting a degree of appropriate abasement. None of them are particularly positive terms

TOP Weil's military-issued identification card as part of her work in the French Resistance during the Second World War.

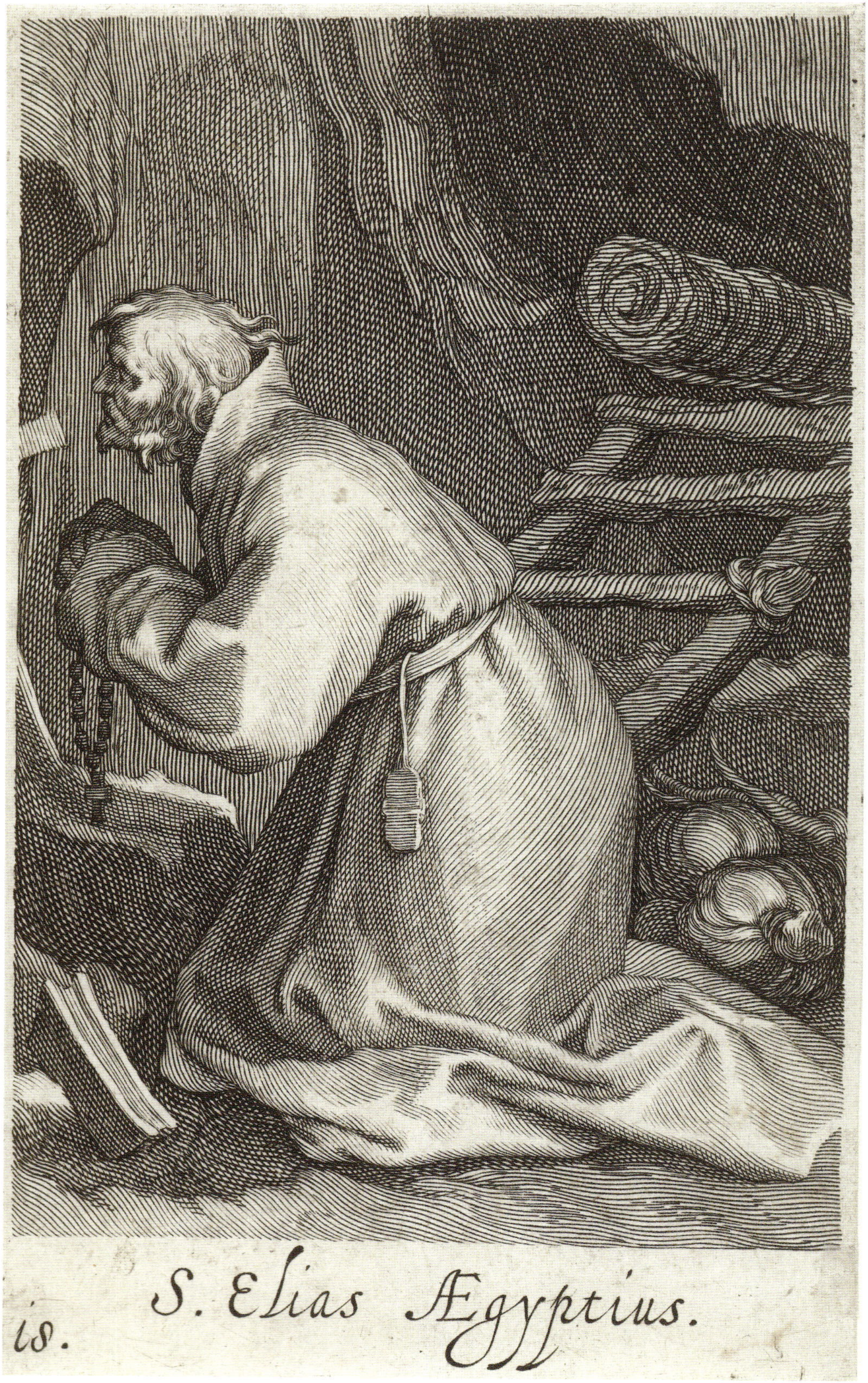
18.
S. Elias Ægyptius.

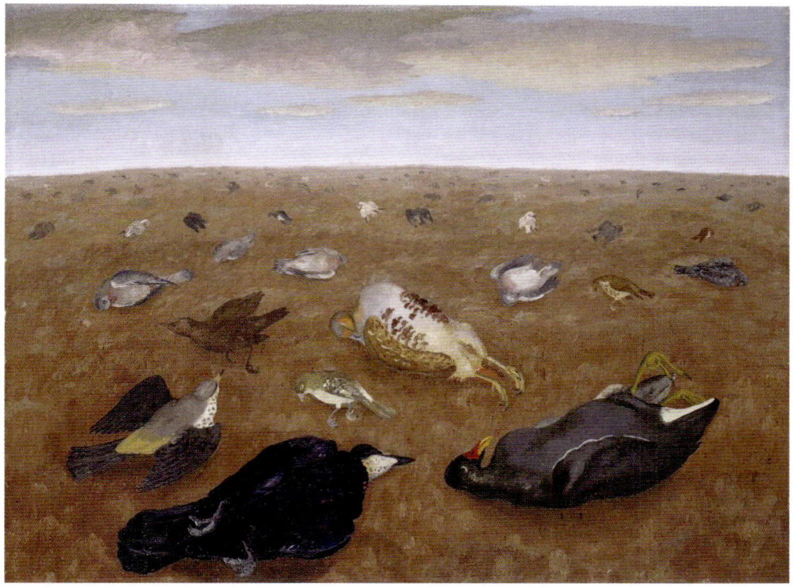

OPPOSITE Late-medieval Netherlandish visionary genius Hieronymus Bosch brings his own deeply eccentric sensibility to his 1493 composition *The Hermit Saints*, original held at the Gallerie dell'Accademia in Venice. St. Anthony, St. Jerome, and St. Giles, each famed hermits, are depicted in each one of the triptychs, with the dangers of Hell on the far left, torturing the mystic Anthony. The abasement of such men is understood by Bosch as being the means to acquire the kingdom of Heaven, with Anthony writing in *Apophthegmata Patrum* that just "as fish die if they stay too long out of the water, so the monks who loiter outside their cells or pass their time with the men of this world lose the intensity of inner peace."

TOP British painter Cedric Morris's 1960 *Landscape of Shame*, original held by the Tate Modern, enigmatically matches its title to an avian massacre, a beachfront of decomposing birds a natural calamity equivalent to the emotional register of guilt.

in contemporary culture, with humility paid the most lip service to, but even that virtue is largely passed over in disdain. Shame, for example, is something that's simultaneously coveted and avoided today; in the former case the mob loves disgracing others, but the individual avoids feeling it himself at all costs. Much editorial space is devoted to bemoaning "cancel culture" or "consequence culture," and while there is more than enough truth to the fact that mob justice can often exhibit more of the spectacle than of fairness, not enough time is also spent considering the pedagogical import of shame. To put it bluntly, shame teaches people something; it is purgative, it can even be salvific and redemptive. Writing in the *Analects* two and a half millennia ago, Confucius argued that if we're led "through moral force," then we will develop a "sense of shame and will also correct" ourselves. Because we so often associate shame with those unpleasant physiological characteristics—the red-cheeked flush of embarrassment, the sinking feeling in the stomach—we can ignore its profound utility. Shame is a rigorous form of introspection, a variety of inner moral questioning to ever refine our behavior so that we're more just, equitable, and fair with our fellow humans—a means of diminishing the prideful voice for long enough to admit "I was wrong," which if deployed properly leads to contrition and forgiveness. Guilt serves a rather similar purpose; rather than being an exercise in humiliation, it's simply a conscience acknowledging where it is in error. As an experience of being in a fallen world—of being a fallen being—guilt is unpleasant, but such an emotion also indicates a utopian counterexample, because where we can admit guilt, then we can admit that we need not always do things in the failed, unfair, cruel ways that we have before—that another world might be beyond the horizon. The midrash in *Exodus Rabbah* of the Talmud states it well—"Repentance makes virtues almost of the very vices of the penitent sinner."

Guilt and shame are the subjects of all great moral literature. Partially because of the innate drama of both related feelings, the blood pressure spike, the burning face and sweaty palms, there is a degree of psychological

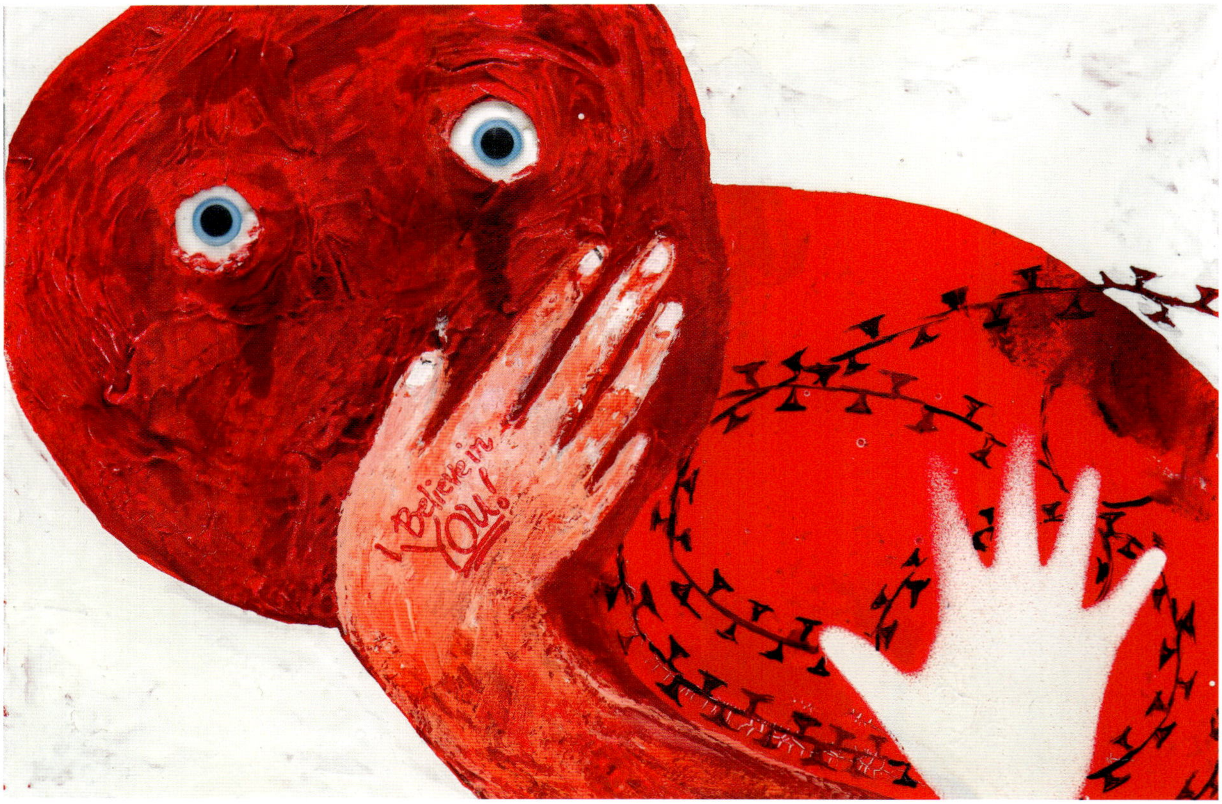

complexity that can be explored. Oft-dismissed by the positive and optimist alike as mere theo-psychological superstition—Eden's masticated apple and the mark of Cain—the universality of guilt actually speaks to the human tendency to disorder. Guilt is a gift, for admitting our culpability as humans is the first step to contrition. The brilliant Soviet poet Anna Akhmatova, witness to the various capitulations and justifications people can make when forced to commit their own bargains with an unjust regime, explored the purpose of shame (among other subjects) in her epic *Requiem*. Writing during the long decades from 1935 until 1961, when Akhmatova's verse was smuggled beyond the Iron Curtain and published in the West, *Requiem* is composed under the backdrop of Joseph Stalin's Great Purge, when millions of Russians were either guilty, complicit, or senselessly punished in an act of national self-abasement. Various types of shame coincide in Akhmatova's verse; the conjured mock-shame of the state, who accused its citizens of various nonsensical thought-crimes such as being counter-revolutionary or bourgeois, and the very-real shame of those who survived by not unfrequently impugning the upstandingness of a colleague, a neighbor, a friend, a family member. The shame of *Requiem* is that of the survivor, the question of why it is that some are arrested, sent to the gulag, summarily executed, and others can continue with their lives in Moscow or Leningrad flats. "Now all's eternal confusion," writes Akhmatova, "Who's beast, and who's man?" The sense of shame at one's survival isn't meant to be nihilistic; rather, it's an acknowledgment of our own finite existence within a universe

ABOVE Contemporary artist Penny Siopis, a South African artist of white Afrikaner descent, explores the intense and complicated emotions that can accompany a sense of collective shame, from denial to guilt. Her 2015 composition *Shame*, with a wide (blue)-eyed figure that appears borderline cadaverous, covering its face with a hand upon which is written "I believe you!," a geometric zip-line of what could almost be the barbed wire concentrating Black South Africans into Bantustans, speaks of the shame and horror of the Apartheid regime.

that contains so many other people, so many other complicated, unthinkable, and yet very human situations. A similar moral complexity is explored in the United States' great novel of reckoning with guilt, Toni Morrison's 1987 *Beloved.* Written in that most American idiom of the gothic, Morrison's tale is fundamentally a ghost story, in which the former enslaved woman Sethe, now living in a Cincinnati farm in 1873, is seemingly haunted by the spirit of the young daughter whom she murdered rather than have be captured into bondage. A mark of moral sophistication in modern literature is the eschewal of easy allegory; Morrison writes not of symbols or synecdoche, but of people. *Beloved* is not a parable, but a novel, thus all the better to actually and squarely look at guilt both national and personal. Echoing the Talmud, Morrison writes, "More it hurt more better it is. Can't nothing heal without pain, you know."

Humility can be the daughter of shame and guilt, but she is not the same thing. Furthermore, humility has little to do (though not nothing to do) with her etymological cognate of humiliation. Fundamentally, humility is a predisposition toward the world, an acknowledgment of the infinitesimal smallness of the individual against the enormity of the cosmos, and most crucially, against the enormity of this mass of humanity. It has nothing to do with lacking confidence, to the contrary. What humility offers is an approach of existence in this world—a self-assured approach—which understands the ways in which the single soul is embedded in a network of mutually reinforcing connections. Humility does not demand, it does not expect, it doesn't yell or pound the table. There is no red-hot cheek or sweaty palms with humility (even if those are the stigmata of the process by which one earns humility), for at its core what it offers is balance, wisdom, and peace. Humility is nothing less and nothing more than confident simplicity, a supplication through the basic things of this moment and of this place, whenever and wherever they might be. By simplicity, this need not mean anything as prosaic as "easy to understand" or "unadorned"; it should not be interpreted in such a literal way. Rather, simplicity is a negotiation with existence, an acceptance of our limited role in this drama that began before us and will complete without us, and the dedication toward helping others in that interim. The prideful man is shamed by having to clean up after himself; the humble sage takes great joy in moving the broom, doing the dishes, weeding the yard. The arrogant person is angered by the waiter who is too slow or the cashier fumbling with her card; the modest shopper just has gratitude for this bit of time spent on earth. None of this is to say that humility countenances a tacit acceptance of that which is wrong with life, but it's not to confuse inconvenience with injustice either. If anything, humility demands an attention to injustice, while understanding that no single woman or man is capable of rectifying this fallen world by themselves. "It is not your duty to finish the work," says Rabbi Tarfon some two millennia ago in *Pirkei Avot*, "but neither are you at liberty to neglect it," and so the humble person awakens and does what is required, going to sleep at the end of the day content to know that they are but a small part of something much larger and more complex.

INTERLUDE—HENRY DARGER

Starting a few months after the 1929 stock market crash up until his death in 1973, the custodian Henry Darger would finish his work at St. Joseph's Hospital, where his existence was maintained in mop heads and rags, measured in sanitizers and disinfectants, and he'd trudge back on the El to his small apartment in Lincoln Park where for forty-three long years, and unbeknownst to anybody, he worked on the longest narrative novel ever composed in the English language. Solitary and friendless, the pious Catholic who attended Mass at least once a day, spent his non-working hours in his cramped Chicago apartment, filled with found objects from old shoes found on the street to balls of twine, impromptu artwork recycled from those materials, and pages and pages of meticulous, scribbled weathered journals, as well as his neatly typed epic fantasy novel *In the Realms of the Unreal*, presumably written for nobody and read by no one, at least not until it was discovered by his landlord several days after Darger's death at St. Augustine's Home for the Aged. During evenings and days off, Darger enveloped himself in the bizarre cosmos of his own creation, a phantasmagoria about the daring Vivian girls, pious Catholics like him, who battle against the cruel Glandelinians, the sisters in part enlisting the assistance of the Blengigomeneans, shape-shifting bat-like creatures. In fifteen volumes, illustrated with carefully constructed fold-out paintings rendered in watercolor and magazine collage, Darger told an oft-disturbing tale about the machinations of evil men who threaten childhood innocence, and the holy war to preserve such purity. Joyce's *Ulysses* is 735 pages, David Foster Wallace's *Infinite Jest* is 1,079, and Samuel Richardson's *Clarissa* unspools across some 1,534 pages. Darger's *In the Realms of the Unreal* is told in an astounding 15,145 pages, completed only because its author died. "Do you think i might be fool enough to run away from heaven if i get there?" Darger asked in his novel, and the question itself implies multitudes.

Fully titled as *The Story of the Vivian Girls, in What is Known as the Realms of the Unreal, of the Glandeco-Angelinian War Storm, Caused by the Child Slave Rebellion*, Darger's novel is a dizzyingly baroque, fabulist, encyclopedic, obsessive accounting of a universe constructed entirely within the head of the man who by day pushed a mop through the halls of St. Joseph's, silent largely to everyone, only uttering a whispered "Amen" to the parish priest at communion. All of his work produced with studied intensity in a cramped and crowded trash-strewn room, exposed metal radiators clanging during a Chicago winter, a rickety wooden desk in front of a bricked-in fireplace, all of it filled top-to-bottom with twine-tied newspapers and bags of bottlecaps, boxes of crayons, and old black Remingtons. From that mess came his bizarre maximalist fantasy with its apocalyptic war between the Christian children and their slave-driving enemies, illustrated on twelve-foot-long scrolls with Darger's vaguely Edwardian drawings, colorized with the artist's own innovative methods using clippings from catalogs and magazines that surpassed even the collage experimentations of the modernist avant-garde. Darger evokes the radicalism and mythos of a William Blake crossed with the homespun midwestern Americana

OPPOSITE, TOP Image from Darger's *Realms of the Unreal*.

OPPOSITE, BOTTOM Image from *Realms of the Unreal* demonstrating Darger's efficiency with techniques from collage and stenciling to intermixing text and image.

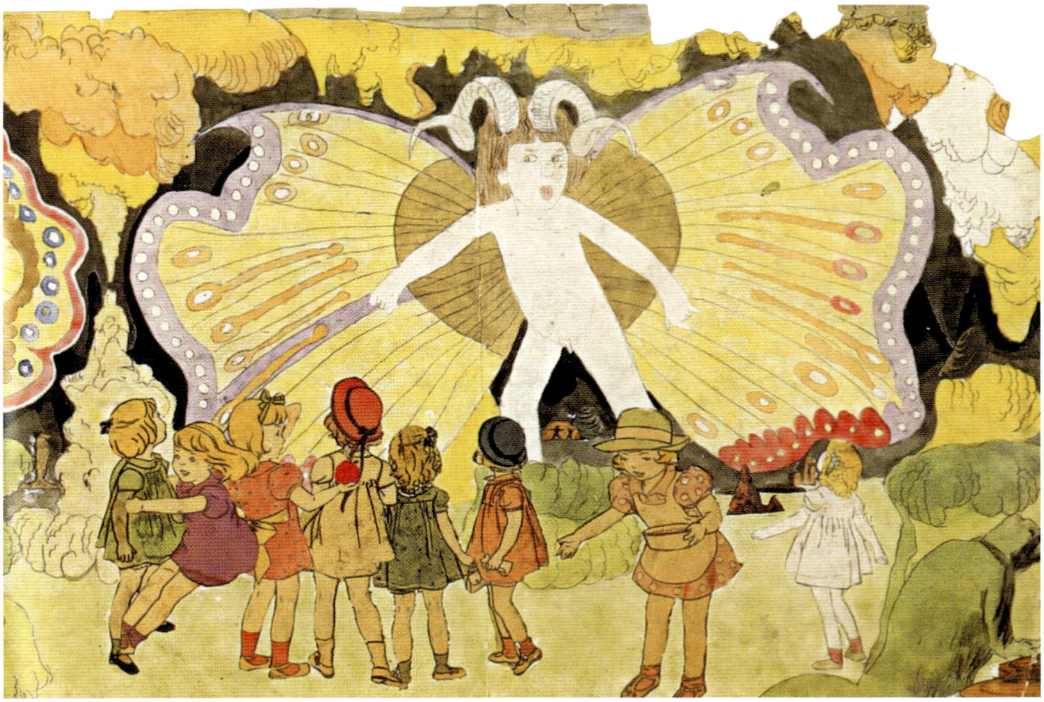

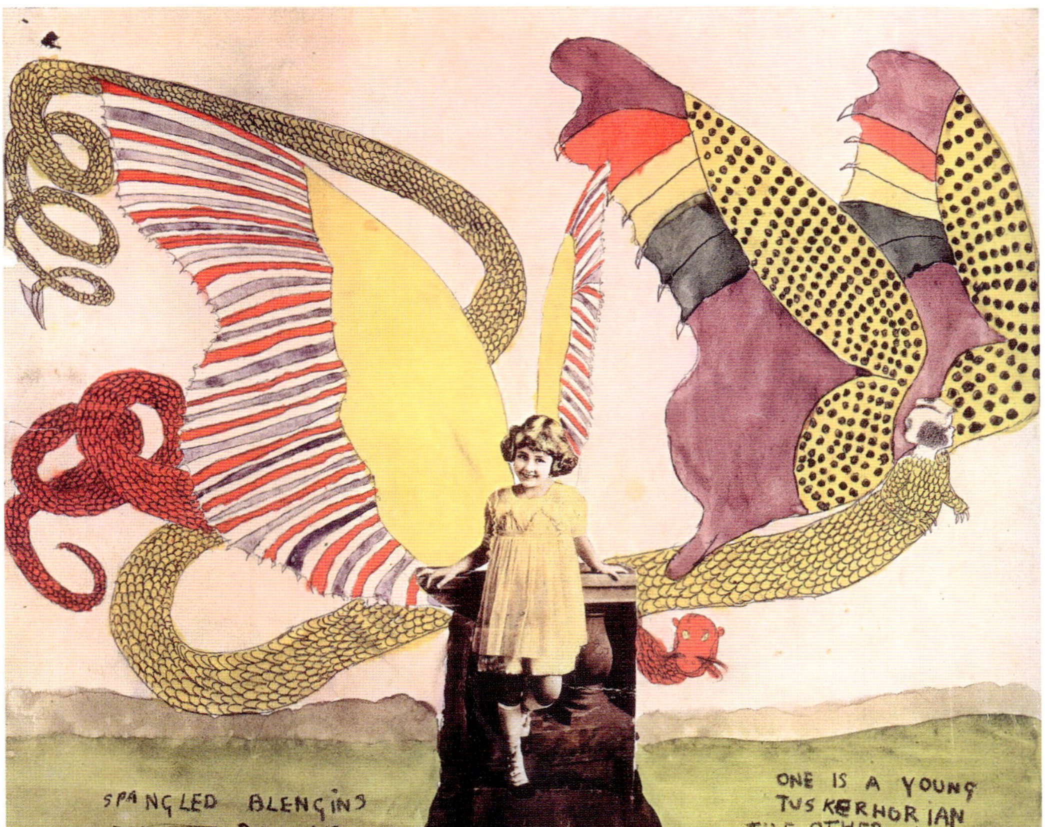
SPANGLED BLENGINS
BOY KING ISLANDS.
ONE IS A YOUNG
TUSKERHORIAN
THE OTHER A HUMAN
HEADED DORTHEREAN

of L. Frank Baum. Witness as a representative example a yellow-hued illustration from *In the Realms of the Unreal*, a catalog photograph of a young girl in bright dress, with coifed blonde curls, who appears almost Victorian; Darger's ink drawings of majestic angelic wings unfurling behind her and serpentine creature slithering in the underbrush. Despite all that labor, despite the 15,145 pages which Darger wrote, he claimed that "There is one really important thing I must write which I have forgotten." In immersing yourself in the tale of the Vivian girls (and how many have actually read the whole thing?), there is the sense that Darger was on the verge of saying a pure truth, but whether because of modesty or fear he took fifteen volumes to not actually be able to utter it.

Whatever his motivations were in producing *The Realms of the Unreal*—schizophrenic compulsion, sexual neurosis, and religious scrupulosity have all been proffered hypotheses—the fame which Darger was unconcerned with during his writing life was acquired upon his death, as the janitor was lauded as an untutored genius, a visionary artist who toiled in anonymity, and where despite his humility (or because of it) he was able to create something of such exquisite, beautiful strangeness. Darger's work is today in collections from the Smithsonian Museum of American Art to the Art Institute of Chicago (and dozens more besides). As an outsider artist, which is to say somebody who didn't benefit from formal education or training, Darger's work set a sales record with compositions going for $750,000. Historian Daniel Wojcik notes in *Outsider Art: Visionary Worlds and Trauma* that the "imaginary world constructed by Henry Darger also was a wholly private endeavor . . . [but] is now considered one of the most significant expressions of outsider art in the twentieth century, praised and studied by critics internationally." None of this, it seems, was ever Darger's intent. While working on *The Realms of the Unreal*, there is no indication that Darger ever queried literary agents or editors, that he ever sent proposals to publishers, magazines, or journals, that he had any desire to ever see his name embossed on the cover of a printed copy of the novel he spent six decades writing. There is no indication even that he ever told anyone about what it was that he was working on. There are many reasons why writers choose to do what they do; esteem, respect, and appreciation being only a few of them (while money is only a goal for the lucky, talented, or delusional). Certainly writing itself is difficult enough that nobody who is engaged in it ever does it only for accolades, for it would not be worth it, and yet authors themselves are rarely lauded as an entirely humble group. There is, for anyone who is true to the title of "writer" at its most genuine and pure, a desire to write because of the joy of singular creation. Darger, it would seem, is something else entirely. For just as a silk moth thinks nothing of money or acclaim but only to produce silk, so did Darger write because he simply couldn't have done anything else.

PRAXIS—A BROKEN AND CONTRITE HEART

Amid the scrubby, dry green hills of Abruzzo where bears interlope among woods of Austrian oak and Italian maple, there is the relatively modest Romanesque Basilica di Santa Maria di Collemaggio of L'Aquila. Built in the thirteenth century by the Celestines, the basilica is a triumph of Italian medieval architecture, an unassuming rectilinear front that nonetheless has a triumphal gothic arch, the entire surface of the church interlaced with a contrasting pink cruciform geometrical design, all of it topped with a small stained-glass rose window. Santa Maria is most celebrated not for its architecture, elegant though it may be, so much as it is for a tomb inside of its

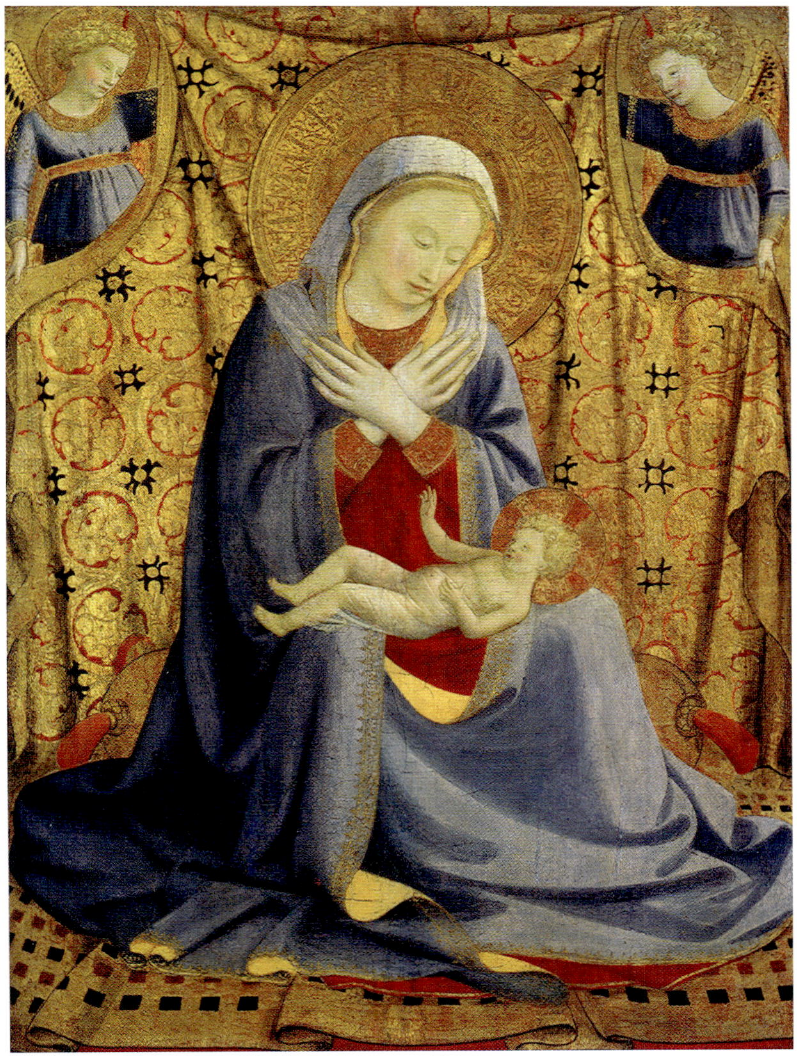

RIGHT Always a model of sanctified humility, here the mother of God's humble countenance radiates through her calm smile. Original of *Madonna of the Pomegranates*, rendered by the Italian master Fra Angelico around 1426, is held by the Prado Museum in Madrid.

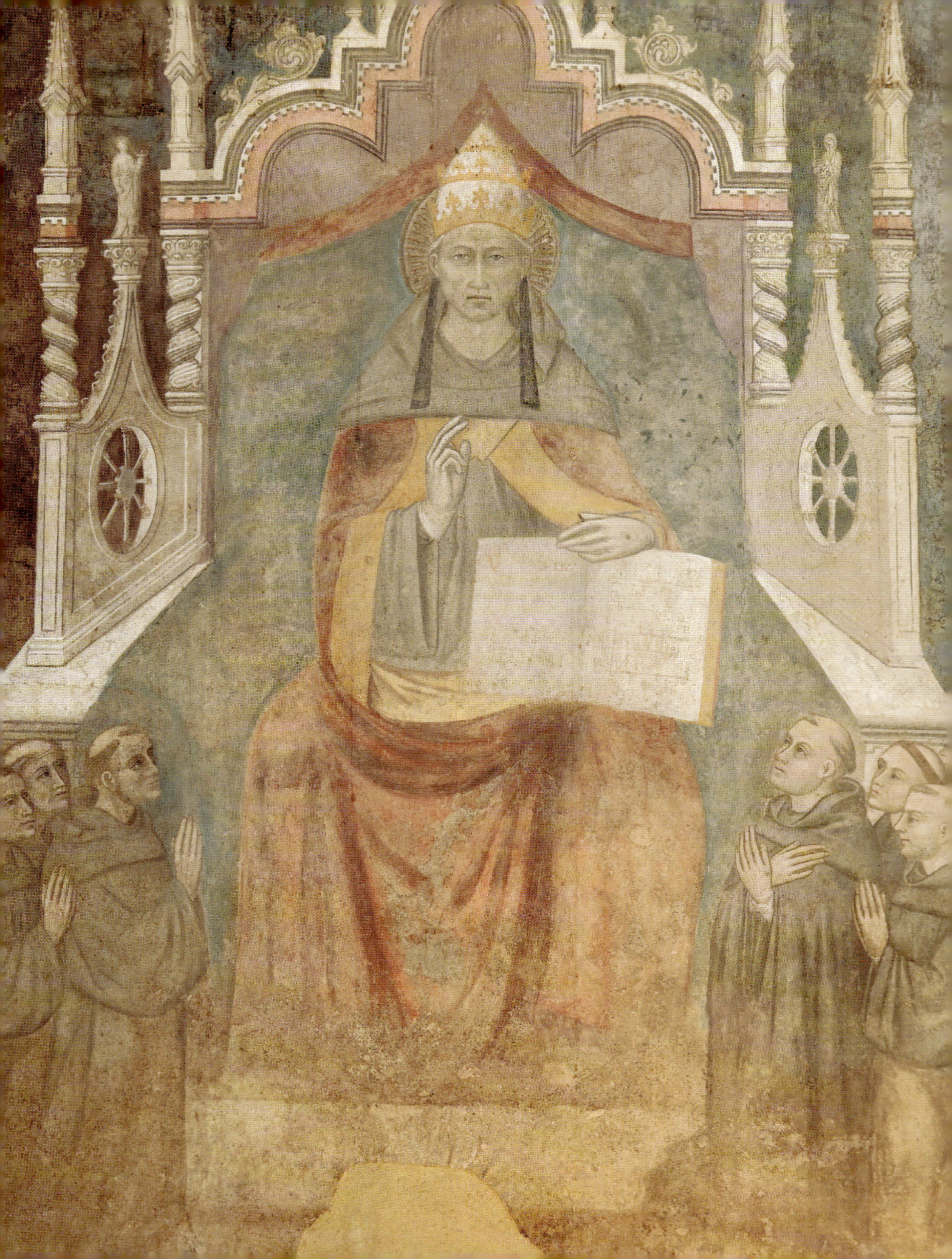

white stone walls, commissioned by a guild of wool workers some three centuries after the 1296 death of the man contained within. Shaped as the body of a man in repose, and wearing the actual ecclesiastical robes, stole, and mitre which his position required, the ossuary of Pope Celestine V—he who made the "great refusal" according to his near contemporary Dante in *The Divine Comedy*—is marked by a three-dimensional relief of the pontiff's face, rendered in silver but startlingly realistic, all deep-lined creases and heavy folds, the visage of a man who was worried in life and is still seemingly anxious in death.

Celestine V's relics are not oft-visited, and though a saint, he is rarely counted as many people's favorite, though that's in keeping with the pope's desires, for he is among the few (only six) to have ever ascended to the majesty of St. Peter's throne, and then after a bit of time deciding that such power and regalia did not suit his own simple necessities, so that he abdicated that responsibility. Founding the monastic order which bears his papal name (and maintains the basilica in L'Aquila) as a branch of the Benedictines, Celestine wore the pope's tiara for only five months in 1294, the already 79-year-old man deciding that his previous life of simple contemplation and prayer could do more good in the world than ruling as Christ's Vicar on earth did. And so he once again became a hermit, no longer Pope Celestine V, but rather once again the simple Abruzzese monk Pietro Angelerio. Such humility is suspect to any who desire temporal power in addition to spiritual power, for the papacy surely embodies both, so that his successor Pope Boniface VIII foolishly feared that he who had stepped down would try and usurp him, ordering Celestine's capture from the woods in Dalmatia where the former pontiff was hiding, and imprisoning him in the Fumone Castle of Lazio. "I desired nothing in the world but a cell," the former pope reflected, "and a cell they have given me."

Because simplicity is unassuming—that's its very purpose—it can be camouflaged against the tumult of that which is larger, flashier, more grandiose. Imagine the saintliness of a man like Celestine, whom far from the rank coward referenced by Dante, was according to the fourteenth-century poet Petrarch a "truly divine spirit." Writing in his 1346 treatise *The Solitary Life*, Petrarch said that he considered Celestine's resignation an "act of a most lofty and free spirit which knew no impositions," a symbolic martyrdom whereby he may have abandoned the eternal city, but he was "going with his spirit." Celestine had to be sacrificed so that Pietro could live; the papal throne had to be destroyed so as to save it. Often castigated for a supposed dereliction of duty, a lack of bravery when faced with the awesome responsibility the Cardinals had entrusted him with, and Celestine's choice to abdicate was actually a stunning and deeply reverential spiritual act. Shown the accoutrement of his position, the tiara and ring, the gilded art and the papal palaces, Celestine rather simply said "No," his preference a cave instead of the Vatican, simple wooden rosaries rather than the full insignia of the papacy. Humility isn't humiliation, though. In descending, there can be an ascension; in reduction, an apotheosis. Petrarch writes that when Celestine sat up and walked away from the papal throne, he "escaped with immense joy, his eyes and his countenance bearing the signs of his spiritual happiness, when, free at last and restored to himself, he went away from the council not as if he had relieved his back of a moderate burden but as if he had freed his neck of a terrible axe." The monk who rejected the keys of heaven

OPPOSITE Niccolò di Tommaso's fourteenth-century depiction of Pope Celestine V in the middle of a triptych held at the New Castle in Naples.

in favor of the Kingdom itself. In humility, the individual is liberated from the tribulations of pride, free to admit that no single individual has it within their power to command a nation, lead a Church, remake the world, alone. As that other great mystic of the thirteenth-century St. Francis of Assisi would say in his *Salutation of Virtue*, commandeered to the page a few decades before Celestine's profound rejection of power, "Pure holy simplicity confounds all the wisdom of this world."

Simplicity is the blessed child of humility, but it's often delivered through those midwives of shame and guilt. There is a difference between those two, the former imposed by outside forces on the individual and the latter arising from within, and while it's true that both can be used as means of social control (indeed any honest accounting must enumerate the oppressive uses of them), they are also important means of reconciling the individual with immoral and unethical actions, with injustice. When the American 4th Armored Division and the 89th Infantry Division arrived at the otherwise bucolic Thuringian town of Ohrdruf on April 4, 1945, they discovered the titular concentration camp abandoned by its German masters and left over to only their dead and dying victims. Part of the Buchenwald complex, the Ohrdruf concentration camp was the first to be liberated by U.S. soldiers, who were horrified by what they witnessed there. Finding twisted piles of emaciated bodies and burnt corpses, the Supreme Commander of the Allied Forces in Europe General Dwight D. Eisenhower cabled back to Washington a description of "starvation, cruelty and bestiality . . . so overpowering as to leave me a bit sick." General George C. Patton, despite being more than conversant with the brutality of war, was so disturbed by the sights and smells of Ohrdruf that he was unable to enter several of the rooms, enumerating the piles of "human bones, skulls, charred torsos on or under the griddle which must have accounted for many hundreds." Thousands of the eleven million dead during the Holocaust were accounted for here at Ohrdruf, almost entirely Jews. Not far from the camp was the town which lent this factory of death its name, a place that by contrast was composed of charming half-timber buildings in the German style and the Baroque castle Schloss Ehrenstein, where everyday women and men went about their everyday tasks, enjoying filling meals of schnitzel and dumplings, fortifying glasses of schnaps, perhaps an evening spent listening to records of Beethoven or Mozart while reading Goethe, all while just across the woods the Nazis murdered in their name. Obviously the wafting smell of decomposing corpses disguised with lye must have drifted into Ohrdruf, the stench of charred bodies sprinkling white ash on the Thuringian countryside, despite the claims from German citizens that they had been unaware of the ongoing Holocaust. And so, when Eisenhower toured the camp, he commanded that the citizens of Ohrdruf travel the few miles themselves, and see what they were guilty of with their German eyes, then committed them to bury the graves of the murdered Jews themselves, with their German hands. Whether or not such necessary shame is enough to gain heaven, I do not know, but perhaps it can stave off entrance to hell, for a bit.

Contrition and redemption, amends and salvation, the theology of how one atones for sins is varied and complicated, far beyond the purview of this simple study, but at the very least it can be affirmed that even if forgiveness ends not in guilt it perhaps needs to begin there. Consider the horrors of partition when in

OPPOSITE Polish painter Teodor Axentowicz imagines the humble supplications of a pious mystic in this 1881 composition *Anchorite*. Often associated with holy women, the position of being an anchorite was as a hermit living amidst the bustle of the world. During the Middle Ages, anchorites often lodged in bricked-up cells within cathedrals, living examples of the peace and humility of seclusion. Original at the National Museum in Warsaw.

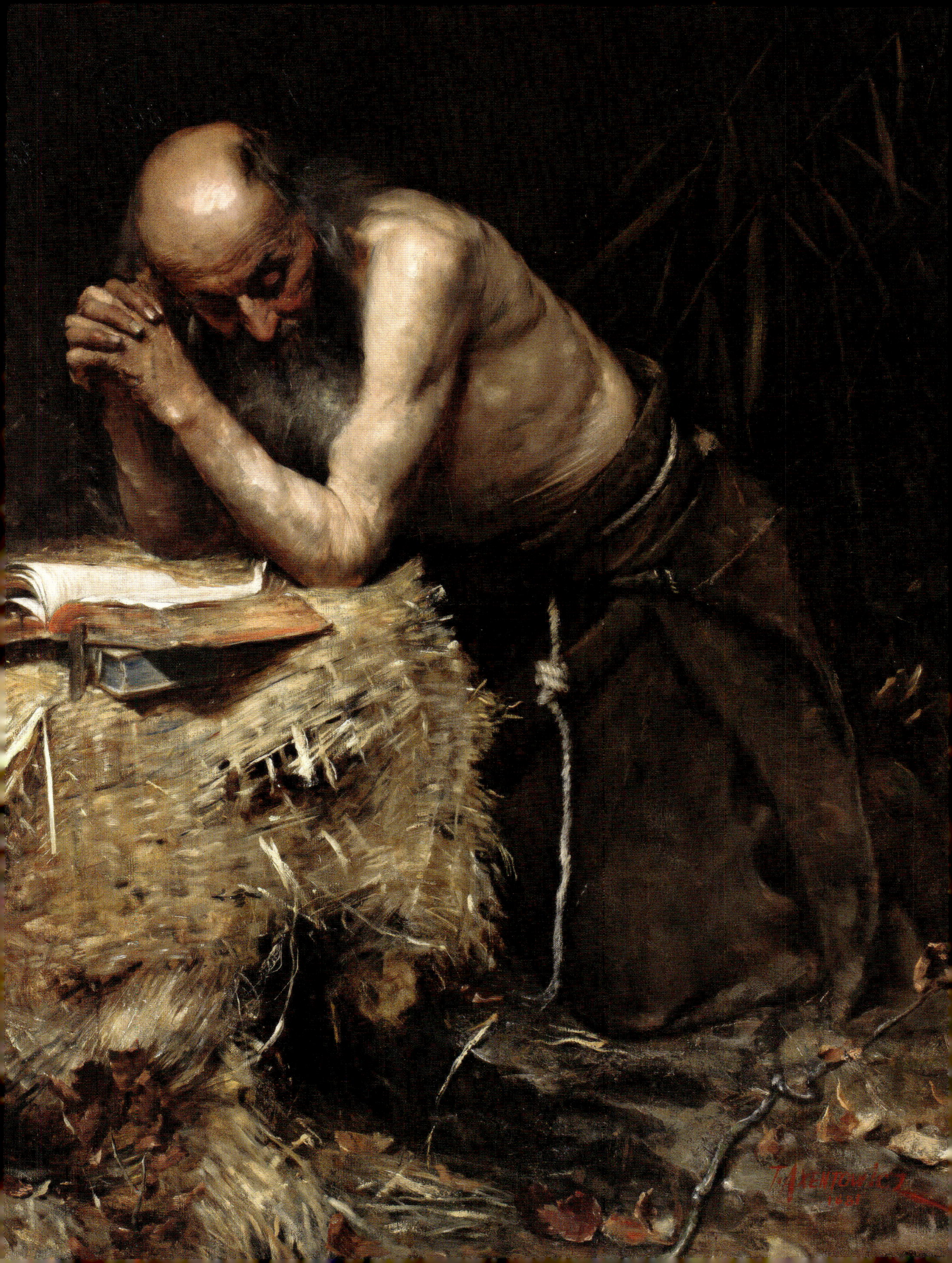

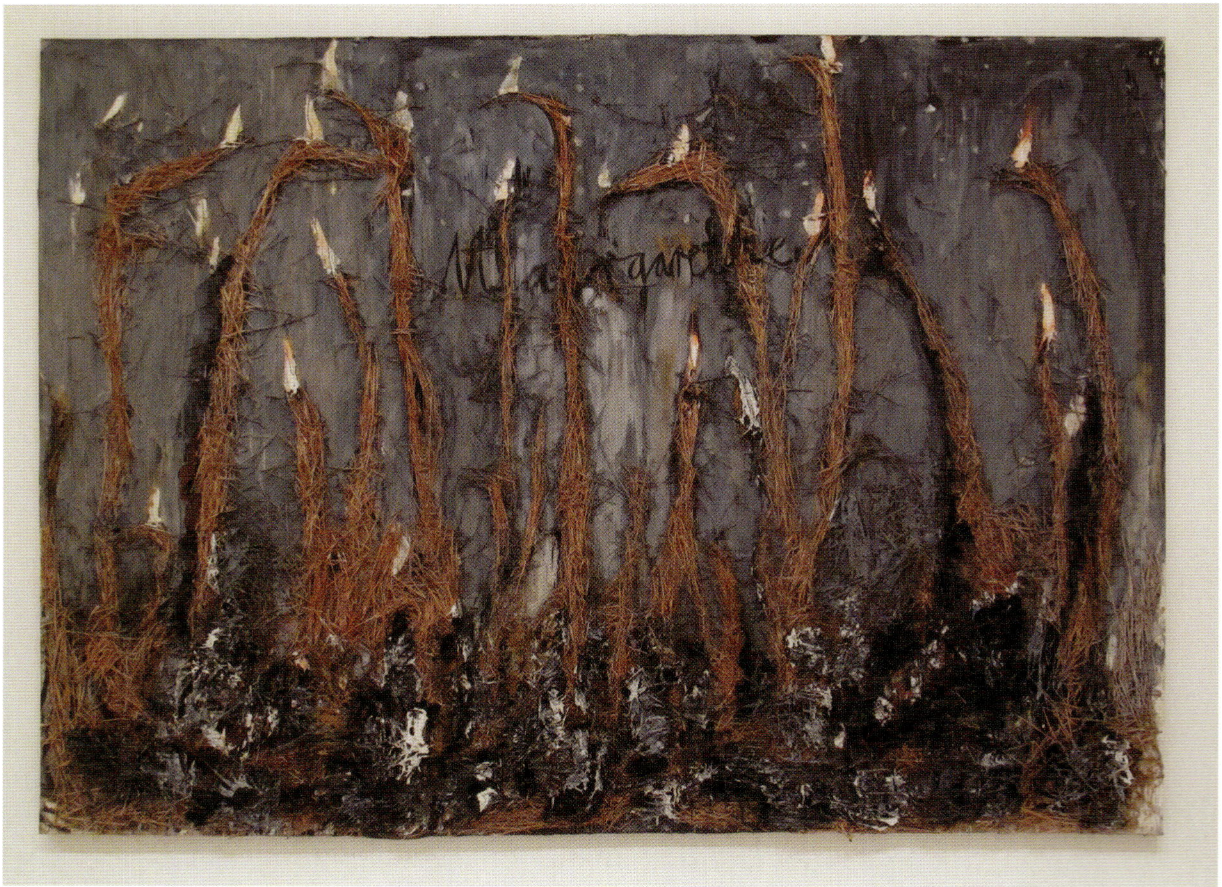

1947 the British Raj was dissolved by its colonial overseers, and rather than aid in the establishment of a newly independent and democratic nation, the Europeans simply placed an arbitrary line between Pakistan and India, Muslims and Hindus, with the respective chaotic transfer of populations leading to incalculable bloodshed. During those months of tumult, perhaps somewhere between two hundred thousand and two million people were killed by their neighbors, communities that had lived inextricably connected for centuries suddenly divided by modern ideology, the result being an intensely personal, intimate, close form of hideous violence. Still not fully reckoned with, thousands of houses were burnt, hundreds of thousands of women and children raped, most likely millions of people murdered in a matter of months, the ground at Ohrdruf still fresh. Sardar Joginder Singh Kholi, a Punjabi teenager during partition, recalls seeing a fellow Sikh immolate herself rather than be raped by a crowd of Muslim men. Nasim Fatima, a Muslim woman, saw her entire family murdered by their Sikh neighbors who'd once promised to protect them. Surinder Shani, a Hindu boy at the time of the violence, recalled to the *Guardian* decades later how his father had decided that their family would forcefully occupy the home of a Muslim family in their neighborhood. Zareena Parveen, twelve years old at the time, tells another reporter from that same British newspaper that "my brother was beheaded in front of me." Guilt seeped into the soil and clay of the subcontinent like the blood of the innocent, a place so overcome

TOP German painter Anselm Kiefer is fascinated by the national guilt of his fellow countrymen following the abyss of the Holocaust, exploring what contrition or redemption could even mean when a culture is capable of such evil. His 1981 *Margarethe*—drawing its name from an allegorical character from the Auschwitz survivor Paul Celan's poem "Death's Fugue"—uses unconventional materials like straw in his expression of German collective guilt. Original at the San Francisco Museum of Art. "Black milk of morning we drink you evenings," wrote Celan, "we drink you at noon and mornings we drink you at night / we drink and we drink."

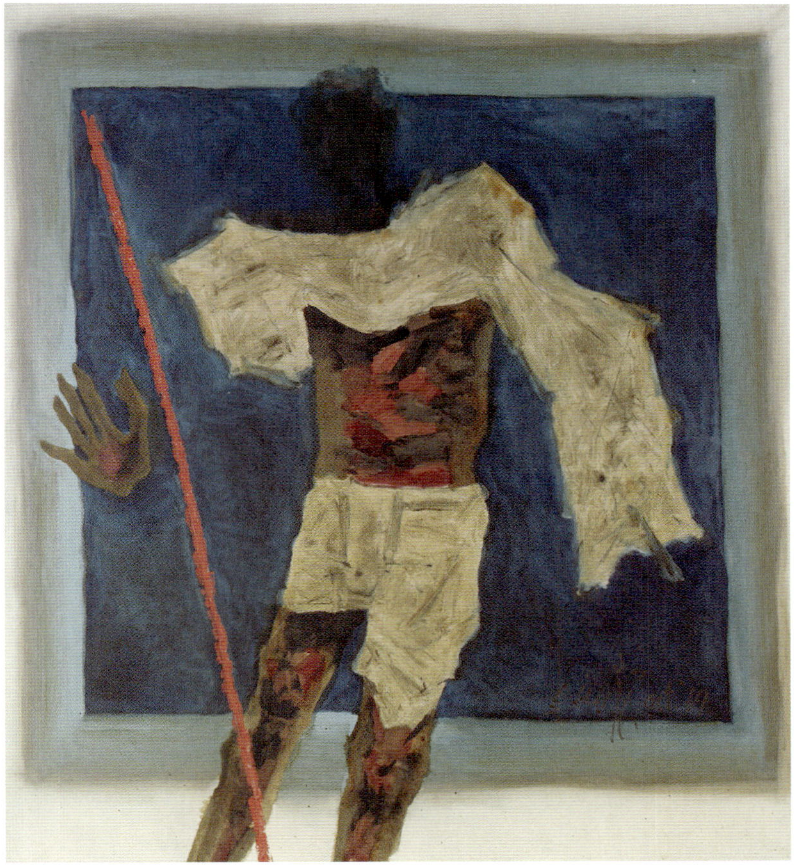

TOP Indian Cubist M. F. Hussain draws from Modernist techniques in his bold 1969 portrait of the national hero Mohandas Gandhi. True to the mendicant's own sense of humility, Hussain presents Gandhi with his features blurred, the man less important than the movement, even while his staff and loincloth are unmistakably iconic. At the core of Gandhi's philosophy wasn't just humility, but indeed failure. Philosopher Costica Bradatan argues in his study *In Praise of Failure: Four Lessons in Humility* that Gandhi sought to "live with failure . . . to make the most of it . . . to turn failure into a more meaningful life."

with violence that forgiveness itself would seem quixotic, paradoxical. Such was the context of the parable which maintains that during this season of bloodletting, when the great Indian pacifist Mohandas Gandhi was undergoing one of his final hunger strikes of protestation, this time not against the British but against his own countrymen, that a Hindu man named Soureen Bannerji came to confess his guilt to the Mahatma. Recounting his revenge lust at his own unspeakable losses which he'd suffered, the man admits that he found an innocent Muslim child, and dashed his head against a wall. Now, fearing hell for such an unspeakable evil, he asks Gandhi what to do. The Mahatma tells the Hindu man that he must find an orphan around the same age as the child that he murdered for simply being a Muslim, and he must raise and provide a good, and safe, and happy life for that boy. The Hindu man agrees. Then Gandhi tells the Hindu that to find forgiveness, he must also make sure to raise the child as a pious Muslim. Which Bannerji did. Grace, the parable tells us, is possible, but it is not cheap.

Paragon of humility, Gandhi told the publication *Harijan* in 1940 that it is "unwise to be too sure of one's own wisdom. It is healthy to be reminded that the strongest might weaken and the wisest might err." Yet the Mahatma's own example was a living embodiment of how, Celestine-like, the abandonment of traditional markers of pride can counterintuitively elevate the individual, how there can be true power in abasement, as the example of Bannerji seeking contrition

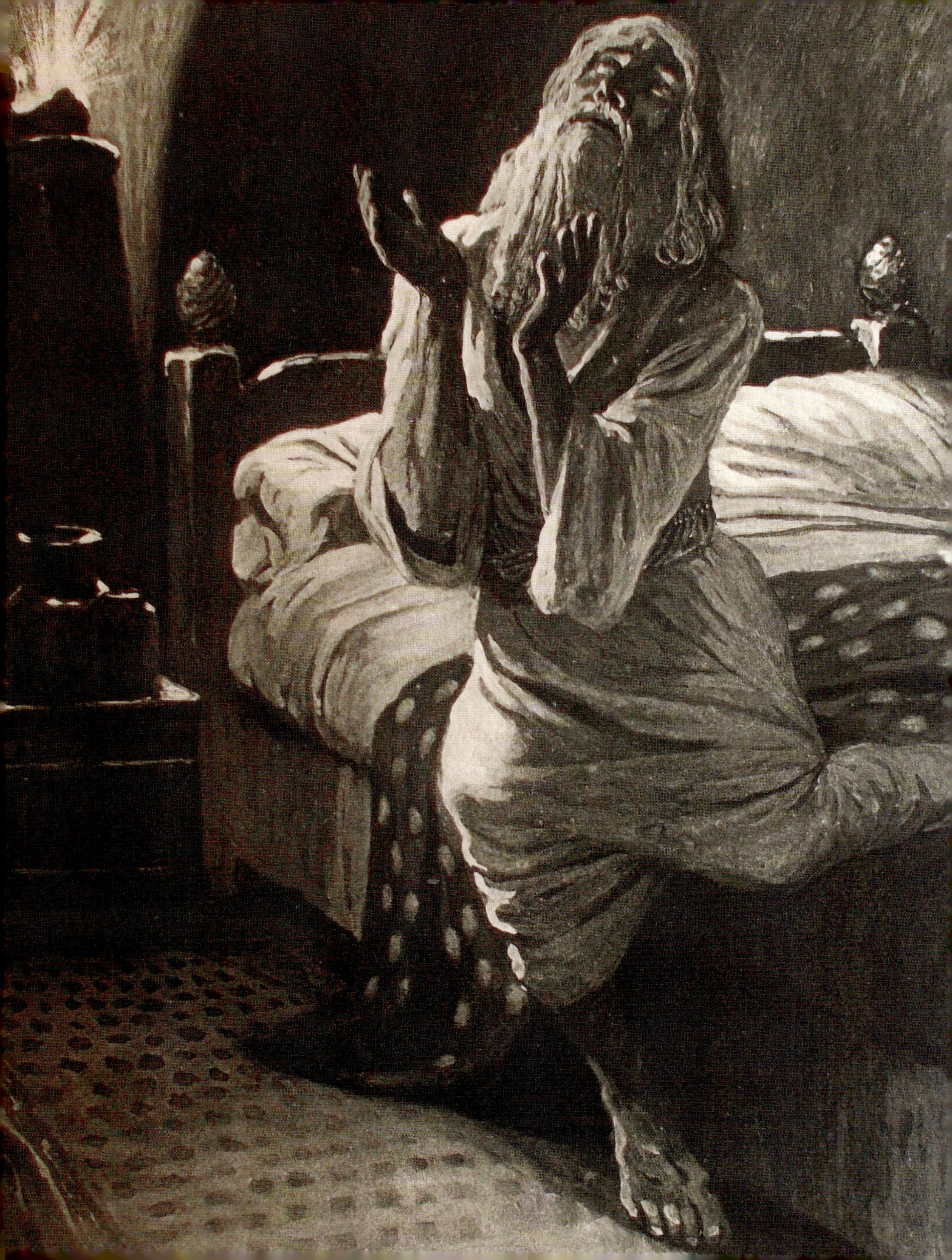

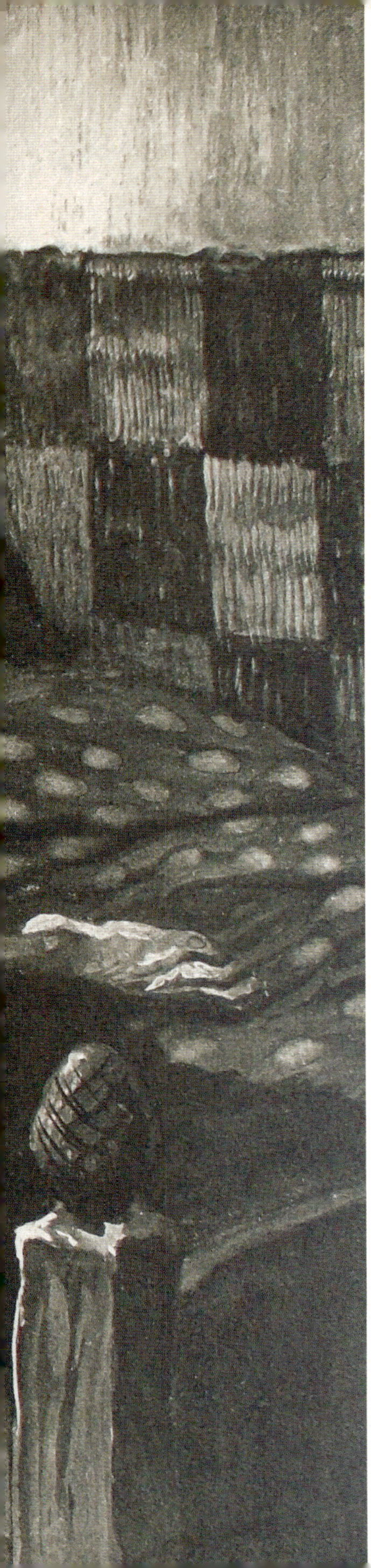

from this modern mendicant demonstrates. When envisioning Gandhi, that pacifist, Indian partisan, and Hindu holy man, there is the image of the emaciated activist wrapped in a simple cotton khadi, frayed sandals on his feet and circular wire-rimmed glasses about his bald head, a man who had seemingly dispatched with vanity, pride, and the very dictates of the self, and in the process had gained a nation. Such a view is, obviously, simplistic. A tremendously complicated man, and like all of us, inevitably a hypocritical one, though Gandhi would admit that himself.

Simplicity—humility—is not perfection, but it is an overture toward the world of humanity so much bigger than any one person. Trained as a lawyer, born into the high Kshatriya caste, and beneficiary of a Western education, Gandhi nonetheless developed a potent theology of simplicity, humility not as humbling but as means of spiritual resistance, writing in his 1920 book *The Doctrine of the Sword* that to be lowly does not mean "meek submission to the will of the evil-doer, but it means the putting of one's whole soul against the will of the tyrant." As a Hindu, Gandhi might not have put it this way, though as a perennialist who saw the mythopoeic wisdom of all faiths it would perhaps resonate, that if the original sin of Lucifer was pride, the only means of engaging with the Prince of this World is to exude the opposite quality, to pair that vice with this virtue. An adamant syncretist, Gandhi astutely drew wisdom from where he could. His intellectual forebearers in this path include the American Transcendentalist Ralph Waldo Emerson, thundering in his 1838 "Divinity School Address" at Harvard College that the "man who renounces himself, comes to himself," and Emerson's great student Henry David Thoreau, noting in his 1849 *A Week on the Concord and Merimak Rivers* that the "wisest man preaches no doctrines." And Leo Tolstoy, writing in his 1892 pamphlet *The First Step* that "to be good and lead a good life means to give to others more than one takes from them." Celestine V, by contrast, figures not at all in Gandhi's thinking, though they are kindred. To be taken to the mountaintop and shown all of the kingdoms of the earth as your bounty, and to turn your back and return to your cave, that's the true measure of greatness, the font of all grace. To this day, Celestine's papal bull of forgiveness issued in 1294 still stands, the pilgrim simply walks under the arches of L'Aquila to regain their soul, for a time.

OPPOSITE French painter of unusual biblical scenes James J. Tissot places the Israelite king in a contemporary nineteenth-century bedroom in this painting made between 1896 and 1902, *David Praying in the Night*, original held by the Jewish Museum in New York City. From the quilt to the four-poster bed, the rug to the nightstand, David's presence in such a singularly Victorian interior only serves to underscore the timeless state which genuine humility can propel the individual soul toward.

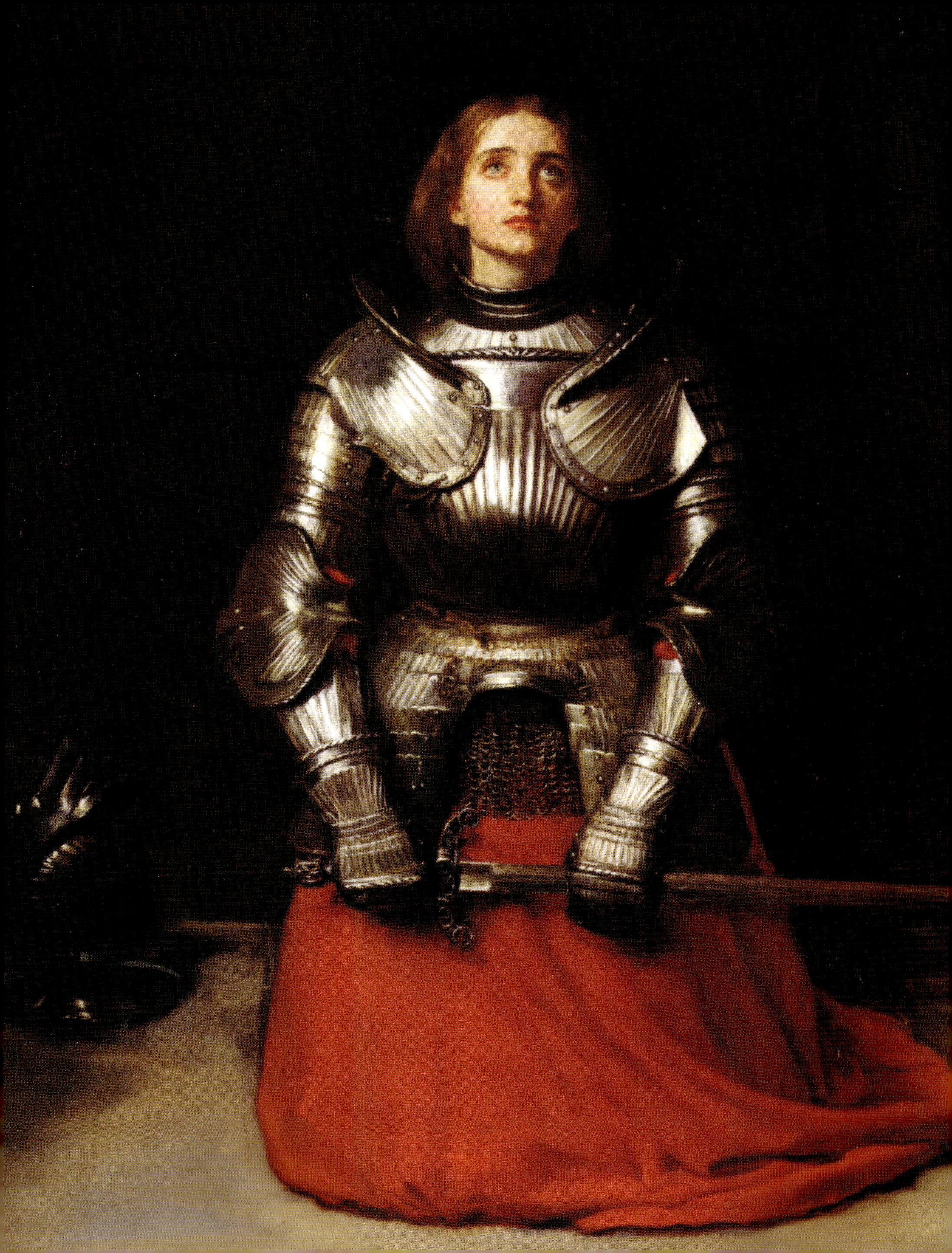

CHAPTER TWO

GROW PURE BY BEING PURELY SHOWN UPON: CHASTITY

". . . there be eunuchs, which have made themselves eunuchs

for the kingdom of heaven's sake."

—Matthew 19:12

"I was beat, incomplete / I'd been had, I was sad and blue,

but you made me feel / Yeah, you made me feel shiny and new."

—Madonna, "Like a Virgin" (1984)

Chastity was oft seen by theologians and Doctors of the Church as on par with temperance and industriousness; not just a state of being which was good in itself, but as a form of renunciation that could be understood as a practice, a means of focusing the mind and soul through denial. While there is a certain fairness in interpreting Christian attitudes toward sexuality as marked by repression, neuroticism, and sublimation, the earliest reasoning about chastity was less in judgment of the physical act of intercourse than it was part of the methodology of the aspiring contemplative, a means along with the aforementioned varieties of holy abandonment to focus the mind toward things divine. In this regard, the desire for sex wasn't necessarily any more intrinsically evil than the desire for food or rest. All were considered idolatries of the body, a prioritizing of individual transient physical pleasure over eternal things. Even scriptural mythology, from the virgin birth to Mary's immaculate conception, need not be read as innately anti-sexuality (though certainly they often are conveyed in that way), so much as they are indicative of profoundly different sorts of people and beings that are transcendent of the humdrum realm of materiality. Understood that way, chastity isn't necessarily just an ideal, it's a *miracle*—which is to admit that it's difficult to the point of aberrance. "Dearest Jesus!" prayed Thomas Aquinas, a lifelong virgin, "I know well that every perfect gift, and above all others that of chastity, depends upon the most powerful assistance of Your Providence." That chastity is about separation from prosaic experience is indicated in its etymology; the English word deriving from the Latin "castus," which more than "pure" means to be "cut away from" or "separated." In its initial meaning, to be chaste precisely meant to no longer be part of regular culture; to reject domesticity and society in favor of a life of lonely introspection. What marks chastity—whither all of the virtues—is a paradox whereby they reflect their attendant vices, where they sustain themselves by an obsession on corporality. When St. Cyprian of Carthage reflected in the third century that "Chastity is the dignity of the body," it could have only been uttered by one who had given great thought to that body (and *bodies*), claiming that the virtue is the "ornament of morality, the sacredness of the sexes, the bond of modesty, the source of purity, the peacefulness of home, the crown of concord."

PREVIOUS SPREAD As with all of his fellow members of the Pre-Raphaelite Brotherhood, English painter John Everett Millais was drawn to the aesthetics of an imagined medieval past, as in this 1865 painting of the fifteenth-century French martyr Joan of Arc, held in a private collection. A prodigious military leader, even though an uneducated adolescent girl, Joan is the only saint to actually be executed by the Church itself (albeit at the prompting of the English occupiers). Celebrated for her chastity, Joan was also an androgynous figure, highlighting the potential subversive import of chastity.

OPPOSITE "When Love within her lovely face appears," writes Petrarch, "Now again and among the other ladies, / As much as each is less lovely than she / the more my wish I love within me grows." French painter Alexander Cabanel's nineteenth-century composition *Petrarch's Laura*, original at the Princeton University Art Museum.

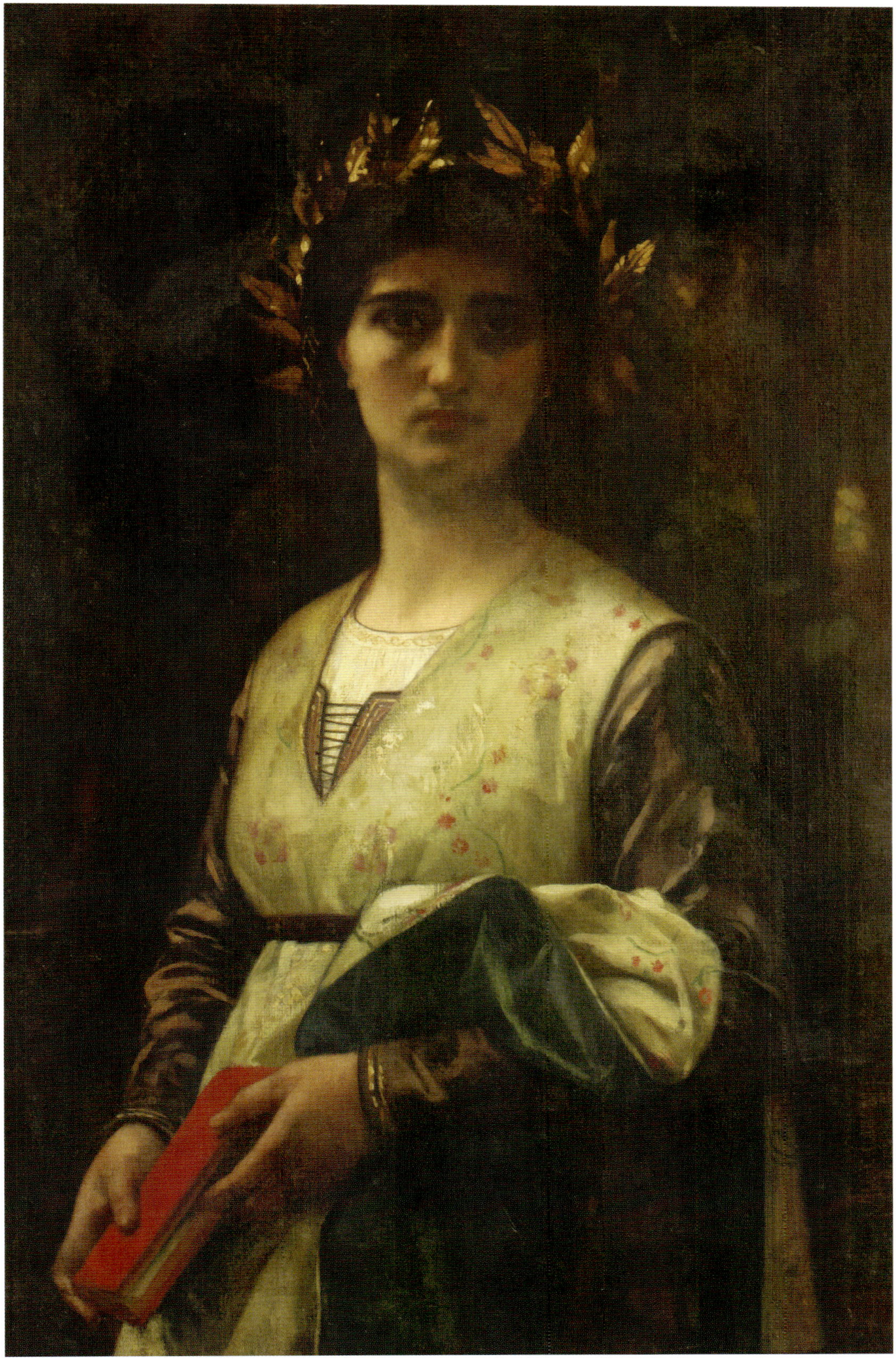

THEORY—AS PURE AS A PEARL

Had Francesco Petrarca ever consummated his passion for his mysterious beloved the French noblewoman Laura de Noves, then perhaps the Renaissance never would have happened. The Tuscan poet Petrarch, subsequently remembered only by his Latin name, first espied Laura underneath the ribbed vault of the Church of St. Claire in Avignon, where the papacy was then in its Babylonian Captivity, on an Easter Sunday in 1327. Laura was modest but striking, slight and beautiful, with curls of blonde down her shoulders like golden rivulets, so that Petrarch, who'd abandoned the priesthood (but affirmed the vow of celibacy), was immediately struck with an intensity of longing for the soon-to-be-engaged woman. As the priest chanted the liturgy of resurrection, Petrarch must have felt a similar rebirth, drawn to this woman at Mass whom he'd never kiss, never caress, never even touch. Despite his own vow of chastity, Petrarch had at least two children with now anonymous women, but Laura was already betrothed to another man, so that this relationship between the poet and the noblewoman which would define courtly love, Western romance, the very idea of secular longing, was consummated only in that long, pregnant stare across a crowded sacristy at Easter Mass, and in 366 immaculate lyrics composed in her honor entitled *Il Canzoniere.* If Petrarch and Laura ever conversed or even met—unknown; how many times he would have seen her—unknown; if Laura de Noves is even the correct identification of the figure of *Il Canzoniere*—is still debated. What is obvious from a reading of those poems is the singular depth of how Petrarch was struck with love, all the more beautiful because it wasn't and couldn't be realized. An idealized, chaste love of the mind, between the father of two children and a woman who delivered eleven. She would be the locus of his desires for the next twenty years, until she perished during the Black Death at the young age of thirty-eight, and even then Petrarch's devotion continued, even as "Life flees and does not stop an hour." Sublimating his love to Laura, Petrarch projected that passion outward into a love of humanity and learning, ironically making the two of them the parents of the Renaissance.

From April 6, 1327, the scholar who had rediscovered the Latin letters of Cicero, the adventurer who had scaled Mont Ventoux, the philosopher who had inaugurated the *humanitas civitas*, would primarily be remembered as Petrarch of Laura, because, as the poet would write, "For your lovely eyes, Lady, bound me." Conveniently her name evoked the laurels which crowned ancient poets (too conveniently to some contemporary critics), and which would sit on Petrarch's brow as he became the first poet laureate of Rome since the distant years of empire. The vast bulk of *Il Canzoniere* was sonnets, that ingenious mechanism for compressing the turns of human emotion in only fourteen lines, which, even if Petrarch strictly hadn't invented it, he did perfect. Pious, Petrarch still wasn't exactly a mystic. Laura in *Il Canzoniere*—*Song Book* in translation—was based on a real woman (despite doubts from some of Petrarch's friends), celebrated not in ecclesiastical Latin but in vulgar Italian. "Whoso list to hunt," writes the English poet Thomas Wyatt in a 1530s version of Petrarch's Sonnet 190, conjuring that field of romantic struggle. Espying a deer—in Petrarch's

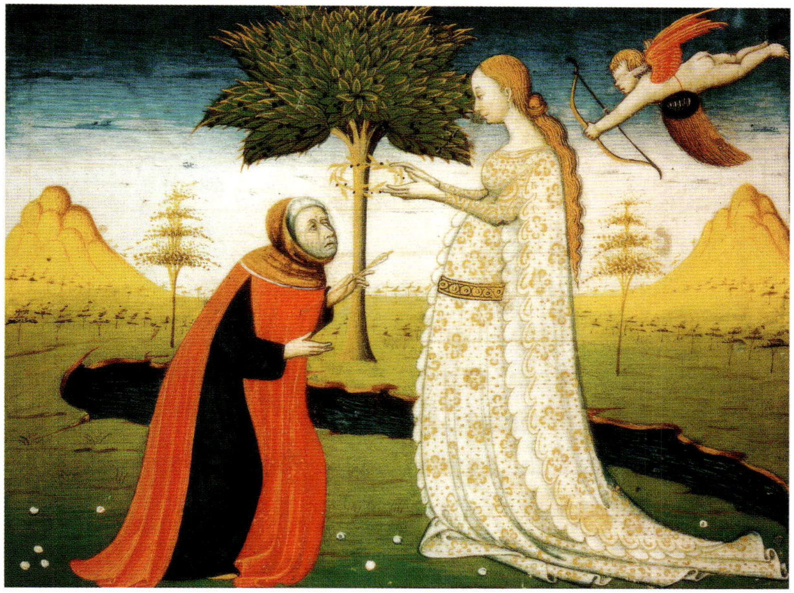

version Laura, in Wyatt's supposedly inspired by Anne Boleyn—and "Who list her hunt, I put him out of doubt, / As well as I may spend his time in vain. / And graven with diamonds in letters plain / There is written, her fair neck round about: / *Noli me tangere*, for Caesar's I am." The Latin—"Touch me not"—uttered in the Gospel of John by Christ to Mary Magdalene after his resurrection, here repurposed as a chaste warning, for this doe is the property of a Caesar, whether Laura's husband or the King of England. If Petrarch was truly the first of the moderns, the first to turn back to the legacy of Greece and Rome, the first to castigate the superstitions of the Middle Ages, the first to elevate poetry—secular poetry—as a vehicle for truth, then it was from the thwarted expectations of his love, the disappointment and heartbreak of unrequited, maybe even unknown, devotion. *Il Canzoniere* collects the first poems written in a modern voice, they heralded a new era of individuality, and more than love poems, they were chastity poems, for as Lord Byron wrote in *Don Juan*, "Think . . . if Laura had been Petrarch's wife, / He would have written sonnets all his life?"

Chastity exists in a reciprocal dialectical tension with lust. The body overfed with ecstasy and the one which is starved of it are equally freakish to the expectations of a society that desires an easily tamable middle path. Both can be extreme, the lech with dozens of paramours and the solitary anchorite and monastic penitent; extreme in that neither comports with what's expected of a domesticated, bourgeois life which countenances sex, just not too much sex. The chaste woman and man, the celibate human, the virgin—all are, in their own way, strangely countercultural, outside of the expectations and norms of regular life. Ironically, they are literally deviants. There is also something obviously erotic in the idealization of chastity; something of the latent, coiled, electric charge about the celibate. Chastity exists as an overlapping but non-reducible category with its related concepts of celibacy and virginity. Technically the first term refers to proper circumscribed sexual conduct, while the second term is

TOP A fourteenth-century Florentine illumirated manuscript showing the divinized Laura crowning Petrarch with the classical laurels of poetic genius.

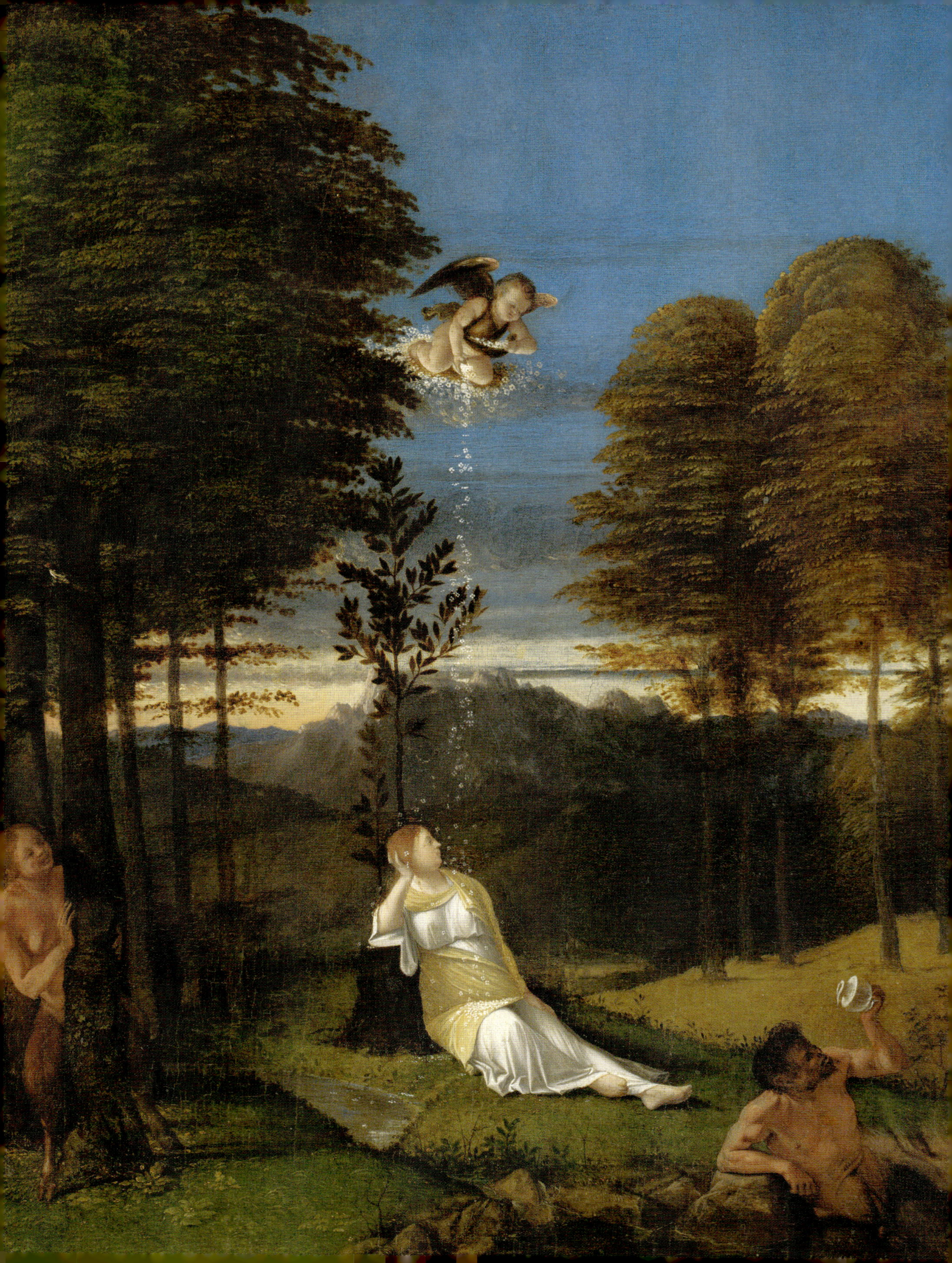

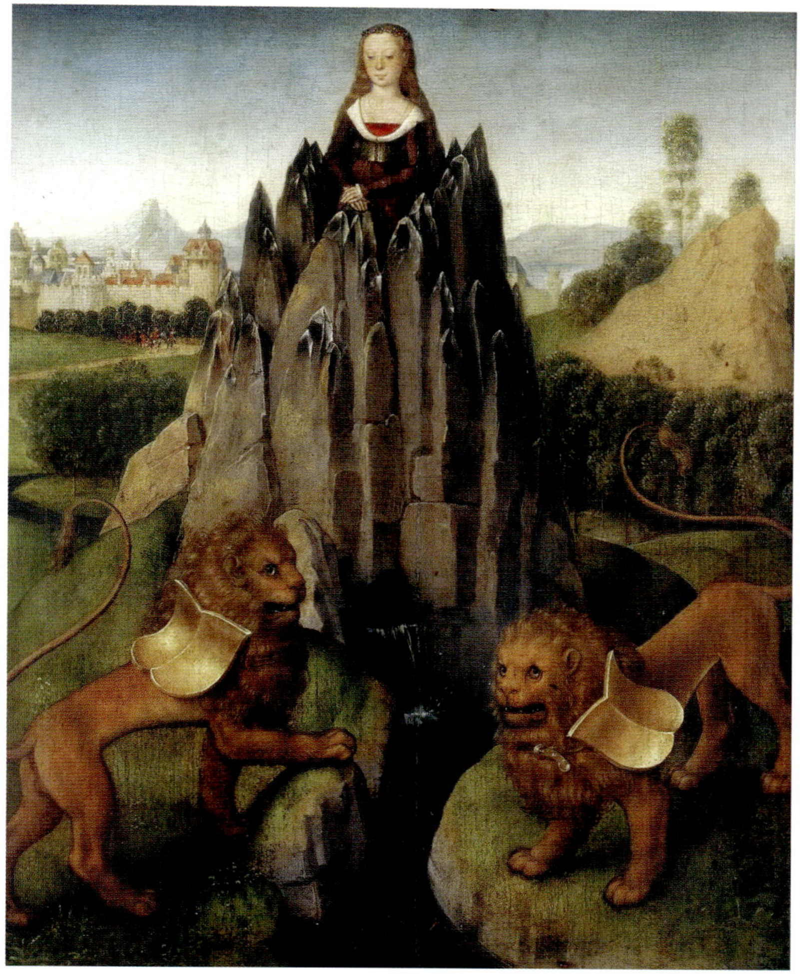

OPPOSITE Italian painter Lorenzo Lotto's *Allegory of Chastity*, painted in 1505 with the original held by the National Gallery of Art in Washington, DC, is another example of the virtue presented as a humble but beautiful woman. Here Chastity is in a sylvan grove where she ignores libidinal satyrs while anointed by a putti flying above.

TOP Flemish painter Hans Memling's enigmatic and arguably ambiguous *Allegory of Chastity*, rendered around 1489 and now held by the Musée Jacquemart-André in Paris, presents two shielded lions guarding the purity of their charge, a beautiful virginal maiden.

the renunciation of all sexual acts, and the final is the person who has never experienced a sexual act. All of these definitions are contingent, arbitrary, relative, and contextual; none are absolutes and all have shades of ambiguity about them, processed through the forge of culture more than that of biology. As a result, in contemporary usages there tends to be a conflation of such things, despite their differences. What all share is a condition of *absence*, of the life devoid of sexuality, whether until virginity is lost or after a vow of celibacy is taken, for those two are the children of chastity. This trinity of sexual abstention resounds through history; as Elizabeth Abbott in *A History of Celibacy* writes, "It was Joan of Arc, Elizabeth I of England, Florence Nightingale. It was Mahatma Gandhi . . . the naked nights he spent with nubile young women, testing his chastity . . . It was Leonardo da Vinci, fearful of a second accusation of sexual impropriety, Sir Isaac Newton mourning his lover's defection, Lewis Carroll looking but not daring to touch." If lust requires an endurance, then chastity is ironically no different.

Celibacy has not always been the standard for clerics, as can be attested to by the sacred prostitutes serving in Sumer's temples dedicated to the fertility goddess Inanna. There are always exceptions to exceptions, since those limber Mesopotamian devotees can be answered by the Vestal Virgins of Rome. Even within Roman Catholicism, there has been woeful inconsistency as regards priestly celibacy, despite current canon law affirming that "Clerics are obliged to observe perfect and perpetual continence for the sake of the kingdom of heaven," arguing that such abstention allows priests to "adhere more easily to Christ with an undivided heart and are able to dedicate themselves more freely to the service of God and humanity." Justifications for the permanent bachelorhood of priests (as well as nuns and monks) range from Christ's suspiciously unmarried status to the argument that if unentangled in domestic affairs, clerics will be better able to shepherd their flock. Regardless, there have always been rather large exceptions to this rule, from those who follow the Byzantine Rite being allowed to marry if it's prior to their ordination, to converted Anglican priests who are already married understandably not having to jettison their wives with divorce papers. Never an issue of dogma in the manner of certain indisputable creedal statements regarding the nature of God, Christ, and the Church, theoretically the papacy could unilaterally reverse priestly celibacy, though this is unlikely to happen for obvious political reasons.

While clerical celibacy has been affirmed in varying ways back to the fourth-century Council of Elvira, it wasn't until 1018 that Pope Benedict VIII formally banned priestly marriage, which was reaffirmed in subsequent synods, most notably the First Lateran Council a hundred and five years later, with the since schismatic Eastern Orthodox Church dissenting in that opinion. Whatever the stated intentions of ecclesiastical authorities, the more pressing issue seems to have been married cardinals, bishops, priests, and so on, willing Church lands to their children, a disagreeable issue of real estate more than sexuality, for the first Pope Peter's status as a husband seems to bother perilously few officials in the Vatican. Protesting clerical celibacy was hardly the only issue that helped to propagate the Reformation—but it certainly was *an issue* which did so. Portly Martin Luther, the former Augustinian monk, in merry matrimony with Katharina von Bora, previously a nun; Father Huldrych Zwingli, who left the Church and brought with him a wife named Anna Reinhart; Archbishop Thomas Cranmer's bride, Margaret, who had to travel in a chest with holes poked in the side as they made their way through the Catholic continent. Then there was the cathedral preacher of Basel with the ridiculous adopted Latinate name of Johannes Oecolampadius, the Catholic humanist transformed into a Calvinist Reformer, taking a wife along the way, to which his former friend Erasmus quipped that he was amazed that the woman in question was actually good-looking.

Chastity's austere son may be celibacy, but virginity is the more popular daughter. Unlike with celibacy, which the majority of people would eschew, all of us are virgins at some point in our lives. While often presented as more of a straightforward condition than either ambiguous chastity or wavering celibacy—*have you ever had sex before?*—virginity is far from the definite state that our culture presents it as. Traditionally interpreted as simply whether an individual has engaged in heterosexual vaginal penetration—a rather anemic definition of the full gauntlet of sexual possibilities—and "virginity" has always been a sociocultural understanding more than a biological fact. "By any material reckoning, virginity does not exist," writes Hanne Blank in *Virgin: The Untouched History*.

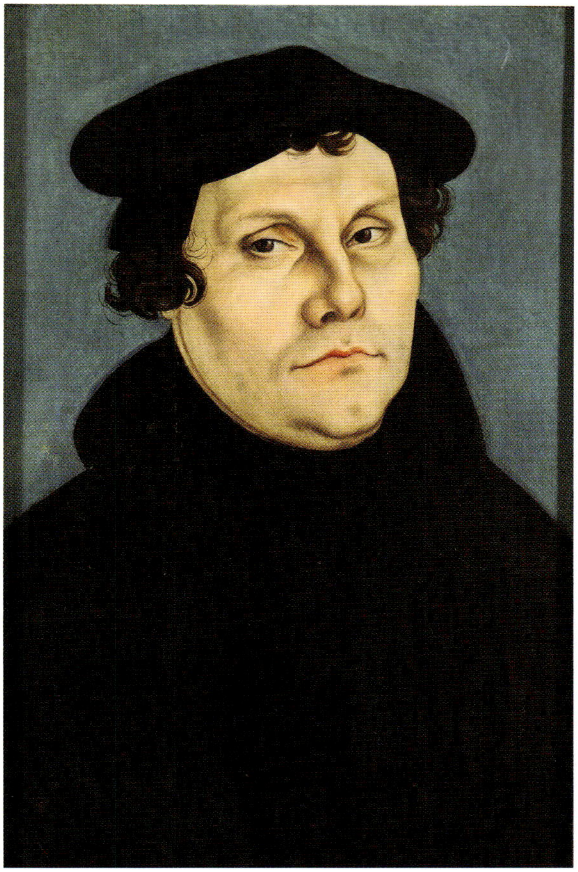

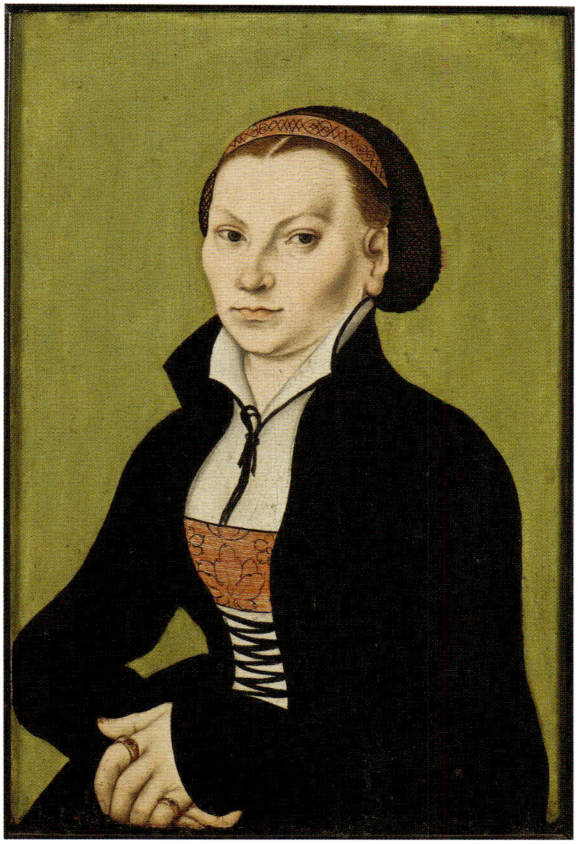

ABOVE German artist Lucas Cranach the Elder, responsible for much of the visual language of the burgeoning Protestant Reformation, paints the former Augustinian monk Martin Luther as a stolid burgher married to the former nun Katharina von Bora, here a respectable wife. Otherworldly mysticism and celibacy would be rejected by Luther and in favor of cozy domesticity, a life both prosaic and comfortable. The painting on the left is from 1525 and held at the Bristol City Museum and Art Gallery, while the one on the right was made a year later and is held in private collection.

"It can't be weighed on a scale, sniffed out like a truffle or a smuggled bundle of cocaine, retrieved from the lost-and-found, or photographed for posterity." So often posited as an objective state that either applies to somebody or doesn't, virginity is rather more complicated. Is a man who has only ever had intercourse with other men a virgin? Is a lesbian? The question itself is bizarre; it reduces the full gauntlet of sexual expressions to the one approved sex act which is potentially procreative, but human eroticism in its full complexity disappears. Concerning virginity, Blank writes that we have "fixed it as an integral part of the experience of our own bodies and selves. And we have done all this without actually being able to define it consistently, identify it accurately, or explain how or why it works." As an example, consider the anatomical indeterminacy of the hymen, used throughout the centuries as predictive of whether a woman was a virgin, a test which ignores individual bodily and biographical variation. As concerns virginity, the hymen has always been a vestige of myth more than reality. The importance of something like the hymen is because virginity itself—however it's ultimately defined—has been understood as *valuable.* More than the particulars of who is or isn't a virgin are the multitude of connotations which the word implies—innocent, pure, untouched, pristine. There are variations to these associations, obviously. Most patriarchal cultures have cared little for masculine virginity, which is why sexual prowess is celebrated in a young man. Those same

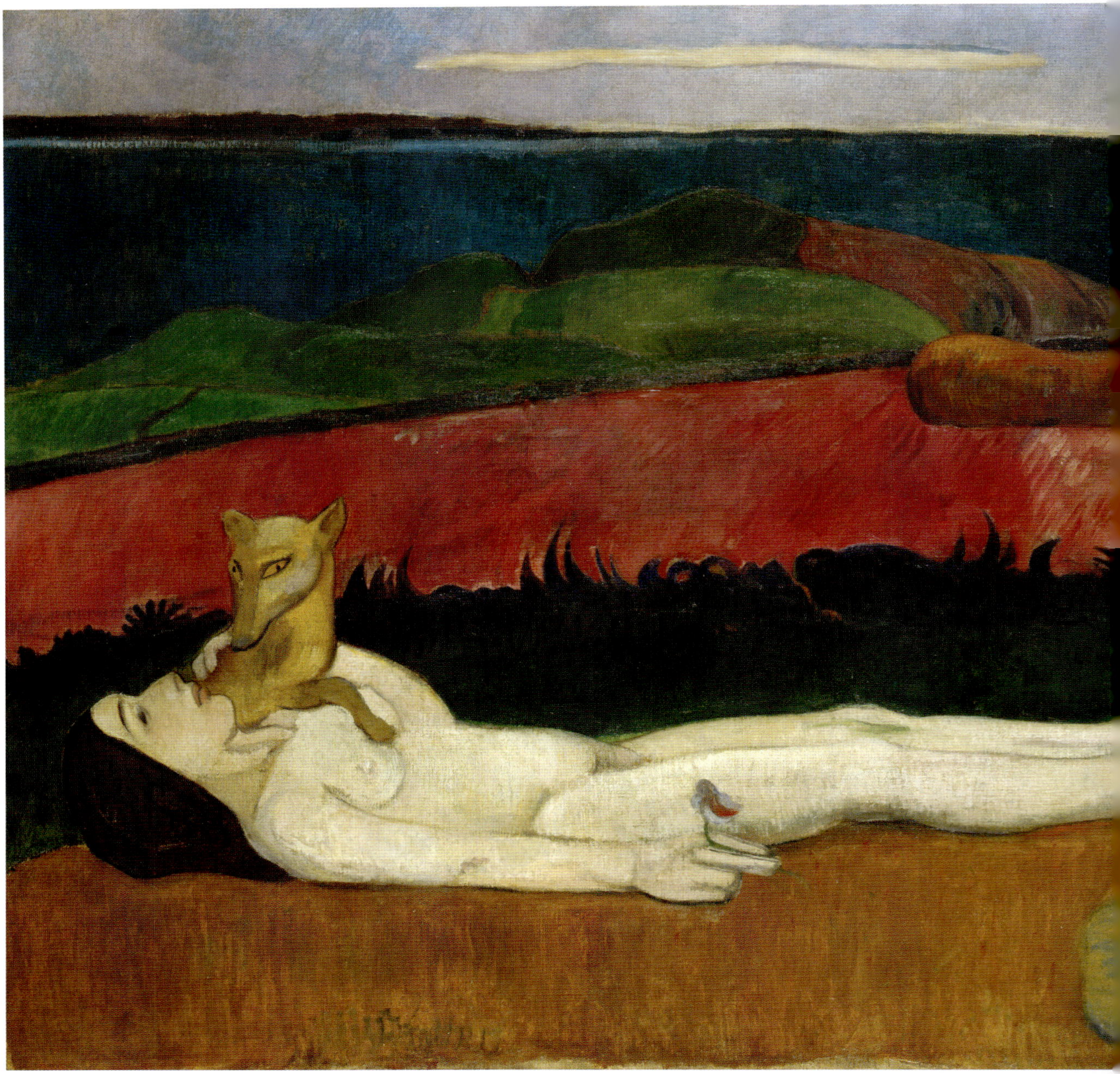

ABOVE French Postimpressionist Paul Gauguin, a man known to have his own complicated relationship to myths of purity and innocence, allegorically depicts the dangers implicit in the moment of sexual consummation in his 1890 work *The Loss of Virginity*, original held by the Chrysler Museum of Art in Norfolk, Virginia.

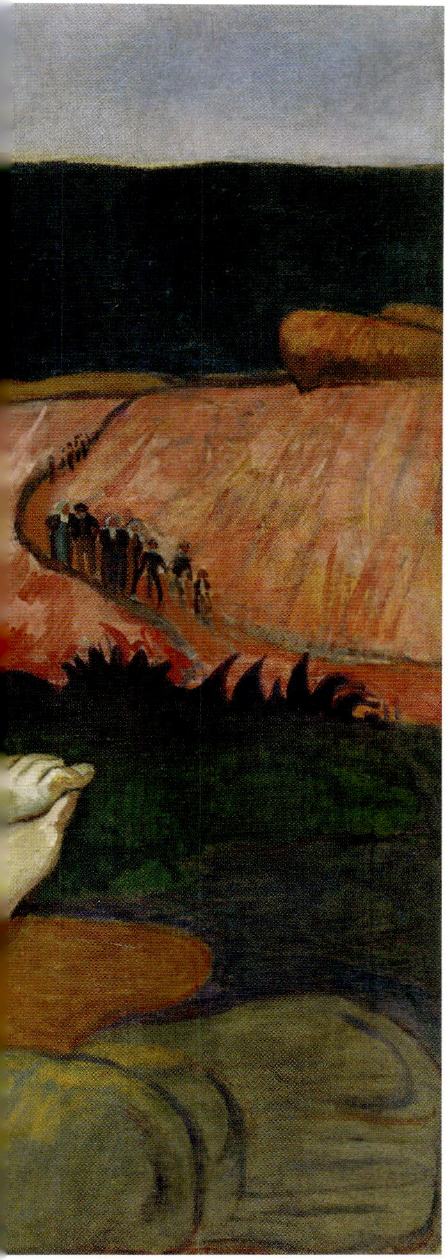

patriarchal cultures categorize women who've reached a certain age (historically thirty) without sexual consummation as spinsters, so that the desirability of virginity at that point disappears. But young female virgins are historically prized, human beings reduced to commodities, discussed in the barbaric rhetoric of being "deflowered."

Virginity, and its preservation unto death, has often been the crux of many hagiographies, women saints valued for their chastity over their own lives. These are complicated stories, often tales of female resistance against rape and sexual trauma, but as is the nature of complicated stories they also tell us something about dominant religious culture values, especially during the Middle Ages, in which celibacy became a devotional ideal. St. Cecelia, a wealthy Roman noblewoman of the third century who had converted to Christianity, was betrothed by her parents to a pagan soldier. While awaiting him on their wedding night, she sang psalms to calm her terrified mind, for which she has been remembered as the patron saint of music. When Cecelia's new husband arrived, she refused his sexual overtures, and told him that if he attempted to rape her, she would be defended by an invisible angel. Upon his demands to see this heavenly creature, Cecelia replied that the angel would only be revealed upon her husband's conversion. He converted, he saw. Ultimately, both newly Christian and chaste wife and husband would be martyred. Agatha of Sicily, executed only a few decades after Cecelia, was but another virgin martyr who died for faith and chastity, refusing the advances of the prefect Quantianus, who among other indignities had her imprisoned in a brothel, with her execution involving hot iron tongs being used to mutilate her breasts. Writing in his thirteenth-century hagiographical compendium *The Golden Legend*, Jacobus de Voragne notes that despite Agatha's horrific death, the saint always "gave honor to God with a free will in all her works, and purchased by her prayers and deliverance to all the country."

At the turn of that same century, another beautiful, young, and virginal Christian noblewoman named Agnes would reject all of the paramours who propositioned her, and as eventual punishment she was stripped naked and dragged through the streets of the Eternal City toward a brothel where she would be forced into sexual slavery. Yet as this grotesque train made its way through Rome, Agnes's hair would grow to cover her nudity; as assorted men attempted to assault or rape her, God would strike them blind. When eventually she was brought to green kindling to be burnt to death, the flames refused to immolate her, so that Agnes was only killed when her head was struck from her shoulders. As reward for her tribulations, she has been canonized as the patron saint of chastity, venerated by the Roman Catholic Church, the Eastern Orthodox Church, and the Anglican Church. Then there is Lucy, a third-century convert of Syracuse who had consecrated her virginity unto the Lord, who was sentenced for her faith to being gang raped in a brothel, but with God striking all of the assailants lame. A popular trope in her martyrology is of Lucy responding to a suitor who complimented the beauty of her eyes by gouging them out and presenting them on a platter, the orbs later miraculously restored. An unnerving aspect of Lucy's iconography are the images of the pretty young girl with otherworldly pupils, holding toward the viewer a plate with another pair of her eyes. All of these women—and other virgin martyrs—are honored in

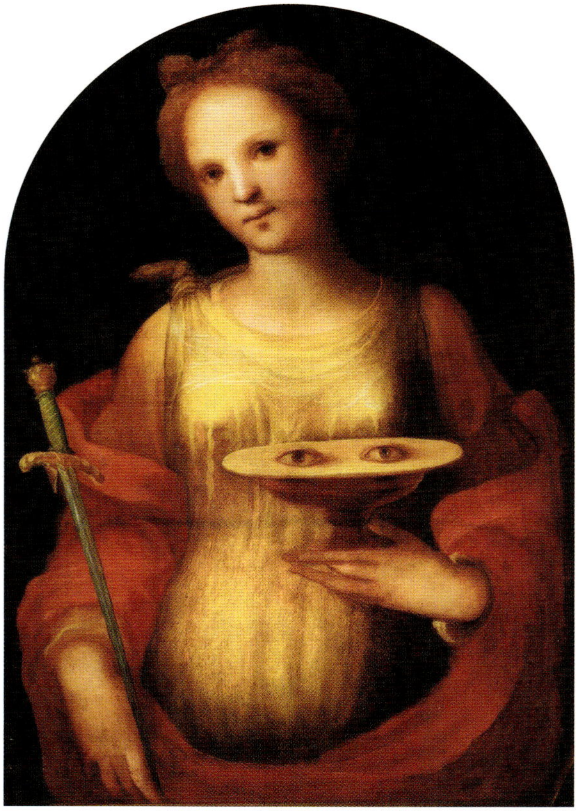

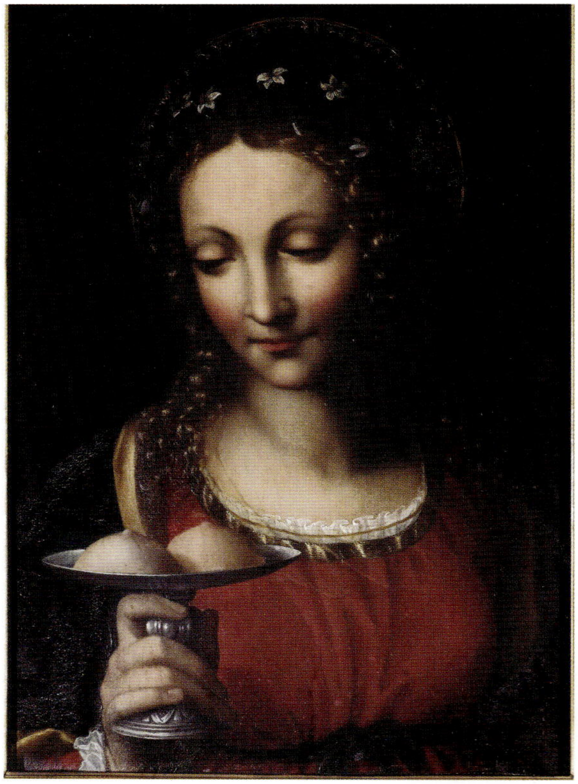

the Roman Rite's Canon of the Mass, their status as being untouched elevating them to godliness.

Secular culture took its cues from Christianity, at least in the West. If chastity was valued by the Church, it's been no less enshrined in other spheres, although the examples can sometimes be less extreme. Well into the Middle Ages, when the faithful read accounts of martyrs in works such as *The Golden Legend*, an equivalent secular cult of chastity simultaneously grew in the form of courtly love. Implicit in the notion of courtly love, this unconsummated, unphysical, unerotic form of supposedly pure romance, is that the sex act itself somehow cheapens affection, even within the marriage bed. Celebrated in the ballads and epics of troubadours from Provence to Aquitaine, Burgundy to Sicily, courtly love was a literary conceit which imagined a knight errant fulfilling duties for a woman whom he couldn't possess, a type of innocent romance beyond the messy particulars of sexuality. Because poems and songs written on the topic of courtly love acknowledge beauty, and thus desirability, the genre is not without the frisson of sexuality; but that such love should always be unconsummated is what made it idealized and thus perfect. The twelfth-century tract *The Skill of Loving Virtuously*, attributed to a Frenchman known only as Andreas Capellanus, enthuses about the "pure love which binds together the hearts of two lovers with every feeling of delight. This kind consists in the contemplation of the mind and the affection of the heart." Still, the treatise maintains that such romance is marked by "omitting the final solace, for that it not permitted for those who wish to love purely."

TOP LEFT Italian mannerist painter Domenico Beccafumi depicts an eerie and disturbing St. Lucy holding her eyes upon a golden platter in this 1521 composition held by the Pinacoteca Nazionale in Sienna. As if offered to the viewer, Beccafumi's painting puts her audience into the uncomfortable position of rapacious suitors. It evokes the legend about the virginal pagan philosopher Hypatia, who brandished a menstrual pad to a potential paramour, chastising him for his love of the debased physical (albeit Lucy's story is both more violent and miraculous).

TOP RIGHT St. Agatha holds her breasts, appearing almost as if desserts rather than body parts, on a silver chalice in this 1693 painting of the Lombard School, after an original by Bernardino Luini, held by the Galleria Borghese in Rome. Such stories about chaste saints removing their body parts have the effect of reducing those same women to those same body parts, an example of the misogynistic dialectic often at the heart of chastity, where risks of sexual violence are the responsibility of women rather than the offending men.

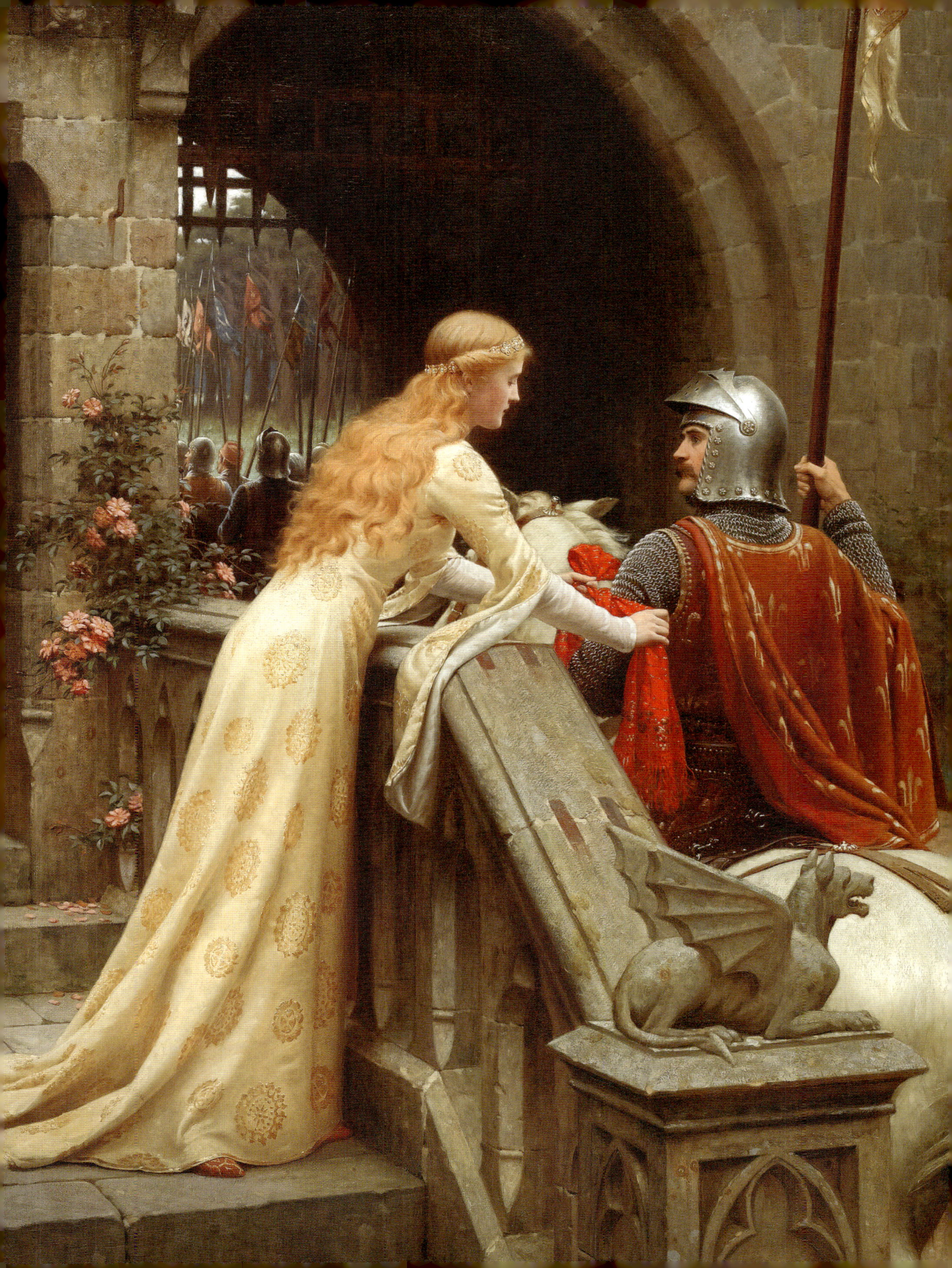

As a standard, the exemplary medieval expression of courtly love was Dante's *The Divine Comedy*, wherein Beatrice Portinari, whom the poet had long loved from afar, even after he married another woman who carried his children, became the conduit for holy, sacred, and transcendent feeling, an intercessory being with God. Having only seen Beatrice twice during the course of his life, Dante nevertheless made her his guide to heaven in "Paradiso," she represented as a luminescent being more angel than saint. Recounting a dream about her in his earlier work *La Vita Nuova*, Dante describes how in "his arms, my lady lay asleep, wrapped in a veil. / He woke her then and trembling and obedient / She ate that burning heart out of his hand." An unconsummated love, yet still a consuming love. Beatrice is more muse than woman; in that regard, she clearly prefigures Petrarch's Laura. So obvious is the similarity that an anxious Petrarch denied having ever even read Dante, the better to dissuade the influence. Whatever the connection, both Beatrice and Laura are more symbol than person, more cipher than woman. They exist to inspire poetry, or to spiritually elevate, but they do not wake and sleep, work and eat, love and sleep with their husbands. They do not experience the pain of childbirth or the joys of motherhood, the affection and frustration of marriage or the limitations of society. They are not people, only objects. Elevated objects, yes, but ultimately tools by which the male protagonist defines himself. Such was the lot of Laura de Noves whom Petrarch made famous, for from the long lineage of her womb would come a rather notorious descendant, her husband Count Hugues de Sade being the direct ancestor of the diabolical Marquis de Sade, a man who knew something about treating women as objects.

INTERLUDE— OUR LADY OF WALSHINGHAM

For five centuries, pilgrims wound their way down the stony paths to the small hamlet of Walshingham upon the southeastern rump of England, drawn to this place where an Anglo-Saxon noblewoman named Lady Richeldis de Faverches was first graced in 1061 with vision of that immaculate Mother, that Queen of Heaven, the incandescent Virgin Mary resplendent in her blue robes. Richeldis, an estimable paragon of devotion, had her soul transported by Mary to Nazareth during the first visitation, where the noblewoman was able to view the holy stable wherein Christ's Nativity occurred. Dedicated in her faith, Richeldis commissioned the building of an exact replica of those modest stables in Walshingham, only to discover that a perfect and beautiful version would be delivered by angels in the middle of the night, this the second of her three visions of Mary. Following the last apparition of the Virgin, Lady Richeldis would pledge to make this English town a site for not just honoring the Mother of God, but also her appearance in this modest village,

PREVIOUS SPREAD Pre-Raphaelite English painter Edmund Leighton gives a particularly idealized view of courtly love and chivalry in his faux-medieval fantasy *God Speed* from 1900, original held in private collection. "Lady of the Mere," imagined William Wordsworth almost a century earlier, "Sole-sitting by the shores of old romance."

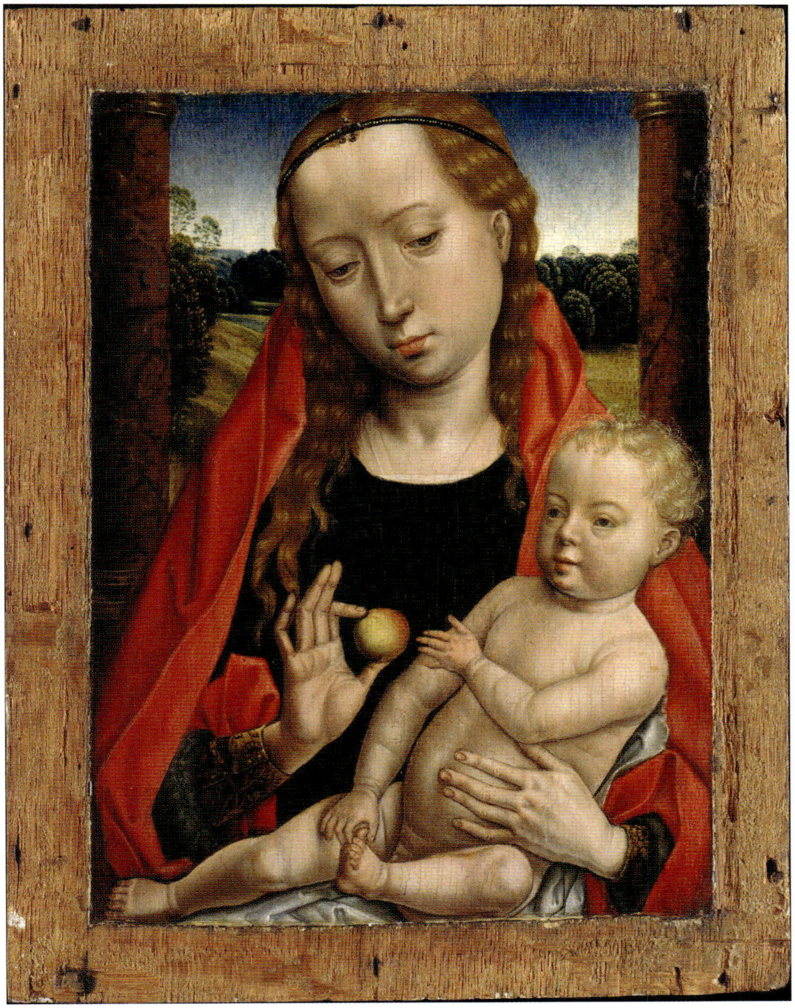

TOP 1490 *Virgin and Child* by the Netherlandish painter Hans Memling, original held by the Metropolitan Museum of Art. As the Middle Ages transitioned into the Renaissance, a more humanistic and naturalistic approach towards representing divinity concurrently developed. Here, a tired Mary distracts the infant Jesus with an apple, which also happens to be a symbol of man's fallen nature. Still, conventions of Medieval art endured, such as depicting the baby Jesus's face as if he were far older, a way of prefiguring the adult Christ, whose sacrifice would redeem the world.

wherefrom henceforth the faithful would commit themselves to the charity and chastity which she embodied, the womb which once contained the entire cosmos. "O gracious lady glory of Jerusalem," reads an account of the apparition printed centuries later in 1485 by the publisher Richard Pynson, "Cypress of Zion and joy of Israel / Rose of Jericho and star of Bethlehem / O glorious lady our asking not repel / In mercy all women ever do you excel." A relic would be kept at the priory which held the shrine to Our Lady of Walshingham, a vial with a few precious drips of breast milk, the pure and chaste physical evidence of a mother's love for her child, yet for the pious Catholics who prayed in this place it was also a miraculous trace of that innocent conception, of that divine birth accomplished without conjugal union. The sacred in the profane, the holy in the quotidian; for the thousands of supplicants who made their way to Walshingham over the centuries, it was the simplicity that was beautiful. "Our Lady stands in the dark at the right side of the altar," wrote the great Dutch humanist Desiderius Erasmus upon visiting in 1513, "a little image, remarkable neither for its size, material or workmanship."

Modesty was no impediment to the miraculous; arguably it was the very point. In his fifteenth-century poem "The Foundation of the Chapel of Walshingham," Pynson enumerates the many healings associated with the Lady, the curative effects of the lame made whole, the blind made sighted, lepers made complete and lunatics made sane, of mariners protected on their voyages. By supposedly delivering Christ in a state of physical and spiritual purity, the Messiah was unimplicated in the original sin that marks the rest of humanity. A being both wholly God and wholly human, but unlike the latter totally extricated from the sullen and debased interconnected affairs to which the rest of us are condemned. Chastity is the Virgin Mary's great miracle, a fact both liberatory and reactionary. As depicted at Walshingham, near as can be reconstituted, the wooden carving of Mary presents her upon a modest throne, draped in robes and a veil, becrowned and hallowed, brandishing a long lily frond while holding the infant Christ, who is clutching a Bible as if a toy. Mary's crown is regal gold, her robes are celestial blue, the globe she sits upon is green. To be sure, there is an ascetic neuroticism to the perseveration on Mary's virginity (Catholics maintain that she was a lifelong celibate, many Protestants only before the birth of Christ), though perhaps it's best to interpret that quality as less austere than simply otherworldly. The idea of a virgin birth—by no means exclusive to Christianity in the ancient world—bestows the numinous into the humdrum. That Christ himself is worshiped not just as a god but *the God* makes the Nativity cosmic. More remarkable in the gospel narratives is that upon learning of the conception from the Archangel Gabriel, Mary consents to the pregnancy, the world's redemption freely chosen by this adolescent girl. There were many visions of Mary over the centuries, many shrines dedicated to her, but in England, Walshingham would count with Canterbury and Ipswich as a place of pilgrimage. "Therefore blessed lady grant thou thy great grace / To all that the devoutly visit in this place," intoned Pynson.

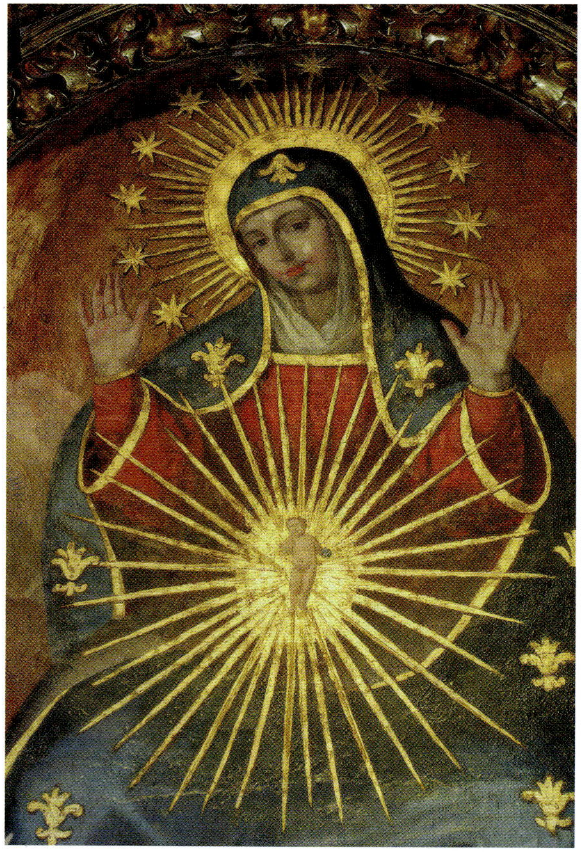

At least until 1538. That was in the midst of King Henry VIII's radical policy of dissolving the monasteries, when the treasures of the Catholic Church were confiscated by the state and redistributed as patronage into the royal coffers and among the monarch's supporters. Statues were pummeled, stained-glass windows were smashed, rood screens were turned over, altars were defiled, manuscripts were burnt. Carried out as part of the Reformation policies of Henry's radical Protestant Chief Minister Thomas Cromwell, the period from 1536 until 1541 saw an unparalleled destruction of England's medieval patrimony, an era of burnt abbeys and demolished cathedrals, of abandoned basilicas and bare ruined choirs. Dismissing much of the cult of saints, relics, and miracles as mere superstitious dross, Cromwell aggressively went about dismantling the Catholic culture of England, much to the resistance of the common folk. The "Black Madonna" of Willesden would be immolated in Chelsea,

TOP Sixteenth-century mural of the Annunciation from the Cathedral of Cordoba in southern Spain, a former mosque. Mary is depicted as an awesome and alien being, a human nonetheless who for nine months carried the creator of the universe within her womb.

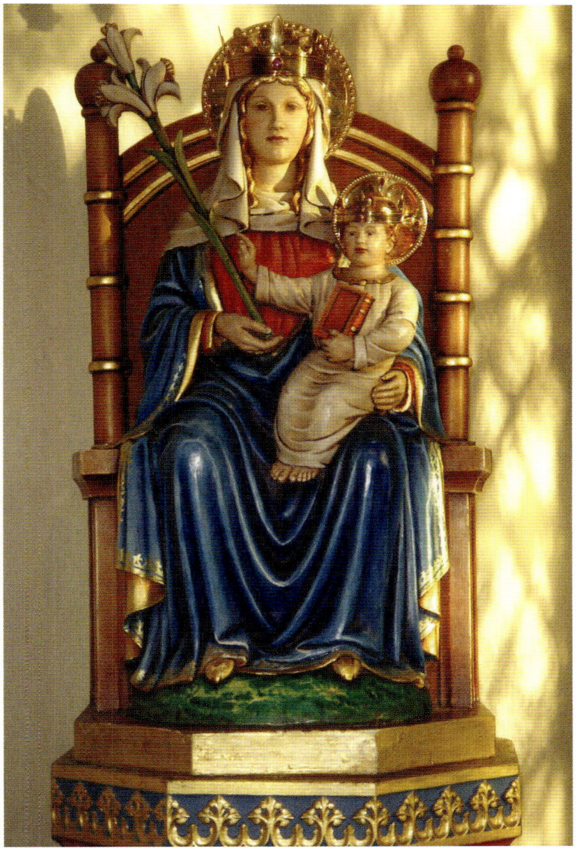

the same location where Our Lady of Doncaster was burnt, as well as Our Lady of Cardigan, all in 1538. Supposedly the same site where Our Lady of Ipswich was destroyed, which Cromwell would write was so thoroughly burnt that there was "nothing about her but two half shoes of silver." It was long believed that the Ipswich statue was cremated alongside Our Lady of Walshingham—despite Henry's once having been a patron of the shrine—the fiery demise of the most popular of Marian devotional objects in England happening only two years before an out-of-favor Cromwell would find his own head on the executioner's block. Not many would mourn for Cromwell, but the populace did for the Virgin Mary, a contemporary ballad lamenting that "Bitter, bitter, O to behold / The grass to grow / Where the walls of Walshingham / So statedly did show."

Something odd would come to replace the Marian symbols throughout the country's churches in the coming generation; rather than the transcendent Lady of Heaven, now the buildings would be decorated with an intricate bit of heraldry, an English lion and a Welsh dragon framing the shield of a new Virgin Queen. Just as the lowly can be made high and the impoverished rich, so there is a paradoxical seduction in chastity, for as the polemicist John Foxe would write about Queen Elizabeth I in *Acts and Monuments*, she was "so good, goodly, and virtuous . . . a chosen instrument of His clemency, so virtuously natured, so godly disposed, so merciful with marring, so humble without pride, so moderate without prodigality, so maidenly without pomp." The English loved Elizabeth because she said that she loved them, as Henry's daughter would go to unseat the Virgin Mary as a kind of cosmic queen, her portrait replacing that of the Mother of God, paintings now depicting her bestriding the world. Not a cult of the Virgin, but a cult of a virgin. This was Gloriana, Elizabeth as a surrogate for the missing Mary, a sublimation of that yearning for the celestial Mother figure once provided by medieval Catholicism now cannily channeled into the ambitions and statecraft of a brilliant monarch, this woman veritably worshiped as one who did "all for love, and nothing for reward," as phrased in Edmund Spenser's epic *The Faerie Queene*. Whether or not Elizabeth was a lifelong celibate, or perhaps if she was infertile (historians disagree on this), there was a profound power of connotation in her advertised chastity, the imputation not just of innocence and purity, but of something vaguely alien and other as well.

In the so-called Ditchley Portrait of the queen painted in 1592 by Marcus Gheeraerts the Younger, Elizabeth isn't in celestial blue but rather an ornate bejeweled pure white dress, her red hair decorated with a pearled tiara. Over her respective shoulders, as if a god mediating between good and evil, are a violent storm on the left and a peaceful day over her right. Elizabeth's slippered feet, as if the Virgin Mary stands athwart the globe, loom over a map of her kingdom itself, the queen configured as the very creator of Britannia. For forty-five years, Elizabeth reigned as if she was the creator of that realm, but being only a human,

TOP An 1897 restoration of Our Lady of Walshingham as crafted by German carpenters at Oberammergau and gifted to the Slipper Chapel in Houghton St. Giles by Pope Leo XIII, who reestablished its significance as a shrine.

she would die in 1603. Centuries later, at the Victoria & Albert Museum (named for descendants of Elizabeth), on a Cromwell Road designated after a cousin of the man who dissolved the monasteries, archivists made a startling discovery. The paint was gone, a hand and the head of the infant Christ were missing, but a careful accounting of description and archival records substantiated that a statue of the Virgin Mary long displayed in the galleries was actually Our Lady of Walshingham, somehow miraculously preserved from the flames, hidden for generations, and resurrected in this museum, long after Elizabeth had perished.

PRAXIS—GET THEE TO A NUNNERY

Barely a few moments on screen—hardly gratuitous, at least by contemporary standards. Cedric Gibbons's 1934 *Tarzan and His Mate*, one of seemingly endless adaptations of the Edgar Rice Burroughs stories about the king of the jungle, implies that his proper English partner Jane sleeps with him in the nude. At one point, the Irish actress Maureen O'Sullivan, who played Jane, is shown naked in obscure silhouette. Most objectionable, however, was a scene in which O'Sullivan's body double, former Olympic swimmer Joseph McKim, performs in a totally nude underwater ballet sequence. When the character of Jane emerges from the water, as once again played by O'Sullivan, there is a brief flash of her bare breast. "The best weapon a woman has is a man's imagination," says Jane in the film, though *Tarzan and His Mate* with O'Sullivan in a halter top and loincloth advocates for sometimes helping the imagination, at least a little bit. Only two years before, Metro-Goldwyn Mayer had released director Jack Conway's *Red-Headed Woman*, starring Jean Harlow in a screenplay by F. Scott Fitzgerald, in which the central character sleeps her way to the top. The film not only features nudity but ends in a violent murder. Barbara Stanwyck starred in the 1933 Alfred E. Green flick *Baby Face*, playing a dissolute burlesque performer who lives by the maxim that "you must use men, not let them use you. You must be a master, not a slave . . . Exploit yourself." Meanwhile, Cecil B. DeMille—as square a director as to ever emerge from Hollywood—filmed the 1930 movie *Madam Satan*, starring Kay Johnson, which included a sex party where characters wore bondage masks and fishnet stockings.

Hollywood had produced hundreds of movies, some of which included premarital sex, homosexuality, prostitution, abortion, infidelity, and drug abuse, yet by the time that *Tarzan and His Mate* was released, a censor would be at the ready to report that "a critical examination of the shot indicated that the woman was stark naked. There were four or five shots of the woman . . . which showed the front of the woman's body." Those scenes would need to

BOTTOM Saucy still from Cedric Gibbon's 1934 film *Tarzan and His Mate*.

OPPOSITE Netherlandish painter Marcus Gheeraerts the Younger's 1592 "Ditchley Portrait" of Queen Elizabeth, named for the nobleman who commissioned it, with the original held at the National Portrait Gallery in London. Gheeraerts's work is a consummate example of the Cult of Elizabeth as it was encouraged during the sixteenth century.

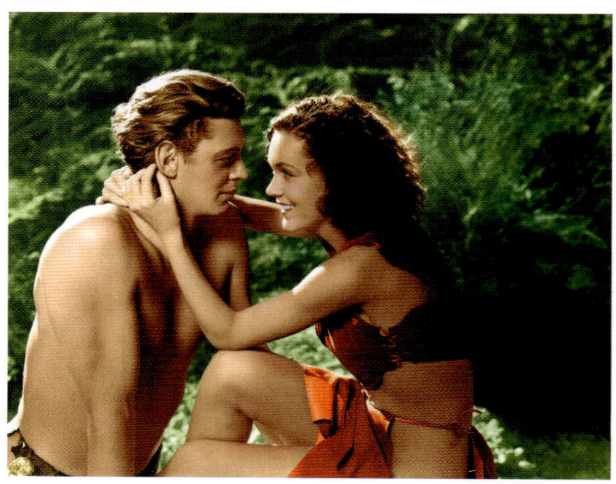

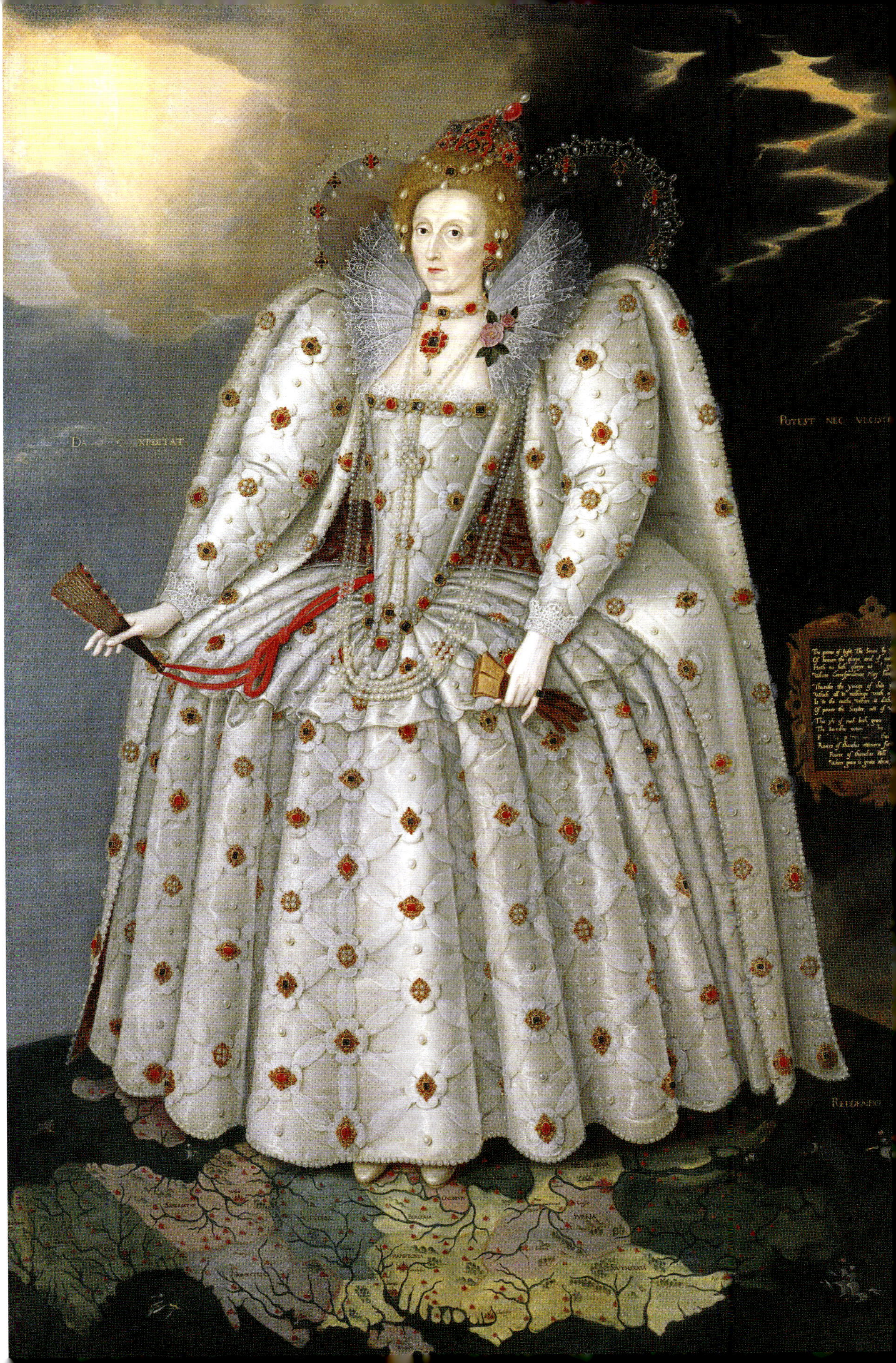
REDDENDO

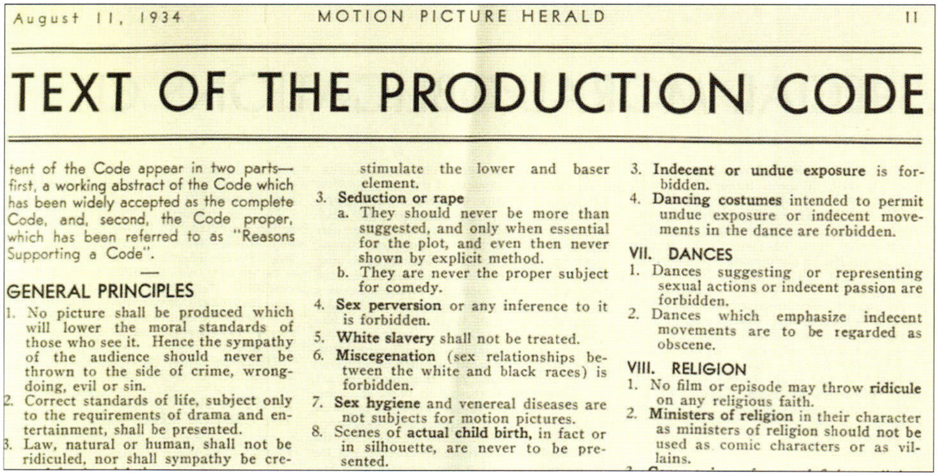

August 11, 1934 MOTION PICTURE HERALD 11

TEXT OF THE PRODUCTION CODE

tent of the Code appear in two parts—first, a working abstract of the Code which has been widely accepted as the complete Code, and, second, the Code proper, which has been referred to as "Reasons Supporting a Code".

—

GENERAL PRINCIPLES

1. No picture shall be produced which will lower the moral standards of those who see it. Hence the sympathy of the audience should never be thrown to the side of crime, wrongdoing, evil or sin.
2. Correct standards of life, subject only to the requirements of drama and entertainment, shall be presented.
3. Law, natural or human, shall not be ridiculed, nor shall sympathy be cre-

stimulate the lower and baser element.

3. **Seduction or rape**
   a. They should never be more than suggested, and only when essential for the plot, and even then never shown by explicit method.
   b. They are never the proper subject for comedy.
4. **Sex perversion** or any inference to it is forbidden.
5. **White slavery** shall not be treated.
6. **Miscegenation** (sex relationships between the white and black races) is forbidden.
7. **Sex hygiene** and venereal diseases are not subjects for motion pictures.
8. Scenes of **actual child birth**, in fact or in silhouette, are never to be presented.

3. **Indecent or undue exposure** is forbidden.
4. **Dancing costumes** intended to permit undue exposure or indecent movements in the dance are forbidden.

VII. DANCES

1. Dances suggesting or representing sexual actions or indecent passion are forbidden.
2. Dances which emphasize indecent movements are to be regarded as obscene.

VIII. RELIGION

1. No film or episode may throw **ridicule** on any religious faith.
2. **Ministers of religion** in their character as ministers of religion should not be used as comic characters or as villains.

be reshot. The difference was the establishment of the Motion Picture Producers and Distributors of America, created by the moguls who ran MGM and Warner Brothers, Paramount and Universal, in an effort at self-policing to prevent government intervention in the film industry. The MPPDA's bible was something called the Motion Picture Production Code, regulating the politics of movies, the violence of movies, and most of all the sexuality in movies. Enforced by William Hays, former Post-Master General, head of the Republican National Convention, Presbyterian elder, and now president of the MPPDA, this rule-book banned "Any licentious or suggestive nudity—in fact or in silhouette; and in any lecherous or licentious notice thereof by other characters in the picture." The Hays Code could be draconian, stipulating that men and women couldn't be seen in bed together and forbidding directorial choices that could leave an opening for "any inference of sex perversion," among other rules. For the equivalent of a little under two million dollars a year, as adjusted for inflation, Hays was the veritable Stationer Register of Hollywood, constraining the antinomian energies of pre-Code film in the bondage of chastity. There is a marked before and after in American movies following the introduction of the Hays Code, a chilling that in some ways wouldn't thaw until the collapse of the infamous studio system of production some three decades later. The purpose of the MPPDA was estimably moral, in part driven by the advocacy of bishops of the Roman Catholic Church who were scandalized by the wanton sexuality in Hollywood films. As Francis Couvares would quip in a 1992 issue of the *American Quarterly* journal, the Hays Code marked Hollywood as an "industry largely financed by Protestant bankers, operated by Jewish studio executives, and policed by Catholic bureaucrats."

Sexuality is marked by rules. Who you're allowed to have sex with, how you're allowed to have sex, in what circumstances you can have sex, and for what purpose you're having sex. Chastity then is a moving target, always defined in relation to whatever the particular set of culturally contingent rules under consideration happen to be. The Hays Code was just one set of those rules; there are certainly different sets. At Mount Kemekus in Java, during the Pon Festival, pilgrims within the indigenous folk religion are encouraged to engage strangers in sex, despite the protestations of the conservative Muslim majority of Indonesia. Among some Shia Muslims, there is a legal union known as *nikah mut-ah*, or

TOP A listing of some of the strict parameters of the recently enacted Hays Code from a 1934 issue of the industry newspaper the *Motion Picture Herald*.

OPPOSITE Detail of a sixteenth-century British embroidery with image of Christ in the Garden of Eden, original held by the Metropolitan Museum of Art. Surrounded by fecundity, the Son of God is nonetheless in a place both prior to and beyond sexual intercourse, where all conception is seemingly virginal.

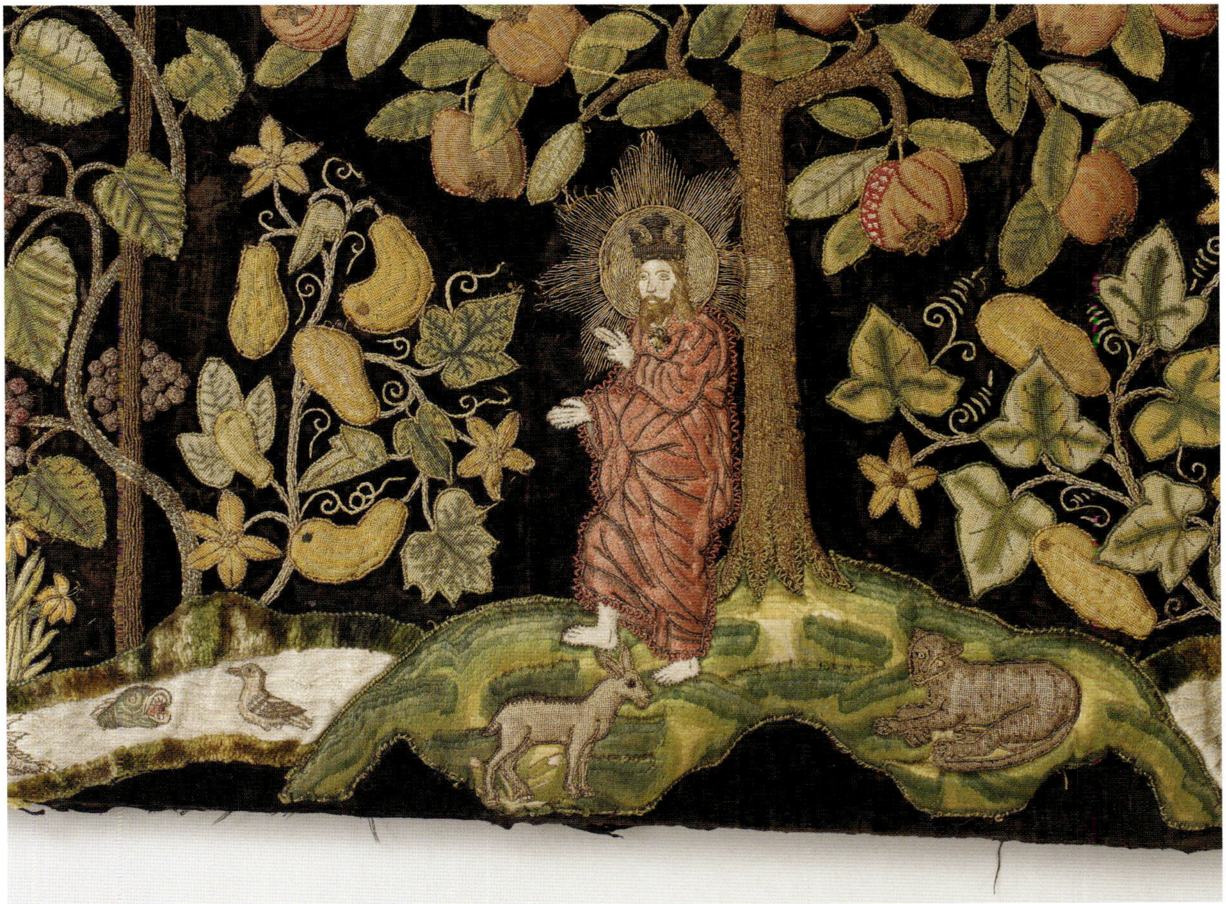

"temporary marriage," a loophole which effectively allows for sanctioned, legal, and therefore supposedly moral prostitution. Among the Mosuo ethnic minority of the Chinese provinces of Sichuan and Yunnan, a strictly matrilinear and matriarchal culture, women practice a form of plural marriage in which they can take multiple husbands, and in which the presence of multiple sex partners is in no way viewed as aberrant or immoral. What is considered chaste or not, licentious or reserved, is a relative issue, ever shifting and mercurial across centuries and cultures. But that there are rules—whatever they may be—which circumscribe sexual activity, well, that's a given. "There is no escaping from power," or codes, or rules, or laws, writes Michel Foucault in his *History of Sexuality*; "it is always already present constituting that very thing which one attempts to counter it with." Chastity and lust are inextricably bound, like two lovers tussling; there is no complete rejection of all rules, for that would describe a nonsensical reality; there is only the replacement of one set with another. "What sustains our eagerness to speak of sex in terms of repression is doubtless this opportunity to speak out against the powers that be," writes Foucault—that fantasy which sustains our "longing for the garden of earthly delights." Eden is a fiction, though. There is no return to any garden of earthly delights, for such a place never existed to begin with, this status just as illusory as virginity.

Because of the reciprocal interdependence of lust and chastity, experience and virginity, there is a strange way in which constraint can be liberating, to which director Michael Curtiz, whose 1942 classic *Casablanca* was produced just a decade after the Hays Code, can attest. The only reason Rick renounces his love for Ilsa is that its consummation would have been considered immoral by the dictates of the MPPDA. This is not to defend the Hays Code, far from it, but it's to note that while censorship is authoritarian, constraint can be liberating. Petrarch's sonnet might be tied up in only fourteen lines, but it's that precise limitation which gives the form such power. In a society which paradoxically both celebrates and condemns sexuality, which is hypocritically titillated by the repressed—and in a far more basic reality where reproduction is the currency of evolution—there is something radical, even subversive, about the personal rejection of sexuality. Whether born from religious commitments or not—and most people who are asexual don't necessarily tie their own orientation to any theological perspective—the individual eschewal of sexuality can be considered a strangely radical act. Amanda Crockett, writing in the journal *New Views on Gender*, argues that "far from doing nothing, asexuals are actually pushing directly against almost every building block of our society," claiming that "asexuals have the potential to radically restructure our lives and perceptions." There are certainly any number of chaste historical figures whose own asexuality was radical, at least in their own lives. As far as biographers have been able to ascertain, physicist Isaac Newton and philosophers Immanuel Kant both died as bachelors, as well as author Henry James and engineer Nikola Tesla. It would be absurd to attribute the laws of mechanics, the categorical imperative, to *The Portrait of a Lady*, or the induction motor to virginity—probably more accurate to think of the lifelong celibacy as a symptom of such genius rather than its cause—but it's to demonstrate the variety of ways in which the procreative urge can manifest. Blank writes that historically there has been "no shortage of radical young spiritual seekers who had added celibacy, even lifelong celibacy, to their spiritual practice," and perhaps that's a way of understanding unrepentant virgins from Newton to James: as secular spiritual seekers who abdicated a seemingly universal human practice in favor of abstraction, in favor of a more atomistic and contemplative existence. Ironically, such asexuality need not be unerotic. The director of the 1969 film *Blue Movie*, the first widely distributed art house flick to contain explicit sex, who was also the creator of the 1964 video art piece *Blow Job*, not to mention the creator of hundreds of seminal queer pornographic sketches, was a lifelong virgin by the name of Andy Warhol.

Because he is such an icon of homoerotic imagery and style, it's surprising that the openly queer Warhol was also asexual; given how cool and aloof he was, it shouldn't be. If part of chastity is the refusal to give over to the Dionysian frenzies of orgasmic ecstasy—for in that way celibacy is not dissimilar to the same

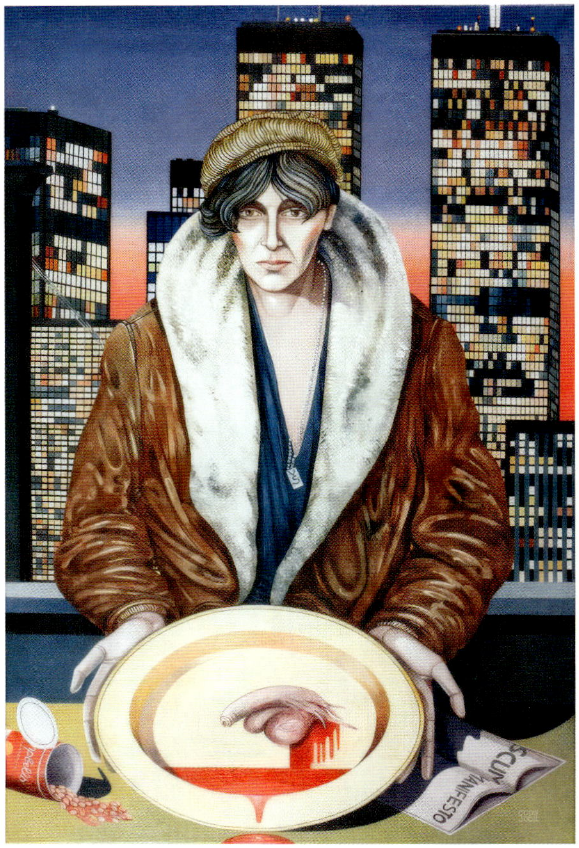

TOP Provocative English artist Caroline Coon revises the Western art canon from a feminist perspective, as in her 2002 *Valerie Solanos*, in which Warhol's attempted assassin is rendered by the conventions of Christian iconology. Standing in front of a stylized 1970s Manhattan skyline, her *S.C.U.M. Manifesto* open as if scripture and a can of Warholian baked beans spilled in front of her, Solanas offers upon a platter not her own breasts as does St. Agatha or her own eyes as St. Lucy, but rather the offending organ of patriarchy, a sacrament of St. Valerie the Castrator.

OPPOSITE A lifelong dedicated Catholic of the Byzantine Rite who attended Mass daily, Andy Warhol made art that was often religious, even when not explicitly so, his famed celebrity pop portraits evoking the icons he would have seen as a child worshiping at St. John Chrysostom Church in working-class Pittsburgh. Detail is from *The Last Supper*, screen-printed in 1986, with the original in a private collection.

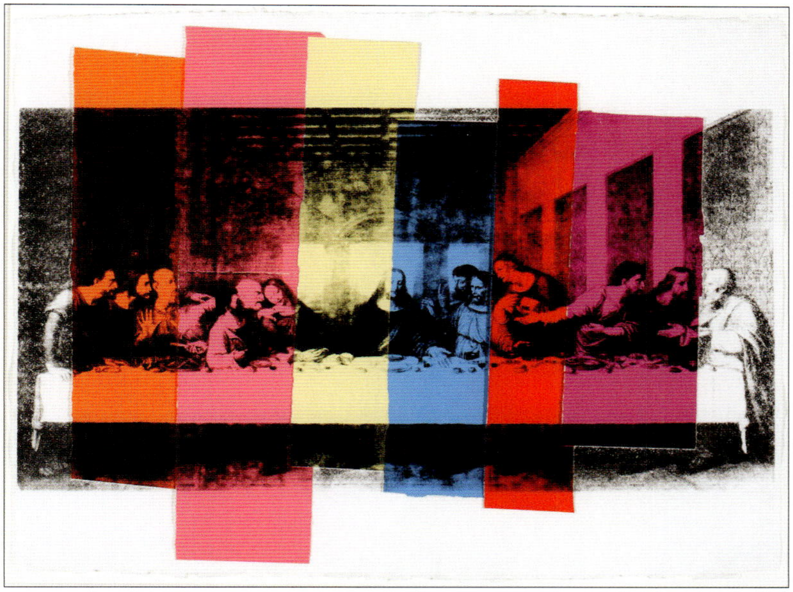

imperatives of temperance—then it makes sense considering Warhol's personality that the artist would find the sweaty exertion, the lollygagging orgasmic grimaces, and the sticky aftermath of intercourse to be distasteful, embarrassing even. For the most part, if biographers are to be believed, Warhol was always a spectator, never a participant. "The most exciting thing is not doing it," wrote Warhol in *No Title.* "If you fall in love with someone and never do it, it's much more exciting." Arguably the most erotic moment of Warhol's life, if eroticism is marked by passion and emotion, tension and release, was when the playwright and radical feminist Valerie Solanas shot him in 1968. A hanger-on in the downtown Factory scene that had accrued around Warhol, Solanas's reasons for the attempted assassination which nearly killed the artist and rendered for him a lifetime of pain and trauma are inscrutable—the result of a disordered consciousness as much as anything she could clearly articulate. Yet because of the stunning violence of her act, Solanas has often been dismissed as a writer and thinker in her own right, a profoundly unfair interpretation of somebody who was able to satirically (and perhaps more than that) examine the peccadillos of predatory male desire and make a vociferous argument for women's self-determination. At the moment in which mainstream second-wave feminists from Betty Friedan to Gloria Steinem were building a powerful and influential mass movement for women's liberation, Solanas was every bit the conservative politician's straw-woman fantasy of the radical feminist as man-hating lesbian. For those feminists making inroads into mainstream discourse, somebody like Solanas was at best irrelevant and at worst dangerous, but her often funny observations about the violence of masculine desire, which she makes in the *S.C.U.M. Manifesto* (of the "Society for Cutting Up Men"), are trenchant and in the best tradition of philosophy grounded in radical chastity. Taking the Christian valuation of chastity but draining it of the theology, Solanas rather repurposed it into a powerful feminist critique. "To call a man an animal is to flatter him," writes Solanas. "He's a machine, a walking dildo. It's often said that men use women. Use them for what? Surely not pleasure." Cutting and acerbic, Solanas's prose almost demands the knee-jerk defensive to respond "But #NotAllMen!," which somehow both misses and makes her point. Whatever her actions, or the severity of her argument, Solanas's point about how often heterosexual sex is about power and control, rather than pleasure and love, should be listened to.

If there was any answer to Solanas's argument, perhaps it's in the example of another chaste eccentric from deep in American history, the radical preacher who went by the name of the Public Universal Friend. Born Jemima Wilkinson in Cumberland, Rhode Island in the midst of the First Great Awakening, when revival and religious fervency burnt across the eighteenth-century colonial frontier, they would prove to be among the most revolutionary of forgotten gender theorists America ever produced. Raised by dissenting, non-conforming Quaker parents and strongly influenced by the celibate offshoot of that denomination known as Shakers, Wilkinson would have a mystical theophany while convalescing from typhus, so that in 1776 they would ascend to heaven and return as the Public Universal Friend. Upon their experience, for with this apotheosis the Public Universal Friend would fuse the masculine and feminine, the male and female, and transcend gender and sexuality altogether, a pair of archangels would declare that there was "Room, Room, Room, in the many Mansion of eternal glory for Thee and for everyone." The abolishment of gender, in the teachings of the Public Universal Friend, were concurrent with their pacificism, for the harsh, domineering, and cruel sexuality which Solanas rightly castigated could be overcome with the liberation of not just women but men, accomplished by demolishing the false binary that separates and oppresses both.

Living chastely was crucial to this ministry, for in making the usual strange and the strange usual there was a critique of the status quo, of the princes of this world who so often do such damage. As unusual as the mission of the Public Universal Friend might seem, they had tremendous popularity throughout Rhode Island and Massachusetts, Connecticut and New York, Pennsylvania and New Jersey, following the same route that doctrinaire preachers like Jonathan Edwards and George Whitfield did, but rather bringing a new dispensation of the spirit, of liberation from the body, even while facing the abjuration and mockery of conservative critics. Echoing the ancient Gnostics and their suspicions of matter and the tyranny of biology, the Public Universal Friend rather imagined a reality of mind, of soul, and of liberation from the socially constrained fictions which we impose on men and women, and everybody else. Taking the words of Paul to their logical conclusion, the Public Universal Friend argued that if in God there is no Jew or Gentile, then neither is there male or female. In the words of a convert named Ruth Pritchard, the "Friend of Sinners began to serve in the year 1777 when this Nation was still in arms and America had embroiled her hands in human blood," describing this "Messenger of Peace going from City to City and from Village to Village proclaiming the News of Salvation . . . The Friend was not staid by guards of armed men. She went through to visit the poor condemned prisoners in their chains . . . No storms or severity of weather could hinder the Friend's journey to speak unto Souls"—not bodies, but souls. In the decades following the Public Universal Friend's conversion and the start of his ministry, skeptics would ask the gentle preacher with ambiguous features and masculine dress as to whether or not they were a man or a woman, to which the visionary would respond with God's words from Exodus—"I am that I am."

OPPOSITE Radical Peruvian artist Giuseppe Campuzano imagines himself as the Virgin Mary in this photographic collage *Letania* or *Litany*, from the 2012 publication *Art & Queer Culture*. Catherine Lloyd and Richard Meyer write in their annotations to the piece that for "Campuzano, the body of the transvestite subject is a primary source of political power," envisioning "transvestites as both sacred, mystical figures and figures subject to the violence and limitations imposed upon them" by both Church and state.

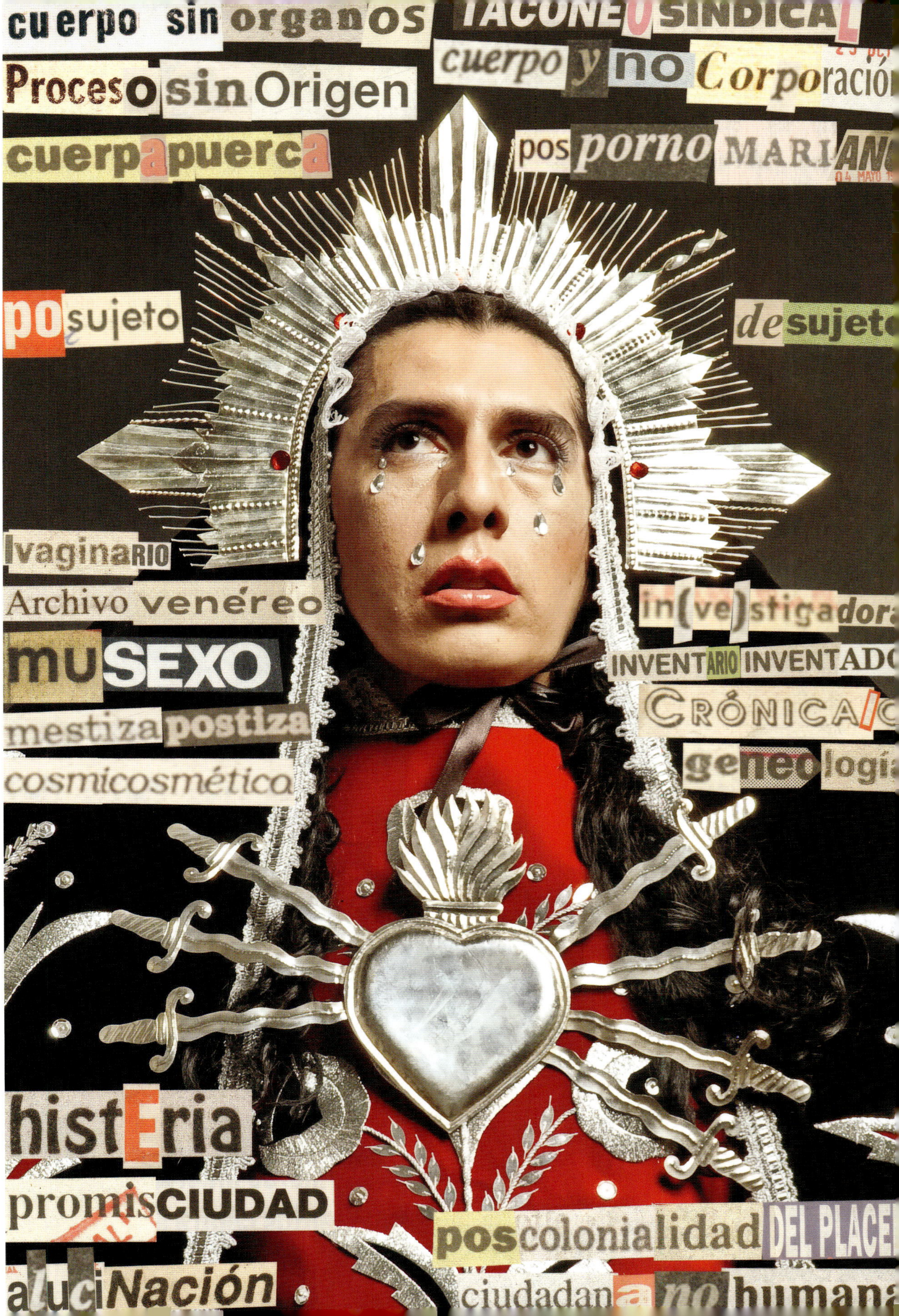

cuerpo sin organos
TACONEO SINDICAL
cuerpo y no Corporación
Proceso sin Origen
cuerpapuerca
pos porno MARIAN
posujeto
desujet
Ivaginario
Archivo venéreo
in(ve)stigador
muSEXO
INVENTARIO INVENTAD
CRÓNICA/
mestiza postiza
geneologí
cosmicosmética
histEria
promisCIUDAD
poscolonialidad DEL PLACE
aluciNación
ciudadana no humana

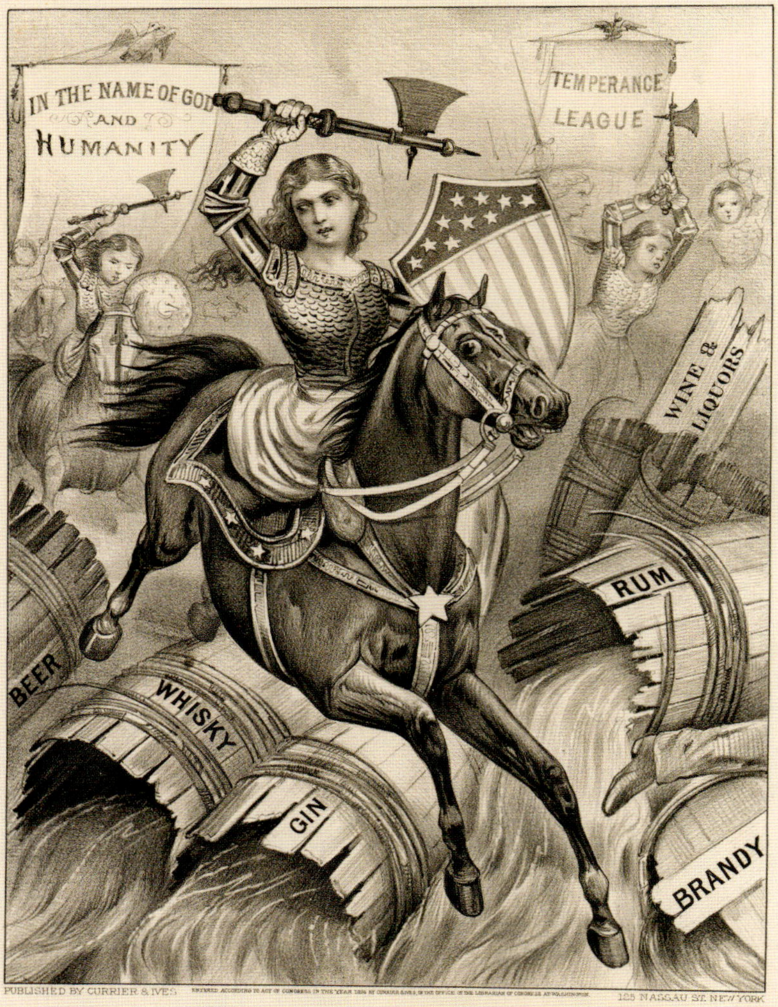

PUBLISHED BY CURRIER & IVES   125 NASSAU ST. NEW YORK

WOMANS HOLY WAR.

Grand Charge on the Enemy's Works.

CHAPTER THREE

DRINK NOT THE THIRD GLASS: TEMPERANCE

"He who is not satisfied with little, is satisfied with nothing."

—Epicurus, *Sovereign Maxims* (c. 300 BCE)

"One drink is too many for me, and a thousand is never enough."

—Brendan Behan, interview on the BBC (1959)

The Renaissance's greatest humanist, who lived, worked, and thought amidst the religious tribulations of Reformation France, was the sixteenth-century essayist Michel de Montaigne. A prophet of humanism's virtues of equanimity, skepticism, and moderation, Montaigne was weary of all zealotry, including an excess of experience. No prohibitionist—he was, after all, a vintner—Montaigne nonetheless maintained that "Greatness of soul consists . . . in knowing how to govern and circumscribes itself; it takes everything for great, that is enough, and demonstrates itself in preferring moderate to eminent things." Student of both Jerusalem and Athens, the Hebraic and the Hellenic, the Christian and the pagan, Montaigne could draw on ample precedent from both strains of the Western tradition in order to justify temperance. Judaism and Christianity had long counselled moderation in eating and drinking, while classical stoics such as the Roman Emperor Marcus Aurelius would proscribe that the ethical man is not "overpowered either by the motion of the senses or the appetites." Temperance, in this way, was understood as a form of self-mastery, as demonstrating a rigor in the control of one's own baser instincts. To live an abstemious life meant to choose the rational human faculties over the bestial animalistic ones. Temperance has a venerable pedigree, from the sages of scripture advising self-regulation and control to Aristotle's claim that the "virtue of justice consists in moderation" and the Buddha's establishment of the Middle Path, which eschewed both excess and asceticism. As a virtue, temperance is ideally intended not to involve excessive self-denial, but rather an embrace of harmony, balance, order.

PREVIOUS SPREAD Groups advocating for prohibition, such as the Women's Temperance League, borrowed from martial and medieval imagery as in this Currier & Ives poster from 1874 entitled *Woman's Holy War.* Featuring a maiden in knight's armor, evoking Joan of Arc, both she and her assorted sisters march their horses through a barroom, destroying casks of rum, whiskey, gin, and brandy, the central figure holding aloft not just an axe but a patriotic star-spangled shield. Because of the political and moral failures of prohibition as enacted by the eighteenth amendment more than a generation later, it's easy to slur groups such as the WTL as schoolmarmish killjoys, ignoring the deadly human cost that alcoholism played (and continues to play) in domestic abuse, a central reason for the creation of these organizations.

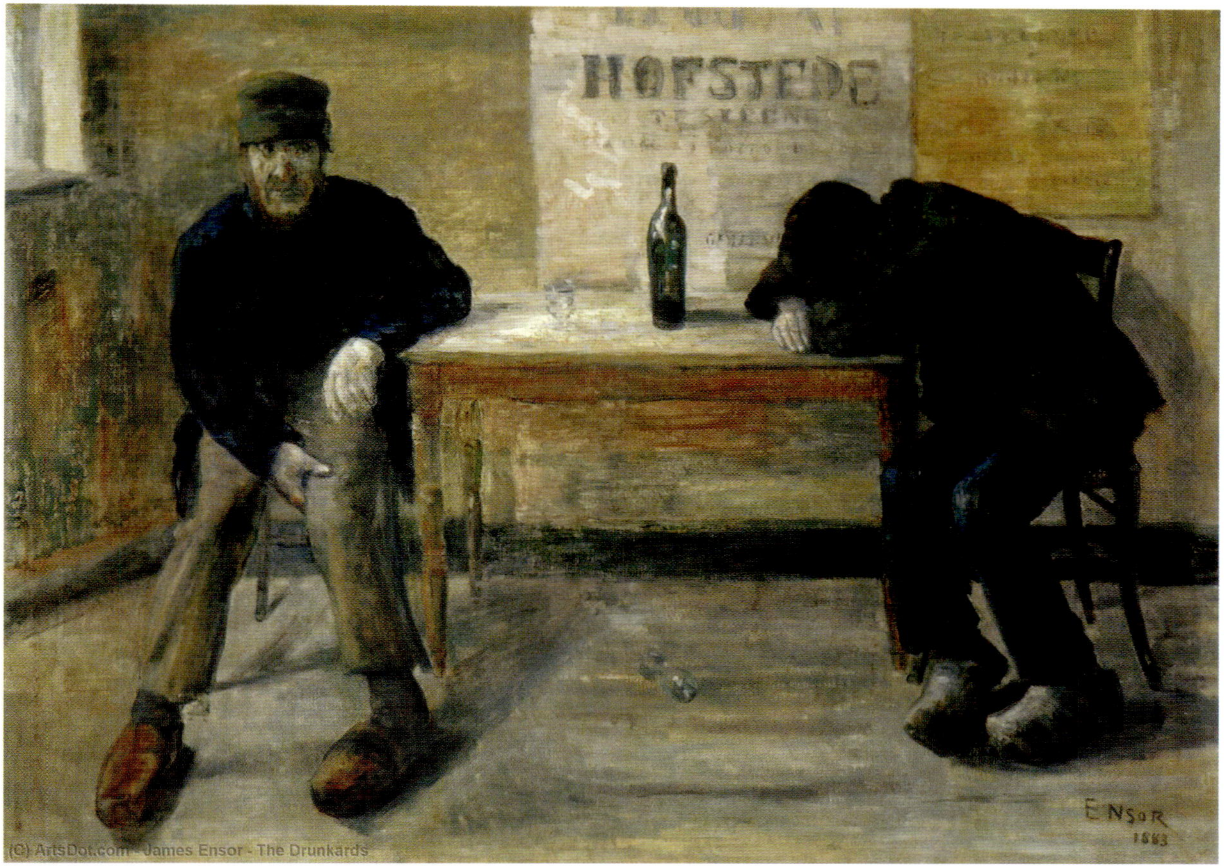

THE FIRST STEP—THEORY

ABOVE Artists, not a particularly abstemious lot, have long depicted the drinking life as one of conviviality and joy, which it certainly can be. Yet Belgian artist James Ensor's 1883 painting *The Drunkards*, completed at the same moment that groups like the Washingtonians were finding success across the Atlantic, accurately depicts late-stage alcoholism as a dreary cycle of lonely addiction, the figures by themselves even when they're together. Original in private collection.

On a cool spring day in 1840, six drinking buddies named William Mitchell, David Hoss, Bill McCurdy, Tom Campbell, Charles Anderson, and George Steer, a fraternity of drunkards long conversant with intoxication and embarrassment, fighting and vomiting, blackout and passing out, hangover and delirium tremens, gathered in the dark, red-bricked, saw-dust-floored environs of Chase's Tavern on Liberty Street in Baltimore, and did something unexpected for both who they were and where they were—they vowed *not to drink*. Two of the men had recently attended a sermon delivered by the temperance reformer Reverend Matthew Hale and, having experienced some sort of spiritual awakening, decided that they wished for a redemption of the soul, but one which could be facilitated only through connection, empathy, and solidarity with their fellow dipsomaniacs who desired to put down the bottle.

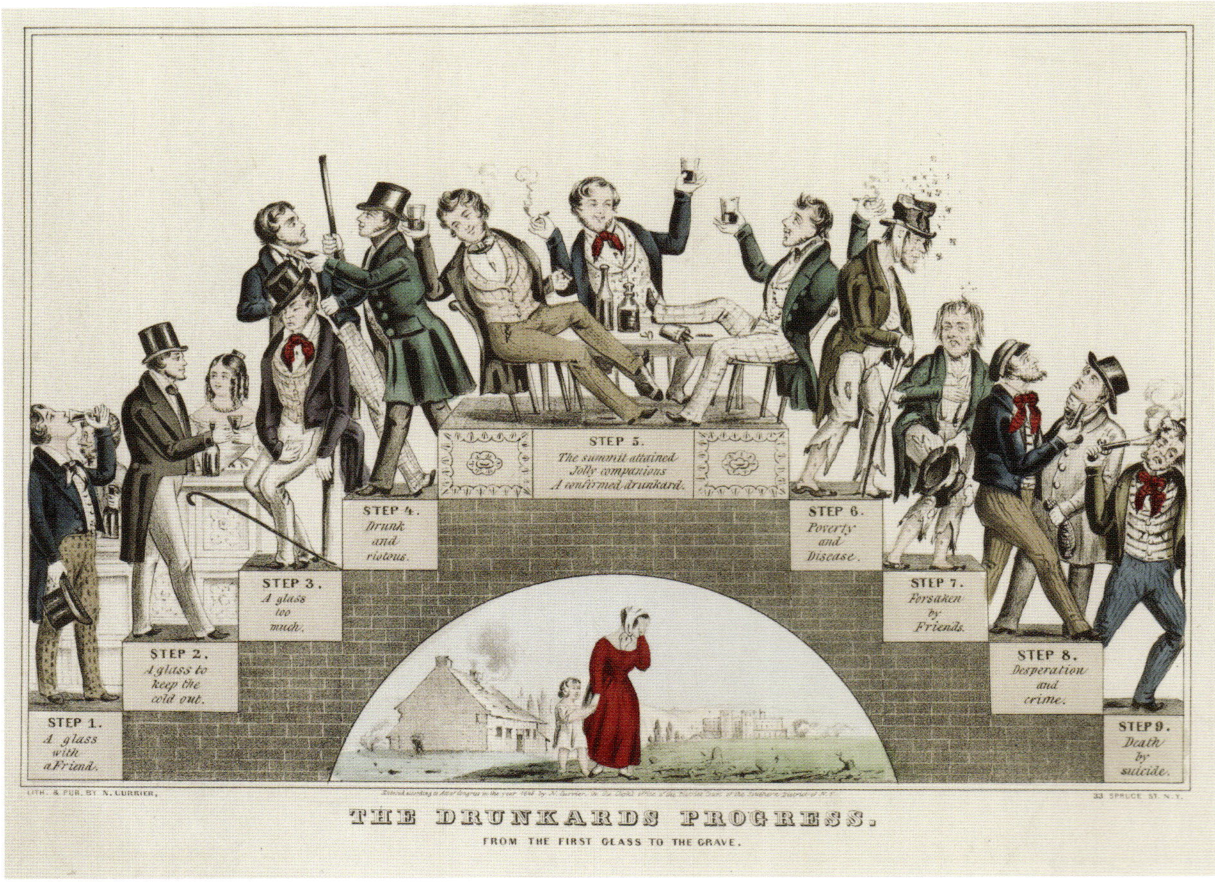

Quite an irony that the six founded their nascent addiction-treatment society at Chase's, surrounded by pewter tankards of frothy warm ale and lager, glasses of astringent rye and whiskey, odor of oysters and boiled crabs, but perhaps an appropriateness as well as they challenged the dragon of their own appetites in the very cave where it waited in repose. As their own account would read two years later, such men were "the *victims*, the *unwilling victims*, rather than the mere *votaries* of the pleasures of the bowl"—not people of loose character, but those who suffered from a disease. But here, in the place that inculcated that illness, they'd find a cure, a hair-of-the-dog if you will. These were men who "had found themselves in the power of a monster, bound hand and foot in chains,—the slave of their own appetites." Historian Christopher M. Finan concurred, arguing in *Drunks: The Story of Alcoholism and the Birth of Recovery* that the Washingtonians are a chapter in one of the "great liberation movements" of American politics and history.

From their initial conversation in which they vowed to not only abstain from intoxicating liquor, but indeed all forms of alcohol be they wine or beer, so that they would be "Capital-T teetotalers" for total abstinence, there would be established the Washingtonian Temperance Society. Unlike more lackadaisical groups, the Washingtonians gave no exceptions for supposedly "soft" beer and wine, understanding that the effects of ethanol were for them consistent, regardless of the delivery mechanism. There were other differences between the Washingtonians and the varied temperance societies proliferating through the United States at the time, often under the influence of evangelical religious revival which marked the Second Great Awakening. For example, the Washingtonians were adamantly *not religious*, as their meeting in a bar rather than a church would indicate. Secondly, they were established by and for alcoholics who desired sobriety rather than being staffed by moralizing Protestant ministers policing behavior. Thirdly, the Washingtonians opened their ranks to men of any station, both rich and poor, and in the antebellum South most amazingly both Black and white. Fourthly, at least initially, the Washingtonians were not a prohibitionist organization, recommending not the banning of alcohol for society at large, but rather the self-regulation of it for the individual alcoholic. Finally, and most crucially, these alcoholics understood addiction not to be a moral issue, not a failure of willpower or character, but as a medical problem. Their solution was the care which they could lend to their brothers, the understanding that only an alcoholic can offer to another alcoholic.

By 1842, the group published *The Foundation, Progress and Principles of the Washington Temperance Society of Baltimore*, venturing forth a program by which alcoholics, in conversation and tutelage with one another, could mutually support their progress in attempting sobriety. More than half a million men would join the society in the decade before the Civil War, affirming their "mutual benefit, and to guard against a pernicious practice, which is injurious to our health, standing and families," pledging themselves "not to drink any spirituous or malt liquors, wine or cider." A certain irony in being named after the first president of the United States, who operated several whiskey stills at his Mount Vernon plantation; but the Washingtonians saw theirs as a revolutionary movement similar to the Continental Army, fighting a tyranny which controlled their lives in the addictions which ravaged them. As part of this program, the Washingtonians committed to not just their abstinence pledge, but also to weekly meetings to hold themselves accountable. Within a year of being founded, the Martha Washingtonian Society would be established for women, an acknowledgment that alcoholism affected both genders. When he was a thirty-three-year-old Illinois state representative in 1842, Abraham Lincoln was invited by a local chapter of the Springfield Washingtonian Temperance Society to address them. Personally, Lincoln had no problem with liquor. Child of the Kentucky and Illinois frontiers that he was, Lincoln was familiar with beer and cider, whiskey and bourbon, but he was asked to speak to the group not as a drunkard but as an interested outsider. The future president would tell the Washingtonians that "In my judgment . . . such of us who have never fallen victims have been spared more by the absence of appetite than from any mental or moral superiority over those who have." He understood how liquor was seemingly omnipresent in both personal and professional life, contributing to the massive public health crisis of rampant alcoholism.

Historian Daniel Okrent explains in *Last Call: The Rise and Fall of Prohibition* that in the "early days of the Republic drinking was as intimately woven into the social fabric as family or church." Okrent writes that by "1830 American adults were guzzling, per capita, a staggering seven gallons of pure alcohol a year," which in modern terms are the "equivalent of 1.7 bottles of standard 80-proof

OPPOSITE American lithographer Nathaniel Currier's 1848 print *The Drunkard's Progress*, which depicts the expected course of biography for a man from casual drinking through several steps that lead to total ruin and destitution. Note the crying wife at the bottom of the diagram.

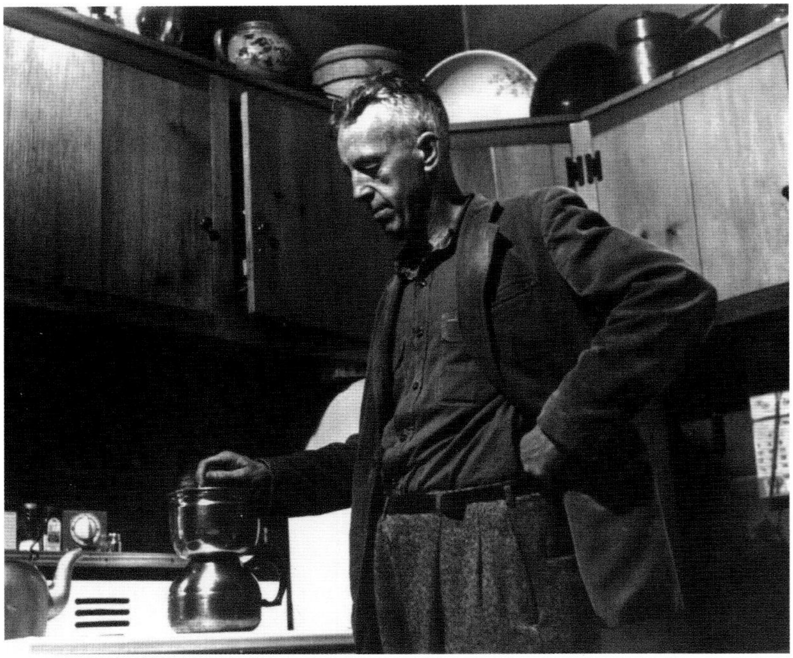

liquor per person, per week—nearly 90 bottles a year for every adult in the nation." Despite that environment, like most people (then and now) Lincoln had no physical dependence on alcohol, no addiction, no inability to temper his own drinking. But unlike many people (then and now) Lincoln didn't attribute his lack of that malady to moral fortitude. Instead, like the current medical consensus, Lincoln believed addiction is a disease rather than failure of willpower. "On this point," Lincoln said, "the Washingtonians greatly excel the temperance advocates of former times . . . They know [alcoholics] are not demons." The future president argued that alcoholics should be treated as anyone would approach "the heirs of consumption and other hereditary diseases." The belief that addicts were "utterly incorrigible" was a dangerous and deadly fallacy that Lincoln argued must be abandoned. What the Washingtonians understood was that addiction is a form of imprisonment, and recovery can be a type of liberation, or as Lincoln told the assembled, "we shall find a stronger bondage broken . . . a greater tyrant deposed." The Washingtonians would endure for a decade before disappearing.

By 1935, when a failed stockbroker named Bill Wilson (remembered as Bill W.), who was undergoing a shaky recovery, sat down in an Akron kitchen with a drunk surgeon named Robert Smith (whom posterity calls Dr. Bob) in what's considered the first meeting of Alcoholics Anonymous, the Washingtonians were all but forgotten. Bearing a startling similarity to that earlier program, the steps and traditions of AA were formulated by Bill W. and Dr. Bob without any awareness of the Washingtonians, proving that the alcoholic in need of desired recovery can rediscover those principles anew, innate as they are in the human spirit. Recovery, though it need not have any spiritual gloss to it, does have its origins within religious thinking. The tale of damnation and redemption which is often an intrinsic part of any individual recovery story is a narrative about a variety of salvation. Narrative

TOP Due to his itinerant drinking, Bill Wilson was a failure at business, but in his recovery as the founder of Alcoholics Anonymous, he would become legendary as the first sponsor to share his strength, experience, and hope. Here, Bill W., as he is fondly remembered in AA, prepares coffee for a meeting. According to the Twelfth Step of the fellowship, recovering alcoholics, having "had a spiritual awakening . . . [are to] carry this message to alcoholics, and to practice these principles in all our affairs."

OPPOSITE In contrast to the hard-drinking antics of hardscrabble men, the Italian Renaissance painter Piero del Pollaiuolo depicts temperance as a woman in this 1470 composition held at the Uffizi.

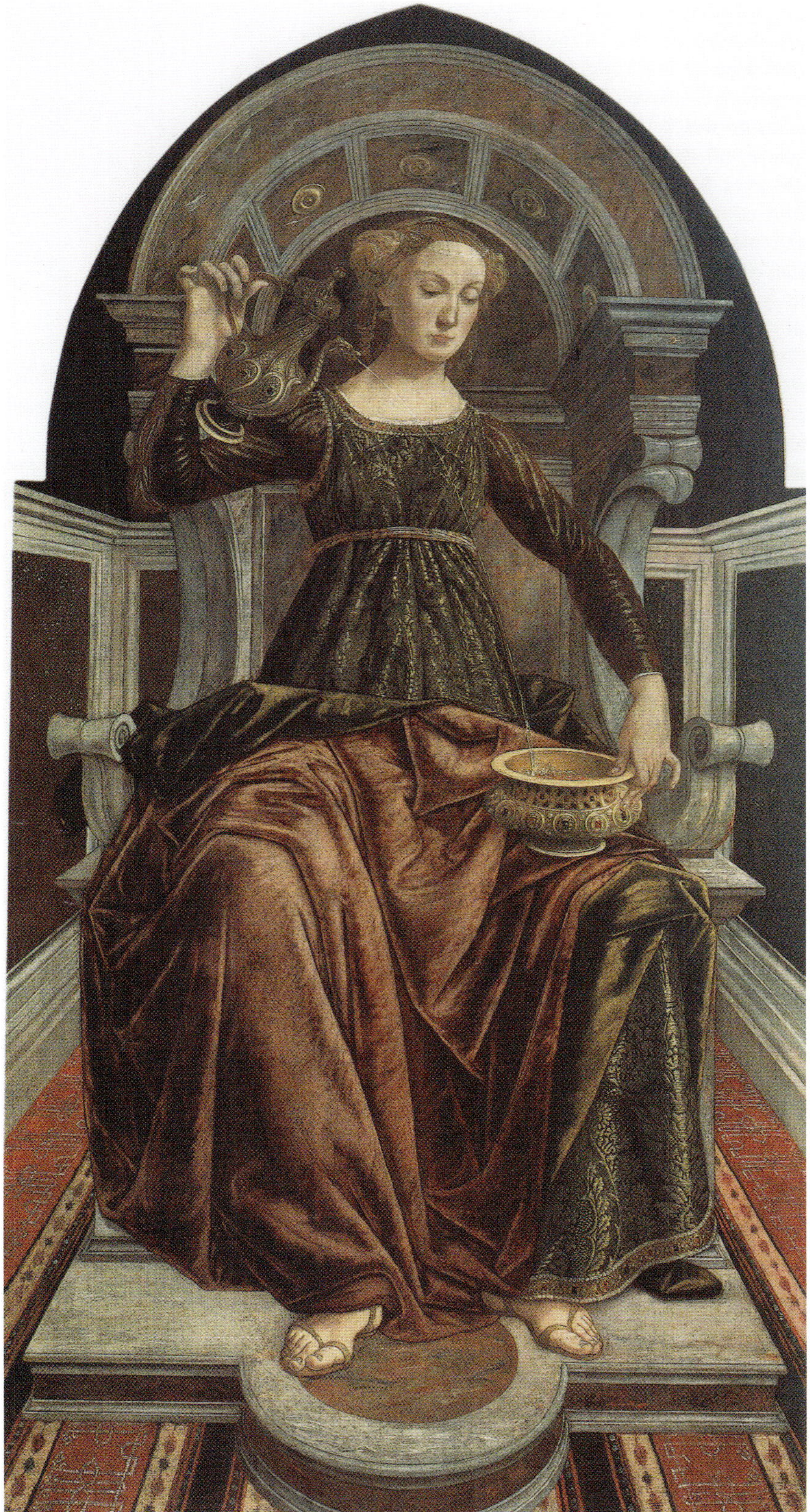

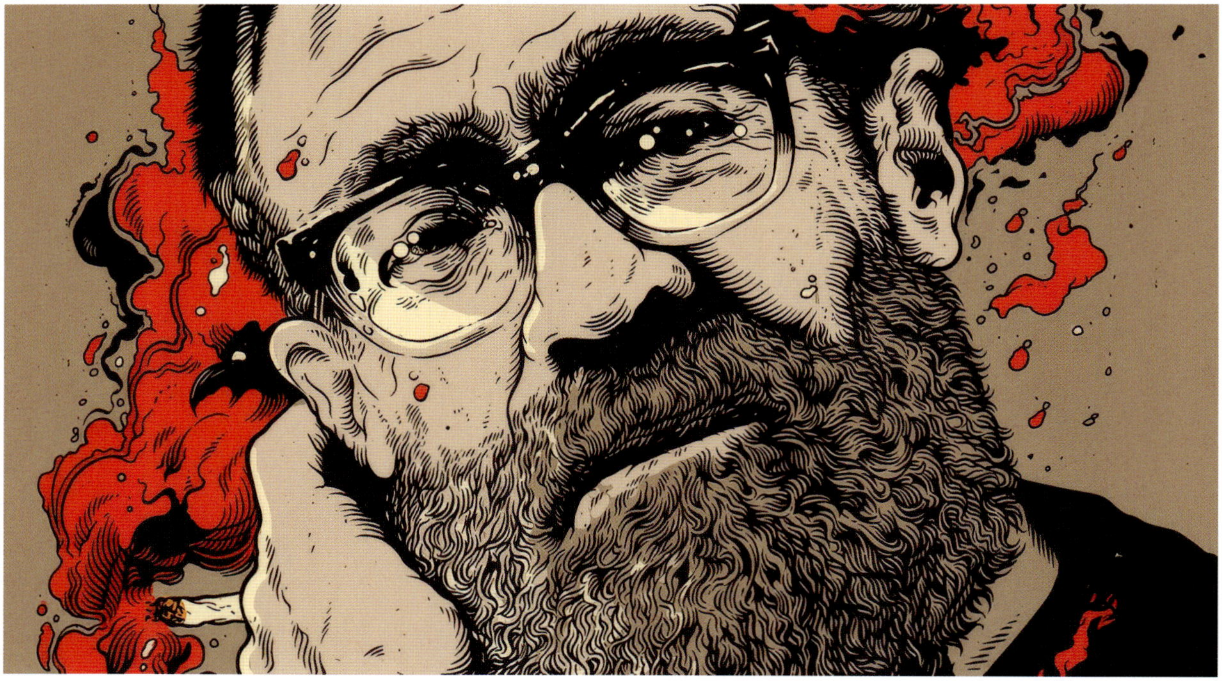

is intrinsic to the process of recovery, whether in the form promulgated by the Washingtonians or in the contemporary Twelve Steps, what's sometimes either affectionately or dismissively called "The Drunkelogue." Naturally, with story at its center—whether in the form of inebriated bar-stool boasting or in earnest church basement public confession—writers have filled the ranks of the alcoholic. Leslie Jamison in her memoir *The Recovering: Intoxication and Its Aftermath* investigates the damaging myth that creativity can only be fueled by booze, and that writers are a holy intoxicated tribe. A graduate of the esteemed University of Iowa Writers Workshop, Jamison imbued this legend with every whiskey, beer, and vodka tonic she drank, writing that Iowa City "surged with dreamlike tales of dysfunction," that there was "Raymond Carver and John Cheever tire-squalling through early morning grocery-store parking lots to restock their liquor stash" (both men, incidentally, went onto productive sobriety). She considers "Denis Johnson getting drunk at the Vine and writing short stories about getting drunk at the Vine" (also went onto sobriety), and "John Berryman opening bar tabs on Dubuque Street and ranting about Whitman till dawn, playing chess and leaving his bishops vulnerable" (attempted sobriety; suicide). "Great Drinkers" shot glasses, literary-themed cocktail books, and not one but two Boston bars named "Bukowski's" all attest to this presumed connection between creativity and alcoholism—and thus the need to feed the latter in service of the former. Reading Ernest Hemingway's *Garden of Eden*, written while he suffered from late-stage alcoholism, should dissuade anyone of this causal connection, though the link between writers and drinking endures for a reason, especially in the United States. Of the nine Americans to have won the Noble Prize in Literature, only three (Pearl Buck, Saul Bellow, and Toni Morrison) were not addicts at some point in their lives. Psychiatrist David Goodwin in his 1990 study *Alcohol and the Writer* concluded that after bartenders, writers were the occupation with the highest incidences of cirrhosis. A fifteen-year study conducted in the late eighties at the University of Iowa Writers Workshop by psychiatrist Nancy J. Andreasen discovered that among both the faculty and students of the program, fully 30 percent would qualify as alcoholics when compared to a little under 7 percent for the wider public.

The full human cost of alcoholism is obscured in a shaky haze of recounted anecdotes, embodied in drained pint glasses and filled ash trays. Examining a *Life* magazine spread about Berryman's readings in Dublin and his subsequent whiskey-and-Guinness-fueled pub crawl, Jamison writes of the connection made between whiskey as the "fluid he ingested" and ink as the "fluid he produced" as being simplistic and damaging. She reminds us that rather than having ink flowing in his veins, Berryman was actually "full of ordinary human blood . . . that his drinking slowly poisoned." Drinking didn't give us *The Dream Songs*, but it did give Berryman thousands of blackouts and hangovers, as well as embarrassment. Romanticize impromptu bar-stool lectures that go on 'til dawn all you want, but it's much harder to valorize drunkenly shitting your pants in public. Berryman didn't write because of his drinking, he wrote in spite of it. The alcohol merely made something unendurable inside of him endurable, until it couldn't any longer. Olivia Laing's *The Trip to Echo Spring: On Writers and Drinking* examines the mythos of the drunken American writer as she looks into the lives of iconic authors and drinkers, some of whom—like Cheever and Carver—got sober, and some of whom—like Hemingway—didn't. There is, for all of its complexity, a celebrated "shimmering link between drinking and darkness, between drinking and *knowing*." Easy enough to forget that vomiting and the shakes aren't just for Nobel laureates; that teachers, plumbers, lawyers, doctors, cops, and accountants suffer too.

This is a fraternity (and sorority) with millions of members, meeting in the basement of the Capitol building and in Anacostia homeless shelters; in a third-floor walk-up at the corner of Eighth and Forty-Second, and in an oak-paneled library in an Episcopalian cathedral on Madison; in Salt Lake City churches and on the Las Vegas Strip. As destructive as Sister Morphine might be, America is still the kingdom of John Barleycorn, and where there is disease there is need for a palliative. So culturally enmeshed is booze and with individuals' possibility of becoming addicted so low when compared to substances like heroin, alcohol and alcoholism remain surprisingly overlooked as a public health issue. With 88,000 annual deaths a year due to alcohol-related causes (as reported by the National Institute of Alcohol Abuse and Alcoholism), drinking remains the third-highest cause of preventable death in the country, after tobacco use and obesity. More than a quarter of adults are monthly binge drinkers, and fully 6.7 percent of adults—that's 15.1 million people—qualify as having "alcohol use disorder," the DSM-V's new designation for alcoholism. The public is rightly wary of the puritanical disaster that was Prohibition, and cognizant that the vast majority of drinkers imbibe without any problem. Yet in part because of that position, alcoholism is often obscured in the public imagination, being viewed as either romantic or an issue of willpower. A general ignorance surrounds its etiology, the ways in which a complex combination of genetics, acculturation, and experience can render some people addicts while others can drink without issue.

Whether drinking to the alcoholic is like finding a missing puzzle piece, turning the volume on the stereo down, or opening a pressure gauge on one's head, it's

OPPOSITE The poet as depicted in Tim McDonagh's illustration for a 2015 article in the *Atlantic* entitled "The Genius and Excess of John Berryman." With a halo of cigarette smoke and glassy-eyed drunken stare, this is the Berryman who in 1971 would say, "Will power is nothing. Morals is nothing. Lord, this is illness."

through language that something as cunning, baffling, and powerful as alcoholism can be conveyed. Narrative is at the center of the alcoholic's self-understanding, whether in the romanticizing of drinking or the denial of its destructive results. Stories of drunken heroism and misadventure and stories of abject humiliation are strangely united in this sense. What makes narrative so potent is that it also conveys the possibility of redemption, with the drafting of new stories. Ironically, it's both addiction and recovery that makes all alcoholics storytellers, in the first instance as means of rationalization and in the second as a method of salvation. Both the Washingtonians and AA are based on the open sharing of trauma and redemption, a network of empathy designed to help the white-knuckling alcoholic in early sobriety to hold on just one more day at a time. *What it was like, what happened, what it's like now.* Drunkalogues tell versions of the same story. There are certain generic touchstones: the unquenchable, almost metaphysical thirst and the unremitting guilt; the missed appointments and shirked responsibilities; the secretive drinking and the hiding of empties; the horror of blackout and the dangers of withdrawal. The list of all of those whom the drinker has hurt. A set typology to the alcoholic's life, both before and in recovery. The ultimate irony in trying to divorce literary creativity from alcoholism is the discovery that the fundamental units of narrative are in many ways central to recovery.

Inevitably AA generates criticism as being fundamentally religious. For these denigrators there is the taint of the numinous about AA—the Big Book as a type of scripture, its founder Bill W. as quasi-messianic, meetings a form of secularized confession and the steps an equivalent form of contrition; the sobriety tokens as relics and the traditions as rituals, the mention of a "Higher Power" speaking for itself. As with most secular critiques of anything which has sublimated theology at its core, this appraisal is both correct and irrelevant—in part because modernity is defined by sublimated theology. Some defenders of AA will say that the "Higher Power" talk is "spiritual and not religious," or that it speaks not of the Abrahamic God, but a "God of your own understanding." There is a bit of the dodge about it, for the brilliance of letting the member define that God in their own terms is a combination of Jamesian Pragmatism with behavior modification which notably *works.* Like the Washingtonians, Bill W. forged AA out of a particularly Protestant understanding of the world, drawing inspiration from evangelical lay societies like the Oxford group, but if the Twelve Steps are a type of religion, then they are one that is distinct from the faith which birthed it. One that by the very pluralistic logic of American religious promiscuity can be combined with any number of other faiths, or no conventional faith at all. That is the sectarian brilliance of this religion, the appearance of not being one at all. And yet millions have been saved in the sanctuaries beneath cathedrals as much as they have been in the pews above. Something radically transgressive in a group like this: anarchically organized with absolutely no established hierarchy, requiring no dues to attend, and structured in an entirely horizontal way. Abstinence almost takes on a radical import. So often mocked as the lifestyle of a scold or a puritan, there is something transgressive in teetotaling, something subversive in sobriety. It is to willfully opt out of at least one of those endless cycles which defines the postmodern condition.

For alcoholics, there is a particularly predictable manifestation of at least one aspect of this condition. If you read Cheever's masterpiece "The Swimmer"

OPPOSITE Scottish painter Peter Howson, known for his sometimes controversial scenes of hideous brutality, underwent a religious conversion necessary for his own sobriety. Howson's 2000 series *The First Step*, which explores each of the twelve steps of AA, simply but with incredible difficulty requires the alcoholic to admit the nature of their addiction and depicts the exhaustion and pain of the drunk as they reach their rock bottom.

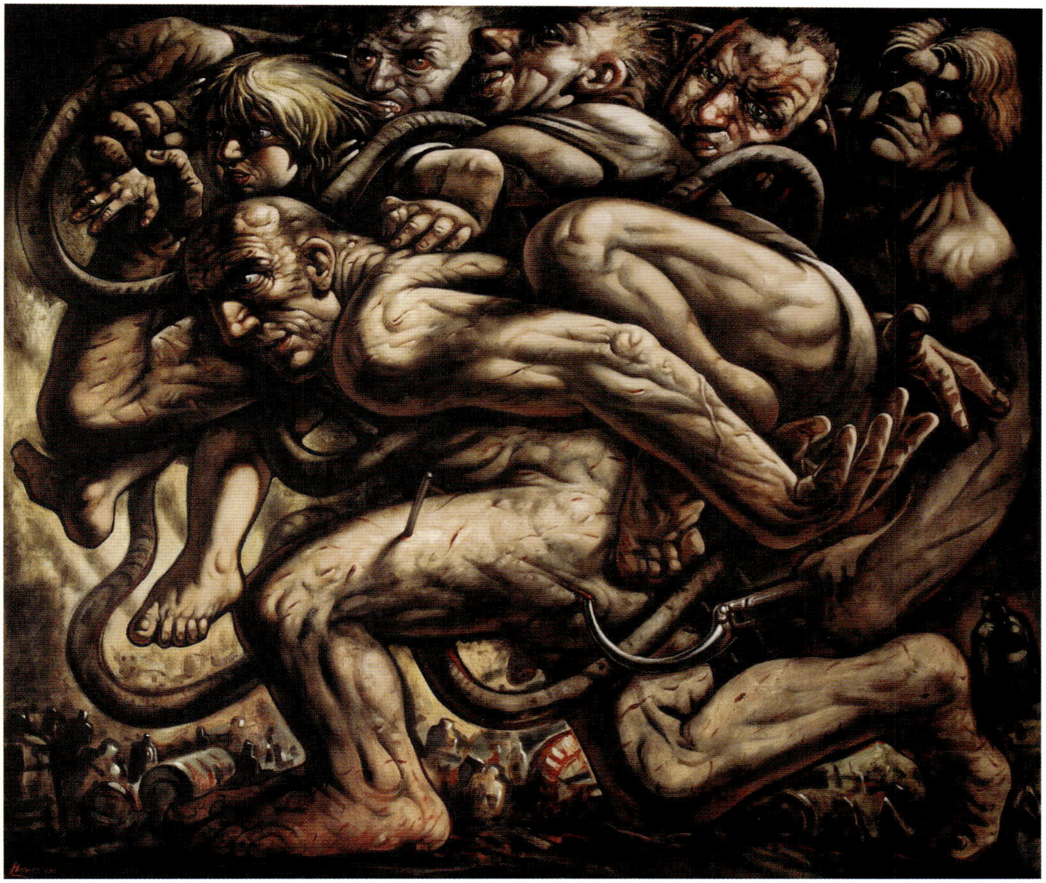

from a 1964 edition of *The New Yorker*, a sense of this process is conveyed. Suburban husband Ned Merrill decides that he'll journey back to his house by swimming through the pools of his neighbors' homes, stopping off for cocktails on the way. Yet at the narrative progresses, so too does Ned's affliction. A tone of subtle, yet malevolent, surrealism permeates the story, as Ned loses track of time, eventually the very seasons coming unwrenched from his consciousness. By the time he arrives home, disheveled with seemingly years of his life lost, he finds it abandoned and overgrown, his wife having long since left. Where exactly things went wrong for him, and why they didn't seem to go wrong in the same way for others doing the same thing, was of course the great mystery of Ned's disease. But that mystery is also irrelevant to the tragedy of it. Cheever writes, equally of himself, that Ned "had done what he wanted, he had swum the county, but he was so stupefied with exhaustion that his triumph seemed vague." Sick and tired of being sick and tired, it would seem. The story's author was deep in his cups that season of '64. But a decade later and even John Cheever could get sober. There are millions of identical stories, for while there is something inevitable about the thirteenth drink after the first, nothing need be inevitable about that first.

INTERLUDE—BOBBY SANDS

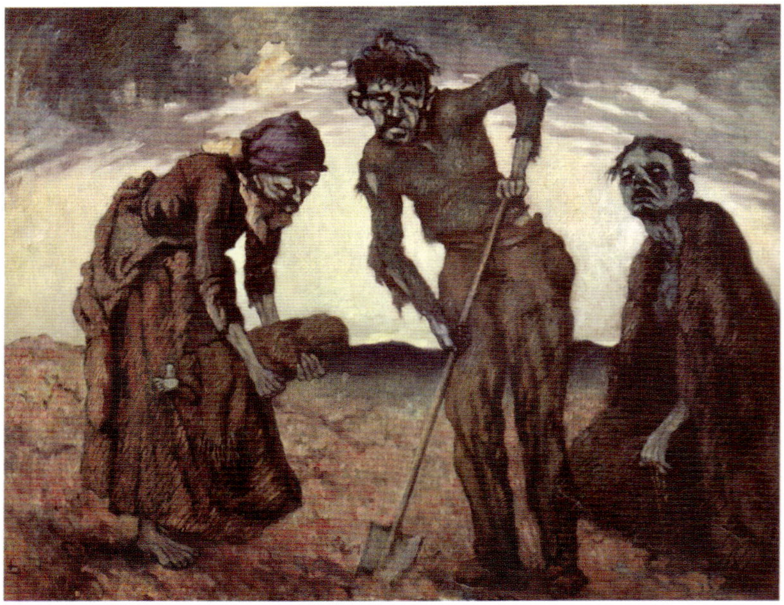

Three days into his hunger strike, Bobby Sands weighed 137 pounds. Six weeks later, on the day that he'd receive the last rites, the Provisional Irish Republican Army soldier was a little over a hundred pounds. He'd live for another three weeks, before dying at the age of twenty-seven on May 5, 1981, in H-block, the Maze Prison hospital, County Down, Northern Ireland. Literary scholar Terry Eagleton in *Radical Sacrifice* notes that to be "martyred is to allow one's death to be taken into public ownership," and for insurgents from Belfast to Bethlehem, Sands resonated as a symbol of post-colonial resistance, the young IRA soldier, improbably elected to Parliament while in the midst of his hunger strike, dying for national self-determination. Fasting has long been a tool of both spiritual purification and political agitation, a humble self-denial which shuts down the body as a means of paradoxically extending its influence. Fasting is the prerogative of the Jew on Yom Kippur, of the Muslim during the holy month of Ramadan, of the Catholic on Good Friday. For Sands it was a political act, whereby his withering body would gain the attention of the public, a living (and dying) demonstration of the ways in which Britain had drained her colony.

In a photo from shortly before he died, one sees a man whom hunger has transformed into a living cadaver; Eagleton might explain that Sands had undergone a "form of semiosis in which one's body is converted into a sign." Gone is the vitality in the iconic photograph of Sands as a young man, the same image seen in Belfast Republican murals, the long-haired child of the sixties in red sweater with handsome, hopeful smile. Before his death, rather, Sands is skeletal, his hair long, dark and unkempt, scraggly thick beard framing his angular face, and

TOP Irish painter Lilian Lucy Davidson's 1946 *Gorta*, previously known as *Burying the Child*, conveys the horrors of the Irish Potato Famine when British policy intentionally starved a million women, children, and men, nearly a quarter of the nation's population, with more emigrating as a result. The nightmare of the Gorta, as it's known in Gallic, directly led to related injustices in the twentieth century. Original at Ireland's Great Hunger Museum at Quinnipiac University in Hamden, Connecticut.

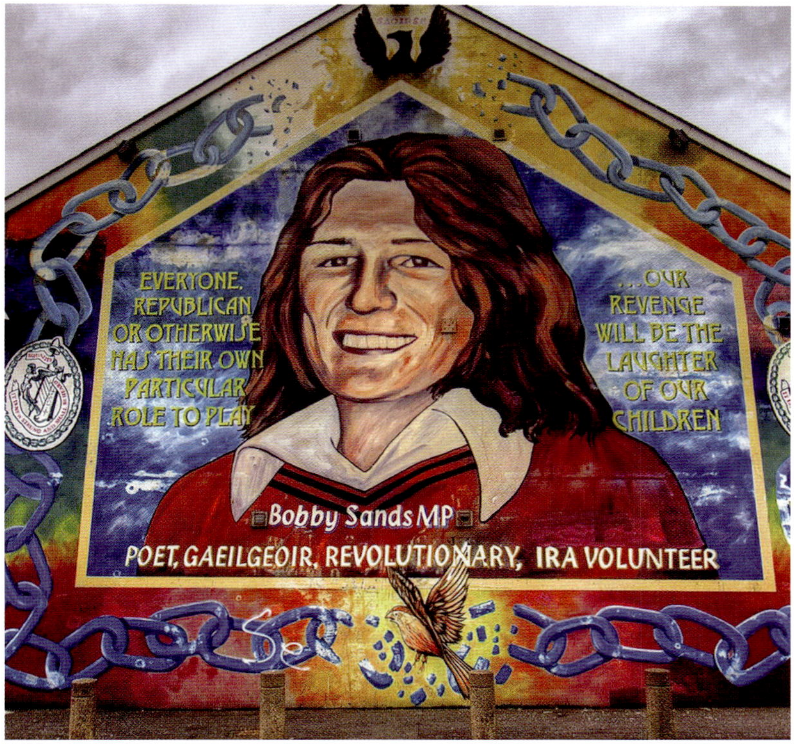

eyes distilled to hungry, pure intensity. An aura—the presence of that original icon. Sands appearing in life before death nothing so much as a breathing *pietà*. Which in part was precisely the purpose of his sacrifice, regardless of whether you think his cause was righteous. For men like Sands, the "act of dying becomes an eloquent piece of discourse, as the flesh speaks more persuasively than any voice," and so this death makes a particular argument about sacrifice and the sacred, oppression and the state. For his Irish Republican audience, Sands's "eloquent piece of discourse" spoke loudly, and his argument was clear in international resistance movements from Palestine to Peru. The reaction of Margaret Thatcher, she who did not believe that society was real, was predictable. Thatcher remained firm that "a crime is a crime." British newspapers were not much more nuanced; *The Daily Mirror* wrote in an editorial a month before he died that "the death of Sands would add another martyr to a history which has a surplus of them." A columnist for that paper, John Edwards, wrote that Sands's death was a "pathetic end for a man," and a cartoon from the *Daily Mirror* mocked the Christian iconography of Sands's death by claiming that he "died that others might die."

Sands's death was interpreted in variable ways depending on audience and political conviction, an ambiguous semiotics of extinction. For republican sympathizers, Sands's death verified Eagleton's claim that "martyrdom is a way of reaping sense from what is otherwise a mere fact of Nature, turning one's mortality into a kind of rhetoric." By contrast, 10 Downing Street and its media apparatus exoticized Sands's protest as barbaric sacrament, Catholic theater for the credulous. An undercurrent in editorials was that there was something unseemly in Sands's sacrifice, whose logic was more pagan than it was

TOP Contemporary Belfast mural of Bobby Sands in life, with his hopeful claim that "our revenge will be the laughter of our children" featured prominently.

political. Dismissal of Sands was of the same sort that allowed Winston Churchill to describe Mahatma Gandhi's hunger strikes as the act of a man who was a "half-naked . . . fakir of a type well known in the east." A nation that had pored over the gory stories of Protestant martyrs at Tyburn as described by John Foxe in his *Acts of Monuments* was no longer conversant in that particular tongue. Corporal mortification speaks not with an English accent. Sacrifice, it should be said, was neither logical nor fashionable to Thatcher nor to the readers of the *Daily Mirror*, but Eagleton warns that to "see the custom [of martyrdom] in orthodox Enlightenment fashion as a species of savagery" that has been "consigned by liberal modernity to the ashcan of history" is a limited, complacent understanding of its significance and efficacy.

As a protest it evoked everything from *toscad*, the ritual fasting of ancient Ireland, to the *Gorta Mór* of 1845 to 1849, when the government Sands was protesting allowed a quarter of Ireland to starve to death. Toscad was a practice which went deep into the past primeval, a pagan remnant of a ritual by which the aggrieved would demand justice by starving themselves in front of the house of those who had wronged them; the potato famine was the man-made deep hunger imposed on the Irish by the British, whose bigotry and enthusiasm for Malthusian economics led to almost a quarter of the former nation dying or emigrating. Hunger was a curse of Sands's countrymen, yet he paradoxically used that same affliction to great power, a tradition of fasting from saints like Aidan, Brigid, Patrick. Sands drew on a reservoir of history, dream, and *mythos* far more profound than an editorial designed for the proverbial man on the Clapham omnibus. Eagleton argues that we must embrace sacrifice, that we can understand it in a "positive or political light." Religion can operate on a frequency that ears congratulating themselves on their rationality are deaf to hear, with an odor and flavor far beyond what any human nose or mouth can detect.

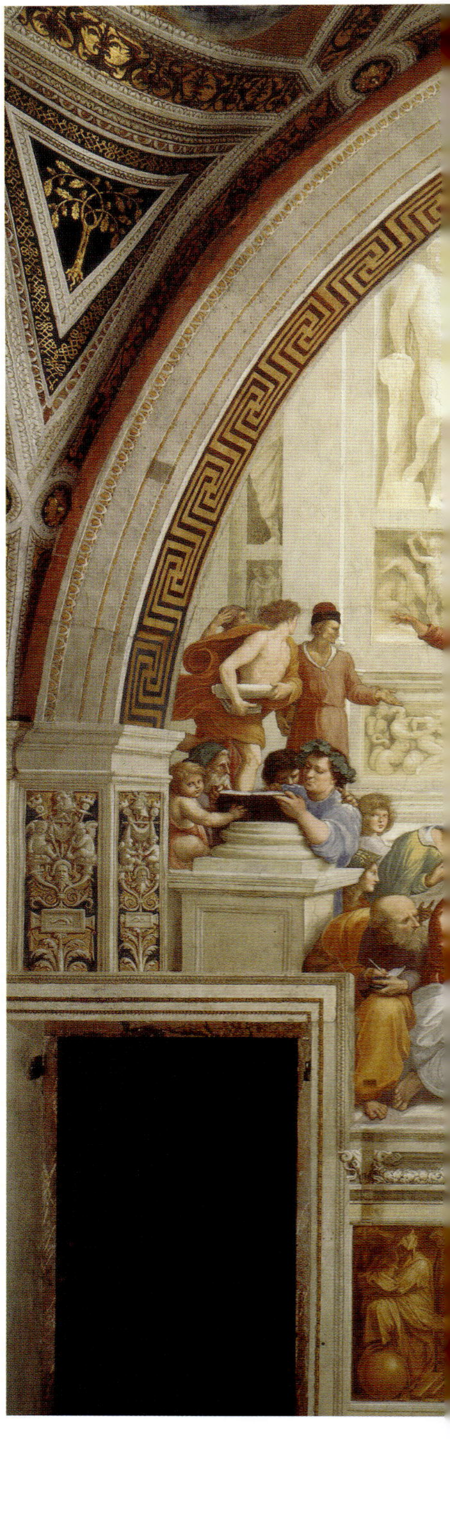

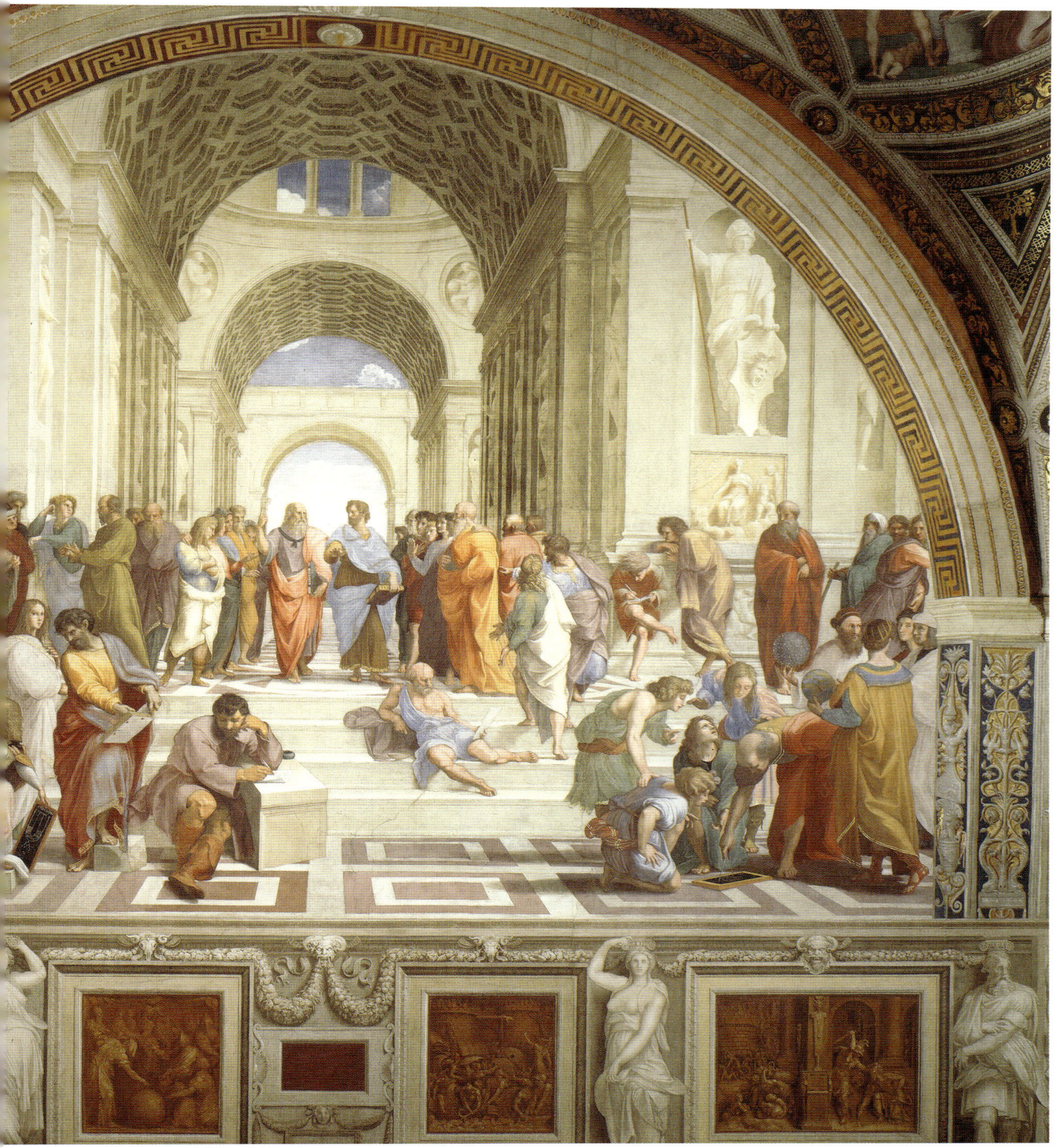

ABOVE Pythagoras does some calculations in this detail from Michelangelo's *The School of Athens*, painted between 1509 and 1511, with the fresco housed in the Apostolic Palace of the Vatican.

PURE BODY, PURE MIND, PURE SPIRIT—PRAXIS

Pythagoras's martyrdom by the edge of a Calabrian bean field which he refused to cross is so antique that it is now impossible to separate his biography from myth. Simultaneous father of rationality and mysticism, Pythagoras had convened a gathering of acolytes in the Greek colonies which lined the toe and heel of Italy's boot, teaching that behind the chaos and drum of our material existence there was a reality defined entirely by mathematics, by the gods of infinite number. He was an oracle as much as a scientist. "Reason is immortal," Pythagoras supposedly said; "all else is mortal." From this hermetic metaphysic—which made a faith from logic—would result any number of tangible and useful innovations, most famously his celebrated theorem, from whose abstraction came the ability for architects to draft buildings, engineers to construct them, carpenters to make their furniture. Two generations before Plato would systematize much of Pythagoras's original thought into academic philosophy, this first man to actually call himself a philosopher, that is, a "lover of wisdom," had envisioned a harmony and perfection beyond this world, a bolstering and fortifying reality that was as distant from us as our waking life is from dreams. Pythagoras followers lived communally and simply, devoting their hours to the parsing of mathematics, the movement of the heavenly spheres, the congruency between cosmology and music. Central to Pythagoras's ethics was a spartan, austere life, including prohibitions on eating meat. As for many religious traditions, the Pythagoreans made a connection between the mind and matter at the nexus of the mouth, whereby what we ingest can affect our disposition, can affect our very spirit. "Sobriety is the strength of the soul, for it preserves its reason unclouded by passion," taught Pythagoras. Yet most infamously, and perhaps confusingly for their largely vegetarian diet, the Pythagoreans are remembered for a very particular dietary restriction—"Abstain from beans," as the master wrote in *The Symbol*. It was this distaste for legumes that directly led to Pythagoras's death.

For if his later biographers Iamblichus and Diogenes Laertius are to be trusted—and much about Pythagoras, including his historical existence, veers between fact and allegory—the philosopher had escaped from a nighttime attack on his house by political enemies, running into the Italian wild. Pursued by his assassins through olive and grape fields, silhouetted in the Calabrian moonlight as he ran past fragrant scented groves of orange and lemon, the only sound his rapid breathing, the hum of crickets, and the hitting of branches off of his body, Pythagoras finally reached the perimeter of a farm for fava beans. True to his own teachings, the master stopped, for he could not cross the field. He waited patiently for his adversaries to arrive, which they did, ultimately thrashing Pythagoras to death, his blood mingling into the brown soil from whence the despised beans were harvested. Dietary restriction unto death. It's a strange story, the tale of the man who prized rationality above all else choosing to die for what seems to us a supremely ridiculous matter of principle. Why exactly the sect

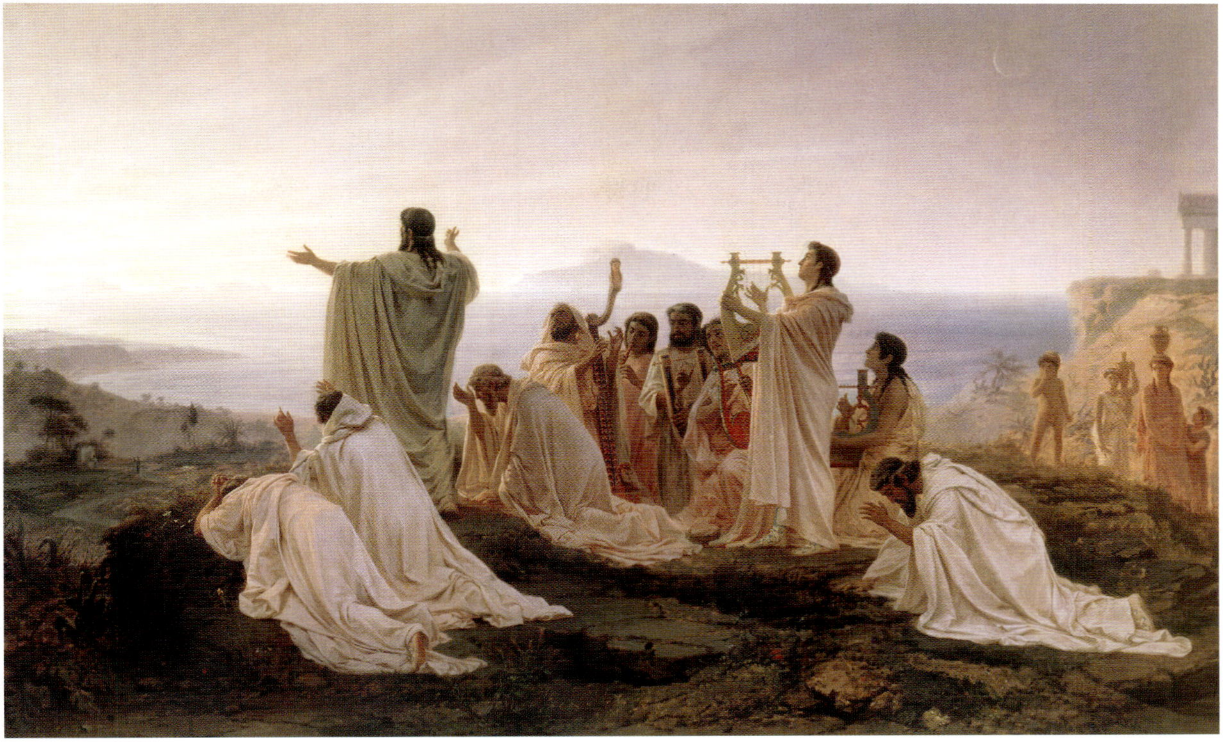

were so resistant to the eating of beans is a matter of some debate. Supposedly Pythagoras, a committed believer in metempsychosis, whereby the souls of the departed would reincarnate as various beings both animal and vegetable, held that beans were particularly susceptible to such a process, so that a serving of falafel could actually be your recently deceased grandmother. Waggishly it could be conjectured that Pythagoras thought the flatulent results of said beans were unbecoming of a school devoted to parsing the secrets of existence, though in *The Symbols* he does claim that the "wind is blowing, adore the wind." Historians of a scientific bent have surmised that the prohibition had something to do with Glucose-6-phosphate dehydrogenase deficiency, that is, an allergy to fava beans which remains common among Greeks, Italians, and Sephardic Jews. Regardless of the exact *why* of the Pythagorean dietary restriction, there is the simple fact that it was apparently so important that the guru was willing to die so as to not violate it. As bizarre as the reasoning of the father of philosopher might be to a jaded modern, the venerable connection between what we eat and who we are is well-expressed in the story of his death. Religion, so often mischaracterized as only concerning belief, is also very much about what we eat.

Temperance has about it the connotation of abstention from drinking, but as a virtue it's more all-encompassing than just whether or not one indulges in alcohol. As the opposite of gluttony, temperance arguably includes practices as varied as fasting and dieting, dietary restrictions and vegetarianism. These are all different sorts of activities, obviously; the food addict and the alcoholic, after all, differ in the important regard that the latter can completely abstain from the substance that is destroying his life, whereas for the former, to do so would

TOP Russian genre painter Fyodor Bronnikov imagines a gathering of the master's disciples charting the relationship between the lyre's melody and that of the cosmos in this 1869 composition *Pythagoreans' Hymn to the Rising Sun*, original at the Tretyakov Gallery in Moscow.

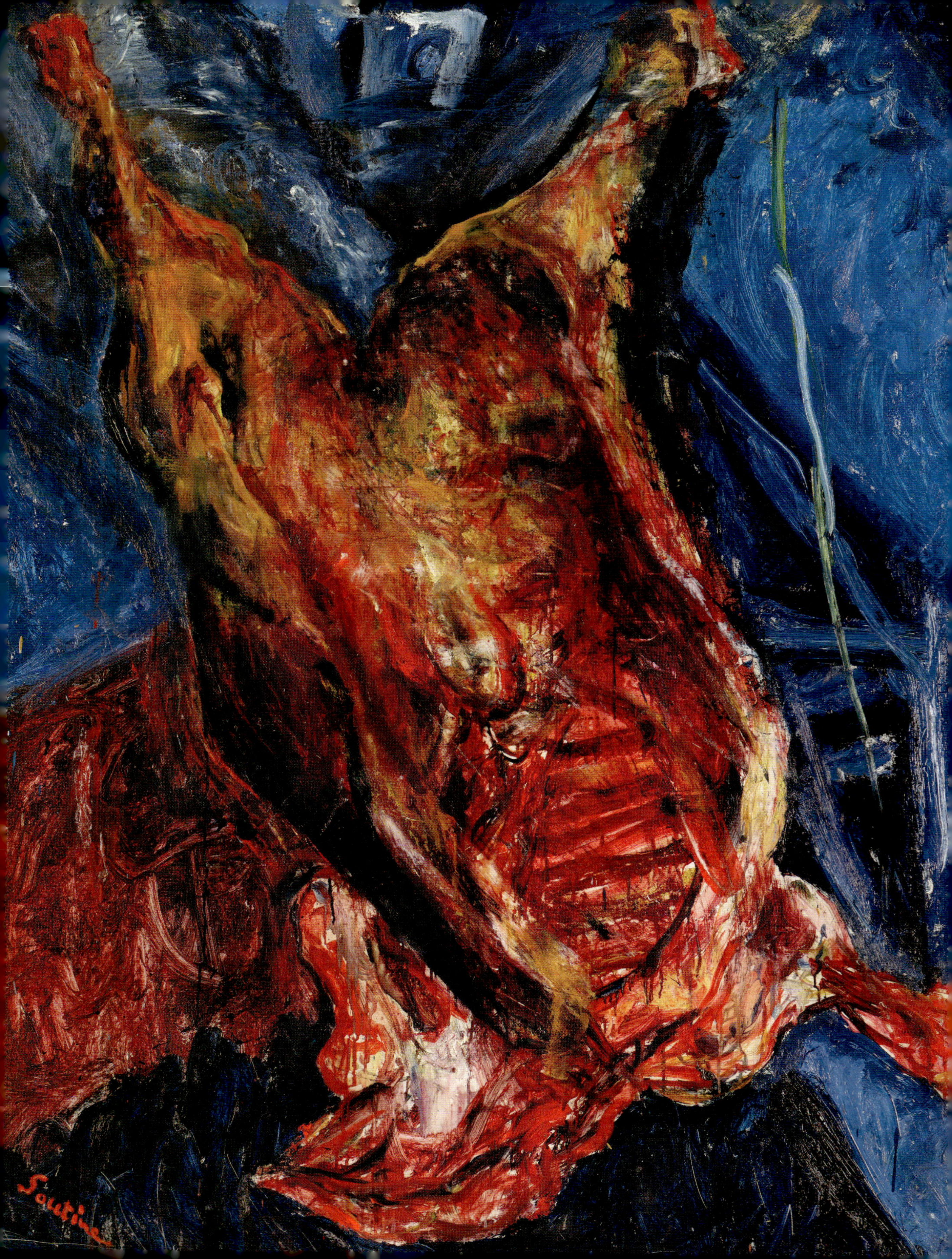
Soutine

result in death (and swiftly). What all of these things share—from teetotaling to veganism—is a sense that the regulation of what goes into your body is crucial to your psychology and to the greater world. That nothing is incidental, whether wine or meat, that a conscientious attitude toward the physical reality of your body is directly related to the nature of your mind. Alcohol, because of how physiologically powerful it is, has naturally often been at the core of what temperance means, even as religions themselves have had a varied relationship to spirits (which are, after all, called that for a reason). The mind-altering nature of alcohol has often given it a central sacramental place within faith, from the Dionysian rites to the Catholic Eucharist, though most Abrahamic religions have counseled for its regulation, from the Talmudic injunctions for moderation in Judaism to the Koranic complete prohibition on drinking in Islam. A Jew or a Muslim avoiding treyf and that which is haram, a Hindu or a follower of Jainism abstaining from meat, a Pythagoras avoiding beans—this too is temperance. When religion is defined only through *orthodoxy*, that is, "proper belief," we ignore the importance of *orthopraxy*, that is "proper practice." Faith is constructed by an edifice of rules, which from one contemporary perspective can be understood as draconian or stultifying, but which is perhaps more properly conceived of as a means of conditioning the body and mind, a type of rigorous practice more akin to spiritual training than it is to killjoy prudery. The religious Jew or Muslim doesn't believe that a slice of bacon will condemn the transgressor to hell—dietary restrictions have nothing to do with anything so simplistic. Rather, the purpose of systems like Kosher and Halal law is to separate the believer from the outside world, to create a temple of the faithful within the wider culture; to bind oneself to an ancient and mysterious system of practice which connects the adherent to a community and to history. Such temperance is about defining a state of purity, and the rigor to try and maintain it. More than a system of arbitrary rules, it's better to think of this variety of temperance as akin to a spiritual exercise, to meditation, even to prayer.

Throughout the Abrahamic traditions, it's *kashrut* or Kosher law within Judaism that is the most iconic of religious dietary regulation. According to tradition, the prohibitions on certain foods and requirements for others was imparted by God to Moses at Mt. Sinai along with the rest of the 613 laws which constitute *mitzvoth*. The bulk of kosher law is given within the biblical book of Leviticus, the middle portion of the Torah, but it's in the massive compendium of oral law composed millennia later, which is known as the Talmud, where the full intricacy of kashrut (including potential loopholes) would be exegetically parsed by the rabbis. The Torah is clear on certain prohibitions—no carnivorous birds or insects, anything from a land animal must chew its cud and have a cloven hoof (cows, yes; pigs, no), anything from the water must have scales (sturgeon and salmon are good; mussels and catfish are bad). Leviticus rather specifically states that a kid must not be cooked in its own mother's milk; beyond the literalism of that injunction, the compilers of the Talmud rather sweepingly interpreted that commandment to mean that meat and milk should not be comingled in the same meal, with a rather intricate system regulating everything from the storage and cooking of those ingredients, to the period of time somebody must wait so that eating one after the other doesn't constitute a violation of that rule. Furthermore, there are regulations on not just the variety of food, but how it's

OPPOSITE French Jewish modernist painter Chaim Soutine's still life *Carcass of Beef*, painted in 1925 with the original at the Albright-Knox Art Gallery in Buffalo, New York, evokes the strictures of handling meat in kosher law, where even an animal deigned as pure, such as the cow, must be treated in a particular way to ensure it matches the specifications of ritual law.

actually prepared, including the manner in which an animal is slaughtered (to minimize pain) and how it should be prepared (to eliminate blood). As much as outsiders tend to react with studied bafflement at kosher law, and even while the Talmud can get quite baroque in the details, the overall system is relatively easy to understand based on the handful of rules given above, even while acknowledging certain other rules, such as the prohibition on leavening during Passover. Almost any potential food you can imagine can be rather quickly evaluated in terms of whether or not it's treyf. Eagles are carnivores, so not kosher; chickens are not, so they are; blue whales, lacking in scales, so not kosher; camels chew their cud—that is, they have a double stomach—but they've got no cloven hooves, so you can't get them in a kosher restaurant; lambs both have a double stomach and cloven hooves, so you can (but not at Passover, long story).

Because two millennia of Christian anti-Judaism has slurred that faith as being a paragon of legalistic, stiff-necked obstinacy, there is often within the wider culture a mocking tone that is detectable as concerns all of these rules, even more so for all of the midrashic interpretations of extensions and exceptions. Even while Catholicism may have historically prohibited meat on Lenten Fridays, and many branches of low church Protestantism forbid alcohol, the maximalist perspective of kashrut, and to a lesser extent halal law, can seem foreboding to the point of absurdity. In defense of such practice, only a boring hobgoblin thinks that the purpose of religion is anything as mundane as mere belief, as simple affirmation of a creed. What practices and rituals do is to solidify membership in a community which approaches the divine collectively. Since few things are as personal and intimate as what we eat, adherence to kosher law is a way to focus the mind toward God during even the most prosaic of situations—it makes it not just possible, but necessary, to contemplate the divine while making gefilte fish or preparing brisket. "Many explanations have been offered for those laws," writes Melvin Konner in *Unsettled: An Anthropology of the Jews*: "hygiene, familiarity, separation from neighboring peoples, totemic identification, and the animals' habits, among others." There is an obvious ethical component to kosher law, a nascent sense of animal rights whereby it is forbidden to cause needless suffering in the slaughter of an animal, so that even gentiles are bound by the Noahide Covenant to not eat from a still-living creature. Then there are the clear health benefits, for avoiding poorly cooked pork in the desert is an ideal way to avoid trichinosis, as surely as not cooking dairy and meat together can prevent the spread of listeria, or the obvious gastrointestinal reasons in eschewing bottom-feeding mollusks and crustaceans. But even while rationalist theologians like Maimonides justified kosher law by recourse to health, the mystic-minded fifteenth-century Sephardic rabbi Abarbanel quipped that if such

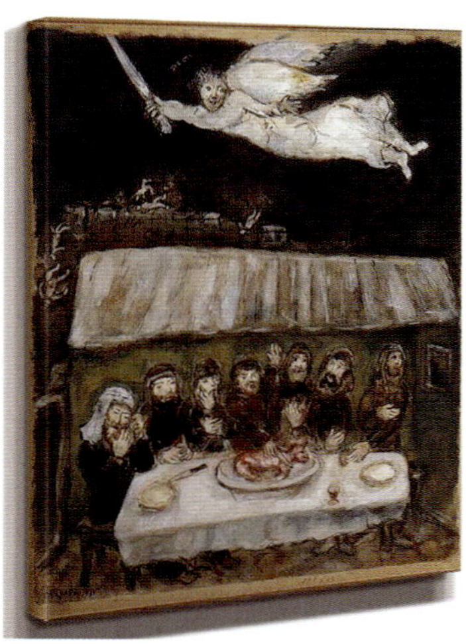

LEFT French painter Marc Chagall's 1931 watercolor *The Israelites Are Eating the Passover Lamb*, a composition with messianic overtones painted on the eve of the Holocaust.

OPPOSITE Islamic painting of 1430 made by an anonymous artisan of the Timrud Empire entitled *Wine Drinking in a Spring Garden*. Original held by the Cora Timken Burnett Collection of Persian Miniatures and Other Persian Art Objects.

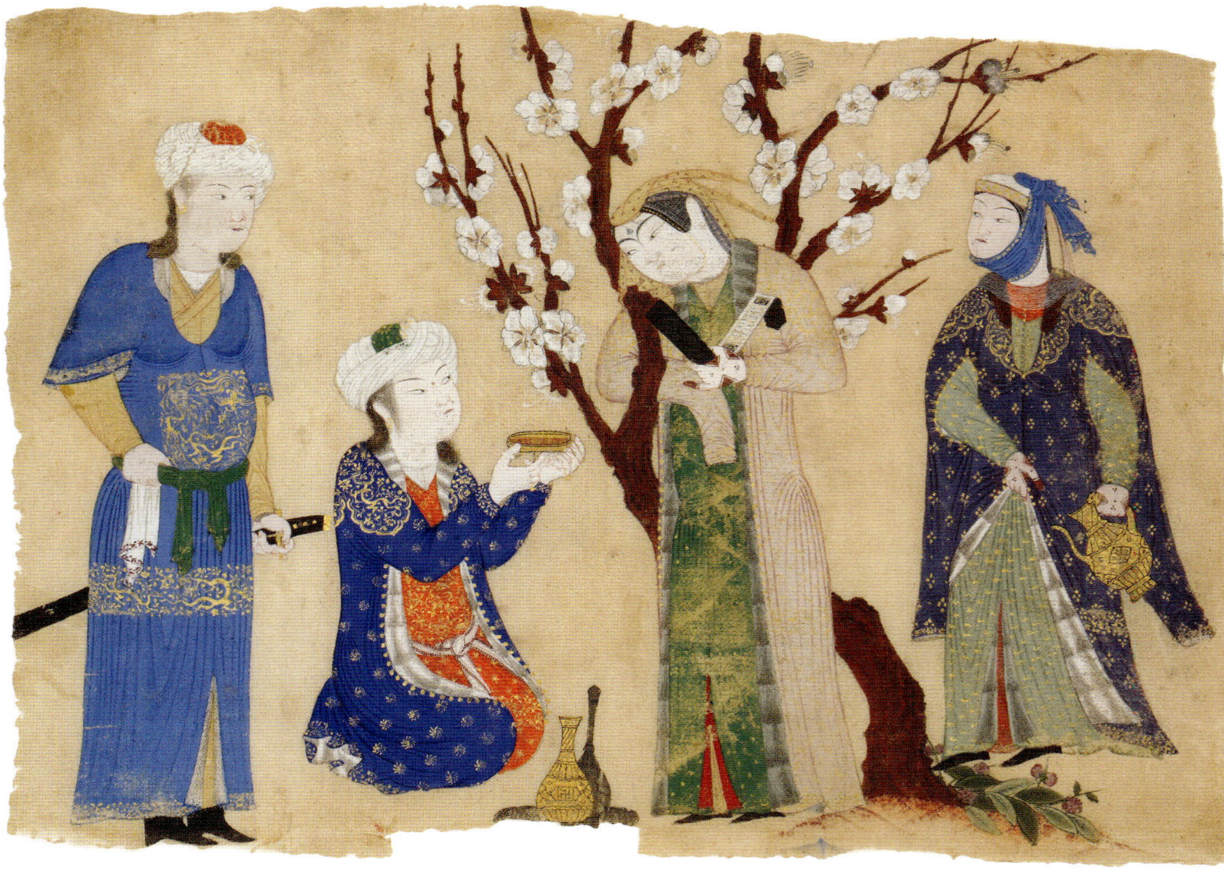

justifications "were the case then the Torah of the Lord would be no more than an insignificant and overly concise medical treatise." Ultimately, Konner concludes that the "common thread" among prohibited foods is that they "violate intactness, completeness, or wholeness," which is why they're considered impure. A dietary code which separates the pure from the impure serves to interject the profane with the sacred, for in positing certain foods as being elevated—a Pesach seder, kiddush wine, the apple and honey of Rosh Hashana—is to make that which we eat (and don't) a question not of dinner, but of the divine.

Judaism's brother faith of Islam has a similar set of dietary restrictions in the form of halal, which while in some respects is less strict, does feature a notable difference—the prohibition of alcohol. "Satan's plan is to stir up hostility and hatred between you with intoxicants," reads Qur'an 5:91. "Will you not then abstain?" Within an ancient world more than familiar with the vagaries of drunkenness, the Prophet's shunning of alcohol was radical, a command to keep a clear head so as to better approach God. By contrast, within Christianity teetotaling was nonsensical until the Reformation, for the transubstantiation of Eucharistic wine (which, it should be noted, only the priest was allowed to drink) would make a blanket condemnation of alcohol an impossibility. Even after the emergence of Protestantism, temperance most often meant moderation rather than complete abstention, for even Martin Luther was a fan of (copious) drafts of German beer and the Calvinist Pilgrims disembarked in Massachusetts in

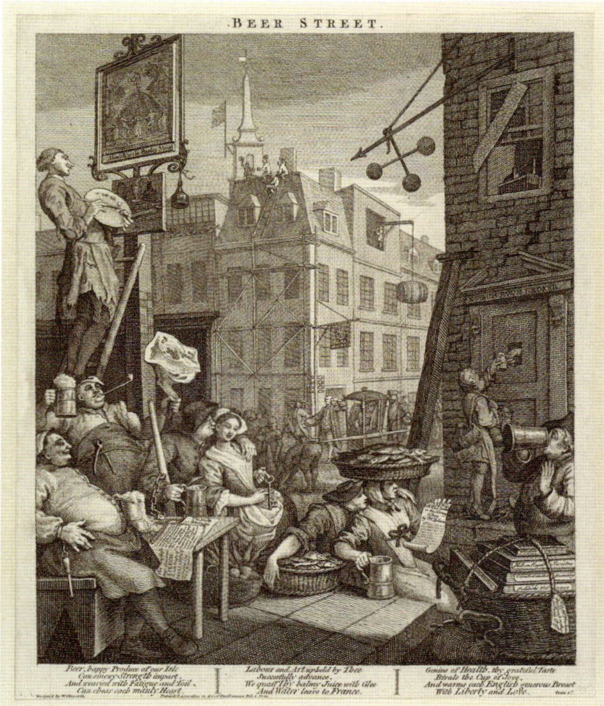

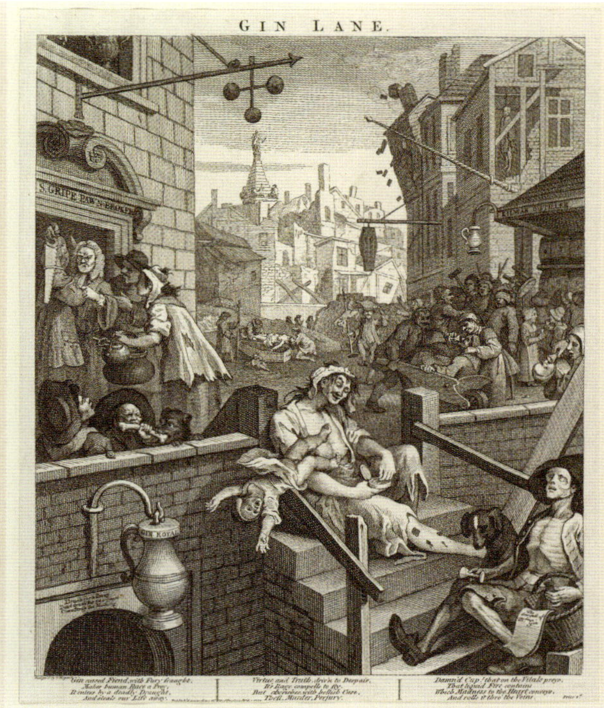

part to brew more ale. A material circumstance was partially the reason for a new fervency against alcohol, as during the seventeenth and eighteenth centuries Europeans were introduced to ever more potent liquors in what's arguably the Western world's first major drug crisis. The population having long been familiar with relatively weak beer and wine, the sudden widespread proliferation of Dutch gin, Scotch whisky, and Caribbean rum lent itself to lurid tales of the impoverished passed out in the streets or prostituting themselves just for another dram. Whether or not this reflected reality, moral hysteria, or some combination is debatable, but that liquor came to be seen as not just a drink but as a drug, at least for a period, is unassailable. Gin, whiskey, and rum would come to be replaced within the public imagination with even more powerful ways of altering your consciousness in the form of opium, cocaine, and heroin, but that alcohol is a drug can't be doubted. If invented today, the physiological affects alone would be enough to have alcohol classified in the United States as a Class 1 narcotic. It has been preserved from such a fate only because of its cultural omnipresence and relatively low addiction rates (though whether civilization would have even begun or not without the fermentation of wheat, barley, grapes, and corn is another question).

By the nineteenth century, when reform movements like the Washingtonians were spreading their own variation on religious awakening, dietary restrictions such as kashrut and halal were evocative for Americans who began to believe that clean living could inculcate a pure mind and even purer spirit. Temperance was only the most obvious of these manifestations, but some evangelical groups embraced codes not dissimilar to kosher law. The Protestant denomination of Seventh-Day Adventists, for example, specifically

ABOVE William Hogarth's 1751 print *Beer Street and Gin Lane* was agitprop done on behalf of the brewers' guild then advocating for legislation to regulate heavy liquor (and their nearest competition). Gin Lane features drunken, disorderly, malnourished, immoral women and men whose faculties have been destroyed by hard spirits, while Beer Street is full of industrious, patriotic, diligent, and (sort of) sober subjects.

OPPOSITE Self-trained radical Quaker Edward Hicks continually returned to one of his favorite themes, illustrating the biblical passage about the lion lying down with the lamb, as in his 1837 composition *Peaceable Kingdom*, with its depiction of a future millennium. With a variety of carnivorous beasts including a lion, a bear, and a leopard mingling together peacefully with beasts who would normally be their prey, Hicks places the treaty between his coreligionists William Penn and the Indians of the Pennsylvania Colony in the background. Such a paradisical dream logically entailed not just pacifism, but vegetarianism as a form of pacificism, for man and beast alike. Original held by the Carnegie Museum of Art in Pittsburgh.

emphasizes the keeping of kosher law, as well as encouraging vegetarianism. For an American culture obsessed with beef and pork, chicken and turkey, not to mention eggs and cheese, the rejection of meat for lettuce and lentils, cabbage and cauliflower, was jarring, still viewed askance by many even as it's become more common and acceptable. America's great prophet of vegetarianism was Sylvester Graham, a nineteenth-century, Connecticut-born Presbyterian minister who was convinced that both meat and the over-processing of food were making people either into sluggish dullards or into excitable and dangerous hysterics, so that he advocated the replacement of sausage-and-chop heavy meals with an ascetic and tasteless herbivore's diet. Famed for his invention of his eponymous flour, composed of coarse-grained whole wheat and the primary ingredient in the cracker which bears Graham's name, the minister maintained that any honest accounting of the various diets of different nationalities would lead one to conclude that those predisposed to vegetarianism are "much better formed races than the flesh-eaters," as he claimed in his *Lectures on the Science of Human Life*.

Moving perilously close to the stereotype of the noble savage, or a kind of reverse eugenics, Graham maintained that "It is only among those tribes whose

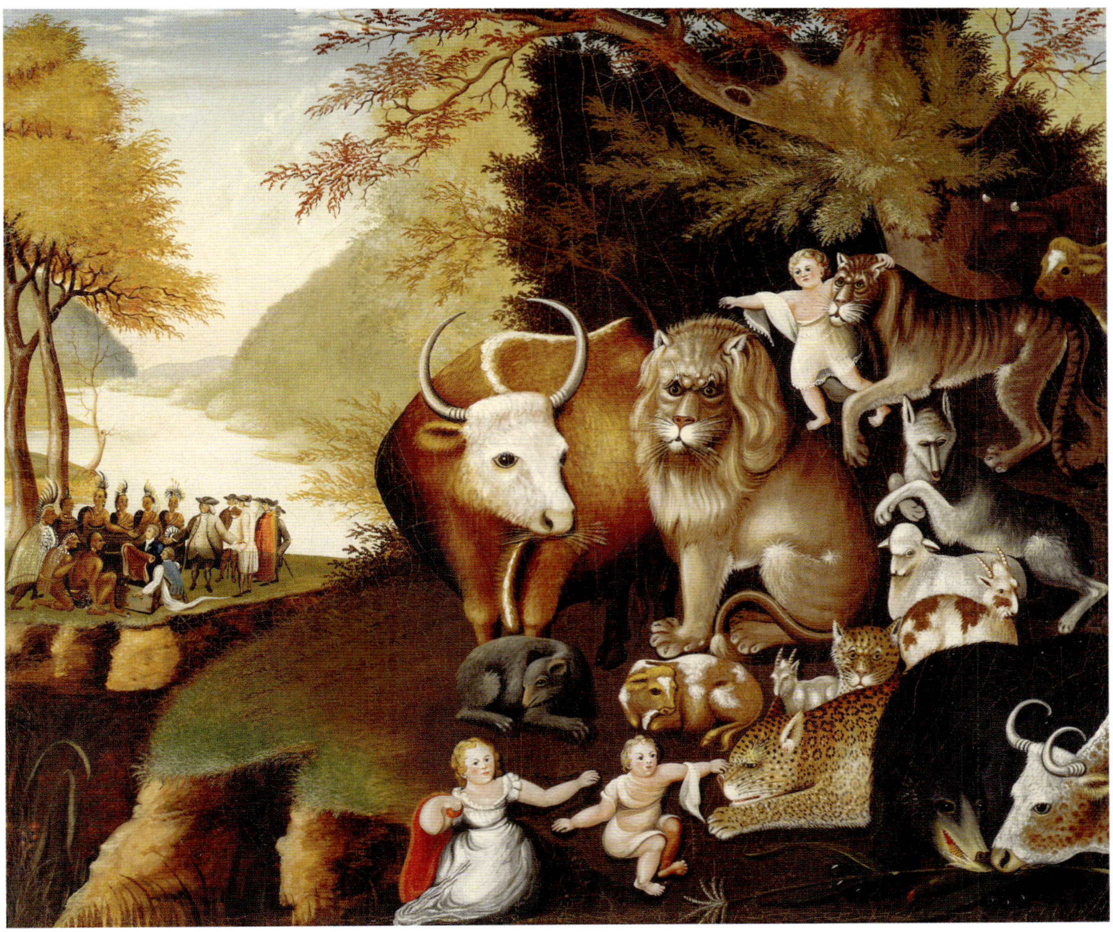

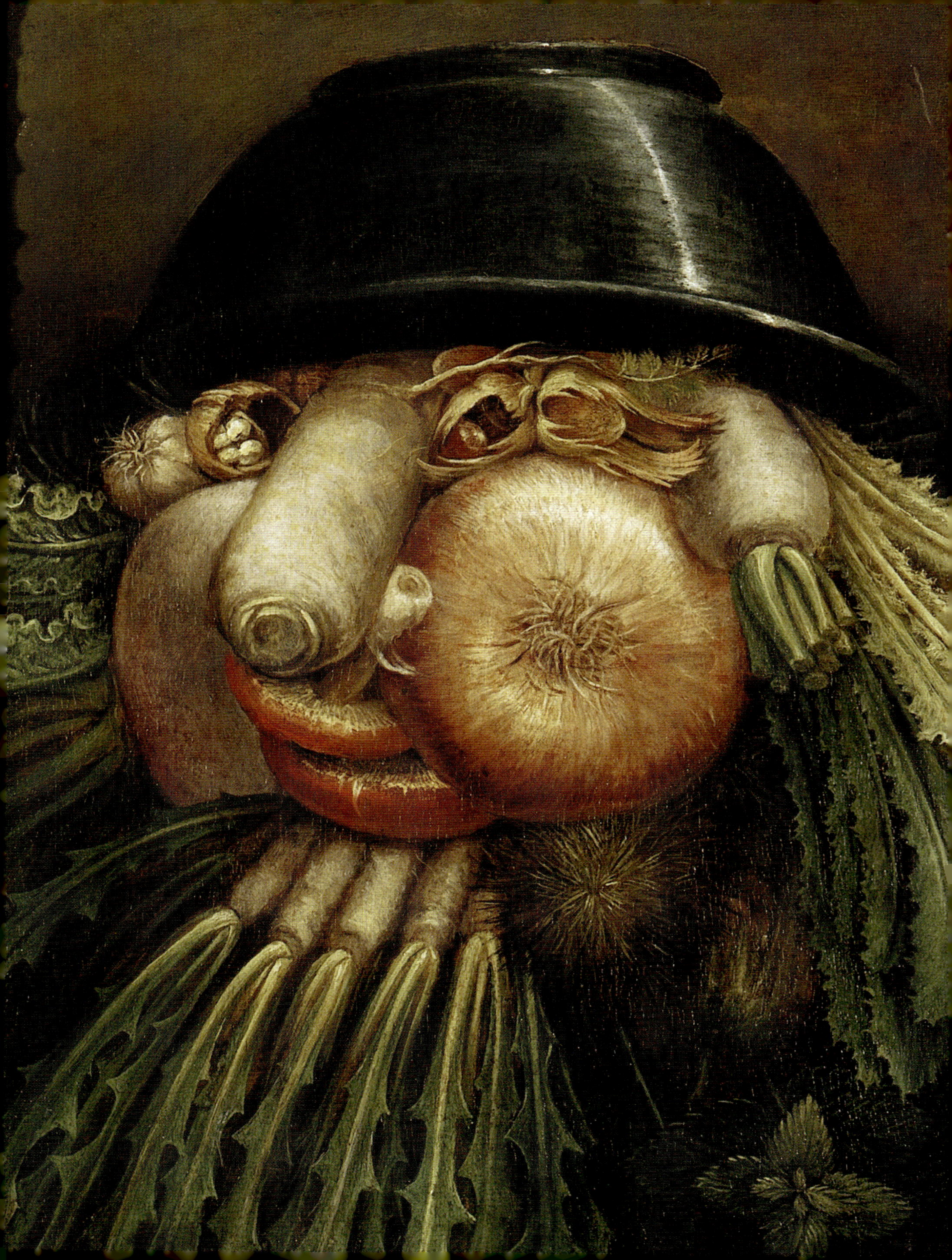

habits are temperate, and who subsist on the non-flesh diet, that the more perfect specimens of symmetry are found." Graham's doctrine of vegetarianism was carried further than it might be expected, bolstered by the desire for clean living inculcated by evangelical religious revival, as well as the Orientalist obsessions of bohemians like the Transcendentalists. All of those bowls of stewed spinach and boiled peas appealed to another enthusiast who believed that man's onanistic energies could be tempered by such fare, and who also gave his name to a beloved American grocery product: John Harvey Kellogg. "The body calls for bread, for life-giving food," wrote Kellogg in his 1903 *The Living Temple*, "but how often we supply, instead, such indigestible, unwholesome rubbish as pickles, green olives, fried foods, and various abominable mixtures which bring into the body death rather than life." A Seventh-Day Adventist who would leave the sect over disagreements about the nature of the Trinity, as well as an acolyte of Graham, the inventor of cornflakes was a physician who directed Michigan's Battle Creek Sanitorium, where he emphasized purity through a very particular vegetarianism, vigorous exercise, and enemas. Kellogg's own medical advice was a combination of common sense (vegetables impart nutrients) and quackery (so do daily enemas), and he was arguably an early prominent example of a particular American type, the expert who decries other experts, the advocate for one-easy-solution, the quixotic prophet who knows all answers and will supply them for just several small payments. Existing at the nexus of doctrinaire evangelicalism and New Age sophistry—a surprisingly thick middle to that Venn Diagram—Kellogg was a keen student of Graham's, as well as the father of the fad diet. As different as they are, fad diets from Atkins to Paleo, Keto to Veganism, South Beach to Nutrisystem, at least all share with Kellogg the faith that the fixing of a disordered life is as simple as fixing a meal, salvation acquired simply by pouring cold, low-fat milk over a bowl of brittle cornflakes.

Not that Graham and Kellogg deserve only snark, far from it. Their claims that a diet heavy in fruits and vegetables is healthier than the boiled meat which crowded American tables is unassailable; the vegetarian axiom that

OPPOSITE AND FOLLOWING SPREAD As court painter to the hermetic-minded Holy Roman Emperor Rudolf II in Prague, the Italian Giuseppe Arcimboldo brought a surreal touch to his Renaissance portraiture, which in its humor evokes the avant-garde of the twentieth century. *Vertumnus*, on the left and painted in 1591, with the original held at the Skokloster Castle in Sweden, is a portrait of Arcimboldo's patron as composed of a cornucopia of produce, some of it from the New World. *The Vegetable Gardener*, on the right and painted sometime between 1587 and 1590 and now displayed at the Museo Civico Ala Ponzone in Cremona, is here shown upside down, showing the face of he who harvested this display. Reflecting Renaissance medical theory, such pictures explicate the vigorous health benefits of the diet represented.

abstention from flesh preserves the life of a sentient being is obvious, regardless of how tasty said animals might be. Adam Shprintzen in *The Vegetarian Crusade: The Rise of an American Reform Movement, 1871–1921* notes that for nineteenth-century progressives, "vegetarianism was visualized as a catalyst for total social reform, including the emancipation of slaves, the extension of suffrage to women, and the end of oppressive economics." For the most radical of vegetarians, abstaining from meat wasn't just an issue of diet, but one of morality. The raising of chickens and cows, sheep and pigs (the last smarter than the average dog), all to be slaughtered and eaten, was a moral stain. A people predisposed to devouring creatures with feelings and thoughts will think little of oppressing their fellow humans as well. These vegetarians borrowed much from the loosely appropriated Vedic and Upanishadic thinking, seeing a code in millennia-old writings of Hindu and Buddhist sages which emphasized the prevalence of suffering and the means to overcome it, in part through acknowledging the sentience in all life. No faith has a more total regard for consciousness among all rungs of the ladder of life, and a revulsion toward eating animals, than the Jains. Derived from the same ancient sources which sustain Hinduism and Buddhism, the Jains hold to a belief in reincarnation that Pythagoras would have recognized, seeing all of the network of life as also being a matrix of consciousness. As a result, the pious Jain takes great care in not killing anything—*anything.* For Jain nuns and monks, beyond even strict vegetarianism, this involves using a broom to sweep their path, so as to ensure that no wayward insects are crushed due to carelessness. The most-exalted potential spiritual path for any Jain is the practice of Sallekhana, whereby at the end of one's life the ascetic slowly reduces their intake of even vegetarian food, until they eventually consume nothing. Finally, as a willing sacrifice, the body withers away, the penitent starves to death, having refused to eat and so instead having been eaten by the universe.

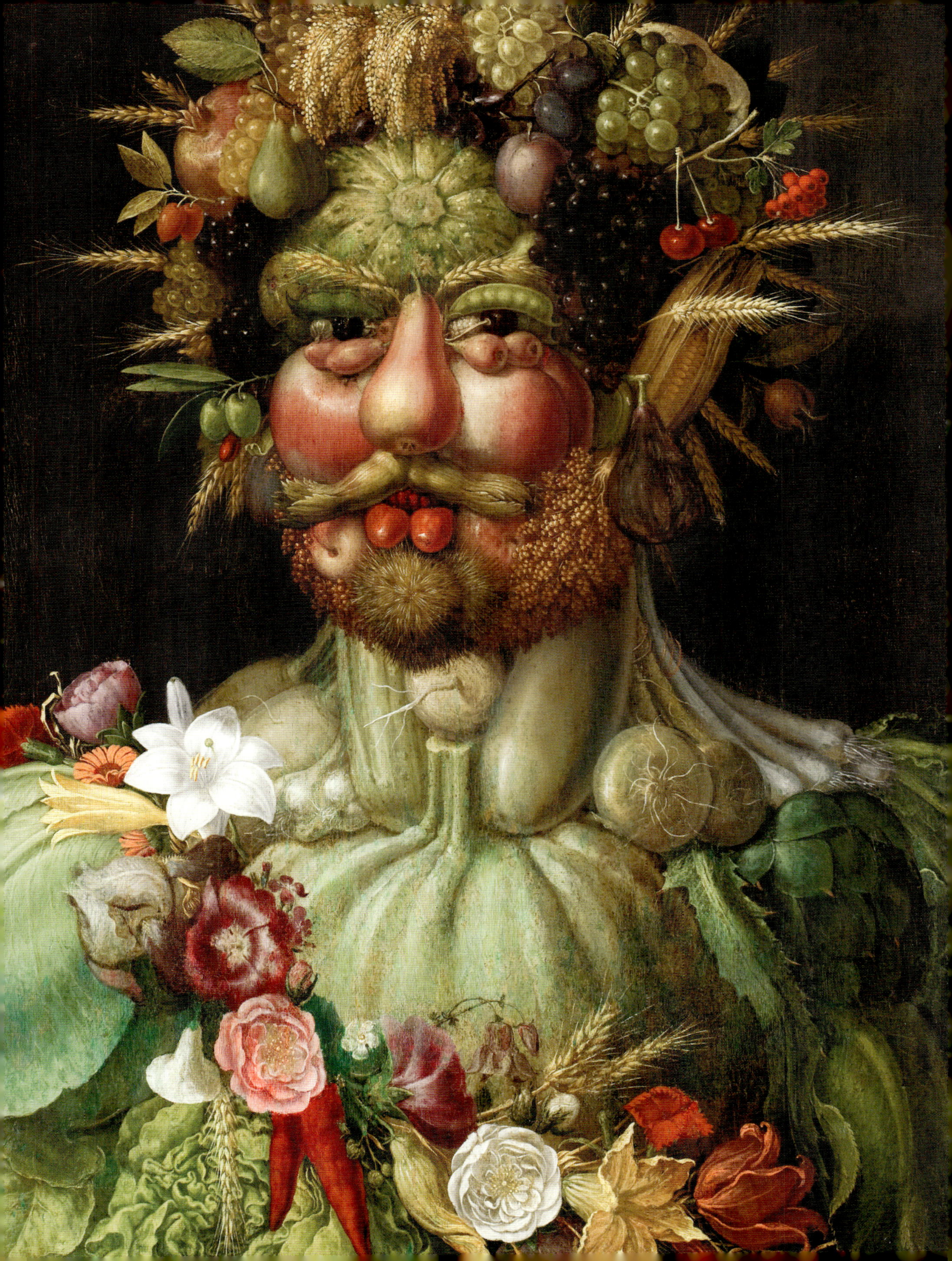

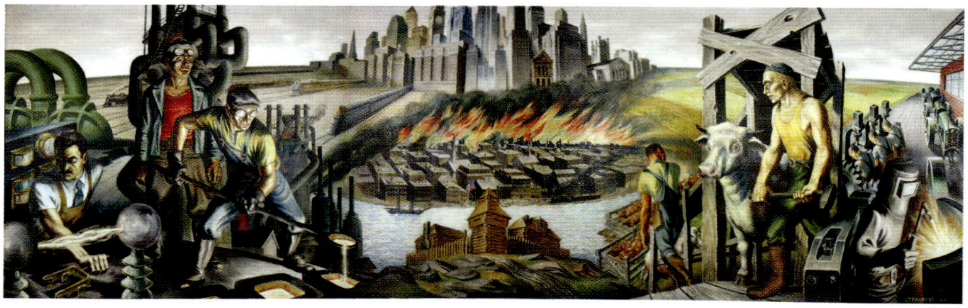

CHAPTER FOUR

THE MOTHER OF GOOD FORTUNE: DILIGENCE

"Zeal is proper for a task, time-wasting is taboo;
anyone who wastes time on his task is neglecting his task."
—Anonymous, *Advice of a Sumerian Scribe to His Student* (c. 2000 BCE)

"You load 16 tons, what do you get?
Another day older and deeper in debt
St. Peter, don't you call me 'cause I can't go
I owe my soul to the company store."
—Merle Travis, *Folk Songs of the Hills* (1947)

Diligence can't be reduced to productivity. While the mavens of both the assembly line and the cubicle may define the virtue purely in terms of hours put in on the job, diligence is not exactly the same as work ethic, studiousness, or industriousness. While related to all of those attributes, diligence is primarily an issue of *intentionality*, of *thoughtfulness*, of *presence*. The diligent person is hard-working, but this is more of a symptom than the cause; the underlying condition is focus. The diligent is compared to the slothful because the former exemplifies full immersion in the present, a commitment to singular attention paid for a task, whether building a steam engine or sweeping the floor, unclogging a toilet or painting the Sistine Chapel ceiling. For the Church Fathers and the Scholastics, diligence was obviously an attribute of piety, for it is not the lackadaisical who takes to daily prayers and sacraments, contrition and amends. "Thus, in the midst of our work can we fulfill the duty of prayer, giving thanks to him who has granted strength to our hands," wrote Saint Basil the Great in the fourth century, "for that which is in the instruments we use and that which forms the matters of the art in which we may be engaged, praying that the work of our hands may be directed toward its goal, the good pleasure of God." What a theologian like Basil understood was that good works are a form of faith; that the hands which are clasped in prayer can just as well be used to harvest grain, to prepare food, to change an infant's soiled linens. The through-line from both good works to faith is precisely diligence, for either to labor hard or to believe intently are both difficult things. As a spiritual exercise, diligence is estimably crucial, a means of fortifying the soul, of conditioning the mind. But there is also an empty form of diligence which upholds labor not as a mere medium of work, but as the purpose in and of itself. Such is soulless, empty labor—of alienated work—where the connection between a task's meaning and those involved therein is severed in favor of rote, profit-driven, valueless business.

PREVIOUS SPREAD Sharing a visual idiom with the proletariat-focused artwork of then popular socialist realism as practiced in the Soviet Union, the murals supported by the federal Works Progress Administration established as part of President Franklin Roosevelt's New Deal extolled the dignity of working-class labor in the midst of the Great Depression. Harry Sternberg's 1937 mural *Chicago: Epoch of a Great City* features a notably interracial trio of workers, including an electrician with a Tesla sphere and a molten iron puddler, framed by the machinery of steel mills and in the distance the rising towers of the metropolis itself, a locomotive dividing the historical city (and its famous conflagration) from the new downtown rising toward a prosperous and equitable future. As fundamentally a reformist capitalist project, the New Deal's politics emphasized workers' rights and its aesthetics had a proletariat sensibility, though WPA-funded art was always more than simple agitprop, offering nuanced and complicated takes on the ambiguities of American life.

OPPOSITE American painter Edward Hopper's 1940 composition *Office at Night*, original held by the Walker Art Center in Minneapolis, conveys a multitude about diligence in its very title.

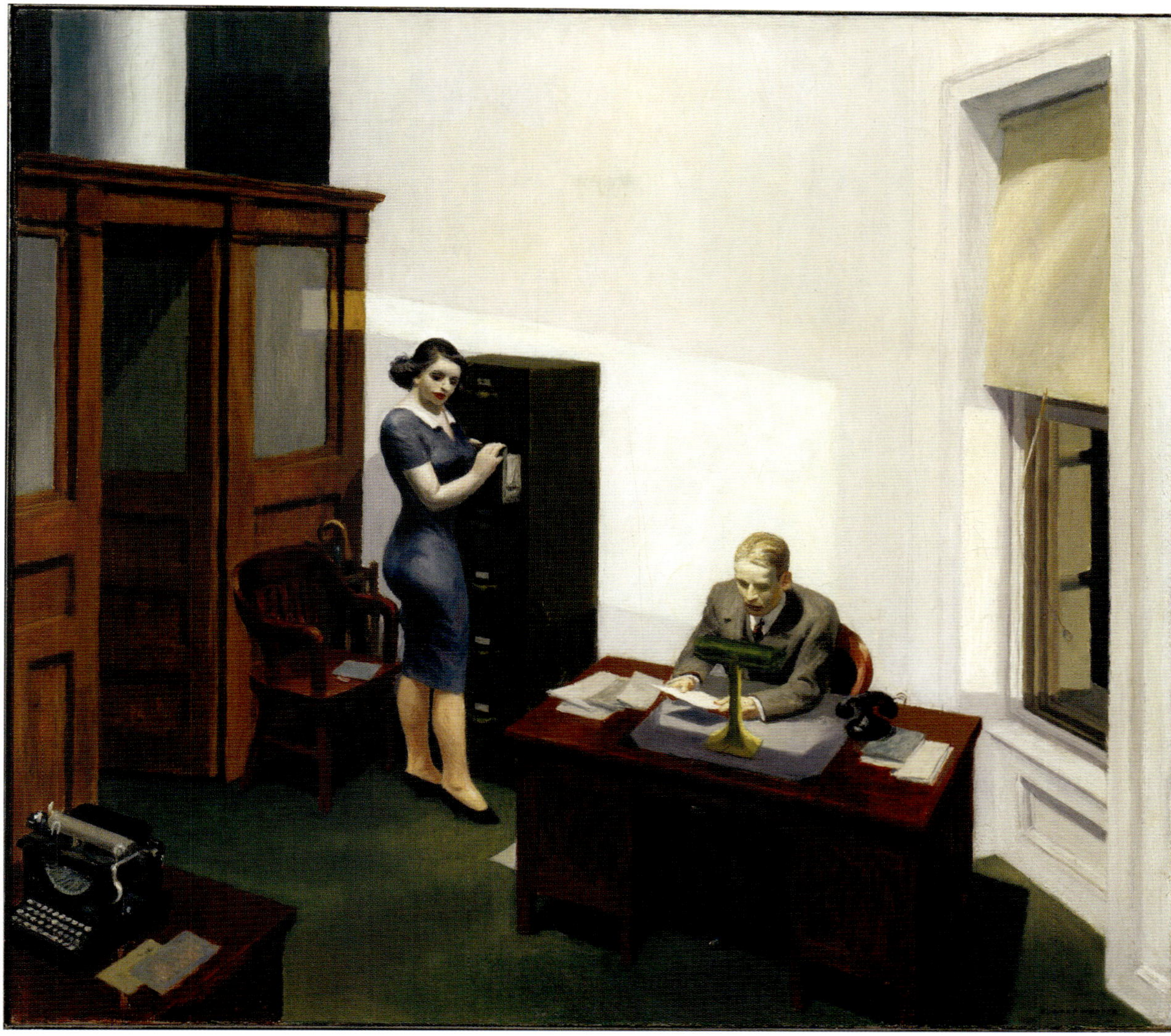

THE IRON CAGE—THEORY

As Franz Kafka awoke one morning from uneasy dreams he found himself transformed into something that might as well have been a loathsome insect, which is to say that as always, he had to shower, drink his coffee, and then scurry across Prague to his stultifying job at the Assicurazioni Generali insurance company. Kafka despised the ten daily hours from Monday through Friday that he spent at his wooden desk, and he only made it a year at the firm until he quit, moving to the slightly more flexible environs of Workers Accident Insurance Company, where he was tasked with evaluating how much compensation workers were owed if they gouged an eye out with a factory lathe or sliced a finger off with a wayward rotary saw. Policies on how much a hand was worth, a foot, a life; Kafka dutifully filled out and filed annual reports on these revenues for the faceless managers upstairs. Look at Kafka in his wheeled captain's chair and his secretary's desk with its individual wooden compartments for filing bills and invoices, the angular, gaunt, yet handsome little man with his swept-back black hair furiously calculating risk and diligently tabulating reward, an insurer involved in the mind-numbing boredom of a soul-denying task. Among the greatest writers of the twentieth century, Kafka examined in *The Trial* the faceless absurdity of modern bureaucracy because he was familiar with the indignities of an office job; *The Metamorphosis* stared with unblinking ferocity at the irrationality which defined our existential condition, because its author knew what it meant to be attached to a desk from nine to five every day of the week. If the dream of the early labor movement was eight hours for work, eight for sleep, and eight for "What thou wilt," then a third of the great author's life was dedicated to filling out requisitioning forms and status reports, the vast bulk of words composed by Kafka dedicated not to literature, but to loathsome commerce. "What a fate: to be condemned to work for a firm where the slightest negligence at once gave rise to the gravest suspicion," wrote Kafka in *The Metamorphosis*, for it's worth remembering that despite the protagonist Gregor Samsa's having been transformed overnight into a massive, quivering cockroach with mucus oozing from his mandibles, this creature's manager was still annoyed that he wouldn't be able to make it into work that morning.

Diligence is a conflicting virtue, for it necessarily raises the question of whom our diligence benefits. As with all of the virtues, what diligence connotated was different before secularism. For the Church Fathers and the Scholastics, a good work ethic was less important for the material benefits which it might accrue than it was for the ways in which work served to glorify God. According to this worldview, the monk and the nun in their cloister were as diligent as any worker, the notches upon their punch-card the assigned times for prayer throughout the day, from matins to compline. An understanding of such diligence shares a sense of *physicality*; as the serf hoists bales of hay into a loft or drives their hoe into the hard earth, so a cleric is on bended knee fingering rosary or supplicating himself before the altar. "We want each of you to show this same diligence to the

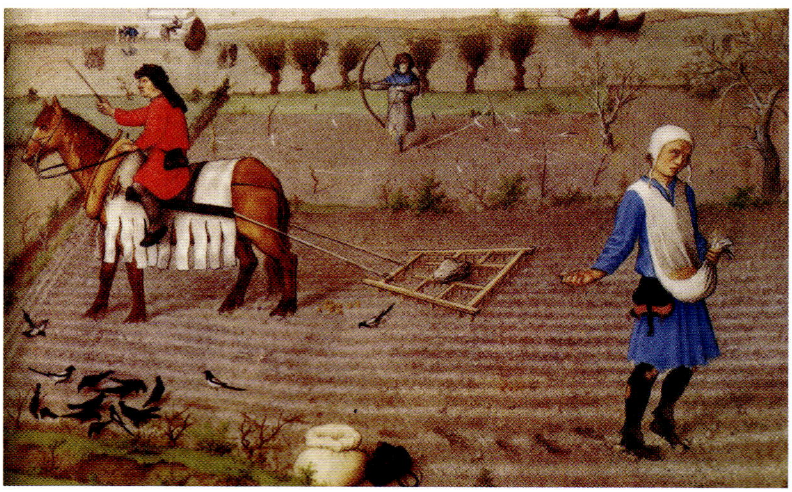

LEFT The medieval calendar was defined by the rhythms of not just liturgy, but also agriculture. From day to day, peasants had a variable schedule, marked not by consistency in the manner of contemporary workers, but by the needs of planting and harvesting. Illustration is from the 1412 manuscript *The Very Rich Hours of the Duke of Berry*, lushly rendered for their patron by the Gothic master illustrators the Limbourg Brothers. Original held by the Condé Museum at the Château de Chantilly.

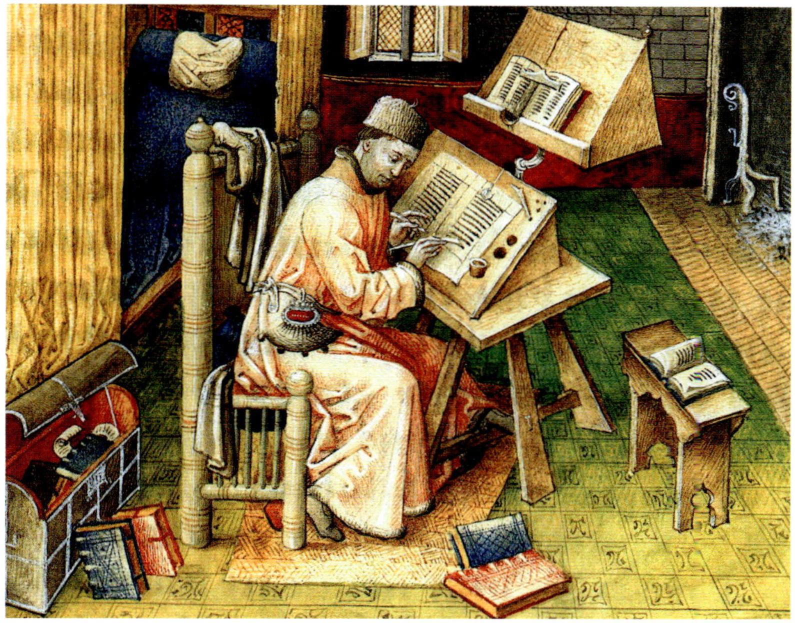

very end," reads Paul in his epistle to the Hebrews, "in order to make your hope sure. We do not want you to become lazy, but imitate those who through faith and patience inherit what has been promised."

Less than a means unto an end, work was understood as a harmonious, balanced, and ordered reflection of that transcendent realm where every being plays its role as surely as fishermen fish and tanners tan. The medieval world didn't separate the sacred and profane; thus, the work of the simple cobbler and regular cooper could be as if a prayer unto itself, in the same way that monastic life also echoed the commercial, with all of those monks brewing beer and making cheese in between their prayers. "May all work, O Lord," prays Aquinas, "delight me when done for Your sake." Notably there was no discussion of profession, but only of vocation; not of career, but of calling—whether one was the pope or a cheesemonger. Of course, the utility of such diligence can't be ignored. Wheat isn't cut, apples picked, and cows milked purely for poetic possibilities, for even if man can't live on bread alone, bread still must be eaten. Virtuousness is an attribute of such diligence on behalf of Christendom, the kingdom, the village, the family, and the individual, for nobody can survive without growing, harvesting, and preparing food, sewing clothes and building homes. Diligence to our neighbor is diligence to ourselves, while both are diligence to God.

Now our diligence is owed to somebody else: to the manager, to the boss, to the owner, to Mammon. Like Kafka hard at work in his dismal little office overlooking the beautiful red terra-cotta roofs of Prague, so too are we chained within paradise, forced to labor for the benefit of somebody not ourselves, or our family, or our neighbors. Obviously, such a shift is itself theological, for that more novel ideology of diligence called capitalism, in which the deity is an Invisible Hand and our prayers to that being are referred to as *profit*, didn't emerge sui generis. Economist R. H. Tawney in his 1926 classic *Religion and Capitalism* argued how Reformation Protestantism, and in particular its most austere formulations in

TOP An anonymous miniaturist of the fifteenth century honors an exemplar of his field in this illustration of the great scribe Jean Mielot, secretary to Philip the Good, Duke of Burgundy from 1449 until 1467. An apt depiction of the eye-straining, wrist-cramping, back-twinging work of the manuscript copyist and illustrator, hunched over their desk in a scriptorium and laboriously rendering every single letter of a book. Original held at the Royal Library in Brussels, Belgium.

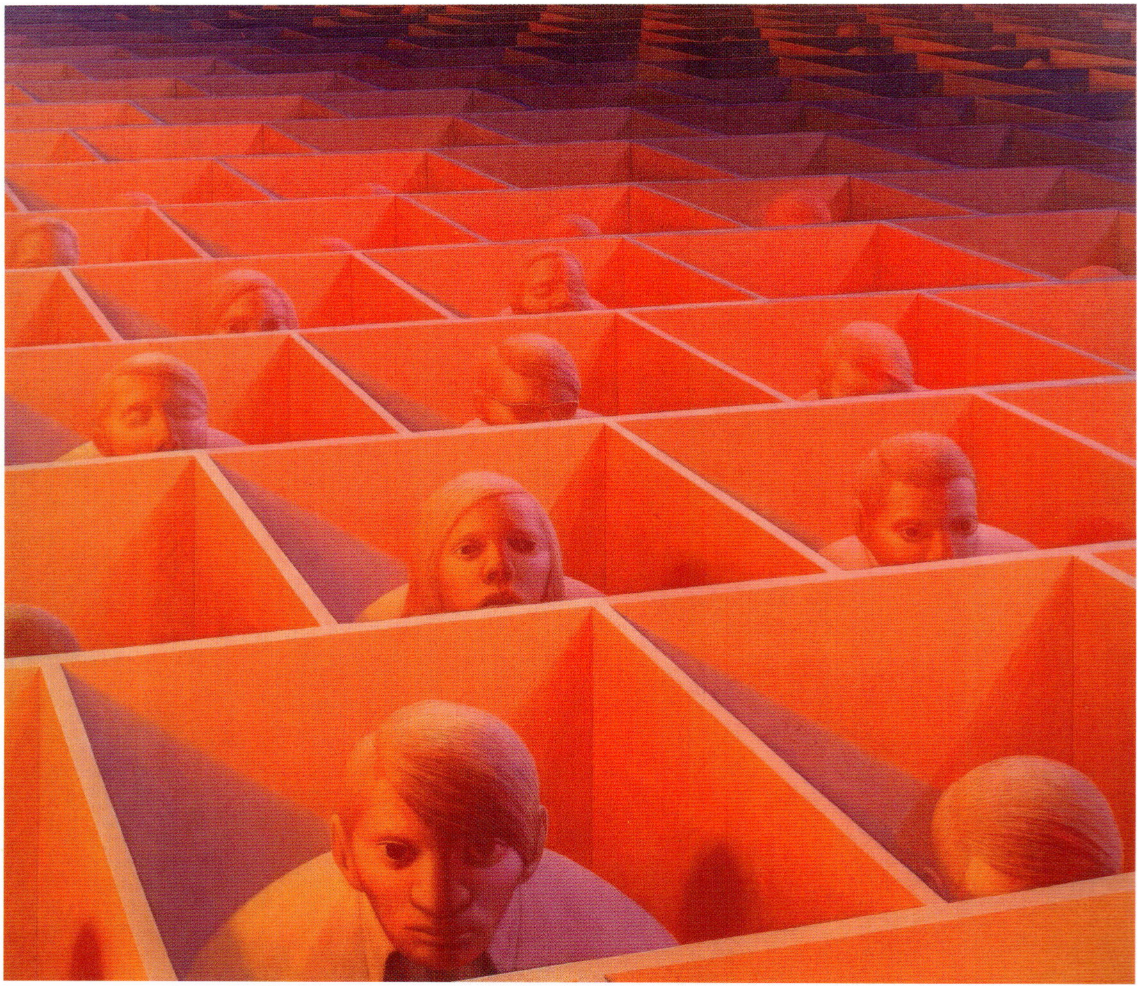

the form of Calvinism, contained an element "which was conservative and traditionalist, and an element which was revolutionary; a collectivism which grasped at an iron discipline, and an individualism which spurned the savorless mess of human ordinances; a sober prudence which would garner the fruits of this world, and a divine recklessness which would make all things new." Capitalism was a secularized form of a new understanding of diligence, one which allowed for efficiency and wealth, instrumentalization and technocratic utilitarianism.

Suddenly work became a means unto an end, or a means unto profit in and of itself. Tawney drew much of his own thinking from the master sociologist Max Weber, who in his landmark 1905 work *The Protestant Ethic and the Spirit of Capitalism* argued that the Reformation inculcated the values of the free market. Claiming that the individual Protestant believer had been severed from the assurances of salvation offered by the rituals of Catholicism, and that the stern doctrines of predestination taught by Calvin (among others), which argued that issues of redemption and damnation were solely the purview of God, Weber argued that evangelical believers judged their worthiness in terms of their good fortune, in particular their financial good fortune. If the Lord's providence

TOP American painter George Tooker was a master of conveying an unnerving synthesis of the real and the surreal. His earliest work is evocative of Hopper, but he would come to develop a more unsettling aesthetic vocabulary, even while still exploring the alienations of modern working life. His 1965 painting *Landscape with Figures* evokes in a more abstract sense the atomized, lonely, individual facets of contemporary existence, even while the cordoned-off silos in which his women and men are trapped remind the viewer of an office's cubicles (similar to prison cells).

should grace the Protestant merchant with wealth, their duty wasn't, however, to spend it on frivolous vanities, but rather to reinvest it and to produce more wealth. Thus an idolatry of diligence would come to hold dominion, where work became a purpose for producing wealth, all of that upon the divine ledger done for its own sake.

Now God is dead, but the Market remains. Capitalism, once animated by the Protestant God, is fully self-sufficient. "The Puritan wanted to work in calling; we are forced to do so," writes Weber. According to Weber, Protestantism had made this restrictive capitalism possible, but economics had come to replace Christianity. Just as Christianity was a totalizing, complete worldview which dominated every experience of medieval life, so is capitalism the faith of our world, our gods' moods now traced in the rise and fall of the market. Wall Street's bronzed bull represents the vagaries of a successful market; this beast appears as if that horned Canaanite demon Moloch. Their Puritanism has secularized and God is now but a divisionary remainder; all which is preserved is an obsessive individualism, the joyless need to accumulate, and the ceaseless fetishizing of work. Now the dominant faith of our age holds that those who are rich are deserving because they've worked hard (an empirically falsifiable claim), and that the only meaning which can be derived in a godless universe is from the sort of work which is capable of generating money. Weber was succinct—we find ourselves now imprisoned in an "iron cage," compelled to work.

Much of how we describe *work*, the unambiguously material reality of *labor*, is inextricably bound with cultural detritus. We speak of working class and middle class, we imagine the blue collar and the white collar, we parse the narcissism of small differences between the *nouvelle riche* and faded gentry, between the wealthy plumber and the poor professor. Then, discussions of work as fueled by diligence will focus on the mythopoesis of labor, the valorization of either the backbreaking work of the builder soldering beams and rivets together in the triumphant castles of steel and glass arising over skylines, or of the supposed

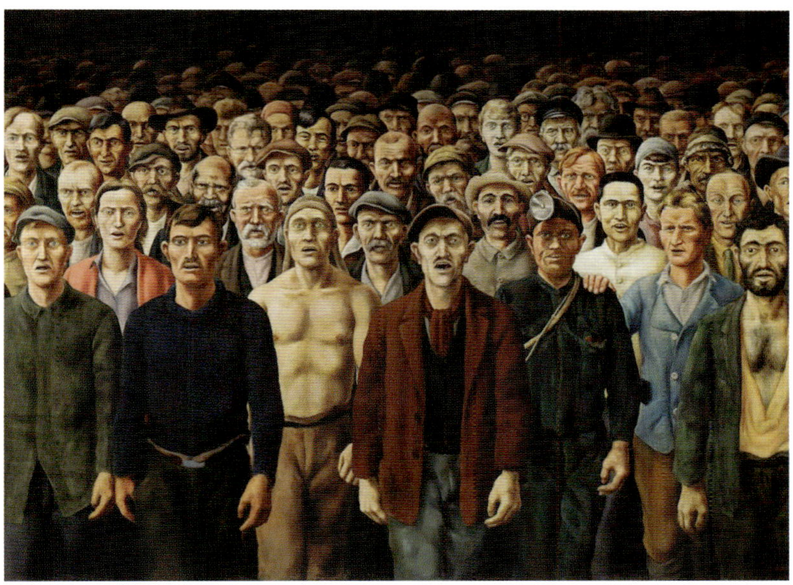

RIGHT German painter Otto Griebel's 1930 *The International*, original held by the German Historical Museum in Berlin, both explored the degradations of industrial capitalism and expressed its creator's communist sympathies.

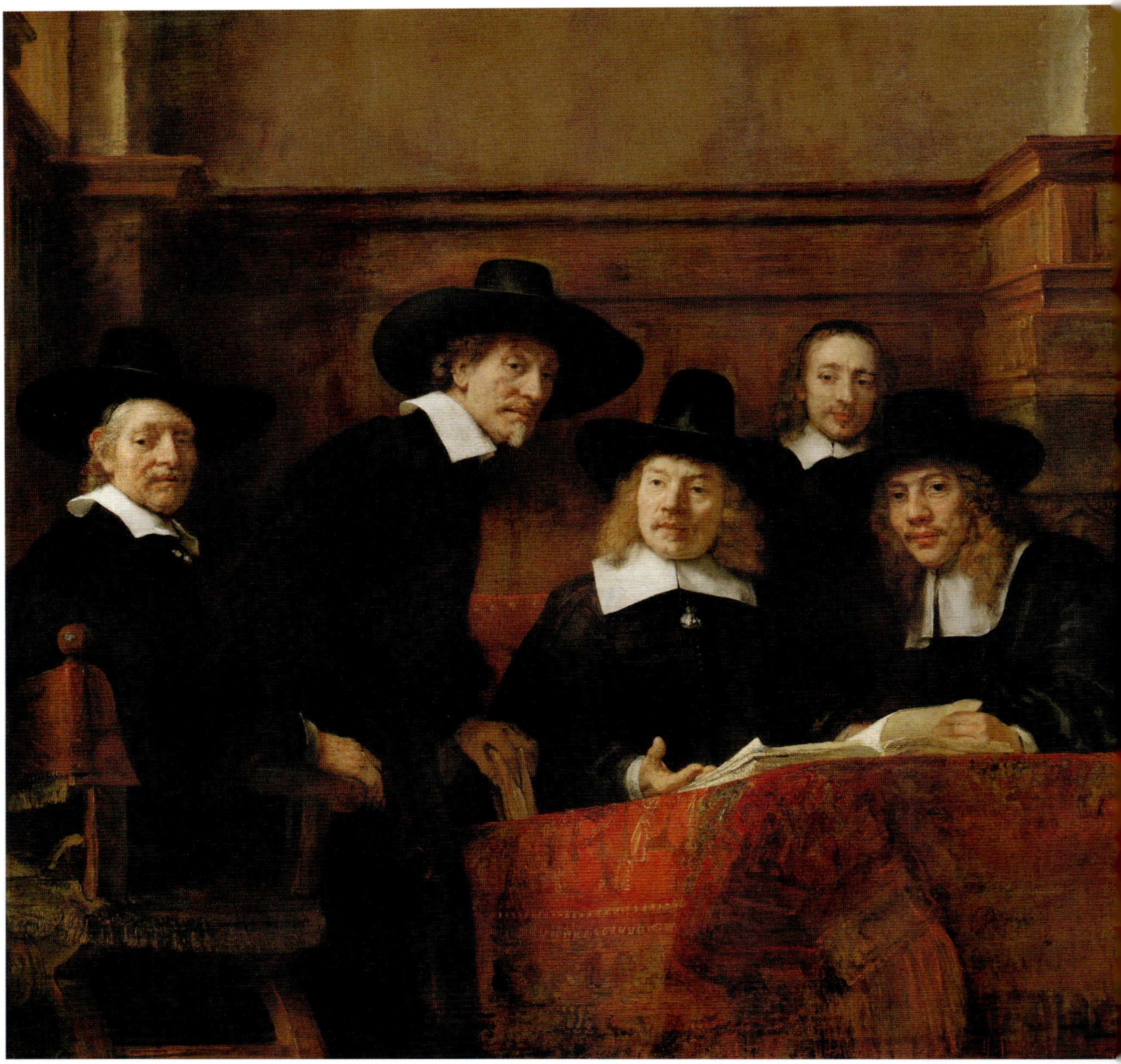

ABOVE Dutch master Rembrandt van Rijn captures an intense moment when these Dutch merchants eternally return the stare of the viewer in his 1662 painting *Syndics of the Draper's Guild*, original held by the Rijksmuseum in Amsterdam.

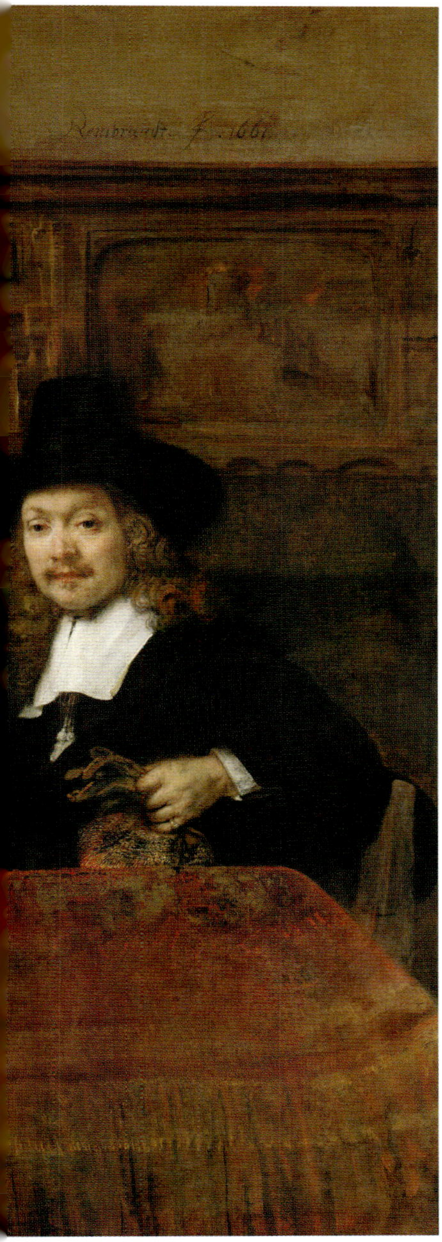

acumen and brilliance of the executive who gets the corner office in that completed skyscraper. In other words, we reduce everything to issues of *class*, but the blunt reality is that if you must work to stay alive, then you're working class. Terms like "working class" and "bourgeoisie," and all the more so the stereotypes which surround such groups, serve to only obscure the major division between those who own everything and everybody else. This is Weber's "iron cage," the world in which we're compelled to labor and unemployment is only a luxury for the rich. What means of resistance could there possibly be? The liberal countenances gentle reform, the conservative gleeful acquiescence, the radical quixotic revolution, the reactionary a furthering of stratification. Short of the millennial revolution which is always just beyond the horizon (for dialectics tells us so), there is at least a small form of resistance in the form of imaginative play, in the way in which workers can reclaim their diligence for themselves. In other words, through art.

As the science fiction novelist Ursula K. Le Guin infamously noted in her 2014 speech given in receipt of the National Book Foundation Medal for Distinguished Contribution to American Letters, "We live in capitalism, its power seems inescapable—but then, so did the divine right of kings. Any human power can be resisted and changed by human beings. Resistance and change often begin in art—very often in our art, the art of words." A utopian possibility, for Le Guin sees in writing—and all creative actions—not mere labor, but vocation. More than that, she intuits the raw material of societal transformation, of envisioning different ways of doing things before enacting them, where there can be a reclamation of diligence away from capital, away from Moloch, and back toward pure, unadulterated, non-instrumental, anti-positivist creation for its own sake.

"I hear America singing, the varied carols I hear," wrote Walt Whitman in *Leaves of Grass*, "Those of mechanics, each one singing his as it should be blithe and strong, / The carpenter singing his as he measures his plank and beam, / The mason singing his as he makes ready for work, or leaves off work," joined by the boatman, shoemaker, wood-cutter, "Singing with open mouths their strong melodious songs." Whitman's great contemporary Emily Dickinson, scribbling on envelopes in her cloister, opined how "Life's little duties do—precisely / As the very least / Were infinite—to me—." Even in our own jaundiced age—call it the era of neoliberalism or late capitalism, of the Anthropocene or apocalypse—there is beauty to be found in the task. Poet Richard Cole in *The Glass Children* perambulates through the charred wasteland of a strip mall, but he ruminates that every "unremarkable donut shop / is somebody's act of faith, / and somewhere almost and / never quite, in the last miles / of aging neon and plastic / backlit signage, here / too is poetry." The purest of poetry is done only for the poet's benefit. Kafka, during the eight hours he was free from sleep or work, dedicated himself to that private muse, creating his own universes in total freedom, a diligence pure and holy. On his deathbed, Kafka made his friend Max Brod promise to immolate all of that private writing which remained, to spar it from the grubby realm of commerce. Obviously, Brod broke his promise. It was a manuscript of *The Trial* which Brod saved from the flames that would be auctioned off in 1988 for two million dollars.

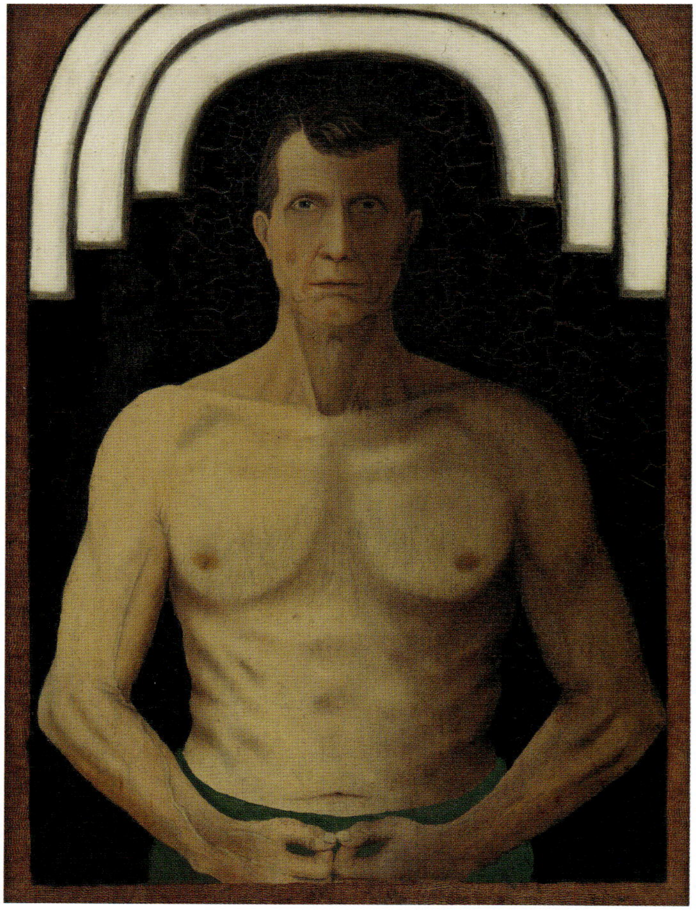

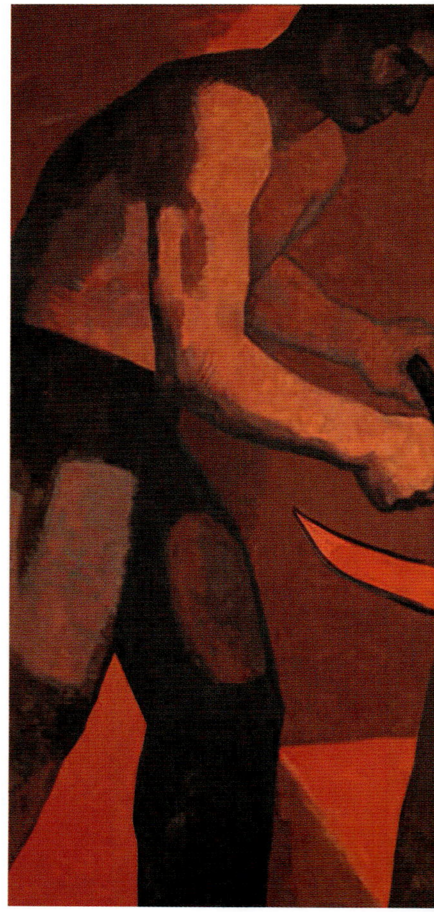

INTERLUDE—ISAAC ASIMOV

Born to Russian-Jewish émigrés some four hundred miles south of Moscow and subsequently raised amid the brownstones and alleyways of Park Slope in Brooklyn, Isaac Asimov ostensibly reached the pinnacle of his education when granted a PhD in biochemistry from Columbia University in 1948, but in reality the writer's training was forever ongoing. Among the most celebrated of science fiction novelists, author of such canonical works as the *Foundation* series, the muttonchopped and bolo-tie-wearing chemist who prodigiously labored away at his Remington in a windowless office (because of his fear of heights) on the thirty-third floor of his Upper West Side apartment didn't affect the romantic disposition of the stereotypical writer. Rather than perching on some Greenwich Village barstool and scribbling half-lyrics in a black leather Moleskine, Asimov was toiling away putting one word after the other, to the eventual number of an astounding five hundred published titles. From Asimov's typewriter ribbon came hundreds of volumes of science fiction, but the chemist also considered topics as far from his ostensible field of academic

TOP LEFT Scottish immigrant, steel and rail worker, self-taught artist—folk painter John Kane brilliantly explored the gritty environs of working-class industrial Pittsburgh. Kane conveys in his 1929 self-portrait displayed at the Museum of Modern Art stoic nobility without necessarily idealizing reality, his imperfect body one that has been used as a machine.

TOP RIGHT Wojciech Fangor's 1954 mural *Forging the Scythes*, painted for the Museum of Warsaw but then plastered over for decades until renovations revealed it in 2020.

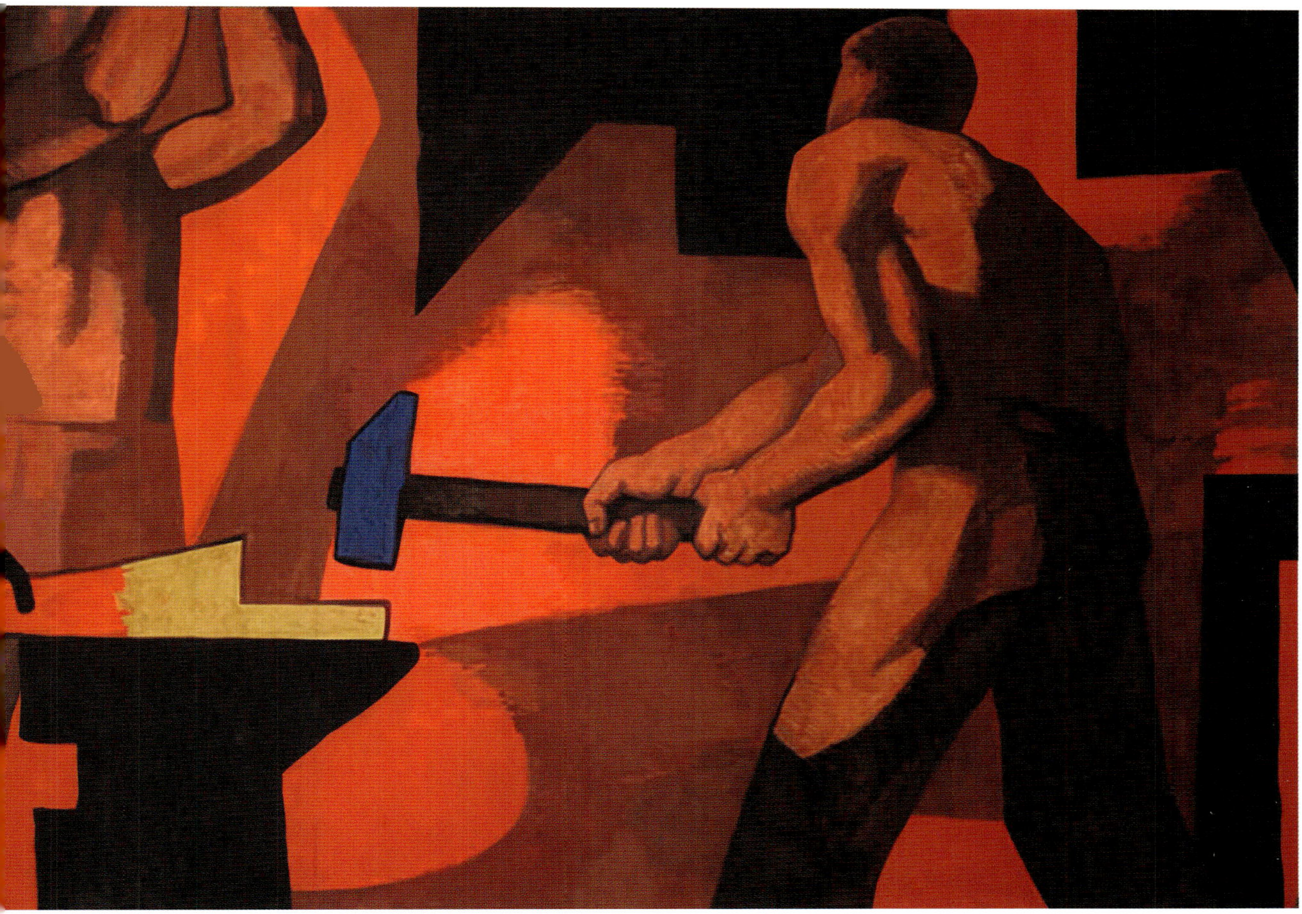

expertise as Shakespeare criticism and Bible translation. "Writing is hard work," Asimov explained in his memoir *In Joy Still Felt*. "The fact that I love doing it doesn't make it less hard work. People who love tennis will sweat themselves to exhaustion playing it, and the love of the game doesn't stop the sweating."

Read any of the dozens of dialogues that constitute the "Writers at Work" series collected across *The Paris Review Interviews*, a celebrated feature conducted largely by George Plimpton for nearly half a century, in which authors elaborated on how they organized their desks, or what brand of typewriter ribbon they used, or when during the day they most often labored. Worth more than a whole shelf of post-structuralist literary criticism, the "Writers at Work" series proves that theory and praxis are identical. Everything depends on where you work, what tools you use, and your schedule. It's no different from a sink full of dishes. Writing requires the same dutiful regularity, for a person "must sit down and get the words on paper, and against great odds," says E. B. White. "This takes stamina and resolution." Raymond Carver emphasizes the same, saying "When

I'm writing, I write every day," in the same way that if a household lets receipts gather on the table and circulars in the mailbox, the situation becomes unmanageable. John Ashbery countenances against falling into bad habits, bemoaning the sloppiness that ensues if one happens to "stay up too late and sleep in too long," while Gabriel García Márquez concurs that any writing requires "extraordinary discipline." Just as the goal of housework is parsimony and economy, Louise Erdrich recommends overwriting the ending of a piece and then going back "to decide where the last line hits." Perhaps most crucially, that which separates the happy writer from the tortured, the joyful gardener from the merely muddy, the zestful carpenter from one who keeps hitting his thumb with a hammer, is that the "most important thing is to be excited about what you are doing," as James Dickey says.

Asimov, like any writer so diligent to produce title after title, didn't write five hundred books of equal worth, of course. Also, as with so many authors who are prolific, Asimov's reputation sometimes suffered by dint of his ethic. Because we endow composition with a certain mysticism, there can ironically be a valorization of the unproductive writer, of the poet or playwright who isn't diligent, the assumption being that still waters run deep, or maybe rather that short *curriculum vitae* paradoxically have more to say. By contrast, an Asimov, or an Anthony Trollope or a Stephen King, is dismissed as a workman, as a contractor, as a hack. This has it precisely backwards, however, for if there is something mystical about writing—and there is—it's precisely because it's work. There is a charged enchantment to the *doing of things*, to the *accomplishment of a task*, for as romantic as the vocation of writing might be, it is also by its very definition labor. Such diligence is, as Asimov noted in a 1979 essay in *The Writer* magazine, an issue of working in a manner that is "single-minded, driven, nonstop." The work itself—those five hundred some books—merely the evidence that that struggle has taken place.

FIRST THE LAUNDRY—PRAXIS

It's impossible not to imagine the words of Robert Frost read in that clipped Yankee-via-San Francisco accent, to intuit the blistering cold of a New Hampshire morning or the blinding whiteness of the snow-covered Franconia Range, the damp exertion of sweat under a flannel collar and muddy boots trudging across yellow and brown leaves slick with early morning ice. Frost is forever a poet of loose coffee grounds dumped into boiling water and intricate blue and red quilts, of wooden spoons hanging from hooks next to gas stoves and of curved glass hurricane lamps, of creaking wooden floorboards and doors swollen with summer's humidity. Visit his white clapboard, gable-peaked farmstead in Derry, New Hampshire, and perambulate in the golden woods of sugar maple and red oak, and it's hard not to romanticize the old man, eyeing him along the rough granite stone wall that he mended every spring, the famous structure whereby "Good fences make good neighbors," which he

OPPOSITE Rowena Morill expresses the mysterious connection between the physicality of labor and the imagination of writing in her 2012 illustration for *Time* magazine of Isaac Asimov hard at work.

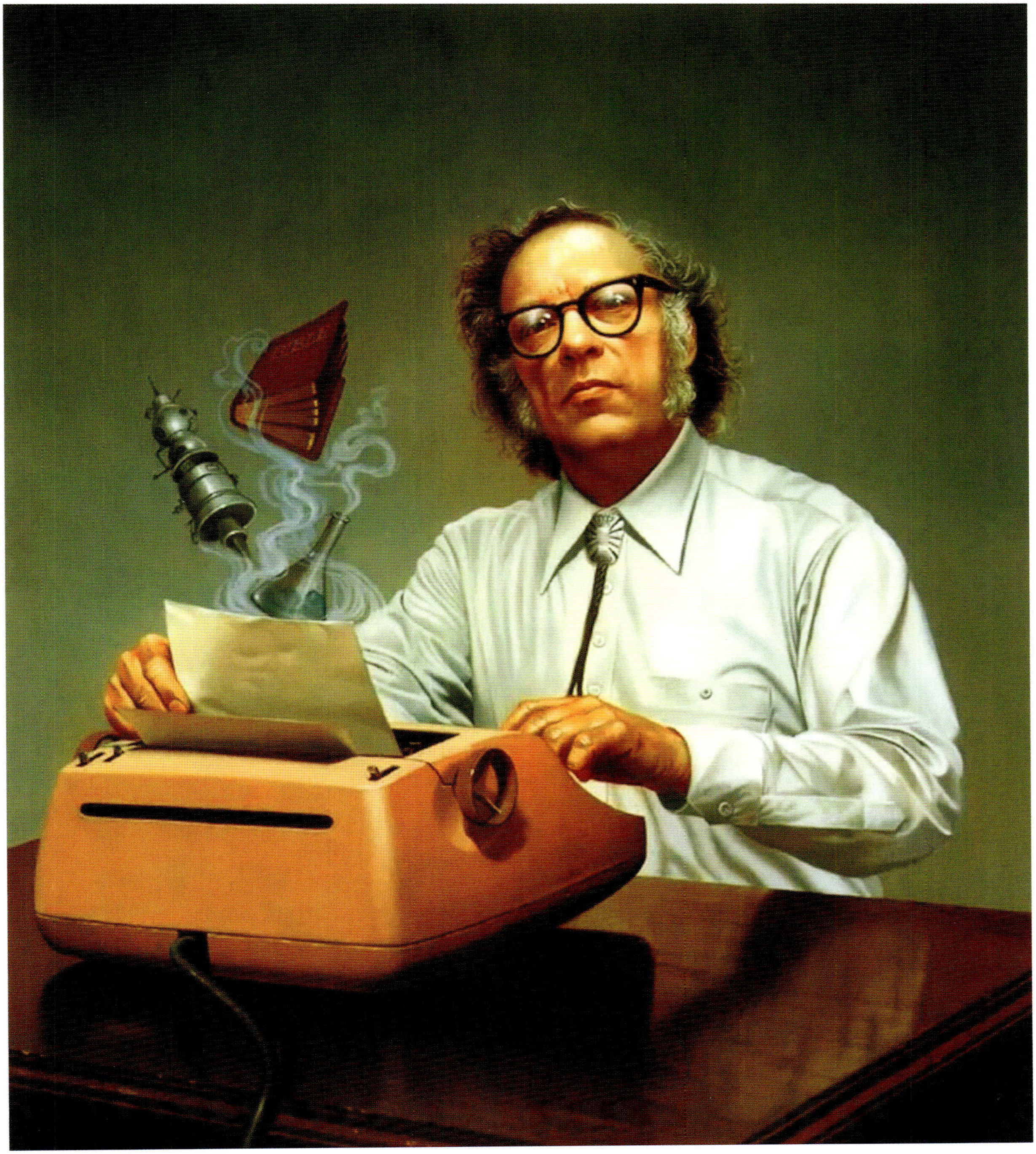

wrote about in his 1914 collection *North of Boston*. The poet was always *fixing things*—mending, building, working. Our greatest singer of chores.

He's at it again in his poem "Two Tramps in Mud Time," which Frost wrote around 1934, five years into the Great Depression. In a cold New England field our narrator chops wood, when he is approached by two hungry vagrants looking for paid labor. There is something vaguely ominous about the unemployed lumberjacks, as "one of them put me off my aim / By hailing cheerily 'Hit them hard!'" Envision the startled narrator wobbling a bit, axe stuck in aborted oak atop a chopping block. "I knew pretty well what he had in mind: / he wanted to take my job for pay." What eventually follows is an ethical rumination, entirely foreign to our current day, where we underpay Uber drivers to deliver pizza or demand Amazon Prime to drone us toilet paper in the middle of the night. "The time when most I loved my task / The two must make me love it more / By coming with what they came to ask." Dignity is such that the tramps won't accept mere charity, but Frost's enjoyment of his housework prevents him from parting with the chopping of timber. "I had no right to play / With what was another man's work for gain. / My right might be love but theirs was need," says the narrator. Ambiguous as to what he does, if the desperate men convince him of the necessity of their task, as indeed Frost knows that their continued presence will eventually move him to turn over the axe. Yet in the chore, here among the warm sun and the chill wind, his "object in living is to unite / My avocation and my vocation . . . where love and need are one." Frost really liked housework.

BOTTOM A writer absorbed in the work of his task from Russian painter Leonid Pasternak's 1899 *The Passion of Creation*, original held in a private collection. Friend of Leo Tolstoy, Pasternak often brought his young son Boris—who would go onto some renown as the author of *Doctor Zhivago*—on his visits to the author.

OPPOSITE There are always chores to be diligently done in this anonymous 1850 painting *New England Farm in Winter*, original held by the Smithsonian Museum of American Art.

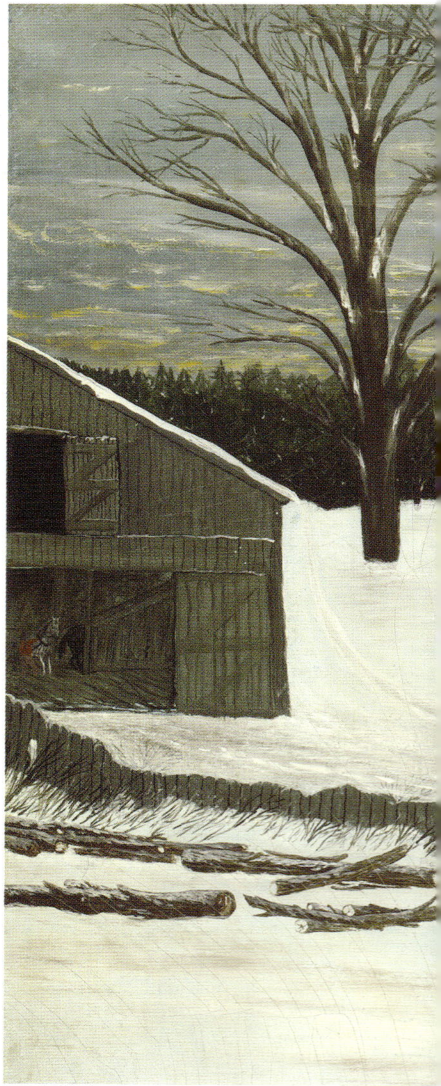

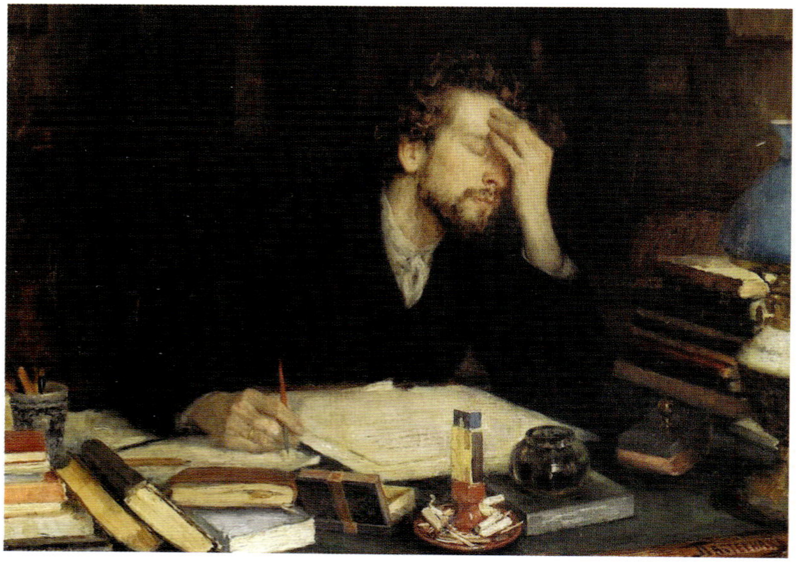

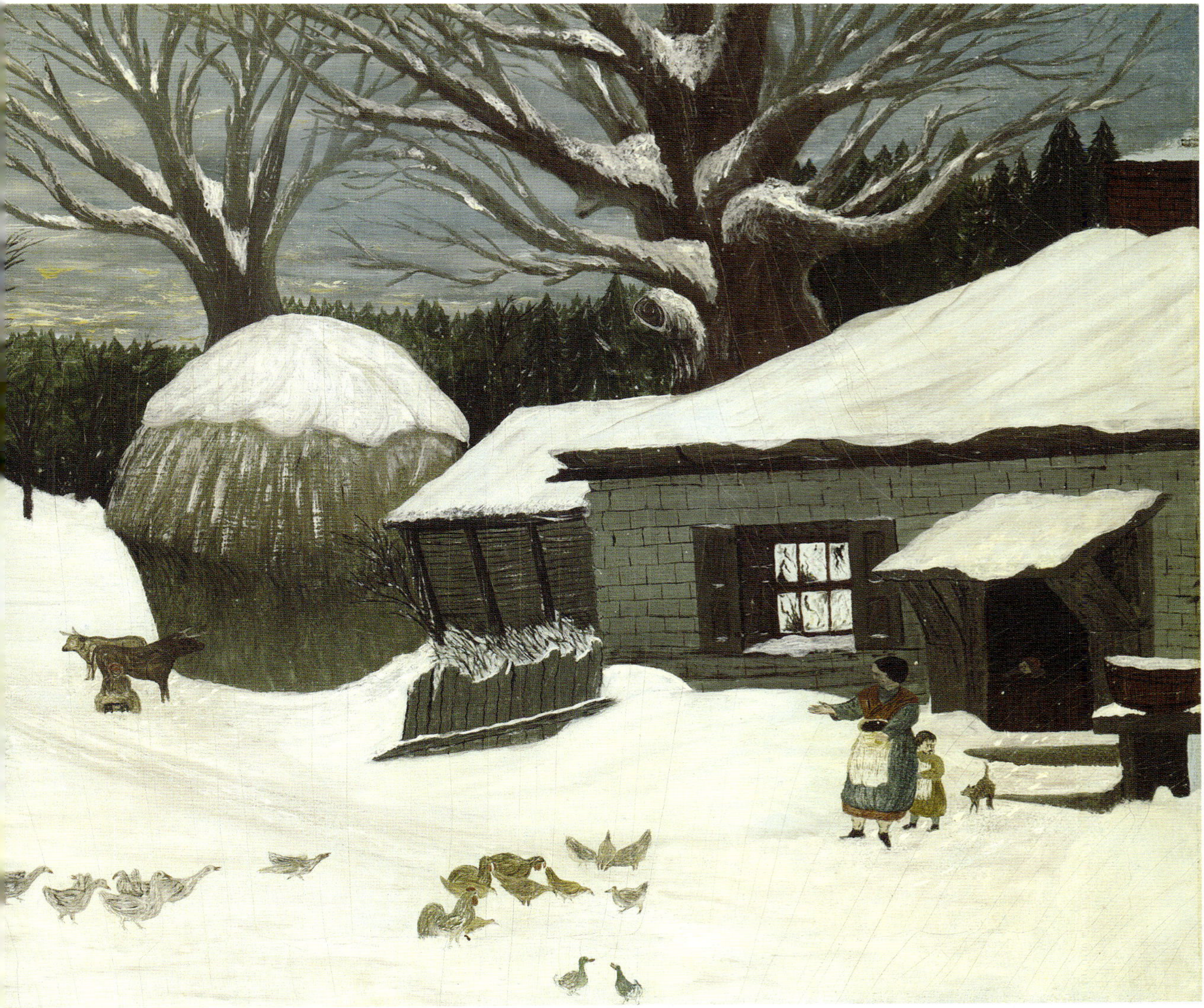

To clean cups, mugs, glasses, and dishes; to soap up a bowl or scrub crusted sauce from a fork, loading up the machine and placing that little alien detergent pod into its compartment; toggling between stream and spray to clean the sink of bread crusts and globs of yogurt. Lithuanian-American poet Al Zolynas describes as much in "The Zen of Housework" from his collection *The New Physics*, how his rubber gloved hand filled up a wine glass with water and soap, "thousands of droplets / of steam—each a tiny spectrum—rising / from my goblet," what he designates the "grey sacrament of the mundane!" Easy to valorize if nobody is making you do it; Frost's hobby was chopping wood apparently, and most of us do our dishes and laundry because the alternative is disgusting, but there is a risk to turning the vacuum into a meditation tool. The narcissistic self-regard of the husband proud of having moved a coffee cup to the sink. Without some self-awareness you might sound like the Berkeley philosopher Paul Feyerabend,

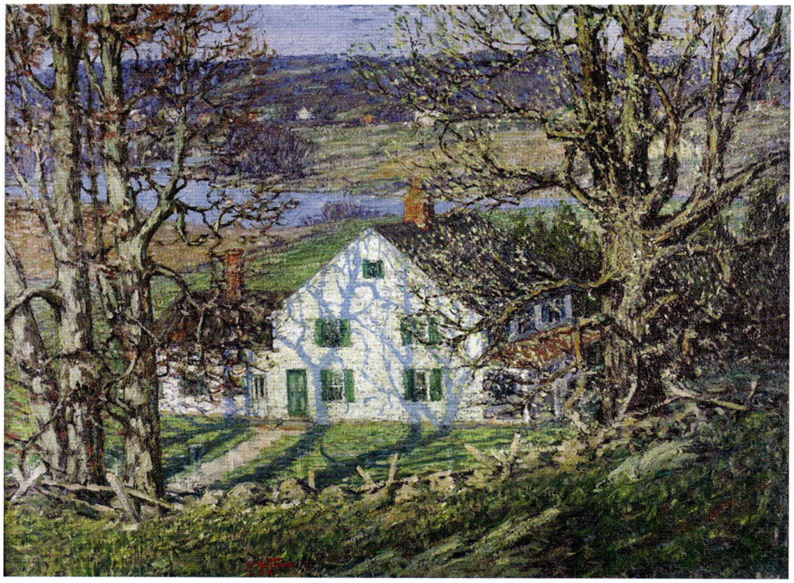

who pretentiously told an interviewer that he most enjoyed doing housework, seeing it as an act of devotion to his wife. After he died, his wife said that Feyerabend had never done any chores. Notice the differing words we use to describe vacuuming or cooking—from meditation to hobby to housework to chore to domestic labor—all of which depends on who is doing it for whom and what's compelling them to do it. By contrast to Zolynas's lyric, former poet laureate Natasha Trethewey writes in a poem from her collection *Domestic Work* about a maid for whom "All week she's cleaned / someone else's house, / stared down her own face / in the shine of copper– / bottomed pots, polished / wood, toilets she'd pull / the lid to." Historically it must be remembered that housework was synonymous with women's work; whether poorly renumerated or not paid at all, the scrubbing, dusting, and washing were marked as feminine. When Frost was outside playing lumberjack, what do you think Elinor Frost was doing? She was inside picking dried johnny cake batter off of the iron stove top, she was washing those musty red flannels with their stink of the woods, she was mixing soap and water in a dented steel bucket and letting the suds flow over a bathroom floor. Betty Friedan describes the score in *The Feminine Mystique*, writing that "As she made the beds, shopped for groceries, matched slipcover material . . . she was afraid to ask even of herself the silent question—'Is this all?'"

Ironically, as the second-wave feminism of the 1960s and '70s smashed through (some) boundaries regarding women's role in the workplace, the onus of domestic labor didn't shift in a more equitable way to male partners. According to a Gallup poll from 2020, even though women now make up more than half the workforce and on average contribute more to their family's finances (even while a gender wage gap endures), they still are responsible for laundry in 58 percent of households and cooking in 51 percent (not to mention childcare). Important, since housework, it must be said, is also often *hard*. Despite those technological miracles of capitalist utopia—the washing machine, the dishwasher, the vacuum

TOP The fences must always be mended at the Old Lyme, Connecticut, homestead depicted in Harry Leslie Hoffman's 1913 painting *A Mood of Spring*, original held by the Florence Griswold Museum in the same community depicted therein.

OPPOSITE Among the most talented and consequential of the Impressionists, American painter Mary Cassatt was too long dismissed by art historians as a "mere" domestic painter, as women's art was as devalued as their household labors. In her 1900 painting *Young Mother Sewing*, Cassatt precisely enlivens such a quotidian scene of diligent household work.

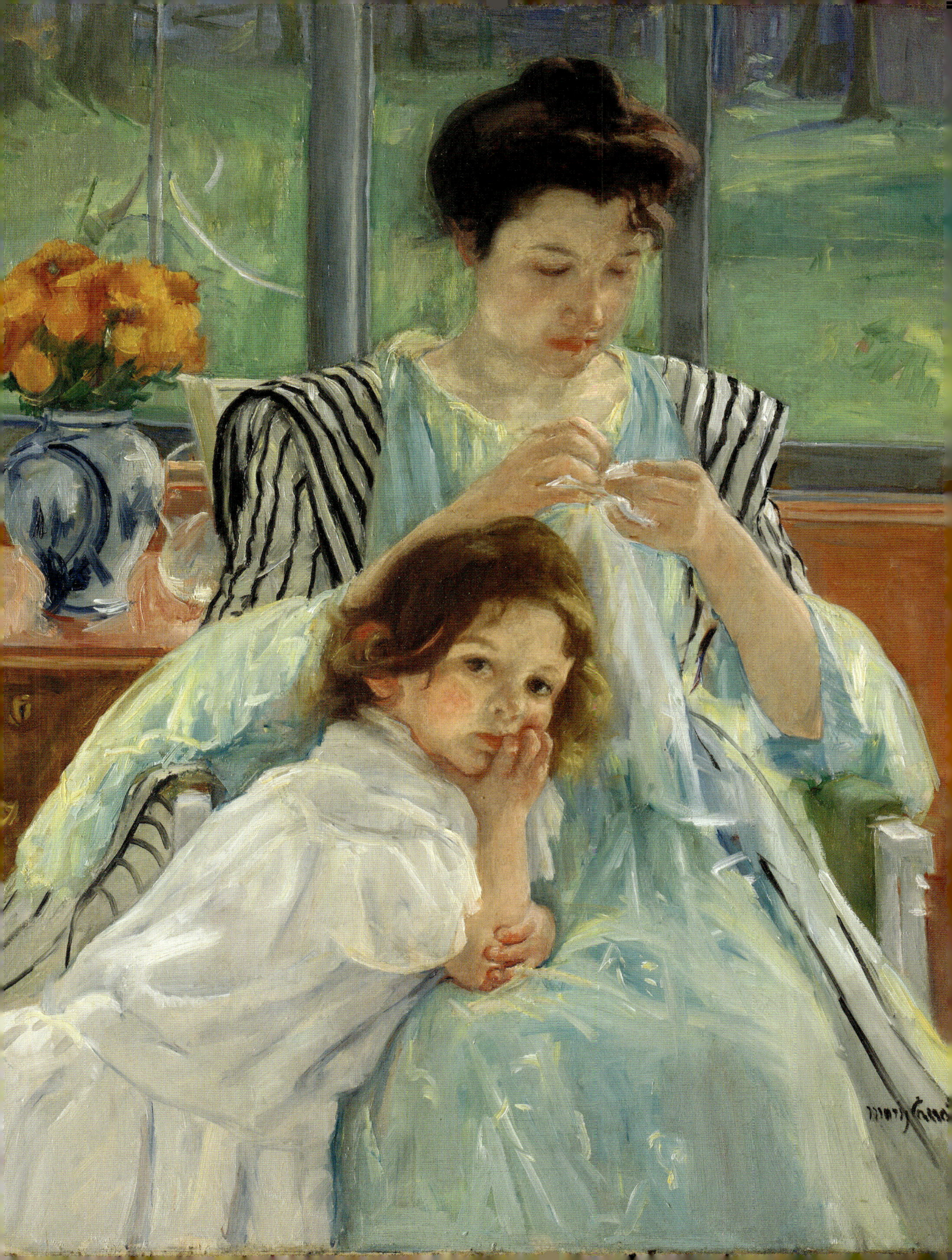

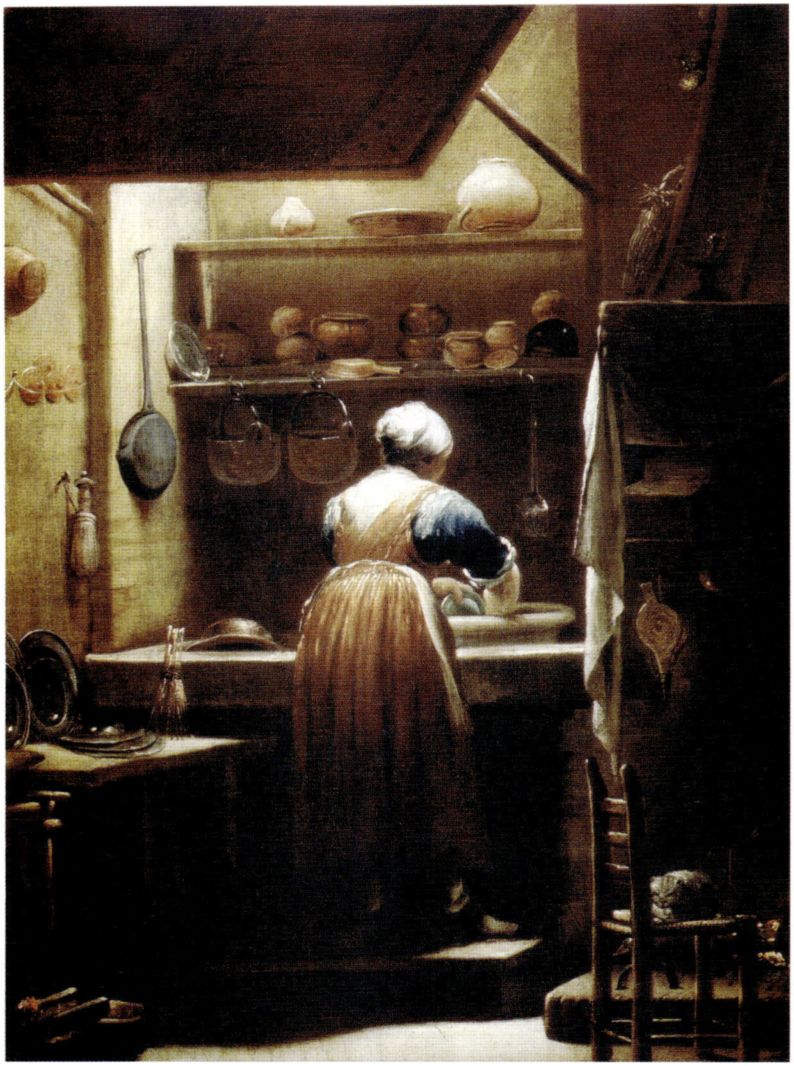

cleaner—chores are time-consuming, monotonous, and frequently unpleasant. There was a reason why activists started the International Wages for Housework Campaign in 1972, a call for a universal basic income that acknowledged that the labor which (at the time almost entirely) women did was indeed labor. Chores can be meditative, but to forget that they're also instrumental is to ignore the people who actually do them.

Strangely it's the same problem that Frost was confronted with, which is just part of an even larger issue concerning the difference between the work we do for ourselves and the work we do for others. Trethewey writes how "Sunday mornings are hers," a still busy day where "church clothes [are] starched" and floors are washed with "buckets of water. Octagon soap." But the language which describes these chores is so much different, joyful even. Rhythmic. There's a "record spinning / on the console, the whole house / dancing" while she cooks on the stove, "neck bones / bumping in the pot" and "a choir / of clothes clapping

ABOVE Italian Baroque painter Giuseppe Crespi's 1712 painting *Kitchen Maid*, with the original at Florence's Uffizi, places his subject not just within the drab confines of her workplace, but illuminated from an unseen source from above.

OPPOSITE English painter Henry Robert Morland's arresting *A Lady's Maid Soaping Linen*, painted sometime between 1765 and 1782 with the original held at the Tate Britain, gives a quiet dignity to the drudgery of domestic labor.

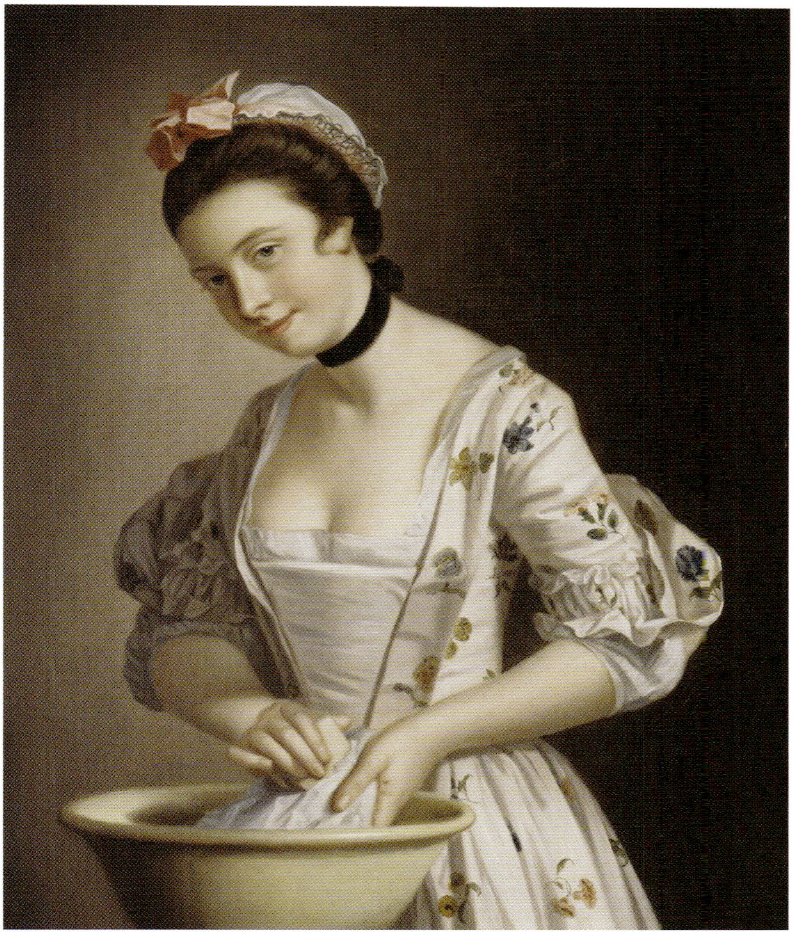

on the line." This maid who still has to clean on her day off is at least cleaning for herself, and, not unlike the narrator in Zolynas's poem, she's got her moments of domestic transcendence as "She beats time on the rugs, / blows dust from the broom / like dandelion spores, each one / a wish." There is a similarity between Trethewey's character and Frost's narrator, that distinction between working for pay and working for yourself. What defines the chore is that it has to be done—for all of us. Cleaning, washing, cooking, gardening—all of these things are crucial to society's functioning more than sitting in a corner office of a glass and steel monolith while moving around imaginary numbers on a screen. Domestic work is defined by the enigma that it's never done, a constant war of attrition against entropy, but also that in a circumscribed way it can be finished perfectly, at least for the time being. A writer can always add another word or a painter another brush stroke, but once a dish is lemony clean it can be as fresh as a new mind.

If there is a danger in forgetting that the chore is work, there is also a loss if we don't remember that Frost and Zolynas and Trethewey have a point. Housework can be a practice, a ritual, a sacrament. The very art of life. Chores can be countercultural, in a way: necessary work for an adequate life rather than for adding a higher number to someone's spreadsheet in the aforementioned glass and steel monolith.

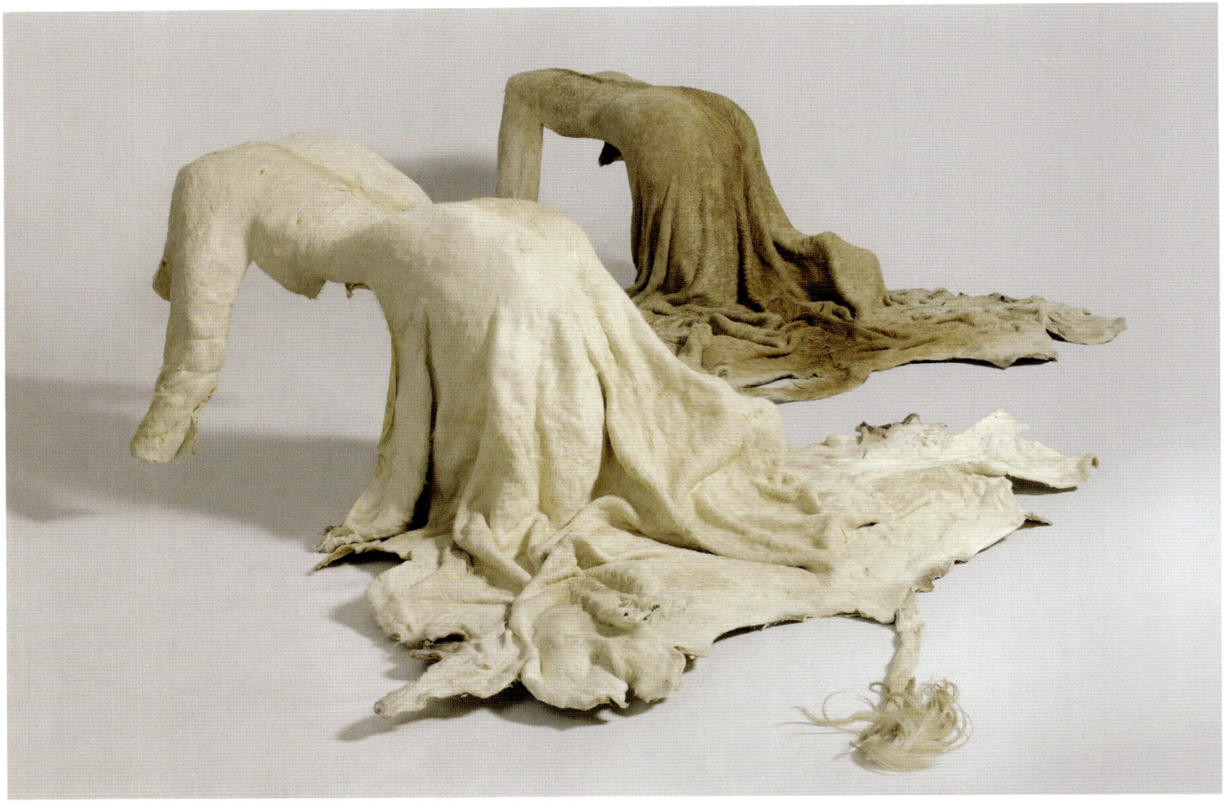

ABOVE South African feminist artist Nandipha Mntambo's 2013 sculpture *Umfanekiso wesibuko (Mirror Image)* is rendered from treated leather shaped in the form of the artist herself, a means of conveying the racialized and gendered ways in which those who perform domestic labor are erased from their own narratives.

Still, it's hard to interpret chores as innately subversive, especially if we rely on Comet and Arm & Hammer, Palmolive and Tide, Kenmore and Dyson, Frigidaire and General Electric. Not long after the 2008 economic collapse, perhaps as part of the general zeitgeist where anarchic self-sufficiency manifested itself in the heady utopianism of Occupy, there was a concruent embrace of doing chores which didn't make Whirlpool or Proctor & Gamble executives wealthier. Suddenly hipsters were homesteaders, hammering espresso machines into plowshares. There followed sticky mason jars filled with pickled tomatoes and acerbic asparagus, frosted growlers of yeasty homemade ale, home-ground coffee, an enthusiasm for strenuous carpentry among women and delicate knitting among men.

Born out of nostalgia, surely; romantic, obviously. The same impulse that mid-decade propelled a thousand fedora-and-clapping bands, from Mumford and Sons to the Lumineers. If anything, the pandemic exacerbated these sentimental desires; or, let a thousand sourdough starters rise. If the American sense of nostalgic chore work harkened to certain (often pernicious) myths of the frontier—rustic cabins and gas stoves, cracked leather and rusted machinery—then across the Atlantic there has been a retreat into a sort of cozy, fantasy Cotswold—warm ale by a hot fire in the cold pub kind of domesticity—the attitude which made *The Great British Bake Off* a hit, soggy bottoms and all.

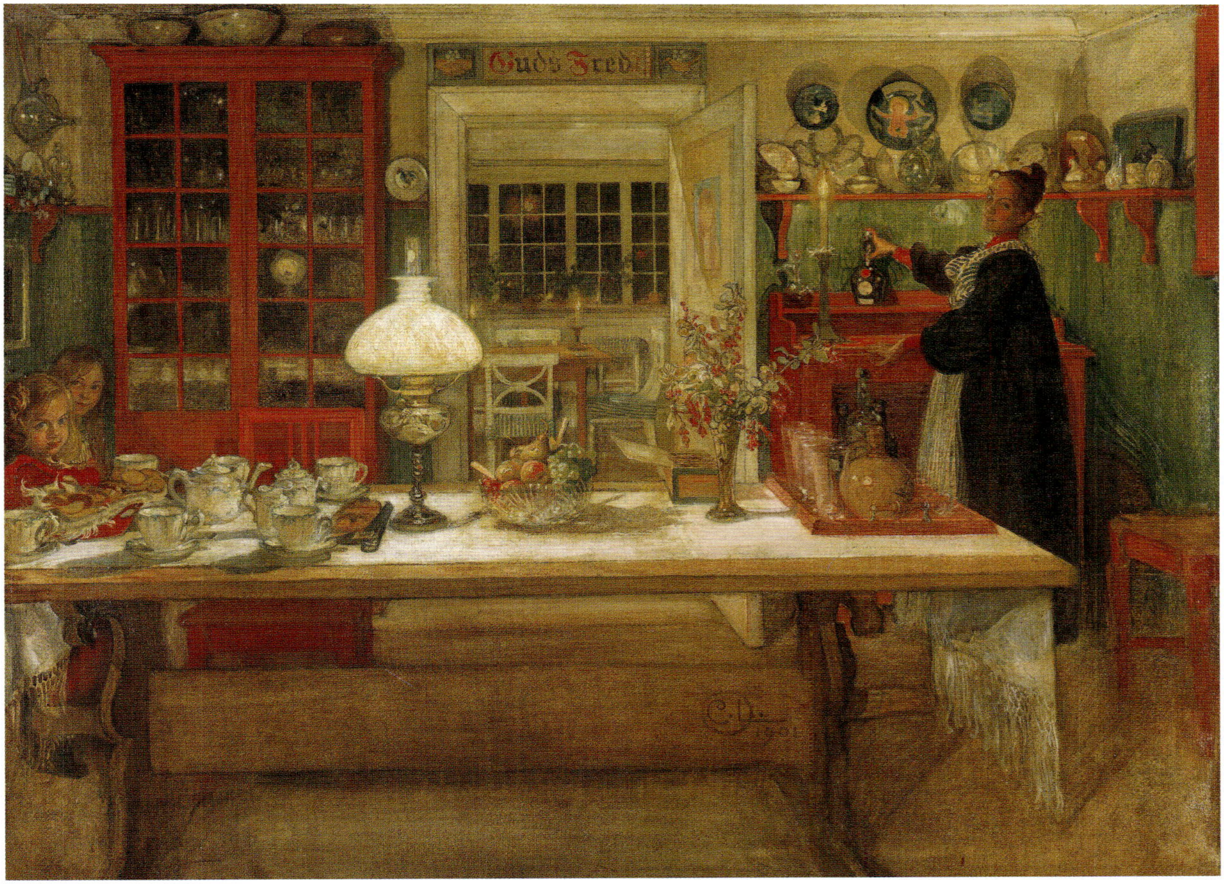

ABOVE A precursor to the aesthetic of domestic nostalgia associated with the cottagecore hipsters of today is the influential Arts & Crafts movement of more than a century ago, when designers, painters, and sculptors in Europe, Britain, and America returned to the pleasures of rustic household diligence. The Arts & Craft work of married Swedish painters Karin and Carl Larsson was more than just sartorial choice: it was lifestyle philosophy as well. Karin's 1901 painting *Getting Ready for a Game*, original held by the National Museum in Stockholm, presents the interior of her and her family's self-designed home in all of its coziness and warmth.

Considering how much time we spend in grocery stores, or vacuuming, or doing laundry, or taking out the trash, chores are often occluded in our literature, albeit we know that Jeeves dusted and somebody was starching Mr. Darcey's collars. Housework exists at the nexus of a whole host of things—race and gender, the personal and the public, the routine and the transcendent. Perhaps it's her midwestern Calvinist practicality, but Marilynne Robinson endows the every-day with charmed straightforwardness, elevating the chore to its rightful place, nowhere as much as in her appropriately named *Housekeeping*, wherein she imagines having "swept the whole floor of heaven," the eschatological work of "reclaiming . . . fallen buttons and misplaced spectacles," whereby chores them-selves are the work of reparation and repair. In cleaning, in organizing, in making that which is disordered ordered, there is a sense that "everything must finally be made comprehensible," as Robinson writes. What "are all these fragments for, if not to be knit up finally?"—the verb itself a conspicuous conflation of feminine housework with fixing the universe. Because we tend to think of domestic work in less grand terms, the physicality stands out more, and yet chores can gesture to a certain beyond as well. Robert Pirsig's countercultural classic *Zen and the Art of Motorcycle Maintenance* makes a case for the mystical possibilities of chores. Pirsig writes that people associate engine metal with "given shapes—pipes, rods, girders, tools, parts . . . as primarily physical," but for those who actually fix such machines, the "motorcycle is primarily a mental phenomenon." Machines are extensions of our mind and can even alter and redefine the mind. Domestic work and technology have always been connected like hand in rubber glove.

Vacuuming, admittedly, doesn't have the same romance as other art, even if it shares the motions of cleaning up, or at least pushing stuff around. Even still, Raymond Carver made something brilliant out of that mundane ritual in his short story "Put Yourself in My Shoes," the genesis of which was just the sentence "He was running the vacuum cleaner when the telephone rang," a line that had appeared as if a mantra in the author's head one day, later unspooling like a cleaner going over a carpet in rigid, tight turns. Despite the vacuum's roar and its slightly electric smell, Carver heard it as muse. Some types of domestic labor have always drawn the attention of writers, been endowed with significance and romanticized. Gardening is celebrated as an artful and (literally) regenerative duty. A sense that in charting tomato vines' progress, basil plants becoming lushly green with spring showers, craggy oregano growing green-brown against the autumn sun, is a bit like seeing a manuscript slowly take form. "If you have a garden in your library," Cicero famously wrote in a letter from before the first century of the Common Era, "everything will be complete." Gardening speaks in a vernacular both primal and cozy, and as such it draws writerly attention more than toilet scrubbing does—we read *The Secret Garden* by Frances Hodgson Burnett and not *The Secret Outhouse*, after all. A garden is a mysterious space, all intertwining vines clinging to a red-brick wall, dirt under fingernails and engorged vegetables, the sense of freshness and safety but also of sexual reproduction and perhaps the erotically illicit, as in that original paradise from which we were all expelled. The realm of what Ovid sings of in *The Art of Love* when he describes how "mid soft green there springs a sacred font" or of Andrew Marvell's nothing being "as am'rous as this lovely green" in "Upon Appleton House." Jamaica Kincaid movingly writes in *My Garden* that her own attempts shall never match her idealized vision, but "for me [that] is the joy of it; certain things can never be realized and so all the more reason to attempt them."

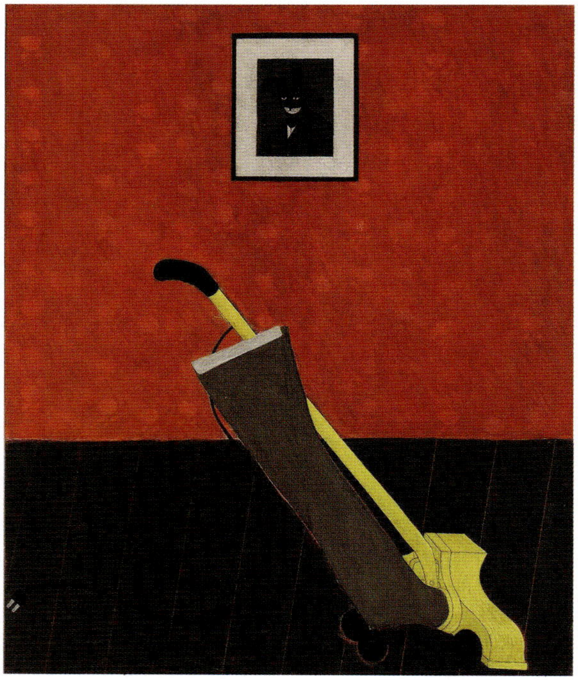

ABOVE American artist Kerry James Marshall brings a bit of ominous humor to his 1981 painting *Portrait of the Artist and a Vacuum*, original held by the Nasher Museum of Art at Duke University in Durham, North Carolina.

OPPOSITE American painter Rembrandt Peale's 1801 depiction of his son with the product of his own gardening in the painting *Rubens Peale with a Geranium*, original at the National Gallery of Art in Washington, DC.

Most of us no longer find such succor in the garden as we do in another place, the supermarket, which requires its own sort of diligence. "This place recharges us spiritually, it prepares us, it's a gate-way," Don DeLillo writes of the supermarket in *White Noise*. This is the sort of place where with "hungry fatigue, and shopping for images" Allen Ginsberg had ecstatic visions of Walt Whitman "poking among the meats" and Federico García Lorca by the watermelons, of "peaches and what penumbras . . . Wives in the avocados, babies in the tomatoes!" Vegetables from a garden are so odd-shaped and dirty; but in the supermarket there are pyramids of oranges whose spherical perfection

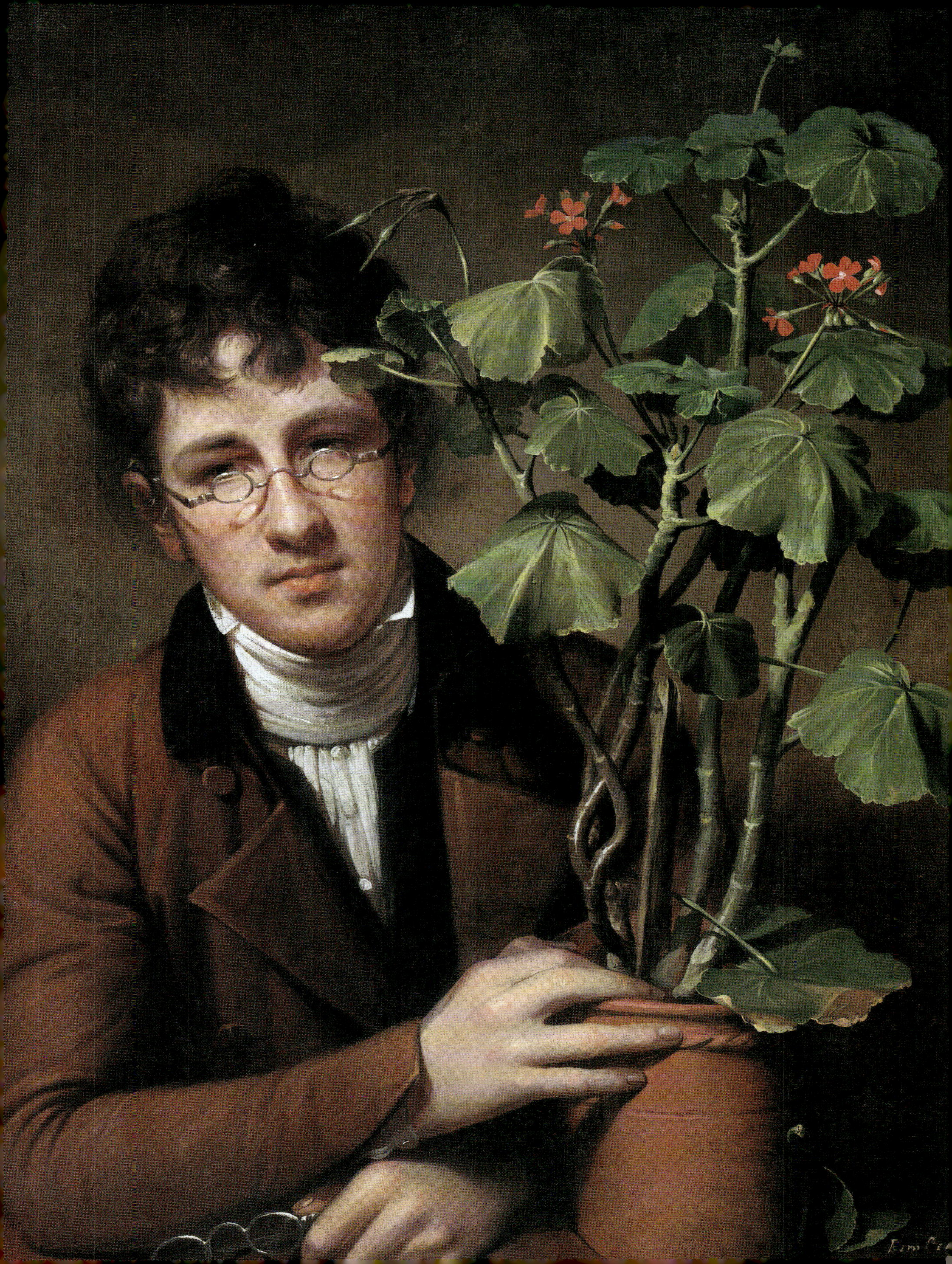

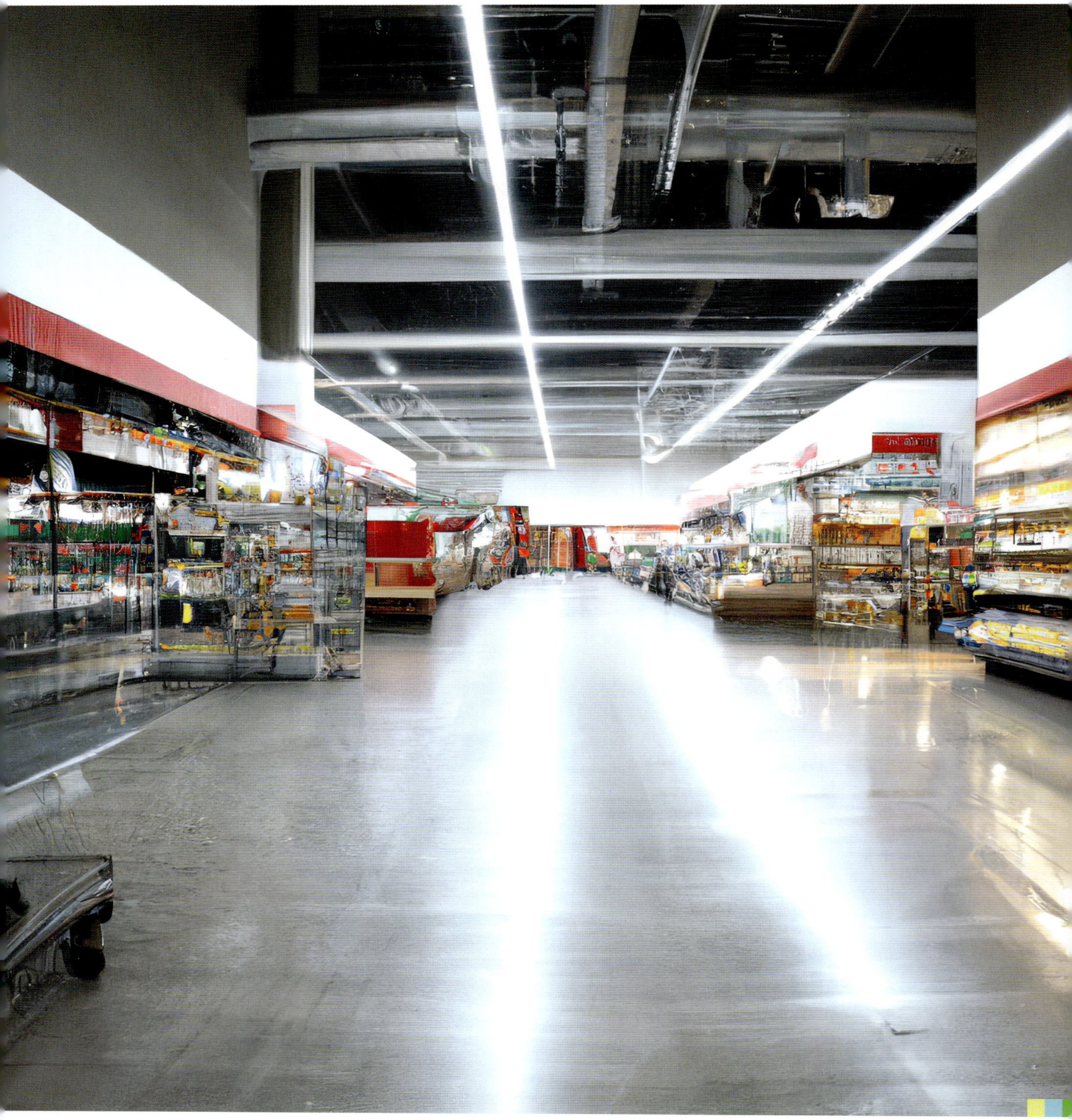

is marred only by the little nipple on top, gleaming McIntoshes and Granny Smiths, jumbled mountains of phallic bananas and crisp heads of lettuce, not to mention all of that shrink-wrapped steak and chicken breasts divorced from any sense that they were cut from a once fleshy creature. Then there are the rows and rows of pre-fabricated chemical American goodness, Oreos and Swedish Fish, Kit Kats and Cape Cod potato chips. Capitalism's illusion of choice is the same as the illusion of freedom. Who cares, though, as long as dinner is on the table?

Yet if preparing food and enjoying it with your family is a devotion of love, then the evidence of that act is the chores left over, the plates with bits of dried ham stuck to them, the slick forks and spoons and the skillet with detritus of browned shallot and garlic affixed within. Because chores are only over when life is, which is part of the diligent wisdom that they impart. Not perfectionism or completism, but the dutiful, continual, never-ending *thisness* of our lives. Housework offers contemplation, yes, but more importantly, it is a reminder of our inescapable physicality, of the materiality of being in this world. There is (or should be) a democracy in that, the often filthy, boring, grueling nature of what it means to simply have the honor of existing in this fallen creation, the joy, beauty, and ecstasy of the whole thing. One can tell the difference between those who never do any housework and those of us who do, for the former have calluses on their souls; they're divorced from such an intrinsic part of what it means to be a human. They're those who never make their bed or take out the trash, change a diaper or wipe a plate, whether because they pay someone else to do it or expect that it's always the responsibility of another person (probably their wife). Most of all, chores wait for no person. Solve a difficult equation, compose perfect measures of music, or craft a beautiful sentence, and afterwards the dog still needs to shit, shoes have to be put away, and the stairs must be vacuumed. As the Zen parable has it, after you've reached enlightenment, ascended to Nirvana, and comprehended the illusory nature of existence, you're still going to have to do the laundry.

OPPOSITE Postmodernity's bounty as depicted in this 2023 artificial-intelligence-generated image of a supermarket display case, nary the human intrusion to be found.

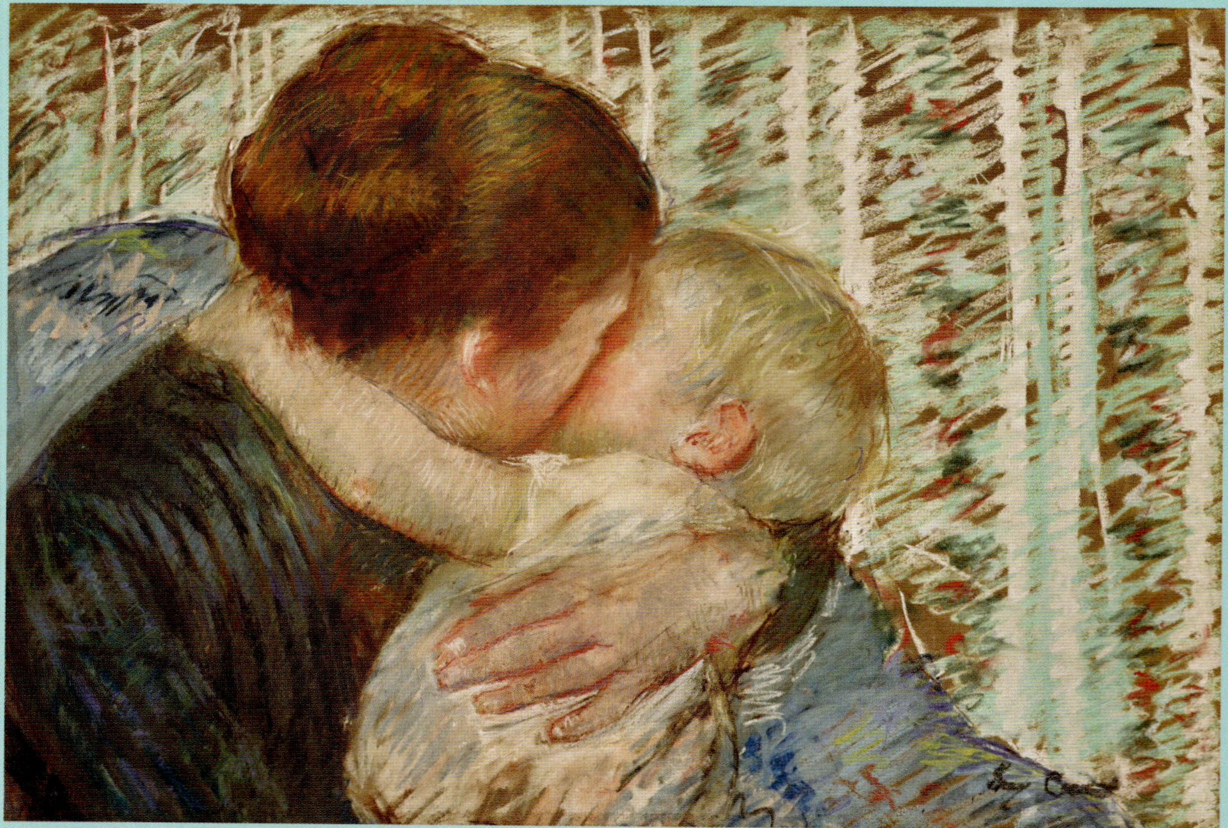

CHAPTER FIVE

A MARK OF FAITH: KINDNESS

"Two things fill the mind with every new and increasing admiration and awe, the more often and steadily we reflect upon them: the starry heavens above me and the moral law within me."

—Immanuel Kant, *The Critique of Practical Reason* (1788)

"Our world hangs like a magnificent jewel in the vastness of space. Every one of us is part of that jewel. A facet of that jewel. And in the perspective of infinity, our differences are infinitesimal."

—Fred Rogers, Dartmouth University commencement address (2002)

Love without kindness is neither. Notable that the apostle Luke counterbalances God's envy and His wrath with His kindness and His love, noting in Acts 14:17 how the Lord "gave us rain from heaven, and fruitful seasons, filling our hearts with food and gladness." Just as the vices other than envy and wrath can seem alien to God, so too do most of the virtues appear separate from the Lord, for what would it mean to speak of an omnipotent being as diligent or an omnipresent entity as humble? Yet that God is kind—at least some of the time—is clearly stated. Despite those divine associations, the word "kindness" itself has a relatively recent history. Traceable in English back to the early fourteenth century, "kindness" has always been related to concepts ranging from the relatively prosaic friendliness to the far more profound compassion and empathy. Unlike its six sister cardinal virtues, "kindness" is the only word whose linguistic root isn't Latinate, derived rather from Germanic Anglo-Saxon, the original form being the Old English "gecynd," which is directly related to the word for "family." Indeed, "kindness" still begins with those first three letters "kin," underscoring the tribal associations of how such loving care was to be extended to blood relations, though perhaps not into the wider realm. Any kindness which ends with the family, however, is no kindness at all. The etymology of the word underscores something rather profound about the concept of kindness; not that it refers to only caring for your own brothers and sisters, parents and children, but that it rather extends toward treating all humans as if they were your kin. The Latin word which appeared in the earliest listing of the virtues was *humanitas*, whose interconnectedness to a multitude of a variety of other words—from "humanity" to the "humanities"—can be easily surmised. There is a universal quality to the concept of *humanitas*, which announces itself in the very word, equating that kindness which we offer to each other to the cause of everyone, everywhere. Yet the more vulgar English association of kindness with family is arguably even more tender. In Latin you are to be kind because everyone is a person; in English you're to be kind because everyone is a brother or a sister. For the German twentieth-century philosopher Max Scheler in *The Nature of Sympathy*, there need not be complex justifications for kindness; it could not be reduced to deduction or induction, syllogism or proof. Rather, our innate sense of "fellow-feeling" exists in the bosom "simply because we are human."

PREVIOUS SPREAD Greatest of the American Impressionists, Mary Cassatt has too often been dismissed by art historians as a painter of "mere domesticity" because of her fascination with family life. Yet few painters have been able to as poignantly and truly capture the moments of private tenderness, comfort, and mutual love as Cassatt, who particularly exulted in the exploration of parenthood. Her 1880 *Mother and Child*, held in a private collection, exemplifies that theme, depicting a woman comforting her child. With subtle technique, Cassatt is able to record an instant in eternity, the background a miasma of pastel that fades into nothingness because the intensity of the emotion is focused on the embrace between the mother and child themselves, an instant elevated into a sublime eternity.

OPPOSITE Franz Kafka as imagined by Andy Warhol in this 1980 portrait, original at the Whitney Museum of Art in New York City, as based on a photograph of the author. Warhol renders Kafka's gaze as intense, though not without friendliness.

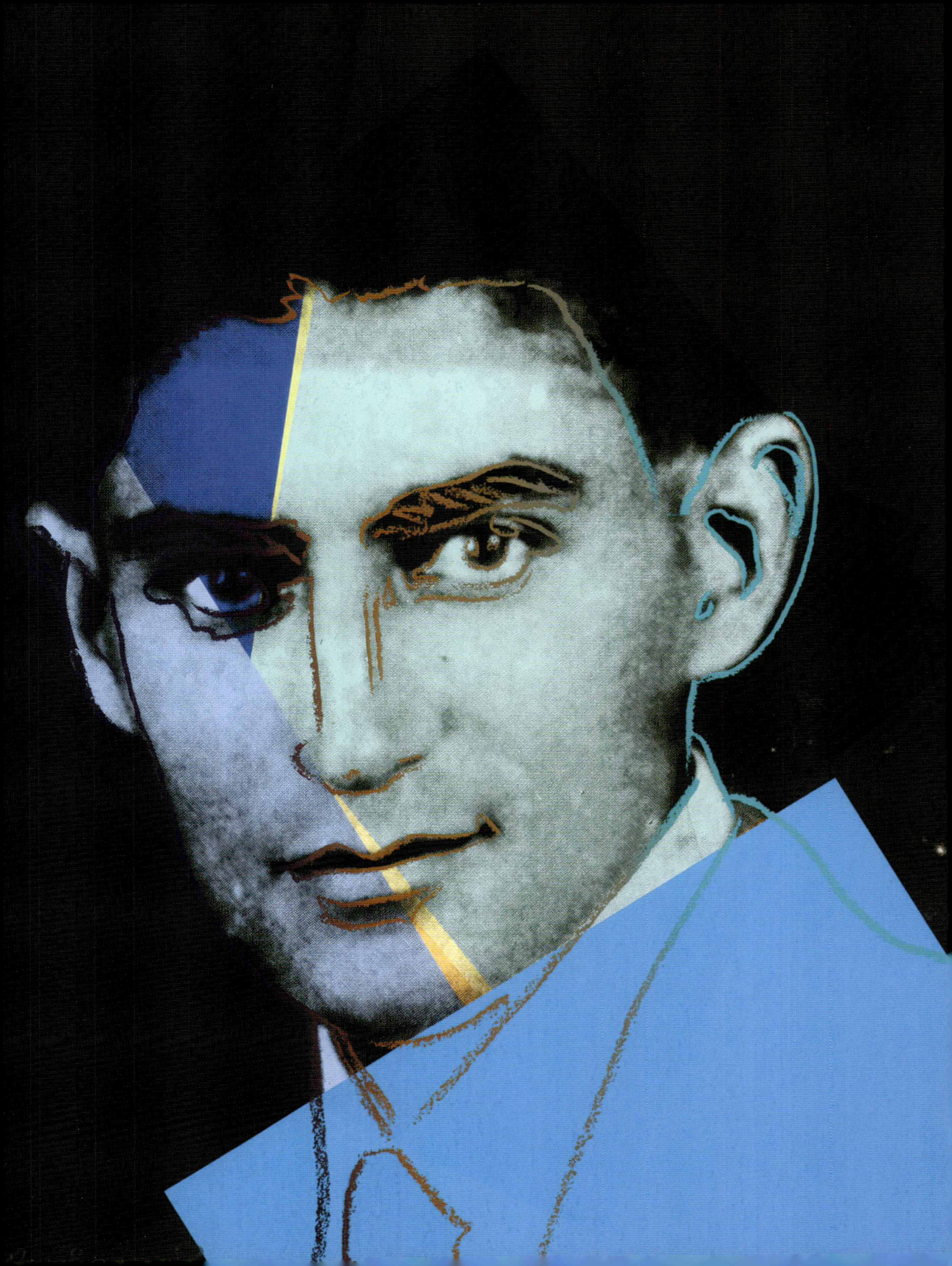

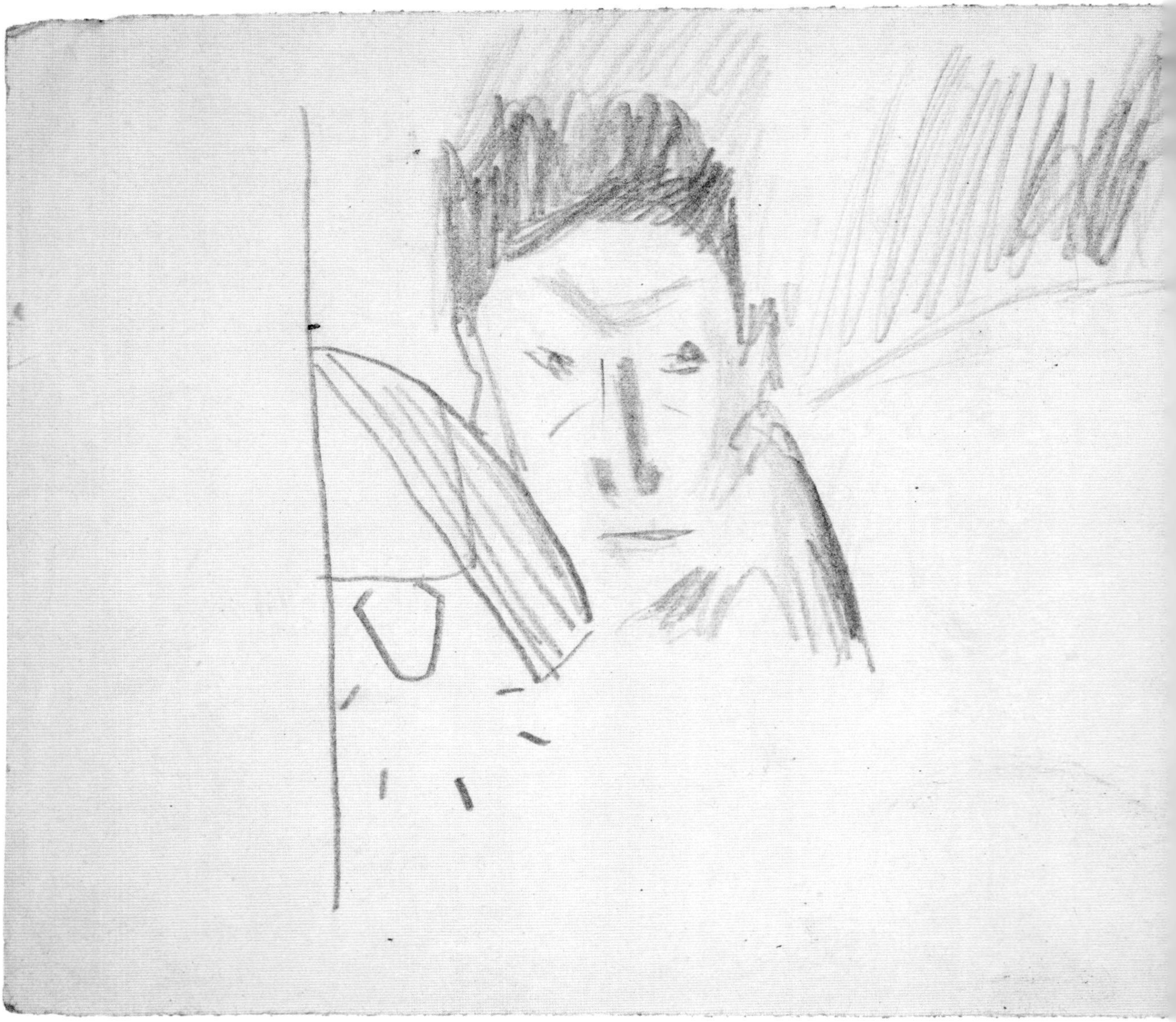

ABOVE Kafka imagines himself—appearing far less friendly—in this self-portrait doodle on the back of an envelope, made between 1905 and 1907. The original is held, appropriately, by the Literary Estate of Max Brod, stored at the National Library of Israel in Jerusalem. As the slightly mocking appearance of the caricature emphasizes, we are often least kind to ourselves.

THE DOLL IN THE PARK

After Franz Kafka died from tuberculosis at the young age of forty while residing in the small Austrian hamlet of Klosteneuburg, his friend Max Brod would posthumously visit upon the writer a most necessary betrayal. "Kafka's writing had afforded him no fame" during his lifetime, writes Benjamin Balint in *Kafka's Last Trial: The Case of a Literary Legacy*. "Public recognition had eluded him, as had any expectation that posterity would be more appreciative than his contemporaries," and so the author entrusted all of his remaining, unpublished papers to Brod. "Dearest Max," wrote Kafka in a signed letter discovered after his funeral in the drawer of his secretary desk, "Everything I leave behind me . . . in the way of notebooks, manuscripts, letters . . . sketches and so on, is to be burned unread and to the last page." There was a kindness in Brod's disloyalty, for rather than as kindling, the friend prepared Kafka's work for publication. At the funeral, Brod had eulogized Kafka as a prophet and an emanation of the Shekhinah, the indwelling presence of the Lord as described by Jewish mysticism. For such a man, there can be no sense in which his creations belong to him, as Brod well understood. Had the wishes of that prophet of the Shekhinah been heeded, then we'd have no *Metamorphosis* with its unclear allegory of Gregor Samsa transformed into an insect, none of the dystopian prophecy of *The Trial*'s Joseph K. heedlessly trying to discover why he was condemned. Because of Brod, those remaining stories and fragments would become the most integral of modernist writings; these prophetic, Kabbalistic works interrogate our alienated condition, the reality of a godless and absurd world. An apt summation of Kafka's body of brilliant work was supplied by Brod in a missive to his friend, who wrote, "Franz—You are happy in your unhappiness." Yet ironically, the most beautiful of stories which Kafka ever wrote is about the possibility of happiness, the possibility of kindness. And it's a story which, unlike the rest of Kafka's œuvre, was successfully erased from literary existence.

Dora Diamant was Kafka's last lover, but arguably the happiest of his romances. The twenty-four-year-old émigrée to Berlin was the descendant of a Polish Hasidic dynasty and a volunteer for the Berlin Jewish Peoples' home; she met the older Czech author while he was being treated in a sanitarium on the Baltic Sea. Their relationship would last only a year before Kafka died, but during that time the young woman was privy to the reaches of the author's soul—that Shekhinah that not even Brod could broach. According to Diamant, who later in life would escape both Nazi Germany and Stalinist Russia alike, she and Kafka would often spend afternoons when he was feeling steady and healthy enough exploring Berlin's Steglitz Park. The hawkish, gaunt, and corpuscular author, despite his wasting, still had those beautiful cheekbones and sad russet eyes and would stroll arm in arm with his short, raven-haired lover. His luck was maybe a few mouthfuls of pumpernickel, perhaps a swallow or two of black tea. Under a canopy of linden and birch, ash and alder, past the fountain and rose garden, in the slight chill of a low-sun autumnal afternoon, Kafka and Diamant encountered a young girl despairing over having lost her doll. The author—childless and a lifelong bachelor—consoled the girl by telling her that "Your doll has

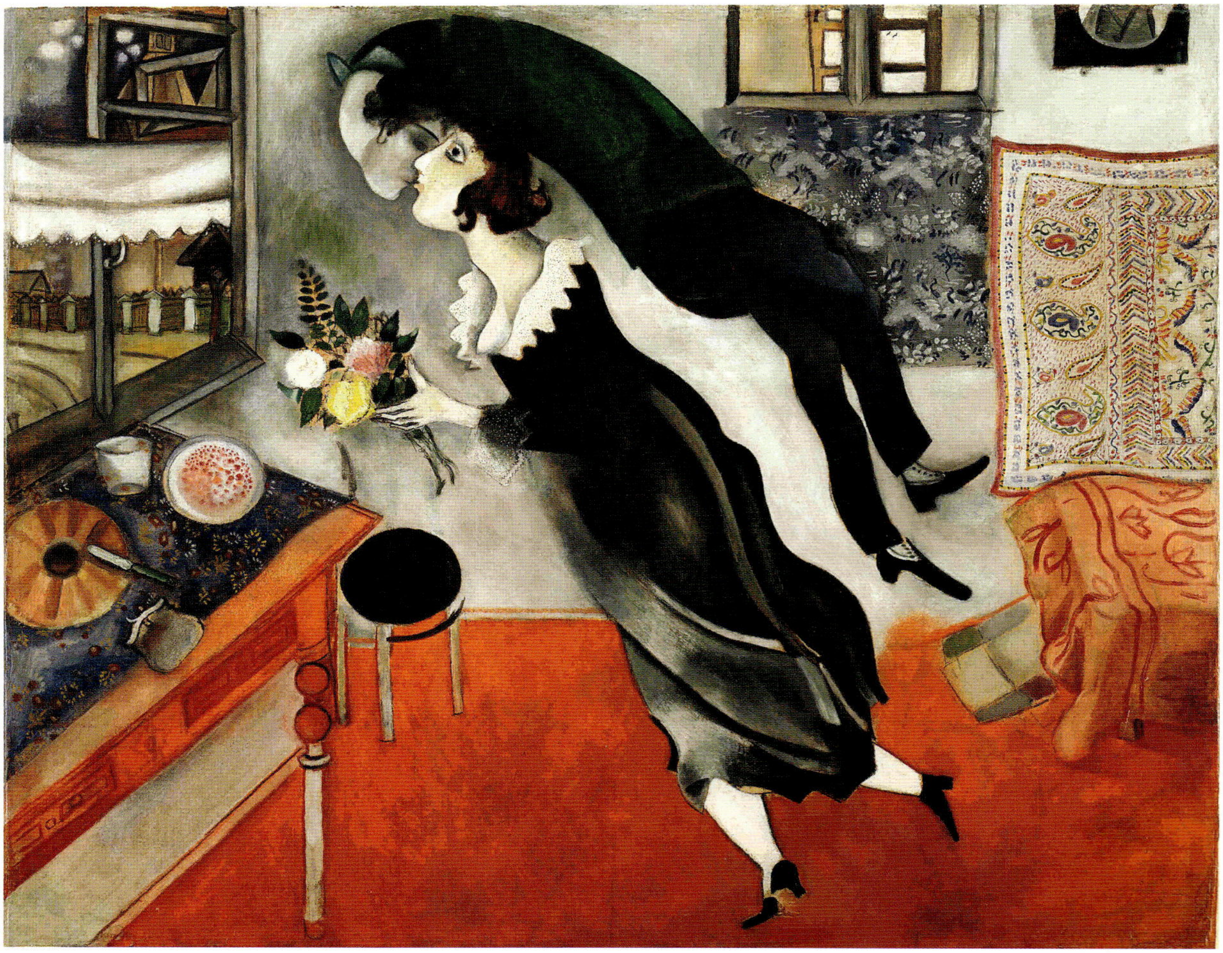

simply gone on a journey—I know because she's written me a letter," according to Diamant, whose account was recorded in a 1984 essay of the *Jewish Chronicle* by critic Anthony Rudolf. According to Diamant, "Franz went home to immediately write the letter," returning to Steglitz the next day with the doll's epistle as a gift for the girl. The girl being too young to read, Kafka read aloud the letter, wherein the doll stated her deep love for the child but said that she was curious about the world and longed to go on adventures; she promised to write home to Berlin every day with stories about all that which she discovered. For three weeks the dying author dedicated his waning energy to composing this new story, wherein the doll meets new friends and attends school, with Diamant remembering that Kafka "set to work with the same seriousness he displayed when composing one of his own works, and in the same state of tension," for it was crucial that the "child at all costs must not be cheated, but truly appeased . . . since the lie must be transformed into the truth of reality by means of the truth of fiction." Nearly sapped of his vitality, Kafka's final letter from the doll described her happy marriage in a foreign country. The girl was now placated despite the loss of her beloved toy. A few short months later, Kafka would die in Diamant's arms.

ABOVE Only four years younger than Kafka, the Franco-Polish artist Marc Chagall was similarly drawn to Jewish themes, though his were often more overtly expressed. His 1915 painting *The Birthday* expresses Chagall's matrimonial bliss on the occasion of his wedding to his childhood sweetheart, Bella. Unlike Kafka, who perhaps wished to be married but was constitutionally incapable of it, Chagall was drawn to the stolid religious values implicit in the kindness of family life, seeing in the love between husband and wife more mysticism than in the meditations of the solitary anchorite.

BELOW "Frog said, 'I wrote, "Dear Toad, I am glad that you are my best friend. Your best friend, Frog."'" Children's book author and illustrator Arnold Lobel's iconic "Frog and Toad" series, done as a series of four titles between 1970 and 1979, was intended to express the simple beauty of companionship and the universal language of kindness. People learn much of what they know about kindness from those loved ones involved in raising them, and the most powerful literature that embodies such virtues is frequently that which is imparted to us in our youth.

Rudolph quotes Diamant as saying that Kafka's intention had been to substitute chaos with order, that he had sought to resolve the "child's conflict through art, the best method he possessed for bringing order into the world." Understandably, the anecdote has proven popular over the last few decades; it appears in American novelist Paul Auster's *The Brooklyn Follies* and in a children's book by Larissa Theule and Rebecca Green entitled *Kafka and the Doll*; it's even been mentioned in a handful of biographies, though generally scholars are more circumspect about its accuracy. No trace of such letters remains; impossible to know if the Berlin child held on to them under a mattress or in a box, if they were consigned to Kafka's desired flames during the violence of Kristallnacht, or if the girl simply disposed of them when she was older, unaware that this was an unsigned tale from the greatest author of the twentieth century. For that matter, there is simply no evidence as to the veracity of the account other than Diamant's own word, though of course memory is culpable to revisions and deletions just as a fictional story is. None of that is of any accounting. Whether or not the story actually happened is incidental; regardless of its factuality, the tale is true. The pathos of such a thing simply can't be underestimated. Part of the anecdote's function, this shadowy, half-remembered account from the borderlands of truth, is to serve the same purpose as those imagined letters from the doll, to bring order out of chaos. That is, incidentally, part of the same after-effect of kindness. With kindness, there is an attribute of restoration, of fixing-the-world, of what the kabbalists call *tikkun olam*. Most importantly, kindness—true kindness—is disinterested. Kafka didn't write the letters for acclaim or for compensation—though prophets seldom do. What he marshalled all of his literary brilliance toward was a freely given gift of beauty, of empathy. He used his otherworldly powers of imagination to craft a better world than one where a beloved doll may have fallen into the bushes or the gutter, never to be seen again. The kindness of Kafka was such that it manifested, even if briefly, a better reality than the fallen one in which we reside. Not all acts of kindness take the baroque form that Kafka's elaborate performed epistolary did, but all acts of kindness are similarly inculcated within the imagination, within the human mind's ability to conceive of sympathy, tenderness, and comfort in ways far larger than the mere individual.

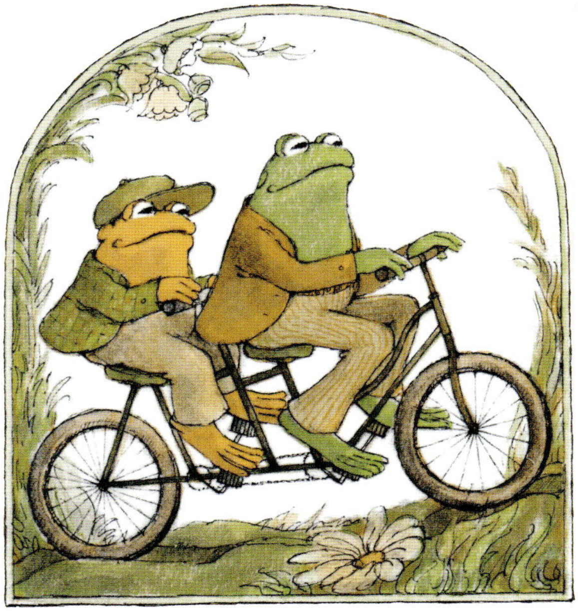

No virtue is as poorly theorized as kindness, and yet no virtue is more crucial. Integral, indispensable, instrumental—queen of human sentiments, for in its absence faith is cold, work is joyless, and life is empty. Kindness is an adjacent neighbor to empathy, compassion, altruism, tenderness, and sympathy, but they are not reducible into one another. Nor should kindness be mistaken for several attributes which often camouflage themselves in the fetters of personability. Niceness is not the same thing as kindness, as the former is a superficial social strategy rather than a virtue. In the thirteenth century the earliest instances of the English word "nice" were in meaning nearer to "stupid," but even today that word's general sense of unassuming agreeableness still evokes a bit of the dullard's character. After all, kindness need not

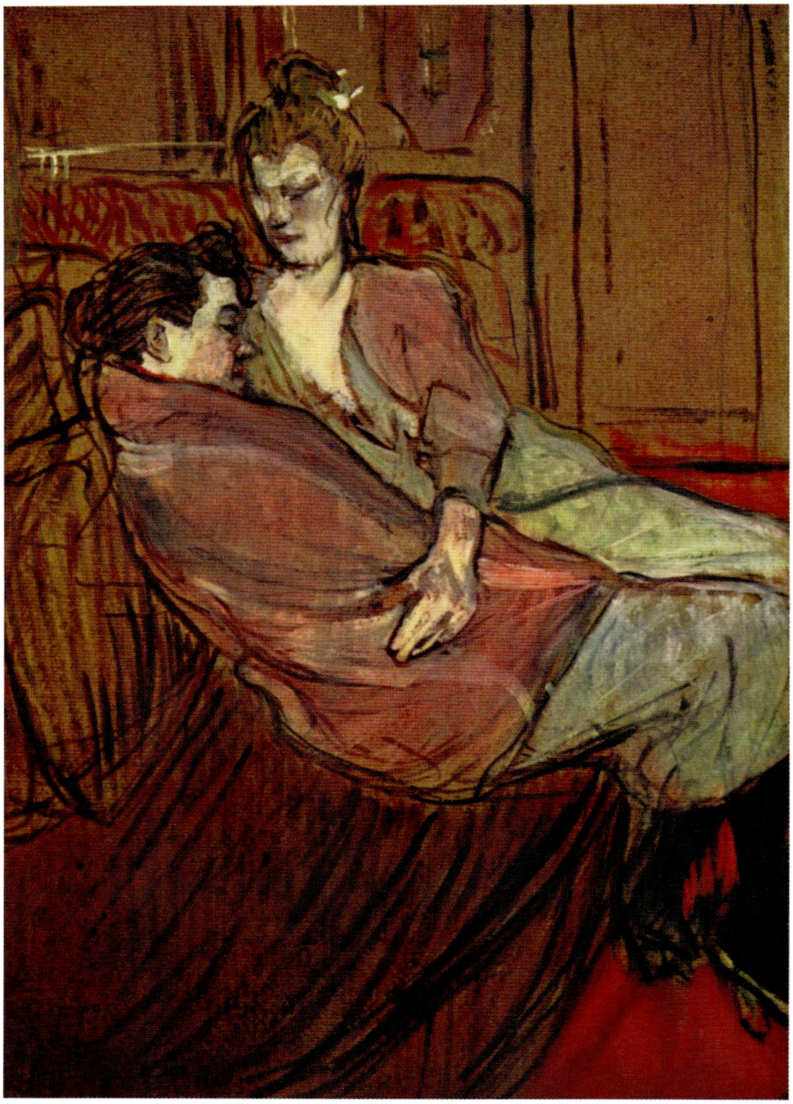

be agreeable (and often the most potent forms are anything but). Friendliness isn't kindness either, though it's nearer to that quality than niceness is. Plenty of cruel people are friendly; folks who think nothing of casual malice in their daily lives can also be polite to their neighbors and they can tip the waitstaff well. Compared to niceness and friendliness, kindness is wholly more mysterious; neither social strategy to ease interactions nor mask to cover wickedness, but a genuine, freely given gift of grace between humans. Crucially, to be kind is not equivalent to being morally good (though the latter are very often the former, even if not always). Because the human soul is a many-layered thing, there are innumerable examples of those who are less than sterling, perhaps even evil, and yet who are capable of a genuine kindness. Both Al Capone and Pablo Escobar established soup kitchens and hospitals; lest the public nature of such endeavors seem as mere marketing, then consider the sadistic, evil serial killer

TOP French post-impressionist Henri de Toulouse-Lautrec was a keen admirer of prostitutes and a frequent denizen of brothels, yet even in such seedy places, dens of commodification and exploitation, he could with keen eye discern genuine kindness among those who plied their trade there. His 1894 *Two Friends* depicts a moment of warm embrace between two of the workers in a brothel. Original held by the Tate Modern in London.

Ted Bundy, who during his murder spree in 1970s Florida simultaneously volunteered as a suicide call center operator, famed among his oblivious colleagues for his success in convincing the desperate and depressed to not kill themselves. If there is a Hell, then surely that brutal murderer of thirty-six women will burn there forever, as there is no weighing the taking of a life against the preservation of one. Still, there is also something uncomfortable, paradoxical, and deeply mysterious about the fathoms deep of a human soul which allows genuine kindness to exist amid the wasteland of evil. The origins of compassion, whether from those who are good or those who are evil, are among the most confounding and beautiful aspects of our fallen nature.

"It is the characteristic of the magnanimous man to ask no favor," writes Aristotle in *Rhetoric*, "but to be ready to do kindness to others," while the Roman Stoic Seneca the Younger noted in *De Vita Beata* that "wherever there is a human being there is an opportunity for a kindness," and yet both sentiments—as admirable as they are—do have a tinge of the tautological about them. Theology, as is its wont, is slightly more helpful, with the various permutations of what's sometimes called the Golden Rule providing a schema for kindness. The Prophet Muhammad is recorded in the Hadith as saying that "kindness is a mark of faith," delineating how belief in Allah is equivalent with loving care toward His creations in the form of our fellow humans, for "whoever has not kindness has not faith."

BELOW Familiar with and welcomed in Amsterdam's vibrant Sephardic community, Rembrandt van Rijn took as his subject a father in the quiet moments before his daughter is to be wed in his 1665 composition *The Jewish Bride*, original held by the Rijksmuseum. Because kindness often lacks in visible drama, it takes a particular genius to relay the incandescence of the virtue radiating outward.

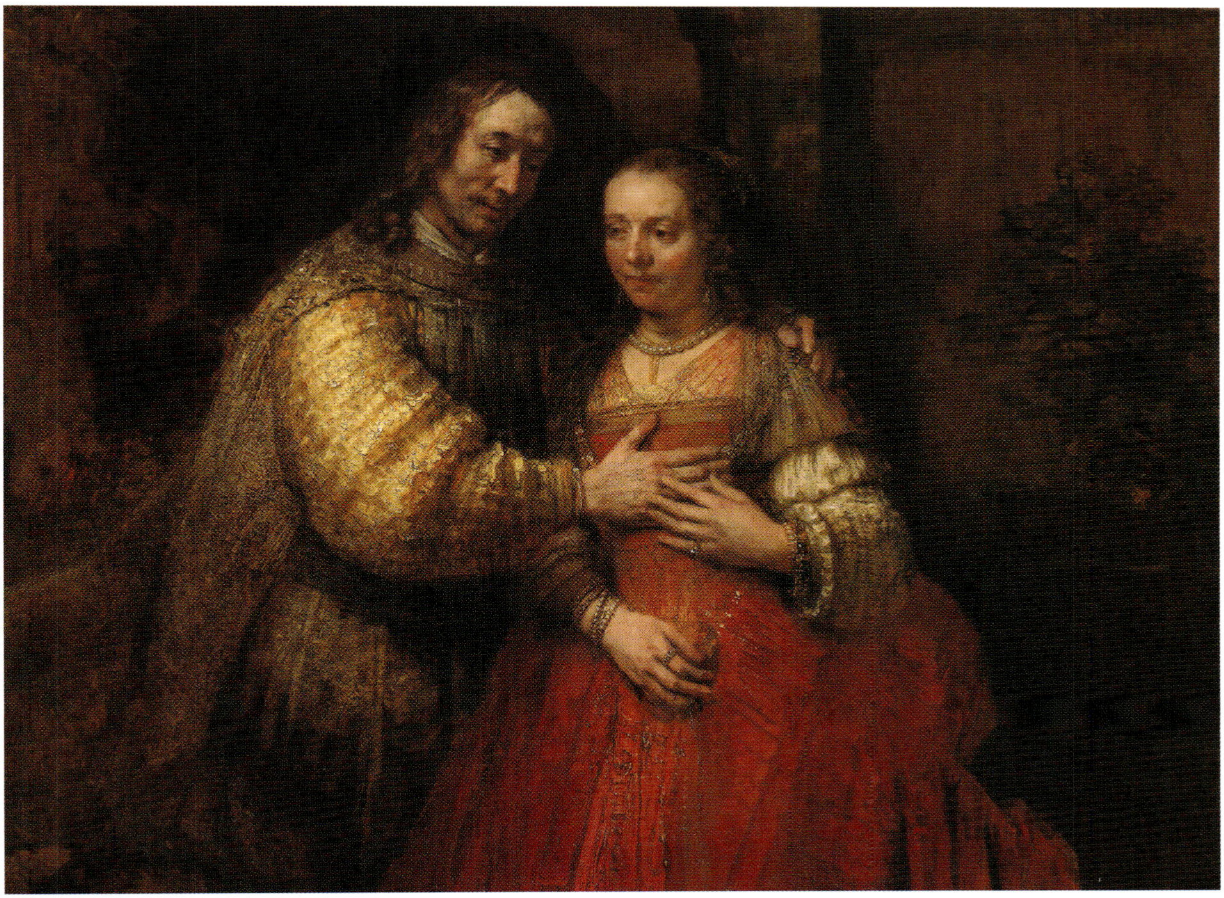

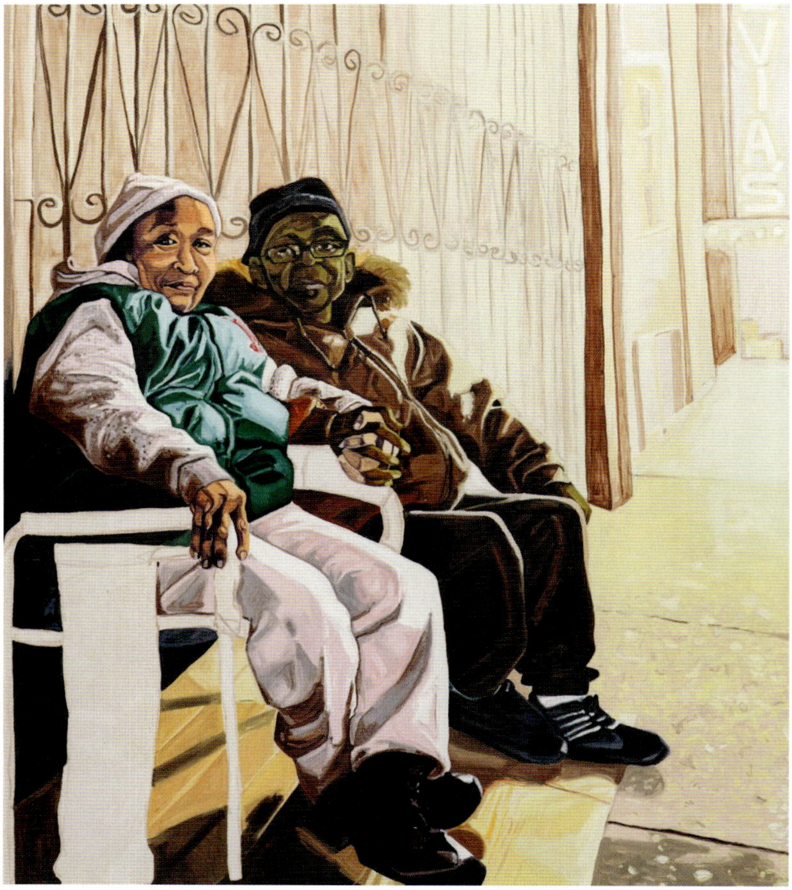

The Apostle Paul defines the quality in cosmic terms in his epistle to the Hebrews, understanding the major force through which God sustains the world as being "underserved kindness" (though it could be argued that "deserved kindness" would be a contradiction). Meanwhile, the Talmud intones with great power that "deeds of kindness are equal in weight to all of the commandments." By not defining what exactly this universally understood but inexplicable virtue *feels* like, the rabbis counterintuitively get closest to actually explicating kindness.

An act of purely given kindness, of tenderness, comfort, love, can't be circumscribed in syllogism or argument; rather, it is felt in an embrace between friends, in consolation given to the grieving, in encouragement imparted to the uncertain, or in a letter written by a doll. Kindness asks not for your deduction or induction, but instead for recognition of each other in the darkness. Literature, as in all things, gets much nearer to the essence of kindness than does philosophy or religion. Literature has long had a reputation as being a mechanism for encouraging empathy, whereby the expression of interiority made possible by forms such as the novel allow for a middle-aged white man to ever so slightly understand the experiences of a young Black girl, or how poetry imparts to a young college student the perspective of being an elderly woman, so that perhaps the very form encourages a type of residual kindness among fellow humans. Suzanne Keen writes in *Empathy and the Novel* that "if empathy can

TOP Contemporary American painter Jordan Casteel's 2017 composition *Yvonne and James I*, original at the Metropolitan Museum of Art, poignantly depicts an elderly married couple after passion has been traded for kindness, a moving evocation of the depth and endurance of love.

OPPOSITE Frequent victim of her husband's infidelities, nevertheless the Mexican Surrealist Frida Kahlo forgave her partner, the muralist Diego Rivera. Because forgiveness—like kindness—is not required, its impartation is freely given as an act of grace. In her 1943 *Self Portrait as a Tehuana*, Kahlo depicts herself in the traditional native dress that Rivera adored, an image of her now ex-husband emblazoned on her forehead, with the artist explaining that her subject was "thinking about Diego." Original held by the North Carolina Museum of Art in Raleigh.

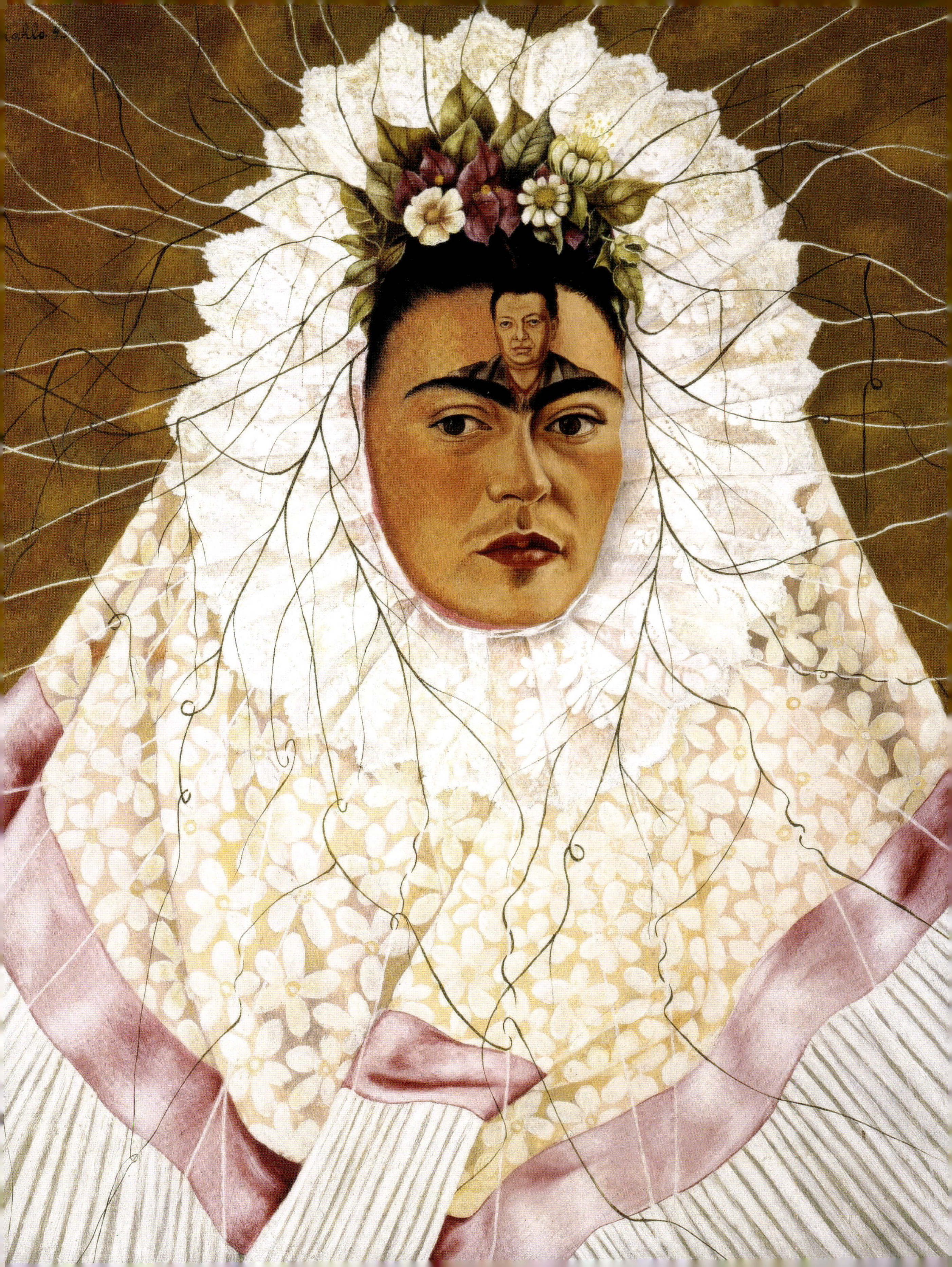

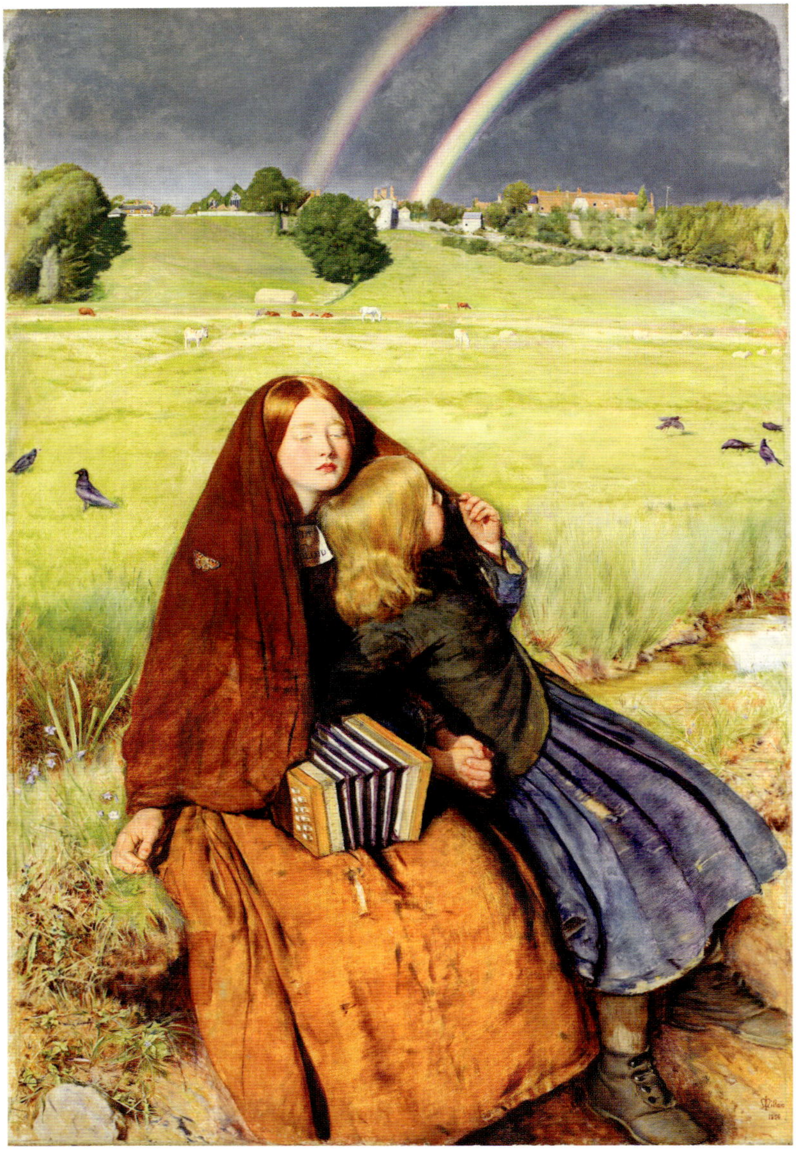

be learned or developed, then novel reading might contribute to the cultivation of empathy" while in *Not for Profit: Why Democracy Needs the Humanities*, philosopher Martha Nussbaum describes how the creation of literature, of immersive fictional worlds, can bolster a certain "moral imagination" which is the wellspring of empathy and then of kindness. Yet this perennial debate over whether or not fiction and poetry inculcate empathy is entirely incidental to this discussion, a critical red herring as to what literature's function regarding empathy and kindness really happens to be. Rather, what's fascinating is the way in which literature can come near to expressing a bit of that intangible light in the darkness, those moments of freely given kindness.

The Southern Gothic and very Catholic writer Flannery O'Connor explained this special skill of literature, this ability to convey that frequently invisible and often inexplicable turn of the soul, the impartation of a grace between humans. She writes in *The Habit of Being: The Letters of Flannery O'Connor* that "all human nature vigorously resists grace because grace changes us and change is painful," the sort of divine kindness that is vehemently not friendly or nice. O'Connor sees this strange and beautiful essence in everything from an old, unrepentant racist briefly giving a perspective of reality's hidden divine nature to the brief second of genuine humanity and kinship between a murderer and the elderly woman who is his victim. Tod Worner at the website Patheos describes O'Connor's vision as expressing "mean grace," explaining that her writing could be "harsh, violent and discomforting. And yet it is also thick with truth, grace and redemption." Far more than a simple didactic method for training people to be empathetic—a dubious hypothesis, despite Keen and Nussbaum's enthusiasm for literature—the moral function of fiction and poetry is simply to express some of the oddity of kindness, the unlikelihood of such selflessness, such tenderness, such human feeling in a world that seems to be dominated by avarice, cruelty, and narcissistic regard. What kindness offers is a respite; it is a keyhole into the kingdom of millennium; what literature then provides is simply a reminder that such acts of compassion and tenderness are possible, despite the nature of the cankered and fallen reality in which we all reside. For example, the Canadian writer Alice Munro's deeply sad and gorgeous short story "The Bear Came Over the Mountain" details without sentimentality the relationship between an imperfect couple, retired university professor Grant and his wife, Fiona, the latter of whom has been stricken by Alzheimer's disease and consigned to an institution. Frequently disloyal to his wife, Grant discovers that Fiona has forgotten who he is, and has thus innocently entered into a romance with another patient suffering from dementia. After assuaging his anguish with the conviction that this predicament is not some form of delayed revenge, Grant embraces the fact that his wife has found some modicum of happiness in her life, so much so that when the wife of Fiona's new lover removes him from the hospital, Grant intervenes to ensure the boyfriend's return. Briefly regaining her faculties, Fiona tells Grant that he could have forsaken her, to which he replies, "Not a chance." A bizarre variety of kindness, and all the more true because of it.

"All these weirdos, and me getting a little better every day right in the midst of them," says the character of Fuckhead in Denis Johnson's novella *Jesus' Son*, an intertwined cycle of stories about an itinerant junkie and drunkard between Iowa City, Seattle, Phoenix, and Chicago, living in neon dive bars and scoring bags of heroin with other addicts. High and sober, in and out of recovery, in the midst of traumatic relationships with lovers and friends, by the end of the novella Fuckhead has scratched together a modest form of happiness, living in a halfway house and finally living with some degree of function, having "never even imagined for a heartbeat, that there might be a place for people like us." Johnson's work is enmeshed in grace, in the enigma of cosmic kindness. Moments of grace for Fuckhead are few and far between, and often hard to discern (as indeed grace must be for any of us). Saving some baby rabbits that he later accidentally crushes to death, seeing the gray shadows of a drive-in movie theater blanketed in snow during a surprise Iowa September squall, cradling a newborn infant to his chest after surviving a car crash that has killed the family who picked him up while hitchhiking, spying on a Mennonite husband washing his young wife's feet in

OPPOSITE English artist John Everett Millais's celebrated 1856 painting *The Blind Girl* depicts two itinerant sisters who perform music for charity in respite from the rain, the older girl cradling her younger sibling beneath her shawl, a concertina on her lap. It's a subject that risks saccharine sentimentality, yet the extreme stillness of the scene (note the butterfly sitting on the older girl's shawl) and the calm beatitude of the main figure's facial expression are poignant in a manner that eschews any cynical interpretation.

supplication. Even in the throes of his addiction there could be a life-saving grace in the very things which are killing Fuckhead, such as in the form of a naive and benevolent bartender, a young woman who "poured doubles like an angel, right up to the lips of a cocktail glass . . . You had to go down to them like a hummingbird over a blossom." The deep and intrinsic difference of kindness is that it can often be hard to identify in the moment, at least intellectually. As a matter of the heart, the situation is completely different (obviously). Johnson learned of such literary kindness, in part, through the tutelage of those master mentors at the University of Iowa Writers Workshop: authors like Raymond Carver, who could imagine the kindness of a man who assists the blind husband of a woman he's been corresponding with in drawing a cathedral, so that the latter could understand these buildings which he'd only ever heard described: "So we kept on with it. His fingers rode my fingers as my hand went over the paper. It was like nothing in my life up to now," a metaphorical description of what empathy feels like as well as an enactment of a profound and intimate kindness. A wisdom which Carver's friend and colleague John Cheever, another professor of Johnson's, described when he claimed that it is not "the smell of corn bread that calls us back from death; it is the lights and signs of love and friendship," lights and signs which are but kindness's stigmata.

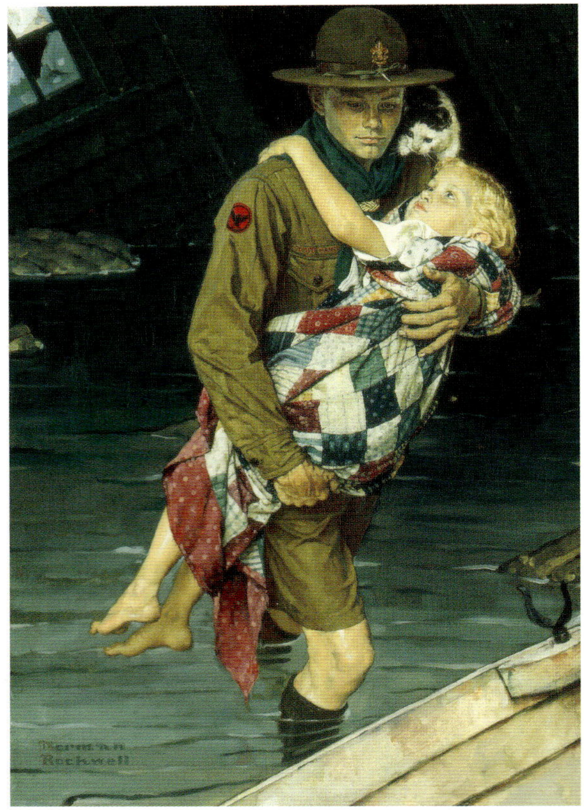

Marilynne Robinson, another daughter of Iowa, explores simple, perfect kindness in her novel *Gilead*, written as a series of epistles by the elderly Presbyterian minister John Ames to his young son who will most likely never know his father as an adult. Expressing an axiom about human ethics, the minister writes to his son, "When you encounter another person, when you have dealings with anyone at all, it is as if a question is being put to you. So you must think, What is the Lord asking of me in this moment, in this situation?" Almost always, invariably, regardless of circumstance or situation, the answer to Ames's question is that the Lord is requiring *kindness*. What that kindness looks like, in what form it shall appear . . . those answers are contingent and relative and contextual, but what kindness necessitates is an acknowledgment that this person whom you are facing, whether familiar or not, friendly or not, a good person or not, is another human being, another universe unto themself, which deserves an acknowledgment of something intrinsic and sacred. *That acknowledgment is what we call kindness.* When a visitor to the second-century Rabbi Hillel asked the master to explain the whole of the Torah while standing upon one leg, the sage hiked up foot to knee and told the man that the entirety of God's command was to treat others as we'd like to be treated, and that the rest was simply commentary. Kurt Vonnegut expressed the same thing in slightly more words and with both feet on the ground in his novel *God Bless You, Mr. Rosewater*, in which a character whispers to two newborn twins, "Hello babies. Welcome to Earth. It's hot in the summer and cold in the winter. It's round and wet and crowded. On the outside, babies, you've got

ABOVE Too often disparaged as a conveyer of kitsch, or as a mere illustrator, the American painter Norman Rockwell was adept at conveying quiet drama with unsparing realism, as in his 1943 composition *Scout Came to the Rescue*. A Boy Scout cradles a young child (with a pet cat upon his shoulder) as they move out from a floodplain, a sunken house in the background. Far from leaning on mere sentimentalism—this is a painting of a violent natural disaster, after all—Rockwell has opted to convey something that is unconveyable in mere words, here expressed in the dignified and stoic determination of the scout and the gratitude of the child.

a hundred years here. There's only one rule that I know of, babies—'God damn it, you've got to be kind.'"

But how to be kind? Surely it's not always easy. It's not always possible to even know what kindness is. To feel it, though, that's a different issue. To reframe the Scripture, kindness is patient, kindness is loving. It does not envy, it does not boast, it is not proud. It does not dishonor others, it is not self-seeking, it is not easily angered, it keeps no record of wrongs Kindness does not delight in evil but rejoices with the truth, where the truth must always be "I see you, you who are in need of this kindness." A kind act is freely given and serves no ulterior purpose. Kindness serves no meaning beyond itself; it is not utilitarian. Kindness is absurd, but all of the most beautiful and important things are. At the beginning of *Gilead*, Ames describes how as a boy he desired to baptize an entire litter of kittens—a pointless exercise to any serious adult who maintains that cats have no souls, yet the purest act of kindness to desire a Heaven for these creatures, the truest act of faith. "I still remember how those warm little brows felt under the palm of my hand," Robinson writes, describing Ames anointing the kittens with water from the river. "Everyone has petted a cat, but to touch one like that, with the pure intention of blessing it, is a very different thing." *The pure intention of blessing*—as apt a summation of kindness as you're likely to find.

INTERLUDE—JONAS SALK

Arsenal Elementary School, its neoclassical, fortress-like, white granite façade as stolid as its name, derived from the former Civil War depot that had sat on this site nearly a century before, loomed over Butler Street in Pittsburgh's Lawrenceville neighborhood, a tightly packed Irish and Polish neighborhood of row houses and nineteenth-century townhomes, of steep, confusing one-way streets and of redbrick cobblestoned avenues lined with trolley car track. Early in 1954, more than a hundred of the students gathered in the gymnasium, formed a queue, and, when it was their turn, rolled up their sleeves in front of the slight and quiet, bespectacled and balding young physician who briefly reassured the children in his New York accent before injecting them with a mixture of three strains of the polio virus that had been deactivated with the chemical formalin. The daughters and sons of steel mill workers, these working-class children were the first beneficiaries of Jonas Salk's revolutionary polio vaccine, the modest physician having first experimented on himself before verifying the safety of the technique and then working toward first vaccinating the children of Pittsburgh, then the rest of the United States, and then the world. As his son later remembered in an interview, Salk "felt that he couldn't ask other parents to let him give this vaccine to their children if he wasn't willing to first try it on his own."

Polio—that horrific disease, often contracted by children and young adults in public pools and swimming holes, restrooms and cafeterias—led to paralysis, the withering of limbs, the atrophying of lungs. The luckiest of those who contracted the feared childhood disease would perhaps walk with crutches or canes for the rest of their lives; the least fortunate would spend their days within the massive circular confines of that metallic prison of the iron lung, their breathing now made possible through the mechanical calculus of pressure differentials, of moving pistons and inflating balloons. At Arsenal, one young girl hobbled in on crutches, having already been infected by one of the three strains of polio, hopeful that Salk's vaccine would prevent further suffering from the remaining two. By the end of that winter, the doctor—employed as the director of the Virus Research Laboratory of the University of Pittsburgh—had vaccinated five thousand students in Pittsburgh. The children's immune systems activated, Salk's vaccination was 70 percent effective in preventing polio inflection. Because of widespread immunity, rates of infection would consequently drop by an astounding 99 percent. The Centers for Disease Control estimates that due to the eradication of polio, some eighteen million incidences of paralysis were prevented and more than two million lives saved. Salk refused to patent the vaccine, understanding it as a public good and leaving it in the public domain. It's estimated by economists that had Salk applied for a patent, he would have made around eight billion dollars. The vaccine "belongs to the people, I say," the doctor told journalist Edward R. Murrow in 1955. "There is no patent. Could you patent the sun?"

We're barely able to visualize such radical (though unassuming) and revolutionary (though modest) kindness. We're so proficient in knowing the grim statistics of those who are evil, the millions murdered by an Adolf Hitler or a Joseph Stalin, the alterity of incomprehensible wickedness, that we barely ever consider its diametric opposite. A man like Salk, and those visionaries of medicine both before and after him, have saved more people than were murdered in Hitler's concentration camps or Stalin's gulags, yet the nature of goodness is such that men of goodness lack the anxious trappings of power. Salk's power, nurtured by curiosity and honed by intelligence, was responsible for millions of young girls and boys being able to live. He was the proverbial savior of not just them, but also their children and grandchildren. Stalin infamously claimed that a single death is a tragedy but a million is a statistic, though ironically something similar is the case with incredible goodness. To pull a man from a burning car or a woman drowning in a river is an act of heroism and bravery, certainly deserving of accolades. Yet did Salk's neighbors—who of course *respected* him—really consider the implications of this skinny man waiting in line for challah at Rosenbloom's Bakery or enjoying dinner with his children at Poli's having been anti-Hitler, anti-Stalin, the man who preserved millions of lives because he was the one who was able to do so?

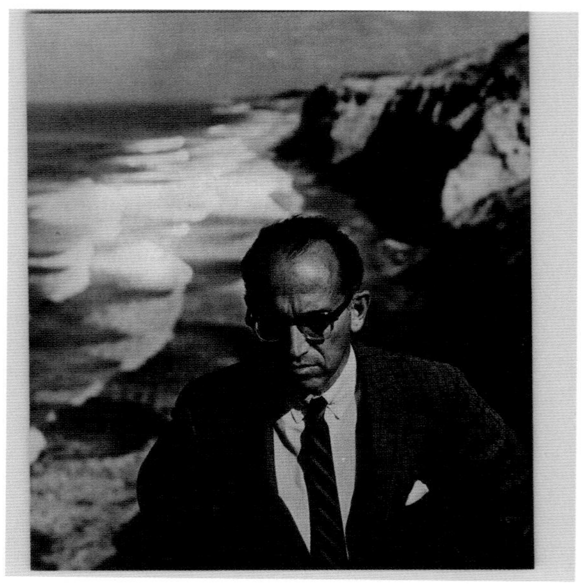

Asked what his central ethic was some three decades after the Arsenal vaccinations, Salk answered that it is to "Learn to live with each other" and to "bring out the best in each other." A cynic would interpret these as clichés, but clichés often come about because they happen to be true. What really must be considered is just how radical,

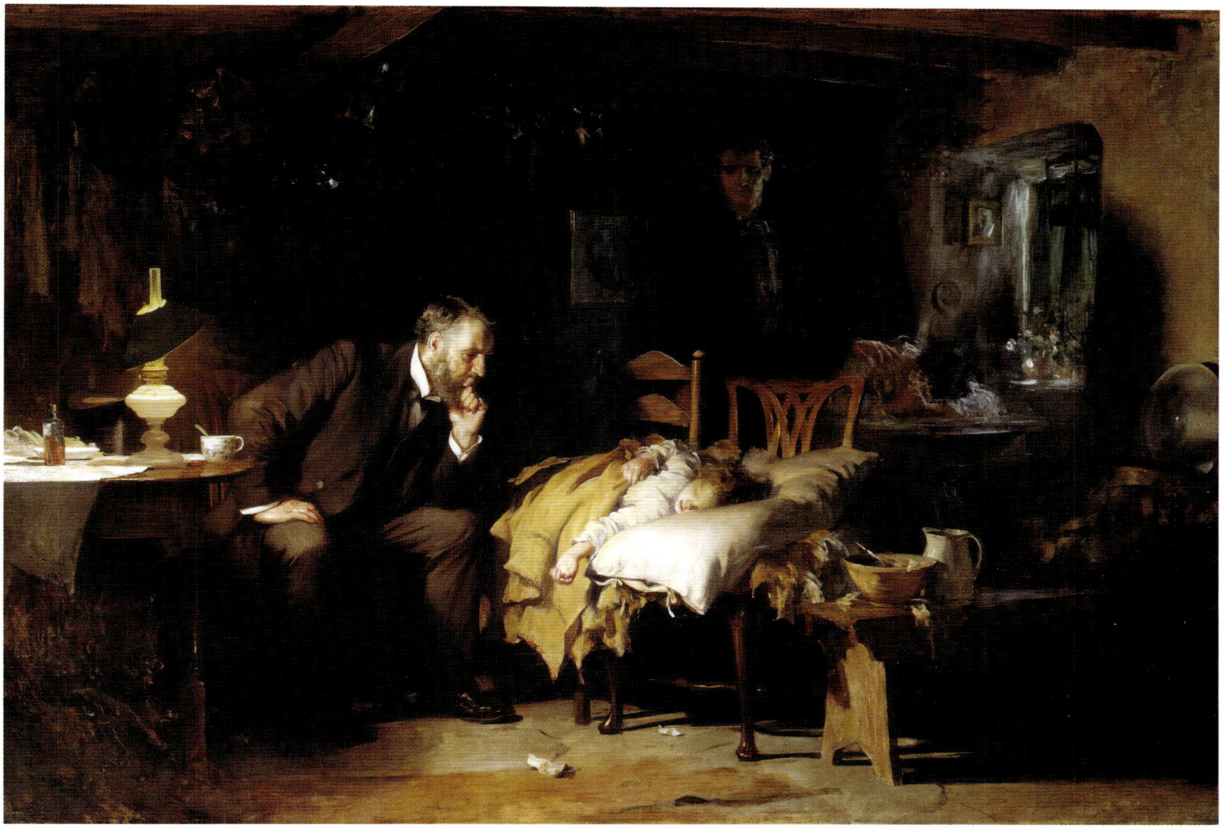

OPPOSITE 1963 photograph of Jonas Salk taken by Philippe Halsman in San Diego, near the institute which he had established three years before. Original at the Smithsonian National Portrait Gallery in Washington, DC.

ABOVE British painter Luke Fildes's 1891 composition *The Doctor* depicts a scene of unimaginable pathos, whereby a physician, having extended every possible solution of medical science to save a septic child, now has only his empathy and kindness to rely on, sitting by the boy's deathbed and consoling him as he passes from this world. Where a priest once would have sat, now it is the doctor's vocation to offer such last rites, the sort of kindness that cannot be paid back, but which is also a burden to bear.

just how *unfamiliar*, such sentiments happen to be, despite their sounding like platitudes. The physician offered a deeper exegesis, saying that such principles bespeak "an entirely different philosophy—a different way of life—a different kind of relationship—where the object is not to put down the other, but to raise up the other." Obviously he's absolutely correct, for though such kindness may not be easy, it really is that simple. Both a genius and a humanitarian, Salk wasn't even awarded a Nobel Prize, yet the legacy of innumerable generations saved is infinitely more precious than any gold disk and certificate handed over by the king of Sweden. Easy to blame science and technology for the predicaments that we currently find ourselves in, from climate change to the sixth great extinction, yet it's also easy to forget that the empirical method and its application are tools, and tools are neutral, only given significance by those who wield them. Salk was able to save millions of lives with his invention, as Louis Pasteur was with his cholera vaccine of 1880 and his rabies vaccine of 1885, as Albert Calmette was with tuberculosis in 1921, George and Gladys Dick for scarlet fever in 1924, Anatol Smorodintsev for influenza in 1937, the eradication of smallpox by Soviet and American partnership in 1980, and Kizzmekia Corbett and the vaccine for COVID-19 in 2021. Billions of human lives have been saved by women and men dutifully putting in anonymous hours at a laboratory somewhere, the depth of such kindness hidden in an unassuming prosaicness, all the more profound as a result.

TIDINGS OF COMFORT AND JOY

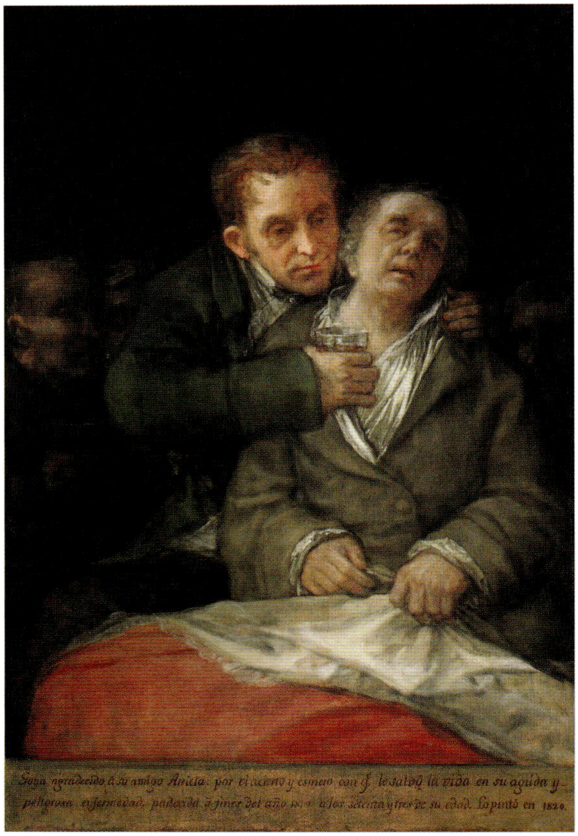

ABOVE The grateful Spanish artist Francisco Goya honors his physician in the 1820 painting *Self-Portrait with Dr. Arrieta*, original held at the Minneapolis Museum of Art. Known for his ability to convey the darker nature of the human psyche, Goya turned toward themes of empathy in this composition, whose subject is drawn from a mysterious 1819 illness which nearly killed the artist, if not for the capable care of Arrieta. Arrieta's expression is concerned but confident, the steady and certain hand of a physician driven by intelligence but compelled by kindness.

OPPOSITE German and British soldiers enjoy a game of soccer on Christmas Day, 1914. How many of these men would survive the war? How many would be dead from one of their athletic opponents' bullets the next day, week, month, year? To what end?

Only a few hours previously, acrid chlorine and sulfur had wafted in blinding invisible mists across the jagged wound of the shrapnel-studded flesh of the Western Front. Now, Allied and German trenches rather traded in projectiles wholly different from artillery bombardment, as soccer balls would be kicked across frozen French fields. From Neuve Chapelle to Messiness and Ploegsteert, Belgium, all along the frigid Yser Front on the evening before Christmas 1914, there was an absence of explosions and screaming, as instead a familiar refrain echoed through the darkness: "Douce nuit, sainte nuit! / Dans les cieux! L'astre luit"—"Stille Nacht, helige Nacht / Alles schlaft; einsam wacht"—"Silent night, holy night / All is calm, all is bright." Where during the day there had been an orchestra of Browning and Winchesters, rifles and machines guns, grenades and flamethrowers, now there was a carol played on an accordion from the German trench, joined in a few hundred yards away by a French concertina or perhaps even a Scottish bagpipe. Tentative at first, these young men whose officers were scarcely out of adolescence walked across the wasteland of battle-scarred earth, all crunch of hard pockmarked soil and tinkling of ice, to shake hands near the corpses of their dead comrades, killed by the very men whom they now nervously joined in holiday celebrations. Prohibited by military leadership, kept secret from the publics of their respective nations, it's estimated that the Christmas of 1914 saw at least a hundred thousand British soldiers lay down their arms alongside an equivalent number of their French allies and German adversaries, for a momentary lull in the violence, an opportunity for shared humanity.

For a few brief hours, the British 18th Infantry Brigade and the 6th Bavarian Reserve Division, King's Shropshire Light Infantry and the German 6th Army, the Royal Welsh Fusiliers and German Battalion 371 all heard the choir of angels rather than the rattle of gatling gun, pausing for an impromptu armistice, a yuletide truce. First a Christmas tree preposterously held by gloved hand over the firing line, a few dirty glass bulbs reflecting the lights of the trenches. Then caroling, the voices of boys singing "Hark! The Herald Angels Sings" and "O Tannenbaum," "God Rest Ye Merry Gentleman" and "Alle Jahre Wieder." Finally, the nervous soldiers would hoist themselves over the reinforced wooden skeletons of the trenches into the battlefield for the singing of songs, the exchanging of gifts—cigarettes and cigars, shots of whiskey and schnapps, tins of shortbread and Lebkuchen—the playing of soccer rather than the fighting of war. "Yesterday the British & Germans met & shook hands in the Ground between the trenches," wrote Private Henry Williamson of the London Rifle Brigade in a letter to his mother. "Yes, all day Xmas day, & as I write. Marvellous, isn't it?" How many of these men enjoying chocolate together or sharing nips of warm liquor were responsible for murdering the others' countrymen the day before? How many would be responsible on December 26? It didn't matter in this moment. Here, on the sacred ground of the Yser Front, there would be a brief respite, an empire of kindness. "Not a shot was fired all night," wrote Captain Robert Miles. He'd die in combat a week later.

A history of the world is not a history of kindness. Ours is a species far more defined by those vices, by avarice and pride, envy and wrath, and most of all, cruelty, than it is by compassion, empathy, tenderness. Yet to only focus on the evil which humans inflict upon each other is to pass far more credit over to the Devil than he possibly deserves. For there is kindness studded throughout time; moments of grace, hidden within the dross of horror which is human history. *These moments are everything.* Goodness is the illumination in the darkness of night, the solid island in the tumult of the tempest. Maybe even more than being rare, kindness is often simply hard to identify, or recognize, exhibiting none of the flashiness of evil, none of the sexiness of wickedness. True kindness need not draw attention to itself; it's the consoling words offered to a depressed stranger at a bar, the last dollar dropped into a soiled Styrofoam cup, the assuaging of the fearful in a hospice bed and the checking beneath mattresses for monsters. Goodness returns dutifully to do the work of existence, which in a crucial way demonstrates a remarkable facet of moral empathy—that far from being prosaic, it's remarkable, it's beautiful, it's inevitable. "Imaginary evil is romantic and varied; real evil is gloomy, monotonous, barren, boring," wrote Simone Weil in *On Science, Necessity, and the Love of God*, while "Imaginary good is boring; real good is always new, marvelous, intoxicating." All evil people are alike; each good person is good in their own way. Kindness is multitudinous; it manifests in surprising forms and is strung through the tapestry of the human story like a gold thread that's often barely visible, but which traverses the entire length of the massive, unfolded fabric.

"People are leading secretly kind lives all the time," write Barbara Taylor and Adam Phillips in *On Kindness*, "but without a language with which to express this," claiming that the "life lived in instinctive sympathetic identification with the vulnerabilities and attractions of others—is the life we are more inclined to live, and indeed is the one we are often living without letting ourselves know that this is what we are doing." Theirs is an interesting hypothesis, the sense that far from our human essence (whatever that is) being inclined toward brutality, we are fundamentally noble creatures, predisposed toward charity. Thomas Hobbes would disagree; Charles Darwin would also quibble; but the entire edifice of Christian Augustinianism with its gloomy predilection toward original sin is the ur-critique of humanity's supposed natural sunniness. As a "Just So" story is to the origins of human cruelty, any number of hypotheses could be proffered, from the stress of resource scarcity toward the maximizing of exploitation in the various unjust political

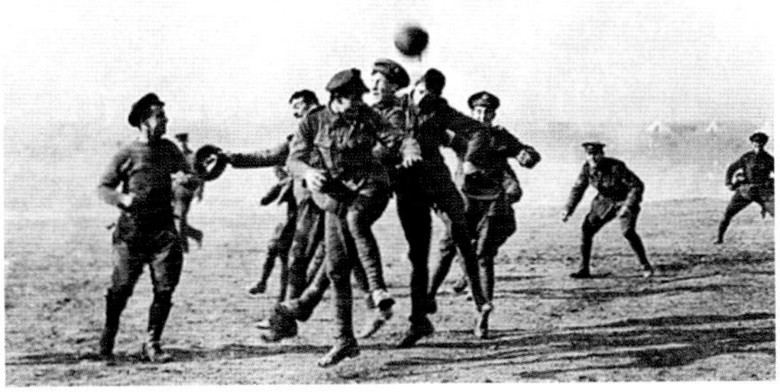

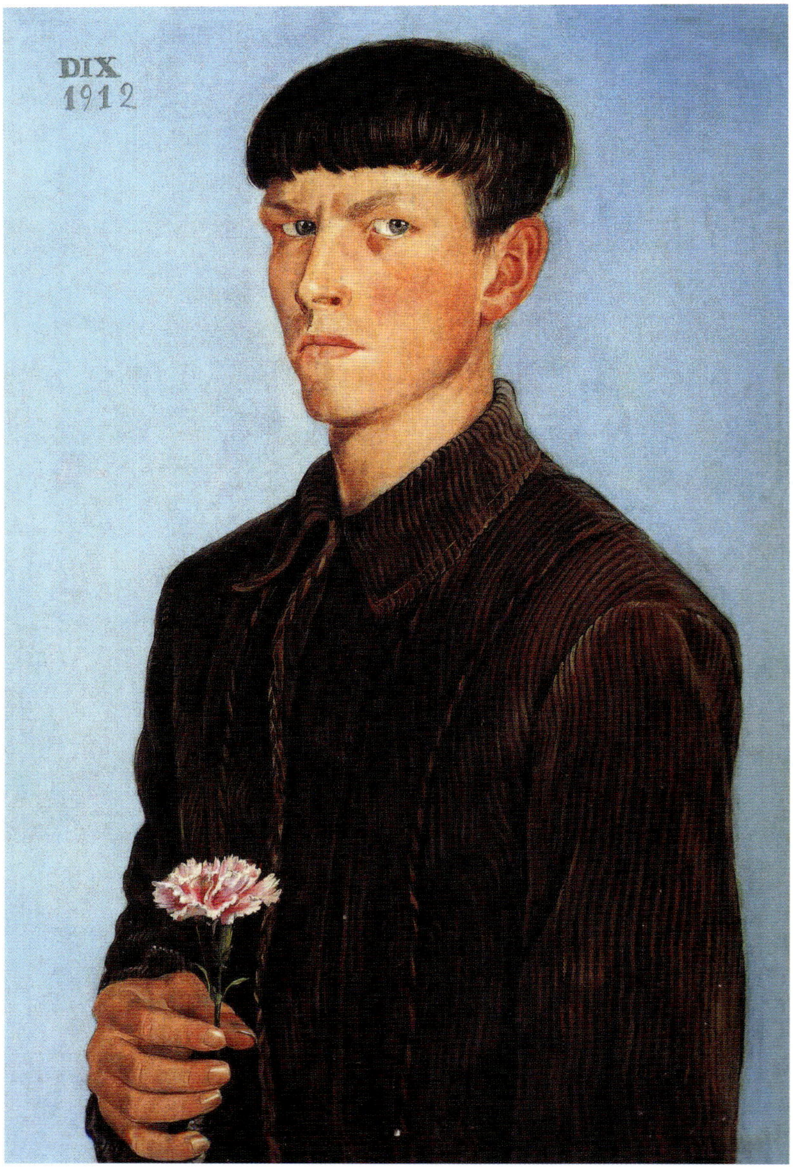

and economic arrangements that have dominated society since civilization first emerged from the sandy soil between the Tigris and Euphrates. All of that is incidental, however; whether or not we're all secretly good or the opposite, the existence of kindness itself is certainly verifiable, practiced a million ways by millions of people every day for time immemorial. What unspoken-of moments of tenderness, of comfort throughout history, have come to pass? What hidden monuments to kindness have been erected, less marked than those sites of atrocity, but all the more crucial? There are particulars of kindness—between those who hate one another and those who love one another, between friends and strangers, between the healthy and the ill. Sparks of generosity shared amid those who dwell in human bodies upon this planet, at least for a bit.

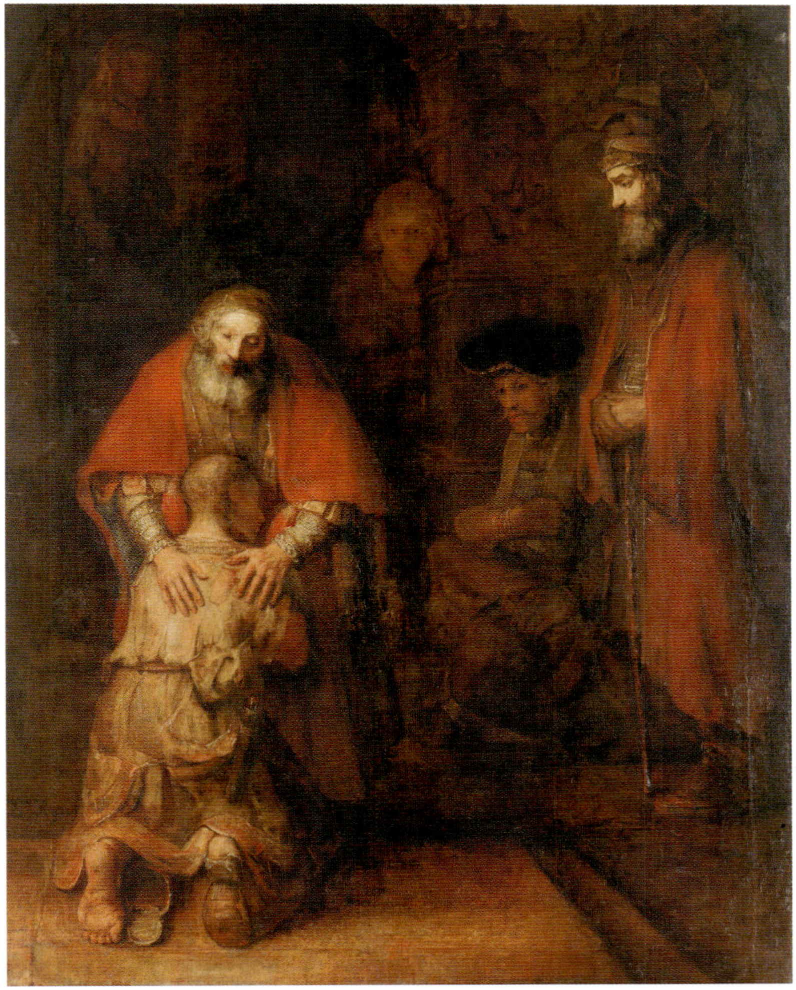

OPPOSITE A working-class enlistee into the Kaiser's army, the German realist painter Otto Dix had seen ferocious fighting during the Great War and survived the Battle of the Somme, which would forever alter his political perspectives. This 1912 self-portrait—painted three years before Dix would join the army—almost foretells the haunted fate of its creator, the grim visage and intense stare of the figure seeming to have already seen more than Dix himself at the time, the flower the only intimation of anything beautiful in the world, though notably none of his fingers seem to actually grasp the self-supporting stem.

TOP An ungrateful son, a spurner of goodness and profligate sinner who abandons his family, and yet when he has lost everything and returns to his father, "his father saw him, and had compassion, and ran, and fell on his neck, and kissed him," as the Gospel of Luke records. Christ's parable of the prodigal son, a narrative meant to inflect a moral teaching rather than the recounting of something which actually occurred, is among the New Testament's most arresting tales of kindness. An important lesson is imparted: the loyal son who stays behind is jealous, for he feels that his sibling has done nothing to deserve such kindness, but that is precisely the point—kindness and love aren't rewards, they're gifts. *The Return of the Prodigal Son* by Rembrandt, painted between 1661 and 1669 with the original at the Hermitage Museum in St. Petersburg, immaculately captures the tenderness between father and son.

There are few examples of cruelty based in hatred and division more extreme than the Crusades, the hideous sectarian war waged against Muslims, Jews, Orthodox Christians, and those labeled as heretics, it being said that during the first siege of Jerusalem so much blood was spilled that it flowed through the narrow stone streets as high as the stirrups upon the sides of the martial horses. Even in the midst of such overweening hatreds, there could be brief glimmers of genuine kindness, regardless of everything. During the twelfth century, when Jerusalem was occupied by Frankish Christians and converted into a Crusader kingdom, the Syrian-born Muslim poet Usama ibn Munqidh would make sojourns to what had been the al-Aqsa Mosque, which had since been transformed into a church. Maintained by the fearsome Knights Templar as their headquarters in the Holy City, whom in his autobiography the poet describes as "my friends," Munqidh was given permission to privately use a small chapel adjacent to al-Aqsa for his five-times-daily prostrations toward Mecca. One afternoon in the year 1140, Munqidh began the *Saleh*, laying out his prayer rug and dropping to his knees while facing south, toward the direction of the far-off Kaaba. A recently arrived Frankish knight, seeing the Muslim

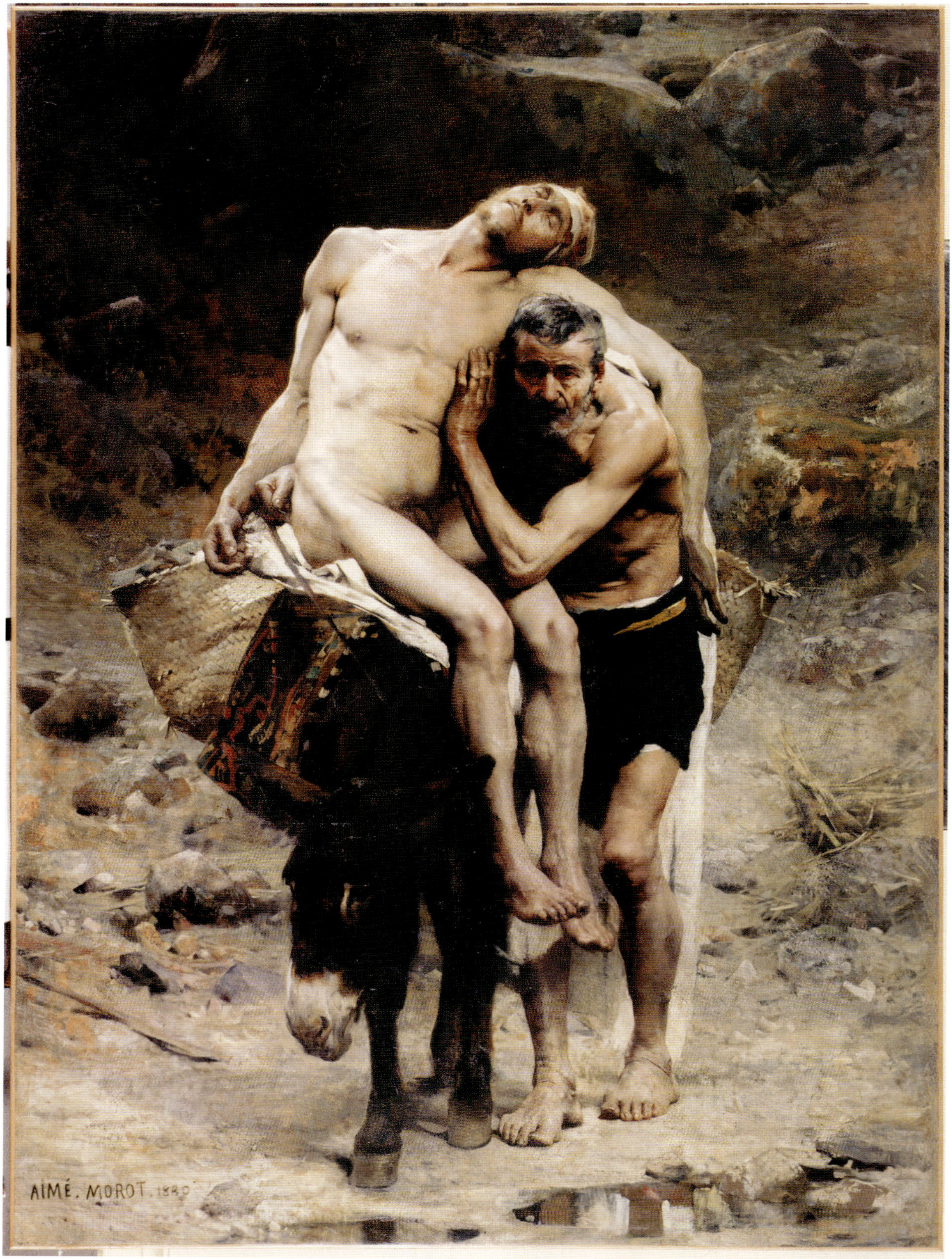
AIMÉ. MOROT. 1880

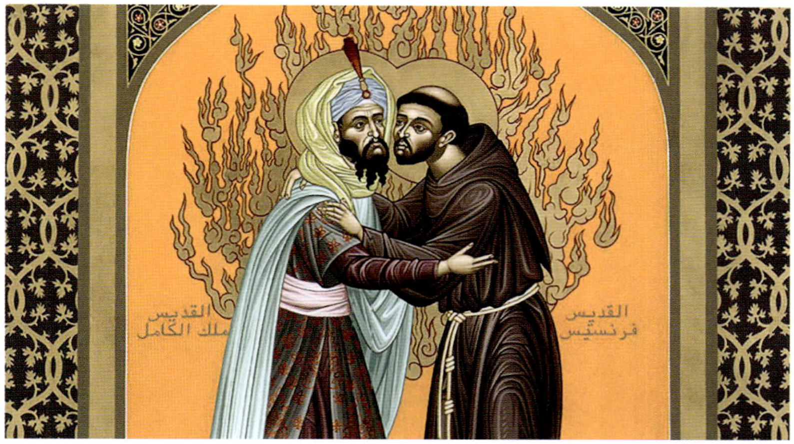

OPPOSITE Another parable of Christ's as recorded by Luke, the perennially moving account of the aged, impoverished, and spurned stranger who helps a man who has been robbed, beaten, and left for dead in the desert between Jerusalem and Jericho. The narrative crux of the tale is that the kind stranger was a member of the hated religious and ethnic community of Samaritans, while the injured man was Jewish. Passed over by his own coreligionists twice, it was a detested Samaritan who actually exhibited the kindness which saved the man's life. The fundamental commandment, as Christ says, was to "love the Lord your God with all your heart, all your soul, with all your strength, and with all your mind; and to love your neighbor as yourself." When a member of the crowd asks "Who is my neighbor?" Christ's answer in the form of the parable makes it clear: "Everybody." *The Good Samaritan* imagines the scene with uncanny realism, as depicted by the French historical painter Aimé Morot in this 1880 composition, original at the Museum of Fine Arts in Paris.

TOP Icon by contemporary artist and Franciscan friar Brother Robert Lentz, painted in Islamic miniaturist style, depicting an actual meeting between St. Francis of Assisi and the Egyptian Sultan al-Malik al-Kamil, a nephew of Saladin's, in the midst of the Fifth Crusade. The sultan had given safe passage to allow the monk to preach to him and was treated as a brother, despite their religious difference, even in the midst of religious war. With both being sons of Abraham and worshippers of Allah, Brother Lentz has appropriately depicted the saint and the sultan as equally crowned with halos.

making his prayers, ran over and grabbed Munqidh but was quickly subdued by the Templars. The Christian knights "came up to him and expelled him," explains Munqidh. "They apologized to me, saying, 'This is a stranger who has only recently arrived from the land of Franks,'" elaborating that the man was ignorant and unfamiliar with Islamic custom. These moments of connection across the iron-forged religious divide demonstrate the possibility of kindness even in the midst of our own cruelties, the same tolerance and compassion that only twenty-five years after Munqidh's prayers in Jerusalem motivated the great Kurdish military commander Saladin to send his personal physician—the brilliant Jewish philosopher Maimonides—to treat the Muslim's adversary, an increasingly ill King Richard the Lionhearted of England, who was thus able to recover (and still lose the Third Crusade).

If those examples show kindness across lines of difference, there is also the thread of solidarity between those who suffer similar afflictions and indignities. For two years starting in 1831, thousands of Choctaw Indians were stripped of their constitutionally recognized rights and forcefully dispossessed of their communally administered homelands in Mississippi and Alabama, forced by the United States Army to march a grueling terrain of five hundred miles of forest, swamp, and scrub on their way to arid Oklahoma. Infamously described by a Choctaw Chief in *The Arkansas Gazette* as a "trail of tears and death," this forced migration would cause some six thousand members of the tribe—nearly a third—to perish. Overseen by President Andrew Jackson, this act was in violation of the Supreme Court and in furtherance of his own genocidal project in the American Southeast, despite the Choctaw being classified by Washington as being among the "civilized tribes" who were in treaty with the federal government. Women and men bundled upon horses and walking on foot, with satchels carrying tvpishuk baskets and nia pots, remembered the Green Corn Festival and the Nanih Waiya mound from whence they believed all of creation emanated. The Choctaw began their walk toward the setting of the sun, driven by white men in U.S. military uniforms. Considering Mississippi and Alabama, the Choctaw attorney George W. Harkins wrote, "Here is the land of our progenitors, and here are their bones; they left them as a sacred deposit, and we have been compelled to venerate its trust; it's dear to us, yet we cannot stay."

A decade after Jackson's removal of the Indians, a different colonial power was subjugating a different oppressed people across the Atlantic Ocean. The Gorta Mór, or Great Hunger, better known as the Irish Potato Famine of 1845 to 1849, was caused by a blight which destroyed the crop. During the famine, one Galway parish recorded 240 congregants who died only a few months in to the dark year known as the Black '47, with the Rev. Timothy Newell noting in the Dublin newspaper *The Freemen's Journal* that "Several instances have occurred in this parish of almost all members of the families being carried off from the effects of the famine." Another victim of the hunger was a woman named Bridget O'Donnell. Enshrined in an iconic drawing of the starving poor of Ireland which appeared in an 1849 issue of *The Illustrated London News*, she was quoted by a journalist recounting how the "whole of my family got the fever, and one boy thirteen years old died with want." Ostensibly the tragedy was the result of the blight, and thus could be attributed to "nature," that impersonal force lacking in agency or conscience, and rhetorically configured as inevitable. But during the exact same time that the potato crop—the staple of poor Irish farmers—was failing, a massive amount of food was actually *exported* to England. It's estimated that fully a million Irish women and men perished—a population drop of almost 25 percent. What do the Choctaw and the Irish have in common, other than both being oppressed by colonial powers that hungrily eyed their land? Human fraternity—for it was in 1847 that the destitute and starving Indians gathered the equivalent of $5,000 to be sent to the citizens of Midleton in County Cork. In response, some seventeen decades later, a massive fundraising campaign was initiated in Ireland to benefit the Choctaw then being decimated by the coronavirus, kindness returning as bread cast upon the waters. The Choctaw Nation officially stated on their website in 2020 that "nothing divides the Choctaw people from the Irish except for the ocean."

BELOW The Cherokee, also consigned to the brutalities of their own trail of tears, as depicted in the American painter Robert Lindneux's 1942 composition, original held by Woolaroc Museum in Bartlesville, Oklahoma. Oppressed by the government and persecuted by the white settlers on their land, the only kindness that they would be granted would come from among each other.

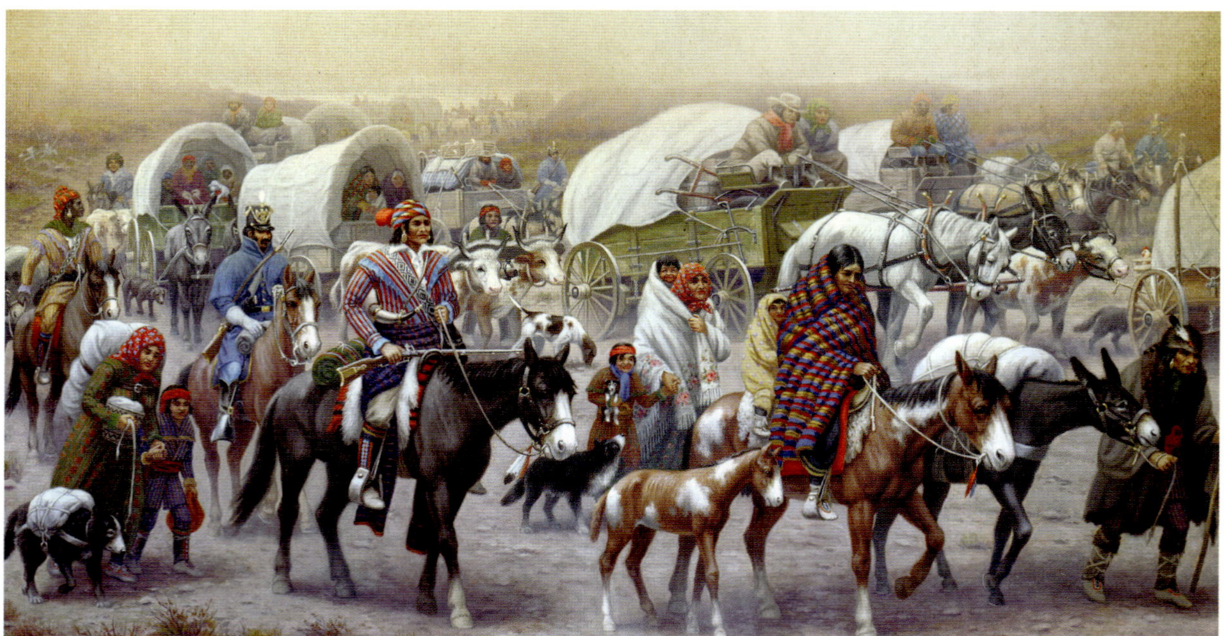

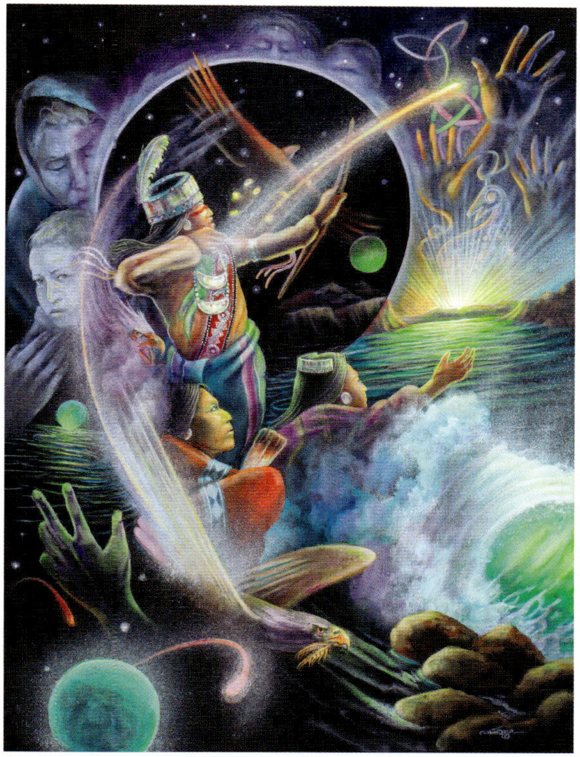

Kindness may ultimately be less than an act, or a statement, or a predisposition, or a sentiment so much as it's simply recognizing another person despite difference; that is, actually seeing them in the totality of their being, in the infinitude of their humanity. The acknowledgment of another beyond the lonely confines of the individual, atomistic human skull. A different word for such kindness is *love*. There are, to be sure, different kinds of love: love of family, romantic love, fraternal love. Love of strangers can be a radical form of the indispensable emotion, that which is necessary for kindness to flourish. A love that leads men to play soccer with military adversaries or hungry people to send food to other hungry people. There are radical implications to love, whereby it can be understood as a breaking down of the wall which defines the narcissistic self, where kindness is the sacrament of such love. The kernel of transcendent love is itself radically transcendent and transformative, regardless of how cultural contexts alter its organization or expression. Love is radical because love removes the locus of attention from the self alone. Love is radically transformative because if one can conceive of oneself as a creature separate from the purely pragmatic realm of economics and biology, then the concept of being part of something bigger than you is diametrically opposed to systems of oppression. The French philosopher Alain Badiou explains in his *In Praise of Love* that, "In today's world, it is generally thought that individuals only pursue their own self-interest. Love is an antidote to that." As such, love is a profoundly political thing (as all things by necessity are), but in that all politics is sublimated theology, love is of course theological as well. Love is at the center of any genuine liberatory politics—love for your fellow human as well as assertion of the right to love. But love must also be at the center of any genuine theology as well, for what is the story of the Gospels but a type of love story? Badiou writes that love is "an individual experience of potential universality," a particularly incarnational perspective. Witness the theological profundity of the statement that "God is love."

In many ways, English suffers a deficiency when it comes to the word "love," which is thought to include romantic, erotic, familial, fraternal, and social varieties under the umbrella of one term. The literary critic Ilan Stavans writes in *Love and Language* that love is "a most amorphous human feeling, capable of extremes: attraction and repulsion, exultation and misery, life and death, Eros and Thanatos." He continues by explaining that "the definition is imperfect, however, perhaps more so than for any other feeling." The Greeks had four for our one: *eros*, *agape*, *philia*, and *storge*. But in many ways, love's very ineffability is part of its power, a signifier not unlike the word "God," which is itself the place in which the dialogue and connection which marks love can be enacted. And as God is frightening, often so too is love. Diane Ackerman writes in *A Natural History of Love* that it "is an emotion that scares us more than cruelty, more than violence, more than hatred. We allow ourselves to be foiled by the vagueness of the word. After all, love requires the utmost vulnerability."

ABOVE Contemporary Choctaw artist and Irish resident Gary White Deer memorialized the gift of his tribe to those suffering during the potato famine in his 2021 painting *An Arrow Through Time*, original held by the Museum of Native American History in Bentonville, Arizona. Combining both Choctaw and Celtic imagery and symbols, White Deer's painting is meant to evoke the inseverable mystic bonds of kindness. "Waylon Gary White Deer will always be welcome in Ireland," wrote Martin McGuinness, the former Deputy First Minister of Northern Ireland, in an introduction to the artist's 2012 memoir *Touched by Thunder*.

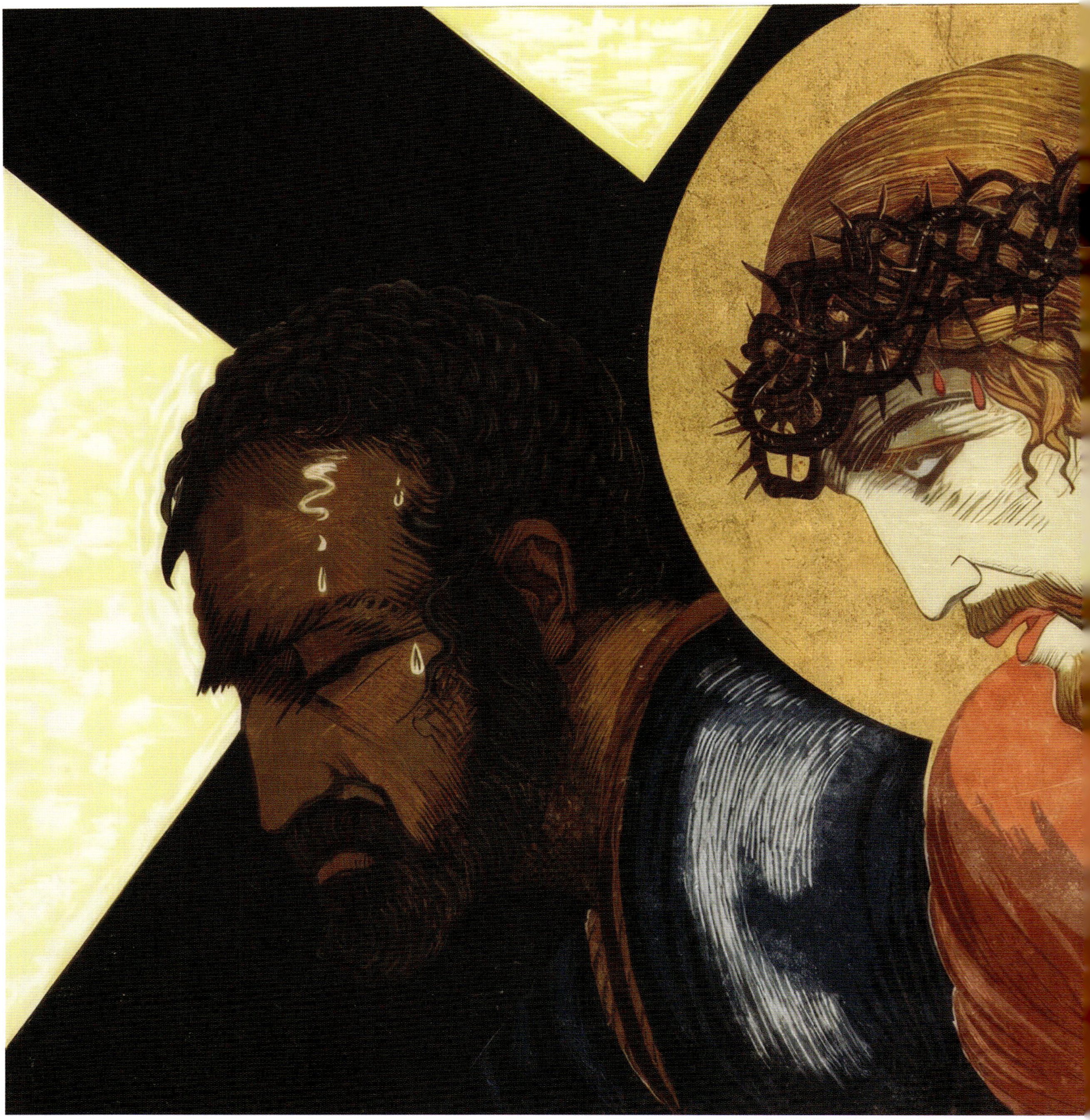

ABOVE After all of his parables about kindness, Christ experienced an expression of its power as he carried toward Golgotha the cross on which he would be crucified. Having stumbled, a man of no accounting whom the synoptic gospels call Simon of Cyrene was compelled by the Romans to assist the Son of God in carrying the cross, and so he did. Knowing not that Jesus was the messiah, that Christ was God, Simon nonetheless visits kindness on one whom he interprets as just another suffering person, with the most profound understanding being that there is no difference between helping another human and helping God. The 1931 illustration is by the French artist François-Louis Schmied.

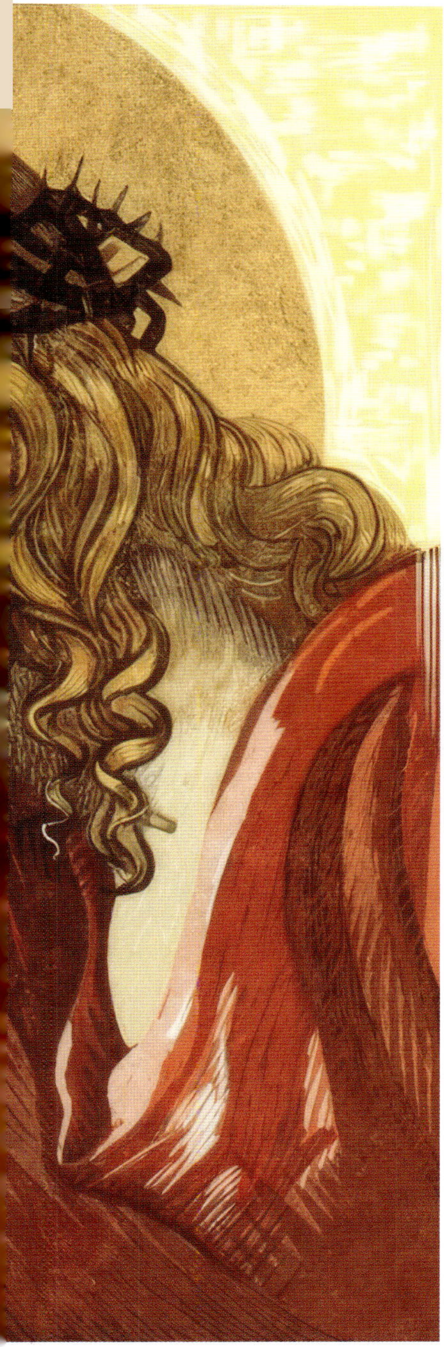

But in our daily reality, so hardened by cruelty and selfishness (same as it ever was), the radicalism of kindness is that it admits to that powerlessness, to that vulnerability. Watch the nightly news—wherever you are—with stories about mass shootings and hate crimes, of wildfires immolating whole towns and cities drowned by hurricanes, of the entire inconceivable sadness of the moment; and then consider how genuine kindness is the only antidote to such despair. As a final visit on that walking tour of human tenderness, consider the graves found at La Chapelle-Aux-Saints in central France, burials made forty thousand years before thousands of young men would put down their arms some two hundred miles north. There, an assortment of Neanderthal skeletons—the remains of hominoids not even considered by anthropologists to be human—were carefully laid out. Most poignant was the body of a two-year-old boy, carefully arranged as if he were sleeping, his skeleton still bearing traces of pollen that had clung to his bones. Whomever had buried the child—parents, family, his tribe—had buried him with flowers. Kindness before we had the word, love existing whether or not there were philosophers and theologians to define it. Always there—from the beginning.

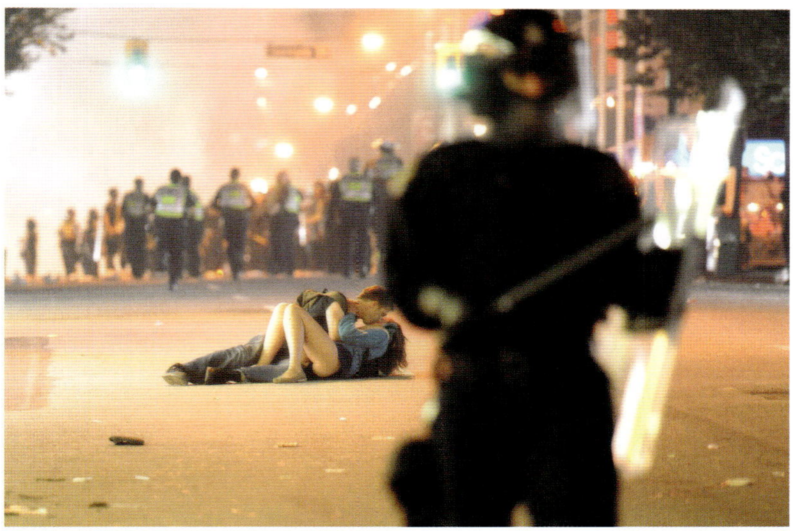

ABOVE In this photograph by Rich Lam for Getty Images, two lovers embrace in the midst of an apocalyptic conflagration during anti-globalization protests held in Vancouver, Canada in 2011. A kernel of kindness in the core of chaos—the secret to liberation.

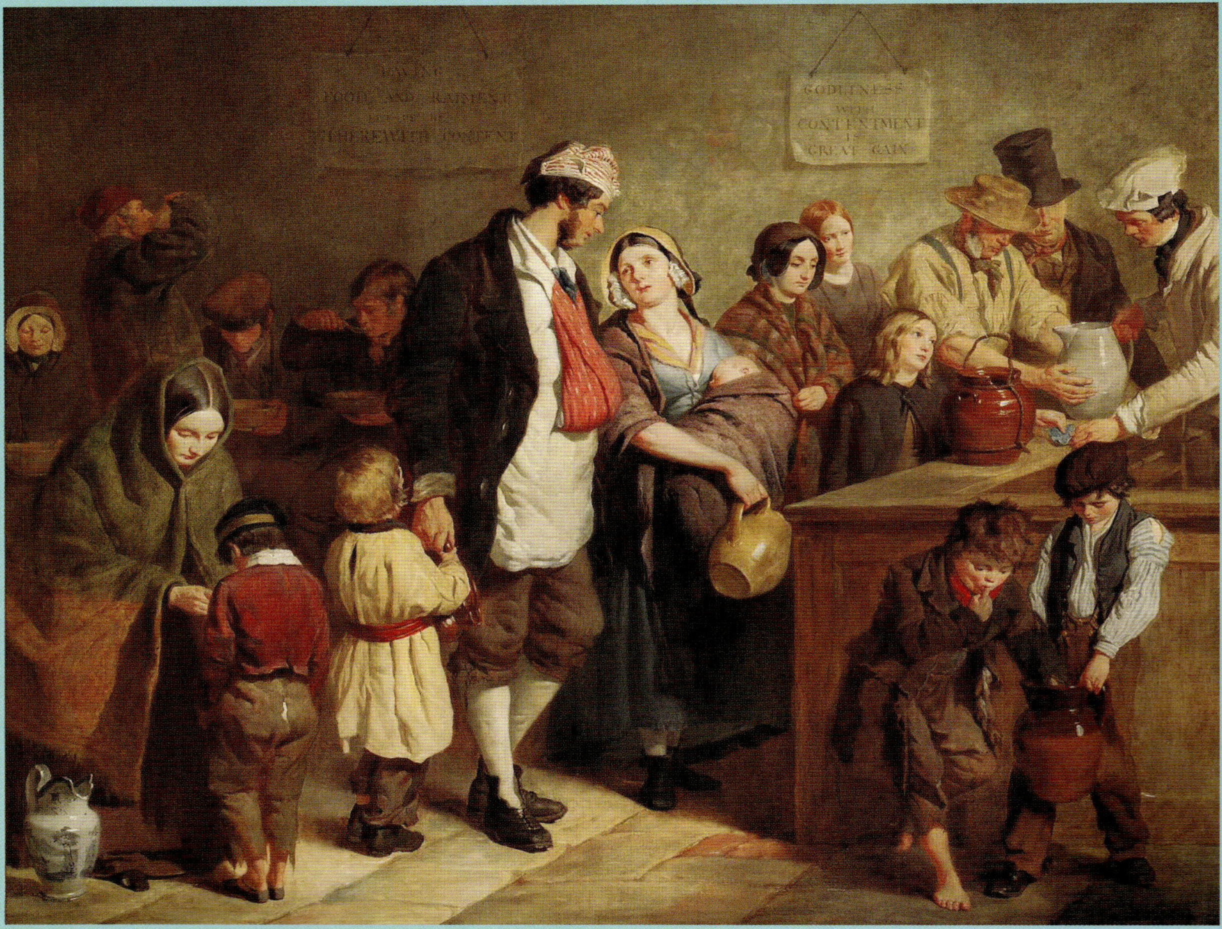
GODLINESS
WITH
CONTENTMENT
IS
GREAT GAIN

CHAPTER SIX

A PERFECT FRIENDSHIP: CHARITY

"Let the rich satisfy the poor implorer,

and bend his eye upon a longer pathway."

—*Rigveda* (c. 1700-1100 BCE)

"Brother, can you spare a dime?"

—Yip Harburg, *New Americana* (1931)

The Latin *caritas*, the etymological root of the Middle English *charite* and thus of the contemporary word *charity*, has a surprising connotation. Its original meaning refers to rareness, costliness, expensiveness—a slightly inverted version of charity, with its associations of soup kitchens and homeless shelters. This is less unusual than might first be presumed, however, as charity has always had the association of *money* about it, as in the question of who has it, who doesn't, and how the former might decide to use it for the latter. After all, charity refers not just to the actual aid which is given to the impoverished (in the form of food, or clothes, or what have you), but also the organizations known as charities who do that giving. Those charities, if they're to be in any way effective, of course, have to have access to money, and preferably a lot of it. There is another way that *caritas*'s connotations of wealth and riches connect to charity, for in the Vulgate that Latin word is sometimes used to refer to God's love, a substance of infinite value. Thus charity and love are intrinsically connected; giving to the less fortunate is seen as an act of fraternal, social, and religious affection, often between strangers. In his thirteenth-century *Summa Theologica*, Thomas Aquinas compared charity to the friendship between humanity and God, calling it the "most excellent of virtues." In this way charity was not investment or pittance, but rather a freely given gift of the self to those who have less, and thus a means of expressing divine love. Even more than that, charity is an enactment of Christ's injunction that how we treat the least of those among us is how we treat Him. If we come with love to the indigent, the vagrant, the refugee, then we are coming to God with love; if we instead approach those in such straits with hate, it's as if we've spurned the Lord Himself. "Do you wish to honor the Body of the Savior?" writes John Chrysostom in his fourth-century *Homilies on the Gospel of Saint Matthew.* "Do not honor it in church with silk vestments while outside it is naked and numb with cold . . .. Honor him then by sharing your property with the poor. For what God needs is not golden chalices but golden souls."

PREVIOUS SPREAD English artist George Elgar Hicks's 1851 painting *The Parish Soup Kitchen*, original at the Royal Academy in London, shows the hectic environs of a religious charity serving food to the destitute. In the era before the emergence of even a perfunctory governmental social safety net, institutions that were administered by churches, like soup kitchens, were often the only thing that prevented mass starvation amongst the lower classes.

OPPOSITE Andrew Carnegie as imagined by his fellow Pittsburgher Andy Warhol in this 1981 portrait commissioned by the Carnegie Museum of Art, Pittsburgh.

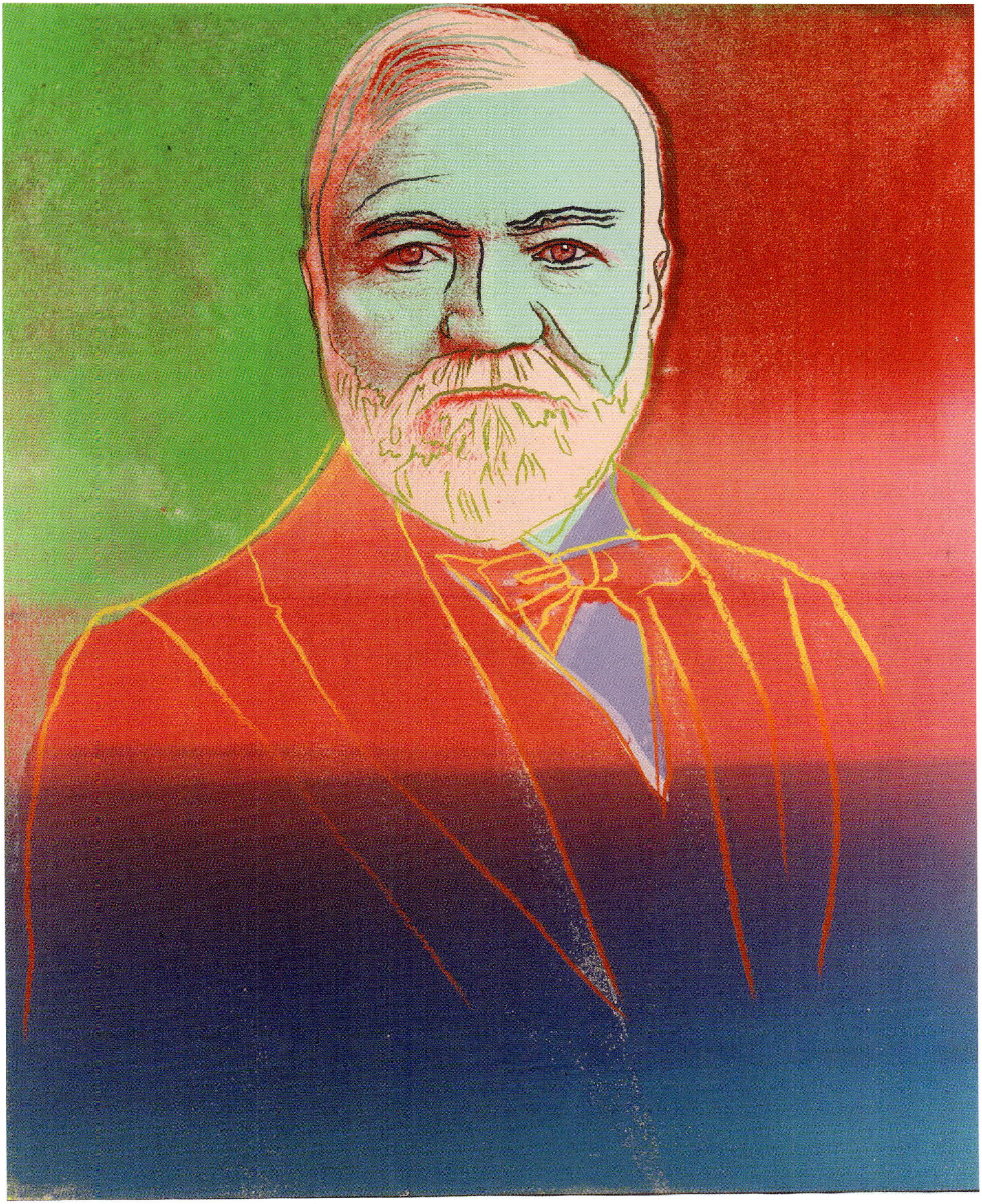

NOBLESSE OBLIGE

On a bluff far above the roiled, brown Monongahela River in Homestead, Pennsylvania, some eight miles southeast of Pittsburgh's downtown, there is a massive, handsome redbrick building of rounded cupolas and a mansard roof whose edifice is ornamented in stone decoration and Victorian wooden trim. A library. More than that, a concert hall, an athletic facility, a swimming pool, even a bowling alley. When dedicated in 1898, the Homestead Library was only the seventh to be endowed by its benefactor—industrialist steel magnate Andrew Carnegie—though over the next few decades it would be joined on a list that included an astounding 2,509 such facilities throughout the globe, in what constituted one of the largest philanthropic ventures in modern history. "The problem of our age is the proper administration of wealth," wrote Carnegie in his 1906 *The Gospel of Wealth*, "so that the ties of brotherhood may still bind together the rich and poor in harmonious relationship."

True to that sentiment, the richest man on earth donated virtually all of his wealth during his lifetime, to a variety of causes ranging from education to world peace, though this rare rags-to-riches industrialist reserved the bulk of his affections for the democratic university which was the public library, recalling the kindness of Colonel James Anderson, who let the young Scotsman borrow books from his personal collection shortly after the Carnegies had immigrated to Allegheny City. Having donated the equivalent of four billion dollars (as adjusted for inflation), Carnegie gave more than 90 percent of his wealth to charity by the time of his death in 1919, the rest put into a trust (as the businessman did not believe in unearned inheritance) that still administers money today. Twenty-five years after its dedication, Carnegie returned to that seventh library in Homestead, overlooking not just the Monongahela below but the massive steel works that had made him his fortune, intoning to the gathered working-class denizens of the gritty town that "when I go on trial for the things down on earth, I think I'll get a verdict of Not Guilty through my efforts to make the world a little bit better than I found it."

There was a rationale for that ambivalence, the reason why Carnegie's conscience may have made him declare that he thought rather than knew that salvation would be his lot. Three decades before that 1914 ceremony honoring the benefactor, but only six years before the Homestead Library opened, that industrial town in the Mon Valley had a rather different experience of Carnegie's largesse. During the 1892 Homestead Steel Strike, Carnegie Steel had vociferously resisted any attempts by the union to try to improve conditions for the workers who produced the robber baron's wealth, and the diminutive, bearded Scotsman absconded to his castle in Scotland during the course of the protests, having dispatched his cruel lieutenant, the coke magnate Henry Clay Frick, to deal with the dissatisfied workers.

Seven days a week, for twelve or more hours at a time, the work in the mill was filthy, dangerous, and poorly renumerated, but despite those conditions, the ostensible friend of the working man Andrew Carnegie refused to

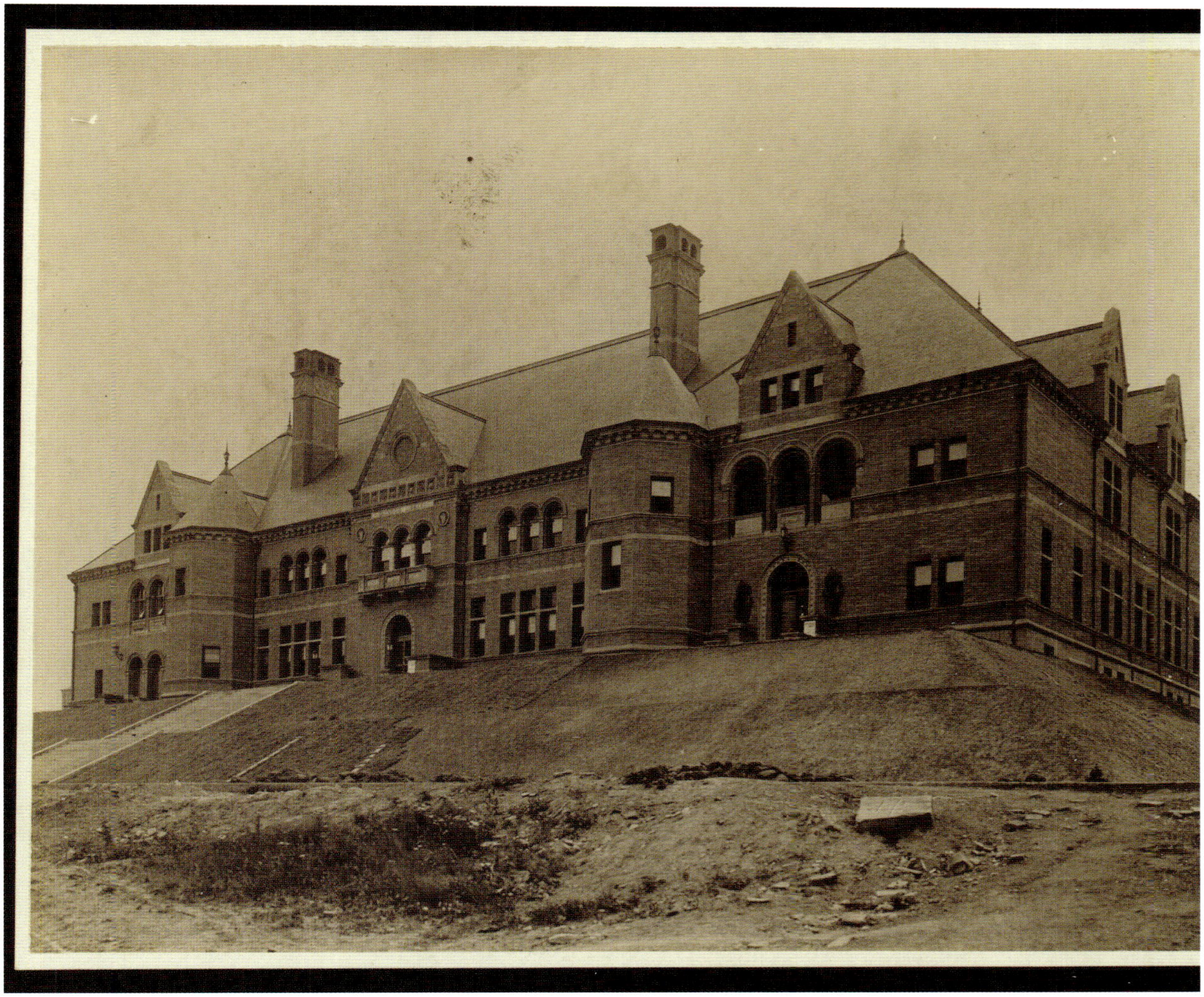

countenance the labor union's demands. And so, several weeks into that strike, Frick sent a contingent of hired mercenaries from the Pinkerton Agency down-river to the banks of Homestead, where workers had gathered by torchlight to defend the locked mill and their own livelihoods; a battle ensued which the union would win at the cost of six deaths. Even while the Battle of Homestead may have been a victory for the union, with the Pinkertons surrendering like a defeated conquering army, the war would ultimately be lost, as strike-breaking would become *de rigueur* for the next several decades. Like the owner of a child-mauling pit bull who blames the dog rather than his own lack of a lock, Carnegie denied any culpability in Frick's decisions, and he hardly felt much sympathy for the men who died. Ostensibly a supporter of labor, Carnegie never quite forgave the Homestead workers who had made him rich, saying, "Our men there are not partners." Even after his donating money for the construction of the Homestead Library, the operations of the institution were administered not by the community (as was the case with the vast majority of Carnegie Libraries), but rather by the steel company itself, a situation that remained the status quo until 1988.

TOP The Carnegie Library of Homestead as photographed around 1900, when it was less than a decade old.

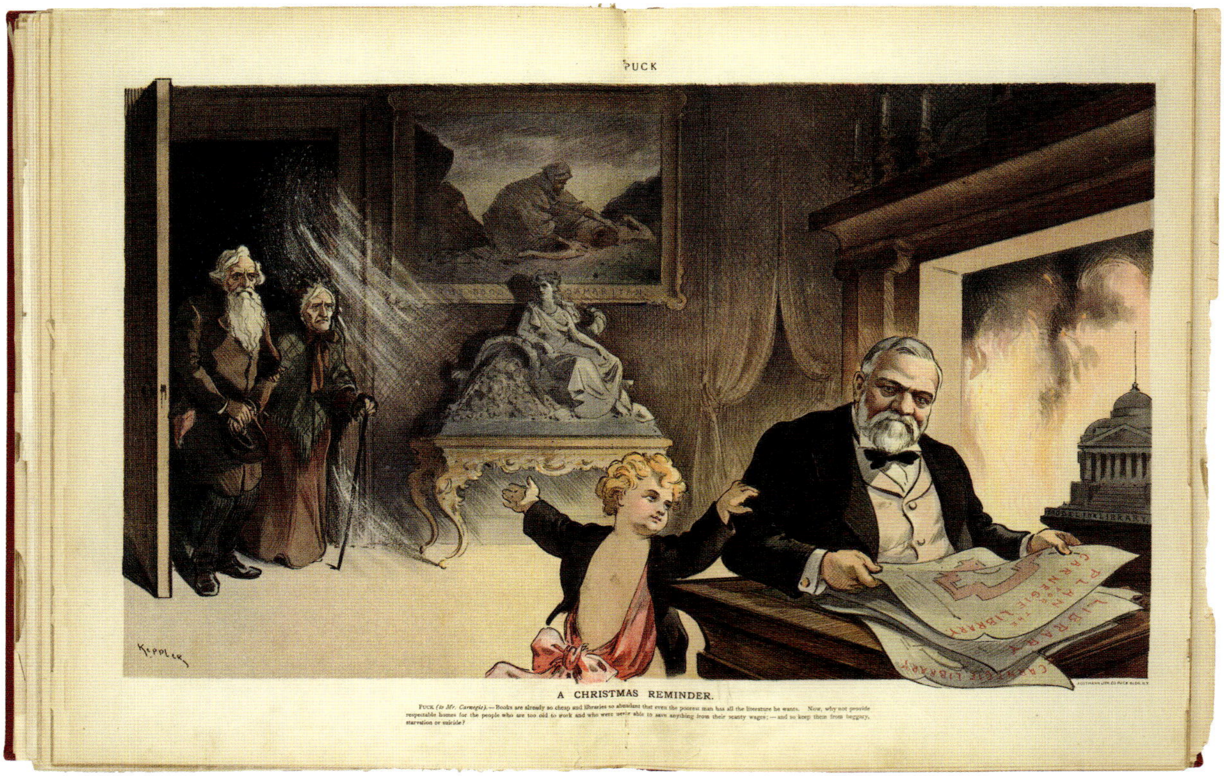

Carnegie libraries would be opened in every U.S. state and several territories, throughout the industrialist's native United Kingdom, and ultimately on several continents, with branches from Serbia to Fiji. His donations provided the nucleus not just for the Carnegie Libraries of Pittsburgh, where he made his wealth, but for the library system of New York City, where he would live, as well as at hundreds of colleges and universities in places like Washington, DC, and Cedar Falls, Iowa. The vast bulk of these institutions are still operational, an enduring act of philanthropy. Because of Carnegie's donations, millions of lives have been altered for the better, educations secured, employment achieved, upward mobility accomplished. In many industrial cities, the Carnegie Library was among the most beautiful buildings in the community, a symbol of dignity and worth in places often considered gritty and ugly. Only a cynic would claim that there was no generosity in Carnegie's donation, but only a fool wouldn't acknowledge that such gifts were always on the industrialist's terms. Critics noted how with their bruising schedules, Carnegie's workers scarcely had the privilege to spend time within the libraries' shelves, and that as much as many towns may have appreciated such largesse, the workers who lived there would have also appreciated increased pay, more days off, rudimentary safety precautions at work, and healthcare. Naturally, the author of *The Gospel of Wealth* had an answer to such criticisms: "If I had raised your wages, you would have spent that money by buying a better cut of meat or more drink for your dinner. But what you needed, though you didn't know it, was my libraries and concert halls."

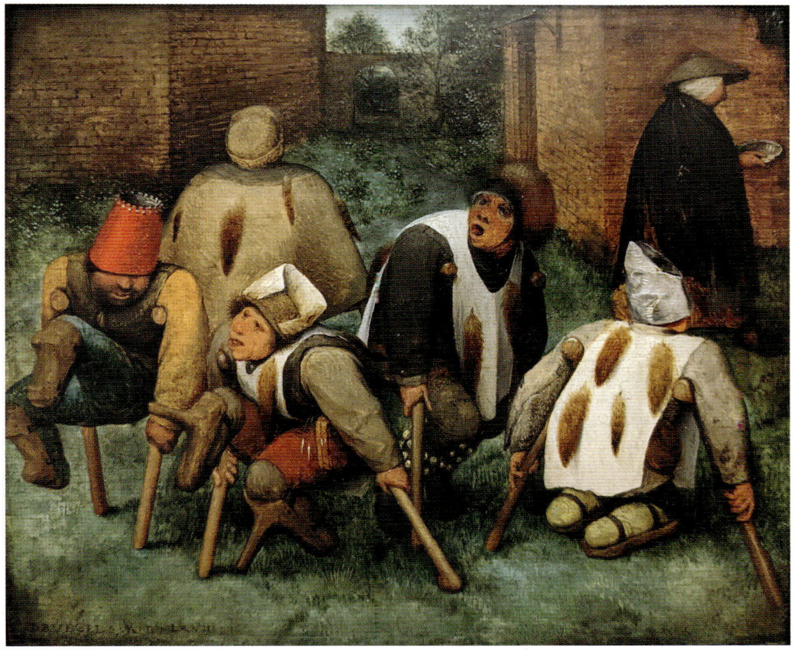

OPPOSITE A cartoon from the satirical newspaper *Puck* published a week before Christmas 1901, which addresses Carnegie's argument about charity functioning best when the "main consideration should be to help those who help themselves." In a Dickensian scene, the industrialist pores over plans for his future libraries, while the magazine's mascot, Puck (the same sprite from Shakespeare's *A Midsummer Night's Dream*), points to an elderly, indigent couple in the doorway to Carnegie's study. Puck says in the caption, "Books are already so cheap and libraries so abundant . . . Now, why not provide respectable homes for the people who are too old to work and who were never able to save anything from their scanty wages; and so keep them from beggary, starvation or suicide?" Carnegie appears annoyed.

TOP Detail from the Netherlandish painter Pieter Brueghel the Elder's 1568 composition *The Beggars*, original at the Louvre. Unlikely that Brueghel meant to evoke sympathy so much as derision, the picture an unflattering portrait of outcasts.

By its very nature—by the connotations of the word itself—"charity" is not revolutionary. Perhaps ameliorator y, or a palliative, maybe even a necessity in an unjust and inequal world, but philanthropy is still evidence of the world's injustices and inequities. Were we in utopia, neither a contributor nor a beggar would any of us be. Because managers don't pay servers enough, we must tip them, but that doesn't mean that it wouldn't be better to live in a just society where people are compensated the way they deserve. Maybe that matters little when hungry or tired; the fact that everyone should have food and lodging doesn't mean that within the moment those with access to such things shouldn't give them as an act of generosity. However, the reality remains that the predicament in which some have nothing, and must thus accept whatever they're given, while others have everything, as well as the choice of whether to give or not, is a feature of this fallen realm. Furthermore, even independent of the American law which allows a philanthropist's generosity to bring a handsome financial reward in the form of tax write-offs, there is also the reality that charity, as a function of monetary wealth, is an ancillary of greed, albeit functioning to better ends. If the significance of massive wealth isn't in gold trifles and gilded treasures but rather in the form of privatized power, charity is just another aspect of that hegemonic magic, albeit funneled not into villas and chalets, sports cars and private jets, but rather into the quasi-divine prerogative to decide who is worthy and just what they might deserve. Perhaps the impoverished would like a fair wage, but by God, if Carnegie thinks they should get a library, a library is what they will get.

Because even the most radical of religious traditions tends not to countenance turning the world upside down, seeing that rather as the Lord's task for millennia, charity has been a central tenet of every major religious tradition. Pray for a revolution, but instead some promised messiah is what you'll eventually get; in the meantime, put a donation in the bucket. "So, give to the poor," exhorted Augustine in a fourth-century sermon; "I'm begging you, I'm warning you, I'm commanding you, I'm ordering you," no doubt uttered with a fervency that may have belabored the echo in the collection plate. Snark though we will, the metaphorical language of financial obligation, monetary repayment, and loan forgiveness permeates religion—"forgive us our trespasses" in the Lord's prayer is more accurately translated as "forgive us our debts," while the so-called Satisfaction Theory of Christ's atonement, which goes back to the first millennium, argued that the debt of humanity's damnation was purchased by the messiah's infinite repayment through His bloody sacrifice. Among the Three Theological Virtues as enumerated by Thomas Aquinas in the thirteenth century, only charity can be counted as also among the Seven Cardinal Virtues, being joined in this numbering by faith and hope. Meanwhile, among Muslims, *Zakat*, or almsgiving, is among the five pillars of the faith, for as the Qur'an notes in sura 2:177, "righteous is he who believeth in Allah and the Last Day . . . and giveth his wealth, for love of Him, to kinsfolk and to orphans and the needy and the wayfarer."

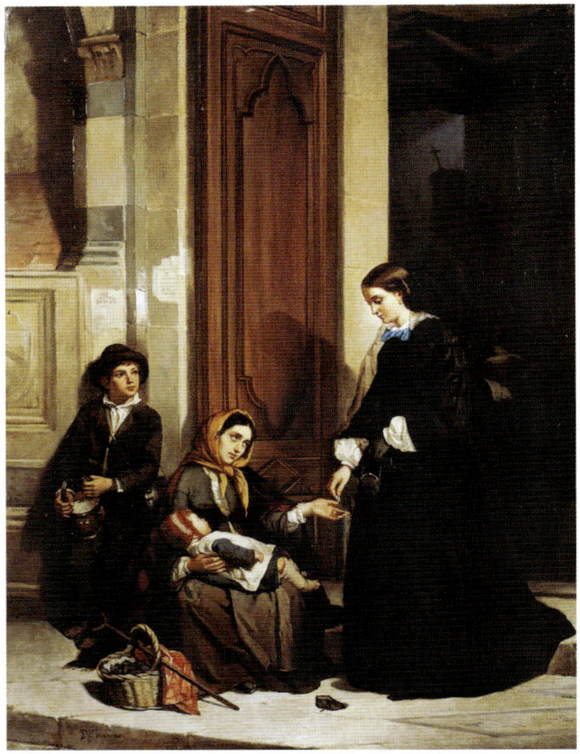

Within Judaism, charity has a more expansive meaning in the Hebrew word *tzedakah*, which can include any gesture of kindness or generosity. This can include the obvious monetary implications of donating to the impoverished, but also volunteering time or lodging or even just attention. The great rabbinic sage Maimonides enumerated an eight-tiered hierarchy of tzedakah in the twelfth century, ranging from the height of charity, which was to give an interest-free loan, all the way down to the least honorable form of generosity, which was to give not out of a sense of obligation or of fraternal love, but merely out of pity. For Maimonides, this last form of tzedakah scarcely counted as charity, because it had about it the sense of psychological coercion, of giving while not really wanting to. By contrast, giving to unknown people, giving anonymously, even giving an inadequate amount, were preferable to generosity, which only serves to salve the conscience of the person doing the giving. This may seem a strange distinction to parse, but Maimonides thus identifies one of the paradoxes of charity, whereby the person giving the money has an obvious power over the person receiving it, so that the act itself is inevitably marked by condescension. It's a paradox riven through any variety of charity, one that perhaps can only be reconciled in Heaven, but nonetheless the identification of it remains troubling.

The administering of donated funds to the poor was, whether in Christian or Muslim lands, or among Jewish communities, an obligation of the clergy and houses of religion. Soup kitchens, food pantries, mutual aid societies,

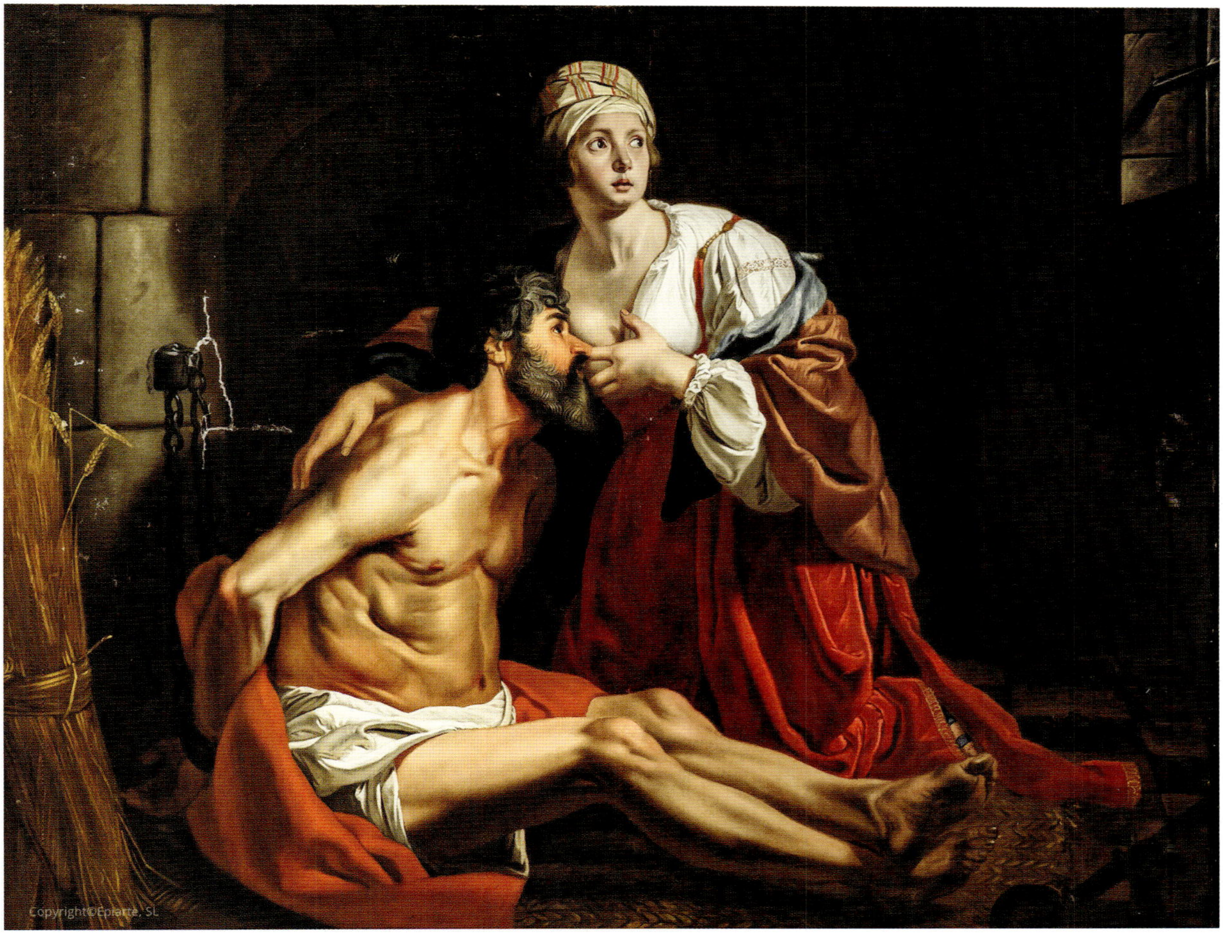

OPPOSITE Italian painter Domenico Induno's 1859 *The Charity*, in which a staid and respectable woman of wealth donates money to an indigent single mother of three. Note the depiction of the begging woman as darker-complexioned (perhaps Romani?) and wearing more colorful (wasteful?) clothing. Regardless of the good intentions of the gentlewoman making a donation, the pose of the beggar woman is by necessity one of supplication, a demeaning position.

TOP An ever-popular subject for painters, the unsettling narrative of "Roman Charity" recounts how an imprisoned father starving to death was nursed to health by breast-feeding from his daughter. The Flemish painter Gaspar de Crayer dramatizes the scene, in a disturbing affirmation of a particular variety of filial piety, in his 1645 composition held in private collection.

orphanages, hospitals: all were first administrated from within an ecclesiastical structure, and even as the long process of secularization descended, those traces of the sacred still remained. "In Catholic and Protestant states alike the rise of the merchant class shifted control of philanthropy from churchmen to lay people," writes Paul Vallely in *Philanthropy: From Aristotle to Zuckerberg*. "All across the continent the state began to involve itself through poor laws in the charity which had once been the exclusive provenience of the Church." Almsgiving was in many ways an Abrahamic replacement of pagan sacrifice. Now, honor was proffered to God not through the act of slitting the throat of a scapegoat, but by giving charitably to the poor (who are, after all, in the image of the Lord). These altruistic motivations which underlie philanthropy differentiate it from classical antecedents in the Greco-Roman world. Whether we consider the Wellcome Trust, the Bill and Melinda Gates Foundation, the Lilly Endowment, or the Open Society Foundations, there is still a sense that such largesse, even if motivated by many divergent and sometimes contradictory interests, is defined within the parameters of a certain religious convention which goes back millennia, one which purports to grant redemption to those who give in support of those with less (and perhaps the secularism of contemporary charities is a moot

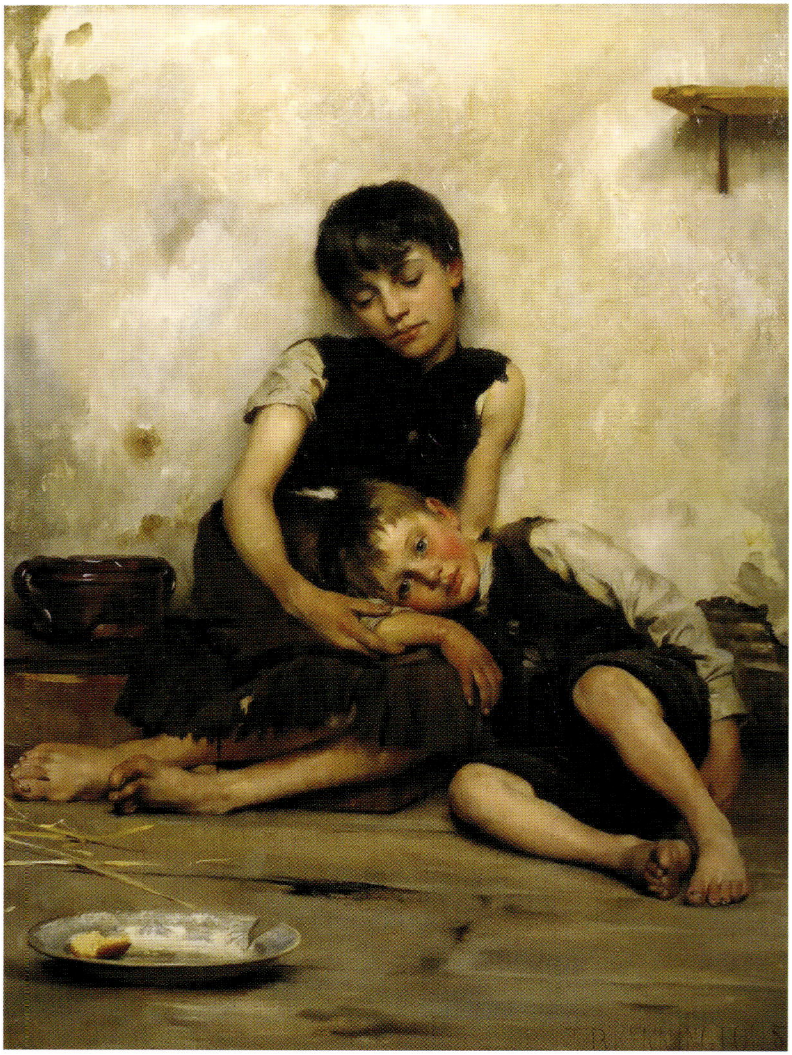

point anyhow, since the single largest donor of such funds globally remains the Rcman Catholic Church).

The modern philanthropic edifice took form in the nineteenth century, as the guilds and hospitals of the distant medieval past gave way to the efficient bureaucratization of charity, so that someone like Carnegie was in the vanguard of generosity, the dispensing of funds made efficient and defined by paperwork just like in any other capitalist venture. For many living on the verge of starvation in the dystopia that was the industrialized Anglophone world, charities were integral to survival, the dispensing of food and the provisions of lodging instrumental in the existence of millions. It should be emphasized, however, that such generosity was often not doled out through the intercession of uncomplicated, virtuous hearts. Donations weren't administered with absolutely no strings attached, and charity also became a potent means of social control and religious conversion. Those who preferred the millennium of revolution over the half-measures of amelioration maintained potent critiques of charity, such as

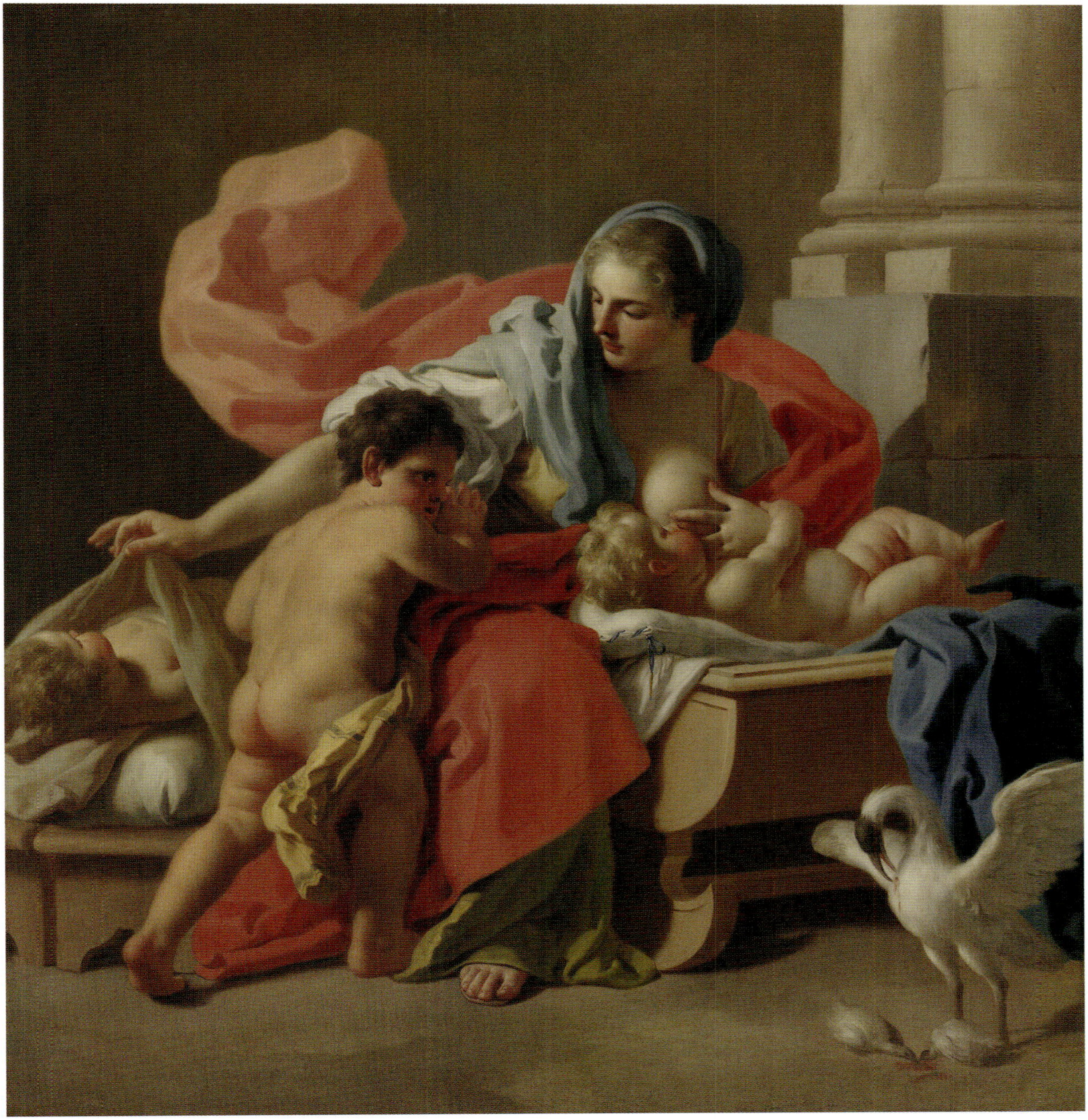

OPPOSITE British painter Thomas Benjamin Kensington's heartbreaking 1885 painting *Orphans*, original held by the Tate Britain.

ABOVE With shades of "Roman Charity," the Italian painter Francesco de Mura's 1743 rococo allegory *Charity* depicts the virtue as being not unlike a mother's feeding of her children, the image of a pelican striking its breast to feed her chicks its blood only reinforcing the connection between philanthropy and maternal duty. Original at the Art Institute of Chicago.

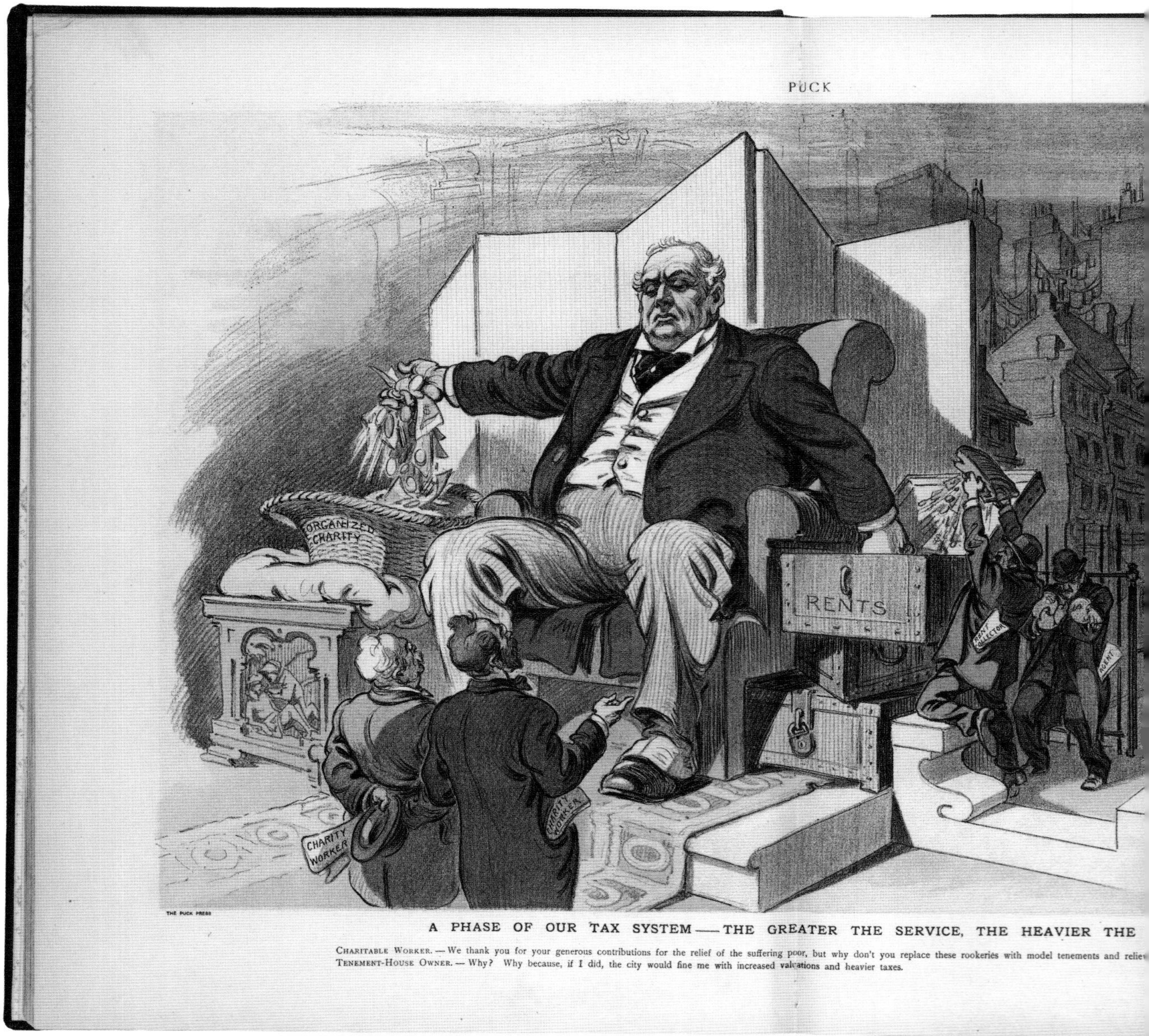

Oscar Wilde, who in his seminal 1891 essay "The Soul of Man Under Socialism" claimed that philanthropy was a "ridiculously inadequate mode of partial restitution . . . usually accompanied by some impertinent attempt on the part of the sentimentalist to tyrannize over private lives." Carnegie may give you a library, but he's not going to recognize your union.

Philanthropy and literature exist in ambivalent relationship. There is the uncomfortable reality that the latter would often not exist without the largesse of the former; in the Renaissance they of course called this patronage, all of those court poets scribbling verse for Medicis or Tudors, but today we've refined the process into the tedium of grant applications and foundation projects. Some of the greatest literary periodicals in contemporary American history—you know their names—have never turned a profit, relying instead on the generosity of interested wealthy patrons. Then, of course, there is the greatest of philanthropic gifts ever bestowed as laurels in the form of the Nobel Prize in Literature, granted to authors as wide-ranging as Ernest Hemingway and Dario Fo, Kazuo Ishiguro and Doris Lessing, Pearl Buck and Bob Dylan, but whose lucre was first generated by the martial glow of a dynamite stick. Despite all of that, there are almost no notable fictional philanthropists in literature, Bruce Wayne and Daddy Warbucks besides. Alone among the virtues, charity is fundamentally rather boring. Certainly its infernal twin of greed is abundantly more interesting in its excess, but even among the vanilla virtues, the mere writing of a check can't compare to the intensity of diligence or the saintliness of patience. Charity can, in some ways, merely seem to be a less honest version of greed, where money is still used as a means for power and control, albeit for more benevolent ends. Despite the relative surfeit of charity as a theme in literature, it's still of course referenced, not least of all by our hungriest of scribes, the poets. A writer of little accounting named May Lewis wrote a damning bit of rhymed verse for a 1927 issue of *Poetry*, asking "What shall we give the old man, / Cast out by the wind and rain? / *A straw bed, and a torn sheet, / And a patched counterpane.* / And what shall we give the old man / To heal his broken heart? / *A plate of soup, and a silver bit, / And a message to depart.*"

Philosophers have had more comfort in evaluating charity, proffering any number of ethical theories on the utility of generosity, on who is worthy to benefit from it, on what its purpose is, and on how it should be administered. In tandem with the rise of philanthropy during the Victorian era, a multitude of ethical theories were formulated to justify the various ways in which wealth could be used. Utilitarianism was a particularly English manifestation of ethical thought that could be applied rather specifically to charity, a system which maintained the axiom that the purpose of life is to maximize happiness among the greatest possible number of people. John Stuart Mills in his 1859 tract *Utilitarianism* argued that a "sacrifice which does not increase, or tend to increase, the sum total of happiness . . . [is] wasted. The only self-renunciation which it applauds, is devotion to happiness, or to some of the means of happiness . . . of mankind collectively." Mills's ethics were estimably liberal and reformist, which is to say conventionally Christian regardless of the content of his own faith, for the philosopher imagined a humane, technocratic, and progressive means of increasing the amount of happiness in the world—by feeding the hungry, clothing the naked, housing the indigent—which was the perfect morality by which to rationalize charity. The modern form of utilitarianism is something called "effective altruism," which equally imagines increasing the greatest amount of happiness across the greatest number of people, in part arguing that the best way to do this is to acquire high-paying jobs and to donate your pay to the impoverished. To make money like a capitalist, in other words, but to spend it like a socialist. "Effective altruism is about asking 'How can I make the biggest difference I can?'" writes philosopher William MacAskill in *Doing Good Better: How Effective Altruism Can Help You Make a Difference*, "and using evidence and careful reasoning to try and find an answer. It takes a scientific approach to doing good." Much like the nineteenth-century Utilitarians, thinkers like Jeremy Bentham who developed an actual equation to deign what was good or not, the effective

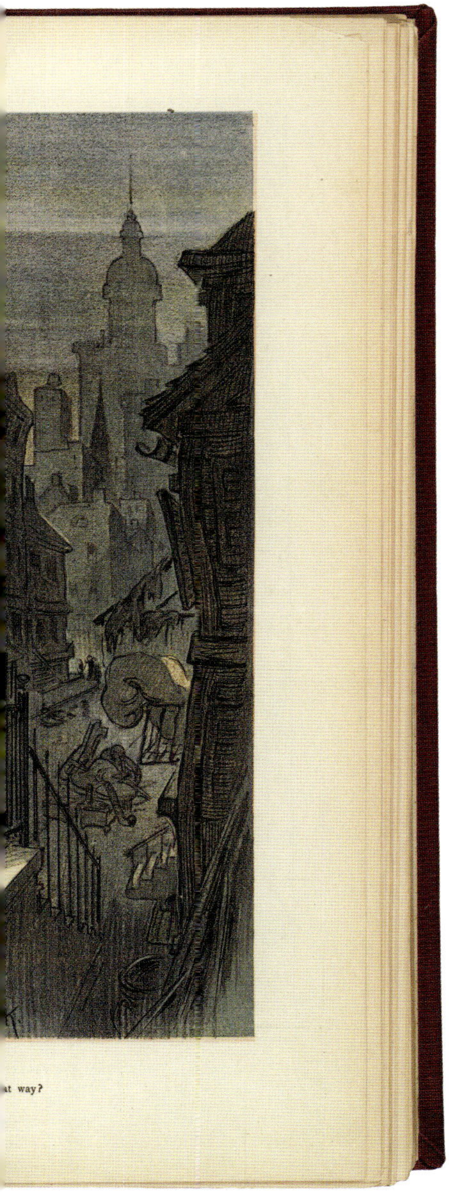

ABOVE A 1911 cartoon from *Puck* magazine depicting a corrupt and negligent landlord, framed by his overcrowded tenements in the background, laundering money out of his box of ill-gotten rents into another box of inadequate charity.

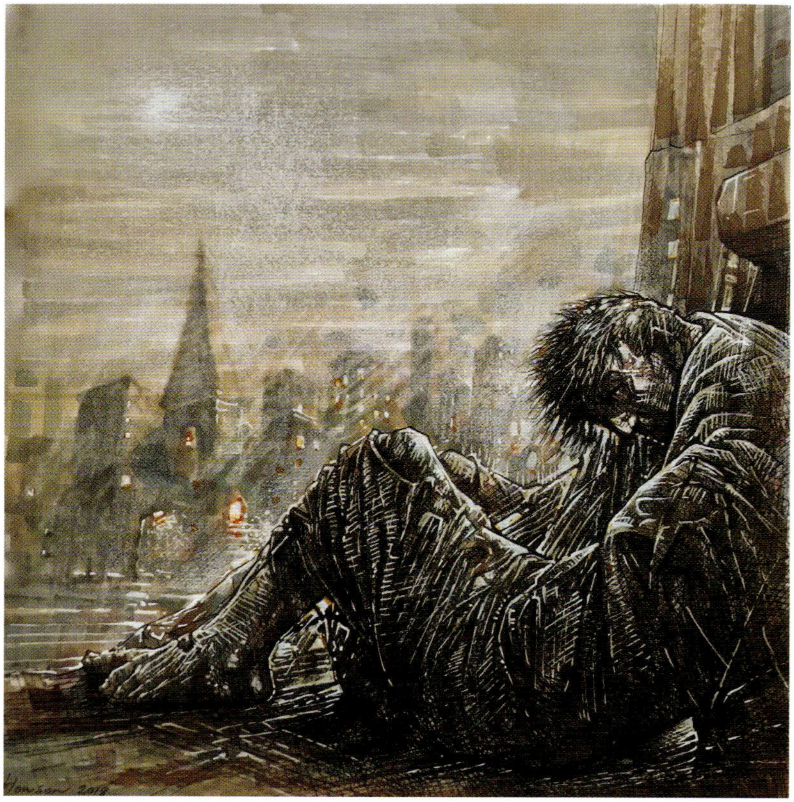

ABOVE Scottish painter Peter Howson's 2018 sketch, part of a series, entitled *Homeless Jesus*. Identifiable from the subtle wounds on his feet, the otherwise anonymous Christ appears to be in a cold, rainy European metropolis, possibly Howson's native Glasgow. Howson's illustration was displayed alongside Canadian sculptor Timothy Schmalz's *Homeless Jesus* statue. Schmalz's sculpture is of a figure draped in a blanket and placed on a public bench, whereby the identity of the sleeping homeless man is again only subtly made manifest through the stigmata on his feet. The statue was displayed publicly in hundreds of cities throughout the world, and in one North Carolina town the minister who had installed it in front of his church ultimately had to have it removed, as parishioners who assumed that it was an actual homeless man kept calling the police to have him arrested.

altruists put their faith in data and the algorithm. They imagine that charity is a simple matter of plugging the numbers, but that the most important thing is who is doing this plugging (them, of course).

As with any theory of charity, there is a hierarchy to who decides what is worthy, how much should be given, and who should be excluded. As with greed, the power to give still relies on a privatization of power; it is mutually exclusive to more democratic means of support. Charity may be necessary for survival in a storm or drought, a famine or a depression. It may be necessary simply for existence in this fallen world. But notably, charity is not the same thing as mutual support, as communal aid, as solidarity. It thrives not on a network, but a ladder. There is, beyond that criticism, a sense in which charity can sometimes obscure the strange alchemy of generosity, the wholly more mysterious nature of giving yourself freely unto somebody in need. Literary critic Lewis Hyde prefers the word "gift" to "charity," arguing that the former is the genesis of any true creative act, any communion between people. He writes in *The Gift: Creativity and the Artist in the Modern World* how the "passage into mystery always refreshes. If, when we work, we can look once a day upon the face of mystery, then our labor satisfies. We are lightened when our gifts rise from pools we cannot fathom. Then we know they are not a solitary egotism and they are inexhaustible." This is very near to what the wisdom of Scripture has always said about charity, that when given as a gift (rather than as a tax dodge) it transforms the altruist as much as the person who receives. This is an alchemy of the soul, a welcoming

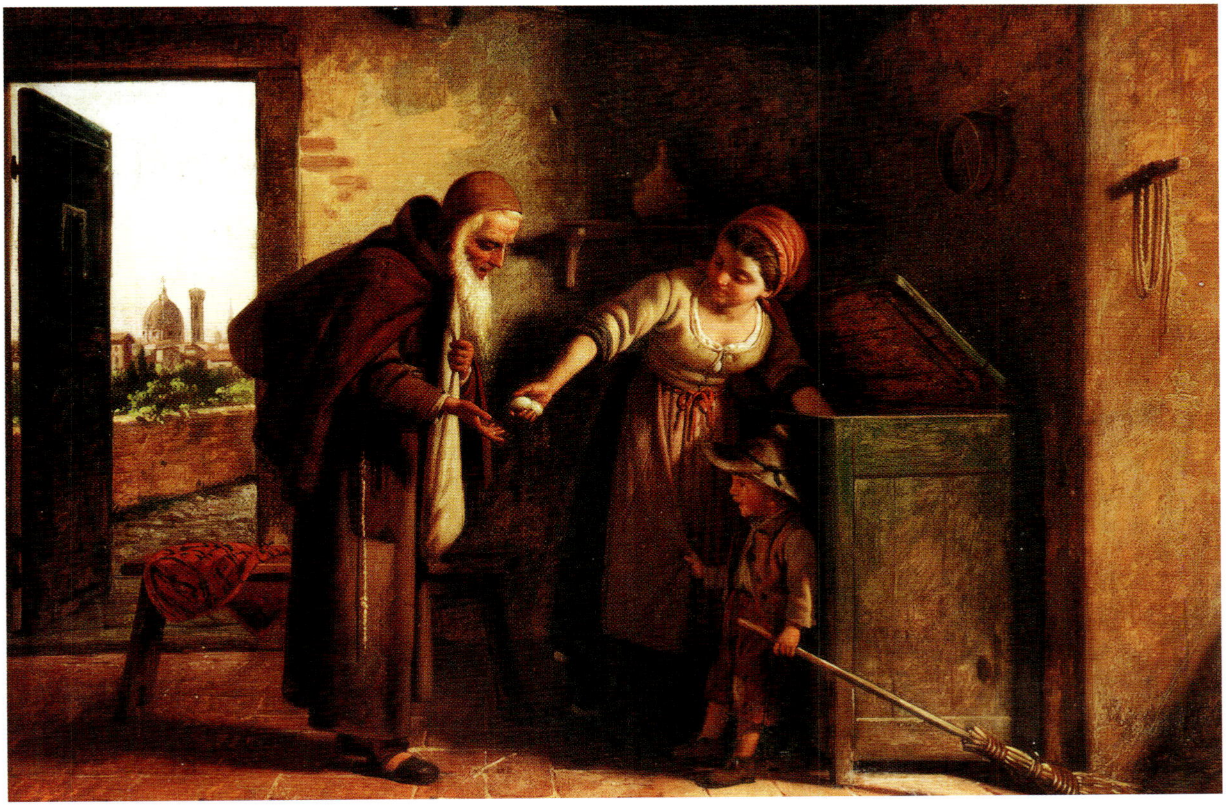

ABOVE Nineteenth-century Italian painter Gaetano Chierici's 1878 *Caritas* conveys some of the humble mystery of genuine charity, as a hardworking mother or servant (but attending to a young child in either case) briefly pauses her own difficult labor to offer a few eggs to a hungry mendicant. Infused with warmth and light, the painting is more about the fellowship of a gift than the condescension of charity. In private collection.

of the insularity of the self into a wider web of individuals, a humbling of the volunteer on behalf of her fellow suffering humans. True charity trades not in condescension, but rather recognition.

One moment in Terry Gilliam's film *The Fisher King* is portrayed with sterling beauty, wherein a character played by Robin Williams describes a version of the eponymous Arthurian legend about a monarch who is gifted a mystical vision of the Holy Grail, only to have it snatched away after he begins to greedily covet the power which it could impart. Punished with a festering wound which only grows more rank and jaundiced, his soul follows the same course as his physical state, and the king begins to die. Williams recounts how a fool arrives at the castle, "And being a fool, he was simple minded, he didn't see a king. He only saw a man alone and in pain." The dying king asks the fool for some water and the jester complies, handing the ruler a cup from his bedside. As the thirsty king drinks, he feels the wound healing, his body being restored, a lightness which he'd forgotten suddenly filling his soul. Looking down at the cup that the fool had handed him, he suddenly realizes that he's been drinking from the Holy Grail. "And he turned to the fool and said with amazement, 'How can you find that which my brightest and bravest could not?' And the fool replied, 'I don't know. I only knew that you were thirsty.'"

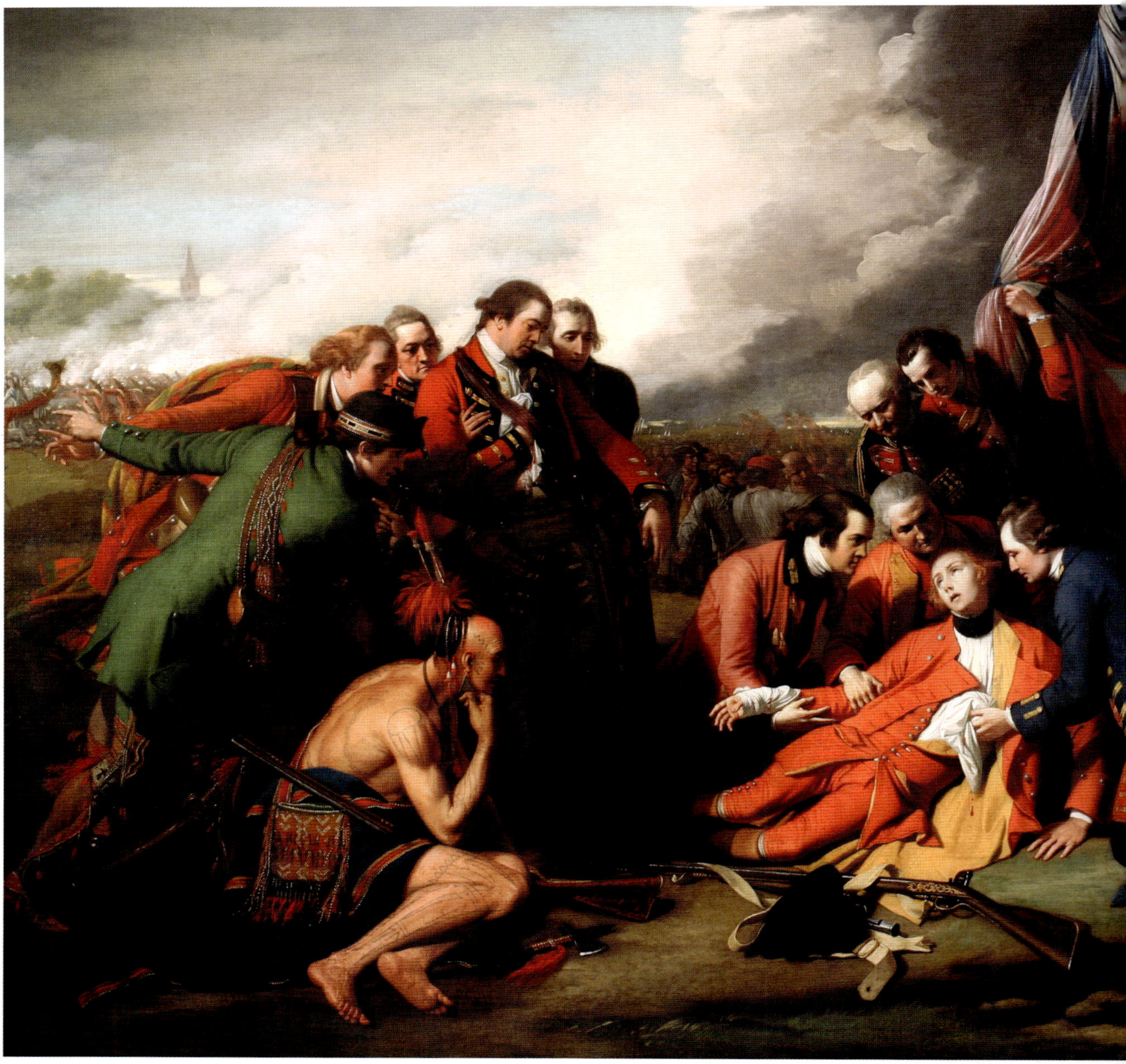

ABOVE American painter Benjamin West's 1770 *The Death of General Wolfe*, original held by the National Gallery of Canada in Ottawa, which depicts an Iroquoian sachem as an idealized "Noble Savage."

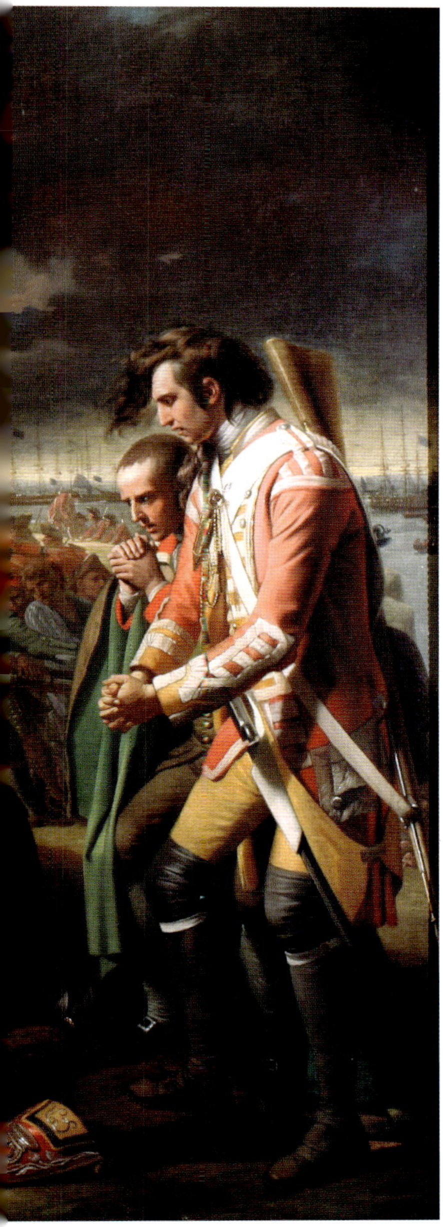

INTERLUDE—KONDIARONK

Within that kingdom of snow and acorns that was New France, along the straits of the Michigan and Huron Great Lakes, there ruled a Wendat sachem whom the French Jesuit Pierre François Xavier de Charlevoix said "possessed greater merit, a finer mind, more valor, prudence or discernment in understanding" than any other foreign princes with whom the Bourbons had relations. Once the enemy of the French, Chief Kondiaronk had led a union of Wendat, Huron, and Petun against the Five Nations of the Iroquois during the Beaver Wars, but had laid down his martial arms and established an amnesty with diplomatic ingenuity in 1701, brokering the Great Peace of Montreal. Affectionately known by his French allies as "The Rat," Kondiaronk bore little similarity to the Hanoverian monarchs in England or the Hapsburgs in Vienna; no contemporary illustration of the sachem survives, but Kondiaronk as imagined by later illustrators is depicted as tall and lean, with his hair on the sides shaved in the middle portion and allowed to grow long on the sides and tied into a top-knot, his torso and arms decorated with tribal tattoos, his frame adorned with feathered necklaces and wampum jewelry. He was, for the French, an object of fascination, of exoticization, even while they celebrated his political genius. Even more enduring was the critique which he offered of European understandings of money and power, a philosophical argument for charity and social reciprocity that when filtered through the mouthpieces of *philosophes* in Paris was in large part responsible for the politics of the Enlightenment, as anthropologist David Graeber proposes.

As Iroquoian speakers, the Wendat were not organized in the hierarchical manner assumed by the French and English; as a sachem, Kondiaronk was strictly speaking not a "king," but a military commander who answered to committees whose composition was both egalitarian and matriarchal. In a manner that evoked Thomas More's fictional land from *Utopia*, the Wendat (as well as their allies and their adversaries) had a sense of common ownership and of equitable and libertarian social arrangements. "They wonder much to hear that gold, which in itself is so useless a thing, should be everywhere so much esteemed," wrote More in 1516 of the Utopians, "that even men for whom it was made, and by whom it has its value, should yet be thought of less value than it is." Notably the philosopher placed his fantastical island in the Western Hemisphere, near the coast of America. Scholarly consensus long held that the ideology which More plays with in *Utopia* was the result of his own contemplations, conveniently projected onto the people of South America, who could be made empty repositories for his own thinking, as opposed to in any way reflecting the actual way in which American Indians may have lived in those Hesperian continents. Kondiaronk, as historians long argued, served a similar purpose, a personage to whom radical political thinkers could attribute their own critiques of European civilization. An explorer and French diplomat such as Louis-Armand de Lom d'Arce de Lahontan would in his 1703 travelogue *New Voyages in North America* formulate his own radical egalitarian philosophies by placing them within the mouth of the sachem, presenting a potent argument on behalf of an imagined Indian

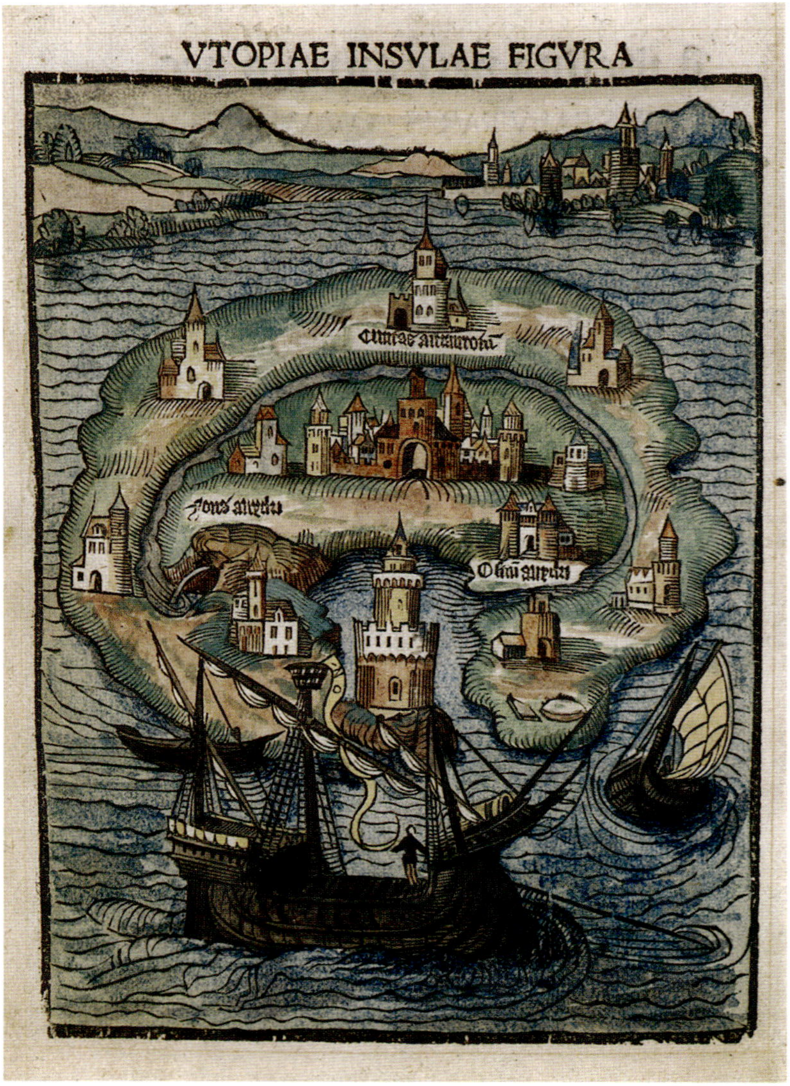

culture built upon reciprocity in contrast to Western greed. Not as well known as later Enlightenment philosophes like Danton and Voltaire, Lahontan's work nonetheless was instrumental in introducing democratic and socialistic ideals, as well as the potent archetype of the "Noble Savage" who countenances those elysian ideologies.

Yet the anthropologists David Graeber and David Wengrow in *The Dawn of Everything: A New History of Humanity* make an argument as revolutionary as it is obvious—maybe Lahontan wasn't using Kondiaronk as a mere mouthpiece; maybe the Frenchman was simply recording what the sachem had actually said (as indeed is literally stated within the *New Voyages in North America* itself), arguing that the reader has "every reason to believe the basic arguments were Kondiaronk's own." Positing that Kondiaronk's "Indigenous critique" wasn't a fiction, but rather a reflection of the Wendat sachem's actual views, Graeber and Wengrow audaciously claim that the Enlightenment politics inaugurated

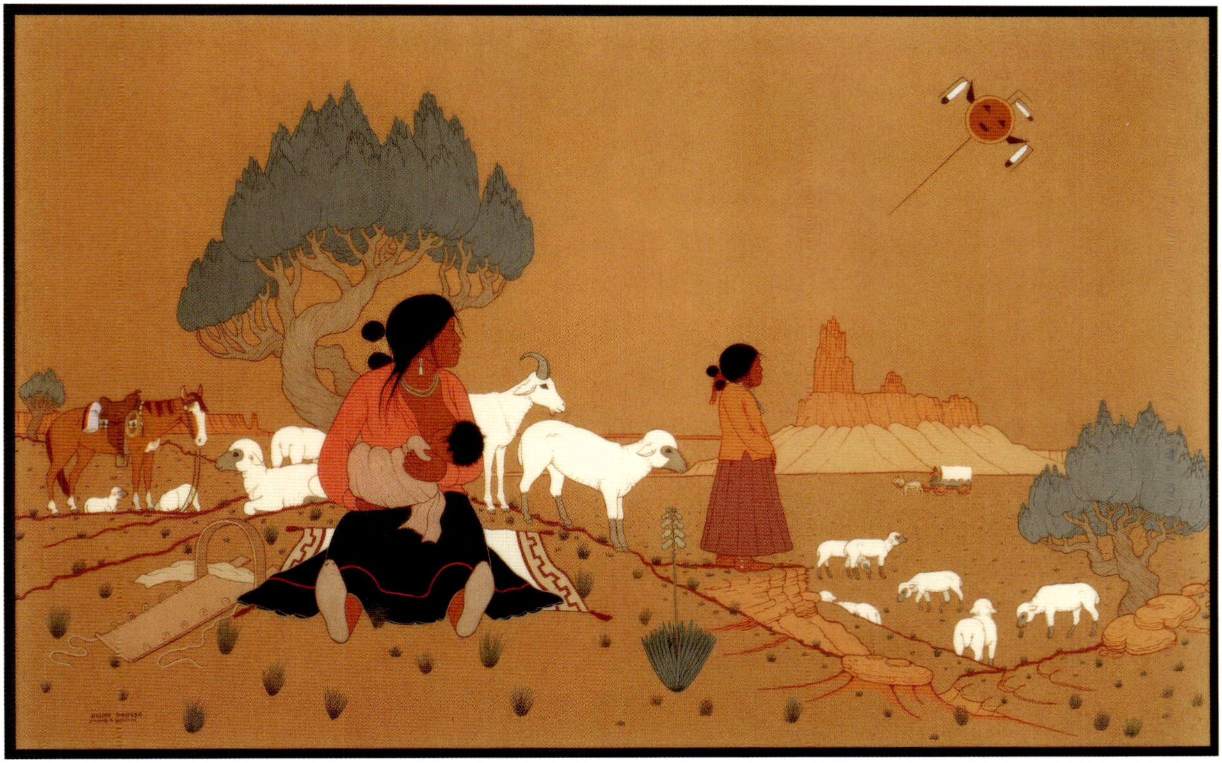

OPPOSITE Colorized frontispiece from More's 1516 *Utopia*, depicting a map of the eponymous island.

TOP Chiricahua Apache artist Allan Houser's 1953 painting *Herding Sheep*, depicting the spirit of consilience to nature and community discussed in the philosophical arguments of the Wendat sachem Kondiaronk. Original held by the Denver Art Museum.

around the turn of the eighteenth century and reaching fruition in the American and French Revolutions wasn't a European novelty, but rather born from an Indian condemnation of Western avarice and power. What Kondiaronk offers is a damning portrayal of French hierarchy, asking Lahontan if he could "seriously imagine that I would be happy to live like one of the inhabitants of Paris? To take two hours every morning just to put on my shirt and make up? To bow and scrape before every obnoxious galoot I meet on the street who happens to have been born with an inheritance?"

Obviously with a bit of Swiftian humor about it, *New Voyages in North America* takes a jocular approach to European civilization, but the contrast with American Indian culture is clear. Kondiaronk's politics is based on mutual support, not greed, the sachem continuing, "Do you actually imagine I could carry a purse full of coins and not immediately hand them over to people who are hungry? That I would carry a sword but not immediately draw it on the first band of thugs I see rounding up the destitute to press into Naval service?" Implicit is the contrast between a culture based in greed and one based in solidarity, for Kondiaronk speaks of something far more radical than mere charity. "For Europeans in 1703, this was heady stuff," write Graeber and Wengrow. Headier still was Kondiaronk's conclusion—that the distinction of "mine" and "thine" had irrevocably stained the soul of Christendom, for "I affirm that what you call 'money' is the devil of devils, the tyrant of the French, the source of all evils, the bane of souls and the slaughterhouse of the living."

THE FISHER KING

Discourse on transcendence and the numinous all you wish, but a white bread sandwich with a rectangle of orange American cheese and slick pink bologna with a thin spread of mayo, all washed down with lukewarm coffee, can be as ecstasy; preach about salvation and redemption, but a warm cot with a thin blanket might as well be Heaven. All men can be mystics with a full belly, but the true sense of vision comes out of a deep hunger, the wisdom that understands a division between spirit and matter is only ever fallacious. Blessed are the hungry, the anxious, the lonely, the tired. That was the politics and theology of a Brooklyn-born-respectable-Protestant-girl-turned-anarchist-journalist-turned-Catholic-convert named Dorothy Day, who along with dozens of her comrades convened on a May Day demonstration in 1933 at lower Manhattan's Union Square Park. Surrounded by the granite sentinels of the skyscrapers, less than a mile from Wall Street, which had plunged the nation (and the world) into the Great Depression, Day and her associate the French activist Peter Maurin sold for a penny cheap-print copies of a newspaper called *The Catholic Worker*. That first of May was the beginning of an attendant movement which shared the newspaper's name, the Catholic Workers understanding themselves as a vanguard operating where Christ and the Proletariat coincided, reading the Beatitudes and the Magnificat as a discourse on how God's Kingdom was of the poor, the weak, the abused, the neglected, the spurned, the persecuted, the low. "We stand at the present time with the Communists," wrote Day in a 1940 issue of *The Catholic Worker*. "The Sermon on the Mount is our manifesto." What, then, did those assembled in the appropriately named Union Square make of the slight, plain, fervent young woman, who to her fellow Catholics must have seemed a godless radical and to her fellow radicals a superstitious zealot?

It doesn't matter what either of those groups may have thought about Day; what mattered was the house which she and Maurin established a few blocks south in the heart of Greenwich Village, based on the principles of apostolic poverty and where lay women and men who cast off their possessions so as to serve the destitute. The drunks and junkies of the Bowery, the prostitutes and runaways on Broadway, the queers and homeless on Canal, the whole multitude of God's kingdom. "The mystery of the poor is this," wrote Day in 1964: "That they are Jesus, and what you do for them you do for Him . . . The mystery of poverty is that by sharing in it, making ourselves poor in giving to others, we increase our knowledge of and belief in love." This was a medieval vision of sacred poverty, of emptying the pocket to fill the heart, the same faith that motivated hospitallers and communards, and which compelled Day and Maurin's Catholic Worker Movement to establish some 240 autonomous collectives across the United States that existed to serve the poor. Not to convert, but to feed, clothe, house, console. Fully a quarter of the population capable of work was unemployed during the most dire days of the Great Depression, what the economist John Maynard Keynes had described as the dawn of a new Dark Ages. Under the visionary leadership of President Franklin Roosevelt, a variety of social welfare programs were inaugurated within the auspices of the New Deal, which served

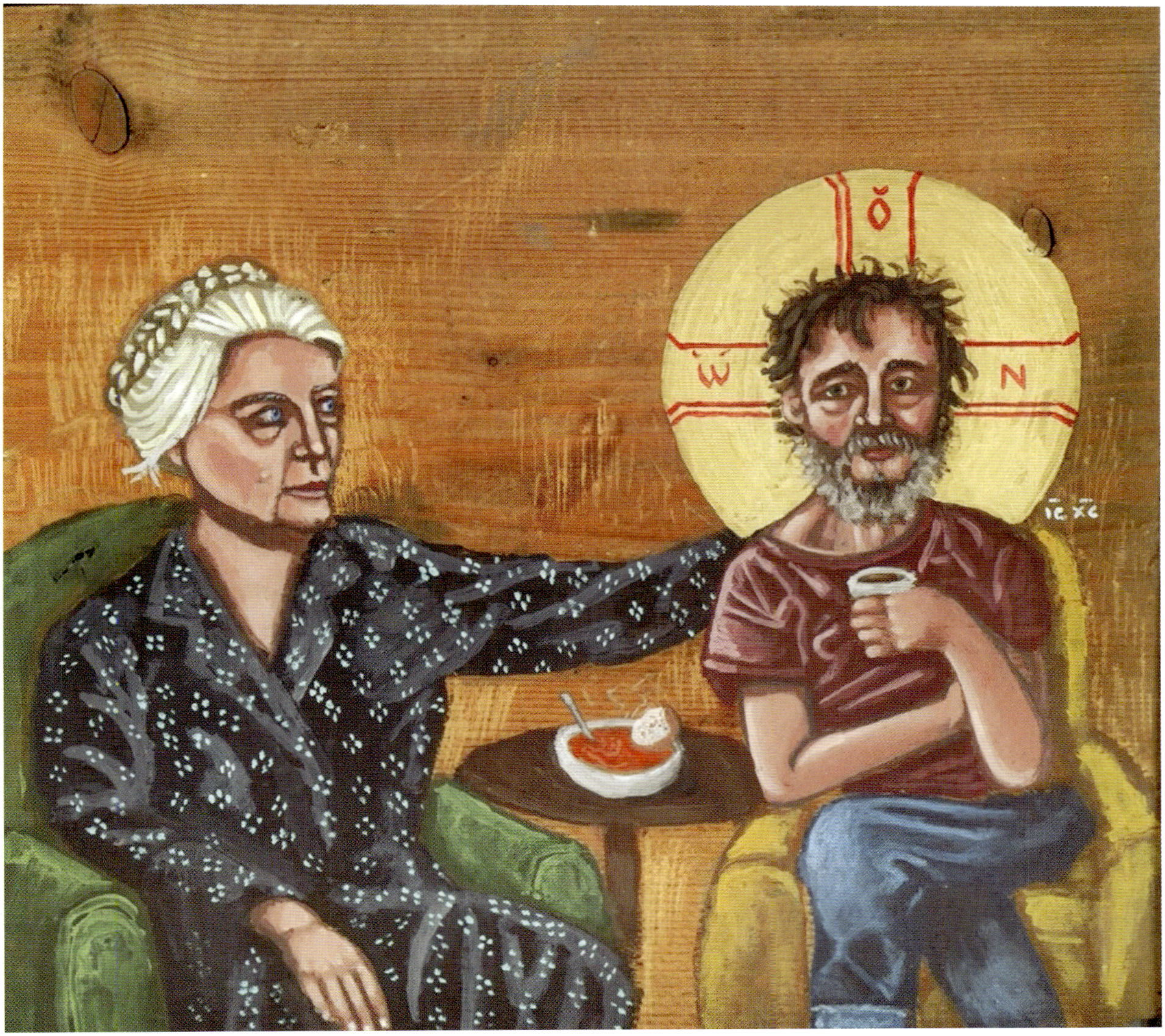

ABOVE Contemporary icon painter Kelly Latimore's 2015 icon of Day with a homeless man whose halo evidences that He is Christ.

to stave off the worst possibilities of mass famine and civil strife. Still, what the Catholic Workers offered was something a bit different, beyond even Day and Maurin being politically much further to the left than Roosevelt. It was a sense of mutual aid, of solidarity between the impoverished. Not charity offered on high by philanthropists or even the government, but within the communion of equals. A form of charity organized not vertically, but horizontally.

This was what was crucial about the "voluntary poverty" which defined the vocation of those saints who worked within the mission houses; not that it made a fetish out of being poor (though the two weren't necessarily mutually exclusive in the Catholic environs of the movement), but that there was an understanding that this would be a type of charity not defined by either condescension or pity. "Most of all, anarchism is just a matter of having the courage to take the simple principles of common decency that we all live by, and to follow them through to

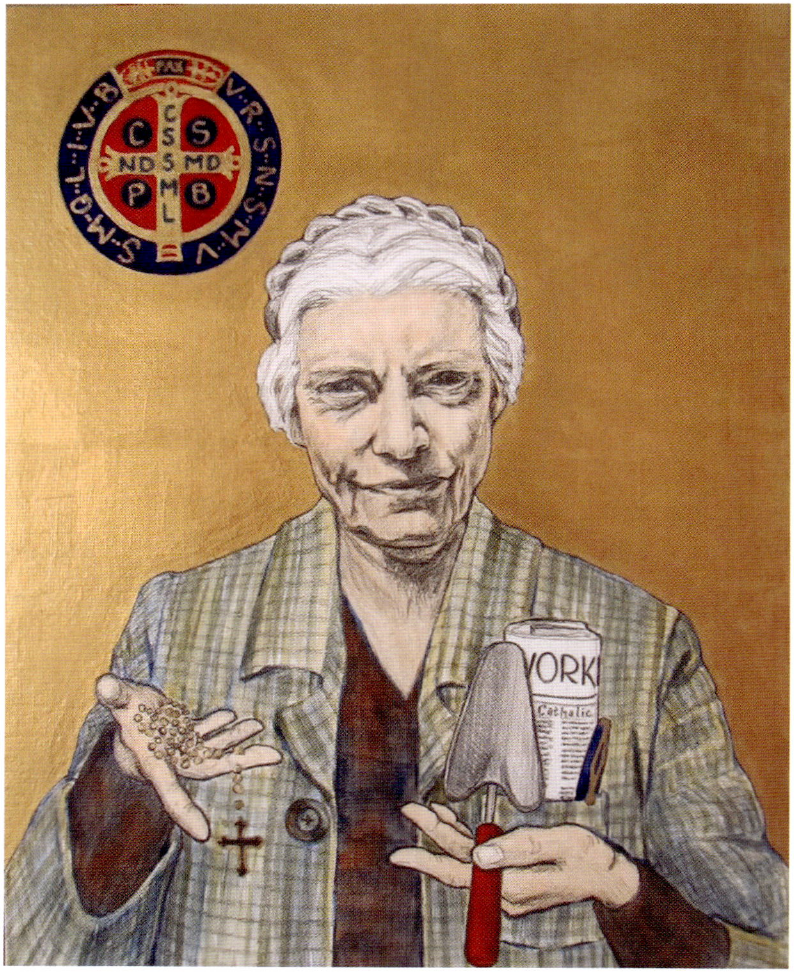

their logical conclusions," as writes David Graeber in *Are You an Anarchist? The Answer May Surprise You!* Day and Maurin didn't consider themselves anarchists; rather, they were Catholics first and communists second, but they adhered to Graeber's principle on following through to their logical conclusion the principles of human decency. If confronted with a starving man, we would not watch him wither away and die; if a child was drowning, we would dive into the water to save her. Why, then, are we so complacent when it's not the matter of a single person perishing, but of thousands, of millions? Graeber writes that "Every time you treat another human with consideration and respect, you are being an anarchist," and this engenders an important type of charity, a mutual charity. Here there are no Carnegies to decide who shall be fed or not. Instead, the people feed each other.

Another group who wouldn't have considered themselves to be anarchists but who abided by Graeber's understanding that respect should be at the core of mutual aid were the Black Panther Party. Black Nationalists as opposed to anarchists, and certainly not pacifists in the mold of Day's Catholic Worker Movement, the Panthers nonetheless had a firm understanding of how respect

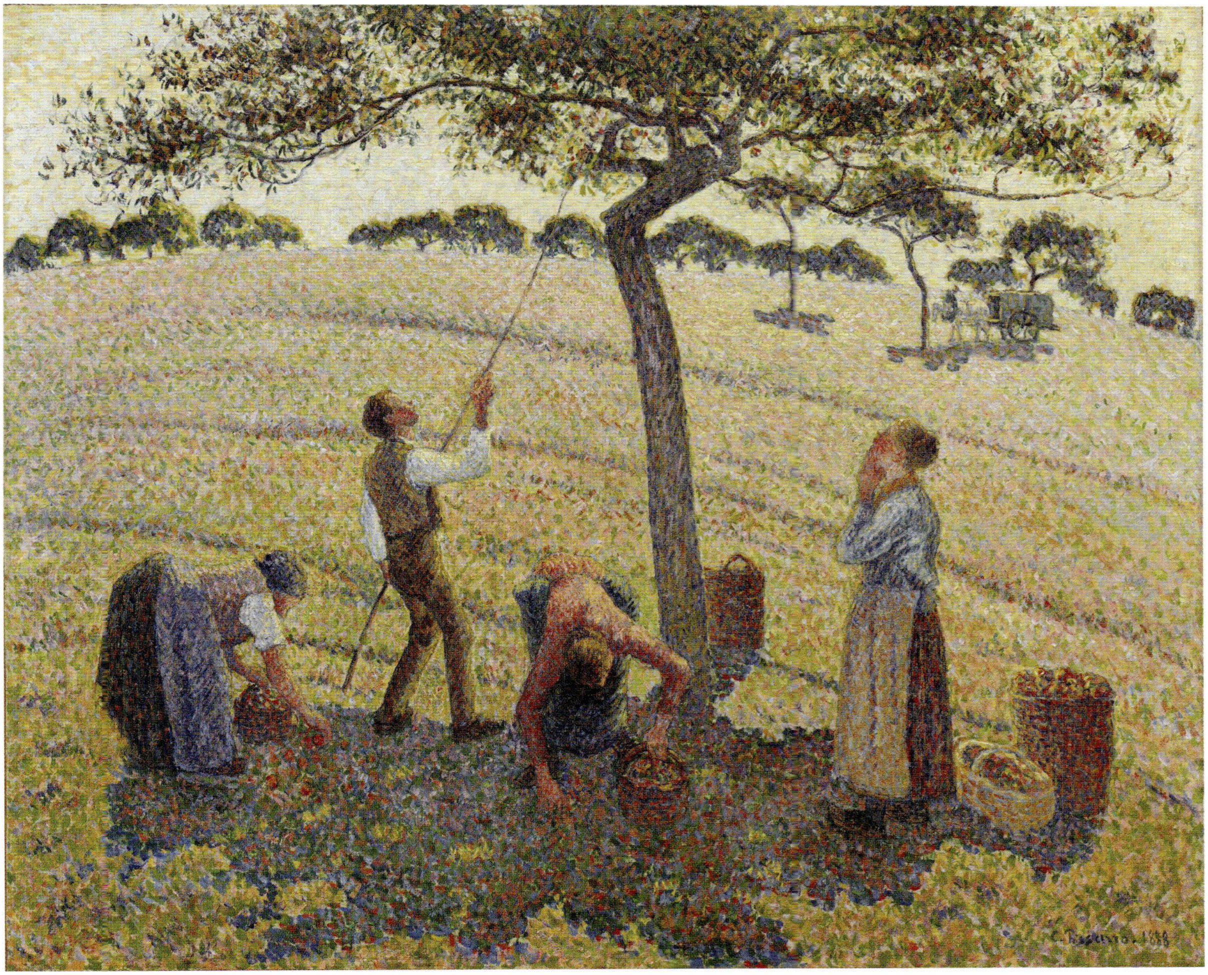

OPPOSITE Iconographer Margaret Brace Willis's 201[illegible] icon of Day, a copy of *The Catholic Worker* in her pocket.

ABOVE Anarchist painter Camille Pissarro's Impressionist 1888 *Apple Harvest at Eragny*, original at the Dallas Museum of Art, depicts the mutual solidarity and labor of a contingent of workers, an illustration of basic communitarian economic principles.

is more than just a strategy, but a metaphysic of recognition between humans, between equals. They rightly demanded respect for the Black communities whom they represented and defended, communities which were continually battered by the structural inequities and racism of American society, but they also enacted respect on the streets of Oakland, Detroit, and Baltimore as well. "We must ally ourselves with the oppressed communities of the world," wrote Huey P. Newton, the founder of the Black Panther Party. "In revolutionary love we must make common cause with these oppressed communities," beginning at home. Stereotype has reduced the members of the Black Panther Party to bandoliers and rifles, berets and leather jackets, but it would be more accurate to see their lasting contribution in powdered eggs and buttered hot cakes, orange juice and milk.

The Free Breakfast for Children Program was established in West Oakland, California in 1969, administered by the Black Panthers and distributing free food to impoverished children throughout the ghettos of the city. Open to children of all racial backgrounds and ethnicities, thirty-six chapters of the program would operate for several years throughout the United States and offer ten thousand

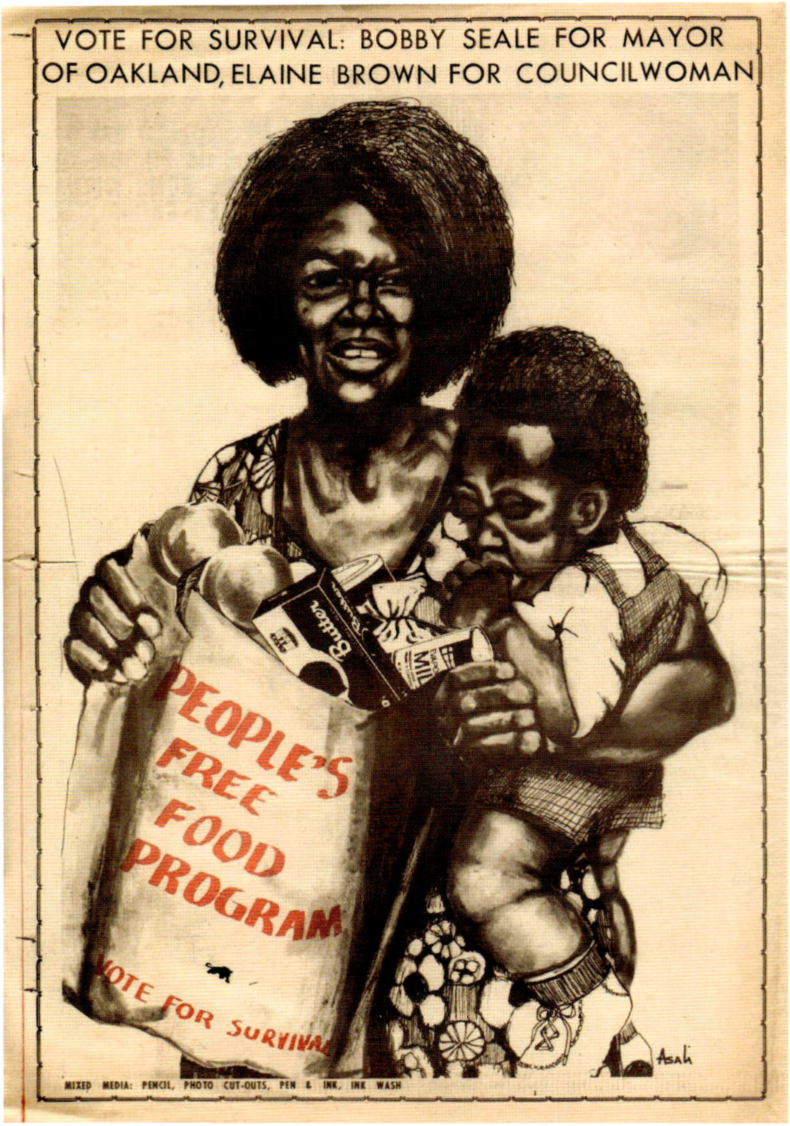

children a day a nutritious, filling, and completely free meal before the start of the school day. Describing the utility and significance of the program, lawyer and activist Dean Spade writes in *Mutual Aid* that the Black Panthers' actions in these cities produced "new ways of living where people get to create systems of care and generosity that address harm and foster well being." Crucially, this was a system dominated not by well-meaning outsiders, but by an organic intercommunity effort of mutual generosity.

Mutual aid can take multiple forms, but what's crucial is this horizontal ordering of power. Yosef Baratz, a founder of the revolutionary kibbutzim movement in first British Palestine and later Israel, wrote in *A Village by the Jordan: The Story of Degania* that what motivated those who established their intentional community was the principle that "there shouldn't be any employers and employed at all. There must be a better way." Inspired by communitarian and

TOP Black Panther Bobby Seale's 1972 campaign poster for Oakland City Council, touting the People's Free Food Program.

OPPOSITE Youths enjoying free breakfast served by the Panthers in New York, 1969.

socialistic values, the kibbutzniks wished to establish in the dry Judean desert a social arrangement built entirely on mutual work and aid. In part drawing from the radical political core of the Hebrew Scriptures, this mostly secular Jewish movement imagined a means of "charity" which wasn't top-down, but rather an interlocking network of equal women and men working together and supporting one another. True to Graeber's and Spade's observations about mutual aid, the operative metaphor for such a community would be as a web, where each node is a person linked to their neighbor, the fabric which is woven being all the stronger because of this network of connections. From that ancient sandy soil then grew olives and dates, pomegranates and almonds, wheat, potatoes and carrots. Women and men were treated equally, children raised communally, private property abolished. "We spoke in the plural," writes Yael Neeman in *We Were the Future: A Memoir of the Kibbutz.* "That's how we were born, that's how we grew up, forever. Our horizons were strange, bent." This was a movement that aimed to convert the singular into the plural, the first person into the third, to turn alienated loner into a locus of community. Most of all, it was based in mutuality, not on the good intentions of a single outsider. The most remarkable instance of such a kibbutz is the rare example of one first founded outside of Israel, on the grim grounds of the death fields of the Buchenwald Concentration Camp, where survivors of the Holocaust formed their own mutual aid community in 1945, welcoming others into their midst with an understanding that, as Rabbi Hillel wrote in the first century, "If I am not for me, who will be for me? And when I am myself alone, who am I? And if not now, then when?"

Another example of refugees from Hitler's Hell who found salvation through mutual aid was the tiny Christian group known as the Bruderhof Community. Because of their plain style of dress—collared white shirts and black pants with

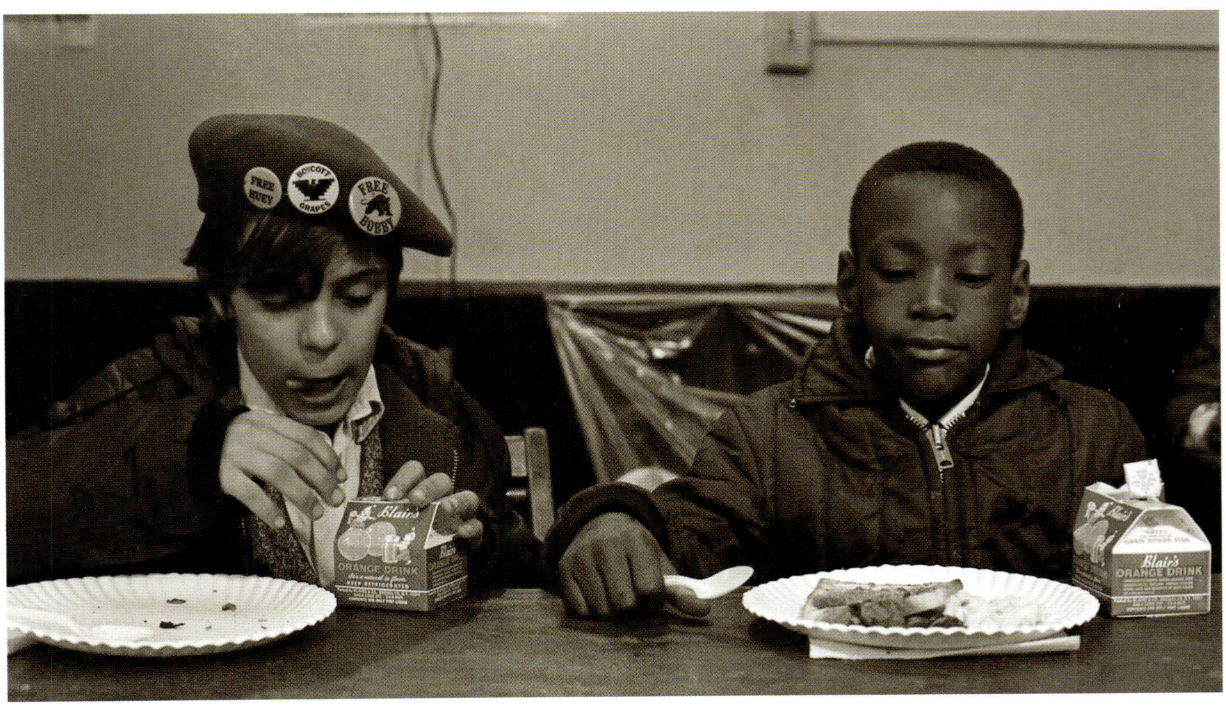

suspenders, straw hats, and beards without mustaches—the Bruderhof are often mistaken for the Amish or Mennonites, though their origins are far more recent. Drawing from the same wellspring of radical Anabaptist thought that had indeed gestated the Amish several centuries before, as well as from Lutheran Pietism and the social gospel of English groups such as the Salvation Army, the Prussian theologian Eberhard Arnold established the Bruderhof in 1920, drawing from his own personal visions about the possibility of creating a utopia on earth, albeit a small one. Inspired by the dictates of apostolic poverty which defined the earliest of Christians, Arnold preached a doctrine of pacifism, mutual support, and common ownership. Every member, following baptism, takes a vow by which "all your faculties, the entire strength of your body and soul, and all your property, both that which you now possess and that which you may later inherit or earn" was to be used in the furtherance of the wellbeing of the community, from each according to their ability and to each according to their need. Building their own society within the larger German nation, a society in opposition to those twin gods of commerce and consumerism and which also disavowed the militarism that defined the Nazi Party, the Bruderhof were in 1937 branded as "un-Aryan" and given forty-eight hours to leave. Some settled in nearby Liechtenstein, while others traveled to an English settlement community which had been founded earlier for the purposes of evangelization. Arnold's group would survive the war. Never a large contingency—today only numbering a little under three thousand members worldwide, spread across thirty-six communities with around half in the United States—the Bruderhof would go on to establish homeless shelters, food pantries, and medical clinics for the most impoverished, funding their activities through a variety of collectively owned business ventures, such as Community Playthings, which specializes in the manufacture of high-quality wooden toys for children.

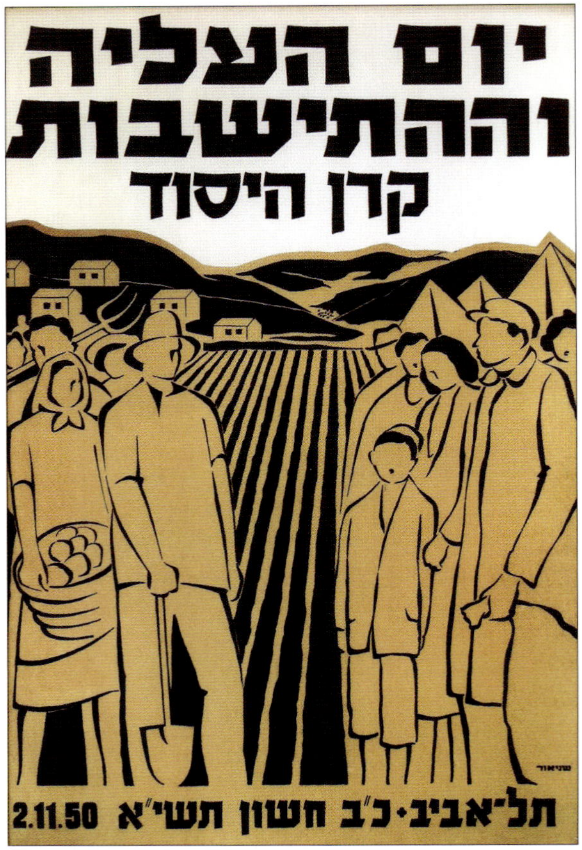

Even more than reorganizing monetary power on this horizontal axis of mutual aid, the most radical forms of charity are those utopian ventures which seek to disestablish the sovereignty of money in its entirety, a genuinely countercultural aim. "Spontaneity, autonomy, seem to be a new type of humanity that's coming about," said the radical American writer Emmett Grogan at London's Dialectics of Liberation Conference in 1967, "and today is the first day in the rest of your lives." During the marijuana- and patchouli-scented summer of love in San Francisco's Haight Ashbury neighborhood, Grogan's radical arts and theater collective known as the Diggers pursued the aim of abolishing money, establishing not just "free stores" where the indigent could secure clothing, furniture, and food, but also founding free ride share programs and medical clinics, in addition to their fervent faith that access to the arts—theater, poetry, music—should also be uncoupled from the machinations of capital. As Peter Berg, another Digger, exclaimed during a protest, "Property is the enemy. Burn it, destroy it, give it

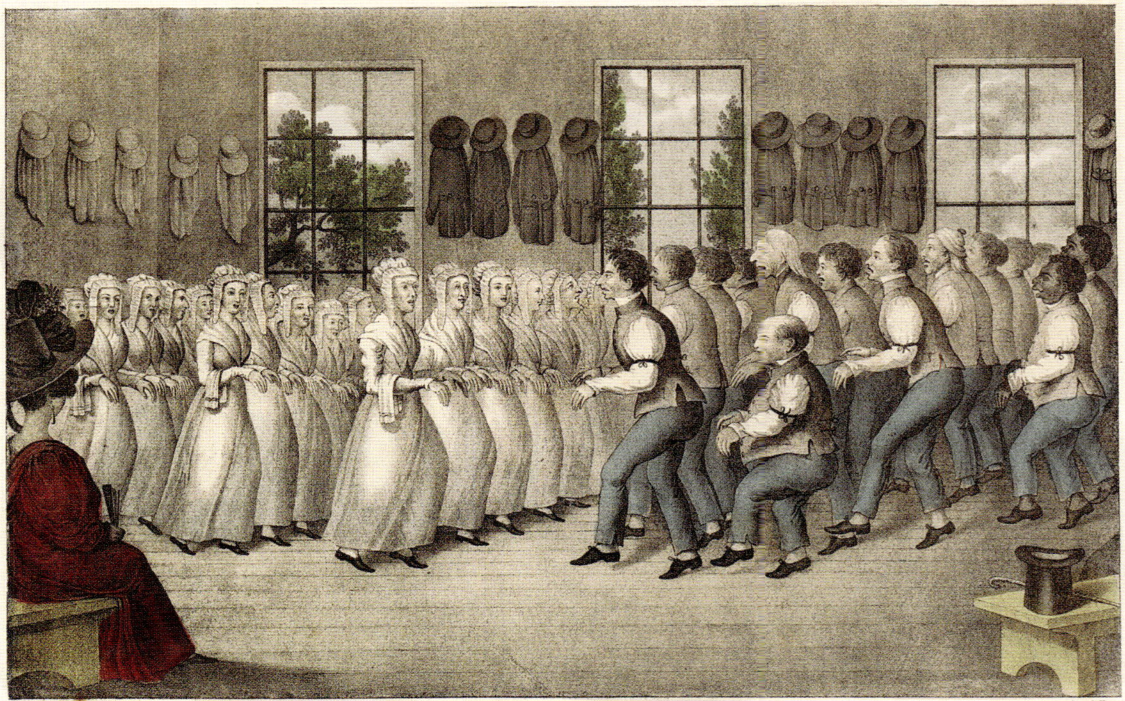

OPPOSITE 1950 United Israel Appeal poster using imagery of the kibbutzim.

TOP Illustration of a New England Shaker church from around 1835, depicting members of the famously celibate denomination dancing during one of their ecstatic worship services. Even more than the Amish and Mennonites, the Shakers adhere to a radically communitarian philosophy of charity and support.

away." This was more than mere agitprop, marketing, or performance art. Every day at four in the afternoon in Golden Gate Park, the Diggers served massive free dinners of stew cooked with fresh meat and vegetables, securing free entertainment for their guests from bands like the Grateful Dead and Jefferson Airplane. At the core of the Diggers' philosophy was this belief that money, even when put to benevolent uses, was oppressive, and that "charity" as such couldn't be extricated from the power of capital—who had it and who didn't. By contrast, they saw genuine charity in mutual aid, in the same voluntary poverty which Day described; not in capitulating to the demands of finance, but abolishing finance altogether. Theirs was a dream enumerated by their historical namesake, the seventeenth-century radical dissenting religious group the Diggers, who in 1649 dug up the hedges which enclosed private land and made the plot at St. George's Hill outside of London into a common treasury to be farmed for the benefit of everyone rather than the profit of a few. Writing that same year in *The True Levellers Standard Advanced*, the Diggers' theoretician Gerrard Winstanley argued that "Those that Buy or Sell Land, and are landlords, have got it either by Oppression, or Murther, or Theft; and all landlords lives in the breach of the Seventh and Eighth Commandments," so that now the task remains to "advance Creation out of bondage."

Yet the Diggers, whether in the 1960s or the 1640s, faced the same conundrum which any utopian group wishing to turn away from the gods of this world

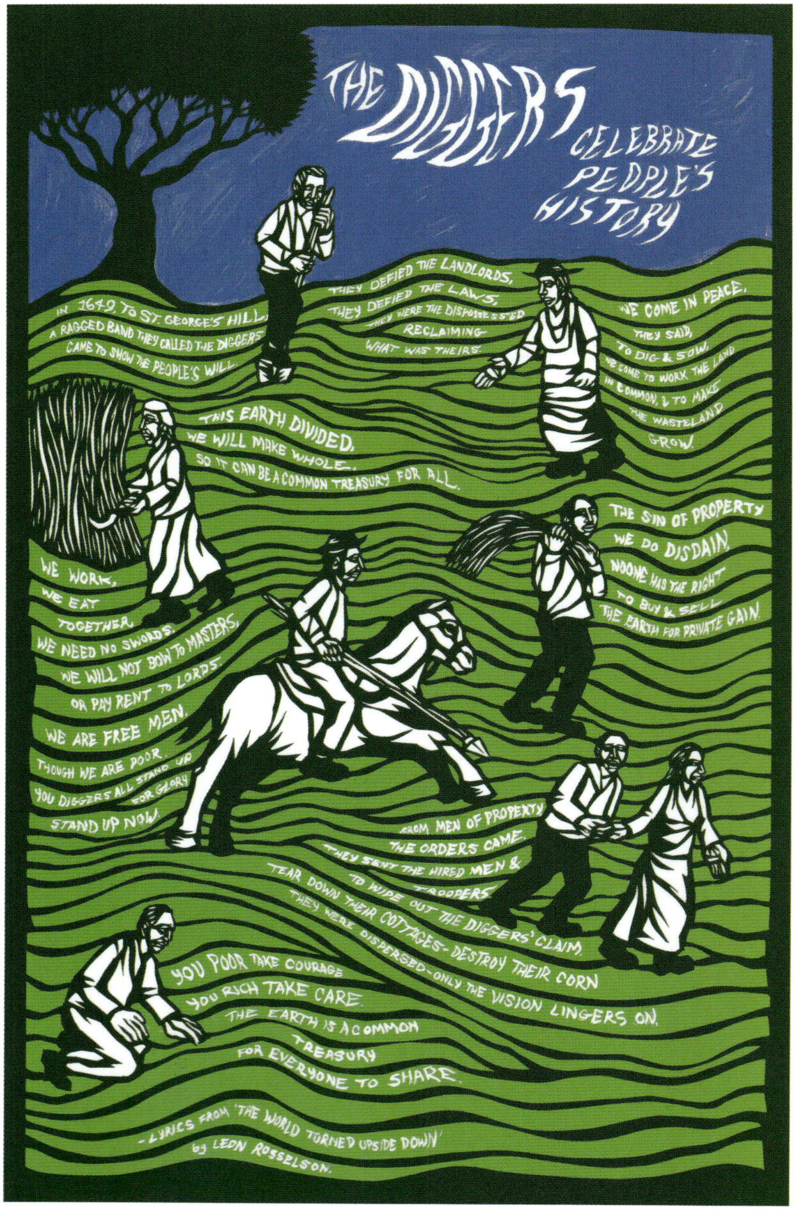

must face—those gods are everywhere. The debate as to whether or not there can be ethical consumption under capitalism—or ethical charity, for that matter—is tired in the sense that it presumes a scenario which is now a hypothetical, an alternative which has not yet been born. Regardless, the model that such groups provide—of generosity, philanthropy, charity—undertaken not by millionaires in order to secure a tax break or to see their family name on a foundation, but rather as a means of mutual support by those consigned to the gutter like the rest of us, deserves more than just admiration, but careful study. Such assistance is not charity in the conventional sense per se, nor is it simple sympathy, or even empathy—it's solidarity.

TOP Artist Erik Ruin celebrates the original English Diggers of the seventeenth century, from whom the artists' collective derived its name, in this 2010 poster included as part of the Celebrate People's History project.

OPPOSITE Byzantine mosaic depicting the parable of the widow's mite from the sixth-century Sant Apollinare Nuovo in Ravena, Italy.

And also a parable, for it's been recounted how in the first century the Temple in Jerusalem encouraged donations for the maintenance of religious ritual and observance, as well as for feeding the hungry, clothing the naked, and housing the indigent. Various dignitaries and merchants gave heavily, pouring money into collection boxes in the courtyard in front of God's temple, though the amounts given were surely a small portion of the overall wealth which they possessed. Finally an elderly woman, who was bent with kyphosis and shuffled with arthritic legs, face grizzled and lined with wrinkles produced by the unforgiving Judean sun, a scattering of wispy gray hairs over her balding pate, deposited within the box a single lepton. Or maybe she was young, recently widowed, an infant she could scarcely feed on her hip. Regardless, whoever she was and whatever she looked like, she gave more than she had.

An eroded copper coin, the face of the Hasmonean king Alexander Jannaeus (an iconographic symbol of the things-of-this-world in opposition to the things-of-Heaven) now a muddled splotch from entropy and friction, the whole unit of currency worth about only six minutes of labor, is said to have constituted the entirety of the widow's fortune. "Verily I say unto you," says Christ in Mark 12:43, "That this poor widow hath cast more in, than all they which have cast into the treasury." Like all of Christ's parables, the meaning is far more obscure than is first implied, a lesson shot through with ambivalence and ambiguity. Those manning the collection plate think that Jesus's message is clear—the Lord loves a healthy giver, and to give more than you're even able to is to give the most of all. Others have said that there is an irony here, that Christ is condemning the economic situation which necessitates such a sacrifice from somebody incapable of making it. Perhaps both are true. And maybe, more than either, what the widow's mite, deposited in Jerusalem, signified was a moment of connection, a statement of understanding, made by one suffering woman unto all of those who share in her afflictions.

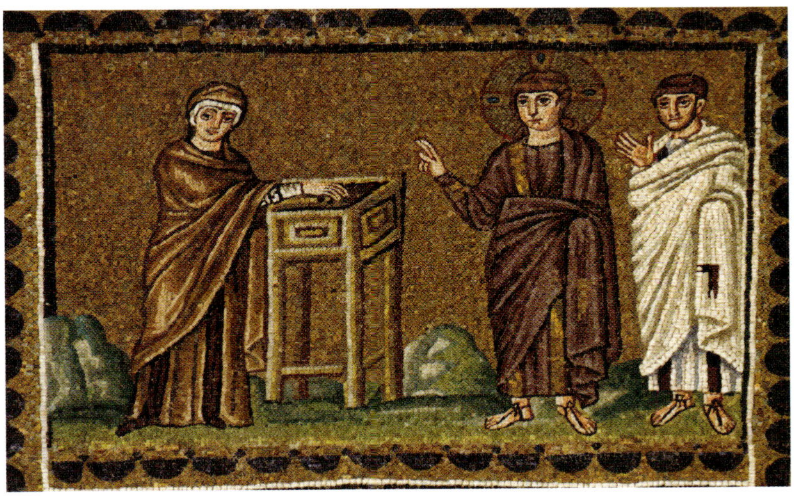

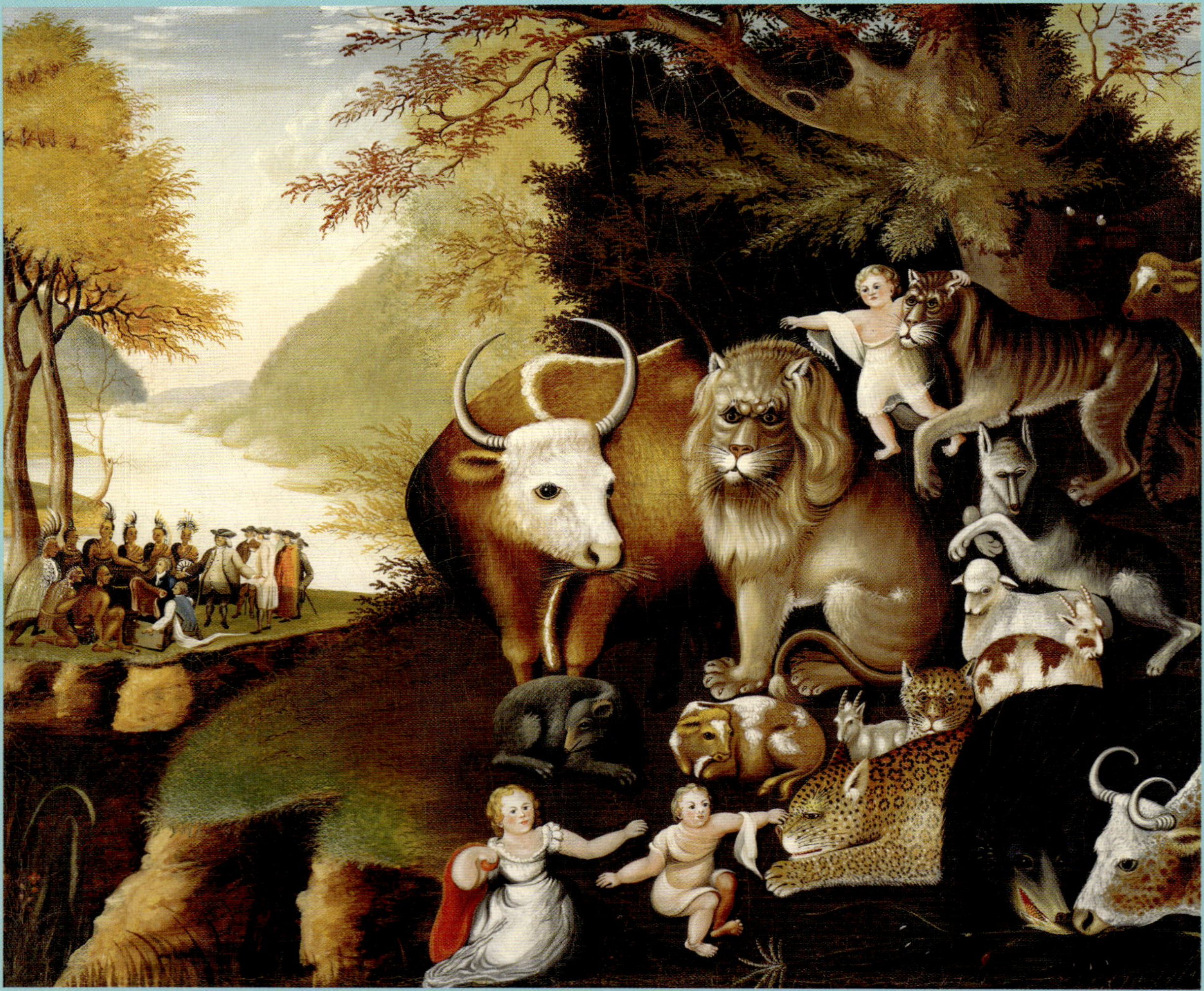

CHAPTER SEVEN

NOTHING VALUABLE LOST: PEACEFULNESS

"All shall be well, and all shall be well, and all manner of things shall be well."

—Julian of Norwich, *Revelations of Divine Love* (c. 1373)

"But above all you should understand that there can never be peace between nations until there is first known that true peace which is within the souls of men."

—Black Elk, *The Sacred Pipe* (1947)

The virtue, in any of the conventional listings, isn't referred to as "peacefulness," but rather as "patience." In a connotative sense, the traditional rendering doesn't do full justice to the concept, to what the Churchmen and Scholastic theologians were speaking of. Patience in a modern context implies the (not unimportant or unadmirable) ability to be calm during the second hour waiting at the Department of Motor Vehicles, to not get angry at an operator when placed on hold with the phone company, to be measured and polite when the waiter at a restaurant is slow with the check. What "patience" really meant in its original context is more a difference of degree than of kind, a species of forbearance where one doesn't just endure a sluggish waiter with equanimity, but a prison and gulag as well. The root of the word—from the Latin *patientia*—is related to the word "suffering," an adjunct to "penitent." What patience refers to is an ability to withstand suffering, to not break under horrible circumstances, to be unbowed and with a countenance of peace even when circumstances are hell. "Peacefulness," then, is a much closer sense of what the word means in those oft-stated clichés referring to the "patience of Job" or the "patience of a saint." What peacefulness promises is the ability to withstand that which you don't control, a strength that isn't physical but rather born from spiritual fortitude. Even more importantly, peacefulness is an intimation, a precursor, to the promised eschaton, when all contradictions are reconciled, when strife and pain are revealed to have been momentarily illusory. As the prophet promises in Isaiah 9:7, and of "peace there shall be no end."

PREVIOUS SPREAD Self-taught American artist Edward Hicks's Quaker faith instilled in him a devotion to that mystical belief in a coming millennium, but one which human devotion and works would be capable of intimating even before the eschaton. A favored theme of Hicks's was that of the peaceable kingdom, drawing from Isaiah 11:6, wherein the prophet foretells how "the wolf shall dwell with the lamb, and the leopard shall lie down with the kid; and the calf and the young lion and the fatling together; and a little child shall lead them," Hicks interpreting the scene literally across several different compositions. In this 1837 rendition *The Peaceable Kingdom*, original held by the Carnegie Museum of Art in Pittsburgh, Hicks's menagerie dwells on an embankment that looks faintly similar to the shores of his own Susquehanna in central Pennsylvania. Indeed the foundational myth of that province is depicted in the upper right corner, where the treaty between Hicks's coreligionist William Penn and the local Lenape Indians is dramatized, the beginnings of the colony as a religious utopia dedicated to pluralism and pacifism a forerunner of that coming millennium.

OPPOSITE Hudson Valley School painter Thomas Cole's most celebrated compositions include the series of five paintings entitled *The Course of Empire*, rendered between 1833 and 1836, with the originals held by the New-York Historical Society. A first-generation inheritor of the young republic's obsession with comparing the United States to Rome, and the potential degradations over time which such similarities might imply, Cole depicted the historical evolution of a fictitious empire (though an undeniably Greco-Roman one) from its very beginnings until after its collapse, with interludes dedicated to republican virtue, imperial decadence, and barbaric collapse itself. *The Savage State* and *Desolation* are respectively the first and last paintings in the series, united in an unexpected symmetry of peacefulness. The first depicts a Bronze Age settlement, a pastoral, sylvan, bucolic scene in which simple farmers worship at a stone monolith. *Desolation* shows the same landscape, dominated by the same Gibraltar-like mountain, but now dotted with the ruins of once-imperial grandeur, marble monuments and temples overgrown with vines and weeds. For those who faced Attila's armies, it would have been a familiar scene, as Cole imagined that it one day could also be familiar to Americans. "Violence and time have crumbled the works of man, and art is again resolving into elemental nature," writes Cole. "The gorgeous pageant has passed—the roar of battle has ceased—the multitude has sunk in the dust—the empire is extinct." And quiet, we might add.

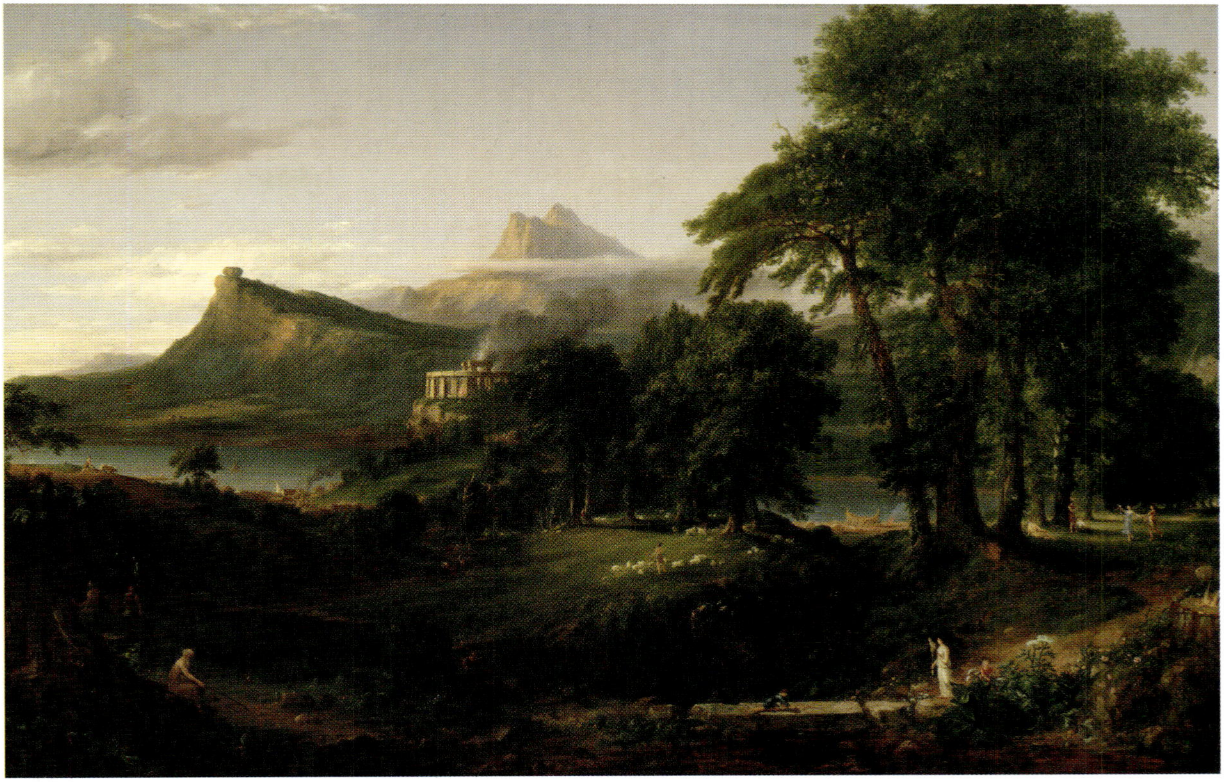

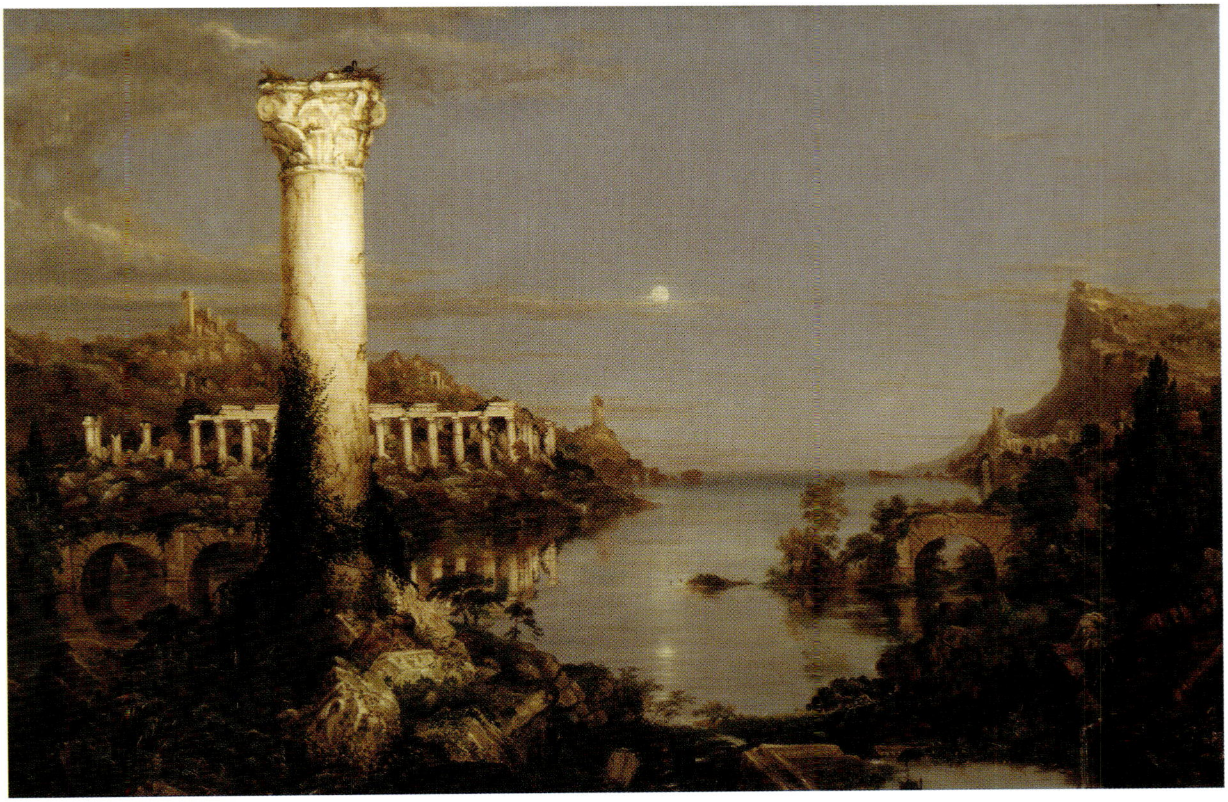

THE LION AND THE LAMB

Along the southern shore of Lake Garda, the long, crooked finger of that body of water probing into the edge of the Italian Alps, the Turkic chieftain and warlord Attila the Hun pitched a camp and made preparations for the coming invasion of Rome in 451. Attila's motley assortment of Huns and Bulgars, Alans and Ostrogoths, rampaged across northern Italy, sacking the countryside around Venetia and Pannonia, while razing the ancient city of Aquila. True to his nomadic origins, Attila was a figure most of all attached to the rigors of martial travel, a creature of the camp and of the mounted horse, bedecked in marmot fur and goat skin, the pointed leather bashlyk the closest the mighty Hun had to a crown. Attila's rough, sunburnt face, framed by his long black handlebar mustache, made him an inescapably foreign figure to these Italians who'd been part of civilized Rome for nearly six centuries by the time the conqueror had pitched his yurt amid the ruins of once-imperial grandeur. Those who awaited the arrival of his hordes told certain legends about Attila, that he brandished the royal sword of the Scythian warriors of the Asian Steppe, or that he'd been blessed by Mars, god of war. Edward Gibbon in his essential eighteenth-century history *The Decline and Fall of the Roman Empire* described Attila as "glorious in his life, invincible in death, the father of his people, the scourge of his enemies, and the terror of the world," while the warlord called himself *flagellum Dei*—the "Scourge of God."

A reputation for barbarism was born not just from Roman xenophobia; Callincus, writing in *Life of Saint Hypatius*, describes how during Attila's excursions into Asia Minor during an (unsuccessful) attempt to conquer Constantinople, there were nonetheless "so many murders and blood-lettings that the dead could not be numbered. Ay, for they took captive the churches and monasteries and slew monks and maidens in great numbers." Now, espying southward down the long boot of the peninsula, Attila dreamed of sacking the Eternal City itself, of lodging his marauders within the marble coolness of the Pantheon, stabling his horses upon Capitoline Hill and pitching his tent on the grounds of St. Paul's. Once the greatest city on earth, the very model of Heaven in the imagination of Augustine, Rome would be reduced to mere vassal. That thousands of people would be murdered, women raped, children orphaned, was of little accounting; that blood would flow through those immaculately constructed stone streets, pooling in the gutters that marked the ingenious series of pipe works through Rome, was irrelevant to Attila. This was a man who, unlike the emperors of Rome, had no interest in *creating* or *building*, also unlike even the other tribal chieftains, who couldn't help but imagine more grandiose purposes to their military campaigns than mere looting. By his nature, Attila was drawn to violence, murder and mutilation, rape and plunder. "For what fortress, what city, in the wide extent of the Roman empire, can hope to exist, secure and impregnable, if it is our pleasure that it should be erased from the earth?" asked Attila. And then, poised to invade, he didn't.

By all contemporary accounts, Attila was one whom modern readers would describe as a sociopath. A successful sociopath, for had he chosen to

OPPOSITE French Neo-Classicist Louis-Jean-François Lagrenée's 1770 *Mars & Venus, Allegory of Peace* depicts the fierce Roman god of war overcome with the beauty of the sleeping goddess of love. Wrath, strife, rage, anger, and war overcome by the peacefulness of slumbering love, a pair of doves (a Jewish and Christian symbol of peace) on the floor alongside. Original at the J. Paul Getty Museum in Los Angeles.

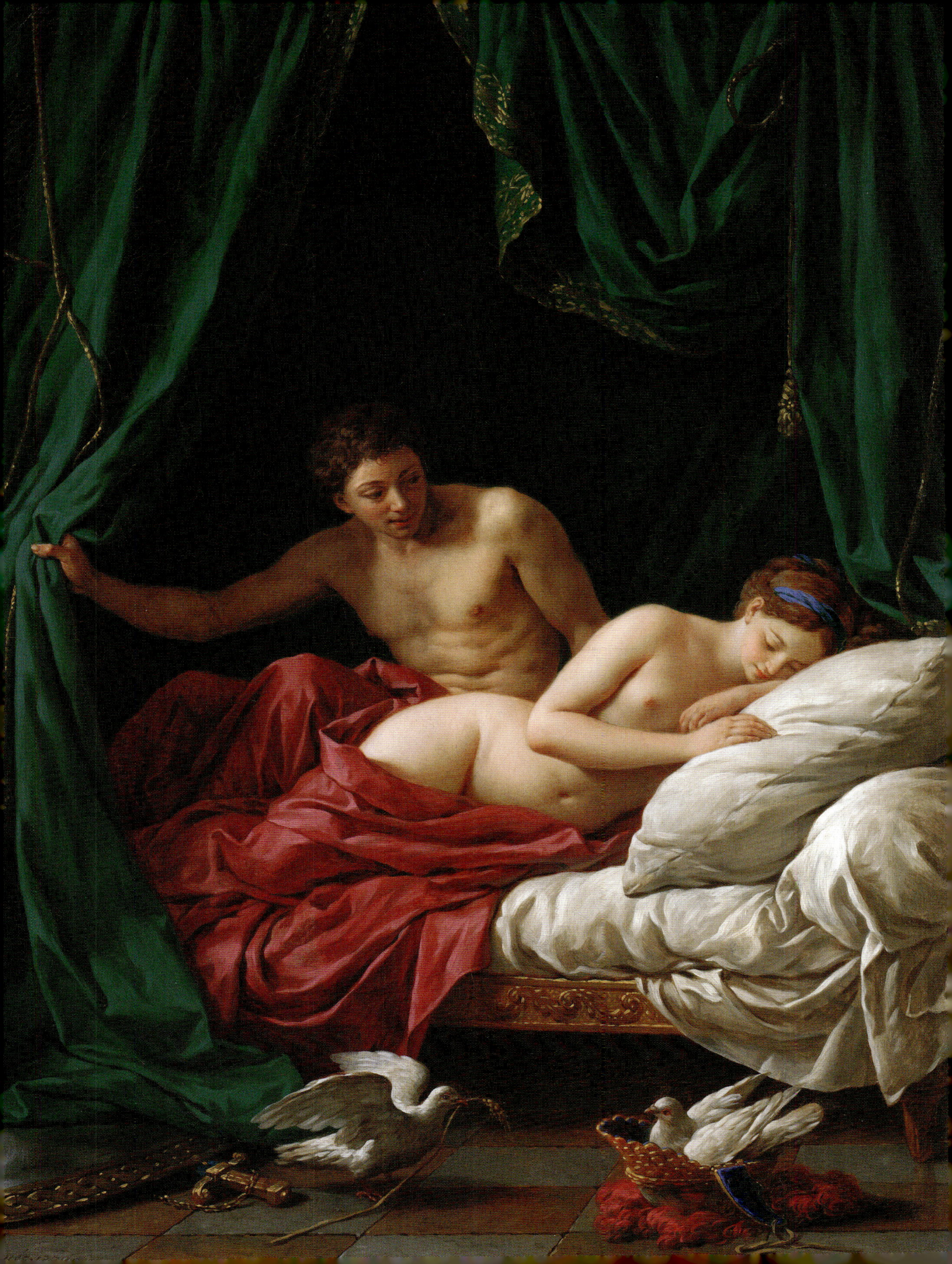

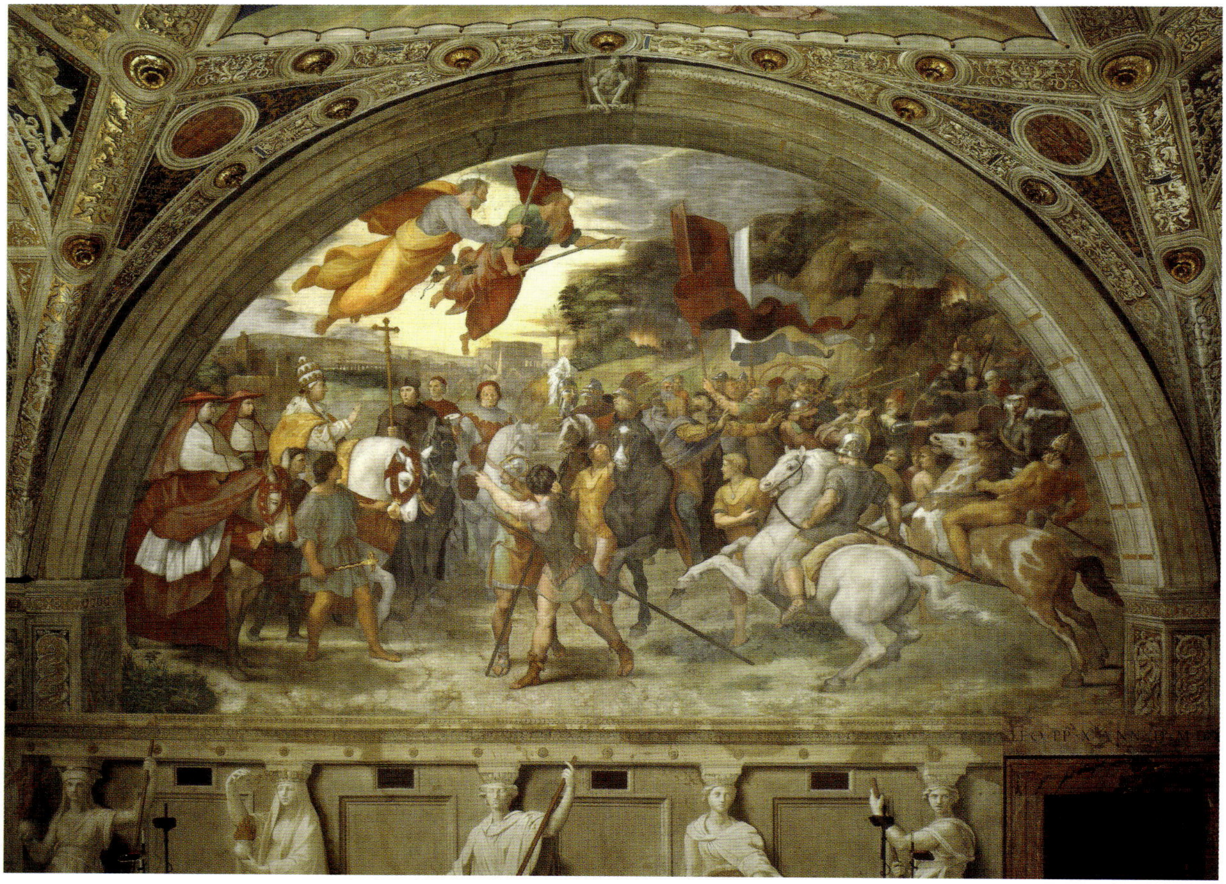

TOP Raphael's 1513 fresco *The Meeting of Leo the Great and Attila*, original at the Apostolic Palace in Vatican City.

OPPOSITE French painter Louis Janmot's idiosyncratic 1854 *Divine Generation (Formation of the Soul)* represents an idiomatic and visually symbolic expression of the artist's metaphysical speculations. Imagining the creation of a human soul within the peaceful perfection of paradise, Janmot shows that individual spirit nurtured by a mystical Trinity, composed of God the Father, Christ the Son, and a feminine Holy Spirit (for the mystical being of wisdom Sophia is a woman, as is the Jewish indwelling presence of the Lord called the Shechinah).

sack Rome, there is little doubt that that once-mighty city—at one point the largest city on earth—would simply fall into his calloused and rough hands like an overripe fruit. Yet he would turn back after meeting with an envoy of three men dispatched by the emperor of Rome, one of whom was Pope Leo I, the first pontiff after whose name the adjective phrase "the Great" would be applied. The opposite in every way from Attila, Leo was the effete, aristocratic son of Tuscan nobility, a theologian prized for the acumen of his nimble mind, able to parse exegesis with subtle dexterity. Joined by two high-ranking civilian officers who were dispatched alongside the pope by Emperor Valentinian III, Leo would meet with Attila somewhere along the Garda coast. Picture the pope, in his white stole affixed with gold and bejeweled inlaid scenes from the gospels, the bishop's miter peaked high above his head, conversing with the barbarian in his fur-lined cap and leather riding boots. Or maybe, rather, it was as imagined by Raphael in a sixteenth-century fresco at the Apostolic Palace in the Vatican, both men mounted on their steeds, Leo in the papal tiara offering a pose of benediction while Attila reaches out toward the pontiff, a feathered helmet upon his head. On one side there are monks and priests, clerics brandishing golden crucifixes; on the other there are attendants of the Hun, barbarians with their spears and battle-axes. What was said between the pope and the vandal is unknown. As far as we can gather, there was no epiphany, no

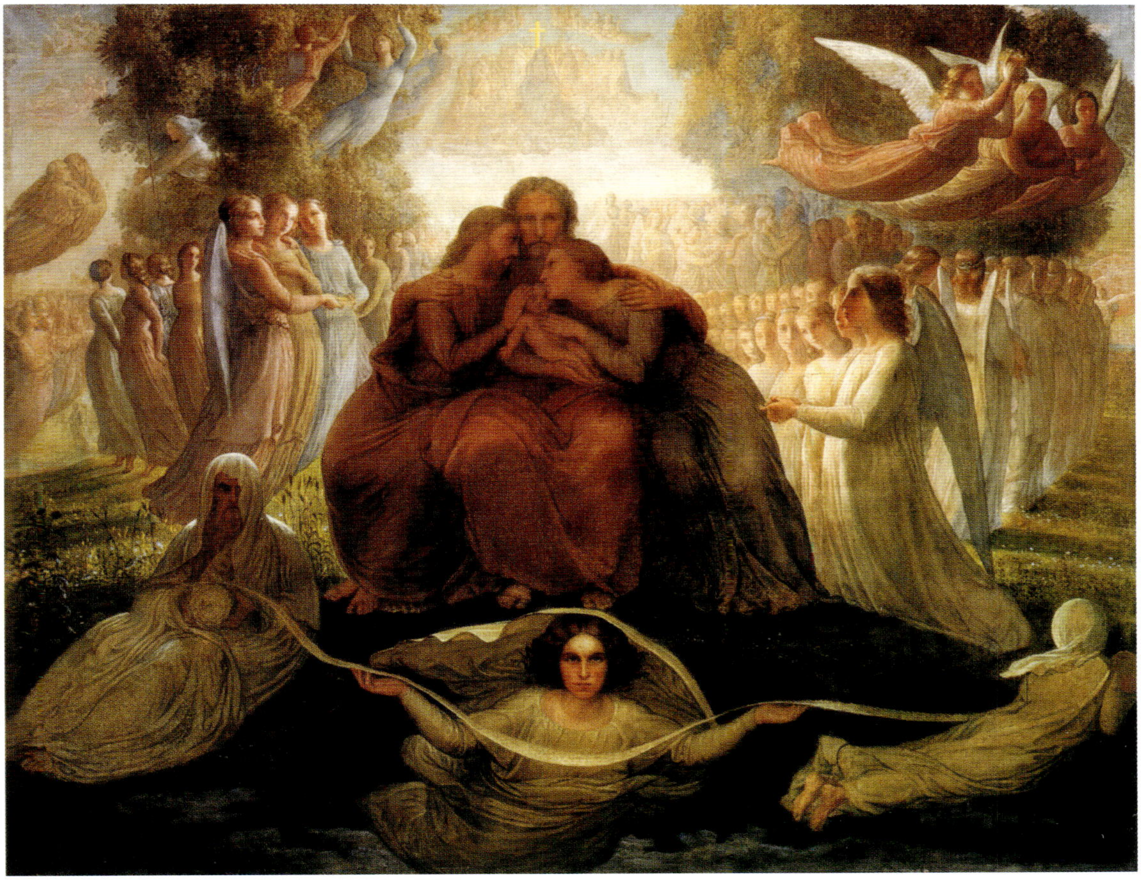

conversion. Yet at some point, in some way, Pope Leo I convinced Attila the Hun not to invade Rome, and so the city would be spared.

"Peace" is a concept of the diseased world, because there would be no need to posit such an idealized state were it not for the obvious fallenness of our cruel and corrupted, barbarous and brutal creation. In paradise, nobody has ever heard of such a thing called "peace"—what would there be to compare it to? As it is, we do not live in paradise, so peace becomes (like God) a standard by which we measure the deficiencies of our own existence. "The wolf also shall dwell with the lamb, and the leopard shall lie down with the kid," says the prophet at Isaiah 11:6, "and the calf and the young lion and the fatling together." This is a vision of millennium, of perfection, when all discord and disunion, violence and vengeance have been expelled, where all contraries have been reconciled in a universal harmony. The mystic core of Scripture is the exultation of this imagined state, where all are in peace with one another so that all are in peace with the Lord. In his epistle to the Philippians, the Apostle Paul describes such a condition as being the peace which "passeth all understanding." More than just the cessation of hostility or the fair and judicious interaction between governments and people, such peace is something else entirely, something as inscrutable and ineffable as God, or Truth, or Love. Yet of course peace also describes a reality in the world of the here-and-now; it can absolutely mean the cessation of

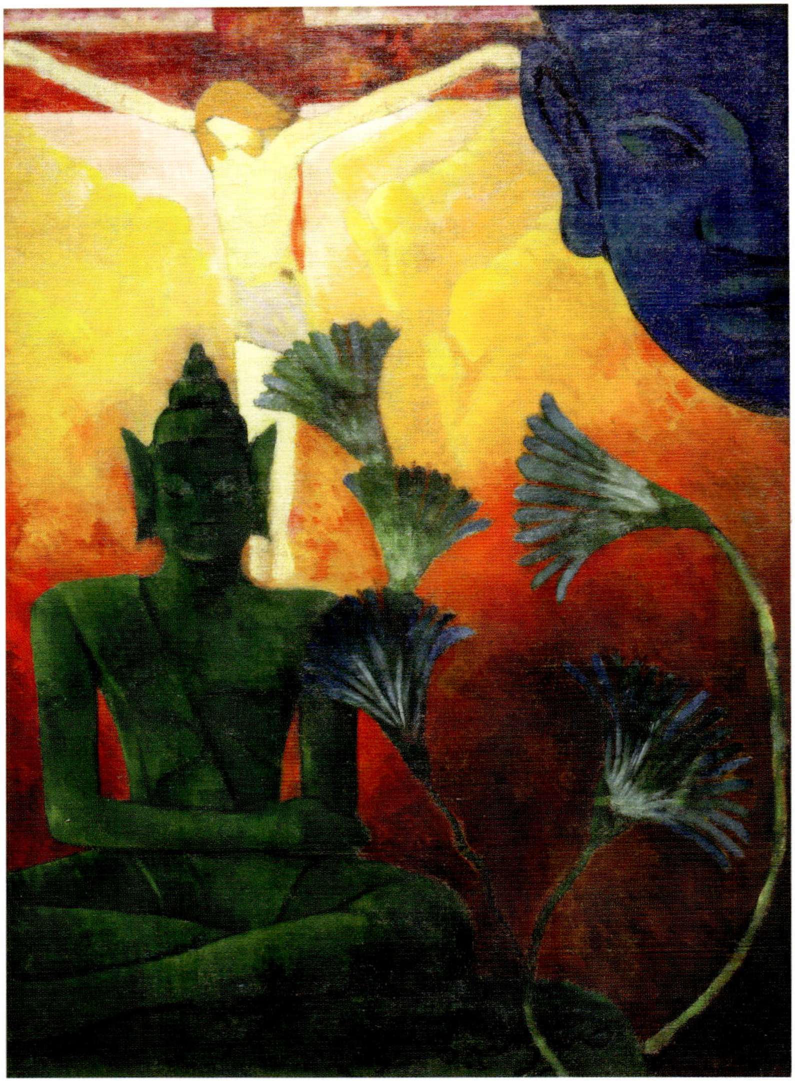

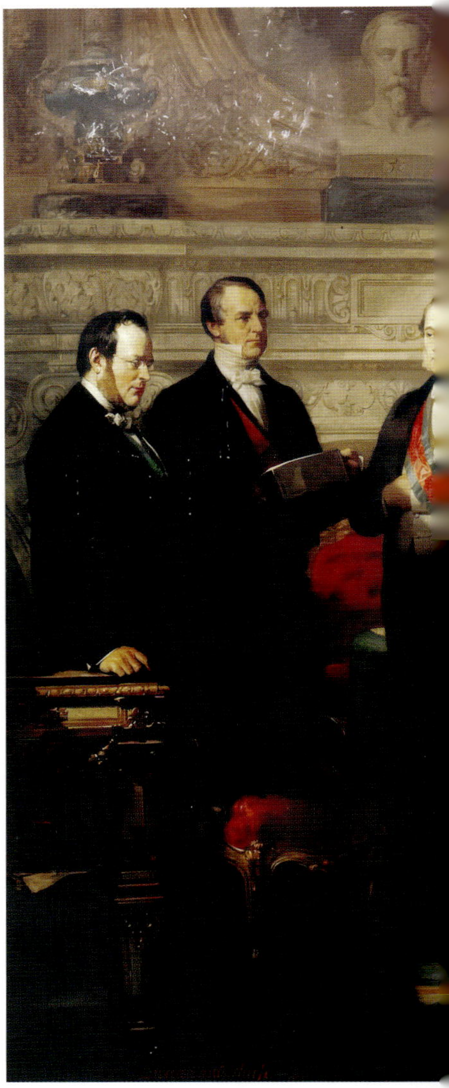

hostilities or the fair and judicious interaction between governments and people. The nature of God's Peace may be spoken of in the devotional poetry of Scripture, but the no less blessed peace of our actual world is conveyed in negotiations, diplomacy, legislation, treaties. Then there is the peace which is internal, the patience the cardinal virtue references, the still mind of the soul at ease and capable of accepting that which is larger than ourselves. All such examples of peace are as shards form the divine Godhead, intimations of that greater and larger Peace in the hereafter, the eternal Beyond. An armistice, treaty, or cease-fire may not be Heaven, but it's a reflection of it. "War is politics by other means," argued the infamous Prussian military strategist Carl von Clausewitz in *On War*. Well then, peace is merely paradise by other means.

"Five enemies of peace inhabit with us," enumerates the early Renaissance poet and humanist Petrarch in his fourteenth-century *The Solitary Life*, "avarice, ambition, envy, anger, and pride; if these were to be banished, we should

LEFT French painter Paul Ranson's 1880 composition *Christ and the Buddha* shows Siddhartha Gautama, the historical Buddha, and Jesus Christ at respectively the moment wherein the former reached the state of Enlightenment known as nirvana and the latter died upon the cross. Very different moments, but sacred moments nonetheless, interpreted by the faithful as portals to peace. Original at the Kunstmuseum in the Hague.

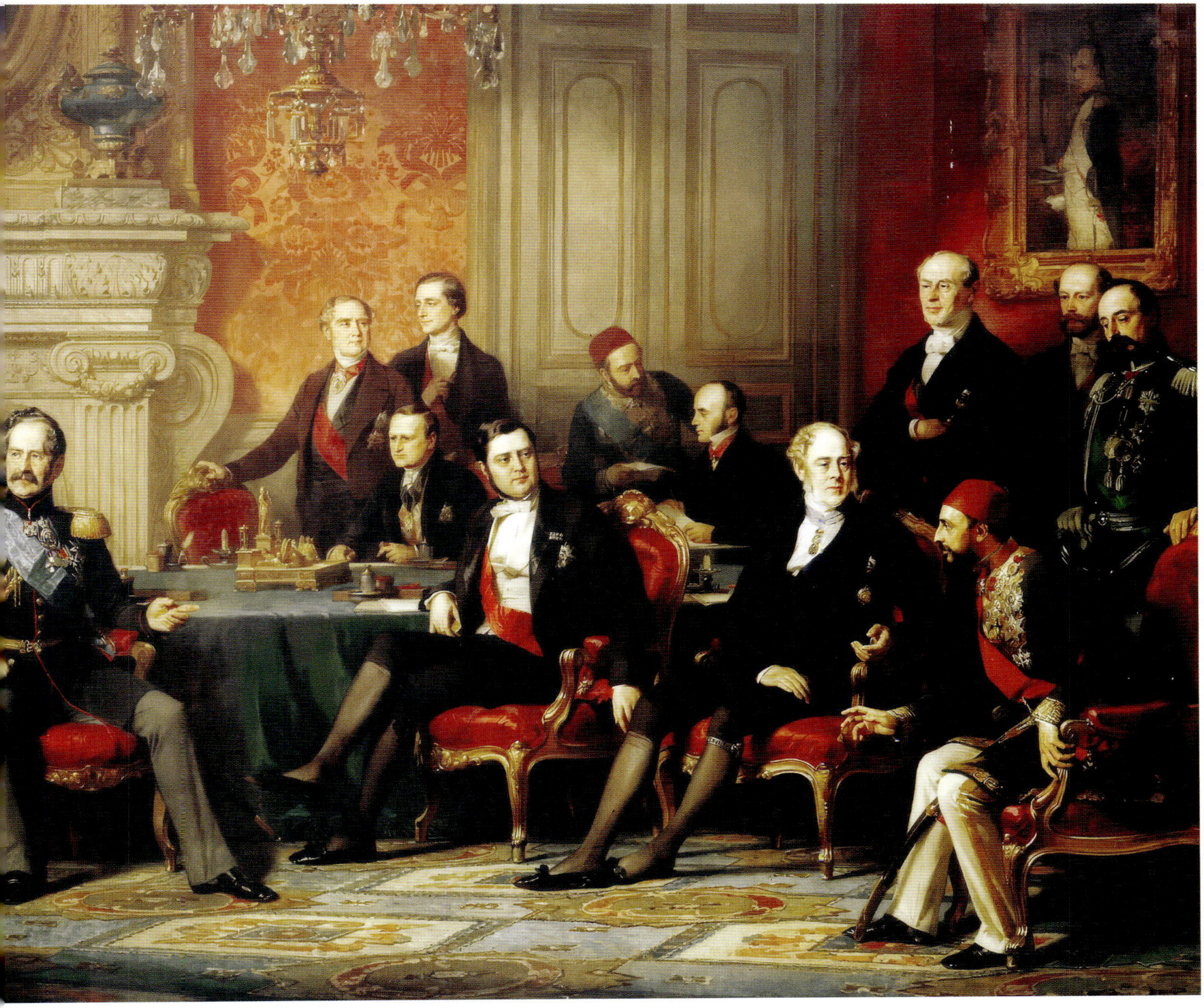

ABOVE Clearly none of these men in Édouard Louis Dubufe's 1856 painting *The Congress of Paris* was a Buddha or a Christ, yet the negotiations of that treaty, signed in the same year that this composition was rendered, brought to a close the chaos and violence of the Crimean War. Original at the Musée d'Orsay.

infallibly enjoy perpetual peace." Telling, that this is a list of the deadly sins with only those appetites of the body—gluttony, sloth, and lust—those lesser transgressions—subtracted. Petrarch implies that the danger of those sins is self-aggrandizement, the calculations of avarice, the puffed-up pomposity of pride, the green-eyed hunger of envy. All of them lead to the degradations of violence, to that infernal kingdom at the opposite end of the cosmos from true peace. What's concluded is that these are sins insomuch that they are sins not against God, or even our fellow humans, but that they violate the sanctity of equanimity, of peace. For this reason, the dreams of faith—which can include, indeed necessitate, justice and judgment—are ultimately in genuflection toward that paradise where the lamb and the lion are partners. Every major religion in history yearns for that peace, the gentle embrace of a reality where all the rough edges have been smoothed, all the crooked lines straightened, all the rips have been mended and the tears have been dried. The Jewish king David sings in Psalm

29:11 that "the LORD will bless his people with peace"; the Christian messiah Jesus Christ says that the peacemakers are the "children of God" in Matthew 5:9; the Prophet Muhammad declares that the "inhabitants of Paradise are busy rejoicing . . . Peace!—such is the greeting, from a Lord All-compassionate." Five centuries before Christ, the historical Buddha—Prince Siddhartha of Gautama—who'd achieved that condition of enlightenment known as nirvana, preached in the *Dhammapada* that "Better than a thousand hollow words / Is one word that brings peace. / Better than a thousand hollow verses / Is one verse that brings peace. / Better than a hundred hollow lines / Is one line of the law, bringing peace."

Otherworldly though the spiritually sanctified dream of millennial peace may be, it's important to note that the priests and prophets of these religious traditions were not without pragmatism. To claim that the peacemakers are the "children of God," as Christ does, is to admit that there are human beings of flesh and blood, fallible and imperfect, who are able to forge a peace. The Buddha's lesson speaks of words—of *laws*—that can reconcile adversaries, that can cease hostilities, that can establish (at least for a time) peace. Only the most dour of defeatists and maudlin of mystics would assume that peace is only a question of poetry or theology, because in the day-to-day existence of women and men it's primarily an issue of politics. Who can live and work freely, who can be guaranteed safety and security, who can share in the relative bounty of a society—all of these are issues of politics more than anything. International agreements on proper conduct during war—not pacifism, but different from an Attila's brutality as well—were conceived of by political philosophers and strategists like the Dutch diplomat Hugo Grotius during the seventeenth century, or the German philosopher Johann Gottfried Leibniz, who imagined a liberal order born out of a community of nations. Both drew inspiration from the Renaissance scholar Desiderius Erasmus, who claimed in his 1508 *Adagia* that the "most disadvantageous peace is better than the most just war," a deeply alien sentiment both then and now, born in part from his own Christian faith, but bolstered even more by his classical humanism.

Yet, if brutality is the biological state of nature (an enormous assumption), then the earliest political agitation to alter that status quo came not just from secular philosophers, but also from theological sources. Scripture may imply that lasting peace is an issue of Heaven, but early modern dissenting non-conformists, such as George Fox and William Penn of the Society of Friends (much more widely known as the Quakers) conceived of peace as not just for Heaven but for earth as well—as a policy statement more than an impossible dream. The Quakers were joined in their nonviolence by Anabaptist groups such as the Amish and Mennonites, or the proto-Protestant denomination of the Moravians. Fox, historically identified as the founder of the Quakers, himself a former military man, recounts in his 1694 autobiography how he wrote a missive to Lord Protector Oliver Cromwell—both a pious and violent leader—of how "I was sent of God to stand a witness against all violence, and against the works of darkness; and to turn people from darkness to light; and to bring them from the causes of war and fighting, to the peaceable gospel." For Fox and those in his stead, peace wasn't an intellectual issue but a practical one. Known for their mystical and allegorical, antinomian and individualist interpretations of Scripture, the Quakers

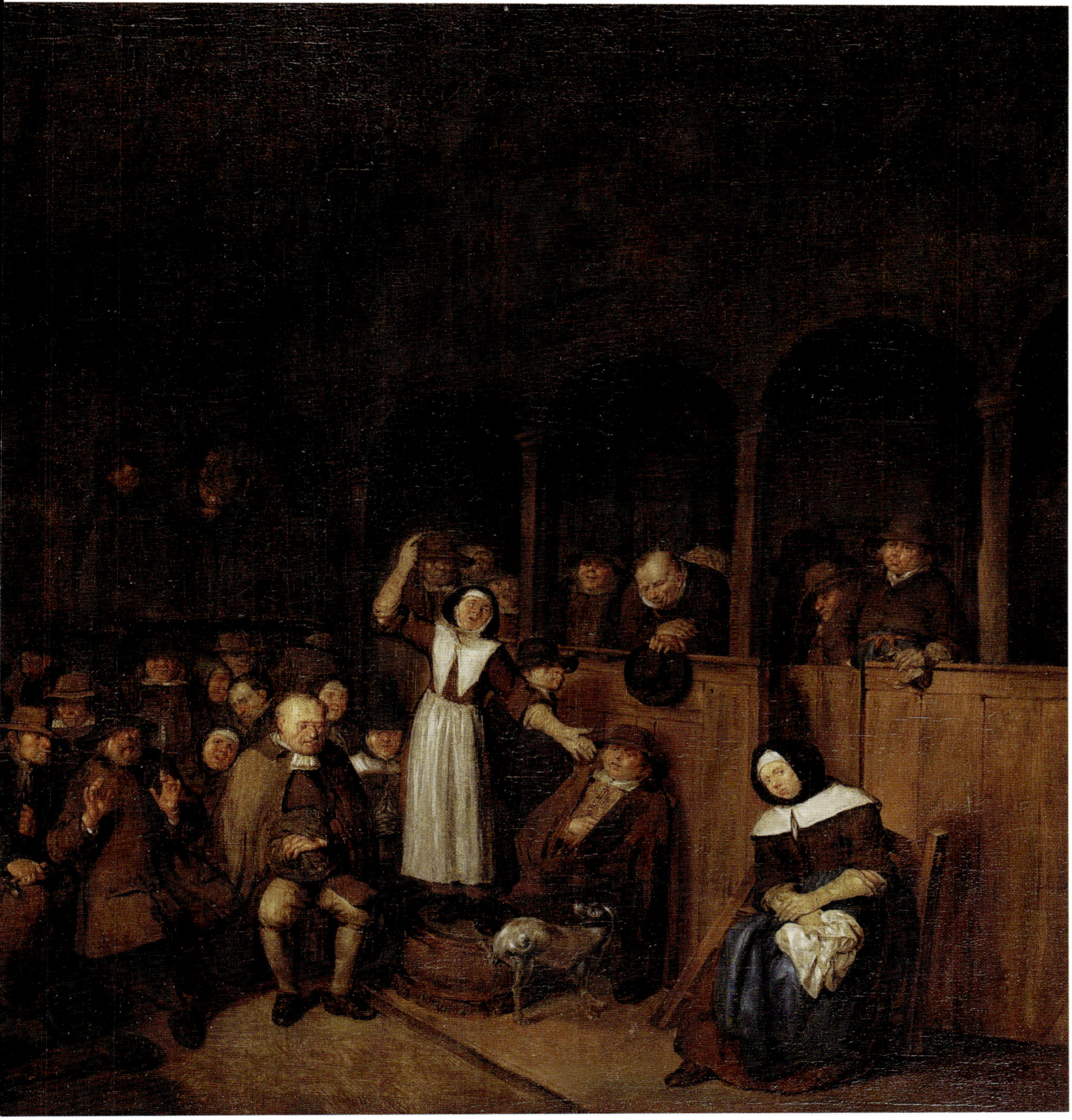

ABOVE Dutch painter Egbert van Heemskerck's *A Quaker Meeting* depicts the idiosyncratic worship services of the Society of Friends, where there was no clergy, ritual, or liturgy, but rather a gathering of the faithful sitting in silence until the "Inner Light" of God motivated some to preach, often new prophecies, often from women. The composition was rendered sometime in the last decades of the seventeenth century and is in a private collection.

were admirably literalist when it came to the most important aspect of Christ's preaching—His pacifism.

"The first clue, lesson number one from human history on the subject of nonviolence, is that there is no word for it," notes Mark Kurlansky in *Nonviolence: The History of a Dangerous Idea.* Kurlansky observes that though every major religion extols the virtues of peace and the lives of those saints who practice nonviolence, "there is no word to express the idea of nonviolence except that it is not another idea, it is not violence." Underscoring the eerie separateness of nonviolence, how anathema it seems to a world which values strength and power, can serve to obscure just how surprisingly frequent the examples of pacifism have been. The Quakers, marginal though they may have seemed, exerted a profound influence on society and politics, at one point administering the largest private land-holding on earth in the form of the colony of Pennsylvania. Leo Tolstoy marshalled all of the wealth and prestige he had as a Russian count in a manner that influenced both Mahatma Gandhi and Martin Luther King Jr., the former having agitated to establish India's independence from the British Empire and the latter disestablishment of the racist Jim Crow laws which oppressed Black Americans. Bertrand Russell, as arid and cold an analytical philosopher as ever produced by the United Kingdom, also founded the movement for nuclear disarmament, while Rabbi Abraham Joshua Heschel advocated for both Black Americans in the United States and the peaceful coexistence of Israelis and Palestinians. At the core of pacifistic thinking is a staunch adherence to martyrdom, the concept that it is better to be a potential victim of violence than a victimizer. It is illogical, irrational, counterintuitive, and wholly beautiful. That such a doctrine is capable, through example and love, of changing the world—as rare as such moments may be—is worth more in proving God's existence than any ontological argument or anthropic principle.

The theologian Dietrich Bonhoeffer, murdered by the Nazis after he risked

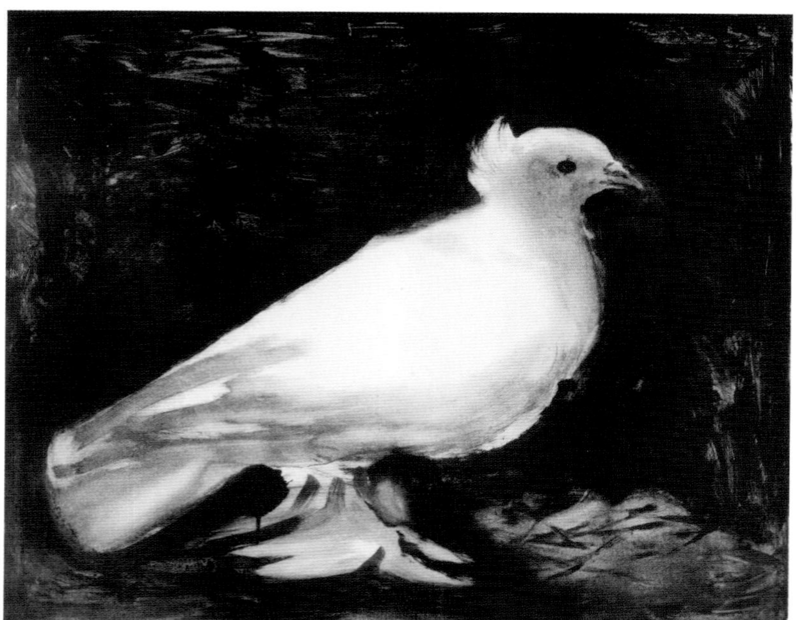

LEFT "And the dove came in to him in the evening; and, lo, in her mouth was an olive leaf pluckt off," reads Genesis 8:6–11, "so Noah knew that the waters were abated from off the earth." Because of her discovery of dry land after the flood, of stability after chaos, the dove has long been a symbol of peace. Picasso imagines the dove in this 1949 painting, made four years after the world's most destructive war. The dove appears as a field of light emerging from the inchoate shadows of darkness. Original at the Tate Modern in London.

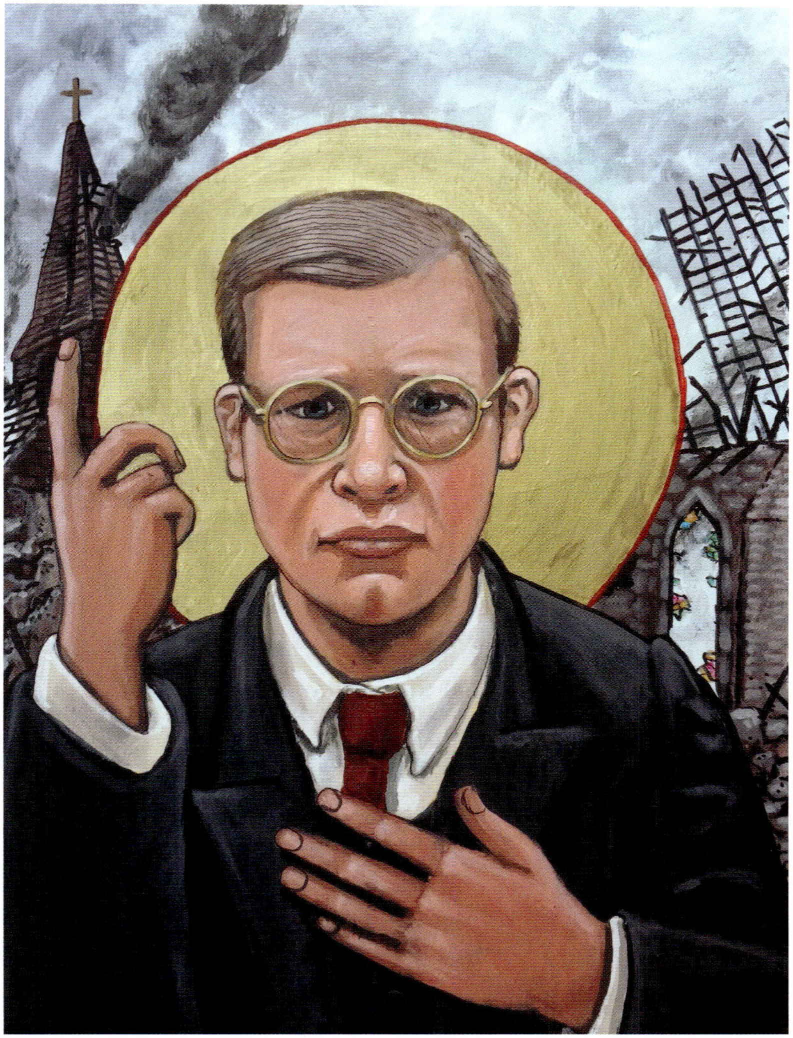

TOP Contemporary iconologist Kelly Latimore's icon of Bonhoeffer surrounded by the devastation of World War II. "The world is overcome not through destruction, but through reconciliation," wrote the theologian. "Not ideals, nor programs, nor conscience, nor duty, nor responsibility, but only God's perfect love can encounter reality and overcome it."

his own soul in the plot to kill Adolf Hitler, wrote in *The Cost of Discipleship* that the "precept of non-violence applies equally to private life and official duty," though the preacher's own decision to help take another life only seems like a paradox in retrospect (albeit a luminous one). Bonhoeffer was a graduate of Union Theological Seminary in New York, where the German was introduced to the liberatory philosophy of the Black church, how when confronted with the indignity and horror of the Prince of this World who maintains oppression and torture, there is a power in peace. After Union, Bonhoeffer would attend Buchenwald, Regensburg, and then Flossenburg, all brutal concentration camps maintained by the Nazis, the final of which would be the site of the minister's martyrdom. He had been a preacher in the Confessing Church, the underground network of Protestant ministers who'd resisted Hitler's obscenity of the so-called Aryan Church. As part of that work, Bonhoeffer—a pacifist—had concluded that even if his mortal soul should be endangered by working to kill a child of God, such a sin could be personally justified, if not theologically,

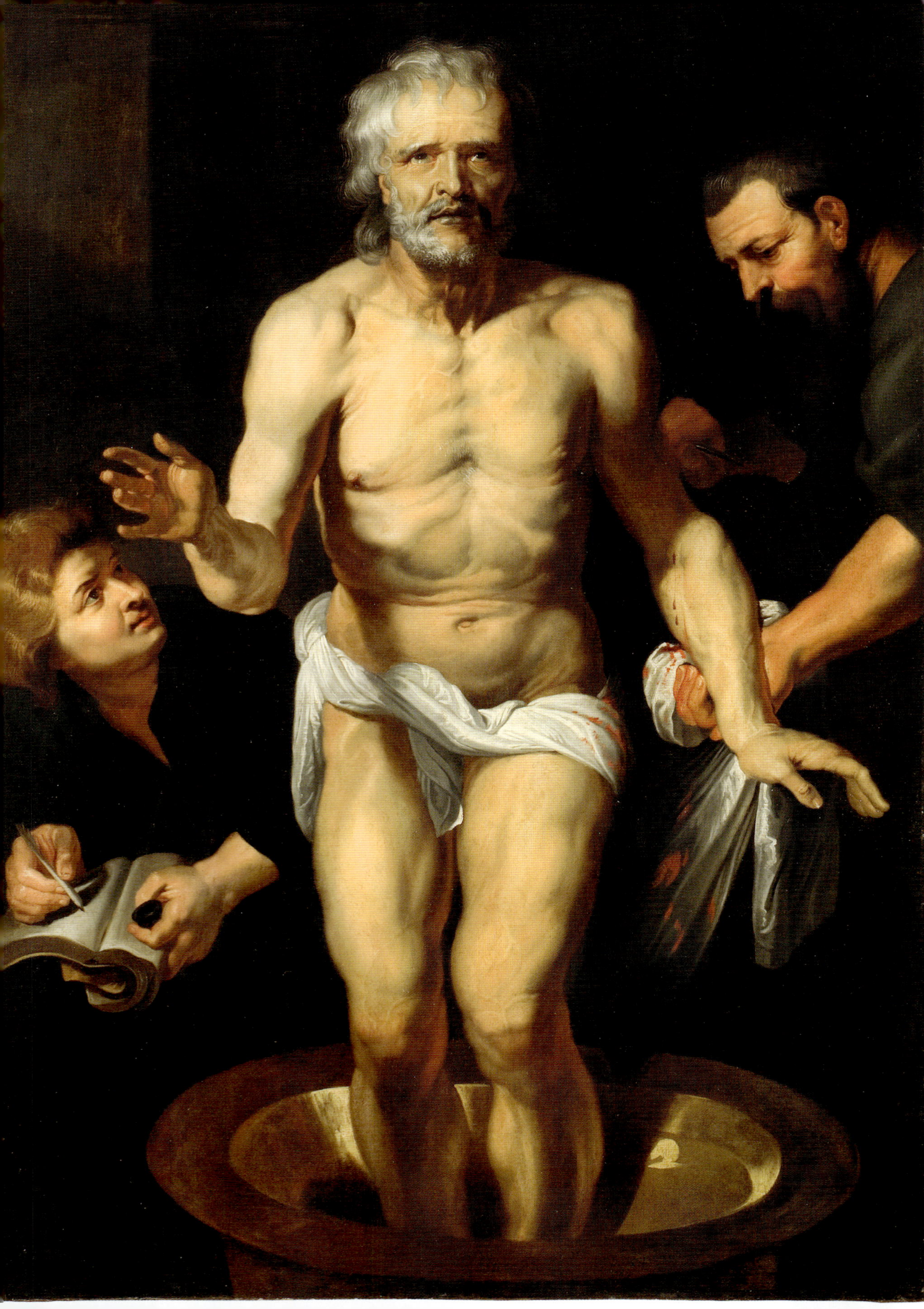

since that child of God happened to be Hitler. And so, after the failure of that assassination attempt codenamed Project Valkyrie, Bonhoeffer found himself upon the scaffold of Flossenburg in April of 1945, ironically the same month that Hitler would die by his own hand, only a few months before the conclusion of this apocalyptic war in Europe. According to a Royal Air Force captain who was imprisoned at Flossenburg the minister calmly preached a sermon as the noose was placed around his neck, Bonhoeffer's last words being "This is for me the end, the beginning of life." Here, in the null point of meaning, the vacuum and abyss which were the Nazi concentration camps, Bonhoeffer created life. This was his agency; independent of the supreme power of his oppressors, he was able to transform his own death. There were no shaking hands, no quivering, no begging, for the preacher existed in a state of utmost peace, the inner still which is the privilege of saints and contemplatives, but which the philosophers tell us is the birthright of every human who is willing to achieve it. Inner peace may seem to be a cheapened version of the actual thing, unless it's all that you have—then it's everything. More than that—*more than everything*—inner peace is a variety of omnipotence at the individual level, a means of enduring, suffering, and exulting despite all of those who have power over you. Bonhoeffer had no ability to overthrow his captors, to slaughter them and liberate the rest of his fellow prisoners, but he could die on his own terms, deny them their sadistic pleasure at his death.

Religion is many things—faith and belief, ritual and custom, even language and food—but it's also spiritual practice, a means of focusing the mind and spirit for precisely those moments, of being able to live a life in the midst of death. There are trains of thought within worldviews commonly thought of as "religious"—elements of Judaism, Christianity, Islam, Buddhism, and so on—which can inculcate a serenity in the face of death, and there are secular philosophies—stoicism, existentialism—which are intended to achieve the same. "It was a great deed to conquer Carthage," quipped the stoic Seneca the Younger, "but a greater deed to conquer death." Like Bonhoeffer, Seneca was executed by a tyrant, in this case the Emperor Nero, in whose stead he'd once disgracefully worked. Yet in learning how to die, in suffering his own execution (which involved poisoning, sitting in a toxic bath, and being stabbed), Seneca exhibited a peacefulness that was capable of harrowing hell. "I am endeavoring to live every day as if it were a complete life," writes Seneca, and therein lay a secret in the peacefulness of cheerfully facing death—every moment is as if a potential doorway to heaven, a portal to paradise, and all of us possess the keys (even if most of us have misplaced them). The Buddha, preaching his own final sermon on his deathbed, explained where these keys can be discovered, teaching that "When the self and external world become one, eternal serenity is enjoyed . . . Become one with no barrier between the self and the outside world." Such inner peace is not Heaven, but it is the experience of Heaven felt by the saints and Bodhisattvas while we await the arrival of millennium.

An overview of current events should demonstrate that ours is still not the millennium, that any lasting peace eludes us, which is perhaps why the narrative-heavy mode of fiction has never been as amenable to stories of peace as has the incantatory unspooling of lyric poetry. "A voice from the dark called out, / 'The poets must give us / imagination of peace, to oust the

OPPOSITE Peter Paul Rubens's *The Death of Seneca* shows the philosopher in mid-argument as well as mid-execution. Painting from 1612, with the original at the Prado in Madrid.

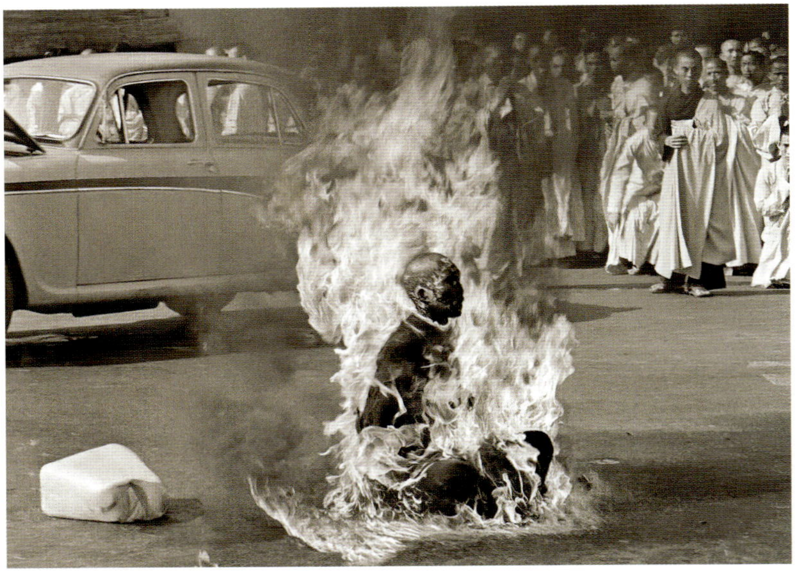

intense, familiar / imagination of disaster,'" writes that great mystic poet Denise Levertov in *Breathing the Water.* This is what poetry can do—imagine the possibilities of another world, of peace, while also engendering within the soul the same disposition that led Bonhoeffer and the Buddha to preach upon the scaffold and from the deathbed. Levertov writes of this "grammar of justice, / syntax of mutual aid," claiming that until the millennium we must subsist by "dimly sensing a rhythm . . . until we begin to utter its metaphors, / learning them as we speak." The grammar of justice can be parsed in the verse of Muriel Ruckeyser, who despite mourning in *The Speed of Darkness* how she has "lived in the first century of world wars," with all of the implications of how perhaps there shall be a third (and then maybe no more), wrote that "As the lights darkened, as the lights of night brightened, / We would try to imagine them, try to find each other, / To construct peace, to make love, to reconcile / Waking with sleeping, ourselves with each other, / Ourselves with ourselves." Reconciliation with others, and the self, a description of that peace beyond peace. This is the dream of the Israeli poet Yehuda Amichai, who writes, "I, may I rest in peace—I, who am still living, say, / May I have peace in the rest of my life. / I want peace right now while I'm still alive . . . I don't want to fulfill my parents' prophecy that life is war. / I want peace with all my body and all my soul. / Rest me in peace." This is the dream of the Palestinian poet Mahmoud Darwish, who writes that "The prophets over there are sharing / the history of the holy . . . ascending to heaven / and returning less discouraged and melancholy, because love / and peace are holy."

ABOVE Among the most infamous photographs of the twentieth century, Malcolm Browne's 1963 World Press Award–winning picture of Buddhist monk Thich Quang Duc in Saigon protesting by self-immolation the persecution of Buddhists in South Vietnam is simultaneously an image of profound violence and of deep serenity. A witness remembered that "as he burned he never moved a muscle, never uttered a sound, his outward composure in sharp contrast to the wailing people around him." "No news picture in history has generated so much emotion around the world as that one," said President John F. Kennedy, only a few months before his own assassination.

OPPOSITE American artist Diane Burko's 2021 painting *Unprecedented*, a work intended to express the emotional register of apocalyptic climate change. From the dreary red and black cracked planetoid shapes on the left to the peaceful blues and whites of what evokes a sunny day on the right, the piece holds in stasis the panic and peace of death, the terror and calm of survival.

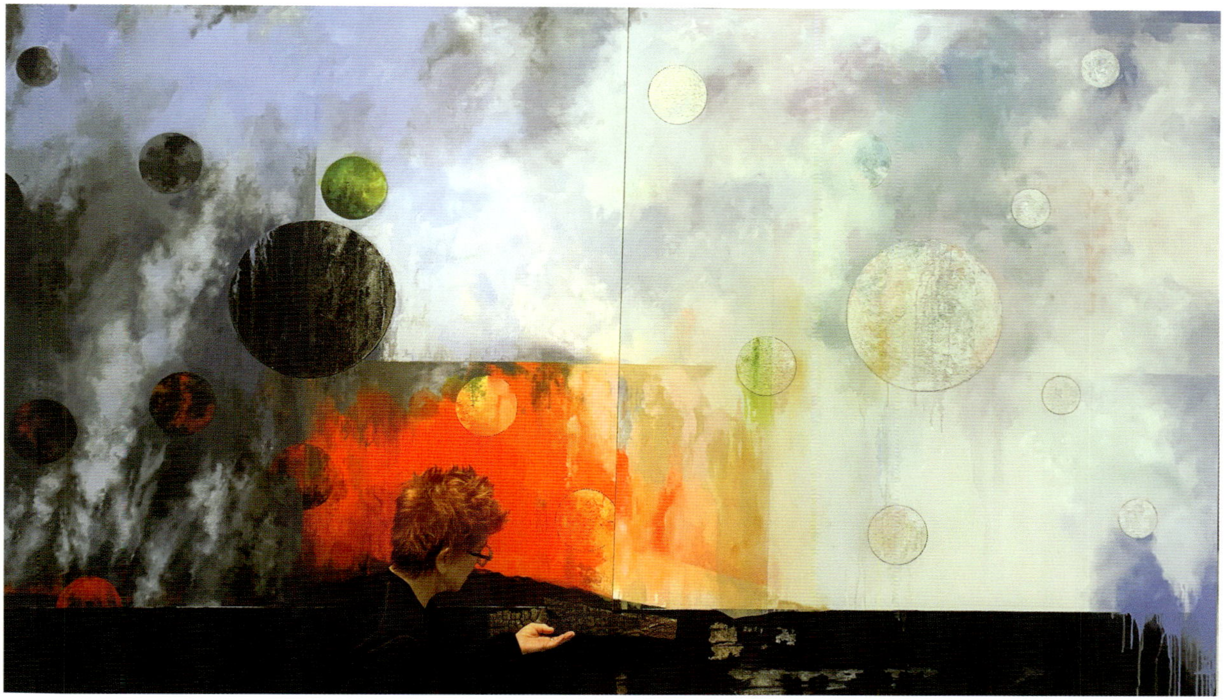

INTERLUDE—DAVID BUCKEL

On an early spring morning in 2018, when the stars were still out and Manhattan glowed in all of its wasteful wattage across the East River, a sixty-year-old retired lawyer named David Buckel made his way past the Grand Army Plaza and the Brooklyn Museum down to Prospect Park. In those hours before the dawn, Buckel dug a shallow circle into the black dirt, which investigators believed he made to prevent the spread of the fire he was about to set, having understood that our collective future would have enough burning. The former attorney paused to send an email to *the New York Times* which read, "Most humans on the planet now breathe air made unhealthy by fossil fuels, and many die early deaths as a result—my early death by fossil fuel reflects what we are doing to ourselves." He doused himself in gasoline and lit a match. Buckel was pronounced dead by 6:30 a.m.

As a civil rights attorney, Buckel's life was one of unqualified success—an early supporter of Lambda Legal, he'd fought doggedly for LGBTQ+ rights not just in New York, but in seemingly inhospitable places from Nebraska to Iowa. As a human being, his life was defined by companionship and love—raising a daughter with his husband of thirty-four years alongside the girl's biological mother and her wife. And as a community member, his life was committed to stewardship and responsibility—rather than using wasteful fossil fuels, he walked several miles every day to the Brooklyn Botanic Garden, where in retirement he organized the center's composting program. By all accounts Buckel's life was

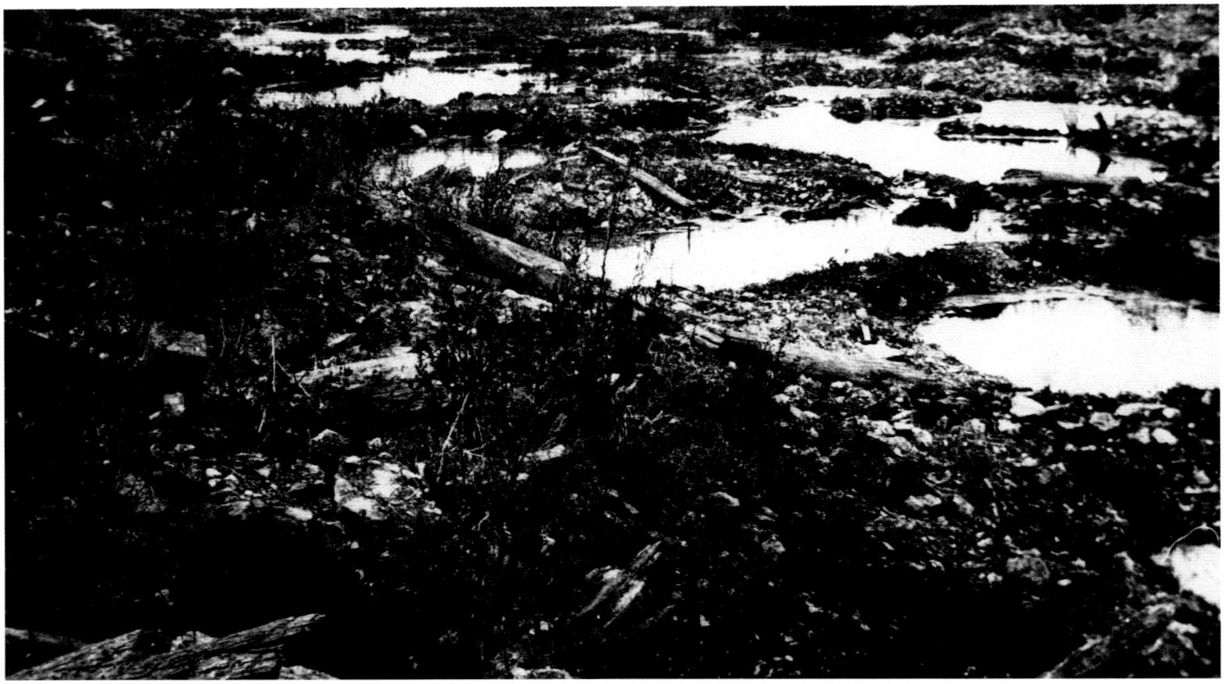

centered around justice, both personal and ecological, which should go to some length in explaining his otherwise unthinkable decision to kill himself on that April 14, though the philosopher Costica Bradatan reminds us in *Dying for Ideas: The Dangerous Lives of the Philosophers* that wherever "self-immolators are going they are not asking anyone with them: their deaths are fierce, but remain exclusively their own."

So, we return to our phones, skimming accounts of collapsing ice shelves and flooding riverbanks, reading articles about how humanity may have less than a few decades left, pushed to the brink by the irrational, insatiable hungers of our economic system and its supporting faith. There is a claim about how some brave souls die for ideas, how their sacrifices are meant to illuminate those malignancies that threaten a society in collapse. Women and men like Giordano Bruno and Hypatia are set aside from the realm of the rest of us. They are, in the original sense of the word, *sacred*, posessing a force that when it "erupts into our lives . . . is unmistakable, its effects lasting, its memory haunting," as Bradatan writes. The martyred, these sacred women and men, are separate from us regular folk who are more content to scroll through Twitter by the pool rather than to die for an idea. If ever a people needed a holy sacrifice uttering parrhesia on the scaffold, a sacred scapegoat shouting the truth from a pyre, it is our own. The media moved on from Buckel's martyrdom in Prospect Park with disturbing promptness—just another horrific story receding deep into our newsfeeds, his radical honesty drowned out in the static of so much otherwise meaningless information permeating our apocalyptic age. Perhaps it's time to listen to him, before it's too late. For, as Seneca wrote, "It was the hemlock that made Socrates great," and, as Buckel said, "Honorable purpose in life invites honorable purpose in death."

TOP A field at Verdun after the battle was over, 1916.

OPPOSITE Remembrance Sunday is held in memory of Armistice every second Sunday in November throughout the United Kingdom. Carel Weight depicted the two minutes of quiet in his 1965 *The Silence*, showing his own Wandsworth, England. Original held by the Royal Academy.

THE REST IS SILENCE

The entire Western front went silent at exactly 11:00 a.m. on November 11, 1918. An armistice had been reached earlier that morning between the Allies and Germany, and it was agreed that hostilities would cease at that precise hour. In 2018, audiologists at London's Imperial War Museum used seismic data which had been gathered in the trenches as part of the war effort to re-create that moment. Now it's possible to listen to what American troops along the River Moselle heard—repeated blasts of artillery fire for two minutes, a final explosion, and then at 11:00 a few gentle bird chirps in the autumn morning as everything falls quiet. An eerie, stunning, beautiful sound. The most sacred thing you will ever hear. Everything and nothing is answered in silence as deep as that. Following such barbarity and horror, the very earth was now enveloped in a deep, blanketing quiet. Novelist Kurt Vonnegut, who had experienced the nightmare of war when he was a POW in Dresden during the Allied bombing campaign of World War II, said of the Armistice that "I have talked to old men who were on battlefields during that minute. They have told me in one way or another that the sudden silence was the voice of God." A strange and moving wisdom understands that when the Lord speaks it may not be through thunderclap and lightning, but rather in the final blast of artillery and a few bird chirps across a scarred and mined field. If dissonance is the question, then silence may be the only answer.

Our present world is not quite as loud as it had been on the Western front (yet), but still we live mired in a never-ending cacophony. A century after God spoke unto the trenches of the Great War, the volume is getting louder and louder; not with artillery shells, but rather the din of chatter, the thrum of status

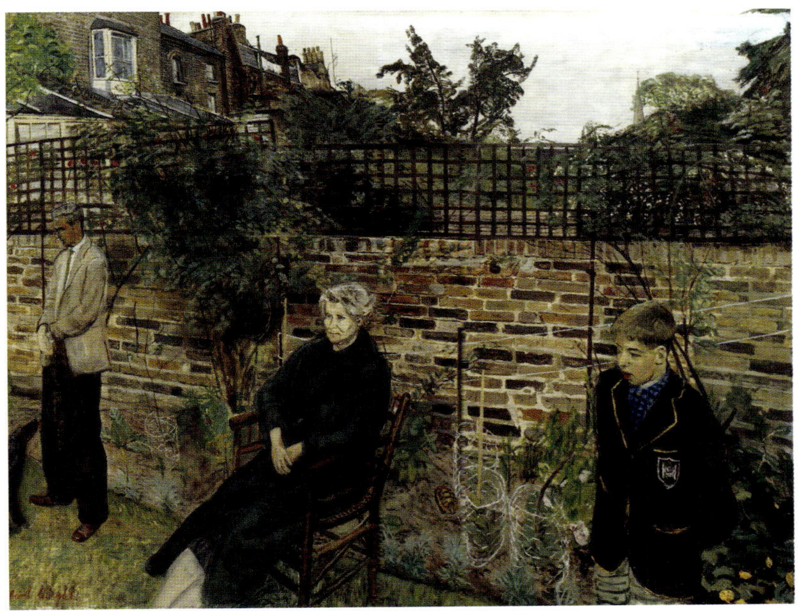

update, the vibration of push notification. Since the omnipresence of the smartphone, we're continually in multiple conversations which often don't deserve our attention. The twenty-four-hour news cycle forces us to formulate hot takes and positions on every conceivable event, from issues of political importance to fleeting pop culture phenomena, and bellicose bloviating announces itself 140 characters at a time from the top on down. If Vonnegut is right that God spoke a century ago, then our current age is too loud to make that voice out today. So loud is our current age, the echo of social media static resounding in our ears, that the French historian Alain Corbin writes that when it comes to silence, "We have almost forgotten what it is." If the industrial revolution heralded a landscape where silence was eliminated, the peace of town and country punctuated by the clank of machinery, then the digital revolution has shifted that very noise into our heads as well. Perhaps that's why there has been a recent spike in interest about silence from philosophically inflected writers. Like Corbin in his *A History of Silence*, we're all looking for a little peace and quiet these days.

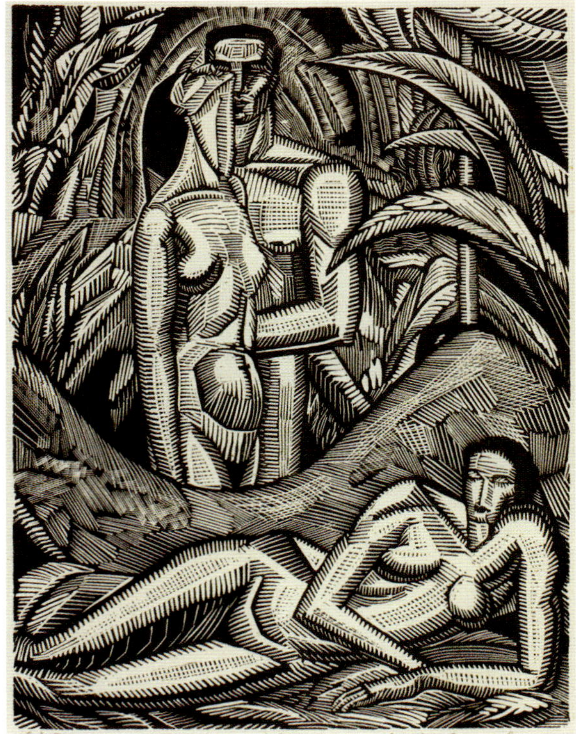

Philosophy is traditionally conveyed through debate and argument. A reliance on disputation and dialogue, syllogism and seminar, would seem to proffer a noisy discipline. Yet philosophy can also be defined by a peaceful undercurrent, a metaphysics of silence. Corbin writes that silence is the "precondition for contemplation, for introspection, for meditation, for prayer, for reverie and for creation." Silence allows us the intentionality required of thought, the presence needed for rumination. If one model of philosophy takes place in the noisy Agora of ancient Athens, long Socratic dialogues among the sellers of lemons and olives, then another way of doing philosophy emphasizes the quiet, the construction of a space in which thought can grow unhampered, where answers may be found among the stillness. Such quiet is its own philosophical method, a mode of thought where answers are not generated through dialectic, but from within the soul of the thinker herself. There is something instrumental in this, where silence is a means to an end. But such an approach still has noise as its ultimate goal, in the form of declared conclusions. However, when parsing the significance of silence there are more radical methods, not just ones where stillness lends itself to future answers, but where wisdom sees silence itself as an answer. In a Western tradition which very much understands logic as a goal unto itself, where truth is a matter of positive statements about objective reality, silence is its own anarchic technique, its own strange approach toward that which we cannot speak. Silence can be both process and result.

From the sixth century before the Common Era, when Lao-Tzu claimed that "the spoken Tao is not the eternal Tao," until Ludwig Wittgenstein's 1924 conclusion that "whereof one cannot speak, thereof one must be silent," silence has been a philosophical counter-tradition. Wittgenstein argued that if all of the questions of science, logic, and mathematics were somehow to be answered,

TOP Evocative of medieval woodcuts, Canadian artist Cecil Buller's 1929 *Contemplation, From Song of Solomon* conveys the counterintuitive solidarity of contemplation, the fellowship of silence, the communion of quiet, the experience of peace among other human beings.

OPPOSITE Mark Rothko's *Green on Blue (Earth-Green and White)* from 1954, original at the University of Arizona Museum of Art.

we'd still have to be silent about that which is most profound. Issues of metaphysics would be passed over in a deep silence, not because they're insignificant, but rather because they're the most important. Perhaps it's pertinent that the Austrian philosopher organized these thoughts while fighting in the loud trenches of World War I. Though separated by millennia, both thinkers believed that when the veil of reality is peeled back, what mutely announces itself is a profound and deep silence. Such an approach shares much with what theologians call the *apophatic*, from the Greek "to deny," an understanding that when it comes to the approximation of ultimate things, it's sometimes more accurate to say what something isn't. We must pass eternity over in silence rather than circumscribe God with the limitations of mere words. Such a perspective holds that there can be more truth in uttering nothing than there is in literal description.

As the ninth-century Irish monk John Scotus Erigena wrote, "We do not know what God is." Anticipating the monk's contention, Jesus's response to Pilate's question of his origins was such that Christ "gave him no answer." Scripture itself conveys that God's silence is often more sacred than his declarations. More than mere humility, apophatic theology is a profound approach which conveys that God isn't just silent, but in some ways *is* silence. What would it mean, in our age of endless distraction and deafening noise, to inculcate silence not just for a bit of peace, but as an answer itself? What would it mean to engender within our lives an apophatic sensibility? To still the ear and mind long enough that we could, as Vonnegut said, "remember when God spoke clearly to mankind"? Not in a booming voice, but rather in the sublime silence which permeates the emptiness between atoms and the space between stars, the very quiet where creation is born.

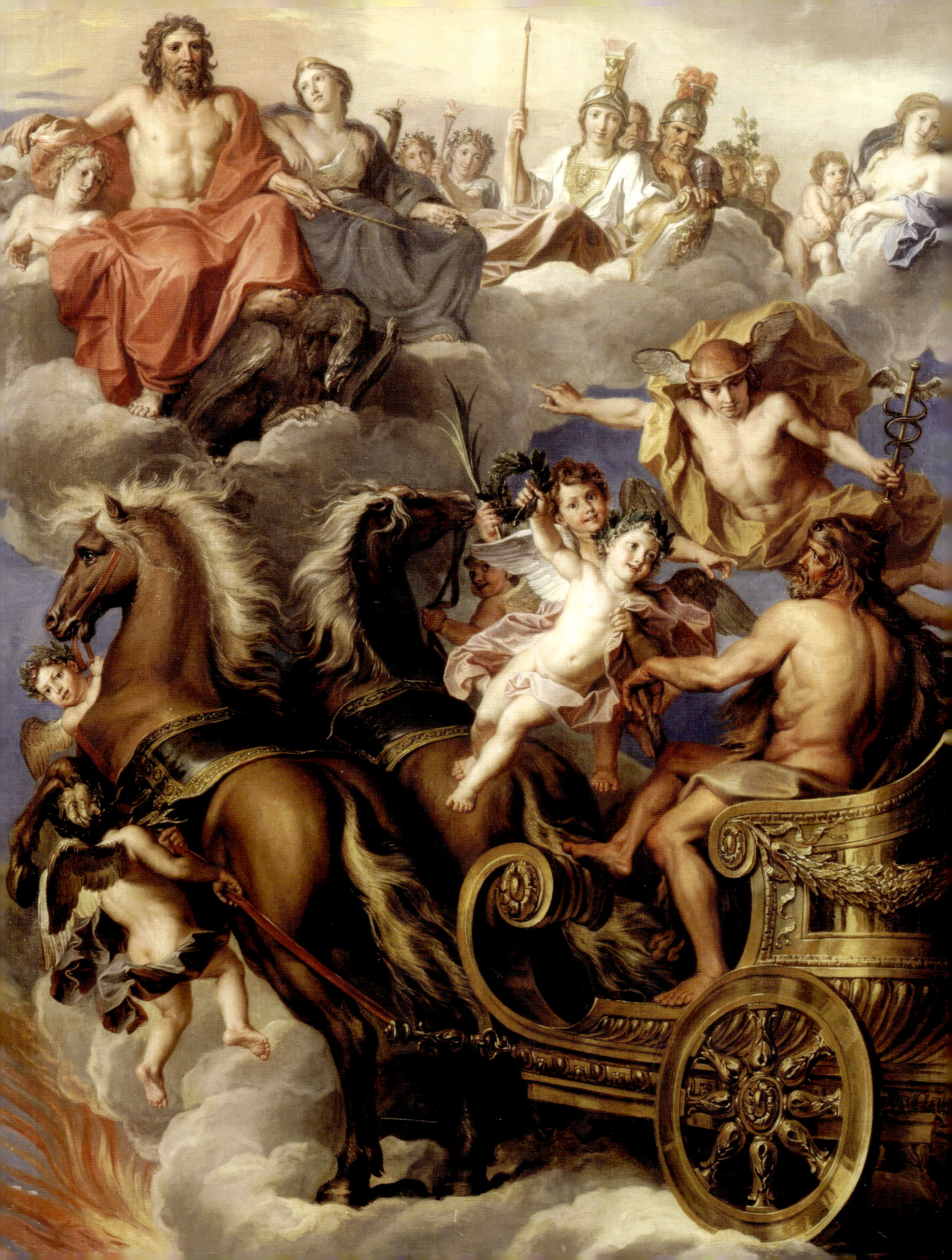

CONCLUSION

THE SEVEN CONTEMPORARY CAPITAL VIRTUES

Far from being archaic remnants of a medieval past, of moralizing censure and pious rectitude, both the Seven Capital Virtues and the Seven Deadly Vices constitute a system which accepts humanity in its variety and complexity, and more importantly, which accepts the human *individual* in their own variety and complexity, all of us in our capacities for both empathy and kindness, hatred and cruelty. Such an ethical calculus trades not in abstraction, but in the very real particulars of lived experience; we have within us all a chorus of saints and sinners, and the task of living a life worth living, especially for others, is to listen to the former more than the latter. Fundamentally, both the virtues and vices describe a limited world, one where we have no choice but to live in a community of others and where goodness and evil are both defined in part by the effects that our actions have on that community. A cursory reading of this volume should demonstrate that the listing of virtues and vices can be estimably ambiguous, that sometimes what appears as one can actually be the other. Despite that, we need not retreat into a noxious relativism, for whatever the particulars may be, virtue is about making room within your soul for the world, about letting that which is outside seep inward. Virtue is always a benediction from the world. In that spirit, then, a suggestion for the Seven Capital Virtues of our current moment.

OPPOSITE French painter Noël Coypel's 1700 *The Apotheosis of Hercules*, original at the Palace of Versailles.

I. **SOLIDARITY**

SUCH A VIRTUE IS CAPABLE OF UNDERSTANDING THAT THE STRUGGLE OF OTHERS IS OUR STRUGGLE, THAT WE ARE UNITED IN OUR NEEDS AND EXPECTATIONS, OUR DREAMS AND DESIRES, OUR LOVES. SOLIDARITY NEITHER CONDESCENDS NOR DICTATES, BUT RATHER SHARES.

II. **EMPATHY**

TO ACT AS IF THE CONCERNS OF THE COMMUNITY ARE YOUR OWN IS SOLIDARITY, BUT TO UNDERSTAND THAT THEY ARE IS EMPATHY. SHE IS THE MOTHER OF JUSTICE.

III. **JUSTICE**

BEFORE PEACE AND PROSPERITY, THERE MUST BE JUSTICE. THE RECTIFYING OF THAT WHICH IS WRONG, THE CORRECTION OF THAT WHICH IS WICKED, JUSTICE IMPLIES THAT EVERY LINE MUST BE STRAIGHTENED AND EVERY TEAR WILL BE WIPED AWAY. JUSTICE REQUIRES NOT JUST A BELIEF IN THE EQUALITY OF ALL PEOPLE, BUT A DEEP FEELING OF IT AS WELL.

IV. **CURIOSITY**

THIS IS THE VIRTUE THAT UNDERSTANDS THAT THE CONTOURS OF THE INDIVIDUAL ARE NOT THE CONTOURS OF THE UNIVERSE, THAT SEES IN THE EXPLORATION AND UNDERSTANDING OF THAT WHICH IS DIFFERENT A POSSIBILITY NOT JUST OF WISDOM, BUT OF SALVATION.

V. **HUMANISM**

WHETHER IT DEFINES ITSELF AS RELIGIOUS OR SECULAR, A FAITH SUCH AS HUMANISM IS THAT WHICH DOESN'T RECOGNIZE ANYTHING INTRINSIC IN BORDERS, IN RACE, IN ETHNICITY, IN DENOMINATION OR SECT. TO BE A HUMANIST IS TO COUNT YOURSELF A CITIZEN OF ALL NATIONS AND AN ADHERENT OF OTHER TRIBES; IT IS THE ANTIDOTE TO RACISM, NATIONALISM, XENOPHOBIA, AND FASCISM.

VI. **CREATIVITY**

THE DESIRE TO CREATE SOMETHING NEW, TO FORGE NOVEL MEANINGS AND EXPRESSIONS, TO SPEAK OF TRUTH, BEAUTY, AND GOODNESS BEYOND THE STULTIFICATIONS OF MARKET AND CONSENSUS REMAINS SUBVERSIVE, REMAINS POWERFUL, REMAINS VIRTUOUS.

VII. **KINDNESS**

NOW, AS THEN, KINDNESS REMAINS THE FONT OF OTHER VIRTUES.

Today, in our desire for equality and for mercy, for justice and for tolerance, let us pray that we can identify the goodness in our fellow humans' eyes, and may such virtue become the watchword of our soul collective.

CREDITS

SEVEN DEADLY SINS

The Allen Memorial Art Museum (pp. 72, 119), Eleanor Antin (p. 190), Uwe Aranas (pp. 182–83), Estate of Jean-Michel Basquiat (p. 174), Will Brown (p. 93), Christie's Images (p. 29), Mathieu Croisetière (p. 80), Dundee Art Galleries and Museums Collection (p. 26), Mark Frederickson (p. 84), Wally Gobetz (pp. 126–27), David Hockney (pp. 134–35), Kunsthistorisches Museum Vienna (p. 75), Maltaper (p. 72), Mentnafunangann (p. 131), Pictor Mulier (p. 43), Museo del Prado (pp. 198–99), The Museum of Fine Arts—Hungarian National Gallery (p. 35), The National Museum in Kraków Digital Collection (pp. 32–33), Odd Nerdrum (p. 80), Oberlin College Library (pp. 144–45), Sucesión Pablo Picasso (p. 188), The Royal Collection Trust (p. 15), Lucas Samaras (pp. 150–51), SaraZen (p. 129), David Shankbone (p. 103), Penny Siopis (p. 20), Estate of Sylvia Sleigh (p. 59), Heinrich Sturzl (p. 50), Karim Tabar (p. 102), VEGAP (p. 188), Noah Verrier (pp. 68–69), Wellcome Images (pp. 192–93)

SEVEN HEAVENLY VIRTUES

ADAGP (p. 120), The Andy Warhol Foundation for the Visual Arts (pp. 57, 145), Artists Rights Society (pp. 120, 145, 166), Basilica of Sant'Apollinare Nuovo (p. 171), Jean-Baptiste Beranger (p. 108), Andreas F. Borchert (p. 11), Jordan Casteel (p. 124), Caroline Coon (p. 56), Erik Cornelius (p. 43), Henry Darger (p. 23), Deutsches Historisches Museum (p. 95), Gayle "Asali" Dickson (p. 166), Flowers Gallery (p. 71), Getty Images (pp. 17, 73, 141, 167), Matthias Griebel (p. 95), John Hammond (p. 190), Leslie Hossack (p. 168), Allan Houser (p. 161), Peter Howson (p. 71), Rich Lam (p. 141), Kelly Latimore (pp. 163, 185), The Estate of Arnold Lobel (p. 121), Tim McDonagh (p. 68), Meanwhile88 (p. 189), Sharon Mollerus (p. 50), Dr. Sean B. Murphy (p. 192), Museum of Warsaw (pp. 98–99), Nationalmuseum (p. 43), Andres Praefcke (p. 99), Royal Academy of Arts (p. 190), Sotheby's (pp. 116–17), Harry Sternberg (p. 88), Tate Images (pp. 19, 107), Thorvaldsson (p. 51), the T. B. Walker Foundation (p. 91), Teen Vogue (p. 167)

Every effort has been made to trace the copyright holders of material quoted in this book. If application is made in writing to the publisher, any omissions will be included in future editions.

7 HEAVENLY VIRTUES 7

Library of Congress Control Number: 2024937748

ISBN: 978-1-4197-7410-2
eISBN: 979-8-88707-302-6

Cernunnos logo design: Mark Ryden
Book design: Benjamin Brard

Printed and bound in China
10 9 8 7 6 5 4 3 2 1

ABRAMS The Art of Books
195 Broadway, New York, NY 10007
abramsbooks.com